Hotels and Country Inns of Character and Charm in Italy

Published in the United States by Fodor's Travel Publications, Inc.
Published in France by Payot /Rivages

ISBN 0-679-00207-3
Third Edition

Hotels and Country Inns
of Character and Charm in Italy
Translators: Mark Ennis, Anne Norris, and Jack Monet
Rewriting: Marie Gastaut
Cover design: Fabrizio La Rocca
Front cover photograph: Castello di Uzzano (Tuscany)
Back cover: Relais Villabella (Veneto)

Special Sales

Fodor's Travel Publications are available at special discounts for bulk purchases for sales promotions or premiums. Special editions, including personalized covers, excerpts of existing guides, and corporate imprints, can be created in large quantities for special needs. For more information, contact your local bookseller or Special Markets, Fodor's Travel Publications, 201 E. 50th Street, New York, NY 10022.

Printed in Italy by Litho Service
10 9 8 7 6 5 4 3 2 1

Fodor's RIVAGES

HOTELS AND COUNTRY INNS of Character and Charm IN ITALY

Conceived by

Michelle Gastaut, Lidia Bieda, and Fabrice Camoin

Project editor

Michelle Gastaut

Fodor's Travel Publications, Inc.

New York • Toronto • London • Sydney • Auckland

www.fodors.com/

WELCOME

Welcome to the world of hotels with character and charm in Italy. This edition contains 436 hotels; 109 properties appear in the guide for the first time. All have been selected for charm, quality of welcome, food, and hotelkeeping. They range from the comparatively simple to the luxurious.

When choosing among them, remember that you cannot expect as much of a room costing 90,000L as you can of one costing 180,000L or more. Please also note that the prices given were quoted to us at the end of 1997 and may change.

When you make your reservation be sure to ask for the exact prices for half board *(mezza-pensione)* or full board *(pensione)* as they can vary depending on the number in your party and the length of your stay. Half board is often obligatory. Note that rooms are generally held only until 6 or 7PM; if you are going to be late, let the hotel know.

STAR RATING

The government's hotel roting organization assigns stars, from one to four, based on the comfort of a hotel, with special weight given to the number of bathrooms and toilets in relation to the number of rooms. This star rating has nothing at all to do with subjective criteria such as charm or the quality of the hospitality which are among our most important criteria. Some of the hotels in this guide have no stars–and that is because the hoteliers have never asked the gouvernment to rate them.

HOW TO USE THE GUIDE

Hotels are listed by region, and within each region by district. The number of the page on which a hotel is described corresponds to the number on the flag that pinpoints the property's location on the road map and to the numbers in the table of contents and index. The phrase "major credit cards" means that Diner's, Amex, Visa, Eurocard and MasterCard are all accepted.

PLEASE LET US KNOW...

If you are impressed by a small hotel or inn not featured here, one that you think ought to be included in the guide, let us know so that we can visit it.

Please also tell us if you are disappointed by one of our choices. Write us at Fodor's Travel Publications, 201 E. 50th St., New York, NY 10022.

RESTAURANTS
LISTING BY REGION

CONTENTS LIST

CONTENTS

Agriturismo, Bed and breakfasts, Villas to rent:

BASILICATA CALABRIA

CAMPANIA

EMILIA ROMAGNA

LATIUM ABRUZZI

M A R C H E

U M B R I A

PIEMONT VALLE D'AOSTA

PUGLIA / APULIA

SARDINIA

S I C I L Y

T U S C A N Y

TRENTINO - DOLOMITES

V E N E T O

KEY TO THE MAPS

Scale : 1:1,000,000

MOTORWAYS

A9 - L'Océane

Under construction
projected

ROADS

Highway

Dual carriageway

Four lanes road

Major road

Secondary road

TRAFFIC

National

Regional

Local

JUNCTIONS

Complete

Limited

DISTANCES IN KILOMETRES

On motorway 10

On other road 10

BOUNDARIES

National boundary

Region area

Department area

URBAIN AREA

Town

Big city

Important city

Medium city

Little city

AIRPORTS

FORESTS

PARKS

Limit

Center

Cartography by

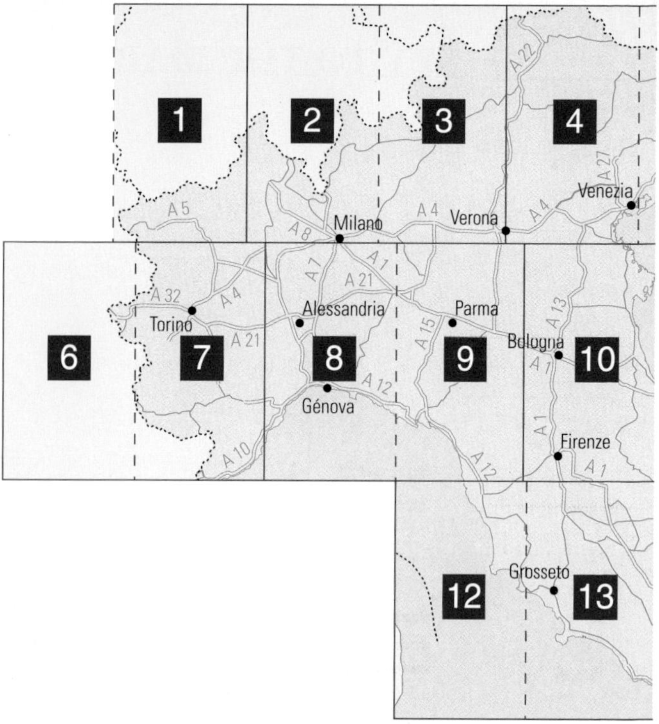

1 2 3 4

A 5 A 22 A 27 A 4 A 8

Milano Verona Venezia

A 1 A 21 A 32 A 4 A 15 A 13

Torino Alessandria Parma Bologna

6 7 8 9 10

A 21 A 12 A 1

Génova Firenze

A 10 A 12 A 1

Grosseto

12 13

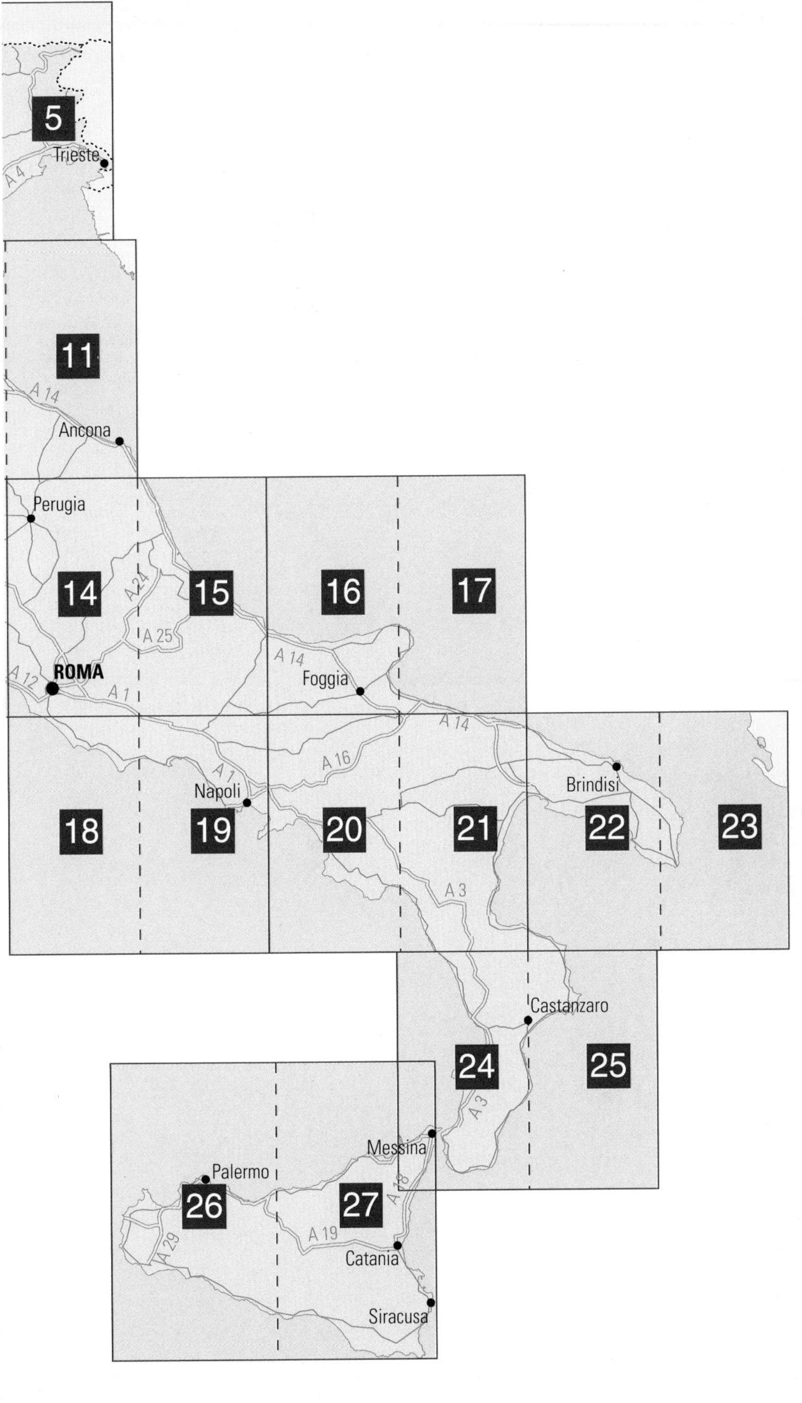
5
Trieste
A 4
11
A 14
Ancona
Perugia
14
A 24
15
A 25
16
17
ROMA
A 12
A 1
A 14
Foggia
18
19
A 1
Napoli
20
A 16
A 14
21
Brindisi
22
23
A 3
Castanzaro
24
25
A 3
Messina
Palermo
26
27
A 18
A 19
A 29
Catania
Siracusa

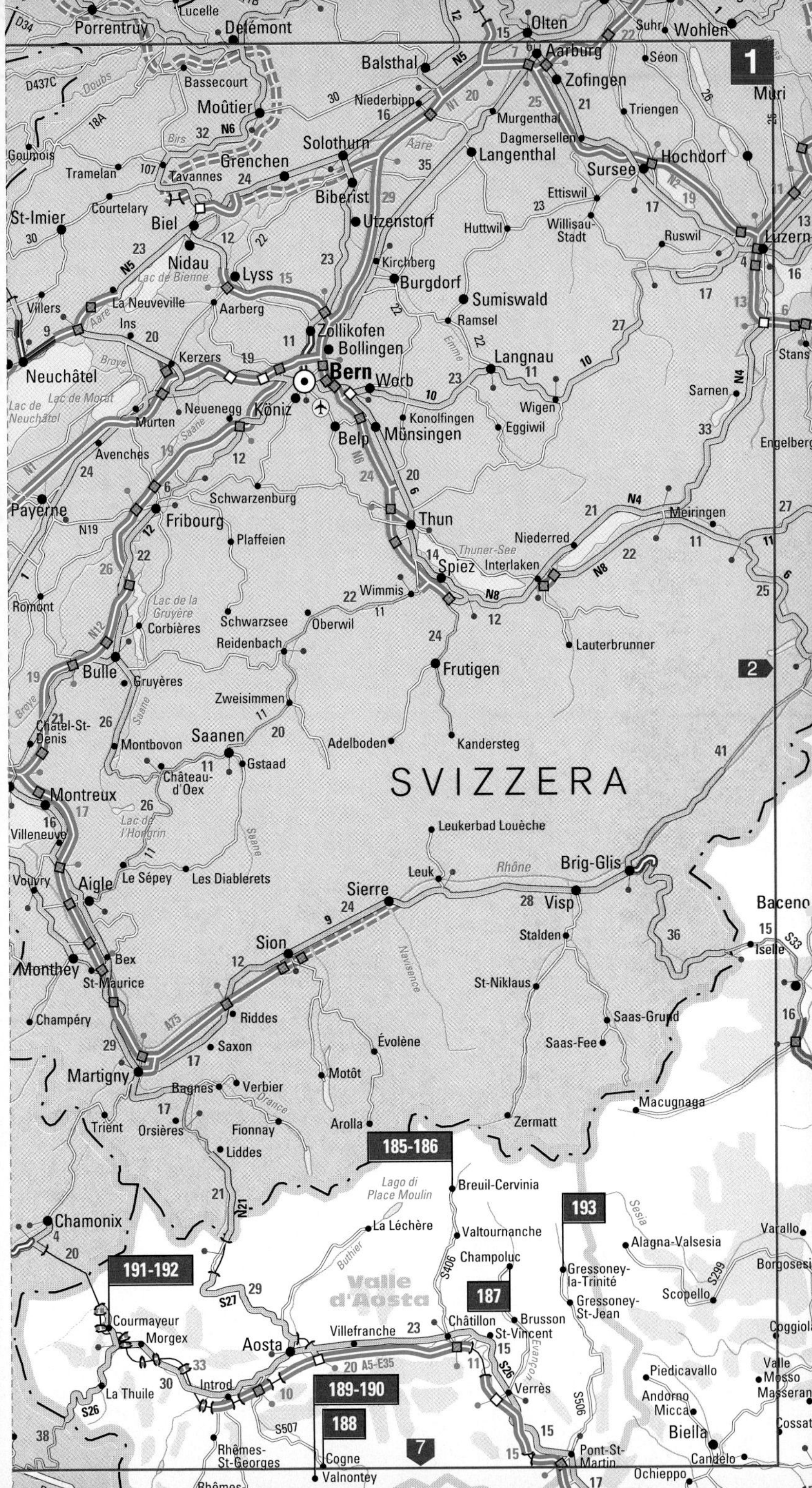
1
2
7
SVIZZERA
Valle d'Aosta
185-186
187
188
189-190
191-192
193
Porrentruy
Lucelle
Delémont
Olten
Aarburg
Zofingen
Suhr
Wohlen
Séon
Muri
Balsthal
Bassecourt
Moûtier
Niederbipp
Murgenthal
Triengen
Hochdorf
Dagmersellen
Langenthal
Sursee
Solothurn
Grenchen
Tavannes
Tramelan
Goumois
Biberist
Utzenstorf
Ettiswil
Willisau-Stadt
Huttwil
Ruswil
Luzern
St-Imier
Courtelary
Biel
Nidau
Lyss
Lac de Bienne
Kirchberg
Burgdorf
Sumiswald
Ramsel
Villers
La Neuveville
Aarberg
Ins
Zollikofen
Bollingen
Kerzers
Neuchâtel
Bern
Worb
Langnau
Wigen
Sarnen
Stans
Lac de Neuchâtel
Lac de Morat
Murten
Neuenegg
Köniz
Konolfingen
Münsingen
Belp
Eggiwil
Engelberg
Avenches
Payerne
Schwarzenburg
Fribourg
Plaffeien
Thun
Thuner-See
Niederried
Meiringen
Spiez
Interlaken
Wimmis
Romont
Lac de la Gruyère
Corbières
Schwarzsee
Oberwil
Reidenbach
Lauterbrunner
Bulle
Gruyères
Frutigen
Zweisimmen
Châtel-St-Denis
Montbovon
Saanen
Gstaad
Château-d'Oex
Adelboden
Kandersteg
Montreux
Villeneuve
Lac de l'Hongrin
Leukerbad Louèche
Vouvry
Aigle
Le Sépey
Les Diablerets
Leuk
Rhône
Brig-Glis
Sierre
Visp
Baceno
Iselle
Sion
Stalden
Monthey
Bex
St-Maurice
St-Niklaus
Champéry
Riddes
Saas-Grund
Saxon
Évolène
Saas-Fee
Martigny
Motôt
Bagnes
Verbier
Drance
Trient
Orsières
Fionnay
Arolla
Zermatt
Macugnaga
Liddes
Lago di Place Moulin
Breuil-Cervinia
Chamonix
La Léchère
Valtournanche
Champoluc
Gressoney-la-Trinité
Alagna-Valsesia
Varallo
Borgosesia
Scopello
Gressoney-St-Jean
Courmayeur
Morgex
Aosta
Villefranche
Châtillon
Brusson
St-Vincent
Coggiola
La Thuile
Introd
Verrès
Piedicavallo
Valle Mosso
Masseran
Andorno Micca
Biella
Cossato
Rhêmes-St-Georges
Cogne
Valnontey
Pont-St-Martin
Candelo
Ochieppo
N1
N2
N4
N5
N6
N8
N12
N21
A5-E35
A75
S26
S27
S33
S299
S406
S506
S507
D34
D437C
Aare
Doubs
Birs
Broye
Saane
Emme
Navisence
Buthier
Sesia
Evançon

2
Adliswil
Uster
Wetzikon
Wattwil
Urnäsch
Feldkirch
Thalwil
Wald
Muri
Zürichsee
Kaltbrunn
Gams
Nerging
Unterwasser
Vaduz
Brand
Cham
Zug
Walensee
Waldenstadt
Zugsee
Näfels
Maienfeld
Schiers
Luzern
Arth
Schwyr
Glarus
Landquart
Kublis
Schwanden
Gersau
Rhein
Chur
Stans
Flims Waldhaus
Reichnau
Altdorf
Arosa
Hinterrhein
Engelberg
Vorderhein
Thusis
Tiefencastel
Bergün
Disentis
SVIZZERA
Savognin
Andermatt
Olivone
Pso d. S. Gottardo
Cresta
Airolo
Maloja
Madesimo
Mesocco
Soglio
Peccia
Biasca
Castasegna
Sonogno
Chiavenna
Formazza
Bignasco
Mosea
Maggia
1
Toce
Bellinzona
Baceno
Lago di Como
Dubino
Gravedona
Locarno
Dongo
Colico
Morbegno
Sta Maria Maggiore
Brissago
115
Malesco
179
116
114
118
Domodóssola
Cannóbio
Porlezza
Bellano
San Mamete
Menággio
Varenna
180
Maccagno
Lugano
119
110-111
Lenno
Luino
Campione
S. Fedele Intelvi
Bellágio
Anzola d'Ossola
L. di Mergozzo
Ghiffa
Lago Maggiore
117
Mandello d. L.
Verbania
112
113
S. Giovanni Bianco
181
Laveno
Morcote
Lago di Lecco
Lecco
Moltrásio
Valmadrera
Stresa
131
Gavirate
Cernobbio
L. di Pusiano
L. di Garlate
Calolziocorte
Erba
Lago d'Orta
Omegna
134
Varese
Cantello
Como
L. di Annone
182-183
Olgiate C.
L. di Alserio
Varallo
Ranco
L. di Varese
Cantù
Castiglione Olona
133
Arona
Orta S. Giulio
Borgosesia
Giússano
Borgomanero
Sesto
Vergiate
Tradate
108-109
Lambro
Coggiola
Somma Lombardo
Trezzo Sull'Adda
130
Saronno
Séveso
Vimercate
Valle Mosso
Romagnano Sesia
Busto Arsizio
Monza
Masserano
Sesia
Legnano
Momo
122 ▸ 129
Bellinzago Nov.
Gorgonzola
Treviglio
Cossato
Rho
8
Inveruno
Sedriano
Milano

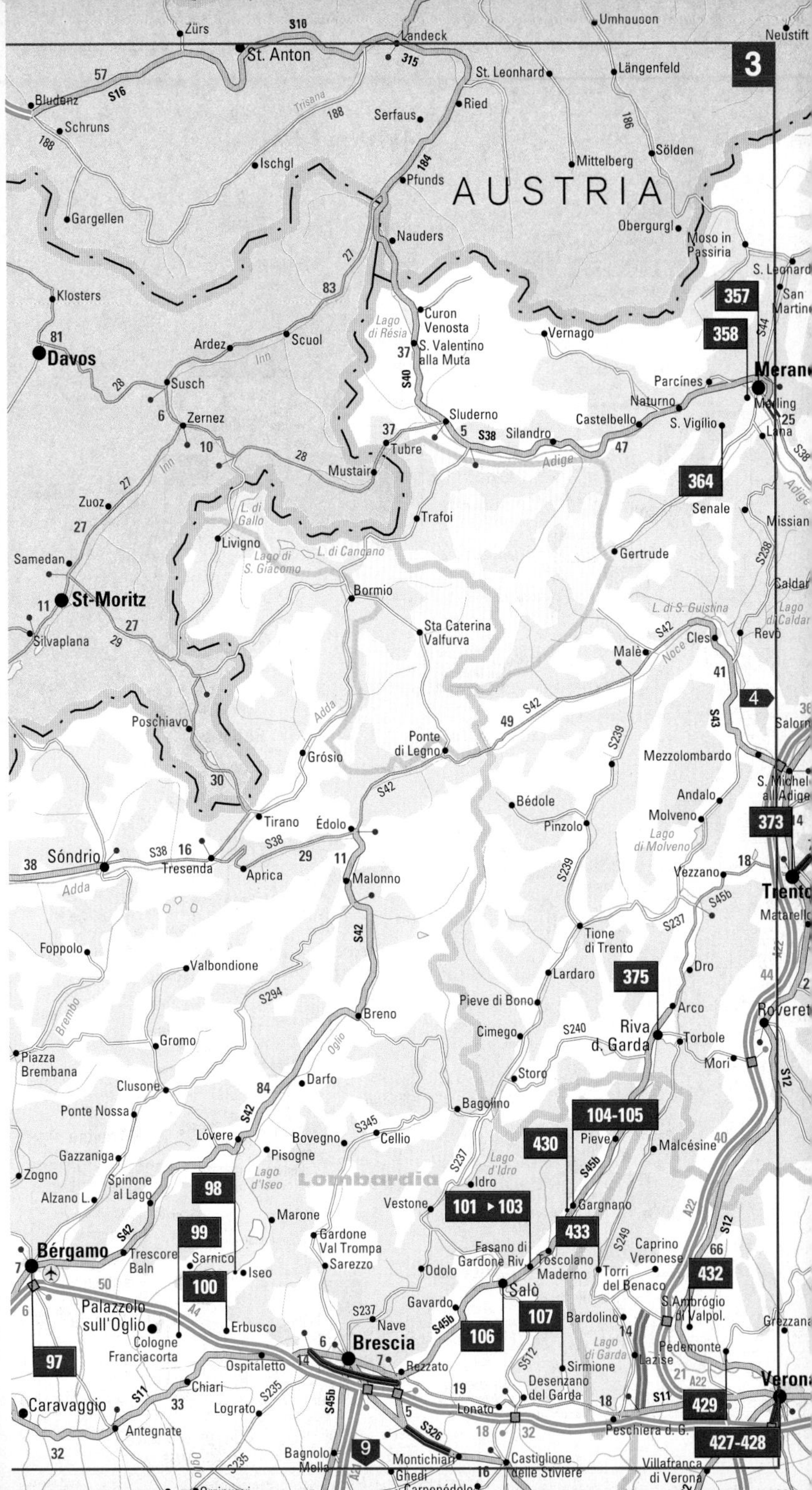
3
AUSTRIA
Lombardia
Zürs
Umhausen
Neustift
St. Anton
Landeck
Bludenz
Schruns
Trisana
Serfaus
Ried
St. Leonhard
Längenfeld
Ischgl
Mittelberg
Sölden
Pfunds
Gargellen
Nauders
Obergurgl
Moso in Passiria
S. Leonhard
San Martin
Klosters
Curon Venosta
Lago di Résia
S. Valentino alla Muta
Vernago
357
358
Davos
Ardez
Scuol
Inn
Susch
Zernez
Parcines
Merano
Naturno
Marling
Castelbello
Sluderno
Silandro
S. Vigilio
Lana
Tubre
Mustair
Adige
364
Senale
Missian
Zuoz
Trafoi
L. di Gallo
Livigno
Lago di S. Giacomo
L. di Cancano
Gertrude
Samedan
Bormio
St-Moritz
L. di S. Giustina
Lago di Caldaro
Caldaro
Silvaplana
Sta Caterina Valfurva
Cles
Revò
Malè
Noce
Poschiavo
Adda
Ponte di Legno
Salorno
Grósio
Mezzolombardo
S. Michele all'Adige
Andalo
Bédole
Molveno
Lago di Molveno
Pinzolo
373
Tirano
Édolo
Sóndrio
Tresenda
Aprica
Malonno
Vezzano
Trento
Matarello
Tione di Trento
Foppolo
Valbondione
Lardaro
Dro
375
Brembo
Pieve di Bono
Arco
Breno
Cimego
Riva d. Garda
Torbole
Rovereto
Oglio
Piazza Brembana
Gromo
Mori
Storo
Clusone
Darfo
Bagolino
Ponte Nossa
104-105
Lóvere
Bovegno
Cellio
430
Pieve
Malcésine
Gazzaniga
Pisogne
Lago d'Iseo
Lago d'Idro
Idro
Zogno
Spinone al Lago
98
Alzano L.
Vestone
101 ▸ 103
Gargnano
Marone
433
Caprino Veronese
Gardone Val Trompa
99
Bérgamo
Trescore Baln
Sarnico
Sarezzo
Fasano di Gardone Riv.
Toscolano Maderno
Torri del Benaco
432
Iseo
Odolo
100
Salò
S. Ambrógio di Valpol.
Palazzolo sull'Oglio
Erbusco
Gavardo
107
Bardolino
Grezzana
Cologne Franciacorta
Nave
106
97
Brescia
Lago di Garda
Pedemonte
Ospitaletto
Rezzato
Sirmione
Lazise
Verona
Chiari
Desenzano del Garda
Caravaggio
Lograto
Lonato
429
Antegnate
Peschiera d. G.
427-428
Bagnolo Mella
9
Montichiari
Castiglione delle Stiviere
Villafranca di Verona
Ghedi
Carpenédolo

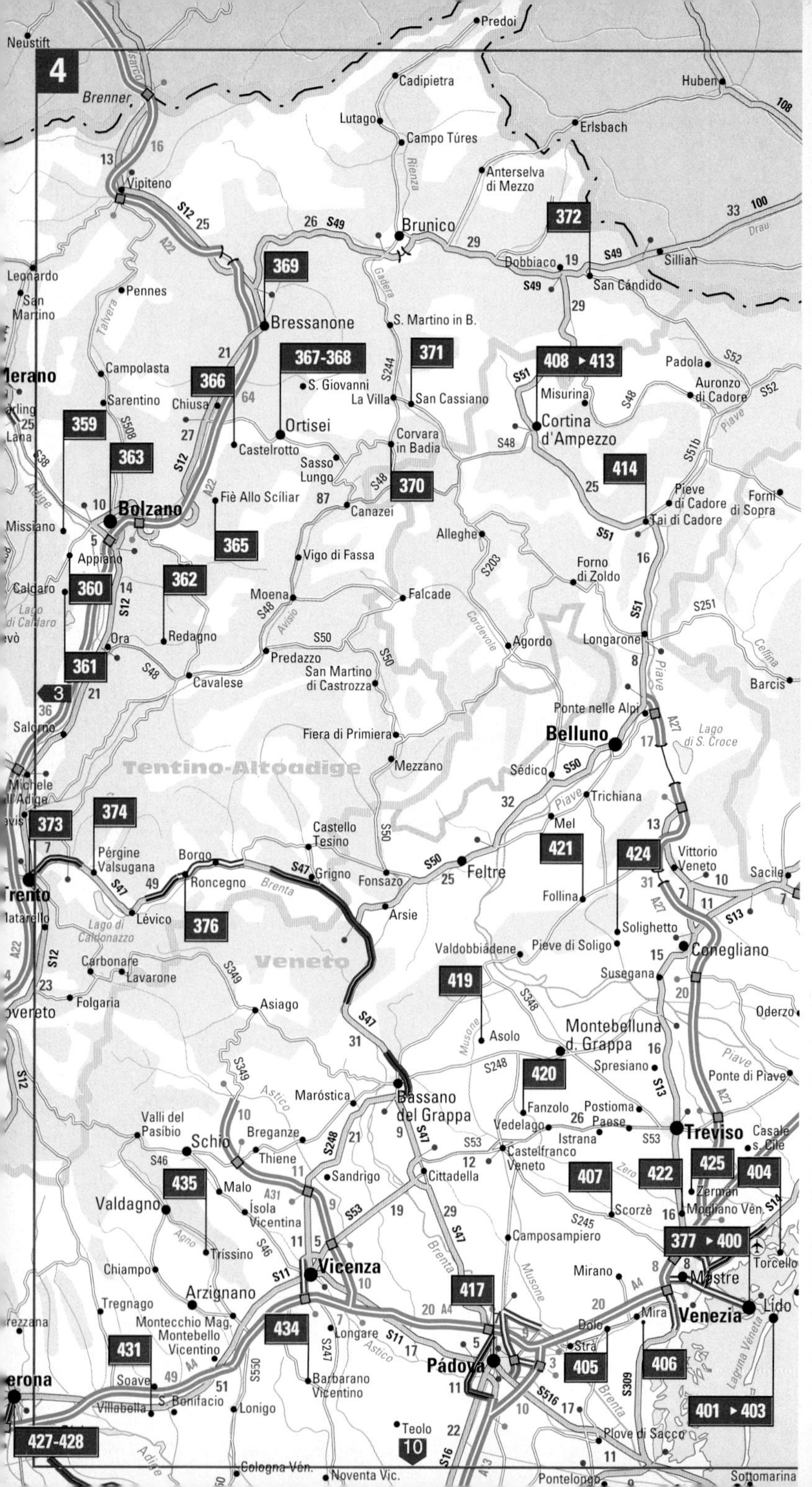

4
Neustift
Predoi
Brenner
Cadipietra
Huben
Lutago
Erlsbach
Campo Túres
Rienza
Vipiteno
Anterselva di Mezzo
372
Brunico
Sillian
Drau
369
Dobbiaco
San Cándido
Leonardo
Pennes
San Martino
Bressanone
S. Martino in B.
Gadera
Talvera
367-368
371
408 ▸ 413
Padola
Campolasta
366
S. Giovanni
La Villa
San Cassiano
Misurina
Auronzo di Cadore
Merano
Sarentino
Chiusa
Cortina d'Ampezzo
359
Ortisei
Corvara in Badia
Piave
Lana
363
Castelrotto
Sasso Lungo
414
370
Pieve di Cadore
Forni di Sopra
Bolzano
Fiè Allo Sciliar
Canazei
Tai di Cadore
Missiano
365
Alleghe
Appiano
Vigo di Fassa
Forno di Zoldo
Caldaro
360
362
Moena
Falcade
Lago di Caldaro
Avisio
Cordevole
Ora
Redagno
Agordo
Longarone
Cellina
361
Predazzo
San Martino di Castrozza
Barcis
3
Cavalese
Ponte nelle Alpi
Salorno
Fiera di Primiera
Belluno
Lago di S. Croce
Tentino-Altoadige
Mezzano
Sédico
S. Michele all'Adige
Trichiana
374
Mel
373
Castello Tesino
421
424
Pérgine Valsugana
Borgo
Vittorio Veneto
Sacile
Roncegno
Grigno
Fonsazo
Feltre
Trento
Brenta
Follina
Mattarello
Lévico
376
Arsie
Solighetto
Lago di Caldonazzo
Valdobbiádene
Pieve di Soligo
Conegliano
Carbonare
Veneto
Lavarone
Susegana
Folgaria
419
Oderzo
Rovereto
Asiago
Montebelluna d. Grappa
Asolo
Musone
420
Spresiano
Ponte di Piave
Astico
Maróstica
Bassano del Grappa
Fanzolo
Postioma Paese
Valli del Pasíbio
Vedelago
Treviso
Casale s. Cile
Schio
Breganze
Istrana
Thiene
Castelfranco Veneto
425
404
435
Sandrigo
Cittadella
407
422
Zerman
Malo
Valdagno
Ísola Vicentina
Scorzè
Mogliano Vên.
377 ▸ 400
Trissino
Camposampiero
Chiampo
Vicenza
Mirano
Torcello
Arzignano
417
Mestre
Tregnago
Lido
Montecchio Mag.
434
Dolo
Mira
Venezia
Montebello Vicentino
Longare
Strà
431
Pádova
405
406
Laguna Veneta
Verona
Soave
Barbarano Vicentino
Villabella
S. Bonifacio
Lonigo
Piove di Sacco
401 ▸ 403
427-428
Teolo
10
Adige
Cologna Vén.
Noventa Vic.
Pontelongo
Sottomarina

5
Obervellach
Möllbrücke
Millstatt
Kleinkirchheim
Winklern
Lienz
Spittal
Feldkirchen
Steinfeld
Techendorf
Weißensee
Drau
Paternion
Ossiacher See
Krumpendorf
Oberdrauburg
Villach
Wörthe
St. Lorenzen
Mauthen
Hermagor
Gail
Arnoldstein
416
Torni Avoltri
Sappada
Pontebba
Kranjskagora
Jesenice
Comegliáns
Lago di Sauris
Moggio Udinese
Na Logu
Villa Santina
Tolmezzo
Ampezzo
Tagliamento
Bovec
Zaga
SLOVENIA
Bohinjska Bistrica
Trnovo
Kobarid
Gemona del Friuli
Robic
Soca
Tramonti di Sopra
Osoppo
Grahovo
Friuli-Venezia
Tarcento
426
Most na Soci
Tricésimo
Zelin
S. Daniele di Friuli
Cividale d. Friuli
Kanal
Maniago
Montereale Cellina
Spilimbergo
415
Idrija
Údine
Dignano
Campofórmido
Godovic
Meduna
6
Aviano
Cellina
Manzona
S. Floriano del Cóllio
Cormóns
Gorízia
Ajdovscina
Mortegliano
Pordenone
Codróipo
Palmanova
Vipava
Casarsa d. Delizia
Gradisca d'Isonzo
San Vito al Tagliamento
Gonárs
Rivignano
S. Giorgio di Nogaro
Monfalcone
423
Azzano Decimo
Cervignano del Friuli
436
Muzzana del Turgnano
Golfo di Panzano
Portbuffolè
Sezana
Latisana
Motta di Livenza
Portogruaro
Laguna di Marano
I. di Grado
I. di S. Andrea
Trieste
Grado
Golfo di Trieste
Kozina
Cessalto
Lignano Sabbiadoro
Múggia
Livenza
Izola
Koper
San Doná di Piave
Cáorle
Piran
Savudrija
Piave
Umag
Buje
Livade
Lido de Jésolo
Vizinada
MAR ADRIÁTICO
Punta Sabbioni
Mirna
Novigrad
Tar
Golfo di Venezia
Porec
Baderna
Vrsar
11
Rovinj

6
FRANCIA
Chambéry
La Motte-Servolex
Grenoble
Voiron
Moirans
Voreppe
St-Egrève
Villard-Bonnot
Domène
Pontcharra
Montmélian
Challes-les-Eaux
Aiguebelle
Bourg-St-Maurice
Aigueblanche
Moutiers
La Plagne
Val-d'Isère
Courchevel
Pralognan-la-Vanoise
Méribel-les-Allues
St-Martin-de-Belleville
Les Ménuires
Val-Thorens
St-Jean-de-Maurienne
St-Julien-Mt-Denis
St-Michel-de-M.
Modane
Valloire
Tunnel du Fréjus
Lanslebourg-Mt-Cenis
Lac du Mont-Cenis
175
176
Bardonecchia
Salbertrand
Oulx
Sauze d'Oulx
Cesana-Torinese
Sestrière
Briançon
Cervières
L'Alpe-d'Huez
Le Bourg-d'Oisans
Les Deux-Alpes
Pont-de-l'Alp
Chamrousse
Vizille
Le Pont-de-Claix
Séchilienne
Laffrey
La Mure
Pierre-Châtel
Monestier-de-Clermont
Entraigues
Valjouffrey
Corps
L'Ailefroide
Vallouise
Brunissard
Abriès
Molines-en-Queyras
L'Argentière-la-Bessée
La Chapelle-en-Valgaudémar
St-Firmin
Clelles
Mens
Lac du Sautet
St-Disdier
St-Étienne-en-Dévoluy
Super-Dévoluy
Les Nonières
La Croix-Haute
Châtillon-en-Diois
St-Bonnet
Les Garnauds
Orcières
Eygliers
Guillestre
Risoul
Maljasset
Laye
Embrun
R. de Serre-Ponçon
Gap
La Roche-des-Arnauds
Veynes
Aspres
Aspremont
Beaurières
Chorges
Savines-le-Lac
Les Orres
St-Paul
Valserres
Tallard
Remollon
Larche
Jausiers
Serres
St-Vincent-les-Forts
Le Lauzet-Ubaye
Barcelonnette
Pra-Loup
Seyne
Eyguians
Monêtier-Allemont
La Motte
Laragne-Montéglin
La Villard d'Abas
Bousiéyas
Verdaches
Barles
Allos
Ribiers
Sisteron
Séderon
Les Omergues
St-Martin-d'Entraunes
Volonne
Digne-les-Bains
Château-Arnoux
Thorame-Basse
Guillaumes
Revest-du-Bion
St-Étienne-les-Orgues
La Colle-St-Michel
Châteauredon
St-Christol
Les Grillons
La Bastie
Les Mées
Mézel
St-André-les-Alpes
Puget-Théniers
Barrême
Le Castellet
La Bégude-Blanche
St-Michel-l'Ob.
Oraison
St-Julien-du-Verdon
La Tuilière
Reillanne
Moustiers-Ste-Marie
Castellane
St-Auban
La Bégude
Volx
Manosque
Lac du barrage de Ste-Croix

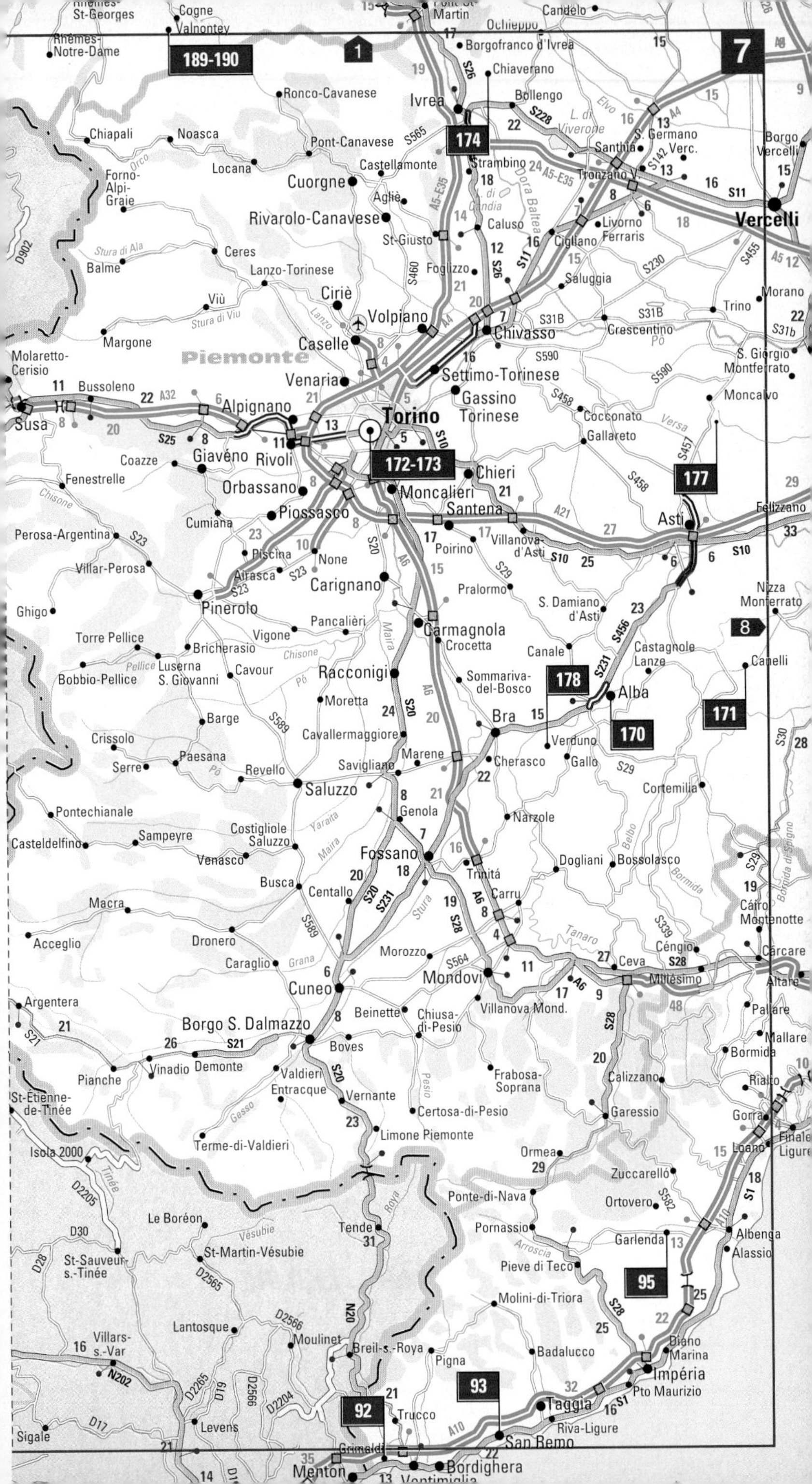

7
189-190
1
174
172-173
177
178
170
171
8
95
93
92
Cogne
Valnontey
Rhêmes-Notre-Dame
Candelo
Occhieppo
Borgofranco d'Ivrea
Chiaverano
Ivrea
Bollengo
L. di Viverone
Ronco-Cavanese
Chiapali
Noasca
Pont-Canavese
Castellamonte
Strambino
Santhià
S. Germano Verc.
Borgo Vercelli
Locana
Forno-Alpi-Graie
Cuorgne
Agliè
L. di Candia
Dora Baltea
Tronzano V.
Vercelli
Rivarolo-Canavese
Caluso
Livorno Ferraris
St-Giusto
Cigliano
Stura di Ala
Ceres
Balme
Lanzo-Torinese
Foglizzo
Saluggia
Ciriè
Viù
Stura di Viu
Volpiano
Chivasso
Crescentino
Trino
Morano
Margone
Caselle
Piemonte
Molaretto-Cerisio
Settimo-Torinese
S. Giorgio Montferrato
Venaria
Bussoleno
Gassino Torinese
Moncalvo
Alpignano
Susa
Torino
Cocconato
Gallareto
Giavéno
Rivoli
Coazze
Chieri
Fenestrelle
Orbassano
Moncalieri
Chisone
Piossasco
Santena
Cumiana
Asti
Felizzano
Perosa-Argentina
Piscina
None
Poirino
Villanova-d'Asti
Villar-Perosa
Airasca
Carignano
Pralormo
Ghigo
Pinerolo
S. Damiano d'Asti
Nizza Monferrato
Pancalièri
Carmagnola
Torre Pellice
Vigone
Crocetta
Bricherasio
Canale
Castagnole Lanze
Canelli
Luserna S. Giovanni
Bobbio-Pellice
Cavour
Racconigi
Sommariva-del-Bosco
Alba
Moretta
Barge
Bra
Verduno
Crissolo
Paesana
Cavallermaggiore
Marene
Cherasco
Gallo
Serre
Revello
Savigliano
Saluzzo
Cortemilia
Genola
Pontechianale
Narzole
Costigliole Saluzzo
Sampeyre
Casteldelfino
Venasco
Fossano
Dogliani
Bossolasco
Trinitá
Busca
Centallo
Carru
Macra
Cáiro Montenotte
Acceglio
Dronero
Morozzo
Céngio
Cárcare
Caraglio
Ceva
Millésimo
Cuneo
Mondovi
Altare
Argentera
Beinette
Chiusa-di-Pesio
Villanova Mond.
Pallare
Borgo S. Dalmazzo
Mallare
Boves
Bormida
Pianche
Vinadio
Demonte
Valdieri
Entracque
Frabosa-Soprana
Calizzano
Rialto
St-Étienne-de-Tinée
Vernante
Certosa-di-Pesio
Garessio
Gorra
Limone Piemonte
Finale Ligure
Terme-di-Valdieri
Loano
Isola 2000
Ormea
Zuccarelló
Ponte-di-Nava
Ortovero
Le Boréon
Tende
Pornassio
Garlenda
Albenga
Alassio
St-Martin-Vésubie
St-Sauveur-s.-Tinée
Pieve di Teco
Molini-di-Triora
Lantosque
Moulinet
Villars-s.-Var
Breil-s.-Roya
Badalucco
Diano Marina
Pigna
Impéria
Pto Maurizio
Taggia
Trucco
Riva-Ligure
Sigale
Levens
San Remo
Grimaldi
Menton
Bordighera
Ventimiglia

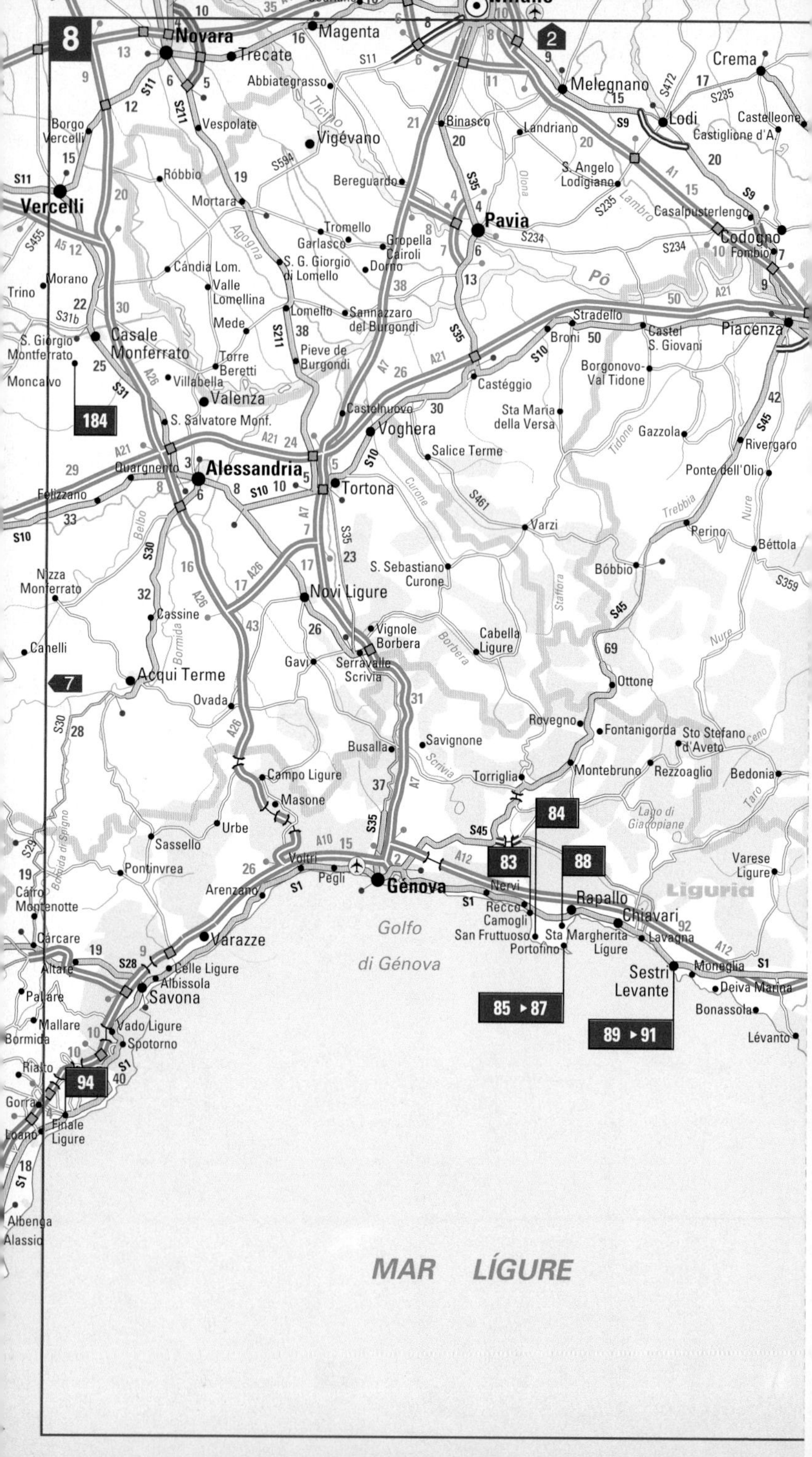
8
2
Milano
Sedriano
Novara
Magenta
Trecate
Abbiategrasso
Melegnano
Crema
Lodi
Castelleone
Castiglione d'A.
Borgo Vercelli
Vespolate
Vigévano
Binasco
Landriano
S. Angelo Lodigiano
Vercelli
Róbbio
Mortara
Bereguardo
Pavia
Casalpusterlengo
Codogno
Fombio
Tromello
Garlasco
Gropella Cairoli
S. G. Giorgio di Lomello
Dorno
Cándia Lom.
Valle Lomellina
Trino
Morano
Lomello
Sannazzaro del Burgondi
Stradello
Broni
Castel S. Giovani
Piacenza
S. Giorgio Monferrato
Casale Monferrato
Mede
Pieve de Burgondi
Torre Beretti
Borgonovo-Val Tidone
Moncalvo
Villabella
Valenza
Castéggio
184
S. Salvatore Monf.
Castelnuovo
Sta Maria della Versa
Voghera
Gazzola
Rivergaro
Quargnento
Alessandria
Salice Terme
Ponte dell'Olio
Felizzano
Tortona
Varzi
Perino
Béttola
Nizza Monferrato
S. Sebastiano Curone
Bóbbio
Novi Ligure
Cassine
Vignole Borbera
Cabella Ligure
Canelli
Gavi
Serravalle Scrivia
Ottone
7
Acqui Terme
Ovada
Rovegno
Fontanigorda
Sto Stéfano d'Aveto
Busalla
Savignone
Campo Ligure
Torriglia
Montebruno
Rezzoaglio
Bedonia
Masone
84
Lago di Giacopiane
Urbe
Sassello
83
88
Varese Ligure
Pontinvrea
Voltri
Pegli
Génova
Nervi
Liguria
Cáiro Montenotte
Arenzano
Recco
Camogli
Rapallo
Chiavari
Cárcare
Varazze
San Fruttuoso
Portofino
Sta Margherita Lígure
Lavagna
Golfo di Génova
Altare
Celle Ligure
Albissola
Sestri Levante
Moneglia
Pallare
Savona
Deiva Marina
85 ▸ 87
Bonassola
Mallare
Bormida
Vado Ligure
Spotorno
89 ▸ 91
Lévanto
Rialto
94
Gorra
Loano
Finale Ligure
Albenga
Alassio
Ticino
Agogna
Olona
Lambro
Pô
Tidone
Trebbia
Nure
Curone
Staffora
Borbera
Scrivia
Belbo
Bormida
Ceno
Taro
MAR LÍGURE

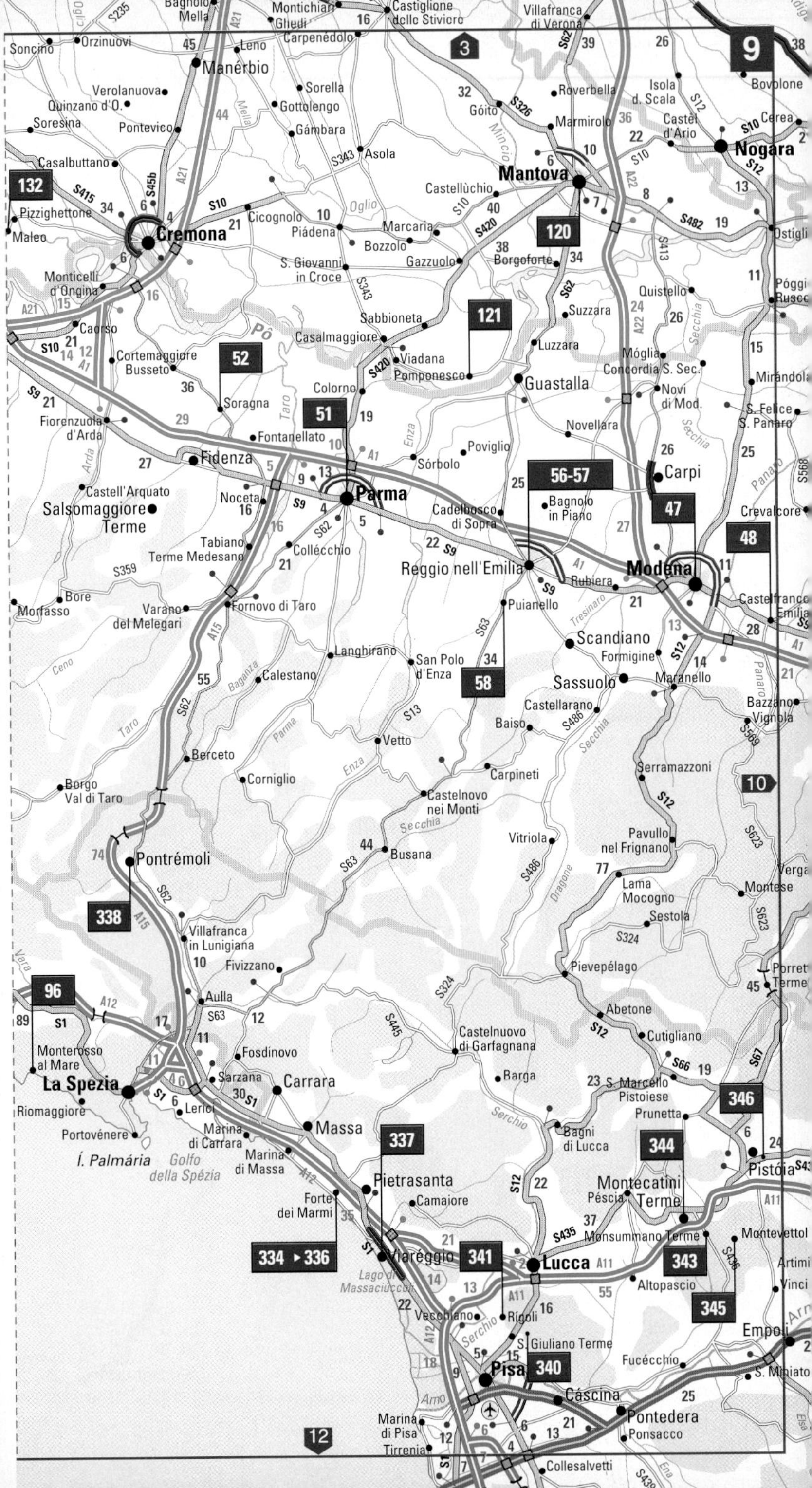

9
3
10
12
132
52
51
121
120
56-57
47
48
58
338
96
337
334 ▸ 336
341
340
343
344
345
346
Bagnolo Mella
Montichiari
Castiglione delle Stiviere
Villafranca di Verona
Ghedi
Carpenedolo
Soncino
Orzinuovi
Leno
Manèrbio
Bovolone
Verolanuova
Sorella
Roverbella
Isola d. Scala
Quinzano d'O.
Gottolengo
Góito
Marmirolo
Castel d'Ario
Cerea
Soresina
Pontevico
Gámbara
Nogara
Casalbuttano
Asola
Mantova
Castellùchio
Pizzighettone
Maleo
Cremona
Cicognolo
Piádena
Marcaria
Bozzolo
Ostiglia
S. Giovanni in Croce
Gazzuolo
Borgoforte
Monticelli d'Ongina
Quistello
Póggio Rusco
Sabbioneta
Suzzara
Caorso
Casalmaggiore
Luzzara
Móglia
Concordia S. Sec.
Cortemaggiore
Busseto
Viadana
Pomponesco
Guastalla
Mirándola
Novi di Mod.
Soragna
Colorno
Fiorenzuola d'Arda
Fontanellato
Novellara
S. Felice S. Panaro
Poviglio
Sórbolo
Fidenza
Carpi
Castell'Arquato
Noceta
Parma
Cadelbosco di Sopra
Bagnolo in Piano
Salsomaggiore Terme
Crevalcore
Tabiano
Terme Medesano
Collécchio
Reggio nell'Emilia
Modena
Rubiera
Bore
Morfasso
Varano del Melegari
Fornovo di Taro
Puianello
Castelfranco Emilia
Scandiano
Formigine
Langhirano
San Polo d'Enza
Calestano
Sassuolo
Maranello
Castellarano
Bazzano
Vignola
Baiso
Vetto
Berceto
Carpineti
Serramazzoni
Corniglio
Borgo Val di Taro
Castelnovo nei Monti
Vitriola
Pavullo nel Frignano
Busana
Pontrémoli
Lama Mocogno
Montese
Vergato
Sestola
Villafranca in Lunigiana
Fivizzano
Pievepélago
Porretta Terme
Aulla
Abetone
Monterosso al Mare
Castelnuovo di Garfagnana
Cutigliano
Fosdinovo
Barga
S. Marcello Pistoiese
La Spezia
Sarzana
Carrara
Riomaggiore
Lerici
Prunetta
Portovénere
Marina di Carrara
Massa
Bagni di Lucca
Pistóia
Í. Palmária
Golfo della Spézia
Marina di Massa
Pietrasanta
Montecatini Terme
Péscia
Forte dei Marmi
Camaiore
Monsummano Terme
Montevettolini
Viaréggio
Lucca
Artimino
Lago di Massaciùccoli
Altopascio
Vinci
Vecchiano
Rígoli
S. Giuliano Terme
Empoli
Pisa
Fucécchio
S. Miniato
Cáscina
Pontedera
Marina di Pisa
Ponsacco
Tirrenia
Collesalvetti
Pô
Oglio
Mincio
Mella
Taro
Enza
Secchia
Panaro
Arda
Ceno
Baganza
Parma
Tresinaro
Dragone
Serchio
Arno
Elsa
Era
Vara
A1
A4
A12
A15
A21
A22
A11
S1
S9
S10
S12
S13
S45b
S62
S63
S66
S67
S235
S324
S326
S343
S359
S413
S415
S420
S435
S436
S439
S445
S482
S486
S568
S569
S623

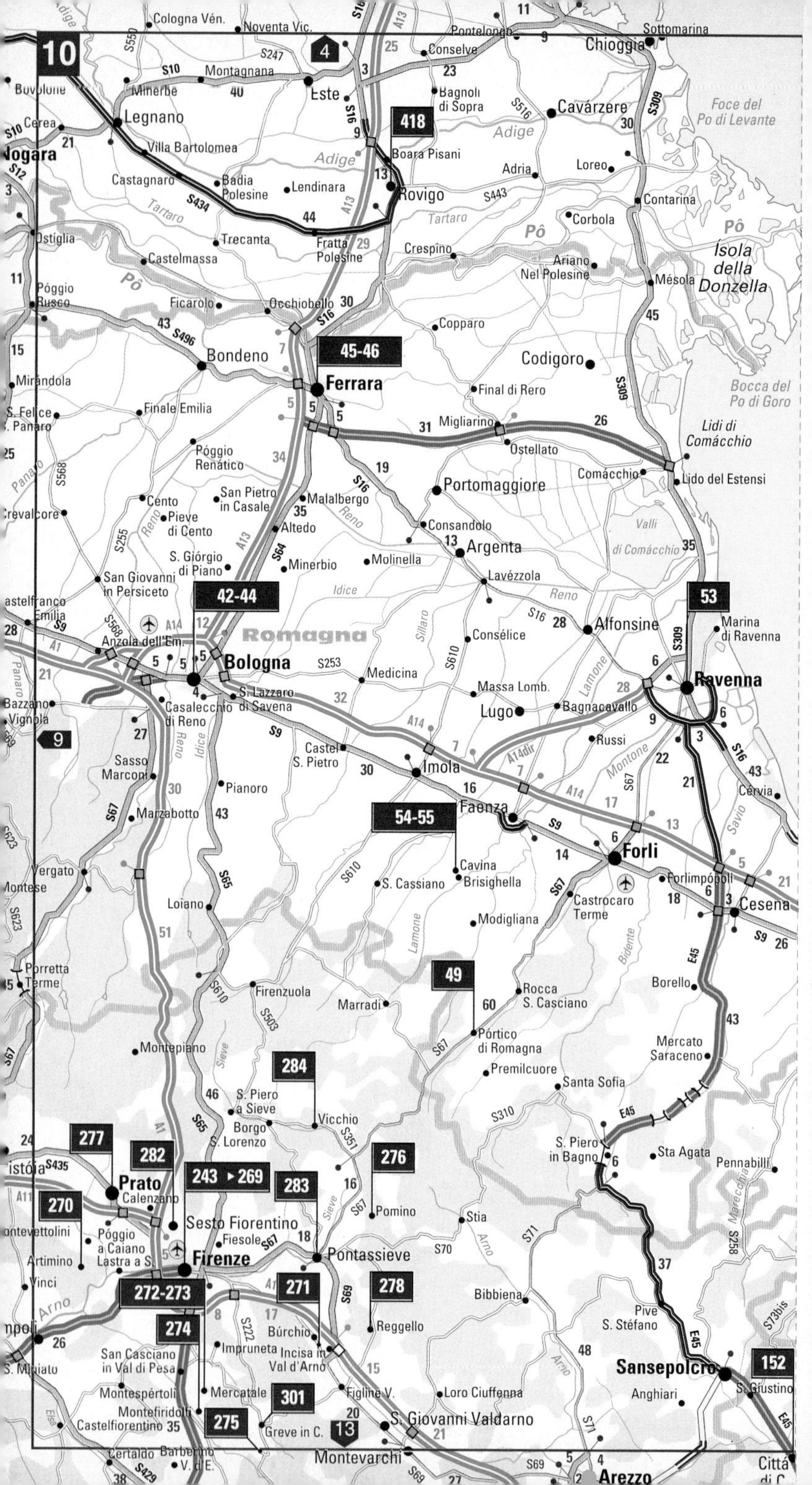
10
Cologna Vén.
Noventa Vic.
4
Pontelongo
Sottomarina
Chioggia
Conselve
Bovolone
Montagnana
Minerbe
Este
Bagnoli di Sopra
Cavárzere
Foce del Po di Levante
Cerea
Legnano
418
Adige
Nogara
Villa Bartolomea
Boara Pisani
Adria
Loreo
Castagnaro
Badia Polesine
Lendinara
Rovigo
Contarina
Tartaro
Corbola
Pô
Ostíglia
Trecanta
Fratta Polesine
Crespino
Ariano Nel Polesine
Isola della Donzella
Castelmassa
Mésola
Póggio Rusco
Ficarolo
Occhiobello
Copparo
Bondeno
45-46
Codigoro
Mirándola
Ferrara
Final di Rero
Bocca del Po di Goro
S. Felice s. Panaro
Finale Emilia
Migliarino
Lidi di Comácchio
Ostellato
Póggio Renático
Comácchio
Lido del Estensi
Portomaggiore
Cento
San Pietro in Casale
Malalbergo
Crevalcore
Pieve di Cento
Altedo
Consandolo
Valli di Comácchio
Argenta
S. Giórgio di Piano
Minerbio
Molinella
San Giovanni in Persiceto
Lavézzola
Castelfranco Emilia
42-44
Reno
53
Alfonsine
Marina di Ravenna
Romagna
Consélice
Anzola dell'Em.
Bologna
Medicina
Ravenna
Massa Lomb.
Bazzano
Vignola
Casalecchio di Reno
S. Lazzaro di Savena
Lugo
Bagnacavallo
9
Russi
Castel S. Pietro
Sasso Marconi
Imola
Pianoro
Cérvia
Marzabotto
Faenza
54-55
Forlì
Vergato
Montese
Cavina
Brisighella
Forlimpópoli
S. Cassiano
Cesena
Castrocaro Terme
Loiano
Modigliana
Porretta Terme
49
Borello
Firenzuola
Marradi
Rocca S. Casciano
Pórtico di Romagna
Mercato Saraceno
Montepiano
Premilcuore
284
Santa Sofia
S. Piero a Sieve
Vicchio
Borgo S. Lorenzo
277
S. Piero in Bagno
Sta Agata
282
276
Pennabilli
Pistóia
Prato
243 ▸ 269
283
Calenzano
270
Sesto Fiorentino
Pomino
Stia
Montevettolini
Póggio a Caiano
Fiesole
Artimino
Lastra a S.
Firenze
Pontassieve
Vinci
272-273
271
278
Bibbiena
Arno
Empoli
274
Búrchio
Reggello
Pive S. Stéfano
Impruneta
Incisa in Val d'Arno
San Casciano in Val di Pesa
S. Miniato
Sansepolcro
152
Montespértoli
Mercatale
301
Figline V.
Loro Ciuffenna
Anghiari
S. Giustino
Montefiridolfi
275
Castelfiorentino
Greve in C.
13
S. Giovanni Valdarno
Certaldo
Barberino V. d. E.
Montevarchi
Arezzo
Città di C.

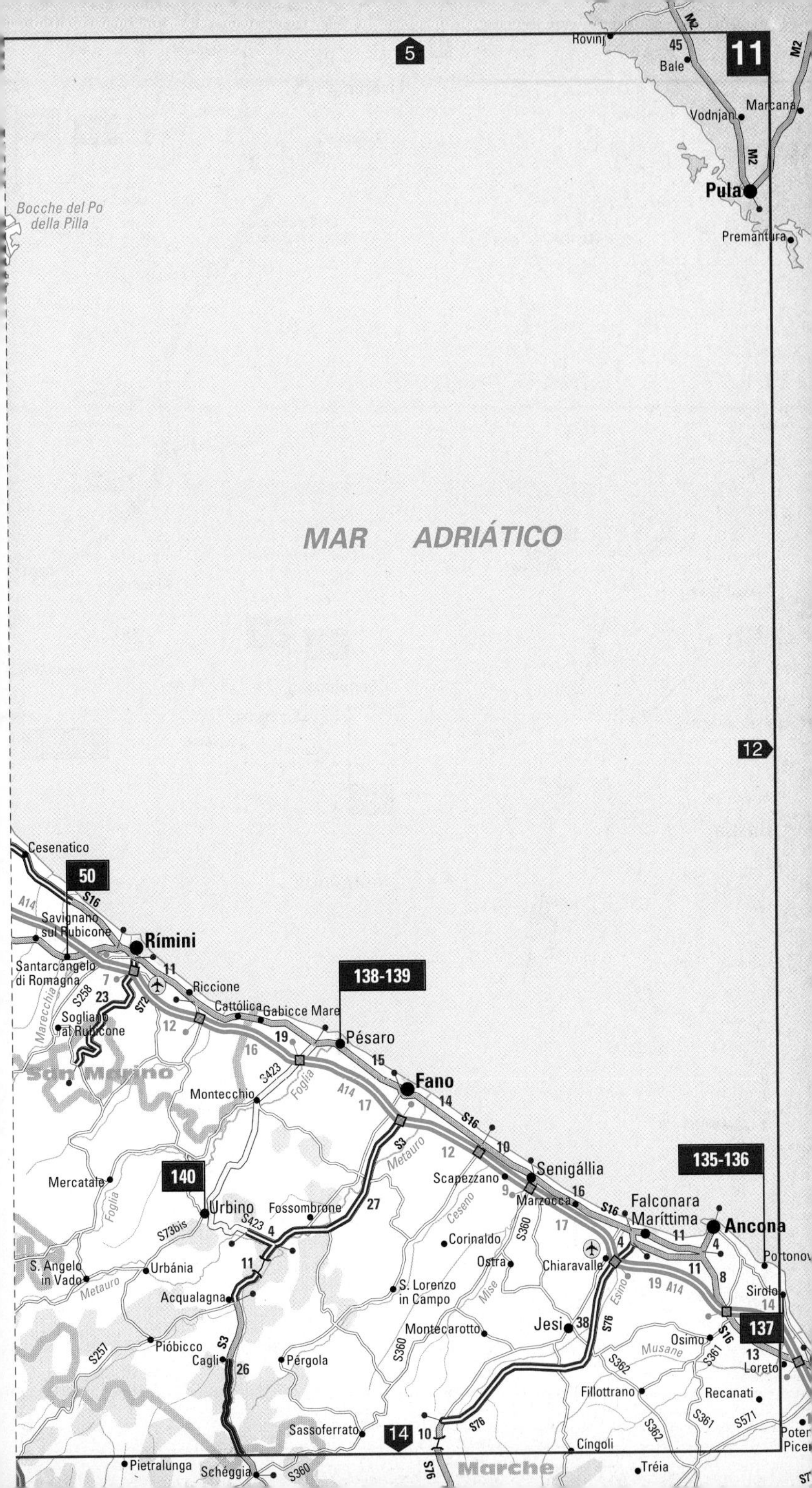

11
5
12
14
MAR ADRIÁTICO
Bocche del Po della Pilla
Rovinj
Bale
Vodnjan
Marcana
Pula
Premantura
Cesenatico
50
Savignano sul Rubicone
Rímini
Santarcangelo di Romagna
Riccione
Cattólica
Gabicce Mare
Sogliano al Rubicone
San Marino
138-139
Pésaro
Fano
Montecchio
Mercatale
140
Urbino
Fossombrone
S. Angelo in Vado
Urbánia
Acqualagna
Pióbicco
Cagli
Pérgola
Sassoferrato
Pietralunga
Schéggia
Senigállia
Scapezzano
Marzocca
Corinaldo
Ostra
S. Lorenzo in Campo
Montecarotto
Chiaravalle
Jesi
Falconara Maríttima
Ancona
135-136
Portonov
Sirolo
137
Osimo
Loreto
Recanati
Fillottrano
Cíngoli
Tréia
Marche
Poter Picer

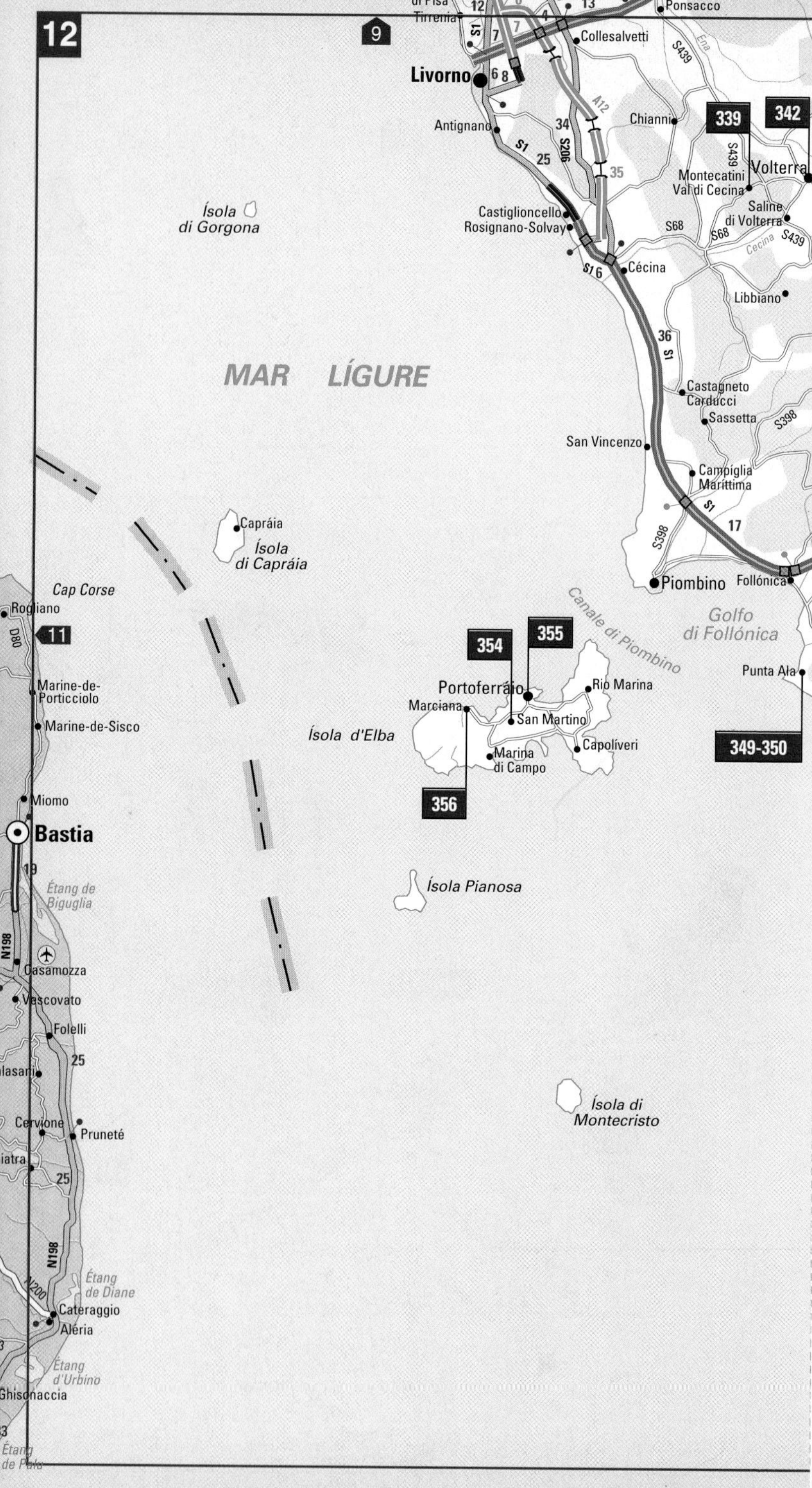
9
Livorno
Collesalvetti
Ponsacco
Tirrenia
di Pisa
Antignano
Chianni
339
342
Volterra
Montecatini
Val di Cecina
Saline
di Volterra
Castiglioncello
Rosignano-Solvay
Cécina
Libbiano
Ísola
di Gorgona
MAR LÍGURE
Castagneto
Carducci
Sassetta
San Vincenzo
Campíglia
Maríttima
Capráia
Ísola
di Capráia
Piombino
Follónica
Golfo
di Follónica
Cap Corse
Rogliano
11
Canale di Piombino
354
355
Portoferráio
Rio Marina
Punta Ala
Marciana
San Martino
Capolíveri
Marina
di Campo
Ísola d'Elba
349-350
356
Marine-de-
Porticciolo
Marine-de-Sisco
Miomo
Bastia
Étang de
Biguglia
Ísola Pianosa
Casamozza
Vescovato
Folelli
Cervione
Pruneté
Ísola di
Montecristo
Étang
de Diane
Cateraggio
Aléria
Étang
d'Urbino
Ghisonaccia
Étang
de Palo

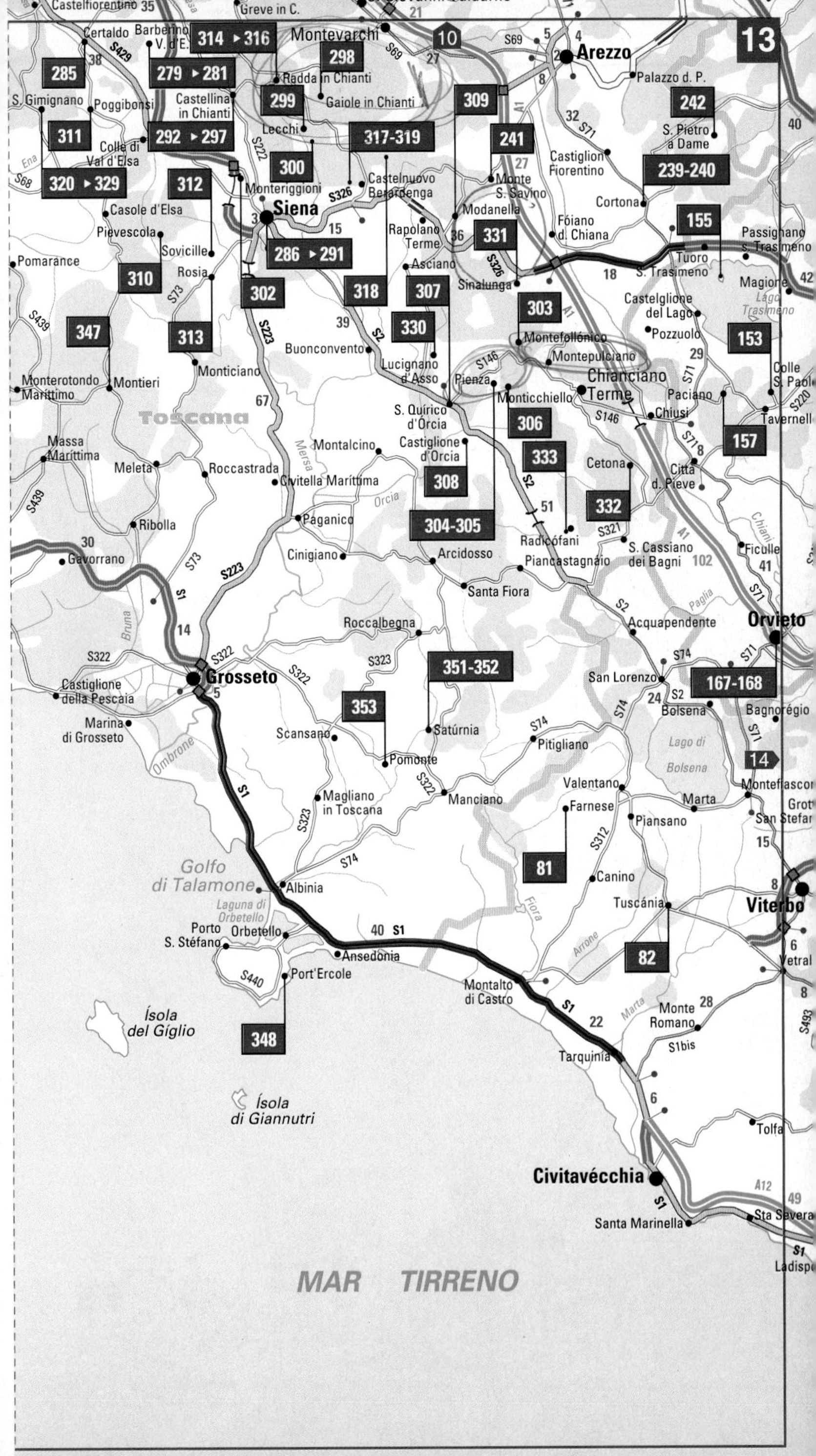

13
Arezzo
Siena
Grosseto
Orvieto
Viterbo
Civitavécchia
Montevarchi
S. Giovanni Valdarno
Greve in C.
Castelfiorentino
Certaldo
Barberino V. d'E.
S. Gimignano
Poggibonsi
Castellina in Chianti
Radda in Chianti
Gaiole in Chianti
Lecchi
Colle di Val d'Elsa
Monteriggioni
Castelnuovo Berardenga
Casole d'Elsa
Pievescola
Sovicille
Rosia
Pomarance
Rapolano Terme
Asciano
Sinalunga
Modanella
Monte S. Savino
Castiglion Fiorentino
Fóiano d. Chiana
Cortona
Palazzo d. P.
S. Pietro a Dame
Passignano s. Trasimeno
Tuoro s. Trasimeno
Magione
Lago Trasimeno
Castelglione del Lago
Pozzuolo
Montefollónico
Montepulciano
Chianciano Terme
Paciano
Colle S. Paolo
Tavernelle
Chiusi
Città d. Pieve
Cetona
Buonconvento
Lucignano d'Asso
Pienza
Monticchiello
S. Quírico d'Órcia
Castiglione d'Orcia
Montalcino
Monticiano
Montieri
Monterotondo Maríttimo
Toscana
Massa Maríttima
Meleta
Roccastrada
Civitella Maríttima
Paganico
Ribolla
Gavorrano
Cinigiano
Arcidosso
Santa Fiora
Radicófani
Piancastagnaio
S. Cassiano dei Bagni
Ficulle
Acquapendente
Roccalbegna
San Lorenzo
Bolsena
Lago di Bolsena
Bagnorégio
Castiglione della Pescaia
Marina di Grosseto
Scansano
Satúrnia
Pomonte
Pitigliano
Valentano
Farnese
Marta
Piansano
Montefiascone
San Stefano
Manciano
Magliano in Toscana
Golfo di Talamone
Albinia
Laguna di Orbetello
Orbetello
Porto S. Stéfano
Ansedonia
Port'Ercole
Canino
Tuscánia
Montalto di Castro
Monte Romano
Tarquinia
Vetralla
Tolfa
Santa Marinella
Sta Severa
Ladispoli
Ísola del Gíglio
Ísola di Giannutri
MAR TIRRENO
314 ▸ 316
298
285
279 ▸ 281
299
309
242
311
292 ▸ 297
317-319
241
300
320 ▸ 329
312
239-240
155
331
286 ▸ 291
310
302
318
307
303
347
313
330
153
306
157
333
308
332
304-305
351-352
167-168
353
14
81
82
348
10

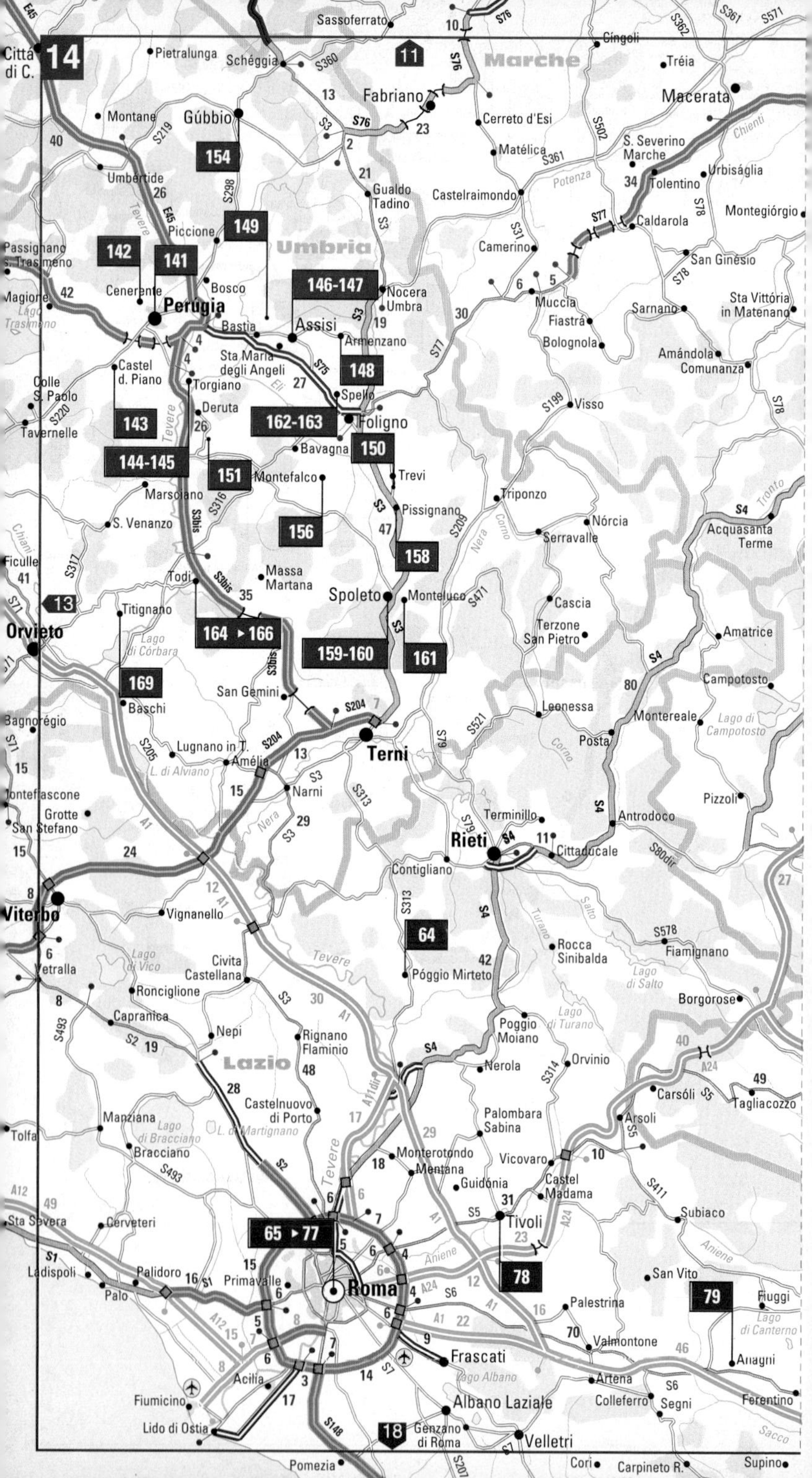

14
11
13
18
Marche
Umbria
Lazio
Città di C.
Pietralunga
Schéggia
Sassoferrato
Fabriano
Cingoli
Tréia
Macerata
Montane
Gúbbio
Cerreto d'Esi
Matélica
S. Severino Marche
Umbértide
Gualdo Tadino
Castelraimondo
Tolentino
Urbiságlia
Caldarola
Montegiórgio
Piccione
Camerino
San Ginesio
Passignano s. Trasimeno
Cenerente
Bosco
Nocera Umbra
Muccia
Magione
Lago Trasimeno
Perúgia
Bastia
Assisi
Sarnano
Sta Vittória in Matenano
Fiastrá
Bolognola
Armenzano
Sta Maria degli Angeli
Castel d. Piano
Amándola
Comunanza
Colle S. Paolo
Torgiano
Spello
Visso
Deruta
Foligno
Tavernelle
Bavagna
Trevi
Montefalco
Marsciano
Triponzo
Pissignano
S. Venanzo
Nórcia
Serravalle
Acquasanta Terme
Ficulle
Massa Martana
Todi
Spoleto
Monteluco
Cascia
Titignano
Orvieto
Lago di Córbara
Terzone San Pietro
Amatrice
Campotosto
San Gemini
Leonessa
Baschi
Montereale
Lago di Campotosto
Bagnorégio
Terni
Posta
Lugnano in T.
Amélia
L. di Alviano
Narni
Montefiascone
Pizzoli
Grotte S. Stefano
Terminillo
Antrodoco
Rieti
Cittaducale
Contigliano
Viterbo
Vignanello
Rocca Sinibalda
Fiamignano
Civita Castellana
Póggio Mirteto
Vetralla
Lago di Vico
Lago di Salto
Ronciglione
Borgorose
Capranica
Nepi
Rignano Flaminio
Poggio Moiano
Lago di Turano
Nerola
Orvinio
Castelnuovo di Porto
Carsóli
Tagliacozzo
Manziana
Lago di Bracciano
L. di Martignano
Arsoli
Tolfa
Bracciano
Palombara Sabina
Monterotondo
Mentana
Vicovaro
Castel Madama
Guidónia
Sta Severa
Cerveteri
Tivoli
Subiaco
Roma
Ladispoli
Palidoro
Palo
Primavalle
San Vito
Palestrina
Fiuggi
Lago di Canterno
Valmontone
Frascati
Anagni
Acilia
Lago Albano
Artena
Fiumicino
Colleferro
Segni
Albano Laziale
Ferentino
Lido di Ostia
Genzano di Roma
Velletri
Pomezia
Cori
Carpineto R.
Supino
Tevere
Chienti
Potenza
Nera
Corno
Tronto
Salto
Turano
Aniene
Sacco
Chiani
Eli
154
149
142
141
146-147
148
143
162-163
144-145
151
150
156
158
164 ▸ 166
159-160
161
169
64
65 ▸ 77
78
79
E45
A1
A12
A24
A1dir
S3
S3bis
S4
S5
S6
S7
S76
S77
S78
S75
S204
S2
S1

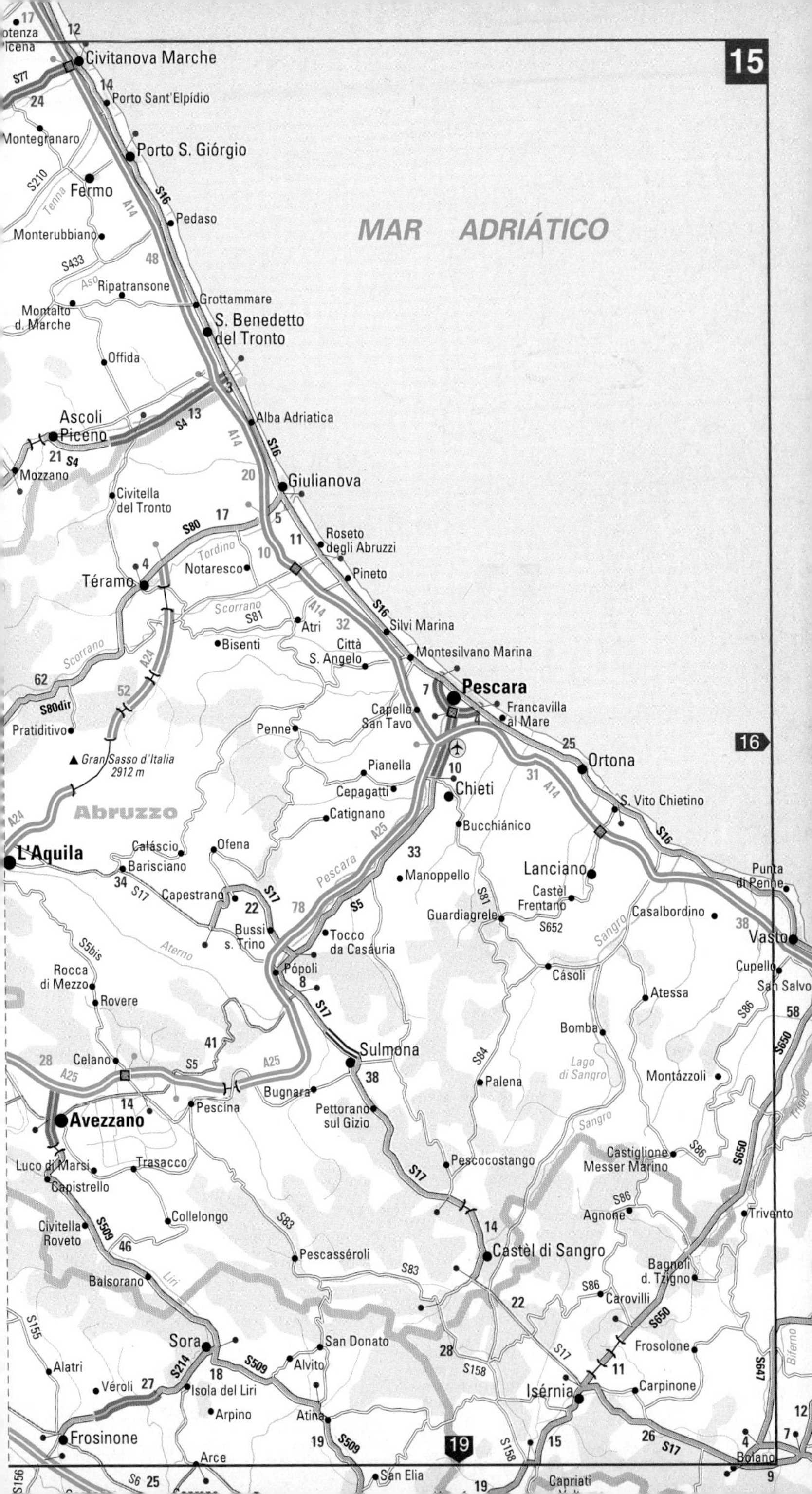
MAR ADRIÁTICO
Civitanova Marche
Porto Sant'Elpídio
Montegranaro
Porto S. Giórgio
Fermo
Pedaso
Monterubbiano
Ripatransone
Grottammare
Montalto d. Marche
S. Benedetto del Tronto
Offida
Ascoli Piceno
Alba Adriatica
Mozzano
Giulianova
Civitella del Tronto
Roseto degli Abruzzi
Notaresco
Pineto
Téramo
Atri
Silvi Marina
Bisenti
Città S. Angelo
Montesilvano Marina
Pescara
Francavilla al Mare
Capelle San Tavo
Penne
Pratiditivo
Gran Sasso d'Italia 2912 m
Ortona
Pianella
Cepagatti
Chieti
S. Vito Chietino
Abruzzo
Catignano
Bucchiánico
L'Aquila
Caláscio
Ofena
Barisciano
Manoppello
Lanciano
Punta di Penne
Capestrano
Castèl Frentano
Guardiagrele
Casalbordino
Bussi s. Trino
Tocco da Casáuria
Vasto
Pópoli
Cásoli
Cupello
San Salvo
Rocca di Mezzo
Rovere
Atessa
Bomba
Celano
Sulmona
Lago di Sangro
Palena
Montázzoli
Bugnara
Avezzano
Pescina
Pettorano sul Gizio
Castiglione Messer Marino
Luco di Marsi
Trasacco
Capistrello
Pescocostango
Collelongo
Agnone
Trivento
Civitella Roveto
Castèl di Sangro
Pescasséroli
Bagnoli d. Tzigno
Balsorano
Carovilli
Sora
San Donato
Frosolone
Alvito
Alatri
Véroli
Isola del Liri
Isérnia
Carpinone
Arpino
Atina
Frosinone
Arce
Bolano
San Elia
Capriati
Tenna
Aso
Tordino
Scorrano
Pescara
Aterno
Sangro
Trigno
Liri
Biferno
A14
A24
A25
S16
S77
S210
S433
S4
S80
S80dir
S81
S5
S5bis
S17
S652
S84
S86
S650
S83
S509
S155
S214
S158
S156
S6
S647
16
19

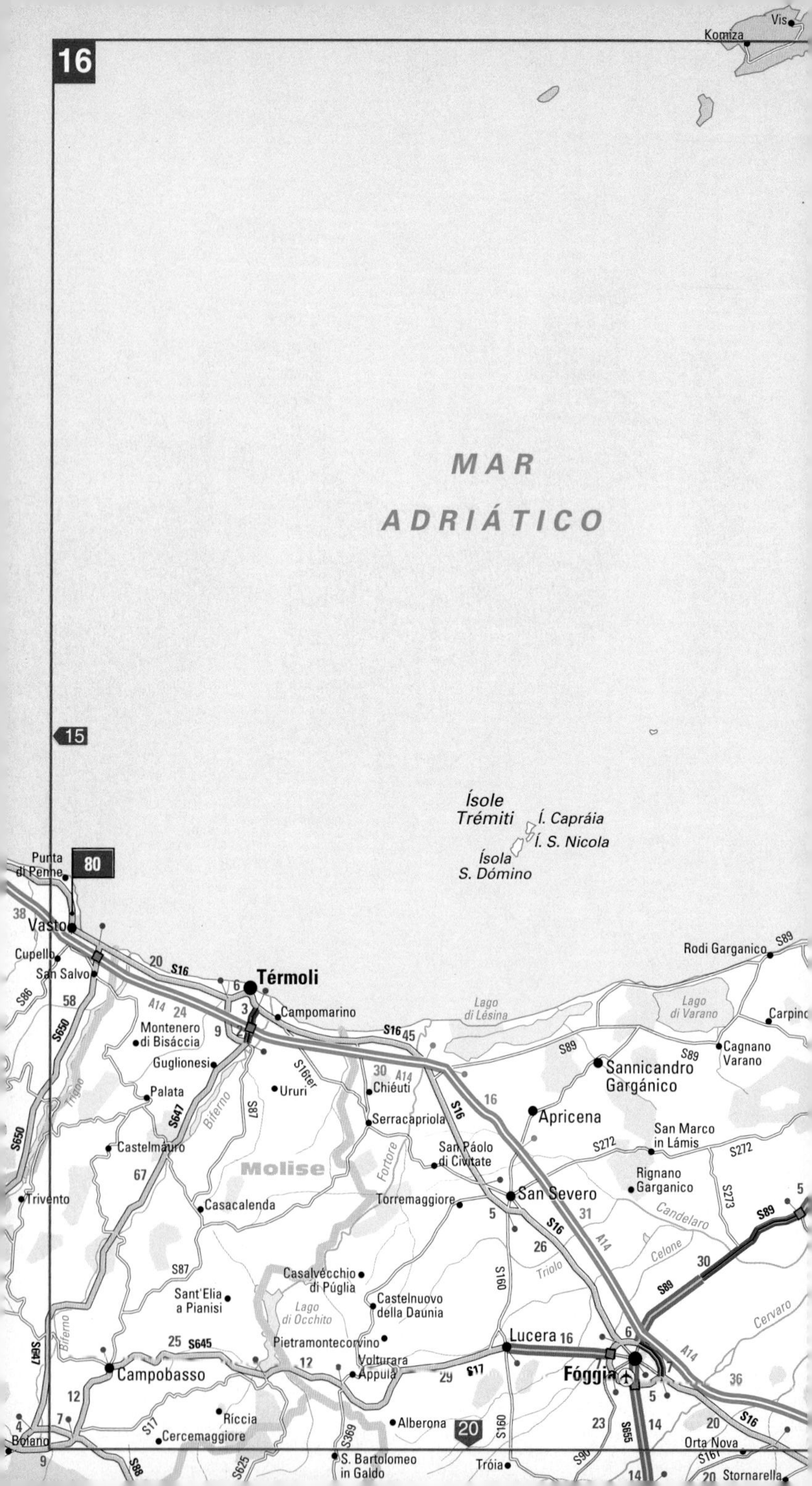

Vis
Komiza

MAR ADRIÁTICO

15

Ísole Trémiti
Í. Capráia
Í. S. Nicola
Ísola S. Dómino

80

Punta di Penne
Vasto
Cupello
San Salvo
Térmoli
Campomarino
Montenero di Bisáccia
Guglionesi
Palata
Ururi
Chiéuti
Serracapriola
Castelmauro
Molise
San Páolo di Civitate
Trivento
Casacalenda
Torremaggiore
San Severo
Rodi Garganico
Lago di Lésina
Lago di Varano
Carpino
Cagnano Varano
Sannicandro Gargánico
Apricena
San Marco in Lámis
Rignano Garganico
Candelaro
Celone
Triolo
Cervaro
Trigno
Biferno
Fortore
Casalvécchio di Púglia
Sant'Elia a Pianisi
Lago di Occhito
Castelnuovo della Daunia
Pietramontecorvino
Lucera
Campobasso
Volturara Appula
Fóggia
Ríccia
Cercemaggiore
Alberona
Bolano
S. Bartolomeo in Galdo
Tróia
Orta Nova
Stornarella

20

A14 S16 S16ter S86 S87 S89 S90 S160 S161 S272 S273 S369 S625 S645 S647 S650 S655 S17 S88

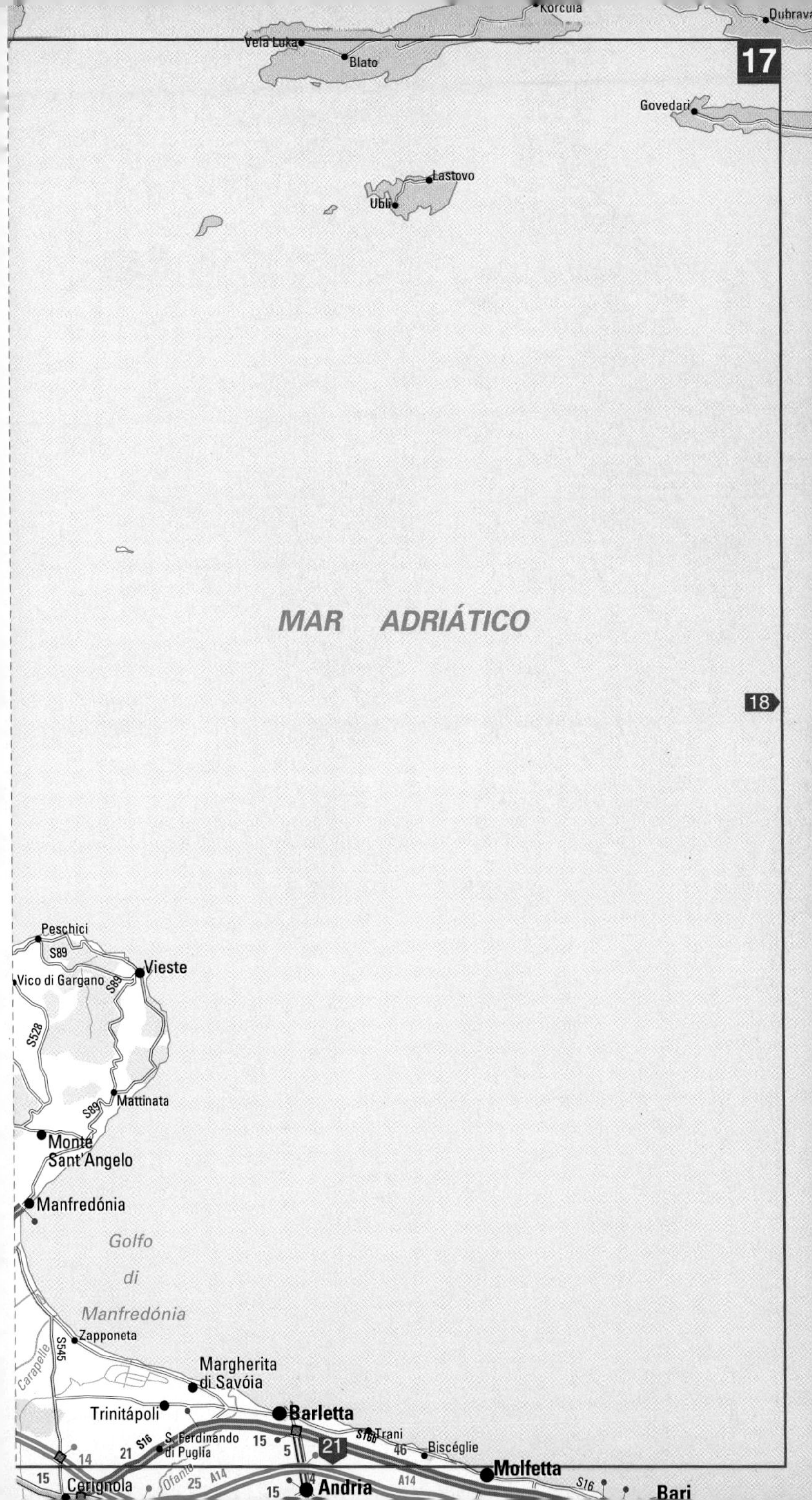
Korčula
Dubrava
Vela Luka
Blato
17
Govedari
Lastovo
Ubli
MAR ADRIÁTICO
18
Peschici
S89
Vieste
Vico di Gargano
S528
Mattinata
Monte Sant'Angelo
Manfredónia
Golfo di Manfredónia
Zapponeta
S545
Carapelle
Margherita di Savóia
Trinitápoli
Barletta
Trani
S160
S16
S. Ferdinando di Puglia
Biscéglie
21
Molfetta
A14
Ofanto
Cerignola
Andria
Bari

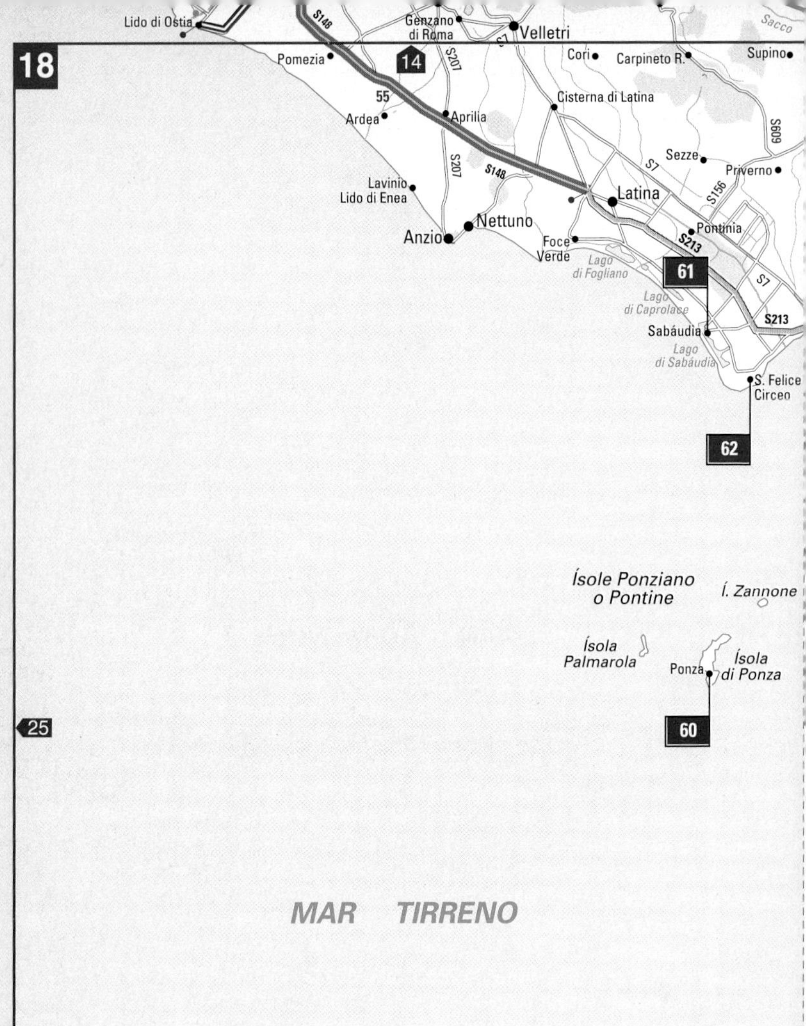

Lido di Ostia
Genzano di Roma
Velletri
Sacco
Pomezia
14
S207
Cori
Carpineto R.
Supino
S148
55
Cisterna di Latina
Ardea
Aprilia
S609
S207
Sezze
S7
Priverno
S148
Lavinio
Lido di Enea
S156
Latina
Nettuno
Pontinia
Anzio
S213
Foce Verde
Lago di Fogliano
61
S7
Lago di Caprolace
S213
Sabáudia
Lago di Sabáudia
S. Felice Circeo
62
Ísole Ponziano o Pontine
Í. Zannone
Ísola Palmarola
Ponza
Ísola di Ponza
60
25
MAR TIRRENO

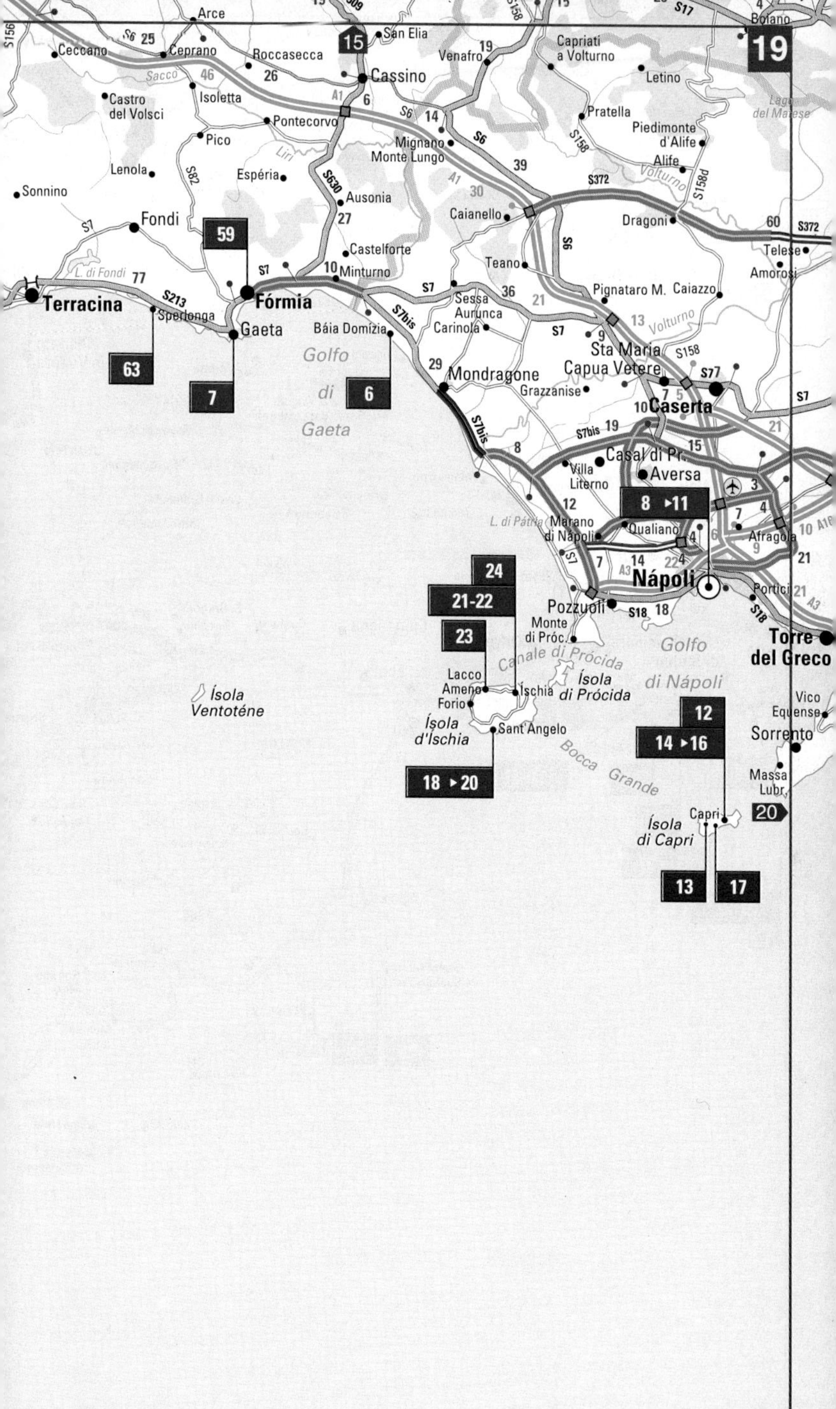

Frosinone
Arce
S6
Ceccano
Ceprano
Roccasecca
Sacco
15
San Elia
Cassino
Venafro
Capriati
a Volturno
19
Letino
Castro
del Volsci
Isoletta
A1
Pontecorvo
Pico
Liri
Pratella
Piedimonte
d'Alife
Lago
del Matese
Mignano
Monte Lungo
Alife
Volturno
Lenola
S82
Espéria
S630
Ausonia
S372
S158d
Sonnino
Caianello
Dragoni
Fondi
59
Castelforte
Telese
Amorosi
S7
L. di Fondi
Minturno
Teano
Pignataro M.
Caiazzo
Terracina
S213
Sperlonga
Fórmia
Gaeta
Sessa
Aurunca
Carinola
S7bis
Báia Domízia
Sta Maria
Capua Vetere
S158
S77
Golfo
di
Gaeta
63
7
6
Mondragone
Grazzanise
Caserta
S7bis
Casal di Pr.
Villa
Literno
Aversa
8 ▸11
L. di Pátria
Marano
di Nápoli
Qualiano
Afragola
A3
Nápoli
24
21-22
23
Pozzuoli
S18
Portici
Monte
di Próc.
Torre
del Greco
Canale di Prócida
Golfo
di Nápoli
Ísola
di Prócida
Lacco
Ameno
Forio
Íschia
Ísola
Ventotène
Ísola
d'Ischia
Sant'Angelo
12
14 ▸16
Vico
Equense
Sorrento
Bocca Grande
18 ▸20
Massa
Lubr.
Capri
20
Ísola
di Capri
13
17

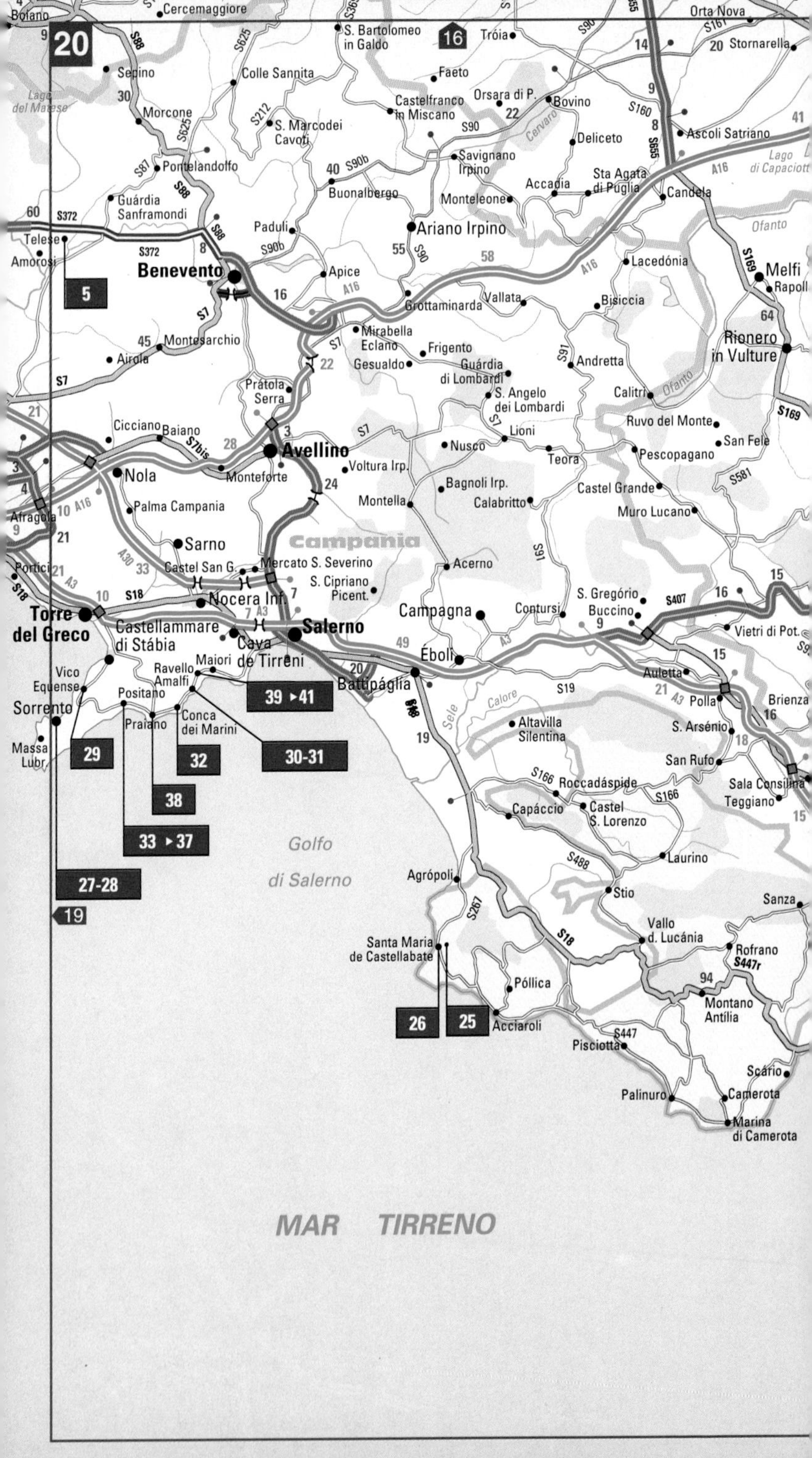
20
16
Bojano
Cercemaggiore
S. Bartolomeo in Galdo
Tróia
Orta Nova
Stornarella
Sepino
Lago del Matese
Colle Sannita
Faeto
Morcone
S. Marcodei Cavoti
Castelfranco in Miscano
Orsara di P.
Bovino
Deliceto
Ascoli Satriano
Lago di Capaciotti
Pontelandolfo
Savignano Irpino
Buonalbergo
Accadia
Sta Agata di Puglia
Candela
Guárdia Sanframondi
Monteleone
Paduli
Ariano Irpino
Ofanto
Telese
Amorosi
Benevento
Apice
Lacedónia
Melfi
Rapolla
5
Vallata
Grottaminarda
Bisiccia
Montesarchio
Mirabella Eclano
Frigento
Rionero in Vulture
Airola
Gesualdo
Guárdia di Lombardi
Andretta
Prátola Serra
S. Angelo dei Lombardi
Calitri
Ruvo del Monte
Cicciano
Baiano
Lioni
San Fele
Avellino
Nusco
Teora
Pescopagano
Nola
Monteforte
Voltura Irp.
Bagnoli Irp.
Castel Grande
Palma Campania
Montella
Calabritto
Muro Lucano
Afragola
Campania
Sarno
Portici
Castel San G.
Mercato S. Severino
Acerno
S. Cipriano Picent.
Nocera Inf.
S. Gregório
Buccino
Torre del Greco
Campagna
Contursi
Castellammare di Stábia
Cava de Tirreni
Salerno
Vietri di Pot.
Vico Equense
Ravello
Maiori
Amalfi
Éboli
Battipáglia
Auletta
Positano
Polla
Brienza
Sorrento
Praiano
Conca dei Marini
Altavilla Silentina
S. Arsénio
Massa Lubr.
39 ▸41
29
32
30-31
San Rufo
Sala Consilina
Roccadáspide
Teggiano
38
Capáccio
Castel S. Lorenzo
33 ▸ 37
Golfo di Salerno
Laurino
27-28
Agrópoli
Stio
19
Sanza
Vallo d. Lucánia
Santa Maria de Castellabate
Rofrano
Póllica
Montano Antília
26
25
Acciaroli
Pisciotta
Scário
Palinuro
Camerota
Marina di Camerota
MAR TIRRENO

Bari
Molfetta
Andria
Cerignola
Canosa di Púglia
Corato
Ruvo di Puglia
Terlizzi
Bitonto
Modugno
Palo del C.
Bitetto
Mariotto
Grumo Appúla
Toritto
Sannicandro di Bari
Casamássima
Capurso
Mola di Bari
Conversano
Trani
Biscéglie
S. Ferdinando di Puglia
Minervino Murge
Puglia
Acquaviva delle Fonti
Sammichele
Cassano del Murge
Gióia del Colle
Lavello
Spinazzola
Venosa
Poggiorsini
Palazza S. Gervásio
Altamura
Santéramo in Colle
Ripacámida
Genzano di Lucánia
Gravina in Puglia
Forenza
Acerenza
Irsina
Mottola
Castellaneta
Matera
Laterza
Oppido Lucano
Bradano
Lago di Giuliano
Ginosa
Avigliano
Tolve
Bilioso
Tricárico
Grassano
Grottole
Miglionico
Potenza
Basento
Montescaglioso
Albano di Luc.
Calciano
Garaguso
Ferrandina
Tito
Anzi
Accettura
S. Máuro Forte
Bernalda
Liolo di Metaponto
Calvello
Laurenzana
Pisticci
Craco
Cavone
Basilicata
Stigliano
Montalbano Jónico
Guárdia
Scanzano
Viggiano
L. di Pietra d. Pertusillo
Agri
Tursi
Policoro
Tramútola
Sinni
Rotondella
Valsinni
Montesano s. Marcellana
Moliterno
S. Chírico Raparo
Senise
Rocca Imperiale
Teana
Chiaromonte
Latrónico
Francavilla in Sinni
Oriolo
Montegiordano
Sapri
Rivello
Lauria
San Severino
Castelluccio
Marina di Amendolara
Maratea
Rotonda
Golfo di Policastro
Trebisacce
Cerchiara di Cal.
Mormanno
Frascineto
Praia a Mare
Morano Cal.
Castrovillari
Cassano Allo Ionio
Le Vigne
Sibari
Scalea
Lao
Coscile
Crati
Marina Schiavonea
Mirto Crosia
Altomonte
Spezzano Albanese
Corigliano Calabro
Rossano
Trionto
Diamante
Roggiano Gravina
Tarsia
Belvedere Marittimo
Bisignano
Acri
Longo-
Ofanto
A14
A16
A3
S16
S93
S97
S170
S98
S378
S96
S100
S172
S171
S96b
S169
S7
S407
S175
S106
S277
S92
S103
S598
D653
S653
S481
S19
S18
S585
S534
S106b
S106r
S560
S177
4
1
3
17
22
24

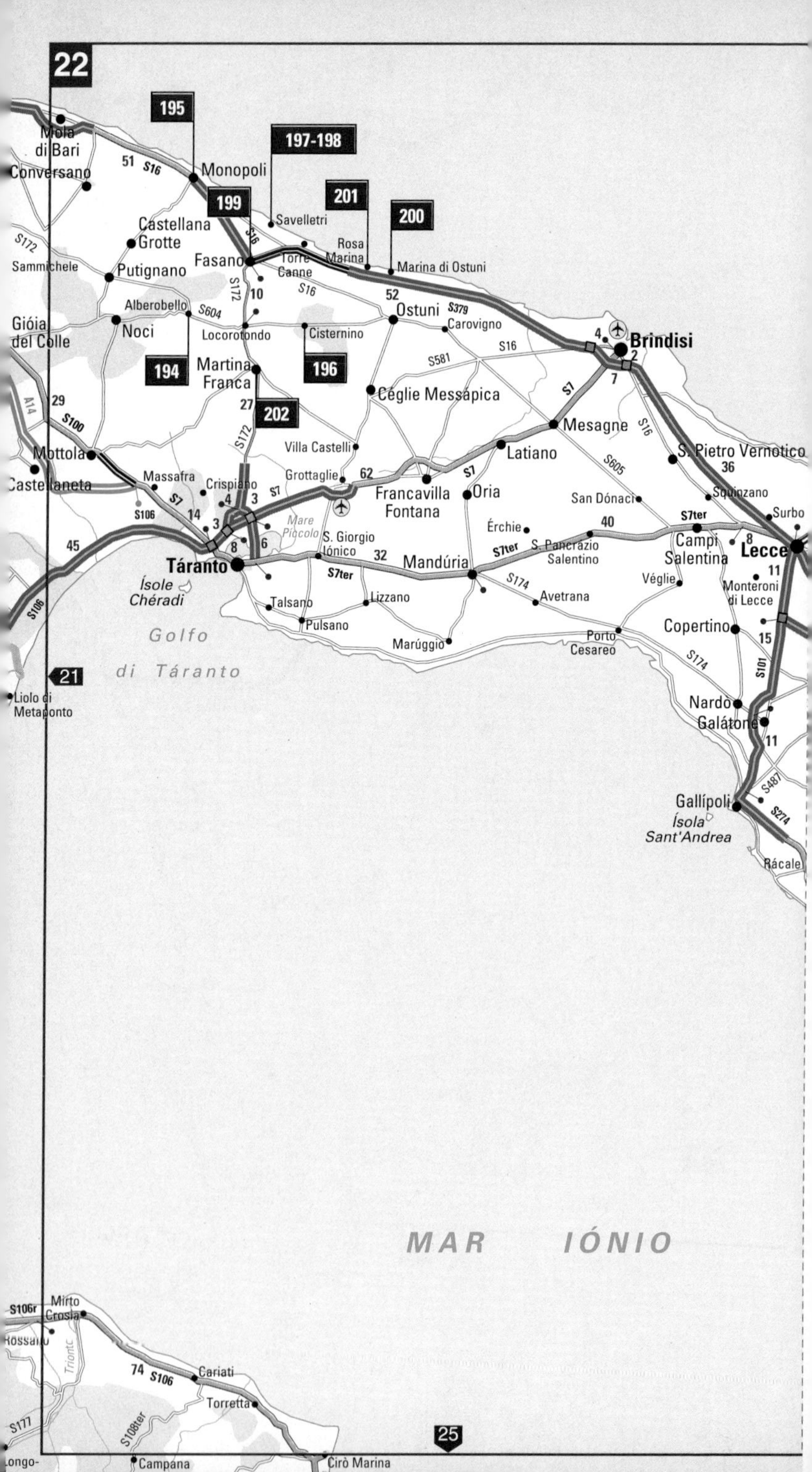
195
197-198
201
200
199
194
196
202
Mola di Bari
Conversano
Monopoli
Savelletri
Castellana Grotte
Rosa Marina
Marina di Ostuni
Fasano
Torre Canne
Sammichele
Putignano
Alberobello
Noci
Gióia del Colle
Locorotondo
Cisternino
Ostuni
Carovigno
Brindisi
Martina Franca
Céglie Messapica
Mesagne
Mottola
Castellaneta
Massafra
Crispiano
Villa Castelli
Grottaglie
Latiano
S. Pietro Vernotico
Francavilla Fontana
Oria
San Dónaci
Squinzano
Surbo
Mare Piccolo
S. Giorgio Iónico
Érchie
S. Pancrazio Salentino
Campi Salentina
Lecce
Táranto
Mandúria
Véglie
Monteroni di Lecce
Ísole Chéradi
Talsano
Lizzano
Avetrana
Pulsano
Marúggio
Porto Cesareo
Copertino
Golfo di Táranto
21
Liolo di Metaponto
Nardo
Galátone
Gallípoli
Ísola Sant'Andrea
Rácale
MAR IÓNIO
Mirto Crosia
Rossano
Trionto
Cariati
Torretta
Campana
Cirò Marina
Longo-
25
S16
S172
S604
S379
S581
S7
S16
S100
A14
S106
S605
S7ter
S174
S101
S487
S274
S106r
S177
S108ter

ALBANIA

Novosele

Vlore

MAR ADRIÁTICO

24

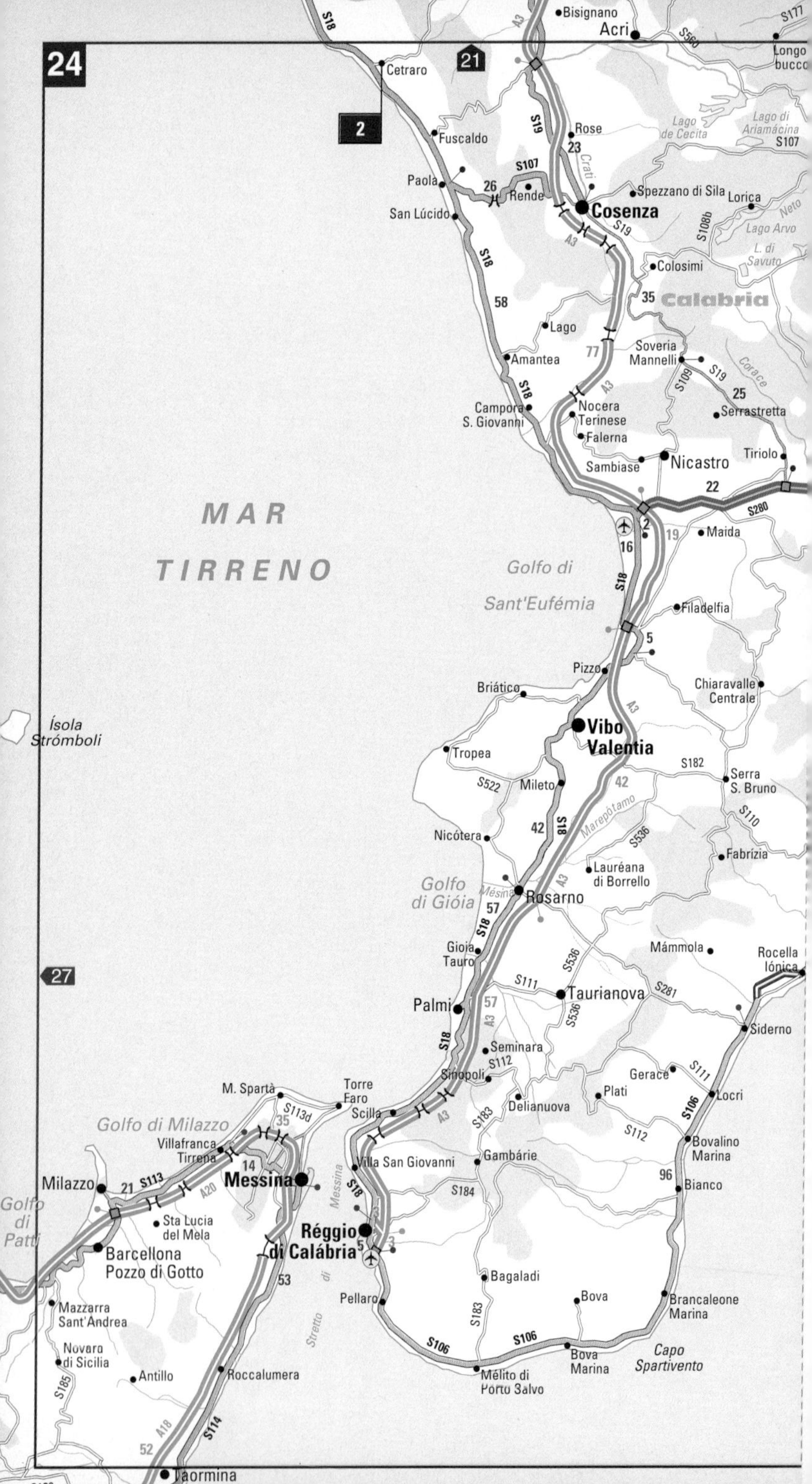

21
2
27
MAR
TIRRENO
Calabria
Bisignano
Acri
Longo bucco
Cetraro
Fuscaldo
Rose
Lago de Cecita
Lago di Ariamàcina
Paola
Rende
Cosenza
Spezzano di Sila
Lorica
San Lúcido
Lago Arvo
L. di Savuto
Colosimi
Lago
Amantea
Soveria Mannelli
Serrastretta
Campora S. Giovanni
Nocera Terinese
Falerna
Sambiase
Nicastro
Tiriolo
Maida
Golfo di Sant'Eufémia
Filadelfia
Pizzo
Briático
Chiaravalle Centrale
Vibo Valentia
Tropea
Mileto
Serra S. Bruno
Nicótera
Fabrízia
Lauréana di Borrello
Golfo di Gióia
Rosarno
Gioia Tauro
Mámmola
Rocella Iónica
Palmi
Taurianova
Siderno
Seminara
Sinopoli
Gerace
Locri
Delianuova
Platì
M. Spartà
Torre Faro
Scilla
Golfo di Milazzo
Villafranca Tirrena
Messina
Villa San Giovanni
Gambárie
Bovalino Marina
Milazzo
Bianco
Golfo di Patti
Sta Lucia del Mela
Réggio di Calábria
Barcellona Pozzo di Gotto
Bagaladi
Bova
Brancaleone Marina
Pellaro
Mazzarra Sant'Andrea
Novara di Sicilia
Antillo
Roccalumera
Mélito di Porto Salvo
Bova Marina
Capo Spartivento
Stretto di Messina
Taormina
Ísola Strómboli
Crati
Neto
Corace
Marepótamo
Mésima
S18
S19
S107
S177
S560
S108b
S109
S280
S522
S182
S110
S536
S111
S281
S112
S113
S113d
S183
S184
S106
S114
S185
A3
A18
A20

Torretta
S108ter
Campana
Cirò Marina
22
Savelli
Pallagorio
S492
S106
Vitravo
S. Giovanni in Fiore
Lago Ampollino
S107
S107
Neto
S179
Cotronei
Crotone
Petília Policastro
Tácina
11
Capo Colonna
Mesoraca
S109
Cutro
25
Taverna
Sersale
Isola di Capo Rizzuto
S109
S180
36
S106
Capo Rizzuto
S179b
Capo Rizzuto
S106
8
Catanzaro
12
S280
Corace
S384
Catanzaro Lido
Squillace
Golfo di Squillace
Staletti
Soverato
S106
47
Badolato
Stilo
S110
Monasterace Marina
S106
33
MAR IÓNIO

Ísola di Ústica

MAR TIRRENO

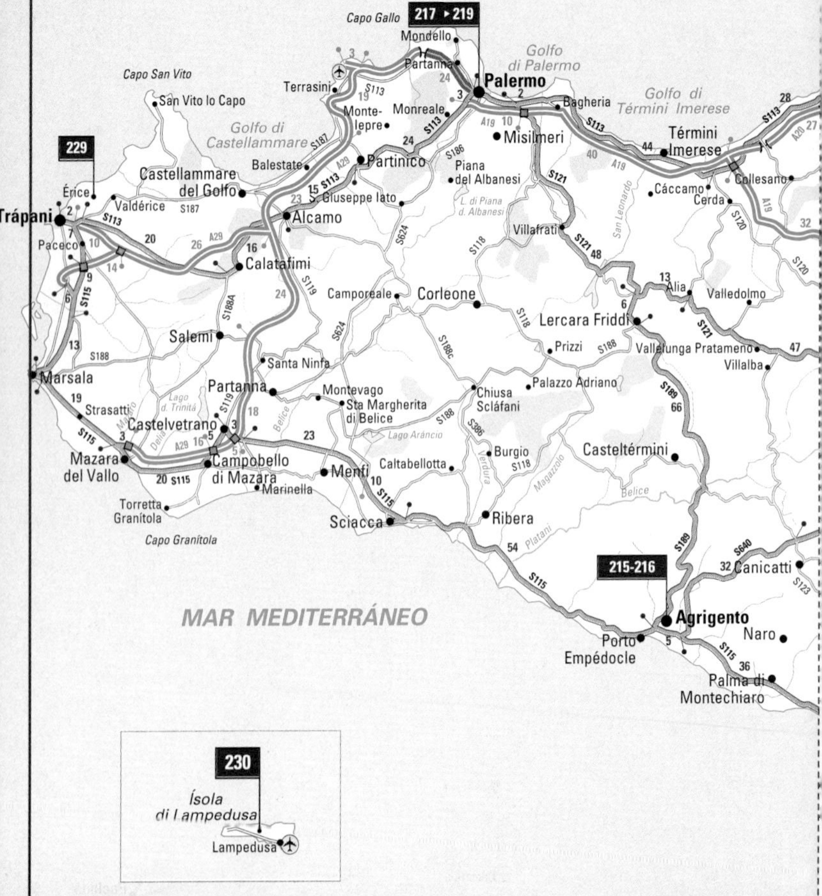

MAR TIRRENO
MAR IÓNIO
MAR MEDITERRÁNEO
Ísole Eolie o Lípari
Ísola Strómboli
Ísola Panarea
Ísola Salina
Ísola Filicudi
Ísola Alicudi
Ísola Lípari
Ísola Vulcano
Lípari
Pollara
Acquacalda
234
235
236-237
231 ▸ 233
238
24
222
223 ▸ 228
220-221
Messina
Réggio di Calábria
Milazzo
Golfo di Milazzo
Golfo di Patti
Villafranca Tirrena
M. Spartà
Torre Faro
Barcellona Pozzo di Gotto
Sta Lucia del Mela
Mazzarra Sant'Andrea
Novara di Sicilia
Antillo
Roccalumera
Pellaro
Gioiosa Marea
Capo d'Orlando
Castell'Umbrie
Sta Agata di Militello
Tortorici
Galati Mamertino
San Fratello
Caronía
Cefalù
Castèl di Tusa
Tusa
S. Stefano di Camastra
Mistretta
Castelbuono
Castel di Lúcio
Geraci Siculo
Gangi
Petralia Sottana
Nicosia
Troina
Cesarò
Randazzo
Taormina
Giardini -Naxos
Fiumefreddo di Sicilia
Giarre
Acireale
Trecastagni
Adrano
Belpasso
Paternó
Mascalucia
Misterbianco
Catánia
Golfo di Catánia
Lago di Pozzillo
Simeto
Agira
Regalbuto
Catenanuova
Leonforte
Alimena
Resuttano
Enna
Sta Caterina Villarmosa
Valguarnera
Grottacalda
Caltanissetta
Raddusa
Ramacca
Piazza Armerina
Barrafranca
Mirabella Imbàccari
Militello in Val di Cat.
Palagonia
Lentini
Augusta
Golfo di Augusta
Francofonte
Melilli
Priolo Gargallo
Sortino
Siracusa
Floridia
Buccheri
Délia
Mazzarino
Caltagirone
Grammichele
Campobello di Licata
Niscemi
Palazzolo Acréide
Licata
Golfo di Gela
Gela
Acate
Cómiso
Vittória
Ragusa
Noto
Avola
Golfo di Noto
Módica
Rosolini
Ispica
S. Croce Camerina
Scicli
Marina di Ragusa
Capo Scaramia
Pozzallo
Pachino
Portopalo

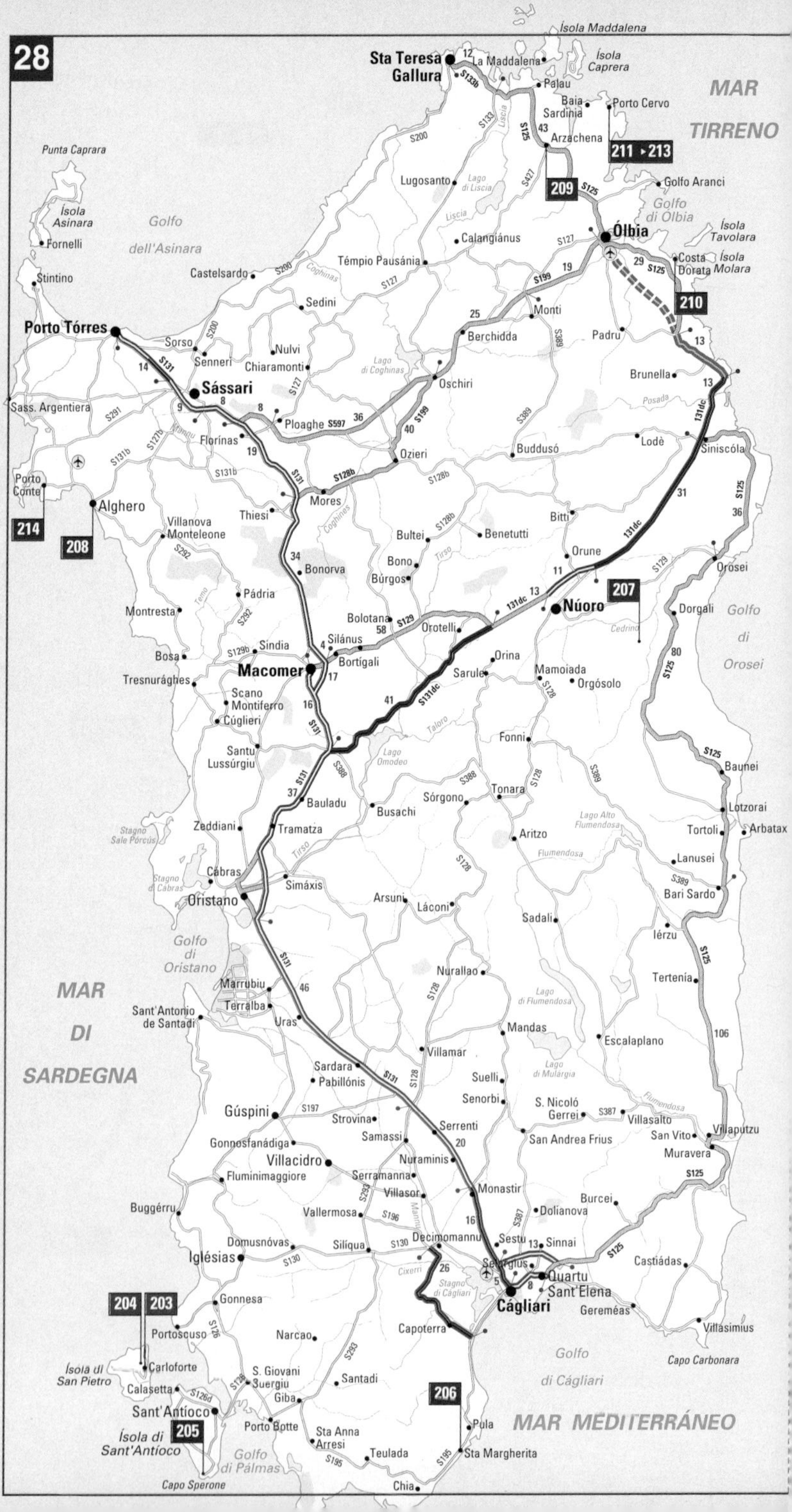

28

Ísola Maddalena
Sta Teresa Gallura
La Maddalena
Ísola Caprera
Palau
MAR TIRRENO
Baia Sardinia
Porto Cervo
Arzachena
211 ▸ 213
Punta Caprara
Lugosanto
Lago di Liscia
209
Golfo Aranci
Golfo di Olbia
Ísola Asinara
Golfo dell'Asinara
Fornelli
Calangiánus
Ólbia
Ísola Tavolara
Témpio Pausánia
Costa Dorata
Ísola Molara
Stintino
Castelsardo
Sedini
210
Monti
Porto Tórres
Sorso
Senneri
Nulvi
Chiaramonti
Lago di Coghinas
Berchidda
Padru
Sássari
Oschiri
Brunella
Sass. Argentiera
Ploaghe
Posada
Florínas
Ozieri
Buddusó
Lodè
Siniscóla
Porto Conte
Alghero
214
208
Mores
Thiesi
Villanova Monteleone
Bultei
Benetutti
Bitti
Bono
Bonorva
Búrgos
Orune
Pádria
Orosei
Montresta
207
Bolotana
Núoro
Dorgali
Golfo di Orosei
Silánus
Orotelli
Sindia
Bosa
Bortígali
Orina
Macomer
Sarule
Mamoiada
Orgósolo
Tresnurághes
Scano Montiferro
Cúglieri
Santu Lussúrgiu
Lago Omodeo
Fonni
Baunei
Bauladu
Sórgono
Tonara
Busachi
Lotzorai
Zeddiani
Tramatza
Lago Alto Flumendosa
Tortolì
Arbatax
Stagno Sale Porcus
Aritzo
Lanusei
Cábras
Stagno di Cabras
Simáxis
Bari Sardo
Oristano
Arsuni
Láconi
Sadali
Golfo di Oristano
Iérzu
Nurallao
Tertenía
MAR DI SARDEGNA
Marrubiu
Terralba
Lago di Flumendosa
Sant'Antonio de Santadi
Uras
Mandas
Escalaplano
Villamar
Sardara
Pabillónis
Suelli
Lago di Mulárgia
Senorbì
S. Nicoló Gerrei
Villasalto
Gúspini
Strovina
Serrenti
San Andrea Frius
San Vito
Villaputzu
Samassi
Muravera
Gonnosfanádiga
Nuraminis
Villacidro
Fluminimaggiore
Serramanna
Villasor
Monastir
Burcei
Buggérru
Vallermosa
Dolianova
Domusnóvas
Sílíqua
Decimomannu
Sestu
Sinnai
Iglésias
Cixerri
Selargius
Quartu
Castiádas
Stagno di Cágliari
Sant'Elena
Cágliari
Gereméas
204 203
Gonnesa
Capoterra
Villasimius
Portoscuso
Narcao
Capo Carbonara
Golfo di Cágliari
Ísola di San Pietro
Carloforte
S. Giovani Suergiu
Santadi
Calasetta
Giba
206
Sant'Antíoco
205
Pula
MAR MEDITERRÁNEO
Ísola di Sant'Antíoco
Porto Botte
Sta Anna Arresi
Teulada
Sta Margherita
Golfo di Pálmas
Capo Sperone
Chia

Hotel Barbieri

Via San Nicola, 30
87042 Altomonte (Cosenza)
Tel. (0)981-94 80 72 - Fax (0)981-94 80 73 - Sig. Barbieri
Web: http://www.telsa.it/mercato/barbieri:barbieri./it

Category ★★★ **Rooms** 30 with air-conditioning, telephone, shower, WC, minibar and TV. **Price** Single 75,000L, double 130,000L. **Meals** Breakfast included, served 6:30-10:00; half board 100,000L, full board 1320,000L (per pers., 3 days min.). **Restaurant** Service 12:30-15:00, 19:30-23:00; menus 65-75,000L. Specialties: Pasta fatta in casa, funghi, salumi tipici, legumi. **Credit cards** All major. **Pets** Dogs allowed. **Facilities** Swimming pool in casa Barbieri, tennis (5,000L), parking. **Nearby** Altomonte (with Cathedral tomb of Filippo Sangineto XIVe and "Saint Ladislas" attributed to Simone Martini), excursions to Monte Pollino from Castrovillari, old Calabrian villages (Stilo, Sibari and Paola as well as Altomonte). **Open** All year.

Behind the unprepossing facade of this hotel hides one of the best restaurants in Calabria. You can savor excellent regional dishes while enjoying a marvelous view of the town of Altomonte, a vista framed by a fifteenth-century monastery and splendid houses. Italian-style breakfast is a real delight. You can, if you like, have it by the shores of Lago del Fareto: the first bite of your day will be delicious if you have the warm ricotta cheese on lightly toasted bread, topped with home-made berry confiture, also available in the gift shop next door. Rooms are spacious, pleasant and unpretentiously decorated (some have small balconies with great views). The hotel has a family atmosphere.

How to get there *(Map 21): 50 km north of Cosenza via A3, Altomonte exit.*

Grand Hotel San Michele

87022 Cetraro (Cosenza)
Tel. (0)982-91 012 - Fax (0)982-91 430
Sig.ra Siniscalchi
E-mail: sanmichele@antares.it

Category ★★★★ **Rooms** 73 with air-conditioning, telephone, bath or shower, WC and TV. **Price** Single 120-230,000L, double 190-350,000L, suite 250-450,000L. **Meals** Breakfast included, served 7:30-10:00; half board 160-270,000L, full board 180-290,000L (per pers., 3 days min.). **Restaurant** Service 13:00-14:30, 19:30-21:30, menu 40-60,000L, also à la carte. Specialties: Regional cooking. **Credit cards** All major. **Pets** Dogs allowed. **Facilities** Swimming pool, tennis, golf (40,000L) and private beach with restaurant service in summer. **Nearby** Old Calabrian villages (Stilo, Sibari, Paola, Altomonte). **Open** All year (except Nov.).

This enchanting turn-of-the-century villa, in a small beach resort on the Tyrrhenian Sea was built at the beginning of the century by the owner's father. Today it is a luxury hotel with many facilities and excellent service–it's one of the few places in Calabria with visible charm and personality. In addition to the well-decorated villa, there are several small houses on the 124-acre estate you can rent. Fresh produce for the hotel kitchen is grown on the property.

How to get there *(Map 24): 55 km northwest of Cosenza via A3, Lagonegro-North exit, towards Praia, then SS18 direction south.*

Locanda delle Donne Monache

Via Carlo Mazzei, 4
85046 Maratea (Potenza)
Tel. (0)973-87 74 87 - Fax (0)973-87 76 87
Sig. Raffaele Bruno

Category ★★★★ **Rooms** 30 and 6 suites with air-conditioning, telephone, bath and satellite TV, minibar. **Price** Single 150-255,000L, double 240-420,000L. **Meals** Breakfast included (buffet), served 7:30-10:00; half board 140-330,000L (per pers.). **Restaurant** Service 12:30-14:30, 20:00-23:00; à la carte. Specialties: Italian and regional cuisine. **Credit cards** All major. **Pets** Dogs not allowed **Facilities** Swimming pool, private beach, parking. **Nearby** Sanctuario Monte San Biagio, Rivello, S. Lorenzo in Padula, Monte Pollino. **Open** 1 week before Easter to end Oct..

This charming hotel between the mountains and the sea, is in Maratea, a village nestled in a cove on the Tyrrhenian coast. Once an old monastery in the center of the village, it has been completely refurbished and decorated with sobriety and elegance, except for the slightly Baroque-like lobby. The rooms, which have kept a monastic air, are very comfortable, with canopy beds and simple, tasteful furniture in the best tradition of modern Italian design. In front of the house there is a secluded garden with a nice swimming pool. The hotel's private beach is even better; a boat at your disposal can take you out to view the Gulf of Policastro. Those who prefer to go hiking and horseback riding will want to head for the back country: the Basicilata is mostly mountains and hills, with beautiful wildlife preserves.

How to get there *(Map 21): 176 km southeast of Salerno via A3, Lagonegro-North Maratea exit, S585 and Maratea.*

Hotel Sassi

Via San Giovanni Vecchio, 89
75100 Matera
Tel. (0)835-33 10 09 - Fax (0)835-33 37 33
Sig.ra Cristallo

Category ★★★ **Rooms** 12 with telephone, bath, WC, TV, minibar. **Price** Single 80,000L, double 140,000L, triple 190,000L. **Meals** Breakfast included, served 8:30-9:30. **Restaurant** See p. 438. **Credit cards** All major. **Pets** Dogs allowed. **Nearby** Les Sassi: Sassi road, le duome in Matera, Chiese rupestri on theTarento road. **Open** All year.

The main points of interest in Matera are the cave dwellings and shrines of Sasso Caveoso that have just been listed by UNESCO as a World Heritage site and the rock-hewn churches of the Basilian monks nearby. This little hotel has been installed by the Cristallo family in one of these ancient dwellings. It reflects all the architecture of Sassi: a succession of vaulted rooms on different levels, small terraces offering surprising views of the nearby Duomo. Although great care has been taken to preserve the typical look and feel of the place, the owners have in no way neglected modern comforts. No two rooms are alike, in size or appearance, but all are well-decorated and comfortable. For years the Italians used to represent Dante's "Inferno" as a kind of Sassi, inhabited by the wretched of the earth (as described by Carlo Levi in "Christ Stopped at Eboli"). Today the houses tend to be occupied by architects, intellectuals and hotels of charm.

How to get there *(Map 21): 67 km south of Bari.*

Grand Hotel Telese

Via Cerreto, 1
82037 Telese Terme (Benevento)
Tel. (0)824-94 05 00 - Fax (0)824-94 05 04
Sig. Montagna

Category ★★★★ **Rooms** 110 with telephone, bath or shower, WC, TV and minibar. **Price** Single 120,000L, double 205,000L, suite 386,000L. **Meals** Breakfast included, served 7:00-9:30; half board 110-140,000L, full board 130-150,000L. (per pers., 3 days min.). **Restaurant** Service 12:30-14:30, 19:30-21:30; à la carte. Specialties: Risotto con brocoli, agnello. **Credit cards** Amex, Visa, Eurocard, MasterCard. **Pets** Small dogs allowed. **Facilities** Swimming pool, tennis (8,000L), parking. **Nearby** Telesia, Faicchio, Cerreto Sannita, Benevento. **Open** All year.

The Grand Hotel Telese built at the turn of the century has preserved the old-fashioned charm typical of the spas of this resort town. Ouside, its neoclassical facade is chic. Inside, you will be impressed by the grand staircase, the beautiful ground-floor rooms with painted ceilings and the second-floor–Louis XV lounge. All the guest rooms are luxurious. The restaurant is in the cellar between the billiard and chess rooms. All in all, it would be a perfect hotel, except for its proximity to a highway, which sometimes disturbs the prevailing tranquility.

How to get there *(Map 20): 65 km north of Napoli via A1, Caserta-South exit, then S265 towards Maddaloni to Telese.*

Hotel Della Baia

Via dell' Erica
Baia Domizia - 81030 Cellole (Caserta)
Tel. (0)823-72 13 44 - Fax (0)823-72 15 56
Sig.ra Sello

Category ★★★★ **Rooms** 56 with telephone, bath or shower and WC. **Price** Single 85-105,000L, double 130-160,000L. **Meals** Breakfast 15,000L, served 7:30-9:30; half board 130-155,000L, full board 140-165,000L (per pers.). **Restaurant** Service 12:30-14:15, 19:30-21:00; menu: 50-60,000L, also à la carte. Specialties: Tonnarelli freddi con crema di trota affumicata, coquilles Saint-Jacques farcite di gamberi. **Credit cards** All major. **Pets** Small dogs allowed (except in the restaurant). **Facilities** Tennis (20,000L), parking. **Nearby** Gaeta, Caserta, Napoli, Pompeii. **Open** May 11 – Sept. 29.

Elsa, Imelde and Velja Sello are three charming sisters who have been running this hotel since the 1970s. After living in Venice and in Rome, they decided that this would now be their family home and have put into it all their sisterly care and attention. It is a modern Mediterranean-style building that stands with its white walls in the midst of a large green lawn planted with bamboo and many other exotic species. Both in the guest rooms and the public areas, the interior decoration is spare and meticulously done. Terra cotta and pastel colors create a fresh, summery appearance. Among other assets are the home-cooked meals and the proximity of the sea.

How to get there *(Map 19): 67 km northwest of Napoli. Via A1 (Rome-Napoli), Cassino exit, towards Formia and Napoli to the stoplight of Cellole, then on the right.*

Grand Hotel Le Rocce

Via Flaca, km 23,300
04024 Gaeta (Latina)
Tel. (0)771-74 09 85 - (0)771-74 16 33
Sig. Viola

Category ★★★ **Rooms** 47 and 7 suites with telephone, bath or shower, WC, TV (air-conditioning and minibar in suites). **Price** Single 130-200,000L, double 160-330,000L, suite 280-350,000L. **Meals** Breakfast included, served 8:30-10:00; half board 100-190,000L and full board 115-200,000L (per pers., 3 days. min.). **Restaurant** Service 12:30-20:00; also à la carte 55-60,000L. **Credit cards** All major. **Pets** Dogs not allowed. **Facilities** Private beach, parking. **Nearby** Gulf of Gaeta. **Open** March - Oct.

This is an ideal spot for those who dream of a holiday close to the sea. Nestled in a little bay of the Gulf of Gaeta, the hotel has lush Mediterranean gardens on terraces that descend to a solarium just over the private beach. The interior architecture echoes the style of the region, favoring generous dimensions and repeated arcades, with a majolica-tiled floor. Whatever their category, all the rooms have a balcony or terrace facing the sea. Most are spacious, all are comfortable and those called superiore boast air-conditioning as well. Salons and dining room, inside and out, have been arranged so as to provide the best view of the gardens and the sea. A good place to stop on a trip south, or as a base for visiting Rome or Naples. Gaeta is on the autostrada, just about halfway between these two principal cities of the south of Italy.

How to get there *(Map 19): 140 km south of Roma, 95 km north of Napoli. 7 km west of Gaetaon the S 213 road.*

1998

Hotel Santa Lucia

Via Partenope, 46
80121 Napoli
Tel. (0)81-764 06 66 - Fax (0)81-764 85 80 - Sig. Ferraro
E-mail: slucia@tin.it - Web: www.santalucia.it

Category ★★★★ **Rooms** 102 with air-conditioning, tel, bath or shower, WC, satellite TV, minibar; elevator. **Price** Single 320,000L, double 440,000L, suite 600-1 800,000L. **Meals** Breakfast include, served 7:00-11:00. **Restaurant** Service Monday to Saturday 12:30-24:00 and Sunday 19:30-23:00, also à la carte 75,000L. Specialties: tagliatelle broccoli e frutti di mare, pesce fresco del golfo all'acqua pazza. **Credit cards** All major. **Pets** Dogs not allowed. **Facilities** Garage (30,000L). **Nearby** Napoli: Archaeology museum, Capodimonte National Gallery and Museum, Villa Floridiana, Certosa di San Martino, Estate of Napoli, Pompeii, Ercolano, Cuma, la solfatara in Pozzuoli, Capri, Ischia, the Amalfi coast, Paestum. **Open** All year.

The Bay of Naples, with Vesuvius rising out of the mist and the peninsula of Sorrento in the background, is certainly one of the most famous panoramas in the world. The hotel is right on the bay, near the little port of Santa Lucia, facing the Castel dell'Ovo, and taking in this whole breathtaking sight, like a Neapolitan painting. The neoclassic facade and Liberty-style interior were renovated in 1990. The maze of little salons are tastefully furnished in elegant tones of gray and blue, which beautifully set off the magnificence of the marble, moldings and stuccos. The bedrooms have the same classical decor, brightened with cheerful prints, comfortable amenities, and those on the front have a view of the bay. The Santa Lucia offers its guests the luxury of a grand hotel combined with a feeling of intimacy.

How to get there *(Map 19): Along the bay, between Castel dell'Ovo, the port of Santa Lucia and the Palazzo Reale.*

Hotel Excelsior

Via Partenope, 48
80121 Napoli
Tel. (0)81-764 01 11 - Fax (0)81-764 97 43
Sig. Vincenzo Pagano

Category ★★★★ **Rooms** 136 with air-conditioning, tel, bath or shower, WC, satellite TV, minibar, safe; elevator. **Price** Single 370,000L, double 470,000L, suite 700,000 - 800,000 - 1,100,000L. **Meals** Breakfast included, served 7:00-10:30. **Restaurant** Service 12:30-15:30, 19:00-23:30, à la carte 60-90,000L. Specialties: Pesce - Regional cuisine. **Credit cards** All major. **Pets** Dogs not allowed. **Facilities** Garage (32,000L). **Nearby** Naples: Archaeology museum, Capodimonte National Gallery and Museum, Villa Floridiana, Certosa di San Martino,Estate of Napoli, Pompei, Ercolano, Cuma, la solfatara in Pozzuoli, Capri, Ischia, Amalfi coast, Paestum. **Open** All year.

The recent renovations in the center have at last made Naples an easier and more pleasant city to explore. Many of its monuments, like the Capodimonte Museum, with its treasures of Italian art, have become more accessible. The world-famous Excelsior, with its mirrors and stuccos and turn-of-the-century splendor, has all the charm of its bygone era. The salons have preserved their flamboyant style, but the bedrooms are not always as tasteful, and the bathrooms, though large, could sometimes do with a little renovation. Still, on the whole, the hotel has the quiet feel of its time. The bedrooms face the Bay and the Castel dell'Ovo. In clear weather you can see Capri and the majestic silhouette of Vesuvius. In the restaurant you can appreciate the local specialties, with their subtle combinations of pasta and fish.

How to get there *(Map 21): Along the bay, between Castel dell'Ovo, the port of Santa Lucia and the Palazzo Reale.*

Grand Hotel Parker's

Corso Vittorio Emanuele, 135
80121 Napoli
Tel. (0)81-761 24 74 - Fax (0)81-663 527
Sig. Italico Rota

Category ★★★★ **Rooms** 83 with air-conditioning, tel, bath or shower, WC, satellite TV, minibar, safe; elevator. **Price** Single 210-260,000L, double 310-365,000L, suite 750-1 500,000L. **Meals** Breakfast included, served 7:00-10:00. **Restaurant** Service 12:30-14:30, 19:30-22:30; closed Sunday; à la carte 60-90,000L. Specialties: Pesce, regional cuisine. **Credit cards** All major. **Pets** Dogs not allowed. **Facilities** Garage (20,000L). **Nearby** Naples: Archaeology museum, Capodimonte National Gallery and Museum, Villa Floridiana, Certosa di San Martino,Estate of Napoli, Pompei, Ercolano, Cuma, la solfatara in Pozzuoli, Capri, Ischia, Amalfi coast, Paestum. **Open** All year.

For 120 years now, this hotel has been synonymous with elegance and chic. An imposing entrance hall with wood paneling, marble and club chairs gives it a rather English look, as does the Napoleone Bar, a piano-bar where guests meet for cocktails in the evening. The bedrooms are classical and comfortable, and each floor is in a different style, ranging from Louis XVI to Charles X. The building is on a small hill in the center of Naples and overlooks the bay. The best place to see the view is the Bellevue, the gastronomic restaurant that serves candle-lighted dinners in an atmosphere of great refinement. An additional feature at the Parker's is the availability of a fine library with a nice collection of old books.

How to get there *(Map 21): In the town center.*

1998

Hotel Paradiso

Via Catullo, 11
80122 Napoli
Tel. (0)81-761 4161 - Fax (0)81-761 3449
Sig. Vincenzo di Donato

Category ★★★★ **Rooms** 83 with air-conditioning, tel, bath or shower, WC, satellite TV, minibar; elevator. **Price** Single160-180,000L, double 240-280,000L, suite 350-400,000L. **Meals** Breakfast included, served 7:00-10:30; half board 160-180,000L. **Restaurant** Service 12:30-14:45, 19:15-22:30; closed Sunday; menu, also à la carte 45,000L. Specialties: Italian and Napolitan cuisine. **Credit cards** All major. **Pets** Dogs not allowed. **Facilities** Garage (25,000L). **Nearby** Naples: Archaeology museum, Capodimonte National Gallery and Museum, Villa Floridiana, Certosa di San Martino,Estate of Napoli, Pompei, Ercolano, Cuma, la solfatara in Pozzuoli, Capri, Ischia, Amalfi coast, Paestum. **Open** All year.

The Hotel Paradiso is an ideal choice for anyone looking for a quiet haven away from the storms of Neapolitan life. Perched on the Posillipo hill, an airy residential quarter of Naples ten minutes from the historic center, it has a wonderful view of the Bay, Mount Vesuvius and the islands of Ischia and Capri. It is a totally modern hotel, whose main assets are calm, comfort and the view. At the panoramic restaurant you can taste the local dishes, with an emphasis on all the products of the sea.

How to get there *(Map 21): Posillipo hill.*

Villa Brunella

Isola di Capri
Via Tragara, 24
80073 Capri (Napoli)
Tel. (0)81-837 01 22 - Fax (0)81-837 04 30 - Sig. Ruggiero

Category ★★★★ **Rooms** 8 and 12 suites with air conditioning, telephone, bath, WC, satellite TV and minibar. **Price** Double 370,000L, suite 470,000L. **Meals** Breakfast included, served 8:30-12:00. **Restaurant** Service 12:30-15:30, 19:30-23:00; menus: 37-42,000L, also à la carte. Specialties: Ravioli alla caprese, frutti di mare, linguine al cartoccio. **Credit cards** Amex, Visa, Eurocard, MasterCard. **Pets** Dogs not allowed. **Facilities** Swimming pool. **Nearby** Capri (Certosa di San Giacomo, Villa Jovis, Punta Tragara, Blue Grotto, Villa Malaparte) Monte Solaro, Napoli, Pompeii, Herculaneum, Cuma, Pozzuoli sulphur springs, Vesuvius, Ischia, Amalfi coast. **Open** Mar. 19 – Nov. 6.

This hotel, near the road that leads to Villa Tiberio, has a nice family atmosphere. Its terraces, which are on several levels and are protected from the wind by berry bushes, jut excitingly out over the sea. It's a marvelous place to enjoy the relaxing lunchtime buffet. The rooms are spacious and comfortable. The ones facing the sea are nicer than those facing the courtyard. The suites have individual terraces. There is no elevator, and it is necessary to climb stairs to even get to the rooms on the ground-floor due to Capri's hilly terrain.

How to get there *(Map 19): Ferry services from Napoli (40 min-70 min), from Sorrento (35 min); in Capri, from Piazzetta towards Villa Tiberio, via Camerelle and via Tragara.*

Europa Palace Hotel

Isola di Capri
80071 Anacapri (Napoli)
Tel. (0)81-837 38 00 - Fax (0)81-837 31 91 - A. Cacace and A. Mantegazza

Category ★★★★ **Rooms** 90 with air-conditioning, telephone, bath, WC, minibar and TV, (4 with private swimming pool). **Price** Single 215-260,000L, double 370-530,000L, suite 650-830,000L (with private swimming pool). **Meals** Breakfast included, served 7:00-12:00; half board +50,000L (per pers.). **Restaurant** Service 12:00, 19:30; menus 60-70,000L, also à la carte. Specialties: Tagliolini al limone, ravioli caprese, risotto al melone. **Credit cards** All major. **Pets** Dogs not allowed. **Facilities** Swimming pool. **Nearby** Anacapri (Villa San Michele, Monte Solaro), Capri (Certosa di San Giacomo, Villa Jovis, Punta Tragara, Blue Grotto, Villa Malaparte), Napoli, Pompeii, Herculaneum, Cuma, Pozzuoli sulphur springs, Vesuvius, Ischia, Amalfi coast. **Open** Apr. – Oct.

The Europa Palace Hotel is situated at Anacapri, the wildest part of the island, but its guests will enjoy the experienced service offered by members of the Mariantonia family, well-known for their cooking and hospitality. To these two basic assets, they have now added a certain well-controlled luxury. The hotel has a number of suites with their own private garden and swimming pool but also very comfortable rooms with terraces where you can have your breakfast and enjoy the healthy sea air every morning. The restaurant carries on the family tradition by providing tasty Mediterranean dishes, with barbecued fish and regional specialties. In the evening, candlelight dinners are served amid the palm trees, the air heavy with the scent of the sea pines. There is also a health club that offers fitness sessions — nothing new, for weren't the emperors Augustus and Tiberius already praising the health-giving climate of Capri?

How to get there *(Map 19): Ferry services from Napoli (40 min-70 min), from Sorrento (35 min); in Capri, at the port, take a taxi or the private bus of the hotel.*

Hotel Luna

Isola di Capri
Via G. Matteotti, 3 - 80073 Capri (Napoli)
Tel. (0)81-837 04 33 - Fax (0)81-837 74 59 - Sig. Vuotto
E-mail: luna@capri.it - Web: http://www:capri.it/it/hotels/luna/home.htlm

Category ★★★★ **Rooms** 48 with air-conditioning, telephone, bath, WC, satelliteTV, safe and minibar; elevator. **Price** Single 180-220,000L, double 250-475,000L. **Meals** Breakfast included, served 7:30-11:30; half board 180-295,000L (per pers.). **Restaurant** Service 12:30-14:30, 19:30-21:30; menus: 60,000L, also à la carte. Specialties: Italian and Neapolitan cooking. **Credit cards** All major. **Pets** Dogs not allowed. **Facilities** Swimming pool. **Nearby** Capri (Certosa di San Giacomo, Villa Jovis, Punta Tragara, Blue Grotto, Villa Malaparte), Anacapri (Villa San Michele, Monte Solaro), Napoli, Pompeii, Herculaneum, Cuma, Pozzuoli sulphur springs, Vesuvius, Ischia, Amalfi coast. **Open** Apr. 1 – Oct. 31.

This is a delightful hotel in an exceptional location. The rooms are large and freshly decorated in a classical style. They are a touch overdone, but very comfortable. Irresistible attractions for visitors are the terraces jutting out over the sea, the large floral garden and the pool close to the Carthusian monastery. Though only a few minutes from the center of Capri, it is a perfect place to get away from it all.

How to get there *(Map 19): Ferry services from Napoli (40 min-70 min), from Sorrento (35 min); in Capri, from the Piazzetta towards Giardini di Augusto via Vittorio Emanuele and via F. Serena.*

Hotel Punta Tragara

Isola di Capri
Via Tragara, 57
80073 Capri (Napoli)
Tel. (0)81-837 08 44 - Fax (0)81-837 77 90 - Sig. Ceglia

Category ★★★★ **Rooms** 47 with air-conditioning, telephone, bath or shower, WC, TV and minibar; elevator. **Price** Double 380-520,000L, suite 530-800,000L. **Meals** Breakfast included, served 7:00-11:00; half board +60,000L, full board +100,000L (per pers.). **Restaurant** Service 13:00-15:30, 20:00-22:30; menu 75,000L, also à la carte. Specialties: Mediterranean cuisine. **Credit cards** All major. **Pets** Dogs not allowed. **Facilities** 2 swimming pools. **Nearby** Capri (Certosa di San Giacomo, Villa Jovis, Punta Tragara, Blue Grotto, Villa Malaparte), Anacapri (Villa San Michele, Monte Solaro), Napoli, Pompeii, Herculaneum, Cuma, Pozzuoli sulphur springs, Vesuvius, Ischia, Amalfi coast. **Open** Apr. – Oct.

The last place you might except to find a project designed by Le Corbusier is on Capri, but this group of ochre-colored brick houses–built into a stone cliff, hanging over the sea–bears the signature of the celebrated 20th-century architect. Today, it is a luxury hotel with more suites than rooms. The entire hotel is sumptuously decorated with antique furniture, paintings, rugs and old tapestries. Its two restaurants are very pleasant; La Bussola has a terrace for outside dining and a marvelous view. The tropical garden overflowing with giant bougainvilleas and other exotic plants, contains two beautiful salt-water pools continually heated to 94°. You can expect a luxury hotel-style welcome and service.

How to get there *(Map 19): Ferry services from Napoli (40 min-70 min), from Sorrento (35 min); in Capri, from the Piazzetta, towards the Villa Tiberio, via Camerelle and via Tragara.*

Hotel Villa Sarah

Isola di Capri
Via Tiberio, 3/A - 80073 Capri (Napoli)
Tel. (0)81-837 06 89/837 78 17 - Fax (0)81-837 72 15
Sig. de Martino

Category ★★★ **Rooms** 20 with, telephone, bath or shower, WC and cable TV. **Price** Single 120-170,000L, double 180-280,000L. **Meals** Breakfast included, served 8:00-10:00. **Restaurant** See p. 441. **Credit cards** All major. **Pets** Dogs not allowed. **Facilities** Solarium. **Nearby** Capri (Certosa di San Giacomo, Villa Jovis, Punta Tragara, Blue Grotto, Villa Malaparte), Anacapri (Villa San Michele, Monte Solaro), Napoli, Pompeii, Herculaneum, Cuma, Pozzuoli sulphur springs, Vesuvius, Ischia, Amalfi coast. **Open** Easter –Oct.

Typical of the villas built in the Capri hills, the Villa Sarah has, just beyond its garden, its own vineyard and orchard that supply all the delicious jams served at breakfast. Though it is located near the center, the quarter is a quiet one and the crowds are not too bad even in midsummer. The atmosphere is friendly and it's nice to relax in the garden or the solarium. The rooms are all equipped with the usual amenities. The beauty of Capri has made it a chic and expensive holiday spot. The Villa Sarah allows you to enjoy it in good conditions and at a reasonable price.

How to get there *(Map 19): Ferry services from Napoli (40 min-70 min), from Sorrento (35 min); in Capri, from the Piazzetta towards the Villa Tiberio, via Camerelle and via Tragara.*

Pensione Quattro Stagioni

Isola di Capri
80073 Marina Piccola (Napoli)
Tel. (0)81-837 00 41
Sig.ra Salvia

Category ★ **Rooms** 12 with bath or shower, WC. **Price** 140-160,000L. **Meals** Breakfast included, served 8:00-10:00; half board 120,000L (per pers.). **Restaurant** Service 20:00; menu. Specialties: Pasta alle zucchine, pollo caprese. **Credit cards** Visa, Eurocard, MasterCard. **Pets** Dogs not allowed. **Nearby** Beach, Certosa di San Giacomo, Villa Jovis, Punta Tragara, Blue Grotto, Villa Malaparte), Anacapri (Villa San Michele, Monte Solaro) Napoli, Pompeii, Herculaneum, Cuma, Pozzuoli sulphur springs, Vesuvius, Ischia, Amalfi coast. **Open** Mar. 15 – End Oct.

Italy is gradually losing its famous *pensioni* where the traveler was enveloped in family warmth and fed on the generous home cooking of la *mamma*. Capri, sophisticated though it may be, still has one. And it is located right at the Marina Piccola, the place where everyone goes to swim by day and dine by night in the little restaurants facing the sea. The Quattro Stagioni occupies one of those flower-clad houses that overlook the bay between Mount Solaro and Mount Castiglione. Today all the rooms have their own bath. As is customary in a real *pensione,* the half-board is obligatory and dinner is at 8. But this is a minor constraint when you consider the prices you pay. There is a lovely promenade that links Marina Piccola with the center of Capri, through the garden of Augustus and with a splendid view.

How to get there *(Map 19): Ferry services from Napoli (40 min-70 min), from Sorrento (35 min).*

Park Hotel Miramare

Isola d'Ischia
80070 Sant'Angelo (Napoli)
Tel. (0)81-99 92 19 - Fax (0)81-99 93 25 - Sig.ra Calise
Web: http://www.ischiaonline.it/hotels/miramare - E-mail: miramare@metis.it

Category ★★★★ **Rooms** 50 with bath or shower, telephone, WC, satellite TV, minibar and fan. **Price** Single 263,000L, double 316,000L. **Meals** Breakfast 18,000L, served 7:30-10:00; half board 205-215,000L (per 1 pers.), 230-240,000 (per 1 pers., in double). **Restaurant** Service 13:00-14:00, 19:30-21:00; menu and carte 75,000L. Specialties: Regional cooking. **Credit cards** Diners, Visa, Eurocard, MasterCard. **Pets** Small dogs allowed. **Facilities** Thermal baths «Giardini Aphrodite». **Nearby** Ischia (Boat or car tour of the island, Castello, Mont Epomeo (788m) from Serrara-Fontana (1h), Beach of Citara in Forio, Lacco Ameno), Lido S. Montano, Capri, Napoli, Pompeii, Herculaneum, Cuma, Pozzuoli sulphur springs, the Amalfi coast to Salerno, Paestum. **Open** Apr. – End Sept.

The short ferry ride to the island of Ischia is delightful. On the way, you will cross the sumptuous Gulf of Naples below the majestic silhouette of Vesuvius, and sail along the Procida peninsula. The Hotel Miramare is in Sant Angelo, one of the few unspoiled places on the island. Directly overhanging the sea, it is just a few steps from the small port and the pretty piazzetta. The hotel has a pleasant atmosphere of longstanding tradition. The rooms are comfortable and warmly decorated, some with balconies with a spectacular panoramic view. A restaurant on the terrace will entice you with classic island seafood. A few steps away, a private flower-lined path leads to the marvelous Aphrodite-Apollo Thermal Garden, which has twelve pools of varying temperatures that are built into the cliff in a series of descending terraces.

How to get there *(Map 19): south of Napoli via A3, Castellammare di Stabia exit, then towards S 145. Ferry service from Napoli (70 min) and from Pozzuoli (40 min).*

Pensione Casa Sofia

Isola d'Ischia
80070 Sant'Angelo (Napoli)
Via Sant'Angelo,29 B
Tel. (0)81-99 93 10 - Fax (0)81-99 93 10 - Sig.ra Bremer-Barricelli

Rooms 8 and 2 apartments (balcony and terrace) with shower and WC. **Price** With half board 120,000L (per 1 pers.). **Meals** Breakfast included, served from 8:00. **Restaurant** Service 18:30 (19:30 in summer), menu. Specialties: Regional cooking. **Credit cards** All major. **Pets** Small dogs allowed. **Facilities** Thermal baths. **Nearby** Ischia (Boat or car tour of the island, Castello, Mont Epomeo (788m) from Serrara-Fontana (1h), Beach of Citara in Forio, Lacco Ameno), Lido S. Montano, Capri, Napoli, Pompeii, Herculaneum, Cuma, Pozzuoli sulphur springs, the Amalfi coast to Salerno, Paestum. **Open** Mar. 16 – early Nov.

Signora Dolly Bremer-Barricelli has made her large and beautfiful house with its incomparable sea view a perfect place for anyone seeking a quiet family holiday. The rooms are all attractively decorated and from the terrace, where you have your very copious breakfast, you can look out over the entire Bay of Sant'Angelo. This ancient fishing village is only one that has kept the charm that must have once been everywhere on Ischia and is today sadly spoiled by tourism. Close by the hotel you can unwind in the thermal pools of the Garden of Aphrodite (there are 12 pools and you go from one to the other.) If your vacation takes you to Ischia, don't miss this invigorating spot. Signora Bremer-Barricelli, who is of German origin, serves dinner at 6.30 p.m. If this is too early for your taste, you may be able to negotiate for a later hour.

How to get there *(Map 19): south of Napoli via A3, Castellammare di Stabia exit, then towards S 145. Ferry service from Napoli (70 min) and from Pozzuoli (40 min).*

Casa Garibaldi

Isola d'Ischia
Via Sant'Angelo, 52
80070 Sant'Angelo (Napoli)
Tel. (0)81-99 94 20 - Fax (0)81-99 94 20 - Sig. Di Iorio

Rooms 20 with shower and WC. **Price** Single 53,000L, double 95,000L, suite 115,000L. **Meals** Breakfast 7,000L, served 8:00-10:00. **Restaurant** See p. 442. **Credit cards** Not accepted. **Pets** Dogs allowed. **Facilities** Swimming pool. **Nearby** Boat or car tour of the island, (32 km), Castello, Mont Epomeo (788 m) from Fontana (1 h), Beach of Citara à Forio, Lacco Ameno, Lido San Montano, Capri, Napoli, Pompeii, Herculaneum, Cuma, Pozzuoli sulphur springs, the Amalfi coast to Salerno, Paestum. **Open** Easter - Nov.

The village of Sant'Angelo, some 300 yards from the dock, is accessible only on foot, but you will find porters and parking facilities the moment you get off the boat. This unpretentious white house, surrounded by fig trees, overlooks the beach and the picturesque fishing village. The rooms are in small individual houses linked by terraced roofs. On the highest terrace is a swimming pool. Despite its sobriety of style, Casa Garibaldi is a pleasure to be in. The atmosphere is welcoming, the view superb and the rooms, simply furnished, are all equipped with showers. No dining room, but a large kitchen where guests may prepare a meal for themselves whenever they like.

How to get there *(Map 19): South of Napoli viar A 3 to Castellammare di Stabia, then S 145. Crossings daily from Napoli (1 h 10) and Pozzuoli (40 mn).*

La Villarosa

Isola d'Ischia
Via Giacinto Gigante, 5
80077 Porto d'Ischia (Napoli)
Tel. (0)81-99 13 16/98 44 90 - Fax (0)81-99 24 25 - Sig. Pepe

Category ★★★★ **Rooms** 33 (10 with air conditioning) and 4 suites with telephone, bath, WC, satellite TV and minibar, elevator. **Price** Single 110-160,000L, double 180-240,000L. **Meals** Breakfast included, served 7:00-10:00; half board 120-175,000L, full board 135-190,000L (per pers.). **Restaurant** For residents, service 13:00-14:00, 19:30-21:00; menus 40-60,000L. **Credit cards** Amex, Visa, Eurocard, MasterCard. **Pets** Small dogs allowed. **Facilities** Swimming pool, thermal baths, hydrotherapy. **Nearby** Ischia (Boat or car tour of the island, Castello, Mont Epomeo (788 m) from Serrara-Fontana (1 h), Beach of Citara in Forio, Lacco Ameno), Lido S. Montano, Capri, Napoli, Pompeii, Herculaneum, Cuma, Pozzuoli sulphur springs, the Amalfi coast to Salerno, Paestum. **Open** Mar. 22 – Oct.

La Villarosa is a hard place to say goodbye to. You will see this as soon as you arrive. This enchanting hotel is set in the middle of a lush tropical garden. Good taste and the best of everything prevail: simplicity, discretion and refinement are evident down to the last detail. An elegant salon opens onto a garden with a springfed swimming pool. The rooms, some with a terrace or a flowering balcony, all have the discreet charm of an old-fashioned country house. You can enjoy your meals in the rooftop restaurant or, in summer, on the marvelous wisteria-covered terrace. The hotel spa is discreetly located in the basement.

How to get there *(Map 19): Ferry services from Napoli-Molo Beverello (75 min by ferry, 40 min by hydrofoil).*

La Bagattella Hotel

Isola d'Ischia
Spiaggia di San Francesco - Via Tommaso Cigliano
80075 Forio d'Ischia (Napoli)
Tel. (0)81-98 60 72 - Fax (0)81-98 96 37 - Sig.ra Lauro

Category ★★★★ **Rooms** 56 with air-conditioning, telephone, bath, WC and TV. **Price** With half board 140-160,000L, full board 160-190,000L (per pers., 3 days min.). **Meals** Breakfast included, served 7:30-9:30. **Restaurant** For residents, service 13:00-14:00, 19:00-20:30; menus, also à la carte. Specialties: Seafood. **Credit cards** Visa, Eurocard, MasterCard. **Pets** Dogs not allowed. **Facilities** Swimming pool, hydrotherapy, parking. **Nearby** Ischia (Boat or car tour of the island, Castello, Mont Epomeo (788 m) from Serrara-Fontana (1 h), Beach of Citara in Forio, Lacco Ameno), Lido S. Montano, Capri, Napoli, Pompeii, Herculaneum, Cuma, Pozzuoli sulphur springs, the Amalfi coast to Salerno, Paestum. **Open** Apr. – Oct.

La Bagatella looks like an oversize Moorish wedding cake dropped into a tropical garden ablaze with oleander bushes and bouganvilleas. The fresh-looking rooms are very luxurious. Some are slightly overdone but are nonetheless pleasant and some have flowering balconies. A modern wing has been added, with simple, functional rooms and efficiency apartments. The new wing and the restaurant open onto a garden with a springfed swimming pool, surrounded by hibiscus bushes and palm trees. There is also a beautiful sand beach just five minutes away on foot.

How to get there *(Map 19): Ferry services from Napoli-Molo Beverello (75 min by ferry, 20 min by hydrofoil); 10 km from Porto d'Ischia.*

Albergo Terme San Montano

Isola d'Ischia
80076 Lacco Ameno (Napoli)
Tel. (0)81-99 40 33 - Fax (0)81-98 02 42
Sig. Farace

Category ★★★★★ **Rooms** 65 and 2 suites with telephone, bath, WC, satellite TV and minibar. **Price** Single 180-260,000L, double 360-540,000L, suite +100,000L. **Meals** Breakfast included, served 7:30-10:30; half board 220-310,000L, full board 240-360,000L (per pers. 8 days min. in August). **Restaurant** Service 13:00-15:00, 20:00-22:00, à la carte. **Credit cards** All major **Pets** Small dogs allowed only in the room. **Facilities** 2 swimming pools, tennis, private beach, water-skiing, sauna, private bus, parking. **Nearby** Ischia (Boat or car tour of the island, Castello, Mont Epomeo (788 m) from Serrara-Fontana (1 h), Beach of Citara in Forio, Lacco Ameno), Lido S. Montano, Capri, Napoli, Pompeii, Herculaneum, Cuma, Pozzuoli sulphur springs, the Amalfi coast to Salerno, Paestum. **Open** April – Oct.

This hotel enjoys one of the most beautiful locations on Ischia. It sits on the top of a hill, overlooking the countryside on one side and the sea on the other, with a great view of the Vivara and Procida Islands, and the slightly hazy outline of Vesuvius in the distance. The San Montano tends to be austerely modern in both its appearance and personality, but the great luxury and comfort of the place more than compensate. The rooms, all with superb view, are decorated in a nautical style. Some have a balcony, others a private garden. On the terraced hillside grounds are two swimming pools and a tennis court. A shuttle bus will take you to the private beach. The prices are high, but well worth it.

How to get there *(Map 19): Ferry services from Napoli-Molo Beverello (75 min by ferry, 20 min by hydrofoil). 6 km from Porto d'Ischia.*

1998

Hotel Residence Punta Chiarito

Isola d'Ischia
80074 Sorgeto - Panza d'Ischia (Napoli)
Tel. (0)81-908 102 - Fax (0)81-909 277
Sig. Impagliazzo

Rooms 8 and 7 studios with air-conditioning, tel, shower, WC, TV, minibar. **Price** Double 95-105,000L (per pers.), studio for 1 week 1,200,000-1,500,000L (2 pers.). **Meals** Breakfast included, served 8:00-10:00, half board 110-140,000L (per pers.). **Restaurant** Service 12:45-14:15, 20:00-21:30, à la carte. **Credit cards** Visa, Eurocard, MasterCard. **Pets** Dogs not allowed. **Facilities** Swimming pool, sauna, parking. **Nearby** Boat or car tour of the island, Castello, Cartaromana, Mont Epomeo (788 m) from Fontana (1 h), beach of Citara in Forio, Lacco Ameno, Lido S. Montano, Capri, Napoli, Pompei, Ercolano, Cuma, La Solfatara in Pozzuoli, Ischia, the Amalfi coast to Salerno, Paestum. **Open** All year.

If you're looking for a break from your busy round of sightseeing and want a retreat alone with the sea, try the Punta Chiarito. Perched on a rocky promontory just over the sea, it is a wonderful place to rest and catch your breath. You can swim at the hotel in a pool filled with mineral water from a nearby spring or at the beach (access by a steep stairway), where the water is warm even in winter. The bedrooms are modern and simple but comfortable and your sleep is lulled by the sound of the waves. Ask for a room facing the Sant'Angelo peninsula. If you're traveling with your family, each bedroom can have a private kitchenette. In the summer, when the entire island may be in a state of effervescence, Punta Chiarito is one of the rare spots where it always feels like "low season."

How to get there *(Map 19): Ferry services from Napoli-Molo Beverello (75 min by ferry, 40 min by hydrofoil); tel (0)81 551 32 36 towards Forio, Panza and Sorgeto.*

1998

Giacaranda

Cenito 84071 Santa Maria de Castellabate (Salerno)
Tel. (0)974-96 61 30- Fax (0)974-96 08 00
Sig.ra Cavaliere

Rooms 4 and 8 apartments with bath, satellite TV. **Price** With half board: 156,000L (1 pers.), 280,000L (2 pers.), apartments 280,000L (2 pers.), 560,000L (4 pers.). **Meals** Breakfast included, served 9:00-11:30. **Restaurant** Service 13:00-15:00, 19:30-22:00; vegetarian menu. Specialties: Mediterranean cooking. **Credit cards** All major. **Pets** Dogs allowed. **Facilities** Tennis, parking at hotel. **Nearby** The Amalfi coast, Napoli, Pompeii, Paestum, Velia, Capri, Padula. **Open** All year (except Dec 24, 25 and 26).

The back country of the Gulf of Salerno offers some extraordinary Greek temples, like Paestum (if you're staying in the area, make sure to go back and see it again at sunset) and the monumental Porta Rossa de Velia, less visited but famous for being the only example of a Roman arch in Greek architecture. These two monuments will help to situate Giacaranda, which is halfway between them. It is a beautiful estate, where the hosts' constant preoccupation is to make their guests feel at home. The rooms and apartments are perfectly kept: fine bedding, comfortable bathrooms, antique furniture and lovely household linens make for a decor that is simple yet refined. As much care goes into the cooking, based on the classic Italian recipes, with all the flavors of the region. You will sample a variety of pastas including homemade ravioli, and for the last night's dinner, the famous local pizza. You will get help and advice for all your outings, be it bathing, walking or sightseeing. A place you'll want to come back to.

How to get there *(Map 20): 120 km south of Napoli. Via A 3 (Salerno/Reggio) Battipàglia exit, then SS 18 (towards Agropoli) bis Santa Maria de Castellabate.*

Palazzo Belmonte

84072 Santa Maria di Castellabate (Salerno)
Tel. (0)974-96 02 11 - Fax (0)974-96 11 50
Sig.ra Wilkinson

Suites 20 with telephone, bath, WC and mini-kitchen. **Price** Suite 250-510,000L (2 pers.), 515-850,000L (4 pers.). **Meals** Breakfast included. **Restaurant** Service 13:00-14:30, 19:30-22:00, à la carte. Specialties: Regional and Italian cuisine. **Credit cards** All major. **Pets** Dogs not allowed. **Facilities** Swimming pool, private beach, parking. **Nearby** Napoli, Pompeii, Paestum, Capri, Amalfi Coast, Padula Vietri. **Open** May – Oct.

Several months a year, the prince of Belmonte opens up his palace to the outside world. This beautiful historical monument was built in the 17th century in the small fishing village and is still used by his family as a hunting lodge to receive royal visitors from Spain and Italy. The prince and his family live in one wing and there are suites for guests in another part of the palazzo. They are unpretentiously but elegantly decorated in light colors and have nice bamboo furniture. Certain guest rooms open onto a pretty courtyard full of fragrant Chilian jasmine; others overlook a garden of fragrant pine trees, magnolias, hibiscus and oleanders; and still others have a terrace on the sea with views of the island of Capri when the weather is clear. The regional specialties served in the restaurant are made with fresh produce from the palace's vegetable garden. The swimming pool and private beach at the edge of a pine forest may make you want to take it easy, but the enticements of Naples, Pompeii and the Amalfi coast are so close by!

How to get there *(Map 20): 120 km south of Napoli via A3, Battipàglia exit, then towards Paestum, Agropoli and Castellabate.*

Grand Hotel Excelsior Vittoria

Piazza Tasso, 34
80067 Sorrento (Napoli)
Tel. (0)81-807 10 44 - Fax (0)81-877 12 06 - Sig. Fiorentino
E-mail: exvitt@exvitt.it - Web: http://www.exvitt.it

Category ★★★★ **Rooms** 106 (with air-conditioning) telephone, bath or shower, WC., TV, safe and minibar. **Price** Single 315,000L, double 392-536,000L, suite 717-1,191,000L. **Meals** Breakfast included, served 7:30-9:30; half board 369-401,000L (per pers. 3 days min.). **Restaurant** Service 12:30-14:00, 19:30-22:00; menu 75,000L, also à la carte. Specialties: Italian and Neapolitan cuisine. **Credit cards** All major. **Pets** Dogs allowed (extra charge). **Facilities** Swimming pool, parking. **Nearby** Bay of Sorrento, Napoli, Paestum, Capri. **Open** All year.

Overlooking the Gulf of Naples from the top of a rocky crag, this palace-hotel is one of the most prestigious in Sorrento. The garden, with a terrace facing the open sea, is an enchanting mixture of fragrant flowers, rose bushes and vines. A highlight is the winter garden overflowing with dwarf palm trees and turquoise flowers. The interior of the palace still has its original frescoes, stucco trimming and ceilings painted in Liberty style. The salons and rooms are all spacious and comfortable and furnished with beautiful antiques. In summer, meals are served on the panoramic terrace, and on Sundays you can join in a *buffet dansant*. Many illustrious personages have stayed here, including Goethe, Wagner and Verdi. The most requested room is the one Caruso lived in at the end of his life, a stay immortalized in a renown song often sung by Luciano Pavarotti.

How to get there *(Map 20): 48 km south of Napoli via A3 to Castellammare di Stabia, then S145.*

Hotel Bellevue Syrene

Piazza della Vittoria, 5
80067 Sorrento (Napoli)
Tel. (0)81-878 10 24 - Fax (0)81-878 39 63
Sig. Russo

Category ★★★★ **Rooms** 73 with telephone, bath or shower, WC, TV, minibar, safe; elevator. **Price** Single 150-250,000L, double 250-400,000L, suite 500,000L. **Meals** Breakfast included (buffet), served 7:00-10:00, half board +50,000L per pers. **Restaurant** Service 19:00-21:00; menu 70,000L, also à la carte. Specialties: Spaghetti con cozze, gnocchi, pesce. **Credit cards** All major. **Pets** Dogs allowed in the rooms only. **Facilities** Private beach, parking. **Nearby** Bay of Sorrento, Napoli, Paestum, Capri. **Open** All year.

On the site of an ancient Roman villa where Virgil and Tiberius once lived, there now stands a handsome 18th-century building, perched just over the sea. Not all the rooms are equally interesting: The large dining room was recently redecorated, but the two small sitting rooms that follow it have frescoes and mosaics that recall its long eventful history. There is an elevator that takes guests down to a private beach. But just for fun, try the old staircase and vaulted passage which are both, along with the columns in the garden, vestiges of the Roman villa. Our favorite room is number 4, one of the few with a balcony facing the sea.

How to get there *(Map 20): 48 km south of Napoli via A3 to Castellammare di Stabia, then S145.*

Hotel Capo La Gala

Via Luigi Serio, 7
Vico Equense (Napoli)
Tel. (0)81-801 57 58 - Fax (0)81-879 87 47
Sig.ra Savarese

Category ★★★★ **Rooms** 18 (9 with air conditioning) with telephone, bath or shower, WC, TV and minibar. **Price** Single 170,000L, double 250,000L, suite 450-600,000L. **Meals** Breakfast included (buffet), served 8:00-10:30; half board 175-220,000L, full board 215-260,000L. **Restaurant** Service 13:00-15:00, 20:00-22:00; menu 60,000L, also à la carte. Specialties: Seafood, frutti di mare. **Credit cards** All major. **Pets** Dogs allowed in the rooms only. **Facilities** Swimming pool, sauna (+1,500L), health center, parking (+20,000L). **Nearby** Gulf of Salerno and Amalfi coast, Napoli, Paestum, Capri. **Open** Apr. – Oct.

Designed around a series of terraces and small stairways cut into the stone hillside, the Capo La Gala blends so well into its surrounding that it seems more a part of the sea than of the land. The rooms, few in number, are all identical. Each one, distinguished by the name of a wind instead of a number, has a balcony facing the sea. You will find a homey atmosphere here, and will enjoy relaxing beside the sulphur-water swimming pool. The restaurant serves mainly seafood and fresh vegetables.

How to get there *(Map 20): 39 km south of Napoli via A3 to Castellammare di Stabia, then S145, towards Sorrento.*

Hotel Luna Convento

Via P. Comite, 19
84011 Amalfi (Salerno)
Tel. (0)89-871 002 - Fax (0)89-871 333
Sig. Milone

Category ★★★★ **Rooms** 48 with telephone, bath or shower, WC and TV. **Price** Single 180-230,000L, double 230-280,000L, suite 330-380,000L. **Meals** Breakfast 20,000L, served 7:30-10:00. **Restaurant** Service 12:30-14:30, 19:30-21:30; menus 70,000L, also à la carte. Specialties: Cannelloni del convento, crespoline, risotto pescatore, gamberoni alla griglia. **Credit cards** All major. **Pets** Dogs not allowed. **Facilities** Swimming pool, private beach, parking. **Nearby** Amalfi (Duomo, "Cloisters of Paradise," Emerald Grotto), Gulf of Salerno and Amalfi coast (Positano, Ravello, Salerno), Paestum, Capri, Napoli, Pompeii, Herculaneum, Cuma, Pozzuolo sulphur springs, Ischia. **Open** All year.

Above the Saracen Tower that looks out over the Gulf, the Luna Convento, clinging to a rock facing the sea, occupies a historic building, an old Franciscan convent mainly known for its superb Byzantine cloister. This magnificent hotel has been in the same family for several generations. It underwent some transformations in the 1950s, namely, an annex that was added to provide more rooms. The amenities vary from room to room. Those in the main house, of course, benefit from the old-fashioned charm of their ancient walls. Over the years, the house has hosted famous guests — there exists, in particular a whole correspondence between Ibsen and the hotel's first owner, Signora Barbano. Although certain improvements could be wished, this is still a delightful spot.

How to get there *(Map 20): 25 km west of Salerno via A3, Vietri sul Mare exit, then S163 along the coast.*

Hotel Santa Caterina

84011 Amalfi (Salerno)
Tel. (0)89-87 10 12
Fax (0)89-87 13 51

Category ★★★★★ **Rooms** 68 with air conditioning, telephone, bath, WC, TV and minibar. **Price** Single 350-400,000L, double 390-540,000L, suite 680-1 100,000L. **Meals** Breakfast 25,000L served 7:30-10:00, half board +75,000L, full board +140,000L. (per pers., 2 days min.). **Restaurant** Service 13:00-15:00, 20:00-22:00, menus 65,000L, also à la carte. Specialties: Linguine al limone, limoni farciti Santa Caterina, crespoline all'amalfitana, penne alla saracena. **Credit cards** All major. **Pets** Dogs not allowed. **Facilities** Swimming pool, private beach, parking. **Nearby** Amalfi (Duomo, "Cloisters of Paradise," Emerald Grotto), Gulf of Salerno and Amalfi coast (Positano, Ravello, Salerno), Paestum, Capri, Napoli, Pompeii, Herculaneum, Cuma, Pozzuolo sulphur springs, Ischia. **Open** All year.

For three generations now, the Hotel Santa Caterina has belonged to a family which understands and enjoys the art of hospitality. The furniture, mostly antiques, has been meticulously selected, giving each room a particular flavor. The bathrooms, are very modern–some even have a whirlpool bath. An elevator will take you down to the sea or the salt-water swimming pool. Ask to stay in the "chalet," a small house tucked away among the lemon trees in the garden.

How to get there *(Map 20): 25 km west of Salerno via A3, Vietri sul Mare exit, then S163 along the coast.*

Hotel Belvedere

84010 Conca dei Marini (Salerno)
Tel. (0)89-83 12 82 - Fax (0)89-83 14 39
Sig. Lucibello

Category ★★★★ **Rooms** 36 with telephone, bath and WC; elevator. **Price** Single 105-135,000L, double 160-210,000L, suite 240-290,000L. **Meals** Breakfast 15,000L, served 7:00-10:00; half board 170-210,000L, full board 190-240,000L. (per pers., 3 days min.). **Restaurant** Service 12:30-14:00, 19:30-21:00; menu 50,000L, also à la carte. Specialties: Crespolini, timballo di maccheroni. **Credit cards** All major. **Pets** Dogs not allowed. **Facilities** Swimming pool, private beach, parking. **Nearby** Amalfi (Duomo, "Cloisters of Paradise," Emerald Grotto), Gulf of Salerno and Amalfi coast (Positano, Ravello, Salerno), Paestum, Capri, Napoli, Pompeii, Herculaneum, Cuma, Pozzuolo sulphur springs, Ischia, . **Open** Apr. – Oct.

You may be impressed by the classical facade of the Belvedere, or by the fact that it is built into a cliff over the sea, but what is truly extraordinary is its view of the entire Amalfi coast with its steep hillsides and beautiful lemon tree orchards. The rooms are modern and very comfortable, with either a balcony or terrace overlooking the sea. An interior elevator will take you down to the pool on the rocks and to the walkway to the sea. The Belvedere is a singularly professional hotel, the cuisine excellent, and the service impeccable yet friendly, and the atmosphere of warm, unimposing hospitality.

How to get there *(Map 20): 65 km southeast of Napoli via A3, Castellammare di Stabia exit, then N336, towards Amalfi.*

Hotel San Pietro

84017 Positano (Salerno)
Tel. (0)89-87 54 55 - Fax (0)89-81 14 49
Sig. Attanasio

Category ★★★★★ **Rooms** 60 with air-conditioning, telephone, bath, WC, minibar and TV. **Price** Single 600-680,000L, double 620-700,000L. **Meals** Breakfast included, served 7:00-11:30. **Restaurant** Service 13:00-15:00, 20:00-21:30; à la carte. Specialties: Italian and Napolitan cooking. **Credit cards** All major. **Pets** Dogs not allowed. **Facilities** Swimming pool, private beach, tennis, windsurfing, parking. **Nearby** Gulf of Salerno and Amalfi coast (Positano, Amalfi, Ravello, Salerno), Paestum, Capri, Napoli, Pompeii, Herculaneum, Cuma, Pozzuolo sulphur springs, Ischia. **Open** Apr. – Oct.

From the sea, the San Pietro looks like a cascade of greenery flowing from terrace to terrace down the slope of Mount Lattari. It is a model of architecture integrated with its environment, covered with bougainvillea and Virginia creeper so thick they nearly invade the rooms. From inside, the view is stupendous. Each room is more sumptuous than the next, and the bathrooms are like something out of a Hollywood fantasy. Each room has a sea view and a ceramic tile balcony. An elevator shaft has been carved out of the rock wall for a height of 88 meters, to take the guests down to a private beach at the foot of the cliff. There is a snack bar down below and a tennis court in another cove nearby. The hotel restaurant serves excellent Italian food and the welcome is exceptional. For safety reasons, the hotel does not accept children under 12.

How to get there *(Map 20): 57 km south of Napoli via A3, Castellammare di Stabia exit, towards Sorrento, Positano.*

Le Sirenuse

Via C. Colombo, 30
84010 Positano (Salerno)
Tel. (0)89-87 50 66 - Fax (0)89-81 17 98
Sig. Sersale

Category ★★★★★ **Rooms** 60 with air-conditioning, telephone, bath or shower, WC, TV and minibar. **Price** Single 360-700,000L, double 400-740,000L, suite 690-850,000L. **Meals** Breakfast included, served 7:00-11:00; half board +85,000L, full board +135,000L. (per pers., 3 days min.). **Restaurant** Service 13:00-14:30, 20:00-22:00; à la carte. Specialties: Pasta, seafood. **Credit cards** All major. **Pets** Dogs allowed except in the restaurant and in the swimming pool. **Facilities** Heated swimming pool, parking. **Nearby** Gulf of Salerno and Amalfi coast: Positano, Grotta di Smeraldo, Ravello, Salerno, Paestum, Capri, Napoli, Pompeii, Ercolano, Cuma, Pozzuolo sulphur springs, Ischia. **Open** All year.

Behind the red-ochre facade of Le Sirenuse you'll find one of the best hotels on the Amalfi coast. This former 18th-century palace looks out over the bay of Positano. It has been modified and expanded over the years, and today the hotel appears to be an odd but charming series of angles, often extended by terraces. The rooms are extremely comfortable and decorated with lovely Venetian and Neapolitan furniture. Certain rooms in the oldest part still have their original ceramic tile floors. You can have lunch and dinner at tables set around the pool. The new chef offers innovative cuisine based on traditional Neapolitan recipes. The staff is friendly and efficient.

How to get there *(Map 20): 57 km south of Napoli via A3, Castellammare di Stabia exit, towards Sorrento, Positano.*

Hotel Poseidon

Via Pasitea, 148
84017 Positano (Salerno)
Tel. (0)89-81 11 11 - Fax (0)89-87 58 33 - Famiglia Aonzo

Category ★★★★ **Rooms** 45 and 3 suites with air-conditioning, telephone, bath or shower, WC, TV and minibar. **Price** Double 270-390,000L, suite 370-600,000L. **Meals** Breakfast included, served 8:00-11:00; half board +65,000L (per pers.). **Restaurant** Service 13:00-14:30, 20:00-22:00; à la carte. **Credit cards** All major. **Pets** Dogs allowed in the rooms only. **Facilities** Swimming pool, health center (20-80,000L), parking (35,000L). **Nearby** Sorrento, Gulf of Salerno and Amalfi coast (Positano, Amalfi, Ravello, Salerno), Paestum, Capri, Napoli, Pompeii, Herculaneum, Cuma, Pozzuolo sulphur springs, Ischia. **Open** April– Nov. 15.

As the Aonzo family likes to recall, the initial idea, back in the 1950s, was to build a nice little place to spend the holidays... Today it is a friendly hotel which, despite its stars, has kept a certain simplicity and conviviality that make guests feel right at home. The attentive hospitality adds to this feeling. Like the rest of the village, the house is built right onto the hill overlooking the bay, an exceptional location which means a wonderful view from the bedrooms, each with an individual terrace. The rooms are spacious and elegant, with all the comfort you expect from a 4-star hotel. The salons have the same refined sobriety. The panoramic terrace has been organized like a large living space — during the summer the restaurant is set up under the bougainvillea and a bit farther on is the swimming pool and the solarium. The hotel has recently opened a fitness center where you can treat yourself to a real cure, provided you can resist the attractions of Positano night life.

How to get there *(Map 20): 57 km south of Napoli via A3, Castellammare di Stabia exit, towards Sorrento, Positano.*

Hotel Palazzo Murat

Via dei Mulini, 23
84017 Positano (Salerno)
Tel. (0)89-875 177 - Fax (0)89-81 14 19 - Famiglia Attanasio
E-mail: hpm@starnet.it - Web: http://www.starnet.it/murat/welcome.html

Category ★★★★ **Rooms** 30 with air conditioning, telephone, bath, WC, TV and minibar. **Price** Single 230-250,000L, double 290-390,000L. **Meals** Breakfast included, served 8:00-11:00. **Restaurant** Solo la Sera, à la carte **Credit cards** All major. **Pets** Dogs allowed. **Nearby** Sorrento, Gulf of Salerno and Amalfi coast (Positano, Amalfi, Ravello, Salerno), Paestum, Capri, Napoli, Pompeii, Herculaneum, Cuma, Pozzuolo (sulphur springs), Ischia. **Open** Easter – Oct., Dec. 26 – Jan. 10.

Built as the summer home of Joachim Murat, Marshal of France and King of Naples, the *palazzo* was converted into a hotel several years ago. It is in Baroque style and has preserved the greater part of its original features, including an enchanting patio where chamber music concerts are sometimes held. The nicest rooms are those in the old part of the building (they are also the most expensive), in particular rooms 1 to 5, which have a balcony facing the Bay of Positano. However, most of those in the newer part of the house also have a balcony with a view of the sea. A few of the rooms have air conditioning. There is no access directly to the hotel by car, but you can park in the Piazza dei Mulini, some 50 meters away.

How to get there *(Map 20): 57 km south of Napoli via A3, Castellammare di Stabia exit, towards Sorrento, Positano. In the old town.*

Albergo Casa Albertina

Via Tavolozza, 3
84017 Positano (Salerno)
Tel. (0)89-87 51 43 - Fax (0)89-81 15 40 - Sig. L. Cinque
E-mail: alcaal@starnet.it

Rooms 21 with air conditioning, telephone, bath and shower, WC and minibar; elevator. **Price** Half board in single 150-240,000L, in double 150-170,000L, in suite 170-240,000L (per pers.). **Meals** Breakfast included, served 7:30-12:00. Half board 130-160,000L (per pers.). **Restaurant** Service 20:00-21:30; à la carte. Specialties: Risotto alla pescatore, penne all'impazzata, zuppa di pesce, pesce alla griglia. **Credit cards** All major. **Pets** Dogs allowed. **Facilities** Parking (30-35,000L). **Nearby** Sorrento, Gulf of Salerno and Amalfi coast (Positano, Amalfi, Ravello, Salerno), Paestum, Capri, Napoli, Pompeii, Herculaneum, Cuma, Pozzuolo sulphur springs, Ischia. **Open** All year.

Take a few steps up a steep little street and you will discover the simple but charming Albergo Casa Albertina. This old village house is run by the son of a fisherman, a former employee of the nearby Sirenuse. Apart from the marvelous 18th-century wooden doors, most of the hotel has a rakish 60's-style decor. However, the dishes, chairs and knick-knacks crafted by local artisans give the place an atmosphere typical of the region. Most of the rooms have a sea-view balcony–it's the perfect place to have breakfast. The service is particularly warm and friendly. You cannot reach the hotel by car, but porter service is available.

How to get there *(Map 20): 57 km south of Napoli via A3, Castellammare di Stabia exit,then S 145 to Meta and S 163 to Positano.*

Grand Hotel Tritone

Via Campo, 5
84010 Praiano (Salerno)
Tel. (0)89-87 43 33 - Fax (0)89-87 43 74 - Sig. Gagliano
E-mail: tritone@xcom.it - Web: http://www.xcom.it/tritone

Category ★★★★ **Rooms** 42 and 14 suites with air-conditioning, telephone, bath or shower, WC, satellite TV, minibar; elevator. **Price** Single 180-250,000L, double 270-360,000L, suite 420-480,000L. **Meals** Breakfast 18,000L, served 7:00-10:30; half board 175-290,000L, full board 215-330,000L. **Restaurant** Service 13:00-14:30, 19:30-21:30; menu 60,000L, also à la carte. Specialties: Risotto, seafood. **Credit cards** All major. **Pets** Dogs allowed. **Facilities** 2 swimming pools, private beach, parking. **Nearby** Sorrento, Gulf of Salerno and Amalfi coast (Positano, Amalfi, Ravello, Salerno), Paestum, Capri, Napoli, Pompeii, Herculaneum, Cuma, Pozzuolo sulphur springs, Ischia. **Open** Apr. 10 – Oct. 15.

This hotel, magnificently sited on a series of terraces dramatically descending to the sea, has long attracted politicians, sports and show business celebrities such as Madonna. You, too, will enjoy it all: the private beach (accessible by elevator), the two salt water swimming pools, the impeccable service and the hotel's grotto-level restaurant.

How to get there *(Map 20): 65 km southeast of Napoli via A3, Castellammare di Stabia exit, towards Sorrento, Positano.*

Hotel Palumbo - Palazzo Confalone

Via San Giovanni del Toro, 16
84010 Ravello (Salerno)
Tel. (0)89-85 72 44 - Fax (0)89-85 81 33 - Sig. Vuilleumier

Category ★★★★★ **Rooms** 21 with air-conditioning, telephone, bath or shower, WC, TV, safe and minibar. **Price** Half board in the palazzo 350-400,000L, in the annex 215-240,000L, full board in the palazzo 400-450,000L, in the annex 240-310,000L. **Meals** Breakfast included, served 7:30-10:30. **Restaurant** Service 12:30-14:30, 20:00-21:30; menu 95,000L, also à la carte. **Credit cards** All major. **Pets** Small dogs allowed. **Facilities** Parking (20,000L). **Nearby** Ravello (Villa Rufolo and Villa Cimbrone), Gulf of Salerno and Amalfi coast (Positano, Amalfi, Ravello, Salerno), Paestum, Capri, Napoli, Pompeii, Herculaneum, Cuma, Pozzuolo sulphur springs, Ischia. **Open** All year.

When Pasquale Palumbo came here from Switzerland in the 19th century, he opened a hotel in the Episcopal Palace, which quickly became the aristocratic rendez-vous of the whole Amalfi coast. When he opened his hotel in the Palazzo Confalone, his fame grew greater yet. This superb 18th-century mansion in Arab-Norman style has majolica-tiled floors, a patio with arcades of pointed arches and five labyrinthine stories opening on the sea. The interior decoration is beautiful, with antique furniture and paintings, including a large canvas from the school of Caravaggio in an alcove of the main salon. Each room has a particular character, as witnessed in the names they bear: *Suite Blu, Torre* or *Romantica*. The less expensive rooms are in the annex. Situated between mountains and sea, there is a wonderful view from every side. The garden is as romantic as can be, with rosebushes, arbors and trellises. The grandeur of the site adds to the luxury of the place, especially the endless view of the sea broken only by the white cliffs of the Cilento coast and the ruins of Paestum.

How to get there *(Map 20): 65 km southeast of Napoli.*

Hotel Caruso Belvedere

Via San Giovanni del Toro, 52
84010 Ravello (Salerno)
Tel. (0)89-85 71 11 - Fax (0)89-85 73 72 - Sig.ra Caruso

Category ★★★★ **Rooms** 24 with telephone, bath or shower and WC. **Price** With half board 250-344,000L, full board 330-420,000L (per 2 pers.). **Meals** Breakfast included, served 7:30-10:00. **Restaurant** Service 12:30-14:30, 19:30-21:00; closed 15 days in Feb.; menu 45,000L, also à la carte. Specialties: Crespolini al formaggio, spaghetti alla contadina, soufflé al limone e cioccolata. **Credit cards** All major. **Pets** Dogs allowed (fee). **Nearby** Ravello (Villa Rufolo and Villa Cimbrone), Gulf of Salerno and Amalfi coast (Positano, Amalfi, Ravello, Salerno), Paestum, Capri, Napoli, Pompeii, Herculaneum, Cuma, Pozzuolo sulphur springs, Ischia. **Open** All year.

The Caruso is tucked away in a quiet garden spot at the end of the little road that links it with the church of San Giovanni del Tore. You enter through a gate flanked by two ancient stone lions and framed by columns and pilasters, then go up one flight to reach the reception. The *palazzo* has well-preserved frescoes and tiled floors in geometric patterns. The walls of the large sitting room are thickly hung with an extensive collection of 19th-century paintings representing landscapes and interiors, and the room is brightened by a number of gaily-colored armchairs. The bedrooms are spacious and most of them offer an extraordinary panorama. The owner is attentive to the needs of his guests, both in the comfort of the surroundings and the quality of the cooking, which he himself supervises. Even though you have to take half-board, the prices here are quite reasonable. So come to Ravello and treat yourself to the unforgettable spectacle of the Gulf of Salerno from your window.

How to get there *(Map 20): 65 km southeast of Napoli via A3, Salerno exit, towards Vietri sul Mare and Ravello.*

Villa Cimbrone

Santa Chiara, 26
84010 Ravello (Salerno)
Tel. (0)89-85 74 59 - Fax (0)89-85 77 77
Famiglia Vuilleumier

Category ★★★★ **Rooms** 18 with telephone, (10 with bath or shower), WC. **Price** Single 250,000L, double and suite 350-550,000L. **Meals** Breakfast 18,000L, served 8:00-10:30. **Restaurant** See p. 443. **Credit cards** Amex, Visa, Eurocard, MasterCard. **Pets** Dogs not allowed. **Nearby** Ravello (Villa Rufolo and Villa Cimbrone), Gulf of Salerno and Amalfi coast (Positano, Amalfi, Ravello, Salerno), Paestum, Capri, Napoli, Pompeii, Herculaneum, Cuma, Pozzuolo sulphur springs, Ischia. **Open** All year except 2 weeks before Easter.

The wonderful gardens of the Villa Cimbrone are, along with those of the Villa Rufolo, one of the recommended sights for tourists visiting Ravello. From its belvedere and its antique-style terraces lined with statues you can admire the view and the spot where, according to legend, God once argued with the devil. But this is a nice place to stay as well as to look at. Periodic renovations have made sure that this historic hotel (Greta Garbo stayed here for some time with Leopold Stokowski) maintains a level of comfort in keeping with the grandeur of the site. Many of the rooms are quite comfortable; all of them have a fine view. Inside there are frescoes, chimneys, majolica tiles and above all a beautiful cloister that adds a touch of magic to the place.

How to get there *(Map 20): 65 km southeast of Napoli via A3, Salerno exit, towards Vietri sul Mare and Ravello.*

Hotel Corona d'Oro

Via Oberdan, 12
40126 Bologna
Tel. (0)51-23 64 56 - Fax (0)51-26 26 79 - Sig. Orsi
E-mail: hotcoro@tin.it

Category ★★★★ **Rooms** 35 with air-conditioning, telephone, bath or shower, WC, cable TV, minibar, safe; elevator. **Price** Single 200-320,000L, double 300-460,000L. **Meals** Breakfast included, served 7:00-11:00. **Restaurant** See pp. 444-445. **Credit cards** All major. **Pets** Dogs allowed. **Nearby** Bologna (Piazza Maggiore and Piazza del Nettuno, Churches of S. Petronio, S. Domenico, S. Francesco, National Picture Gallery), Madonna di San Lucca, San Michele in Bosco, "Giro sulle colline" (car tour around Bologna), Road of the castles (Bazzano, Monteveglio, S. Maria), Golf Course (18-hole) in Chiesa Nova di Monte San Pietro. **Open** All year.

The blend of styles in this small, four-star hotel right in the historical center of Bologna gives it a pleasant, informal atmosphere. Although the building dates from the 8th century, it has been modified several times; You can now admire a Madonna and Child from the 15th century as well as the Liberty-style stucco decoration circa 1900. The hotel continues to improve on what has been its reputation up to now: comfort, service, and quiet.

How to get there *(Map 10): via A14, Bologna-Arcoveggio exit. On the "Tangenziale," number 7 exit towards center and piazza Maggiore.*

Hotel Commercianti

Via de' Pignattari, 11
40124 Bologna
Tel. (0)51-23 30 52 - Fax (0)51-22 47 33 - Sig. Orsi
E-mail: hotcom@tin.it

Category ★★★ **Rooms** 35 with air-conditioning, telephone, shower, WC, cable TV, safe and minibar. **Price** Single 145-200,000L, double 210-300,000L. **Meals** Breakfast included, served 7:00-11:30. **Restaurant** See pp. 444-445. **Credit cards** All major. **Pets** Small dogs allowed. **Facilities** Parking (25,000L). **Nearby** Bologna (Piazza Maggiore and Piazza del Nettuno, Churches of S. Petronio, S. Domenico, S. Francesco, National Picture Gallery), Madonna di San Lucca, San Michele in Bosco, "Giro sulle colline" (car tour around Bologna), Road of the castles (Bazzano, Monteveglio, S. Maria), Golf Course (18-hole) in Chiesa Nova di Monte San Pietro. **Open** March to Dec.

The most convenient feature of this hotel is its location: right next to the San Petronio cathedral in a special traffic-free zone (which, however, hotel guests can enter with car to use the hotel garage). The Commercianti was originally the town hall in the 12th century, and a lot of the original architecture is still intact. The decor is functional and contemporary with air-conditioning and comfortable bathrooms. The nicest rooms in the old tower have a remarkable view of the rooftop stained-glass windows and of the cathedral. The other rooms look out on the Piazza Maggiore.

How to get there *(Map 10): via A14, Bologna-Arcoveggio exit. On the "Tangenziale," number 7 exit towards center and piazza Maggiore.*

Hotel Orologio

40123 Bologna
Via IV November, 10
Tel. (0)532-231 253- Fax (0)532-260 552 - Sig.ra Orsi
E-mail: hotoro@tin.it

Category ★★★ **Rooms** 32 with air-conditioning, telephone, Bath or shower, WC, cable TV, safe and minibar. **Price** Single 145-200,000L, double 210-300,000L. **Meals** Breakfast included, served 7:00-11:00. **Restaurant** See pp. 444-445. **Credit cards** All major. **Pets** Dogs allowed. **Facilities** Parking (30,000L). **Nearby** Bologna (Piazza Maggiore and Piazza del Nettuno, Churches of S. Petronio, S. Domenico, S. Francesco, National Picture Gallery), Madonna di San Lucca, San Michele in Bosco, "Giro sulle colline" (car tour around Bologna), Road of the castles (Bazzano, Monteveglio, S. Maria), Golf Course (18-hole) in Chiesa Nova di Monte San Pietro. **Open** All year.

This small well-located hotel is next to the Piazza Maggiore in Bologna, one of the most visited towns in Italy, where it can be especially difficult to find a place to stay in professional exhibit season. This town is also a great place for tourism and gastronomy. The Hotel Orlogio has been entirely renovated and now offers comfortable, more personalized rooms, most of which have a nice view on the oldest vestiges of the town. The professionalism of the Orsi family, which runs some of the finest establishments in town, is evident in the quality of the service. Don't lose this address.

***How to get there** (Map 10): via A14, Bologna-Arcoveggio exit. On the "Tangenziale," number 7 exit towards center and piazza Maggiore.*

Locanda della Duchessina

Vicolo Voltino, 11
44100 Ferrara
Tel. (0)532-20 21 21 - Fax (0)532-20 26 38
Sig.ra Evelina Bonzagni

Category ★★★ **Rooms** 5 with air-conditioning, tel, bath or shower, WC, satellite TV, minibar, safe. **Price** Single 140,000L, double 180-220,000L, suite 270,000L. **Meals** Breakfast served 7:00-10:00, half board 110-140,000L (per pers.). **Restaurant** See p. 445-446. **Credit cards** All major. **Pets** Dogs allowed (+15,000L). **Nearby** Ferrara (Duomo, Palace of Ludivic the Moor, Castello Estense, Diamond Palace, spectacle of the traditional Palio in May), Abbey of S Bartolo, Cento and Pieve di Cento. **Open** All year (except in August).

Ferrara is well worth a visit, with its Renaissance houses and art treasures, the heritage of its long and splendid past. The Locanda della Duchessina, which has just opened, is a new and much less expensive addition to the luxurious Duchessa Isabella. It is a small building with an interior courtyard and a few quiet, comfortable rooms, though their style (like that of the Duchessa, for that matter) is a bit too "cute" for our taste. Nevertheless, it has a good location near the center of town and makes a nice stopover in a city that still lacks a "hotel of charm." An added plus is that guests who present this guide will get an 8% reduction on the price of a room.

***How to get there** (Map 10): 47 km Northeast of Bologna via A 13, Ferrara-North exit.*

Locanda Borgonuovo

Via Cairoli, 29
44100 Ferrara
Tel. (0)532-21 11 00 - Fax (0)532-24 80 00 - Sig.ra A. Ornandini
Web: www.4net.com/business/borgonuovo

Rooms 4 with air-conditioning, tel, shower, WC, TV, minibar. **Price** Single 95-000L, double 130-160,000L. **Meals** Breakfast included, served 7:30-10:00. **Restaurant** See p. 445-446. **Credit cards** Amex, Visa, Eurocard, MasterCard. **Pets** Dogs not allowed. **Facilities** Bikes. **Nearby** Ferrara (Duomo, Palace of Ludivic the Moor, Castello Estense, Diamond Palace, spectacle of the traditional Palio in May), Abbey of S Bartolo, Cento and Pieve di Cento. **Open** All year.

In the heart of this old city that was once the home of the Dukes of Este, the Borgonuovo offers all the intimacy of a little guest house. Built within the walls of a 15th-century monastery, it is a nice stopping place in a city that really lacks hotels of charm and where all the accommodations tend to be on the expensive side, particularly for someone traveling alone. The four rooms in the house are fairly small, simply decorated, but with all the necessary amenities. One of them even has a kitchenette (5,000 L. extra per person/per day) for guests who plan a longer stay. In fine weather, the copious breakfast is served on the patio of the locanda. Or you can breakfast in the living room you share with the owners, who are both friendly and helpful. They have bicycles for rent to tour the historic center, which is now (like elsewhere in Italy) completely off-limits to cars. A good address to keep in mind to visit a city that deserves to be better known.

How to get there *(Map 10): 47 km Northeast of Bologna via A 13, Ferrara-North exit; in the old city.*

Canalgrande Hotel

Corso Canalgrande, 6
41100 Modena
Tel. (0)59-21 71 60 - Fax (0)59-22 16 74

Category ★★★★ **Rooms** 79 with air-conditioning, telephone, bath or shower, WC, TV and minibar; elevator. **Price** Single 189,000L, double 275,000L, triple. 333,000L, suite 432,000L. **Meals** Breakfast included, served 7:00-10:30. **Restaurant** Service 12:30-13:45, 19:30-21:45; closed Tuesday; menus 35-45,000L, also à la carte. Specialties: Paste modenesi, verdure ai ferri, dolci casalinghi. **Credit cards** All major. **Pets** Dogs allowed. **Facilities** Garage (15,000L). **Nearby** Modena (Duomo, Estense Gallery and Library), Roman churches of San Cesario sul Panano and of Pieve Trebbio near Monteorsello, Abbey of Nonantola, Golf Course (27-hole) in Colombaro di Formigine. **Open** All year.

The Canalgrande is located right in the center of town, and has a large garden with a charming fountain surrounded by enormous several-hundred-year-old trees. Formerly a patrician villa, it is today a hotel with Neoclassical architecture. The foyer and the series of salons around the entry are handsomely done in stucco. Contemporary armchairs and beautiful old paintings give the place a cosy atmosphere. The guest rooms and bathrooms are comfortable. Be sure to check out La Secchia Rapita, the restaurant in the cellar, with its beautiful vaulted brick ceiling.

How to get there *(Map 9): 39 km northwest of Bologna via A1, Modena-South exit, then S9 (via Emilia-East) to Corso Canalgrande and to the left (near by the church).*

Villa Gaidello 

Via Gaidello, 18
41013 Castelfranco Emilia (Modena)
Tel. (0)59-92 68 06 - Fax (0)59-92 66 20
Sig.ra Bini

Apartments 3 with bath or shower, WC, TV and minibar. **Price** 150-310,000L. **Meals** Breakfast included, served 8:00-10:00. **Restaurant** Service 13:00, 20:00; menus 70,000L. Specialties: Regional cooking. **Credit cards** All major. **Pets** Dogs not allowed. **Facilities** Lake in the park, parking. **Nearby** Church in Castelfranco, Modena, Roman churchs of San Cesario sul Panano and of Pieve Trebbio near by Monteorsello, Abbey of Nonantola, Bologna, Golf Course (27-hole) in Colombaro di Formigine. **Open** All year (except Aug., Sunday evening, Monday).

If you plan to stay a while in Bologna or Modena and if you like country living, perhaps you will decide to stay at Signora Bini's lovely farmhouse, several miles away from these two large towns. She has only three apartments, each sleeping from 2 to 5 persons. Somewhere between an inn and a guest house, the appeal of this place lies in the arts of hospitality and a cuisine based largely on homemade products. You must book in advance, whether for lodging or for meals — the lodgings are justly appreciated for their country charm and Signora Bini's cooking for the quality and freshness of the products: her pasta is made the day it is used, fruits and vegetables come from her garden and the wine is grown in the estate vineyards. An appealing spot.

How to get there *(Map 9): 13 km southeast of Modena - 26 km northwest of Bologna via S9 (the hotel is in the country, 1 km from the city).*

Hotel Al Vecchio Convento

Via Roma, 7
47010 Portico di Romagna (Forli)
Tel. (0)543-96 70 14 - Fax (0)543-96 71 57
Sig.ra Raggi

Category ★★★ **Rooms** 14 with telephone (9 with bath or shower and TV.). **Price** Single 90,000L, double 120,000L. **Meals** Breakfast 15,000L, served at any time; half board 120,000L (per pers. 3 days min.). **Restaurant** Service 12:30-14:00, 19:30-22:00, closed Wenesday except in summer; menus 35-55,000L, also à la carte. Specialties: Funghi tartufi, cacciagione. **Credit cards** All major. **Pets** Dogs not allowed. **Facilities** Parking. **Nearby** Church of Polenta, Biblioteca Malatestiana in Cesena, Abbey of Madona del Monte near Cesena, Ravenna. **Open** All year.

This former convent now converted into a hotel adjoins the palace of Beatrice Portinari — the famous "Beatrice" who so inspired Dante. Here all the skills of local artists and craftsmen were put to use to restore the antique furniture — wooden or iron beds, period chests and chairs — and the original architecture of the building. In the cooking as well, tradition is respected: Many dishes are based on vegetables, rice or pasta and you can end the meal with a glass of *laurino,* the local liqueur. Breakfast is now served in a new dining room near the garden and the jams and preserves on the breakfast table are also homemade. Hospitality is another tradition and you won't be disappointed here, either. An address that's worth a detour to sample the charm of old Italy.

How to get there *(Map 10): 97 km southeast of Bologna via A14, Forli exit - S67 (towards Firenze).*

Hotel Della Porta

Via Andrea Costa, 85
47038 Santarcangelo di Romagna (Forli)
Tel. (0)541-62 21 52 - Fax (0)541-62 21 68

Category ★★★ **Rooms** 22 and 2 suites with air-conditioning, telephone, bath, WC, TV and minibar. **Price** Single 100-120,000L, double 140-170,000L, suite 240,000L. **Meals** Breakfast included, served 7:00-10:30. **Restaurant** See p. 448. **Credit cards** All major. **Pets** Dogs allowed. **Facilities** Sauna (15,000L), parking. **Nearby** Santarcangelo (museum, Rocco Malatestiana, San Michele), Verruchio, Longiano, Rimini, San Marino, Amalia Golf Course (9-hole). **Open** All year.

The Hotel Della Porta is in Santarcangelo, several miles from Rimini, in Montefeltro, between Romagna and the Marches. This region was the cradle of the famous Malatesta family, and is dotted with splendid Renaissance monuments, along with traces of the forbidden romance of Francesca and Paolo, which Dante immortalized in his "Divine Comedy." It consists of two houses in the old village. The spacious salon-reception area serves as a tourist information office. It is illuminated by a sizeable skylight, and decorated in contemporary style. The guest rooms are large and very comfortable and have a more traditional decor. A nice touch is that each one has a work or living area. Our favorite rooms are in the adjoining house, with its antique furniture and ornate frescoes of flowers on the ceiling. There is no restaurant, but the hotel will help make arrangements with the best ones in the village.

How to get there *(Map 11): 15 km west of Rimini; via A14 Rimini-North exit, then towards Santarcangelo.*

Hotel Verdi

43100 Parma
Viale Pasini, 18
Tel. and Fax (0)521-29 35 39 - Sig Dondi

Category ★★★★ **Rooms** 20 with air-conditioning, telephone, bath and shower, WC, TV, minibar, safe; elevator. **Price** Single 220,000L, double 290,000L, suite 330,000L. **Meals** Breakfast 15,000L, served 7:00-12:00; half board +35,000L (per pers., 3 days min.). **Restaurant** «Santa Croce». Service 12:00-14:00, 20:00-22:00; closed Sat. lunch and Sun.; menu and carte 50-60,000L. Specialties: Regional cooking. **Credit cards** All major. **Pets** Dogs not allowed. **Facilities** Parking, garage. **Nearby** Parma (Duomo, Baptistery, Abbey of St. John, National Gallery, Farnese Theater, Arturo Toscanini's Birthplace), House of Verdi in Roncole, Verdi Theater in Busseto, Villa Verdi in Sant'Agata, Mantova, Sabbioneta. **Open** All year except 2 weeks in Aug.

Surprisingly little known, the city of Parma shines like a little Mannerist jewel set into northern Italy with its palaces and churches that so many illustrious painters (Corregio and Parmigiano, among others) adorned with their works. The city is also known for its cooking and boasts more fine restaurants than it does hotels of charm. The Hotel Verdi is one of the rare ones. Near the gardens of the Ducal Palace, it started out as a Liberty-style villa. It was recently restored and is now a pleasant, charming place to stay for anyone who wants to explore Parma. Just a few steps from the hotel, you mustn't miss the famous restaurant Santa Croce where you can taste the specialties: *culatello* and the homemade tortelli and lasagna. One drawback: as the hotel is near the road, the rooms on that side are a bit noisy. However, they were recently soundproofed, which should have solved the problem.

How to get there *(Map 9): 13 km southeast of Modena - 96 km northwest of Bologna via S9.*

Locanda del Lupo

Via Garibaldi, 64
43019 Soragna (Parma)
Tel. (0)524-59 71 00 - Fax (0)524-59 70 66 - Sig. E. Dioni
E-mail: locanda@polaris.it

Category ★★★★ **Rooms** 46 with air-conditioning, telephone, bath or shower, WC and satellite TV. **Price** Single 140,000L, double 200,000L, suite 270,000 L. **Meals** Breakfast included, served 7:30-10:30; half board 140-160,000L (per pers.). **Restaurant** Service 12:00-14:00, 19:30-22:00; menu : 55,000L, also à la carte. Specialties: Salami tipici, formaggi di Parma, tortelli di ricotta. **Credit cards** All major. **Pets** Dogs allowed in the rooms only. **Facilities** Parking. **Nearby** Parma; Verdi pilgrimage tour: Arturo Toscanini's birthplace in Parma, House of Verdi in Roncole, Verdi Theater in Busseto, Villa Verdi in Sant'Agata; La Rocca golf course (9-hole) in Sala Barganza. **Open** All year (except Aug. 10-20).

For years, Locanda del Lupo was famous locally for its fine cuisine, and appreciated as well by Parisian gastronomic critics. It has now expanded operatious to become a hotel. The rooms and salons are simply decorated but refined and comfortable. The main attraction, however, remains the restaurant where early recipes from the archives of Prince Meli Lupi, a former resident, are brilliantly prepared and served. The wine cellar is well stocked. You may count on a warm welcome here.

How to get there *(Map 9): 33 km northwest of Parma via A1, Fidenza exit.*

Bisanzio Hotel

Via Salara, 30
48100 Ravenna
Tel. (0)544-21 71 11 - Fax (0)544-32 539
Sig.ra Fabbri

Category ★★★★ **Rooms** 38 with air-conditioning, telephone, bath or shower, WC, cable TV, safe and minibar, elevator. **Price** Single 140,000L, double 160-210,000L. **Meals** Breakfast included (buffet), served 7:00-10:00. **Restaurant** See p.446-447. **Credit cards** All major. **Pets** Dogs allowed. **Facilities** Swimming pool, sauna, parking. **Nearby** Ravenna (The Neoiam Baptistery, Archiepiscopal Museum and Church of St. Andrea, Church of San Vitale, Basilica of St. Apollinare Nuovo, Dante's Tomb), Basilica of St. Apollinare in Classe (about 4 miles south of the city, bus no. 4), The Adriatic coast, Adriatic Golf Course (18-hole). **Open** All year (except Dec. – Jan.).

Don't be misled by the unimpressive facade of the Hotel Bisanzio. Once you cross the threshold you will find yourself in a charming lounge-reception room that is as comfortable and inviting as could be. It is furnished in 1920s style and opens onto a little garden. The rooms are small but pleasant and tastefully decorated. The bathrooms are modern and well-designed. In short, the Bisanzio has benefited from a true professionalism without losing any of its provincial charm. Ideally located in the center of Ravenna, the hotel is just behind the Cathedral San Vitale and the mausoleum of Galla Placidia with its deservedly famous mosaics. From this location, you can visit the whole town on foot. Ever since the town authorities limited traffic in the Via Salara, the rooms facing the street are as quiet as those in the rear.

How to get there *(Map 10): 74 km east of Bologna.*

Il Palazzo 

Via Baccagnano, 110
48013 Brisighella (Ravenna)
Tel. and Fax (0)546-803 38
Sig. Matarese

Rooms 4 with shower. **Price** Double 80,000L. **Meals** Breakfast included, served 8:30-10:00. **Restaurant** Service 12:30-20:00; menu 25,000L. Specialties: Organic cooking. **Credit cards** Not accepted. **Pets** Dogs not allowed. **Facilities** Parking. **Nearby** In Brisighella: La Rocca, sanctuary of Monticino, Termes, Pieve del Tho (S.Giovanni in Ottovano), Park Carnè (walks), Park della Vena del Gesso (la Tanaccia), Modigliona, Faenza (museum), Ravenna, Rimini, Riolo Terme golf course (18-hole). **Open** All year.

Brisighella, a charming medieval village in the foothills of the Appenines, is also a health spa with thermal springs. The Adriatic beaches are close by and an excursion to Rimini is a must: One should make sure to see the Temple Malatestino for the grandiose architecture of Leon Battista Alberti and for the lovely fresco by Piero della Francesca. Ravenna, with its celebrated mosaics, is also nearby. If you plan to visit this region, this simple inn is a nice place to stay. Its architect/owner has designed the rooms in a style that is modern and rustic at the same time, with a charm of their own. Their windows look out over the vineyards and orchards all around. In May, impressive numbers of fireflies will accompany your evening strolls. If you eat on the premises, you will be pleased to know that the bread and all the specialties are made by the mistress of the house, with organically-grown products.

How to get there *(Map 10): 6 km of Faenza. A 14, Faenza exit. In Brisighella, towards Terme/Modigliona.Il Palazzo is on the left after the Hôtel Terme.*

Relais Torre Pratesi

Cavina 48013 Brisighella (Ravenna)
Via Cavina, 11
Tel. (0)546-845 45 - Fax (0)546-845 58
Sig.ra and Sig. Raccagni

Category ★★★★ **Rooms** 3 and 4 suites with air-conditioning, telephone, bath or shower, WC, TV, minibar and safe. **Price** Double 200,000L, suite 250,000L. **Meals** Breakfast included, served to 14:00; half board 150-1750,000L (per pers.). **Restaurant** Service 20:00-22:00; closed Tues.; menu and carte 70,000L. Specialties: Regional cooking. **Credit cards** All major. **Pets** Dogs allowed. **Facilities** Golf Club la Torre, Manneggio Villa Corte, thermal baths «Riolo Terme». **Nearby** Faenza, Brisighella, Church of San Pietro in Sylvis, Ravenna. **Open** All year.

This massive hotel towers deep in the lush Romagnian countryside, which is famous for its wine, oil and truffles. It was built in 1510, and a farm was added in the 19th century. Renovated with careful attention to artistic detail, the rooms have the spacious dimensions of days gone by. The elegant simplicity of the furniture highlights the materials, stone and wood. The modern conveniences do not at all detract from the beautiful restoration work. Home-style cuisine allows you to savor products fresh from your hosts‘ farm. This place is magical–it's a great way to experience the beautiful, well-preserved Lamona valley, which extends all the way to Florence.

How to get there *(Map 10): 28 km south pf Faenza, via A14, Faenza exit, then S302 (Brisighella-Firenze) to Fognano, then towards Valletta during 4 km.*

Hotel Posta

Piazza del Monte, 2
42100 Reggio Nell'Emilia
Tel. (0)522-43 29 44 - Fax (0)522-45 26 02
C. Salomon

Category ★★★★ **Rooms** 43 with telephone, bath or shower, WC, TV and minibar. **Price** Single 210,000L, double 270,000L, suite 310,000L, apartment 390,000L. **Meals** Breakfast included, served 7:00-10:30. **Restaurant** See p. 448. **Credit cards** All major. **Pets** Dogs allowed. **Facilities** Parking (20,000L). **Nearby** Church of San Faustino in Rubiera, Church of Novallara, Château of Scandiano, Parma, Matilde di Canossa Golf Course (18-hole). **Open** All year.

This former palace is in an ideal location in the heart of the historic town center, on Cesare Battisti Square. The austere medieval facade conceals the rococo interior which is embellished with old stucco ornaments from the walls of a famous local bakery frequented by the notables of the town. The rooms are highly original and offer all the comforts you would expect from a four-star hotel.

How to get there *(Map 9): 27 km southeast of Parma via A1, Reggio Nell'Emilia exit.*

Albergo delle Notarie

Via Pallazuolo, 5
42100 Reggio nell'Emilia
Tel. (0)522-45 35 00 - Fax (0)522-45 37 37
Dr Stefano Zamichelli

Category ★★★★ **Rooms** 34 with air-conditioning, tel, bath or shower, WC, satellite TV, minibar; elevator. **Price** Single 190-200,000L, double 230-245,000L, suite 270-350,000L. **Meals** Breakfast 20,000L, served 7:00-10:00. **Restaurant** Service 12:30-14:30, 19:30-22:30; closed Sat., (Jun - Sept. closed Sat and Sun.); menu 45,000L, also à la carte. Specialties: Regional cooking. **Credit cards** All major. **Pets** Dogs allowed. **Facilities** Parking (20,000L). **Pets** Dogs not allowed. **Nearby** San Faustino church in Rubiera, Novallara Churche, Chateau of Scandiano, Canossa, Parma, Golf course (18-hole). **Open** All year (except in August.).

The town of Reggio nell'Emilia may not have the splendor if its more famous neighbors, Parma and Modena, but it is still an interesting and pleasant stop. The two basilicas of San Prospero and della Ghiara, near the hotel, bear witness to the artistic treasures of its past. The Albergo delle Notarie is located in the old quarter and shares the town's discreet yet colorful elegance. The recent renovation opted for simplicity and comfort: a spare, refined look determined by the size of the rooms and choice of furniture, whether modern or period. A major asset is a good restaurant where you can sample the pasta, ham and sausages that make the province of Emilia a famous culinary center.

How to get there *(Map 9): 27 km southwest of Parma via A 1, Reggio nell'Emilia exit.*

Albergo Casa Matilda

42030 Puianello (Reggio Emilia)
Via A. Negri, 11
Tel. and Fax (0)522-88 90 06
Famiglia Bertolini

Category ★★★★ **Rooms** 7 with telephone, bath, WC, minibar and TV. **Price** Single 200,000L, double 250,000L, suite 300-400,000L. **Meals** Breakfast included, served from 7:30. **Credit cards** All major. **Pets** Dogs not allowed. **Facilities** Swimming pool. **Nearby** Parma, Verdi pilgrimage tour: Arturo Toscanini's Birthplace in Parma, House of Verdi in Roncole, Verdi Theater in Busseto, Villa Verdi in Sant'Agata; La Rocca golf course (9-hole) in Sala Barganza. **Open** All year.

If you would like to get away from it all in a country setting, where fine dining is time-honored tradition, Casa Matilde is adestination to consider. This friendly inn, in the shady hills of the Parmesan Appenin, is in the middle of a small park full of flowers. The spacious rooms are individually decorated. The large beautiful salons have been carefully laid out to ensure that you have all of the comforts of home. The surroundings are perfect for long romantic walks. Your hostess will be happy to answer any questions you might have. She knows all about this *queen-valkyrie* named Matilda and the mysteries of the region.

How to get there *(Map 9): 35 km southwest of Parma; 10 km of Reggio Emilia. Via A1, Reggio Emilia exit, then towards Puianello-Quattro Castella.*

Hotel Castello Miramare

Via Pagnano
04023 Formia (Latina)
Tel. (0)771-70 01 38 - Fax (0)771-70 01 39
Sig.ra Celletti

Category ★★★★ **Rooms** 10 with air conditioning, telephone, bath or shower, WC, TV, safe and minibar. **Price** Single 100-110,000L, double 130-150,000L. **Meals** Breakfast 16,000L, served 7:30-12:00; half board 130-160,000L, full board 150-180,000L. (per pers., 3 days min.). **Restaurant** Service 12:30-15:00, 19:30-21:30; menu 65,000L, also à la carte. Specialties: Tonnarelli all'aragosta e funghi, cocktail di astice alla catalana. **Credit cards** All major. **Pets** Small dogs allowed. **Facilities** Parking. **Nearby** Cicero's Tomb, Church of San Pietro in Minturno, Abbey of Montecassino, Island of Ponza. **Open** All year.

The Castello Miramare is a good stopping place on the way to the south of Italy. The town of Formia is of no particular interest except for Latin scholars who may want to visit Cicero's tomb, 2 kilometers away along the Appian way. The castle itself has several rooms with modern comfort and old-style decor, handsome gardens and numerous public rooms. These facilities are often used for receptions, but the staff members are very nice and they will go out of their way to make sure that these events do not in any way inconvenience individual clients.

How to get there *(Map 19): 76 km southeast of Latina via A2, Cassino exit, then S630 towards Formia and SS7.*

Hotel Cernia

Isola di Ponza
Via Panoramica
Chiaia di Luna 04027 Ponza (Latina)
Tel. (0)771-804 12/80 99 51 - Fax (0)771-80 99 54 - Sig. Greca

Rooms 60 (40 with air conditioning), telephone, bath or shower, WC, TV and minibar. **Price** Single 150-190,000L, double 220-330,000L. **Meals** Breakfast incl., served 8:30-10:30. **Restaurant** Service 13:00-14:30, 20:00-21:30; menus 60-70,000L, also à la carte. Specialties: Seafood, italian and regional cuisine. **Credit cards** All major. **Pets** Dogs allowed. **Facilities** Swimming pool, tennis, private bus. **Nearby** Beach of Chaia di Luna. **Open** April 1-Oct.

Buried in a dense and fragrant garden, the Cernia is just a five minute walk from the beautiful Chiaia di Luna beach, and near the port where you will find the most famous restaurant on the island, Gennarino a Mare. The hotel is vast and the rooms numerous. Certain rooms-201, 202, 203 and 204–have a large terrace and a rewarding view of the sea. The straw window-shades, wicker furniture, rocking chairs and white couches create a friendly vacation atmosphere in the salon enfilade. The beach isn't far away, but a swim in the large hotel swimming pool set in the shade can also be nice on a hot summer day.

How to get there *(Map 18): Ferry services from Rome, Napoli, Anzio, San Felice Circeo, Terracina, Formia (1:30/2:00) - cars are permitted in summer if you stay 15 days minimum on the island.*

Hotel Le Dune

04016 Sabaudia (Latina)
Lungomare
Tel. (0)773-511 511 - Fax (0)773-55 643
Sig. Zanotti

Rooms 78 with air conditioning, telephone, bath or shower, WC, TV and 10 with minibar. **Price** Single 130-165,000L, double 190-270,000L, suite 450-550,000L. **Meals** Breakfast (buffet) 20,000L, served 7:30-12:00; half board 165-230,000L, full board 190-265,000L (per pers., 3 days min.). **Restaurant** Service 13:00-14:30, 19:30-22:00; menus and carte 50-70,000L. Specialties: Pesce - risotto alla crema di scampi, ravioli con ripieno di scamorza e melanzane, spigola al cartoccio. **Credit cards** All major. **Pets** Dogs not allowed. **Facilities** Swimming pool, tennis (16,000L), sauna, parking. **Nearby** Beach. **Open** Apr. – Oct.

This hotel is in Sarabuda, a vacation spot for the Roman intelligentsia. Some 60 miles from Rome, it has all of the advantages of a beach resort, located in a national park on a peninsula extending all the way into the shade of the majestic Circeo promontory. The spacious comfortable rooms are all on the sea, just in front of the hotel, past the pool and the private beach. When the morning mist lifts, you can see the island of Ponza from your balcony. The restaurant features "elaborate" and (sometimes happy) seafood cuisine. If you would like a break from the hustle and bustle of Rome, don't hesitate to come here and enjoy the sea air, but if its peace and quiet you are looking for, you'd better come in June or September.

How to get there *(Map 18): 20 km south of Latina, on the sea front 2 km of Sabaudia.*

Hotel Punta Rossa

Via delle Batteria
04017 San Felice Circeo (Latina)
Tel. (0)773-54 80 85 - Fax (0)773-54 80 75
E-mail: punta-rossa@panservice.it - Web: italyhotel.com/lazio/punta-rossa

Category ★★★★ **Rooms** 36 and 4 suites and 20 mini-apartments with air-conditioning, telephone, bath or shower, WC, TV, video and minibar. **Price** Double 220-450,000L, suite 420-520,000L. **Meals** Breakfast incl., served 8:00-11:00; half board in high season 275,000L (per pers.). **Restaurant** Service 13:00-14:30, 20:00-22:30; menu 65,000L. Specialties: Tonnarelli seafood, frutti di mare. **Credit cards** All major. **Pets** Dogs allowed. **Facilities** Swimming pool, sauna (+ 20,000L), private beach, health center, parking. **Nearby** Terracina, Abbey of Fossanova, Temple of Jupiter Anxur, National park of Circeo. **Open** All year.

The seven-and-a-half acres of the Hotel Punta Rossa lie within a protected site on the San Felice Circeo peninsula, a truly unique location. The architecture is slightly dated, but the hotel is otherwise fully up-to-date. It looks like a miniature village set into the contours of a hill abounding with lush vegetation. The rooms are vast in size, simply decorated, and very comfortable. They all face the sea, and most of them have landscaped terraces. Several mini-apartments, suitable for four to six people are tucked away in the garden; there can be rented by the week. The hotel has a health-and-beauty center, a nice salt-water swimming pool, a private beach, and a small port at the end of a path that winds through the rocks and plantings. The restaurant is excellent.

How to get there *(Map 18): 106 km southeast of Rome via A1, exit N148, towards Latina then Terracina.*

Parkhotel Fiorelle

Via Fiorelle, 12
04029 Sperlonga (Latina)
Tel. (0)771-540 92 - Fax (0)771-540 92
Sig. Di Mille

Category ★★★ **Rooms** 33 with telephone, bath or shower, WC and safe. **Price** Single 125,000L, double 145,000L. **Meals** Breakfast 10,000L, served 8:00-9:30; half board 95-125,000L, full board 100-135,000L (per pers.). **Restaurant** Only for residents - Service 13:00-14:00, 19:30-22:00; closed Friday, menu 35,000L, also à la carte. Specialties: Seafood, regional cooking. **Credit cards** Visa, MasterCard. **Pets** Dogs allowed. **Facilities** Swimming pool, private beach, parking. **Nearby** In Sperlonga: National Archeological Museum and Tiberius, Grotto; Terracina (Duomo and Piazza del Municipio), Abbey of Fossanova. **Open** Easter – Oct. 1.

The regulars who come to the Fiorelle to unwind year after year tend to keep their distance from newcomers. This works out very well within the overall peaceful ambiance which the owners carefully cultivate for all their guests. No one from outside the hotel is admitted to the bar, the pool, or the private beach. The garden, an important part of the pleasant experience of the hotel, is well kept and has flowers blooming year-round. Meals are prepared with fresh vegetables from the garden, and menus are submitted to the guests the day before for selection.

How to get there *(Map 19): 57 km southeast of Latina via S148 to Terracina, then S213 to Sperlonga.*

Hotel Borgo Paraelios

02040 Poggio Mirteto Scalo (Rieti)
Valle Collicchia
Tel. (0)765-26 267 - Fax (0)765-26 268
Sig. Salabe

Category ★★★★★ **Rooms** 13 and 2 suites with air-conditioning, telephone, bath or shower, WC and TV. **Price** single 350,000L, double 450,000L. **Meals** Breakfast 25-35,000L, served 8:00-10:30; half board 690,000L. (per 2 pers., wine not incl.). **Restaurant** Service 13:00-15:00, 20:00-22:30; menus 100-130,000L, also à la carte. Specialties: Italian cooking. **Credit cards** All major **Pets** Dogs allowed (+suppl.). **Facilities** 2 swimming pools (1 indoor), tennis, sauna, parking, private bus to the station or airport, parking. **Nearby** Roma, Colle dei Tetti golf course (9-hole). **Open** All year.

The Borgo Paraelios is amazing: there are few rooms but many salons of all sizes. It is, above all, a haven of elegance in the Roman countryside. The sumptuous decor of this splendid house compares favorably with the luxury level typically found in palaces. There are very beautiful furnishings and paintings in every room, including the garden-level rooms. Try your best billiard shots under the stony gaze of Roman emperors carved in marble. This place is quiet, luxurious, exquisite.

How to get there *(Map 14): 40 km north of Rome via A1, Fiano Romano exit - until S4 to Passo Corese, S313, Poggio Mirteto, towards Cantalupo Terni.*

Hotel Lord Byron

Via G. de Notaris, 5
00197 Rome
Tel. (0)6-322 04 04 - Fax (0)6-322 04 05
Sig. Ottaviani and A. Savona

Category ★★★★★ **Rooms** 37 with air-conditioning, telephone, bath, WC, TV, safe and minibar; elevator. **Price** Double 400-620,000L, suite 800-1 000,000L. **Meals** Breakfast incl., served from 7:00. **Restaurant** Service 12:30-15:00, 20:00-22:30, closed Sunday and 2 weeks in Aug., à la carte. **Credit cards** All major. **Pets** Small dogs allowed (fee). **Facilities** Parking. **Nearby** Tivoli (Villa d'Este, Villa Adriana), Castelli Romani (Castel Gandolfo, Frascati, Grottaferrata), Anzio and Nettuno, Palestrina, Anagni, Etruscan zone (Cerveteri, Tarquinia), golf course (9-18-hole) in Rome. **Open** All year.

The Lord Byron is located in the heart of the Parioli district–the most fashinable in Rome–facing the Villa Borghese gardens. Amadeo Ottaviani, the owner, has given it a high-style look. Thick luxurious carpeting, capacious white armchairs bearing the initials of the hotel, lacquered white ceilings, sumptuous bouquets and many other details reflect his taste for perfection. The Relais du Jardin restaurant is popular with Romans, who come for the fine dining and the lovely decor. Spend some time at the bar; your companion might turn out to be a countess.

How to get there *(Map 14): Near the Galleria Nazionale d'Arte Moderna - and the Villa Borghese gardens.*

Hotel Giulio Cesare

Via degli Scipioni, 287
00192 Rome
Tel. (0)6-321 07 51 - Fax (0)6-321 17 36 - Sig. Pandolfi
E-mail: guilioce@uni.net - Web: http://www.travel.it/roma/giulioce/giulioce.html

Category ★★★★ **Rooms** 90 with air-conditioning, telephone, bath or shower, WC, satellite TV and minibar, elvator. **Price** Single 310,000L, double 410,000L. **Meals** Breakfast incl., served 7:00-10:30. **Restaurant** See pp. 448-450. **Credit cards** All major. **Pets** Dogs not allowed. **Facilities** Parking. **Nearby** Tivoli (Villa d'Este, Villa Adriana), Castelli Romani (Castel Gandolfo, Frascati, Grottaferrata), Anzio and Nettuno, Palestrina, Anagni, Etruscan zone (Cerveteri, Tarquinia), golf course (9-18-hole) in Rome. **Open** All year.

An atmosphere of elegance pervades this large hotel, the former residence of Countess Solari. Antique furniture, rugs, and tapestries give the rooms a feeling of well-being and comfort. Breakfast is served in the garden as soon as the weather permits. You may want to spend some time there, as it is one of the most charming parts of this lovely hotel.

How to get there *(Map 14): Near the Piazza del Popolo.*

Hotel d'Inghilterra

Via Bocca di Leone, 14
00187 Rome
Tel. (0)6-69 981 - Fax (0)6-699 222 43 - Sig. Ensoli
E-mail: reservation@charminghotels.it - Web: http://www.charminghotels.it

Category ★★★★ **Rooms** 90 and 12 suites with air-conditioning, telephone, bath or shower, WC, TV and minibar, elevator. **Price** Single 340-375,000L, double 460-540,000L, suite 690-1 600,000L. **Meals** Breakfast 30,000L, served 7:30-10:30. **Restaurant** Service 12:30-15:30, 19:30-22:30; menus 60-80,000L, also à la carte. Specialties: New italian cuisine. **Credit cards** All major. **Pets** Dogs not allowed. **Nearby** Tivoli (Villa d'Este, Villa Adriana), Castelli Romani (Castel Gandolfo, Frascati, Grottaferrata), Anzio and Nettuno, Palestrina, Anagni, Etruscan zone (Cerveteri, Tarquinia), golf course (9-18-hole) in Rome. **Open** All year.

Anatole France, Franz Liszt, and Felix Mendelssohn have all stayed at the Hotel d'Inghilterra, a first-class grand hotel and a favorite among celebrities all over the world. It is on a pedestrian cul-de-sac near the Piazza di Spagna, and has recently been carefully restored. The lobby is superb, done in black and white marble, with stucco columns decorated with white palm trees. The salon is decorated with both antique and contemporary furniture, oriental rugs, and marvelous Neapolitan gouache paintings. The rooms are all excellent, but if you want to have the rare pleasure of breakfast overlooking the rooftops of Rome, ask for ones with a terrace on the top floor. Room service is available for light meals. The service is impeccable.

How to get there *(Map 14): Near the Piazza di Spagna.*

Hotel Raphaël

Largo Febo, 2
00186 Rome
Tel. (0)6-68 28 31 - Fax (0)6-68 78 993
Sig. Vannoni

Category ★★★★ **Rooms** 73 with air-conditioning, telephone, bath, WC (9 with terrace). **Price** Single 335-395,000L, double 495-695,000L, suite 660-760,000L. **Meals** Breakfast incl., served 7:00-11:00. **Restaurant** See pp. 403-406. **Credit cards** All major. **Pets** Dogs not allowed. **Nearby** Tivoli (Villa d'Este, Villa Adriana), Castelli Romani (Castel Gandolfo, Frascati, Grottaferrata), Anzio and Nettuno, Palestrina, Anagni, Etruscan zone (Cerveteri, Tarquinia), golf course (9-18-hole) in Rome. **Open** All year.

The Raphaël is one of the best-known hotels in Rome, frequently playing host to international events and world-famous people. It is ideally located, just near the Piazza Navona. Its rooms are all comfortable but some of the bathrooms have not yet been renovated, as some clients have learned to their regret. However, the rooms of "luxury" category have been redone, with furniture of exceptional quality and wonderful decoration by a Venetian artist. Lunch and dinner can be taken at the Relais Picasoon, and snacks are available at any time. In summer, dinners are held for hotel guests (by reservation only) on the marvelous panoramic terrace.

How to get there *(Map 14): Near the Piazza Navona.*

Hotel Sole Al Pantheon

Piazza della Rotonda, 63
00186 Rome
Tel. (0)6-678 04 41 - Fax (0)6-699 406 89
Sig. Giraudini

Category ★★★★ **Rooms** 26 with air-conditioning, telephone, bath or shower, WC, TV and minibar. **Price** Single 340,000L, double 470,000L, suite 560-650,000L. **Meals** Breakfast incl., served 7:00-11:00. **Restaurant** See pp. 448-450. **Credit cards** All major. **Pets** Dogs not allowed. **Facilities** Parking (+35,000L). **Nearby** Tivoli (Villa d'Este, Villa Adriana), Castelli Romani (Castel Gandolfo, Frascati, Grottaferrata), Anzio and Nettuno, Palestrina, Anagni, Etruscan zone (Cerveteri, Tarquinia), golf course (9-18-hole) in Rome. **Open** All year.

This hotel, picturesquely located on the Piazza della Rotonda facing the Pantheon, has recently been completely renovated, with special care taken to preserving its old world charm. There are only twenty-six rooms, all very comfortable (request a quiet back room). Each one bears the name of a celebrity who stayed there, among them Jean-Paul Sartre, who was a regular. The bathrooms are particularly well-equipped. A whirlpool bath can be a real delight after a day out and about in Rome. In addition to the list of restaurants we recommend at the end of this guidebook, try the little trattorias on the square, where on summer evenings you can dine very pleasantly just across from the Pantheon, Imperial Rome's best-preserved monument.

How to get there *(Map 14): In front of the Pantheon.*

Hotel Carriage

Via delle Carrozze, 36
00187 Rome
Tel. (0)6-699 01 24 - Fax (0)6-678 82 79
Sig. Del Sole

Category ★★★ **Rooms** 24 with air-conditioning, telephone, bath or shower, WC, TV and minibar. **Price** Single 215,000L, double 270,000L, triple 330,000L, suite 440,000L. **Meals** Breakfast incl., served 7:00-11:00. **Restaurant** See pp. 448-450. **Credit cards** All major. **Pets** Dogs not allowed. **Nearby** Tivoli (Villa d'Este, Villa Adriana), Castelli Romani (Castel Gandolfo, Frascati, Grottaferrata), Anzio and Nettuno, Palestrina, Anagni, Etruscan zone (Cerveteri, Tarquinia), golf course (9-18-hole) in Rome. **Open** All year.

The Carriage is a small hotel in the heart of a quarter where many of the capital's luxury boutiques are located, near the Piazza di Spagna. The entry, the salon, and the ground-floor breakfast room all have an elegant 18th-century decor. The rooms are comfortable, and air conditioned, which means you won't hear street noise. If you make your reservation in time, ask for Rooms 501 or 601, which are on a terrace with a beautiful view of the rooftops of the Eternal City. Even if you don't get these rooms, you can still have breakfast on the terrace. The suites accommodate up to four people.

How to get there *(Map 14): Near the Piazza di Spagna.*

Mecenate Palace Hotel

Via Carlo Alberto, 3
00185 Roma
Tel. (0)6-44 70 20 24 - Fax (0)6-44 61 354
Sig.ra Capuzzo

Category ★★★★ **Rooms** 62 with air-conditioning (5 no smoking), tel, bath or shower, WC, satellite TV, minibar; elevator. **Price** Single 380,000L, double 500,000L, suite 1,000,000L. **Meals** Breakfast included, served 7:00-10:00. **Restaurant** Service 12:00-14:30, 19:30-23:00; carte 50,000L. **Credit cards** All major. **Pets** Dogs allowed. **Facilities** Garage (40,000L). **Nearby** Castelli Romani, Fracasti, abbey of Grottaferrata, piazza della Republica (le Bernin) in Ariccia.Tivoli (Villa d'Este, Villa Adriana), Palestrina, Anagni, 9- and 18-hole golf course in Rome. **Open** All year.

Situated near the Termini railroad station and facing the church of Santa Maria Maggiore, the Mecenate has just emerged as a luxury hotel after a long renovation. The owner's aim was to give the hotel the atmosphere of a private apartment. This is particularly true for the three suites, each of which is named after a Roman poet: Horace, Virgil and Propertius. One touch, for example, is the kettle in your room, where you can make a cup of tea whenever you like. The decoration is elegant and meticulous and the marble bathrooms are spacious. Half the rooms have a view of the church. Both the roof garden and the Terrazza dei Papi are well-equipped for breakfast all year round. A nice spot to know, lacking until now in this neighborhood.

How to get there *(Map 14): Near the rail station (stazione Termini). La via Carlo Alberto is on the piazza Santa Maria Maggiore.*

Hotel Gregoriana

Via Gregoriana, 18
00187 Rome
Tel. (0)6-679 42 69 - Fax (0)6-678 42 58
Sig. Panier-Bagat

Category ★★★ **Rooms** 19 with air-conditioning, telephone, bath or shower, WC, TV and minibar; elevator. **Price** Single 200,000L, double 320,000L. **Meals** Breakfast incl., served 7:00-11:00. **Restaurant** See pp. 448-450. **Credit cards** Not accepted **Pets** Dogs allowed (fee). **Nearby** Tivoli (Villa d'Este, Villa Adriana), Castelli Romani (Castel Gandolfo, Frascati, Grottaferrata), Anzio and Nettuno, Palestrina, Anagni, Etruscan zone (Cerveteri, Tarquinia), golf course (9-18-hole) in Rome. **Open** All year.

The Via Gregoriana is in an ideal spot: just above the Spanish Steps, near the church of Trinita dei Monti. Fortunately, though, the street is a quiet one, which adds to the intimate atmosphere of the hotel. We don't much care for the decor, which is a mixture of Art Deco and Liberty with a touch of exotica, but it is quiet and comfortable, and some of the rooms have a nice view over the rooftops of Rome. What does make this hotel stand out is the warmth with which you are welcomed as soon as you arrive and the attentiveness of the staff throughout your stay. You are instantly made to feel like a privileged guest, which explains the loyalty of the clientele and hence, the need to reserve your rooms well in advance.

How to get there *(Map 14): From Piazza di Spagna ascend the Spanish Steps.*

Hotel Locarno

Via della Penna, 22
00186 Rome
Tel. (0)6-36 10 841 - Fax (0)6-32 15 249
Sig.ra Celli

Category ★★★ **Rooms** 47 and 1 for disabled persons with air-conditioning, telephone, bath or shower, WC, satellite TV., safe and minibar; elevator. **Price** single 195,000L, double 320,000L, suite 360,000L. Apartment for 1 week 1 750,000L **Meals** Breakfast incl., served 7:00-11:30. **Restaurant** See pp. 448-450. **Credit cards** All major. **Pets** Dogs not allowed. **Facilities** Bikes. **Nearby** Tivoli (Villa d'Este, Villa Adriana), Castelli Romani (Castel Gandolfo, Frascati, Grottaferrata), Anzio and Nettuno, Palestrina, Anagni, Etruscan zone (Cerveteri, Tarquinia), golf course (9-18-hole) in Rome. **Open** All year.

The Hotel Locarno offers a good number of attractive rooms, right in the center of Rome, just a few steps from the Piazza del Popolo. We recommend those that have been renovated: They are furnished in an antique style and the bathrooms are decorated with pretty, handmade tiles. In a small palazzo just across the street there are several apartments for rent by the week, complete with hotel services. In the summer, breakfast is served under large white sun umbrellas on the ground floor patio-terrace. This also doubles as a bar open until midnight. In the winter, you can sit before a roaring fire in the large living room fireplace. There is also a terrace with a bar that affords a wonderful view of Rome. The welcome is always charming, the prices reasonable and the location excellent. All in all, a pleasant place to stay.

How to get there *(Map 14): Next to the Piazza del Popolo.*

Hotel Teatro di Pompeo

00186 Roma
Largo del Pallaro, 8
Tel. (0)6-687 28 12 - Fax (0)6-688 055 31
Sig. Mignoni

Category ★★★ **Rooms** 12 with air-conditioning, telephone, bath or shower, WC, TV, safe, minibar and elevator. **Price** Single 190,000L, double 250,000L. **Meals** Breakfast incl., served 7:00-10:00. **Restaurant** See pp. 448-450. **Credit cards** All major. **Pets** Dogs allowed. **Nearby** Tivoli (Villa d'Este, Villa Adriana), Castelli Romani (Castel Gandolfo, Frascati, Grottaferrata), Anzio and Nettuno, Palestrina, Anagni, Etruscan zone (Cerveteri, Tarquinia), golf course (9-18-hole) in Rome. **Open** All year.

If you are looking for a quiet but centrally located hotel for your Roman vacation, this is the place. Located right in the heart of Rome, with its back to the Campo dei Fiori and close to the Piazza Navona, the hotel is on a quiet little square. All of the rooms, under the roof, have sloping ceilings, and half of them open onto the square. Though the decor is simple, the size of the hotel makes it a warm friendly place, with the charm of an old-fashioned pensione (plus modern conveniences). The adjoining restaurant "Costanza" is independent of the hotel and serves fine cuisine. The arched ruins of the old theatre of Pompeii , inaugurated in the year 55 B.C. provide the decor. The service is discreet but efficient.

How to get there *(Map 14): near Piazza Campo dei Fiori and the church of S. Andrea della Valle.*

Hotel Sant'Anselmo

00153 Roma
Piazza Sant' Anselmo, 2
Tel. (0)6-575 08 45/574 35 47 - Fax (0)6-578 36
Sig. Piroli

Category ★★★ **Rooms** 45 with telephone, bath or shower, WC and TV. **Price** Single 100-140,000L, double 150-190,000L. **Meals** Breakfast incl., served 7:00-10:30. **Restaurant** See pp. 448-450. **Credit cards** All major. **Pets** Dogs not allowed. **Facilities** Parking. **Nearby** Tivoli (Villa d'Este, Villa Adriana), Castelli Romani (Castel Gandolfo, Frascati, Grottaferrata), Anzio and Nettuno, Palestrina, Anagni, Etruscan zone (Cerveteri, Tarquinia), golf course (9-18-hole) in Rome. **Open** All year.

Already prized in antiquity for its quiet (the Romans built their thermal baths here) Aventino Hill is a haven of tranquility from the summer heat of Rome even today. There are three old patrician houses there, submerged in verdant shaded alleyways, which are hotels. The S. Anselmo and the Villa S. Pio are right next door to each other, and the Aventino is nearby. There is one reservation number for all three hotels; ask for the first or second one. The rooms are small but charming. The upper rooms overlooking the whole south side of the town are the nicest ones. Breakfast is simple, but served in a cool interior garden. This is one of the rare places in Rome with quiet, elegance, and reasonable prices.

How to get there *(Map 14): near Termal of Cracalla.*

Hotel Villa del Parco

Via Nomentana, 110
00161 Rome
Tel. (0)6-442 377 73 - Fax (0)6-442 375 72
Famiglia Bernardini

Category ★★★ **Rooms** 31 with air-conditioning, telephone, bath or shower, WC, TV and minibar (2 rooms with wheelchair access), elevator. **Price** single 165-200,000L, double 215-246,000L, suite 257-290,000L. **Meals** Breakfast incl., served 7:00-10:30. **Restaurant** See pp. 448-450. **Credit cards** All major. **Pets** Dogs allowed. **Facilities** Parking (10,000L). **Nearby** Tivoli (Villa d'Este, Villa Adriana), Castelli Romani (Castel Gandolfo, Frascati, Grottaferrata), Anzio and Nettuno, Palestrina, Anagni, Etruscan zone (Cerveteri, Tarquinia), golf course (9-18-hole) in Rome. **Open** All year.

This beautiful turn-of-the-century house, with its gracefully fading pink facade, is located in a quiet residential quarter, a twenty-minute walk from the Via Veneto, just outside of the historic district. The shade trees in the little garden and the park nearby keep it cool in the summertime. You will like the series of small salons (several in the basement remind one of similar rooms you might find in London), the small bar tucked into an alcove, and the tables under the trees where you can have tea and light snacks. This will quickly become your Rome home-away-from-home. Prices vary greatly, and the cheapest rooms are sometimes the most charming. Our favorites are 5, 7, 12, and 22.

How to get there *(Map 14): North of Rome, next to the Porta Bologna.*

Pensione Scalinata di Spagna

Piazza Trinita dei Monti, 17
00187 Rome
Tel. (0)6-69 94 08 96 - Fax (0)6-69 94 05 98
Sig. Bellia

Category ★★★ **Rooms** 15 with telephone, bath or shower, WC, TV, safe and minibar. **Price** Single 350,000L, double 380,000L, triple 450,000L, suite (4-5 pers.) 650,000L. **Meals** Breakfast incl., served 7:30-11:00. **Restaurant** See pp. 448-450. **Credit cards** All major. **Pets** Dogs allowed. **Nearby** Tivoli (Villa d'Este, Villa Adriana), Castelli Romani (Castel Gandolfo, Frascati, Grottaferrata), Anzio and Nettuno, Palestrina, Anagni, Etruscan zone (Cerveteri, Tarquinia), golf course (9-18-hole) in Rome. **Open** All year.

Near the chic shopping streets of the city and famous Spanish steps, this intimate and elegant little hotel has a location every bit as good as its luxurious neighbor, the Hassler Medici. The rooms are very comfortable, with air-conditioning (indispensable in summer) and tasteful decoration. A terrace affords a fine view over the rooftops of Rome, many of which have their own little terraces. You will find a courteous welcome and attentive service. In short, for a pleasant stay in the Eternal City, this is one of the best addresses to be found.

How to get there *(Map 14): Up the stairs of the Piazza di Spagna.*

1998

Hotel Ristorante Adriano

Via di Villa Adriana, 194
Villa Adriana 00010 Tivoli (Roma)
Tel. (0)774-38 22 35 / 53 5028 - (0)774-53 51 22 - Famiglia Cinessi

Rooms 7 and 3 suites with air-conditioning, telephone, bath or shower, WC, TV and minibar. **Price** Double 160-260,000L, suites 260,000L. **Meals** Breakfast included, served 8:30-10:00. **Restaurant** Service 12:30-20:00; also à la carte 70-80,000L. **Credit cards** All major. **Pets** Dogs not allowed. **Facilities** Tennis, parking. **Nearby** Tivoli: duomo, Villa Adriana, Villa d'Este, Villa Gregoriana, Roma. **Open** All year.

Hadrian's Villa, always a tourist highlight, then immortalized by Marguerite Yourcenar's excellent book, has become a must for all visitors to Rome. If you are among these visitors, why not spend a night (or more) at the Adriano, just next to Hadrian's Villa and then take the opportunity also to visit the Villa d'Este and the Villa Gregoriana, both at Tivoli, only six kilometers away. You will never regret either the visit or the hotel: the lovely gardens with their bubbling fountains and waterfalls that inspired Fragonard, Hubert Robert, Corot and even Maurice Ravel, and the hotel-restaurant, both comfortable and gastronomic. It is a beautiful fuschia-colored building standing on a broad lawn shaded by palms and cypress trees. The room are upstairs. Luxurious rather than charming, they are very comfortable and some even have a view of the ancient walls of the famous neighbor. The restaurant is decorated with great elegance, and the white walls beautifully set off the 19th-century furniture and the fine china and crystal on the tables. Excellent cuisine prepared by Gabriella, in charge of the kitchen, and Patrizia, who does the sweets and pastries. Umberto offers a kind and thoughtful welcome. A fine place for a Roman holiday.

How to get there *(Map 14): 36 km from Rome, 6 km before Tivoli.*

Villa La Floridiana

Via Casilina, km 63,700
03012 Anagni (Frosinone)
Tel. (0)775-767 845 - Fax (0)775-767 845/6
Sig.ra Camerini

Category ★★★★ **Rooms** 9 with air-conditioning, telephone, bath or shower, WC and TV. Wheelchair acces. **Price** Single 110,000L, double 160,000L. **Meals** Breakfast included, served 7:00-10:00; half board 140,000L, full board 180,000L (per pers.). **Restaurant** Service 12:00-15:00, 19:30-22:00; closed Sun. evening and Mon. noon; menu 60,000L. Specialties: Traditional cooking. **Credit cards** All major **Pets** Dogs allowed. **Facilities** Parking. **Nearby** In Anagni: cathedral, Palazzo Boniffacio VIII, Palazzo Comunale; Rome, Tivoli (Villa d'Este, Villa Adriana), Castelli Romani (Castel Gandolfo, Frascati, Grottaferrata), Anzio and Nettuno, Palestrina, Anagni, Etruscan zone (Cerveteri, Tarquinia), golf course (9-18-hole) in Rome. **Open** All year (except Aug).

Villa La Floridiana is located about thirty miles south of Rome in Anagni, a beautiful medieval village on the slopes of Mount Ernici, former summer residence of emperors and popes (three were born here!). This recently opened hotel exudes an old country-house charm, with its rough pink facade, green shutters, and large shady terrace. The interior is simply decorated with pretty regional furniture, floral and gingham fabrics, giving the place a cheerful atmosphere. The rooms are spacious and comfortable, the service friendly and attentive. The hotel can provide you with information about when to visit the historical monuments, which are off the usual tourist track. Most of the attractions don't keep very formal hours.

How to get there *(Map 14): 50 km southeast of Rome. Via A2, Anagni exit.*

Villa Vignola

Corso Vannucci, 97
Vignola 66054 Vasto (Chieti)
Tel. (0)873-31 00 50 - Fax (0)873-31 00 60
Sig. Mazzetti

Category ★★★★ **Rooms** 5 with air-conditioning, telephone, bath or shower, WC, TV and minibar. **Price** Single 160,000L, double 280,000L. **Meals** Breakfast incl., served 7:30-10:30. **Restaurant** Service 12:30-14:30, 19:30-22:30; menu 65,000L, à la carte. Specialties: seafood. **Credit cards** All major. **Pets** Dogs allowed (fee). **Facilities** Parking. **Nearby** Vasto. **Open** All year.

The Villa Vignola is a very intimate place, scaled for a limited clientele, as there are only five rooms and about ten tables. You can see the sea from the rooms and the terraces through a multitude of trees growing close to the beach. The place has the air of a private vacation house on the beach. The cozy salon, the small number of rooms, and their intimate, elegant decor certainly have a lot to do with this effect. This is a great place to come for a rest.

How to get there *(Map 13): 74 km south of Pescara via A14, Vasto exit, then towards Porto di Vasto (6 km north of Vasto).*

Il Voltone

Voltone 01010 Farnese (Viterbo)
Tel. (0)761-42 25 40 - Fax (0)761-42 25 40
Mmes Parenti

Rooms 30 with tel, bath, WC. **Price** Single 100-115,000L, double 140-170,000L, suite 200-230,000L. **Meals** Breakfast included, served 8:00-10:00; half board 105-150,000L, full board 135-180,000L (per pers.). **Restaurant** Service 13:00-20:00; menu 40-45,000L; also à la carte 50,000L. Specialties: Regional cuisine. **Credit cards** Visa, Eurocard, MasterCard. **Pets** Dogs allowed. **Facilities** Swimming pool, parking at hotel. **Nearby** Viterbo, Tarquinia, Ortebello, Cerveteri, Véio, Isola Bisantina, Lago di Bolsena, "Le Querce", 18-hole golf course in Viterbo. **Open** Mar 29 - Nov. 14.

Between Latin Rome and Florentine Tuscany, why not stop and see this lovely region of the Etruscans? Il Voltone is a rare find - all alone in the middle of a large agricultural estate in a tiny 17th-century village that has been wonderfully renovated and transformed, this hotel gives you the feeling that you are a guest in a private home. The yellow, ochre and pale pink colors outside and the antique furniture and carpets inside reinforce this gentle, homey atmosphere. The bedrooms are comfortable and each is personalized. You can go horseback riding or mountain-biking on the estate and there is also a lovely swimming pool with a view over the entire valley. The area was the home of the powerful Farnese family and boasts a wealth of historic points of interest. Your hosts will advise you on things to see and itineraries to choose. This place makes a wonderful retreat.

How to get there *(Map 13): 45 km north of Viterbo, via A 1 (Roma-Firenze), Orte exit then Viterbo, Capodimento, Valentano, Voltone.*

Hotel Al Gallo

Via del Gallo, 22
01017 Tuscània (Viterbo)
Tel. (0)761 44 33 88 - Fax (0)761 44 36 28
Sig.José Pettiti

Category ★★★ **Rooms** 10 with tel, bath or shower, WC, TV; elevator. **Price** Single 116,000L, double 166,000L. **Meals** Breakfast 12,000L, served 7:30-10:00; half board 164,000L, full board 198,000L (per pers, 2 days min.). **Restaurant** Service 12:00-14:00, 19:00-22:00; menu 50-80,000L, also à la carte.Specialties: Ventaglio di proscuitto d'oca al pepe nero con carfiofi e peperoni arrostiti, ravioli di petto di anatra e tartufo nero all'olio di canino, involtini di manzo alla brace con basilico ed alloro, stogliatina di ricotta e miele. **Credit cards** All major. **Pets** Dogs not allowed. **Facilities** Tennis, parking. **Nearby** Viterbo, Tarquinia, Ortebello, Cerveteri, Véio, Isola Bizantina, Lago di Bolsena, "Le Querce", 18-hole golf course in Viterbo. **Open** All year.

On the border between Tuscany and Latium, the little town of Tusc^nia is one of those mysterious Etruscan cities, with tumuli and galleries of tombs scattered through the surrounding countryside. In addition, there are vestiges of the Middle Ages: the basilicas of San Pietro and Santa Maria Maggiore are jewels of early Christian and Romanesque architecure. The bedrooms are nicely decorated (except for the apple green carpeting) with blond wood furniture and flowered wallpaper. Choose rooms 7, 8 or 9 which overlook the lower part of town or number 6, which has a balcony. Be careful: Don't take one of the little rooms that are really singles, but sometimes used as doubles. Al Gallo is known for its restaurant, where the menu varies each month with the season and the market. A refined cuisine that features truffles.

How to get there *(Map 15): 20 km of Viterbo, via A 1, Orte exit.A 12, exit Civitavecchia.*

Hotel Cenobio dei Dogi

Via Nicolo Cueno, 34
16032 Camogli (Genova)
Tel. (0)185-72 41 - Fax (0)185-77 27 96 - Sig. Siri

Category ★★★★ **Rooms** 107 with air-conditioning, telephone, bath or shower, WC, TV and minibar; elevator. **Price** Single 160-250,000L, double 240-480,000L, suite 500-600,000L. **Meals** Breakfast included, served 7:30-10:15; half board +60,000L, full board +120,000L (per pers., 3 days min.). **Restaurant** Service 12:45-14:15, 20:00-21:30; à la carte. Specialties: Seafood. **Credit cards** Amex, Visa, Eurocard, MasterCard. **Pets** Dogs allowed. (+15,000 L). **Facilities** Swimming pool, solarium, tennis (+25,000L), private beach, parking. **Nearby** Ruta and Portofino Vetta (Monte di Portofino); Punta Chiappa and the Abbey of S. Fruttuoso by foot or boat; Portofino, Rapallo and the Riviera di Levante; Rapallo golf course (18-hole). **Open** All year.

This large and beautiful villa stands at one end of the Gulf, in the pretty little seaside resort of Camogli, the twin city of Portofino. For a long time it was the property of an eminent family that gave the city of Genoa a number of its Doges. When it was bought in the 1950s and transformed into a hotel, it quite naturally kept the memory of the Doges in its name. Today it is one of the luxury hotels of the Ligurian Riviera. From our point of view, it lacks a certain lived-in feeling. Moreover, the rooms are rather unequal in quality. Considering the prices, to be completely satisfied one would have to get one of the rooms facing the sea. The others are rather ordinary. The facilities are, of course, in keeping with the status of the hotel: a beautifully planted garden, a swimming pool and a private beach right at the foot of the building guarantees absolute tranquility even at the height of the season.

How to get there *(Map 8): 26 km east of Genova via A12, Recco exit, then S333 to Recco, Camogli, along the coast.*

Albergo da Giovanni

Casale Portale, 23
15032 San Fruttuoso - Camogli (Genova)
Tel. (0)185-77 00 47
Famiglia Bozzo

Rooms 7 with shower (indoor). **Price** Single 60,000L, double 90,000L. **Meals** Half board 100,000L, full board 130,000L. **Restaurant** Service 13:00-14:30, 20:00-21:15; menu, also à la carte. Specialties: Seafood. **Credit cards** Not accepted. **Pets** Dogs not allowed. **Nearby** Abbey of S. Fruttuoso, Camogli, Portofino. **Open** June – Sept. (open weekends Oct. – May).

The Albergo da Giovanni is in San Fruttuoso, a magical, forgotten-by-time town dating from Roman antiquity, which most people stop off and visit during boat trips from Camogli and Portofino. The city is set on a small inlet surrounded by woods that border the sea, and has a cathedral, an abbey, a bell-tower and the Andréa Doria tower. Previously regarded as a day-trip destination, San Fruttuoso now welcomes adventurous overnighters, thanks to this beach house. The comfort is basic and the service nonexistent, but the restaurant is great and serves dishes made with fish fresh from the sea. The most magical part is being able to stay behind in this wonderfully evocative place and wave goodbye as the last boat of the day sails away.

How to get there *(Map 8): 26 km east of Genova via A12, Recco exit, then S333 to Recco then Camogli along the coast. Ferry services from Camogli to San Fruttuoso. (Information: 39-185-77 10 66.).*

Albergo Splendido

Viale Baratta, 16 - 16034 Portofino (Genova)
Tel. (0)185-26 95 51 - Fax (0)185-26 96 14 - Sig. Saccani
E-mail: splendido@pn.itnet.it

Category ★★★★★ **Rooms** 69 with air-conditioning, telephone, bath or shower, WC, TV and minibar, elevator. **Price** With half board 600-720,000L (single), 1,190-1,600 000L (2 pers. in double room), 1,820-2,500 000L (2 pers. in suite), with full board +105,000L. **Meals** Breakfast included, served 7:30-10:30. **Restaurant** Service 13:00-14:30, 20:00-21:45; menu, also à la carte. Specialties: Italian cooking. **Credit cards** All major. **Pets** Dogs allowed (except in restaurant and in the swimming pool). **Facilities** Swimming pool, tennis (+40,000L), sauna, health center, parking (+35,000L). **Nearby** Fortezza di San Giorgio in Portofino, Abbey of S. Fruttuoso by foot or boat, Rapallo and the Riviera di Levante, golf course of Rapallo (18-hole). **Open** Mar. 22 – Jan. 2.

The Splendido, nestled amid woods on the heights over Portofino, is part of the landscape of the famous port. It is a real jewel of a place, admirably preserved. If possible, you should avoid coming in July and August, or if you do, at least avoid arriving toward the end of the day — the access from Santa Margherita is really quite difficult. Nevertheless, what a reward when you walk through the leafy gardens, with the scent of flowers in bloom, and catch sight of the port, with the sailboats crisscrossing the bay. It is as romantic as it is luxurious. The lounges are cool and comfortable, and the lovely terrace is used as a dining room in summer. The garden is filled with walks and paths leading to the village or the beach, and there are many quiet places to sit and enjoy the view. Our favorite rooms are those with a balcony in the trees. The rates are quite steep, but it's truly like paradise.

How to get there *(Map 8): 36 km east of Genova via A12, Rapallo exit, S227 along the coast to Portofino.*

Hotel Piccolo

Via Duca degli Abruzzi, 31
16034 Portofino (Genova)
Tel. (0)185 269 015 - Fax (0)185 269 621
Sig. Bologwa

Category ★★★★ **Rooms** 22 with tel, bath, WC, TV, minibar; elevator. **Price** Single 110-200,000L, double 180-320,000L, suite 320-400,000L. **Meals** Breakfast included, served 7:30-10:00; half board 200,000L, full board 240,000L (per pers.). **Restaurant** Service 12:30-14:00, 19:30-21:00; menu, also à la carte 40,000L. **Credit cards** All major. **Pets** Dogs allowed. **Facilities** Parking and garage (10,000L). **Nearby** Fortezza di San Giorgio in Portofino, Abbey of S. Fruttuoso di Camogli by foot or boat, Rapallo golf course (18-hole). **Open** Dec 27 - Nov 3.

The Hotel Piccolo stands just at the last curve, from which you catch your first glimpse of Portofino (anyway, unless you have a resident's pass, you have to wait at the exit of Santa Margherita until a parking place becomes free in the Portofino parking lot). The hotel has been nicely renovated, with a good utilization of all available space, as the house really is piccolo. There is a small but inviting reception area, a few meters from where you park your car. The rooms, (reminiscent of a ship's cabin) are cozy and pleasant to live in, each with a living room corner and a shower room equipped with all you need. Some rooms have terraces and those on the higher floors have a view of the sea. For swimming, you just have to cross the road to reach the little cove (complete with beach chairs) with its own private access, a great plus in this town where access to the beach is not always easy. There is a welcoming atmosphere as well.

How to get there *(Map 8): 3o km east of Genova via A 12, Rapallo exit, then S 227 along the coast to Portofino.*

Hotel Nazionale

Via Roma, 8
16038 Portofino (Genova)
Tel. (0)185-26 95 75 - Fax (0)185-26 95 78
Sig. Briola

Category ★★★★ **Rooms** 12 with air-conditioning, telephone, bath or shower, WC, TV and minibar. **Price** Double 300,000L, suite 400-500,000L. **Meals** Breakfast 25,000L, served 7:30-12:00. **Restaurant** See p. 453. **Credit cards** Visa, Eurocard, MasterCard. **Pets** Dogs allowed. **Nearby** Road from Portofino to Rapallo (8km, not counsel in summer); Abbey of S. Fruttuoso di Camogli by foot or boat, Rapallo and the Riviera di Levante, Rapallo golf course (18-hole). **Open** March 15 – Nov. 30.

If you really want to feel a part of every event that takes place in the life of Portofino, then stay at the Nazionale. It is right smack on the port, in one of those fisherman's houses with their yellow, rose, orange or ochre tints that lend their traditional charm to this village. But be forewarned — the show goes on by night as well as by day. The hotel was renovated a few years ago with a view to comfort (it's true that the rooms are comfortable) rather than appearance. The hospitality is nothing to write home about, either. But hotels are few and rooms are hard to find around here.

How to get there *(Map 8): 36 km east of Genova via A12, Rapallo exit, S227 along the coast to Portofino. (Parking is 300 meters from the hotel).*

Imperiale Palace Hotel

Via Pagana, 19
16038 Santa Margherita Ligure (Genova)
Tel. (0)185-28 89 91- Fax (0)185-28 42 23
Sig. Mura

Category ★★★★★ **Rooms** 102 with air-conditioning, telephone, bath or shower, WC, TV and minibar, elevator. **Price** Single 220-310,000L, double 340-560,000L. **Meals** Breakfast included, served 7:30-10:30. Half board +80-100,000L and full board +140-160,000L. **Restaurant** Service 13:00-14:30, 20:00-22:30; menu 110,000L, also à la carte. Specialties: Italian cooking. **Credit cards** All major. **Pets** Dogs allowed. **Facilities** Swimming pool, parking. **Nearby** Road from Portofino to Rapallo (8km, not counsel in summer); Abbey of S. Fruttuoso by foot or boat, Rapallo and the Riviera di Levante, Rapallo golf course (18-hole). **Open** Apr. – Nov.

The splendors of the past await you at the Imperiale Hotel. Originally the property of a rich Corsican family in 1889, it became a hotel around 1910. Since then it has hosted important historic events–the treaty of Rapallo between Russia and Germany–and many noted movie stars. Rooms are spacious, classically decorated, and luxurious. The ones in the front have a wonderful view of the sea. The salons and dining rooms are superb. In summer, you can enjoy lunch on the terrace just over the hotel's private beach, and in the evening, candlelight dinners and dancing on the large terrace. A truly palatial experience.

How to get there *(Map 8): 30 km east of Genova via A12, Rapallo exit, then S227 along the coast.*

Grand Hotel Villa Balbi

Viale Rimembranza, 1
16039 Sestri Levante (La Spezia)
Tel. (0)185-42 941 - Fax (0)185-48 24 59
Sig. Rossignotti

Category ★★★★ **Rooms** 99 with air-conditioning (on request), telephone, bath, WC, TV and minibar; elevator. **Price** Single 110-200,000L, double 280-320,000L, suite 350-450,000L. **Meals** Breakfast included, served 7:30-10:00; half board 190-250,000L, full board 220-280,000L (per pers. 3 days min.). **Restaurant** Service 12:30-14:00, 19:30-21:00; menu 65-75,000L, also à la carte. Specialties: Italian cuisine. **Credit cards** All major. **Pets** Dogs not allowed. **Facilities** Heated swimming pool and private beach (35-40,000L), parking (+15,000L). **Nearby** San Nicolo Church, Sestri Levante (Baia del Silenzio, coast road from Sestri Levante to Monterosso al Mare), the Cinque Terre by boat or by train, Rapallo golf course (18-hole). **Open** Jan. – Nov.

The Villa Balbi is one of those historic houses built for princes, then later, for want of a king, converted into luxury summer residences. The decor has changed in the course of centuries and the clientele as well, judging from the number of Mercedes parked all over the grounds, but the salons that look out on the *passagiata* of palm trees and the pines in the garden still have their air of mystery. There is some antique furniture in the large guest rooms and the service is what you would expect from a luxury hotel. Although it is right in the center of town, only the street separates you from the private beach, where you will have your cabin, sun umbrella and beach chair. Children seem to prefer the swimming pool. An ideal hotel place if you can afford it.

***How to get there** (Map 8): 50 km east of Genova via A12, Sestri Levante exit.*

Hotel Helvetia

Via Cappuccini, 43
16039 Sestri Levante (Genova)
Tel. (0)185-41 175 - Fax (0)185-457 216
Sig. Pernigotti

Category ★★★ **Rooms** 24 with air-conditioning (on request), telephone, bath or shower, WC, satellite TV, minibar and safe, elevator. **Price** Single 160,000L, double 210,000L, suite 230,000L. **Meals** Breakfast included (buffet), served 7:30-10:30. **Restaurant** See p. 453. **Credit cards** Visa, Eurocard, MasterCard. **Pets** Dogs allowed (+20,000L). **Facilities** Private beach, bikes, parking (+10,000L). **Nearby** San Nicolo Church, Sestri Levante (Baia del Silenzio, coast road from Sestri Levante to Monterosso al Mare), Cinque Terre by boat or by train, Rapallo golf course (18-hole). **Open** Mar. – Oct.

In this pretty little beach resort of the Ligurian Riviera, the Helvetia is our favorite hotel. Sheltered in the little Bay of Silence, it has been lovingly looked after for many years by the Pernigotti family. All the rooms were recently re-done: bright and luminous, with well-equipped bathrooms, they face either the sea or the garden. It would be a pity not to have the sea view, but the salons and the terrace are also a good vantage point from which to see it. The morning is a wonderful time to enjoy the panorama, as you help yourself from the delicious and copious buffet breakfast, served until 10 o'clock. The beach is right at your feet, to go swimming whenever you feel like. The kind, attentive hospitality of Signor Pernigotti makes this the sort of place you want to come back to.

How to get there *(Map 8): 50 km east of Genova via A12, Sestri Levante exit. Pedestrian way but you can used for deposit your luggages.*

Hotel Miramare

Via Cappellini, 9
16039 Sestri Levante (Genova)
Tel. (0)185 48 08 55 - Fax (0)185 41 055
Sig. Carmagnini

Category ★★★★ **Rooms** 43 with tel, bath or shower, WC, satellite TV, minibar; elevator. **Price** Single 130-250,000L, double 190-300,000L, suite 310-380,000L. **Meals** Breakfast 20,000L, served 7:30-10:00; half board 155-250,000L, full board 185-280,000L (per pers. 3 day min.). **Restaurant** Service 12:30-14:00, 19:30-21:00, menu 60-70 000L, also à la carte. Specialties: Pansotti in salsa noci, cima alla genovese. **Credit cards** Visa, Eurocard, MasterCard. **Pets** Dogs not allowed. **Facilities** Private beach, parking (18,000L) and garage. **Nearby** Hotel dei Castelli's park. San Nicolo church, Rizzi museum, Sestri Levante.(Baia del Silenzio, coast road from Sestri Levante to Monterosso al Mare), Cinque Terre; Rapallo 18-hole golf course. **Open** Mar - Oct.

The Miramar has been converted into a luxury hotel, and this is obvious as soon as you walk in. The lobby is busy and inviting. All the common areas are on the ground floor: salons and restaurants, but also shops and meeting rooms. Everything is bright and neat. The rooms have modern style decor. Most are set up as small apartments and they can be combined to accommodate up to six persons. The nicest are those with a sea view. There is a large terrace and a garden just facing the beach of the Bay of Silence. In short, a very comfortable hotel - although the renovation was essential, it is true that it has lost a little of its former charm.

How to get there *(Map 8): 50 km east of Genova via A 12, Sestri Levante exit. Pedestrian street but you can go with your car to deposit luggage.*

1998

Baia Beniamin

Corso Europa, 63
18036 Grimaldi Inferiore - Ventimiglia (Imperia)
Tel. (0)184 38002 / 38027 - Fax (0)184 38002 / 38027
Sig. Brunelli

Rooms 5 with tel, bath or shower, WC, TV. **Price** Double 400,000L. **Meals** Breakfast (at any time). **Restaurant** Service 12:30-14:00, 20:00-21:30, closed Mon. "Déjeuner d'affaire" 65,000L (except national holidays), menu 110,000L; also à la carte. Specialties: Agnolotti di nasello, taglioni ai crostacei e fiori di zucchine, branzino con funghi porcini, medaglioni di pescatrice di timp, piccata di branzino con petali di melone al'acto balsamico. **Credit cards** All major. **Pets** Dogs not allowed. **Facilities** Parking. **Nearby** Menton, Villa Hambury's garden; Monaco, San Remo, San Remo golf course (18-hole). **Open** All year (except in Nov.).

The Baia Beniamin stands amid oleanders, geraniums, eucalyptus and palm trees on a rocky outcrop descending to a little beach, just a few hundred yards from the port of Menton. Carlo Brunelli is first and foremost an excellent cook. His delicate cuisine features fish dishes, and his "business lunch" will give you an idea of his talent. There are five rooms over the restaurant and a stay in one of them makes a nice gourmet holiday. They are comfortable and elegant and open onto a large covered terrace. Our favorite is number 5, with its double exposure. The house is at the water's edge and has its own beach chairs on the little beach. A good stopping place for fine dining while you discover Menton, the last pearl of the French Riviera on the Ligurian coast.

How to get there *(Map 7): 3 km from Menton, 8 km from Vintimille on the inferior cornice.*

Royal Hotel

Corso Imperatrice, 80
18038 San Remo (Imperia)
Tel. (0)184-53 91 - Fax (0)184-61 445
Sig. Mayer

Category ★★★★★ **Rooms** 142 with air-conditioning, telephone, bath or shower, WC, TV and minibar; elevator; wheelchair access. **Price** Single 180-35,000L, double 320-525,000L, suite 510-990,000L. **Meals** Breakfast included, served 7:30-10:15; half board 222-375,000L, full board 263-440,000L (per pers. 3 days min.). **Restaurant** Service 12:30-14:30, 19:30-21:30; menu 95,000L, also à la carte. Specialties: Risotto ravioli di nasello salsa all'astrice-angello Royal-branzino ai carciofi. **Credit cards** All major. **Pets** Dogs allowed (+22,000L). **Facilities** Swimming pool, tennis (25,000L), fitness, sauna, solaruim, minigolf, hairdresser, parking (+17-30,000L). **Nearby** San Remo : Casino et grand marché, Bussana Vecchia, Taggia (San Domenico Church), Ceriana and Baiardo villages, San Remo golf course (18-hole). **Open** Dec. 20 – Oct; 4.

The picturesque historic center of town is at Pigna, on the heights. San Remo (which takes its name from Saint Romolo) only began to spread down to the sea when it became a famed beach resort in the 19th century. The Royal Hotel, along with the luxurious Liberty-style Municipal Casino, bear witness to this luxury life of that era on the *Riviera di Ponente*. The architect Luigi Vetti was in charge of the latest renovations, which aimed at improving the comfort of the hotel while preserving all that gave it its charm. The vast public rooms that open onto the grounds were preserved and the bedrooms were beautifully decorated. The service and hospitality are in high style for a price that clearly shows that San Remo is not as fashionable as it used to be. And yet, the back country is as beautiful as ever.

How to get there *(Map 7): 56 km east of Nice (France) via A10, San Remo exit.*

Hotel Punta Est

Via Aurelia, 1
17024 Finale Ligure (Savona)
Tel. and Fax (0)19-60 06 11
Sig. Podesta

Category ★★★★ **Rooms** 40 with telephone, bath or shower and WC (30 with TV, 30 with minibar); elevator. **Price** Single 100-250,000L, double 300-360,000L, suite 400-800,000L. **Meals** Breakfast 25,000L, served 8:00-10:00 (15:00 in room); half board and full board 170-290,000L (per pers. 3 days min.). **Restaurant** Service 13:00-14:00, 20:00-21:00; menu 50-75,000L, also à la carte. Specialties: Branzino al sale. **Credit cards** Amex, Visa, Eurocard, MasterCard. **Pets** Dogs not allowed. **Facilities** Swimming pool, private beach, parking. **Nearby** Abbey of Finale Pia, prehistoric caves near by Toirano, coast road from Finale Ligure to Savona (Noli, Spotorno), Golf Garlenda Course (18-hole). **Open** May – Sept.

The Hotel Punta Est is perched on a little promontory overhanging the beach. It consists of two buildings–an 18th-century villa and a modern addition–set in the middle of a trellised garden with large pine trees, palms, bougainvillea and hibiscus. The rooms are comfortably furnished and all have a view of the sea. The private swimming pool and reserved spaces on the beach across from the hotel allow you to escape the summer crowds. The large, panoramic terrace with piano bar is a nice place to spend an evening.

How to get there *(Map 8): 30 km south of Savona via A10, Finale Ligure exit.*

La Meridiana

Via ai Castelli, 11
17033 Garlenda (Savona)
Tel. (0)182-58 02 71 - Fax (0)182-58 01 50 - Sig. and Sig.ra Segre
E-mail: meridiana@ab.infocomm.it.

Category ★★★★ **Rooms** 32 with telephone, bath, WC, ssatellite TV, safe and minibar; elevator. **Price** Double 350-400,000L, apart. 450-550,000L. **Meals** Breakfast 28,000L; half board 300-350,000L (per pers. 3 days min.). **Restaurant** In summer, lunch at the swimming pool; dinner 20:00-22:00; menu 90,000L, also à la carte. **Credit cards** All major. **Pets** Small dogs allowed in rooms (+25,000L). **Facilities** Swimming pool, bike, sauna (20,000L), moutain bikes, golf, parking. **Nearby** Vestiges romains et baptistère à Albenga et ses plages, Garlenda golf course (18-hole). **Open** Mar. – Dec.

The road to the Meridiana is not always pleasant, but once you have arrived, you will have no regrets. The atmosphere is one of a large country house, opening on the countryside, with beautiful grounds and a swimming pool. You will find the same airy comfort in the rooms. The hotel restaurant, Il Rosmario, is one of the better ones in the area. Mr. Segre, the dynamic owner, sees to it that only the best local products are used in the fine cuisine. A plus for many is the golf course right next door. This is a great place for a get away; ask about the special weekend package and golf rates.

How to get there *(Map 7): 100 km east to Nice (France) via A10, Albenga exit, then S453 towards Garlenda.*

Hotel Porto Roca

Via Corone, 1
19016 Monterosso Al Mare (La Spezia)
Tel. (0)187-81 75 02 - Fax (0)187-81 76 92
Sig.ra Guerina Arpe - Sig. and Sig.ra Segre

Rooms 43 with telephone, bath or shower, WC, TV and minibar. **Price** Single 220,000L, double 250-350,000L. **Meals** Breakfast included, served 7:30-10:00; half board 180-220,000L, full board 210-250,000L (per pers. 3 days min.). **Restaurant** Service 12:30-13:30, 19:30-21:00; menu 60-70,000L, also à la carte. Specialties: Sfogliatelle Porto Roca, straccetti "paradiso", branzino al sale, crostate di frutta fresca. **Credit cards** Amex, Visa, Eurocard, MasterCard. **Pets** Dogs allowed (+15-20,000L). **Facilities** Private beach in summer, parking in the village. **Nearby** The Riviera di Levante, the Cinque Terre by boat or by rail, Riomaggiore, Manarola, Marigola golf course (9-hole) in Lerici. **Open** Apr. 20 – Nov.

Monterosso rivals the charms of the neighboring villages of "Cinqueterra." The access road was built very recently and you still have to leave your car in the village parking lot. In the summer, it is guarded night and day, and if you inform the hotel of your arrival, they can arrange to have you picked up. The 43-room Porto Roca, the only hotel of this category to be found in these villages, towers over the Bay of Porticciolo and the beach of Monterosso. The interior furnishings are pleasantly kitsch, a mixture of different styles from the medieval to the 18th century. For sunbathing, you have a choice between the beach at the foot of the hotel and the terrace that overlooks the cliffs.

How to get there *(Map 9): 32 km northwest of La Spezia via S370, along the coast.*

Agnello d'Oro

Via Gombito, 22
24129 Bergamo Alta
Tel. (0)35 24 98 83 - Fax (0)35 23 56 12
Sig.Capozzi

Category ★★★ **Rooms** 20 with tel, bath or shower, WC, TV; elevator. **Price** Single 70,000L, double 100-120,000L. **Meals** Breakfast 10-000L, served 7:30, 10:00. **Restaurant** Service 12:30-14:30, 19:30-22:00, closed Mon. and Sun. evening; menu 55-65,000L; also à la carte. Specialties: Regional cooking. **Credit cards** All major. **Pets** Dogs allowed. **Nearby** In Bergamo: Piazza Vecchia, S. Maria Maggiore, Colleoni churche, Galeria Carrara. International Piano Festival, Abbey of Pontida, Treviglio and Rivolto d'Adda church. La Rossera golf course (9-hole) in Chiuduno. **Open** All year.

This small inn stands on a tiny piazza in the upper town of Bergamo. It is first of all a typical restaurant with solid wooden chairs and tables, red checkered tablecloths and shiny brass decorations on the walls. The specialties are the tasty dishes of Lombardy and if you order the risotto al profumo des bosco, you can have your souvenir plate to take with you. The rooms have been renovated and are simple but comfortable enough for a stopover in this town, whose artistic and historic heritage make it one of the most interesting in Lombardy. If no one is there to greet you on arrival, don't hesitate to ring the bell - the owner is undoubtedly busy in his kitchen.

How to get there *(Map 3): 47 km northeast of Milano. Airport di Oria al Serio, 4 km.*

I Due Roccoli

via Silvio Bonomelli, 54
25049 Iseo (Brescia)
Tel. (0)30-982 18 53 - Fax (0)30-982 18 77
Sig. Agoni

Category ★★★ **Rooms** 13 with telephone, bath or shower, WC., TV, safe and minibar **Price** Single 140-150,000L, double 180-210,000L, suite 220-250,000L. **Meals** Breakfast 16,000L, served 7:30-10:00. **Restaurant** Service 12:00-14:00, 19:30-22:00; menu 45-65,000L, also à la carte. Specialties: Agotino di ricotta, code di gamberi, pesce del lago. **Credit cards** All major. **Pets** Small dogs allowed. **Nearby** Lake Iseo, Bergamo, Val Camonica, Church of S. Pietro in Provaglio d'iseo, Brescia, Bergamo, Franciacorta golf course (18-hole). **Open** Mar. 16 – Oct. 31.

Thanks to its mild climate, Lake Iseo has become a tourist haven, bordered by little lakefront resorts. The Mediterranean vegetation and forests that seem to plunge straight into the water give the place an almost Alpine look, although the altitude is only 185 meters. The architecture of the resort houses is not always very attractive. To find buildings of character, it's best to go a bit further from the lake shores. I Due Roccoli is on the heights overlooking the lake. It consists of the old villa and a new building with guest rooms that are comfortable and decorated in a pleasant country style. If you have the choice, take a room facing the water. In short, this is a good spot, slightly off the beaten track but not too far away from the tourist highlights of Lombardy.

How to get there *(Map 3): 25 km north of Brescia (via A4 Milano/Venezia, Rovato exit), towards Lago Iseo, then Polaveno (4 km of Iseo).*

Cappuccini

via Cappucini, 54
Cologne Franciacorta (Brescia)
Tel. (0)30-755 72 54 - Fax (0)30-715 72 57
Sig. Pelizzari

Category ★★★ **Rooms** 7 with air-conditioning, telephone, bath, WC, satellite TV, safe and minibar. **Price** Single 160,000L, double 250,000L, suite 300,000L. **Meals** Breakfast 25,000L served 9:30-11:00. **Restaurant** Service 12:30-14:30, 19:30-22:00; menu 80,000L, also à la carte. Specialties: Manzo all' olio, stracotto con polenta, seafood. **Credit cards** All major. **Pets** Dogs not allowed. **Nearby** Lake Iseo, San Pietro Chirch in Lamosa in Provaglio d'Iseo, Bergamo, Brescia, Sirmione, Franciacorta golf course (18-hole). **Open** All year (except Jan. 1 – 20 and Aug. 1 – 20, and Wednesday).

Austere elegance and refinement, these are the qualities of this former monastery respectfully converted into a hospitable holiday spot. This lovely region on the border of Lombardy and Venetia, with its landscape of rolling hills and vineyards, is still little known by the masses of tourists. A serene landscape with plain stone houses whose only adornment is often their large canvas sunshades. The building still has the long corridors and vaulted passages of its monastic past. They lead to bedrooms that are very comfortable, yet even here the decor is minimal in style. The largest, which open onto the countryside, have a mezzanine and a small living room with a fireplace. A series of small dining rooms make it possible for guests to dine without being inconvenienced by the dinners or receptions that are sometimes held on the convent grounds. The cuisine, based largely on regional recipes and local products, will give you a taste of yet another aspect of the *dolce vita* in Franciacorta.

How to get there *(Map 3): 27 km west of Brescia, towards Bergamo.*

L'Albereta - Ristorante G. Marchesi

Via Vittorio Emanuele, 11
Erbusco (Brescia)
Tel. (0)30-776 05 50 - Fax (0)30-776 05 73
E-mail: albereta@terramoretti.it

Category ★★★★ **Rooms** 44 with air-conditining, telephone, bath, WC, TV and minibar. **Price** Single from 180,000L, double from 295,000L, suite from 550,000L. **Meals** Breakfast 20-45,000L, served 7:30-10:30; half board 210,000L, full board 240,000L (per pers.,3 days min.). **Restaurant** "Gualtiero Marchesi" Service 12:30-14:00, 19:30-22:00; closed Sunday evening, Mon.; menu 100-160,000L, also à la carte. Specialties: Italian "nouvelle cuisine". **Credit cards** All major. **Pets** Dogs allowed. **Facilities** Swimming pool, tennis, sauna, parking, garage. **Nearby** Lake Iseo, Bergamo, Brescia, Lake Garda, Lake Como, Franciacorta golf course (18-hole). **Open** All year (except 20 days in Jan.).

The Albereta is reputed to be the finest country inn in Lombardy, both for the cooking of Gualtieri Marchesi, who offers his own interpretations of traditional specialties, and for the winecellar, made up essentially of Italian and French wines. A stay here will also give you the chance to discover the region, with the softly rounded hills of Bellavista that form a backdrop for the verdant vineyards of Franciacorta. The dining room, under a large portico, faces the pleasant grounds that surround this fine 18th-century villa and its outbuildings. The rooms have comfort and refinement, the meals are delicious and as other distractions there are a library, a billiard room, plus a swimming pool and tennis court for sunny days. All the ingredients for an ideal weekend.

How to get there *(Map 3): 20 km west of Brescia, via A4 (Milano/Venezia) Rovato.*

Hotel Villa del Sogno

Lago di Garda
Via Zanardelli, 107
25083 Fasano di Gardone Riviera (Brescia)
Tel. (0)365-29 01 81 - Fax (0)365-29 02 30 - Famiglia Calderan
E-mail: sogno@mail.gsnet.it - Web: http://www.gesnet.it/sogno

Category ★★★★ **Rooms** 31 with telephone, bath or shower, WC and TV. **Price** Single 190-260,000L, double 320-460,000L, suite 420-500,000L. **Meals** Breakfast included, served 7:30-10:00; half board 190-270,000L, full board 210-260,000L (per pers.,3 days min.). **Restaurant** Service 12:30-14:30, 19:30-21:30; menu 80,000L, also à la carte. Specialties: Trota del Garda, ossibuchi alla gardesana, spaghetti alla trota. **Credit cards** All major. **Pets** Dogs not allowed. **Facilities** Swimming pool, tennis, sauna, parking **Nearby** Botanical garden of Gardone di Sotto, The Vittoriale (D'Annunzio estate), Belvedere San Michele; Verona, Soiano golf course (27-hole). **Open** Apr. – Oct. 20.

A symphony of pale yellow and ochre tones lights the facade of this romantic turn-of-the-century villa, with a terrace like something out of a dream. On a slight rise, it towers over Lake Garda amid the lush vegetation of its wonderful garden. A refined and elegant hotel, it is decorated with antique furniture and paintings of various epochs, with here and there a touch or a detail that is odd or unexpected, but which in no way spoils the ensemble. The rooms are perfect — spacious, some in Liberty style, others Venetian. One room has a small loggia, and others, below the main terrace, have their own private terraces. There is a very pleasant bar. On the grounds overlooking the lake are a nice swimming pool and tennis court.

How to get there *(Map 3): 130 km east of Milano - 36 km northeast of Brescia via S45 bis the left bank (Fasano, 2 km).*

Grand Hotel Fasano

Lago di Garda
Corso Zanardelli, 160
25083 Fasano di Gardone Riviera (Brescia)
Tel. (0)365-290 220 - Fax (0)365-210 54/290 221 - Sig.ra Mayr

Category ★★★★ **Rooms** 87 with telephone, bath or shower, and WC; elevator, wheelchair access. **Price** Double 198-451,000L. **Meals** Breakfast included, served 7:30-10:30; half board +25,000L (per pers.). **Restaurant** Service 12:30-14:30, 19:30-21:30; menu 65,000L, also à la carte. Specialties: Italian cuisine. **Credit cards** Not accepted. **Pets** Dogs allowed (+10,000L). **Facilities** Heated swimming pool and private beach, tennis (25,000L), parking (10,000L). **Nearby** Lake Garda, Villa Martinengo in Barbarno, botanical garden of Gardone di Sotto, The Vittoriale (D'Annunzio estate), Belvedere San Michele; Verona, Soiano-hole golf course (9-18-hole). **Open** Easter – Nov.

The Grand Hotel Fasano used to be a hunting lodge belonging to the imperial family of Austria, which perhaps explains, apart from the origins of the owner, the number of German tourists who come here. The hotel is comfortable, if a little over-decorated. The rooms are all pleasant, but ask for one in the older part. The garden, right on the lake, consists of beautiful plantings of palm trees, flowers, and greenery.

How to get there *(Map 3): 130 km east of Milano - 36 km northeast of Brescia via S45 bis, on the left bank (Fasano Gardone, 1 km).*

Villa Fiordaliso

Lago di Garda
Corso Zanardelli, 132
25083 Gardone Riviera (Brescia)
Tel. (0)365-20 158 - Fax (0)365-29 00 11 - Sig. Tosetti

Category ★★★★ **Rooms** 6 and 1 suite with air-conditioning, telephone, bath, WC., TV and minibar. **Price** Double 300-800,000L. **Meals** Breakfast included, served 8:00-10:00. **Restaurant** Service 12:30-14:00, 19:30-22:00, closed Mon. and Tues. lunch; menus 85-120,000L, also à la carte. Specialties: Season-cuisine. **Credit cards** All major. **Pets** Dogs not allowed. **Facilities** Private embarcadère, parking. **Nearby** Villa Martinengo in Barbarno, botanical garden of Gardone di Sotto, The Vittoriale (D'Annunzio estate), Belvedere San Michele, Verona, Bogliaco golf course (9-hole). **Open** All year (except Jan. 2 - Feb. 28.).

The 4-story Villa Fiordaliso stands on the shores of Lake Garda, the front facing the lake, but the rear of the building is directly on the road. The architecture could be termed eclectic, happily mingling Renaissance loggias and neoclassical Venetian-style windows. In 1985, restoration work was begun, its aim to preserve the original charm of this building that was once the home of Gabriele D'Annunzio (before he moved a little further away) and later, from 1943 to 1945, became the residence of Mussolini's mistress, Clara Petacci. The rooms are all comfortable and some of them have a terrace facing the lake. The Rose Room has a sumptuous bathroom all done in Carrara marble. The restaurant is known for its gastronomic quality and it is well worth stopping for a meal there even if you don't stay at the hotel. The atmosphere is a bit "old-style."

How to get there *(Map 3): 130 km east of Milano - 5 km northeast of Brescia via S45 on the left bank (1 km of Gardone Riviera).*

Hotel Baia d'Oro

Lago di Garda
Via Gamberera, 13
25084 Gargnano (Brescia)
Tel. (0)365-71 171 - Fax (0)365-72 568 - Sig. Terzi

Category ★★★ **Rooms** 12 with air-conditioning, telephone, bath, WC, TV and minibar. **Price** Double 160-240,000L. **Meals** Breakfast included, served 8:00-10:00. **Restaurant** Service 19:30-20:30; à la carte. Specialties: Pasta fatta in casa, pesce del lago e di mare. **Credit cards** Not allowed. **Pets** Dogs allowed. **Facilities** Garage (15,000L). **Nearby** Villa Feltrinelli, Lake Idro, Church of Madonna di Monte Castello, Pieve di Tremosine, Verona, Bogliaco golf course (9-hole). **Open** Apr. – Oct.

The colored facade of the Baia d'Oro, formerly a smallish house belonging to a fisherman, makes it easy to spot on the edge of Lake Garda. A private wharf keeps a *motoscaffo* at the disposal of the guests. On the picturesque lakeside terrace, you can enjoy lunch or dinner based on some of the best cuisine of the region–the hotel even recommends guests choose the half-board option so as not to miss out on the local treats. The rooms are comfortable and most have a small balcony, where you can have a pleasant breakfast while taking in the superb view. On the dining room walls are complimentary letters with famous signatures, notably one from Winston Churchill.

How to get there *(Map 3): 46 km northwest of Brescia via S45 bis, on the left bank.*

Villa Giulia

Lago di Garda
25084 Gargnano (Brescia)
Tel. (0)365-71 022/71 289 - Fax (0)365-72 774
Famiglia Bombardelli

Category ★★★ **Rooms** 22 with telephone, bath, WC, satellite TV, minibar and safe. **Price** Single 120-140,000L, double 260-300,000L. **Meals** Breakfast included, served 8:00-10:00. **Restaurant** Service 12:30-13:30, 19:30-20:30; à la carte. Specialties: Regional cooking. **Credit cards** Visa, Amex, Diners, MasterCard. **Pets** Small dogs allowed (10,000L). **Facilities** Swimming pool, sauna, private beach, parking. **Nearby** Villa Feltrinelli, Lake Idro, Church of Madonna di Monte Castello, Pieve di Tremosine, Verona, Bogliaco golf course (9-hole). **Open** 1 week before Easter – Oct. 10.

Success is often a question of passion and perseverance, two qualities which helped Rina Bombardelli turn the family *pensione* into a hotel of considerable charm. This Gothic-style villa, right on Lake Garda, has a great view of the lake and the Baldo mountains, which appear green or snowy white according to the season. The atmosphere is very cozy. The salon-bar is divided into distinctly different areas by wing and club chairs. The dining room, similarly divided, is lit by two beautiful Murano crystal chandeliers. In summer, the restaurant is set up on the veranda. The well-furnished rooms have a view of either the garden or the lake. Off to one side there is a swimming pool and a solarium on the lawn.

How to get there *(Map 3): 46 km northwest of Brescia via S45 bis, on the left bank.*

Hotel Laurin

Lago di Garda
25087 Salò (Brescia)
Viale Landi, 9
Tel. (0)365-220 22 - Fax (0)365-223 82 - Sig. Rossi

Rooms 36 (18 with air-conditioning) with telephone, bath or shower, WC, TV and minibar. **Price** Single 135-150,000L, double 230-300,000L, suite 250-380,000L. **Meals** Breakfast included, served 8:00-10:00; half board 195-250,000L (per pers., 3 days min.). **Restaurant** Service 12:30-14:30, 20:00-21:30; menus, à la carte. Specialties: Fish. **Credit cards** All major. **Pets** Small dogs allowed. **Facilities** Swimming pool, parking. **Nearby** Villa Martinengo in Barbarano, Garden of Gardone di Sotto, Vittoriale degli Italiani, Belvedere San Michele, Verona, Bogliaco golf course (9-hole). **Open** Feb. – Nov.

A popular vacation spot in the last century, Lake Garda has kept beautiful vestiges of this era. Salo, one of the rare villages to have kept the luster of the old days, is also etched painfully into the history of Italy, having been the last bastion of Mussolini's supporters. The Hotel Laurin is an admirably preserved Liberty-style villa, one of the precious jewels of the area. The salons are decorated with frescoes of voluptuous romantic subjects. The rooms have parquet floors and delicate furniture adding to the elegant harmonious atmosphere. Most of them have an enchanting view of the lake. The staff will welcome you warmly. Be sure to take a walk along the banks up to the village and visit the very unusual "Vittoriale," the palace-museum of the poet Gabriele d'Annunzio.

How to get there *(Map 3): 130 km east of Milano - 35 km northeast of Brescia via S45 on the left bank (1 km from Gardone Riviera).*

Villa Cortine Palace Hotel

Lago di Garda
Via Grotte, 12
25019 Sirmione (Brescia)
Tel. (0)30-99 05 890 - Fax (0)30-91 63 90 - Sig. Cappelletto

Category ★★★★★ **Rooms** 49 with telephone, bath, WC, TV; elevator. **Price** Double 480-620,000L, junior-suite 700-940,000L, suite 800-1,100 000L. **Meals** Breakfast included, served 7:30-10:30. Half board 315-355,000L, full board 385-445,000L (per pers. (obligatory in low season). **Restaurant** Service 12:30-14:15, 19:30-21:15; menus 90-110,000L, also à la carte. Specialties: Italian and international cooking. **Credit cards** All major. **Pets** Dogs allowed (+40,000L). **Facilities** Swimming pool, tennis (15,000L), private beach, parking. **Nearby** Lake Garda, Grotte di Catullo and Castle of Scaliger in Sirmione, Brescia, Verona, Soiano golf course (9-18-hole). **Open** Apr. – Oct. 25.

This lovely house in neo-classical style was built by Count von Koseritz, who was later killed in World War II. Later, a rich industrialist from Milan renovated the property and converted it into a luxury hotel. The interior is adorned with fluted columns and Corinthian capitals, with marble, gilded wood and frescoes. A second building, recently added in order to increase the capacity, has unfortunately spoiled the ensemble. The luxuriousness is all a bit too strident, but the quality of amenities and service is up to the highest expectations. Besides, the site is marvelous: The lovely grounds with ornamental fountains and balconies over the lake confirm what Catullus said so many centuries ago — that Sirmione was the jewel of the entire peninsula.

How to get there *(Map 3): 127 km east of Milano - 40 km east of Brescia via A4, Sirmione exit - San Martino di Battaglia.*

1998

Albergo Terminus

Lago di Como
Lungo Lario Trieste, 14 - 22100 Como
Tel. (0)31 329 111 - Fax (0)31 302 550 - DrPassera
E-mail: larioterminus@galactica.it

Category ★★★★ **Rooms** 38 with air-conditioning, tel, bath or shower, WC, satellite TV, minibar, safe; elevator. **Price** Single 170-210,000L, double 200-300,000L, suite 420-550,000L. **Meals** Breakfast 25 000L, served 7:15-10:30. **Restaurant** Service 12:30-15:00, 19:30-22:30; closed Tue; also a la carte. Specialties: Italian cooking. **Credit cards** All major. **Pets** Dogs allowed. **Facilities** Sauna, parking and garage at hotel (22,000L). **Nearby** Menaggio, Villa Carlotta in Tremezzo, garden of the Villa Serbelloni and Villa Melzi, Villa d'Este golf course (18-hole) in Montorfano. **Open** All year.

All along the Como waterfront the imposing villas stand shoulder to shoulder, but you can't miss the little French-style garden with its lawns and pebbled paths just in front of the Albergo Terminus. The hotel has kept intact its Liberty-style stuccos and woodwork and floral decorations as well as the fantasy of its interior architecture, with a central great hall surrounded by salons and a veranda dining room extending onto a pleasant terrace in summer. All the bedrooms are comfortable, but the prettiest are those facing the lake. One worthy of special mention is La Torretta, a suite with a terrace and a panoramic view of Como.

How to get there *(Map 2): 48 km from Milano; on the harbor.*

1998

Hotel Villa Flori

Lago di Como
Via Cernobbio, 12 - 22100 Como
Tel. (0)31 573 105 - Fax (0)31 570 379 - Famiglia Passera
E-mail: lariotermінus@galactica.it

Rooms 45 with tel, bath or shower, WC, TV, minibar; elevator. **Price** Simple 170-240,000L, double 200-300,000L, suite 380-450 000L. **Meals** Breakfast 25,000L, served 7:15-11:00. **Restaurant** Service 12:30-14:30, 19:30-21:00, menu 65-85,000L; also à la carte. Specialties: Italian cooking. **Credit cards** All major. **Pets** Dogs allowed (except in restaurant). **Facilities** Parking and garage (20,000L). **Nearby** Menaggio, Villa Carlotta in Tremezzo, Bellagio, garden of the Villa Serbelloni and Villa Melzi, Villa d'Este golf course (18-hole) in Montorfano. **Open** Feb. 10. - Dec. 2.

The Villa Flori was originally intended as a wedding present from the Marchese Raimondi to his daughter Giuseppina, who was to marry Garibaldi. But the wedding never took place as the general discovered that the girl's past was not above reproach, and for a long time the house remained uninhabited. Today it is one of Lake Como's very pleasant hotels. The entrance hall gives not a clue to what you will find inside. The salons and dining room are richly appointed in pleasing pastel tones. All the bedrooms face the lake and some have a large living room and balcony. The silky fabrics, thick carpets and large modern bathrooms make them very comfortable to live in. With Milan so close by, the hotel is often used for seminars and receptions, but all is done to see that these events do not inconvenience the guests.

How to get there *(Map 2): 48 km from Milano; 2 km from Como. Cernobbio road.*

Grand Hotel Villa Serbelloni

Lago di Como - Via Roma, 1
22021 Bellagio (Como)
Tel. (0)31-95 02 16 - Fax (0)31-95 15 29 - Sig. Spinelli
E-mail: gh.villaserbelloni@po.bes.it - Web: http://www.fromitaly.it/bellagio/h5/serb

Category ★★★★★ **Rooms** 85 (60 with air-conditioning) with telephone, bath, WC, TV and minibar; elevator. **Price** Single 320-450,000L, double 460-710,000L, junior suite 900-1,100 000L. **Meals** Breakfast included, served 7:30-10:30; half board +85,000L, full board +160,000L (per pers., 3 days min.). **Restaurant** Service 12:30-14:30, 20:00-22:00; menu 95,000L, also à la carte. Specialties: Pasta della casa, pesce del lago. **Credit cards** All major. **Pets** Dogs allowed. **Facilities** Heated swimming pool, tennis (20,000 L), sauna, fitness and beauty, squash, private garage (25,000L), parking. **Nearby** Milano, Lake Como (Villa Melzi, Erba to Bellagio by the Vallassina), Bellagio to Como, Villa Trotti, Grotta verde in Lezzeno, Careno, Villa Pliniana in Riva di Faggetto, Grandola golf course (18-hole). **Open** Apr. – end Oct.

The Serbelloni is one of those historic villas built in the 19th century all along this lovely section of the lake to provide the aristocratic families of Lombardy with all the grandeur they could possibly desire. Others were the Villa d'Este at Cernobbio, the Villa Carlotta at Tremezzo, the Villa Olmo in Como or the Villa Ricordi in Cadenabbia where Verdi wrote part of "La Traviata." The Serbelloni, with its impressive Liberty-style facade stands overlooking the lakefront in its magnificent English-style garden, planted with an incredible variety of trees. Stuccos and columns add a further note of luxury to the public rooms. As for the bedrooms, most of them have retained their volumes, painted ceilings and original furniture; a few of them, however, are not so well-situated. So if you can afford to stay at the Serbelloni, you had best reserve a room facing the lake, and thereby enjoy the wonderful vista that so enchanted Flaubert and Liszt.

How to get there *(Map 2): 31 km north of Como.*

Hotel Florence - "Firenze"

Lago di Como
Piazza Mazzimi
22021 Bellagio (Como)
Tel. (0)31-950 342 - Fax (0)31-951 722 - Sig. and Sig.ra Ketzlar

Category ★★★ **Rooms** 32 with telephone, bath or shower, WC, satellite TV, hairdrayer and minibar. **Price** Single 170,000L, double 225,000L, suite 310,000L. **Meals** Breakfast included, served 7:30-10:15; half board 155-160,000L (per pers.). **Restaurant** Service 12:30-14:30, 19:30-21:30; à la carte. Specialties: Stracci di pasta agli spinaci e pecorino, Cappellacci, Barbabiet, Pesce persico con salsa di porri e tortino di mais. **Credit cards** Visa, Eurocard, MasterCard. **Pets** Dogs allowed (except in restaurant). **Nearby** Milano, Lake Como (Villa Melzi, Erba to Bellagio by the Vallassina), Bellagio to Como, Villa Trotti, Grotta verde in Lezzeno, Careno, Villa Pliniana in Riva di Faggetto, Grandola golf course (18-hole). **Open** Apr. – Oct.

Under the arcades that line Bellagio's port, just near the entrance to the Hotel Serbelloni, one notices a small hotel with a terrace where refreshments are served to tourists waiting for the ferry. This is the Hotel Firenze. It also has a cocktail lounge where jazz concerts are given on Sunday. The dining room and bedrooms are on the upper floors. They are all nicely appointed with antique furniture and fine fabrics. All have a view of the lively port and the lake. The dining room with its fireplace has a convivial atmosphere, but in the summer meals are also served on the terrace facing the lake. The owners will give you a warm welcome. The Firenze is less luxurious than its neighbor but far less expensive as well. It is a hotel of charm and quality, well worth discovering.

How to get there *(Map 2): 31 km north of Como via S583; on the right bank.*

Grand Hotel Villa d'Este

Lago di Como - Via Regina, 40 - 22012 Cernobbio (Como)
Tel. (0)31-348 1 - Fax (0)31-348 844 - Sig. Claudio Ceccherelli
E-mail: info@villadeste.it - Web: http://www.villadeste.it

Category ★★★★★ **Rooms** 166 with telephone, bath, WC, satellite TV, safe and minibar; elevator. **Price** Single 625,000L, double 925,000L. **Meals** Breakfast included **Restaurant** Service 12:00-14:30, 21:30-22:00; à la carte. Specialties: International cooking. **Credit cards** All major. **Pets** Dogs allowed. **Facilities** 2 swimming pools, sauna, tennis, squash, garage, parking. **Nearby** Ossuccio and gardens of the Villa Arconati in Punta di Balbianello, Villa Carlotta in Tremezzo, Mennagio, Lugano, boat for Bellagio in Tremezzo, Villa d'Este golf course (18-hole) in Montorfano. **Open** Mar. 23 – Nov.

The Villa d'Este has always been a favorite of celebrities - those whose names grace the pages of the popular magazines. Built in the 16th century, it was even then favored by the aristocracy and now that the horse-drawn coaches are gone, the Rolls and Mercedes have taken their place in the little village streets of Cernobbio. The interior still bears traces of these illustrious visitors: The Napoleon room has its original silk hangings and a statue attributed to Canova attests to the stay by the famous sculptor. Each room is unique, a personalized decor of silk draperies and antique furniture. But the gardens are even more unforgettable: ruins and columns, rockwork and basins are set amid a vegetation of rare species. To entertain its demanding clientele, the hotel provides such a variety of sports facilities that it is possible to do just about everything without leaving the grounds — a large swimming pool built out over the lake, all the water sports available, a golf course at Montofano, a health center. After an excellent dinner (with dancing, if you wish) you can always end the evening in the private night club. The staff is uniformly excellent.

How to get there *(Map 2): 5 km north of Como*

Grand Hotel Imperiale

Lago di Como
22010 Moltrasio (Como)
Via Durini
Tel. (0)31 346 111 - Fax (0)31 346 120

Category ★★★★ **Rooms** 92 with air-conditioning, tel, bath, WC, satellite TV, minibar, safe; elevator. **Price** Single 160-210,000L, double 230-320,000L, suite 330-420,000L. **Meals** Breakfast included; half board 180-195,000L, full board 180-235,000L (per pers. 3 days min.). **Restaurant** Service 12:00-14:30, 19:30-22:00; carte. Specialties: Italian cooking. **Credit cards** All major. **Pets** Dogs allowed. **Facilities** Heated swimming pool, beach, tennis, squash, garage (15,000L). **Nearby** Ossuccio and gardens of the Villa Arconati in Punta di Balbia, Menaggio, Villa Carlotta in Tremezzo, boat for Bellagio, gardens of the Villa Serballoni and Villa Melzi; Golf Villa d'Este (18-hole) in Montorfano. **Open** All year.

If the Villa d'Este is an impossible dream, drive on for a few more kilometers till you reach Moltrasio. There a beautiful villa that has just been completely transformed stands between its park and the lakefront. At the rear of the old house they have built a new addition linked to the rest by a large and very modern atrium which serves as the reception area. Metallic corridors lead to the modern rooms of the new wing. Although these are perfectly adequate, we recommend you book one of the ten rooms in the Villa Stucchi facing the garden, and if you can afford it, La Romantica, opening onto the lake. There are two restaurants, one overlooking the swimming pool and a man-made private beach on the lake. The prices are not too steep, but you should know that the hotel has several conference rooms, and a seminar might possibly disturb your stay.

How to get there *(Map 2): 7km north of Como.*

San Giorgio Hotel

Lago di Como
Via Regina, 81 - Tremezzo 22016 Lenno (Como)
Tel. (0)344-40 415 - Fax (0)344-41 591
Sig.ra Cappelletti

Category ★★★ **Rooms** 26 with telephone, bath or shower and WC. **Price** With half board and full board 130-160,000L. (per pers., 3 days min.). **Meals** Breakfast 20,000L, served 8:00-11:00. **Restaurant** Only for residents; Service 12:30-13:30, 19:30-20:30; menu. **Credit cards** Amex, Visa, Eurocard, MasterCard. **Pets** Dogs not allowed. **Facilities** Tennis (18,000L), parking. **Nearby** Milano (Lake Como, Villa Carlotta in Tremezzo, Mennagio, Lugano), boat for Bellagio in Tremezzo, golf course (18-hole) in Grandola e Uniti. **Open** Apr. – Sept.

The San Giorgio is a gracious hotel, run as a family affair. It's located in the heart of the Bay of Tremezzina–the dreamiest part of Lake Como. The main building, next to the small old house, was built by the current owner's grandfather. The dining room and the grand salon, which still have the family furniture, 19th-century chairs and couches and a mahogany roll-top desk, open onto a garden-level porch. The rooms are all large and have functional bathrooms, balconies and a view of the bay and the mountains. The grounds, formerly an olive grove, dip gently downward to the lake. They bloom with wisteria and magnolia flowers in the spring, and in the fall are full of the fragrance of exotic plants. The hotel is only a few miles from the wharves of Tremezzo, Cadenabbia and Menaggio–perfect for sailing buffs eager to explore the Italian lakes.

How to get there *(Map 2): 27 km north of Como via S340, on the left bank.*

Grand Hotel Victoria

Lago di Como
22017 Menaggio (Como)
Tel. (0)344-32 003 - Fax (0)344-32 992
Sig. Proserpio - Sig. Palano

Category ★★★★ **Rooms** 53 with telephone, bath or shower, WC, satellite TV and elevator. **Price** Single 145-175,000L, double 220-260,000L, suite 370,000L. **Meals** Breakfast 25,000L (buffet), served 7:30-11:00; half board +55,000L (per pers.). **Restaurant** Service 12:30-14:00, 19:30-22:00; menu 55,000L, also à la carte. Specialties: Italian cooking. **Credit cards** All major. **Pets** Dogs allowed. **Facilities** Swimming pool, parking. **Nearby** Villa Carlotta in Tremezzo, Mennagio, Lugano, golf course (18-hole) in Grandola e Uniti. **Open** All year.

Set on magnificent grounds with enormous trees facing Lake Como, the Grand Hotel Victoria is a late 1880s-style palace. The vast salons have parquet floors, stucco ceilings and a quiet and harmonious atmosphere. As soon as the weather allows, meals are served on the terrace facing the lake under a big striped tent. The most recently refurnished rooms gained in comfort what they may have lost of their former personality.

How to get there *(Map 2): 35 km north of Como via S340, on the left bank.*

Hotel Stella d'Italia

Lago di Lugano
Piazza Roma, 1
San Mamete 22010 Valsolda (Como)
Tel. (0)344-68 139 - Fax (0)344-68 729 - Sig. Ortelli

Category ★★★ **Rooms** 35 with telephone, bath or shower, WC, satellite TV, safe; elevator. **Price** Single 85,000L, double 165-195,000L. **Meals** Breakfast included, served 7:30-10:00; half board 110-170,000L (per pers., 3 days min.). **Restaurant** Service 12:30-14:00, 19:30-21:00; menu 35,000L, also à la carte. Specialties: Seafood, pasta. **Credit cards** All major. **Pets** Small dogs allowed. **Facilities** Private beach, garage (10,000L). **Nearby** Lake Lugano, Villa Favorita, Lugano-Mennagio, Villa Carlotta in Tremezzo. **Open** Apr. – Oct.

On the shores of Lake Lugano, San Mamete is a pretty little village, home to the Stella d'Italia, which has been run by the Ortelli family for three generations. Many readers have written to us about the beautiful interiors adorned with Madame Ortelli's interesting collection of paintings, artistic lighting and comfortable furniture. The rooms have been renovated and the nicest ones, in the front, have large door-windows facing on the lake. The lakeside garden is marvelous and here you can dine pleasantly under a large trellis smothered with Virginia creeper and roses. There is a small beach where you can sunbathe and go for a swim in the lake. The panorama and surroundings are superb, the prices moderate and the service friendly.

How to get there *(Map 2): 42 km north of Como via A9, Lugano-south exit, then towards Gandria-Saint Moritz.*

Villa Giulia Al Terrazo

Lago di Como
23868 Valmadrera (Lecco)
Via Parè, 73
Tel. (0)341-58 31 06 - Fax (0)341-20 11 18

Rooms 12 with telephone, shower, WC, TV, (10 with minibar). **Price** Single 105,000L, double 185,000L, suite 225,000L. **Meals** Breakfast 18,000L (buffet), served 7:00-10:30; half board 160,000L, full board 180,000L (per pers., 3 days min.). **Restaurant** Service 12:30, 19:30; menus 70-90,000L, also à la carte. Specialties: Insalata di gamberi e asparagi mimosa, tagliolini freschi con gamberi aromatizzati al curry, prosciutto d'anatra con finocchio e acquadelle, Croccantino stelato all anice. Crema di vaniglia dorata. **Credit cards** All major. **Pets** Dogs allowed. **Facilities** Parking. **Nearby** Lecco (Villa Manzoni), villa Monastero Mornico gardens, Lecco to Erba (basilicata San Pietro al Monte). **Open** All year.

Trying to find a hotel in Milan (unless you stay in a palace) is doomed to failure if the trip has not been planned a long time in advance. This is why one of our readers told us about the Villa Giulia, about 30 miles from Milan, easily accessible by highway. It is in a late 18th century villa on the shores of Lake Como, (known locally as Lago di Lecco). Several pretty comfortable rooms will allow you to prolong your visit and enjoy the quality of the service and the kindness of the staff. This is a good standby hotel, but is also an ideal place to stay for those interested in exploring the Italian lakes.

How to get there *(Map 2): 56 km north of Milano via motorway towards Lecco.*

1998

Hotel Olivedo

Lago di Como
Piazza Martiri de la Liberta', 4
22050 Varenna (Lecco)
Tel. (0)341-83 01 15 - Fax (0)341-83 01 15 - Sig.ra Laura Colombo

Category HH **Rooms** 15 (6 with bath or shower). **Price** 90-105,000L (without bath), 100-150,000L (with bath). **Meals** Breakfast included, served 8:30-10:30; half board 85-90,000L (without bath.) and full board100-110,000L (with bath.) per pers. **Restaurant** Service 12:30-14:00, 19:30-21:00; menu 40,000L. Specialties: Pesce di lago, antipasti i dolci fatti in casa. **Credit cards** Visa, Eurocard, MasterCard. **Pets** Dogs allowed. **Facilities** Parking. **Nearby** Varenna: Villa Monastero Mornico gardens, (April - Oct.), Lecco (villa Manzoni), Lake Como. **Open** Dec. 15 - Oct.

The nicest way to get to Varenna is to put the car on the ferry and cross the lake from Menaggio or Bellagio - you get a wonderful view of the pretty multicolored houses that descend right down to the water's edge. The hotel is just there, facing the dock. On its shaded terrace stand several tourists, waiting for the boat. The house is a noble yellow building with green shutters, where all is simple but arranged with utmost care. This is clear from the first look at the dining room (with its pretty tablecloths and candles just waiting for the evening meal) or the charming little village bistro. The rooms are extremely well-kept and Laura points out with pride that she still has laundry staff who know how to use starch. However, the rooms are not equally comfortable: not all of them have a private bathroom and some of the furniture has seen better days. To be sure that you won't be disappointed, ask to reserve a room facing the lake. This is a friendly and unpretentious place, in a village a bit off the main tourist paths, which is perhaps something of an advantage.

How to get there *(Map 2): 50 km from Como.*

Villa Simplicitas e Solferino

22028 San Fedele d'Intelvi (Como)
Tel. (0)31-83 11 32
Sig. Castelli

Category ★★ **Rooms** 10 with shower and WC. **Price** With half board 115-150,000L, full board 150,000L (per pers.). **Restaurant** Service 12:30-14:30, 20:30-22:00; menus 40-55,000L. Specialties: Italian and regional cuisine. **Credit cards** Not accepted. **Pets** Dogs allowed (fee). **Facilities** Parking. **Nearby** Cernobbio, Church of Sala Comacina, Val d'Intelvi, Lanzo d'Intelvi, Lugano **Open** Apr. – Oct.

Let us say at the outset, this is a real inn of charm and one of our favorite places of all. First the site: You leave the shores of the lake, which can get a bit too touristy, and head for the mountainous countryside, into a landscape of large chestnut trees, larches and ferns. The villa is built on a rise surrounded by verdant meadowland. The cat and the dogs of the house will be the first to greet you and bid you welcome. The interior is delightfully simple, with worn floorboards, faded curtains and yellowed old engravings, but the rooms are as cozy as can be (with comfortable bathrooms) and the cooking, Trentino style, is excellent. A perfect spot if you're seeking inspiration, or a lovers' retreat, or just a wonderful house for a family vacation.

How to get there *(Map 2): 30 km north of Como via S340, on the left bank to Argegno, then left towards San Fedele Intelvi.*

Albergo San Lorenzo

Piazza Concordia, 14
46100 Mantova
Tel. (0)376-22 05 00 - Fax (0)376-32 71 94
Sig. Tosi

Category ★★★★ **Rooms** 39 with air-conditioning, telephone, bath or shower, WC, satellite TV, minibar and elevator. **Price** Single 125-250,000L, double 150-300,000L, suite 150-350,000L. **Meals** Breakfast included, served 7:00-10:00. **Restaurant** See p. 459. **Credit cards** All major. **Pets** Dogs not allowed. **Facilities** Garage (30,000L). **Nearby** Mantova: Piazza Sordelo, Duomo, Palazzo Ducale, piazza delle Erbe, S. Andrea - Santuario delle Grazie (6 km) où a lieu à la mi-août le rassemblement national des madonnari - Descente du Mincio et du Pô (de mars à octobre, départ devant le Castello di San Giorgio), à bord de l'Andes 2000 pour Venise, retour en pullman pour l'abbaye de San Benedetto Pô et pour le parc du Mincio - Sabbioneta : parc du Palazzo del Giardino, teatro olimpico et palazzo ducale, l'église de Villa Pasquali à 2 km et Viadana à 11 km - Verona. **Open** All year.

The Albergo San Lorenzo is the ideally place for visiting the wealthy town of Mantua (Mantova). It is in the middle of a pedestrian area close to the Duomo and the Palazzo Ducale. Decorated with antique furniture and a rococo decor, it is spacious and comfortable. Breakfast is served on a pretty rooftop terrace. The staff is very discreet and the absence of a restaurant makes this a very restful place. Mantua offers the considerable advantage of being off the beaten tourist track, even though it is undeniably beautiful.

How to get there *(Map 9): 62 km northeast of Parma via S343. 45 km southwest of Verona.*

Il Leone

Piazza IV Martiri, 2
Pomponesco (Mantova)
Tel. (0)375-86 077 - Fax (0)375-86 770
Famiglia Mori

Category ★★★ **Rooms** 8 with air-conditioning in the double room, telephone, shower, WC, TV and minibar. **Price** Single 100,000L, double 135,000L. **Meals** Breakfast 15,000L, served 8:00-10:00; half board 135-145,000L, full board 155-165,000L (per pers., 3 days min.). **Restaurant** Service 12:00-14:00, 20:00-22:00; closed Sun. evening, Mon.; à la carte. Specialties: Salumeria, ravioli al zucca, tartufi, risotto, zabaione e semi-freddo. **Credit cards** All major. **Pets** Small dogs allowed. **Facilities** Swimming pool. **Nearby** Church in Viadana, Church in Villa Pasquali, Sabbioneta, Mantova, Parma. **Open** Jan. 27 – Dec. 26.

Behind the austere facade of this house in the village of Pomponesco–formerly the fiefdom of the celebrated Gonzagua family–you will find a swimming pool and a lovely patio. The salons are impressive: they have superb furniture and high ceilings, and one is decorated with magnificent frescoes. The rooms are large and comfortable. Ask for one by the pool. Breakfasts are copious, the cuisine is perfect and the risotto unforgettable. The wine cellar is well stocked with Italian and international wines.

How to get there *(Map 9): 32 km northwest of Parma via S62 to Viadana, then on the right towards Pomponesco.*

Four Seasons Hotel

Via Gesù, 8
20121 Milano
Tel. (0)2-77 088 - Fax (0)2-77 08 5000
Sig. V. Finizzola

Category ★★★★★ **Rooms** 70 and 28 suites with air-conditioning, telephone, bath, WC, satellite TV, safe and minibar; elevator. **Price** Single 726-859,000L, double 862-995,000L, suite 1,094-5,390 000L. **Meals** Breakfast 45,000L, served 7:00-11:30. **Restaurants** "La Veranda"; service 11:30-23:00; menu: 75,000L, also à la carte. "Il teatro"; service 19:30-23:00; closed Sun. and Aug. 1 – 20; menu 75,000L. Specialties: Italian cooking. "Il Teatro"; service 19:30-23:30; menu 90,000L. Specialties: Mediterranean cooking. **Credit cards** All major. **Pets** Dogs allowed except in restaurant. **Facilities** Fitness club, garage (25,000L). **Nearby** Milano Duomo, Brera-Museum; opening December 7 of the lyric season at the Scala, Piccolo teatro di Milano - Abbey of Chiaravalle; Villa Reale in Monza, Abbey of Viboldone, Lake Como, la Piazza Ducale in Vigevano), Certosa di Pavia, golf course (9-18-hole) at Parco di Monza. **Open** All year.

A superb oasis in the lively triangle of culture and fashion formed by the junction of the Via Montenapoleone, Via della Spiga, and Sant' Andrea, the Four Seasons is in a former Fransiscan monastery built in the 15th century, complete with cloister and intact frescoes. Discreetly luxurious, the hotel features simple, elegant rooms accented with Fortuny fabrics in faded colors, sycamore wood furniture and marble baths. Everything is comfortable, softly lit and very quiet. Room service is available around the clock, so if you prefer to have dinner in your room after your evening at La Scala, all you need do is ring. Otherwise, you can enjoy fine savory cuisine at one of two restaurants before having one last drink at the *Foyer,* the hotel bar.

How to get there *(Map 2): In the center of the town.*

Excelsior Hotel Gallia

Piazza Duca d'Aosta, 9
20124 Milano
Tel. (0)2-67 851 - Fax (0)2-66 713 239
Sig. Occhiolini

Category ★★★★ **Rooms** 237 with air-conditioning, telephone, bath, WC, TV and minibar. **Price** Single 380-440,000L, double 460-510,000L, suite 700-1,300 000L. **Meals** Breakfast 26-38,000L, served 7:00-10:30. **Restaurant** Service 12:30-14:30, 19.30-22.30; menu: 80,000L, also à la carte. Specialties: Italian cooking. **Credit cards** All major. **Pets** Dogs not allowed. **Facilities** Fitness club, garage (25,000L). **Nearby** Milano Duomo, Brera-Museum; opening December 7 of the lyric season at the Scala, Piccolo teatro di Milano - Abbey of Chiaravalle; Villa Reale in Monza, Abbey of Viboldone, Lake Como, la Piazza Ducale in Vigevano), Certosa di Pavia, golf course (9-18-hole) at Parco di Monza. **Open** All year.

Just across from the train station, the Excelsior Gallia is one of the great institutions of Milan. It was built in the 305 and its interior announces comfort and luxury. The elegant, comfortable rooms have 30s, 50s, and contemporary decor. You will find excellent cuisine (one of the best restaurant in Milan) and perfect service here. Night owls can sip a nightcap while listening to the piano music in *The Baboon*. This classic grand hotel is a great find.

How to get there *(Map 2): In front of the station.*

Grand Hotel Duomo

Via San Raffaele, 1
20121 Milano
Tel. (0)2 88 33 - Fax (0)2 864 620 27 - Sig.Gnoni
E-mail: hduomores@telemacus.it - Web: www.duomohotel.it

Category ★★★★★ **Rooms** 153 with air-conditioning, tel, bath, WC, satellite TV, minibar, safe; elevator. **Price** Single 340-410,000L, double 480-570,000L, suite 740-900,000L. **Meals** Breakfast included, served 7:00-11:00. **Restaurant** Service 12:30-14:30, 19:30-23:00; menu 70-90,000L; also à la carte. **Credit cards** All major. **Pets** Dogs allowed. **Facilities** Garage (70,000L). **Nearby** Milan (Duomo, Brera museum, Piccolo teatro di milano; Abbey of Chiaravalle; Villa Reale in Monza, Abbey of Chiaravalle; Villa Reale in Monza; Abbey of Viboldone; lake Como; la piazza Ducale in Vigevano, Certosa di Pavia, golf course (9-18 hole) at Parco di Monza. **Open** All year.

The Duomo is Milan's traditional luxury hotel. Its location just opposite the cathedral has contributed to its reputation. The common areas (lobby and great hall) are still in the modern style of the 1950s, but this look does have a certain allure. The bedrooms, however, have been redone to suit today's taste. They are spacious and elegant and offer good comfort and excellent service. As for the suites, each one is a real duplex with a view of the cathedral. In winter breakfast and meals are served in the large dining room whose windows are under the arcades along the piazza, but in fine weather they are served on the panoramic terrace, just a few yards from the lacy stonework of the towers and spires of the Duomo.

How to get there *(Map 2): piazza del Duomo.*

Hotel Pierre Milano

Via de Amicis, 32
20123 Milano
Tel. (0)2 720 005 81 - Fax (0)2 805 2157

Category ★★★★★ **Rooms** 49 with tel, bath, WC, TV, minibar. **Price** Single 230-350,000L, double 390-550,000L, suite 690-800,000L. **Meals** Breakfast 22-35,000L (brunch) Served 7:00-10:30. **Restaurant** "Petit Pierre". Service 12:30-14:30, 19:30-22:30; menu 50-70,000L, also à la carte. Specialties: Italian and regional cooking. **Credit cards** All major. **Pets** Dogs allowed with a reservation. **Facilities** Parking at hotel. **Nearby** Milan (Duomo, Brera museum, Piccolo teatro di milano; Abbey of Chiaravalle; Villa Reale in Monza, Abbey of Chiaravalle, Villa Reale in Monza, Abbey of Viboldone, lake Como, la piazza Ducale in Vigevano, Certosa di Pavia, golf course (9-18-hole) at Parco di Monza. **Open** All year (except in August).

Near the Ticinese quarter, just behind the Via Lanzone and the Via del Torchio, famous for the antique and fine crafts shops, a stay at the Pierre Milano is a good way to get to appreciate this city, which is the heart of modern Italy. A visit to the Brera is a must, if only for the Christ of Mantegna, but you shouldn't miss seeing the boutiques and galleries that show the latest creations of Italian design. The Pierre is a perfect illustration of the spirit of Milan, which blends tradition with great modernity and technological sophistication. For example, the bedrooms are the height of functional and contemporary style, yet on the beds you will find wonderful old linen sheets. The service is perfect. The elegant atmosphere of the piano bar makes it a favorite meeting place for guests, who often stop here for cocktails before dinner and sometimes drop in for a nightcap as well.

How to get there *(Map 2): Ticinese quarter.*

Hotel Diana Majestic

Viale Piave, 42
20129 Milano
Tel. (0)2-29 51 34 04 - Fax (0)2-20 10 72

Category ★★★★ **Rooms** 94 with telephone, bath, WC, TV and minibar; elevator. **Price** Single 291,500-430,000L, double 401,500-560,000L. **Meals** Breakfast 31-46,200L. **Restaurant** See pp. 455-457. **Credit cards** All major. **Pets** Small dogs allowed. **Facilities** Parking. **Nearby** Milano Duomo, Brera-Museum; opening December 7 of the lyric season at the Scala, Piccolo teatro di Milano - Abbey of Chiaravalle; Villa Reale in Monza, Abbey of Viboldone, Lake Como, la Piazza Ducale in Vigevano), Certosa di Pavia, golf course (9-18-hole) at Parco di Monza. **Open** All year.

Well-situated at the end of the Corso Venezia, this hotel of the Ciga-Sheraton group has now recovered all its authenticity, after a restoration carried out with great respect. The Art Deco architecture and features have been preserved: On the ground floor, the little reception room with its 1930s leather armchairs is leads to the circular grand salon, a lounge with wicker furniture opening onto a garden. This garden is the last trace of the countryside that once began at the Porta Venezia. The statue of Diana the Huntress that still stands here recalls the inauguration on this site of the Diana Baths, the first public swimming pool for women in Italy. In April, when the wisteria is in bloom, it forms an enormous flowering arbor, under which the restaurant is installed. The bedrooms have also kept their original decor, but a further refurbishing project to be carried out this year will enhance both their beauty and comfort.

How to get there *(Map 2): Near the Corso Venezia.*

Hotel Spadari al Duomo

Via Spadari, 11
20123 Milano
Tel. (0)2 720 023 71 - Fax (0)2 861 184

Category ★★★★ **Rooms** 38 and 1 suite with air-conditioning, tel, bath, WC, satellite TV, minibar, safe; elevator. **Price** Single 320-360,000L, double 360-420,000L. **Meals** Breakfast included. **Restaurant** See p. 455-457. **Credit cards** All major. **Pets** Dogs not allowed. **Facilities** Parking. **Nearby** Milano: Brera museum, Piccolo teatro, Abbey of Chiaravalle, Villa Reale in Monza, Abbey of Chiaravalle, Villa Reale in Monza, Abbey of Viboldone, Lake Como, la piazza Ducale in Vigevano, Certosa di Pavia, golf course (9-18-hole) at Parco di Monza. **Open** All year.

With the Duomo as a landmark, the ease with which you can find the Hotel Spadari will reassure all those who feel nervous about finding their way around Milan. All visitors interested in food will appreciate the proximity of Speck's, the well-known gourmet boutique of Milan. Aside from the usual assets of a four-star hotel, the Spadari gets its personality from that of its owners, fervent collectors of contemporary art. The total space of the hotel has been redesigned with a view to showing off the works of young Milanese artists, whose murals, paintings and sculptures adorn the reception rooms. There is some offbeat furniture by Ugo La Pietra in postmodern style. The bedrooms retain a classic look even with the abstract paintings that add a modern but never aggressive touch. The bathrooms are thoroughly modern as well. One of the top-floor suites has a view on the spires of the Duomo. A fine address for all who like or are curious about modern art.

How to get there *(Map 2): Near the Duomo.*

Hotel de la Ville

Via Hoepli, 6
20121 Milano
Tel. (0)2-86 76 51 - Fax (0)2-86 66 09 - Sig. Nardiotti
E-mail: de.la.ville@italyhotel.com

Category ★★★★ **Rooms** 109 with telephone, bath, WC, satellite TV and minibar; elevator. **Price** Single 350,000L, double 460,000L, suite 1,000 000L. **Meals** Breakfast included **Restaurant** See pp. 455-457. **Credit cards** All major. **Pets** Small dogs allowed. **Facilities** Parking. **Nearby** Milano Duomo, Brera-Museum; opening December 7 of the lyric season at the Scala, Piccolo teatro di Milano - Abbey of Chiaravalle; Villa Reale in Monza, Abbey of Viboldone, Lake Como, la Piazza Ducale in Vigevano), Certosa di Pavia, golf course (9-18-hole) at Parco di Monza. **Open** All year.

The elegant Hotel de la Ville is ideal for active vacationers, as it is close to stores, the Duomo and La Scala. The walls and chairs of the salons and the smoking room are monochromatic shades of pink and blue. The very comfortable rooms are carefully decorated with beautiful fabrics on the walls, matching the bedspreads and curtains. The most spacious suites also enjoy the privilege of a view of the spires of the Duomo. There is no restaurant in the hotel, but, you can dine very pleasantly at *Le Canova* nearby.

How to get there *(Map 2): Between piazza S. Babila and piazza della Scala.*

Antica Locanda dei Mercanti

Via San Tomaso, 6
20123 Milano
Tel. (0)2-805 40 80 - Fax (0)2-805 40 90
Sig.ra Paola Ora

Category ★★★ **Rooms** 10 with telephone, shower, WC, (3 with TV). **Price** Single 150,000L, double 180,000L, suite 220-250,000L. **Meals** Breakfast 10,000L, served 7:00-10:00. **Restaurant** See pp. 455-457. **Credit cards** Visa, Eurocard, MasterCard. **Pets** Dogs not allowed. **Nearby** Milan: Duomo, Teatro alla Scala, Pinacoteca di Brera, Piccolo Teatro di Milano, Abbey of Chiaravalle, Villa Reale in Monza, Lake Como, Certosa di Pavia, golf course (9- and 18-hole) at Parco di Monza. **Open** All year.

In Milan, charming often means pricey. The opening of this small hotel will not solve the problem of finding affordable lodging in Italian cities, but perhaps it will be a start in creating a category of hotel that is cruelly lacking. Located in the quarter of La Scala, the hotel occupies the second floor of an old building. Be careful - the Locanda has no street sign, just a name-plate along with others on the list of bells at the front door. The ten rooms available are all nicely decorated. The shower rooms are small but adequate. The building is extremely quiet. Breakfast is served in the rooms because there is only a tiny reception area, no sitting room, and service is kept to a minimum. But we wouldn't dream of complaining - we're delighted to find a charming hotel at a decent price. Excellent value for the price, with charm thrown in, makes the Locanda dei Mercanti a rare find.

How to get there *(Map 2): in the Scala neighborhood. Parking nearby, see with the hotel.*

Hotel de la Ville

Via Hoepli, 6
20121 Milano
Tel. (0)2 86 76 51 - Fax (0)2 86 66 09 - Sig. Nardiotti
E-mail: de.la.ville@italyhotel.com

Category ★★★★ **Rooms** 109 with tel, bath, WC, satelitte TV, minibar, safe; elevator. **Price** Single 350,000L, double 460,000L, suite 1,000 000L. **Meals** Breakfast included. **Restaurant** Le Casanova. See pp. 455-457. **Credit cards** All major. **Pets** Small dogs allowed. **Facilities** Parking (60,000L). **Nearby** Milano: Brera museum, Piccolo teatro, Abbey ofChiaravalle, Villa Reale in Monza, Abbey of Chiaravalle, Villa Reale in Monza, Abbey of Viboldone, Lake Como, la piazza Ducale in Vigevano, Certosa di Pavia, golf course (9-18-hole) at Parco di Monza. **Open** All year.

Monza is famous of course for its Formula One grand prix, but it is also known for the little neo-classic palace built by Archduke Ferdinand of Austria as his country residence while he was Governor of Lombardy. Later, Eugéne de Beauharnais (Josephine's son and Napoleon's stepson) planted the superb park, which is well worth visiting. Located just opposite the Villa Reale, the Hotel de Ville is a small luxury hotel, run by the Nardi family for several generations. Elegance, refinement and comfort characterize this house, which is also as inviting as a private home. Mahogany furniture, Chinese ceramics, woodwork and lighting create a cozy, somewhat English atmosphere. The service is always present but never ostentatious. This fine hotel is a good place to know and it's only 15 kilometers from Milan.

How to get there *(Map 2): 15km northwest of Milano.*

Albergo Madonnina

Largo Lanfranco da Ligurno, 1
Ligurno 21050 Cantello (Varese)
Tel. (0)332 417 731 - Fax (0) 332 418 403
Famiglia Limido

Rooms 14 with tel, bath, WC, TV. **Price** Double 100-140,000L. **Meals** Breakfast 15-000L, half board 135-150,000L (per pers.). **Restaurant** Service 12:30-14:00, 19:30-21:30, closed Mon., menus 55-75,000L. Specialties: Regional cooking. **Credit cards** All major. **Pets** Dogs not allowed. **Facilities** Parking. **Nearby** Lake Como, Lake majeur, Lake Varèse, Monte Campo dei Fiori (view), Castiglione Olona; Castelseprio (S.Maria Foris portas). **Open** All year.

Cantello is a little country village between Lake Como and Lake Maggiore, a few kilometers from Varese. The Madonnina owes its reputation mainly to its restaurant, specially known for its spring menus featuring fresh asparagus. Each season meals are built around a theme, based on local produce. This former coaching inn, covered and surrounded by lush vegetation, also has a few rooms, some in the main building, some in the annex. We prefer the former, for the annex holds the dining room, where receptions are held. The decoration is simple and elegant, which nicely sets off the architecture of the place. The amenities are very good, particularly the bathrooms. A very useful address for its cuisine and refinement in a region rich in tourist attractions.

How to get there *(Map 2): 9 km from Varese.*

Albergo del Sole

Via Trabattoni, 22
20076 Maleo
Tel. (0)377-58 142 - Fax (0)377-45 80 58 - Sig. Colombani
E-mail: de.la.ville@italyhotel.com

Category ★★★★ **Rooms** 8 with telephone, bath or shower, WC, TV and minibar **Price** Single 160,000L, double 260,000L, apartment (4 pers.) 360,000L. **Meals** Breakfast included. **Restaurant** Service 12:15-14:15, 20:15-21:45; closed Sun. and Mon.; menu 60-90,000L, also à la carte. Specialties: spaghetti con pomodori, olive e capperi, fegato di vitello all'uva, seafood. **Credit cards** All major. **Pets** Dogs allowed. **Nearby** Cremona, Piacenza, Certosa di Pavia. **Open** All year (except Jan., Aug., Sunday evening and Monday).

For many years people who appreciated fine dining came to Maleo to enjoy the delicious Lombardian cuisine of Franco Colomani, but after dinner it wasn't always easy to find a place to stay. To answer this demand Franco opened this inn. The rooms are simple, elegant and very comfortable. This is a great place to stop off for a meal or spend a pleasant weekend if you are visiting the Pavia or Crémona monasteries.

How to get there *(Map 9): 60 km south of Milano via A1 Casalfusterlengo exit, towards Codogno, then Maleo at 5 km.*

1998

Hotel Colonne

Via Fincarà, 37
Sacro Monte 21100 Varese
Tel. (0)332-224 633- Fax (0)332-821 593

Category ★★★★ **Rooms** 10 with telephone, bath, WC, satellite TV, minibar. **Price** Single 130-150,000L, double 200,000L. **Meals** Breakfast included, served 7:30-10:00. **Restaurant** Service 12:30-14:30, 19:45-22:00; closed Tue; menu, also à la carte. **Credit cards** Visa, Eurocard, MasterCard. **Pets** Dogs not allowed. **Nearby** Santa Maria del Monte Sanctuary, Monte Campo dei Fiori (panorama), Lake Varese, Lake Lugano, Castiglione Olona: casa Castiglioni, la Chiesa di villa. **Open** All year (except in Jan.).

The Hotel Colonne in on Sacro Monte which, along with Monte Campo dei Fiori, tower over Varese and its lake. The access is by car, of course, but don't miss a walk around the 14 identical chapels built in the 17th century and decorated with frescoes and sculptures by Lombard artists. As for the hotel itself, it is a lovely place combining all the qualities of a hotel of charm: "an elegant and refined decor in an attractive setting, comfortable and well-kept rooms, a good view, an excellent restaurant, a warm welcome, a thoughtful staff... The weak points? Just one: the hotel and the restaurant are closed on Tuesday." This was an opinion we received from a couple of our readers, and it was exactly what we found when we went to check out the Colonne at their excellent suggestion.

How to get there *(Map 2): 56 km northwest of Milano. In Varese, leave town via the viale Aguggiari to Sacro Monte.*

Il Sole di Ranco

Lago Maggiore
Piazza Venezia, 5
21020 Ranco (Varese)
Tel. (0)331-97 65 07 - Fax (0)331-97 66 20 - Famiglia Brovelli

Category ★★★★ **Apart.** 4 and 10 suites with air conditioning, telephone, bath or shower, WC., TV, safe and minibar. **Price** Single 330,000L, double 350,000L, suite 500-700,000L. **Meals** Breakfast included, served 7:30-11:00; half board 285-315,000L (per pers., 3 days min.). **Restaurant** Service 12:30-14:00, 19:45-21:30; menus 85-135,000L, also à la carte. Specialties: Regional cooking. **Credit cards** All major. **Pets** Dogs not allowed. **Facilities** Parking. **Nearby** Santa Caterina del Sasso (sanctuary), Arcumeggia, Stresa, Borromean islands; Villa Bozzolo, Villa Taranto, Casalzuigno, Rocca di Angera. **Open** All year (except Jan.).

For three generations, Il Sole has been famous for its fine restaurant. Eight duplex suites have been added, each with a balcony or terrace on Lake Maggiore. The comfortable furniture is a fine example of the talent of Italian designers. The warm shades of colors used in the fabrics give the rooms a cozy feel. The cuisine is, of course, masterful; the restaurant is still reputed to be among the best in Italy. Carluccio Brovelli, with the help of his son, David, is the family cook, and his wife, Itala, makes wonderful preserves and other homemade specialties, which you can buy at the gift shop. You will find all this–plus beautiful grounds, a delightful terrace and excellent service at Il Sole.

How to get there *(Map 2): 67 km northwest of Milano via A8, Sesto Calende exit; then S33 and S629 towards Laveno, on the right bank; 30 km from the airport Mimano-Malpensa.*

Hotel Fortino Napoleonico

Via Poggio
60020 Portonovo (Ancona)
Tel. (0)71-80 14 50 - Fax (0)71-80 14 54
Sig. Roscioni

Category ★★★★ **Rooms** 30 with air-conditioning, telephone, bath or shower, WC, TV and minibar. **Price** Double 260-300,000L, suite 360-400,000L. **Meals Breakfast** included, served about 7:30-10:30; half board 170-210,000L, full board 200-240,000L (per pers., 3 days min.). **Restaurant** Service 13:00-14:30, 20:00-22:00; menu 60-70,000L, also à la carte. Specialties: Seafood. **Credit cards** All major. **Pets** Dogs allowed. **Facilities** Swimming pool, tennis (15,000L), gym, private beach, parking. **Nearby** Portonovo (Abbey Santa Maria di Portonovo), Ancona, Conero golf course (27-hole) in Sirolo. **Open** All year.

The "Fort Napoleon," erected on Bay of Portonovo in 1808, is now an extraordinary hotel. The road that winds around this former military edifice has been transformed into flowering terraces with laurel and other fragrant plants and the old arms room has metamorphosed into multiple salons and dining rooms filled with Empire-style furniture. Carefully selected antique furniture and contemporary materials coexist in perfect harmony in the guest rooms. The seafood-based cuisine is innovative and excellent.

How to get there *(Map 11): 10 km south of Ancona via A14, Ancona-South exit, towards Camerano.*

Hotel Emilia

Poggio di Portonovo, 149
60020 Portonovo (Ancona)
Tel. (0)71-80 11 45 - Fax (0)71-80 13 30
Sig. Fiorini

Category ★★★★ **Rooms** 27, 3 suites with air-conditioning, telephone, bath or shower, WC, TV and minibar; Wheelchair access. **Price** Double 200-300,000L, suite 250-400,000L. **Meals** Breakfast included; half board 170-210,000L, full board 200-240,000L (per pers., 3 days min.). **Restaurant** Service 12:45-14:00, 20:00-22:00; menus 70,000L, also à la carte. Specialties: Seafood, pasta fatta in casa e verdure. **Credit cards** All major. **Pets** Dogs not allowed. **Facilities** Swimming pool, tennis, parking. **Nearby** Portonovo (Abbey Santa Maria di Portonovo), Ancona, Conero golf course (27-hole) in Sirolo. **Open** All year.

A beautiful green lawn extends from the foot of the hotel to the cliff overhanging the ocean. The twittering of the swallows living on the rooftops will wake you in the morning. The pleasant rooms look out over the sea. This family estate, named after a woman who actively campaigned for the preservation of the region, has an atmosphere of deep tranquility. Today, father and son, continuing the family tradition, manage the hotel and restaurant.

How to get there *(Map 11): 10 km south of Ancona via A14, Ancona-South exit, towards Camerano.*

Hotel Monte Conero

Badia di San Pietro
60020 Sirolo (Ancona)
Tel. (0)71-93 30 592 - Fax (0)71-93 30 365

Category ★★★ **Rooms** 47 with telephone, bath or shower and WC, elevator. **Price** 130-174,000L, with half board 105-135,000L (per pers., 2 days min.). **Meals** Breakfast served 8:00-9:45. **Restaurant** Service 13:00-15:00, 20:00-22:00, closed Sun. evening, Mon., Jan.; menu 60,000L, also à la carte. Specialties: Seafood. **Credit cards** All major. **Pets** Small dogs allowed. **Facilities** Swimming pool, tennis (15,000L), parking. **Nearby** Abbey of San Pietro, Abbey Santa Maria di Portonovo, Ancona, Golf Conero Course (27-hole) in Sirolo. **Open** Mar. 15 – Nov. 15.

At the summit of the regional park bearing the same name, this 12th century Carmaldosian abbey overlooks the sea and the village of Sirolo. Around the abbey the owners have built a comfortable, modern hotel with a panoramic restaurant. The simple rooms are well equipped and face the sea. The rooms over the restaurant have a private terrace. Since the beaches of Sirolo are only two-and-a-half miles away, the Monte Conero is filled with Italian tourists in the summer and at such times, seems like a typical tourist resort. Summer, therefore, is not the best season to visit this beautiful place. There is a large, inviting pool on the grounds, as well as a golf course two-and-a-half miles away.

how to get there *(Map 11): 26 km southeast of Ancona via the coast to Fonte d'Olio, towards Sirolo, then towards Badia di San Pietro to Monte Conero.*

Hotel Vittoria

Piazzale della Libertà, 2
61100 Pesaro
Tel. (0)721-34 343 - Fax (0)721-65 204
Sig. A. Marcucci Pinoli

Category ★★★★ **Rooms** 30 with air-conditioning, telephone, bath or shower, WC, TV, elevator. **Price** Single 100-220,000L, double 120-280,000L, apartment 200-450,000L. **Meals** Breakfast 25,000L (buffet), served 7:30-10:30. **Restaurant** Service 13:00-15:00, 20:00-22:00; menu 30-45,000L, also à la carte. Specialties: Seafood. **Credit cards** All major. **Pets** Dogs allowed. **Facilities** Swimming pool, sauna, garage. **Nearby** Pesaro: Piazza del popolo (Palazzo Ducale), house of Rossini; Villa Caprile, Villa Imperiale, Gradara, Urbino, Civici museum. **Open** All year.

Meeting place for the stars of the Rossini Opera Festival in August, the Hotel Vittoria is on the sea and is one of the best hotels in town. The salon still has its original 1900 stucco finish; it opens onto a restaurant on a large Scandinavian-style porch. In summer, the large windows are opened and you can dine outside with a view of the sea. The rooms are simple, elegant and provide every comfort; the same is true for the bathrooms. The owners have several similar estates in the area, so if you like variety you can enjoy a meal in one these.

How to get there *(Map 11): Between Bologna and Rome via A14.*

Villa Serena

Via San Nicola, 6/3
61100 Pesaro
Tel. (0)721 55 211 - Fax (0)721 55 927
Sig.Pinto

Category ★★★ **Rooms** 10 with air-conditioning, bath or shower, WC, TV. **Price** Double 130-170,000L, suite 190-260,000L. **Meals** Breakfast 15,000L, served 7:30-10:30.half board and full board: 110-160,000L, 130-190,000L (per pers. 3 day min.). **Restaurant** Service 13:30-15:00, 20:30-22:00; menu 65,000L, also à la carte. Specialties: Salmone marinato con rucola, filetto di branzino, carre di vitello in crosta. **Credit cards** All major. **Pets** Small dogs allowed. **Facilities** Swimming pool, parking. **Nearby** In Pesaro: piazza del Popolo (Palazzo Ducale), house of Rossini, Civici museum, Rossini Opera Festival in Aug.; Villa Caprile; Villa Imperiale; Colle San Bartolo o Accio; Gradara; Urbino. **Open** Jan 21 - Jan 2.

If you are coming to Pesaro for the Rossini festival, or for another event, and if you prefer not to stay in the city itself, nor on the rather crowded Adriatic coast, then your only choice is to head for the surrounding hills. Four kilometers from the sea and three from the town center, the summer residence of the Counts of Pinto de Franca (in a landmark building) has been a hotel since the 1960s. Built in 1600, decorated with 17th-century frescoes and ancient paintings and filled with the furniture of the Pinto family (which still runs the place) this hotel is an ideal spot for anyone who seeks peace and quiet. The swimming pool, surrounded by orange and lemon trees, overlooks the peaceful Umbrian plain. Don't be put off by a certain austerity - the rooms and bathrooms are done with great sobriety. The central part of the house, with its three bedrooms and a living room, can be used as an independent apartment with its own private entrance.

How to get there *(Map 11): Between Bologna and Roma via A14.*

Hotel Bonconte

61029 Urbino
Via della Mura, 28
Tel. (0)722-24 63 - Fax (0)722-47 82
Sig. A. M. Pinoli

Category ★★★★ **Rooms** 23 with air conditioning, telephone, bath or shower, WC, cable TV and minibar. **Price** Single 140,000L, double 220,000L, suite 330,000L. **Meals** Breakfast 28,000L, served 7:30-10:30. **Restaurant** Service 20:00-22:30, closed Tuesday; menu 28,000L. Specialties: Antipasti vegetali, passatelli in brodo, ravioli agli asparagi, agnello, filetto G. Cesare. **Credit card** All major. **Pets** Dogs allowed (8-10,000L). **Facilities** Parking. **Nearby** Urbino (Palazzo Ducal, Galleria delle Marche, San Giovanni Battista), Urbania, Sant'Angelo in Vado, Castles and villages of Montefeltro: Sassocoruaro, Macereta, Feltria - Pesado ("Victoria Club" beach). **Open** All year.

The Hotel Boconte is in the historic town of Urbino. This old duchy seems unchanged since the days of splendor of its prince of light, Federico de Montefeltro. He wanted it to be a model for a new society where the refinement of manners would reflect the elegance of thought and taste, as described by Castiglione in *The Perfect Courtisan (Il Cortegiano).* The hotel is on the outskirts of this pink village, close to the Ducal Palace. It has a splendid view of the magical hills of Umbria which illuminate the backgrounds of the paintings of Piero della Francesca. This will make you forget the small size but comfortable rooms.

How to get there *(Map 11): 36 km southwest of Pesaro via A14, Pesado-Urbino exit, then S423*

Locanda della Posta

Corso Vanucci, 97
06100 Perugia
Tel (0)75-57 28 925 - Fax (0)75-57 32 562
Sig. Bernardini

Category ★★★★ **Rooms** 40 with air-conditioning, telephone, bath or shower, WC, TV, minibar; elevator. **Price** Single 150-187,000L, double 200-295,000L, suite 300-350,000L. **Meals** Breakfast included, served 7:30-10:00. **Restaurant** See p. 460. **Credit cards** All major. **Pets** Dogs allowed. **Nearby** Perugia (Corso Vanucci, Duomo, Palazzo dei Priori, Fontana Maggiore), Torgiano (home to the Lungarotti winery and wine museum), Gubbio, Assisi, Bettona, Spello, Spoleto, Ellera golf course (18-hole) in Perugia. **Open** All year.

The Locanda della Posta is an old palace which has been entirely restored. On the Corso Vanucci, one of the most beautiful and famous avenues–which can get pretty noisy–you will have a chance to feel the pulse of the town and enjoy the Peruginian pace of life. The rooms are extremely comfortable. The decor is subtle, elegant and very pleasant. The salons still have their original frescoes. The service is friendly. Be sure to spend some time visiting this historic city, on whose walls you can actually see traces of the Etruscan, Roman and Renaissance periods.

How to get there *(Map 14): In the old city.*

Castello dell'Oscano
Villa Ada - La Macina

Cenerente 06134 Perugia
Tel (0)75-69 01 25 - Fax (0)75-69 06 66 - Sig. Bussolati
E-mail: oscano@krenet.it - Web: http://www.assind.perugia.it/oscano

Category ★★★★ **Rooms** 22 with telephone, shower, WC, TV and minibar. **Price** Double in Villa Ada 170-200,000L, suite in Oscano 300-350,000L. **Meals** Breakfast included, served 7:00-10:00. **Restaurant** Only for residents, Service 20:30; closed Thus.; menu 50,000L. **Credit cards** All major. **Pets** Dogs allowed. **Facilities** Swimming pool, parking. **Nearby** Perugia, Torgiano, Assisi, Bettona, Madonna del Miracoli Church in Castel Rigone , Spello, Spoleto, Ellera golf course (18-hole) in Perugia. **Open** All year (except Jan. 15 – Feb. 15).

Just a few kilometers from beautiful Perugia, the ancient towers and crenellated walls of the Castello dell'Oscano rise up amid a forest of cedars, sequoias and cypresses. It is a historic castle that has preserved its interesting library and large wood-paneled salons. The comfortable and luxurious suites are situated in the castle. Here, the owners have followed a maxim of Cicero, who said that a room without a book was like a body without a soul, and thoughtfully provided a small bedside volume with a selection of writings by Goldoni, Maïakovski and de Maupassant. On this vast estate of some 250 hectares, you can also stay at the Villa Ada, a house dating from the 19th century. The decor is sober but elegant and comfortable, and you can have your meals and breakfast at the Turandot, the restaurant of the *castello*. For a longer stay, you may also choose to rent an apartment at the Macina, a few kilometers away. The furnishing is spare, but there is a swimming pool and you can have the pleasure of buying your wine, cheese and honey on the property.

How to get there *(Map 14): 8 km of Perugia, towards Firenze, Madonna alta exit; stade Renato Curi; railway bridge; south Marco; Cenerente.*

1998

Villa Aureli

via Cirenei, 70
06071 Castel di Piano Umbro (Perugia)
Tel. (0)75-514 04 44 - Fax (0)75-514 94 08 - Dott. L. di Serego Alighieri

Apartments 2 (4-6 pers.) with kitchen, sitting room, 2 rooms, telephone, bath, TV. **Price** For 1 week 1,270-1,790,000L (4 pers.) - 1,370-1,980,000L (6 pers.). **Credit cards** Not accepted. **Pets** Dogs not allowed. **Facilities** Swimming pool, parking. **Nearby** Perugia, Assisi, Spello, Collegio del Cambio (Perugin fresco), Montefalco, Ellera golf course (18-hole) in Perugia. **Open** All year.

Our arrival at the Villa Aureli was like something out of a Visconti film, a scene full of charm that seemed to belong to another time. The old Count di Serego Alighieri was walking in the magnificent garden surrounded by a flock of grandchildren who had come, as they do every summer, from the four corners of Europe to see their grandfather and touch their roots. One of the grandchildren showed us around the villa. It was a marvel. The building dates from the 16th century, but the facilities inside are in the finest tradition of the 18th, the time when the Alighieris acquired the villa. The present descendant and owner has worked hard to find old documents that would enable him to preserve or recreate the decor of the past: decorative rock work, Chinese ornaments, Persian prints, painted furniture and the baroque Italian gardens, making the whole place a sort of museum of the art of living of that bygone age... The villa is large and has two handsome apartments, comfortable and elegant, and marked with the same historic grace. The larger and finer of the two is on the second floor. It goes without saying that if you want to stay at the Aureli, you will have to contact the Count early enough to settle all the details well in advance. A stay at the Villa Aureli is quite an experience.

How to get there *(Map 14): 10 km of Perugia, Madonna Alta exit, statale 220 towards Città della Pieve.*

Albergo Le Tre Vaselle

Via G. Garibaldi, 48
06089 Torgiano (Perugia)
Tel (0)75-98 80 447 - Fax (0)75-98 80 214 - Sig. Margheritini

Category ★★★★★ **Rooms** 48 and 12 suites with telephone, bath or shower, WC, TV and minibar. **Price** Single 195-200,000L, double 295-330,000L, suite 400,000L. **Meals** Breakfast included, served 7:30-10:00; half board +65,000L, full board +130,000L (per pers. 3 days min.). **Restaurant** Service 12:30-14:30, 20:00-22:00; menus: 65-75,000L, also à la carte. Specialties: Medaglioni di vitello alle erbe aromatiche, fiori di zucca gratinati con ricotta di bufala e timo, e piccoli pomodori al torre di giano **Credit cards** All major. **Pets** Dogs not allowed. **Facilities** 2 Swimming pool, sauna, health fitness club, parking. **Nearby** In Torgiano: wine museum (home to the famous Lungarotti winery); Perugia, Assisi, Bettona, Ellera golf course (18-hole) in Perugia. **Open** All year.

Perugia is only 8 kilometers away, so if you like the country, with tradition, refinement and good cuisine, then stay at the Tre Vaselle. The hotel has a handsome stone facade and below it a superb terrace where breakfast and meals are served in good weather. When the weather is not so fine, the living and dining rooms have fireplaces and a nice log fire creates a homey, intimate atmosphere. The rooms are sober and elegant, the service discreet and courteous. Add to all this the interest of the site: The beautiful fortified village of Torgiano is known for its Lungarotti wines, and you will find a wine museum with a nice collection. Other places too will allow you to sample local produce, like the Osteria del Museo where you can taste or buy olive oil, fine wines and honey from the Azienda Lungarotti. Those with a real interest in wine production can visit the estate itself, to see the vines and storerooms.

How to get there *(Map 14): 16 km from Perugia via SS3 towards Todi.*

La Bondanzina

06089 Torgiano (Perugia)
Tel. (0)75 98 80 447 - Fax (0)75 98 80 214
G. Margheritini

Category ★★★★★ **Rooms** 4 and 1 suite with air-conditioning, tel, shower and 1 bath, WC, minibar. **Price** Single 200,000L, double 295-300,000L, suite 400,000L. **Meals** Breakfast included served 7:00-10:30; half board +70,000L (per pers. 3 day min.). **Restaurant** Le Tre Vaselle. See p 144. **Credit cards** All major. **Pets** Dogs not allowed. **Facilities** Swimming pool and health center in the Tre Vaselle hotel, Sauna (30,000L). **Nearby** In Torgiano: Cellar, Wine museum, Perugia, Bettona, Assisi, ad Ellera golf course 18-hole in Perugia. **Open** All year.

Still in Torgiano, La Bondanzina, named after its former owners, is a village house dating from the 19th century. With the same management, the same quality of service and the same refinement as the Tre Vaselle, except that there are only a few rooms, each one meticulously arranged. There are two small singles, two doubles and a suite. Some fine pieces of antique furniture and amazing panoramic murals create a very poetic setting. Meals are served in the main house, just a few yards away, but if you like, breakfast can be brought to you in your room. This is a little hotel of great charm.

How to get there *(Map 14): 16 km from Perugia via SS3bis towardsTodi.*

Hotel Subasio

Frate Elia, 2
06081 Assisi (Perugia)
Tel (0)75-81 22 06 - Fax (0)75-81 66 91
Sig. Elisei

Category ★★★★ **Rooms** 70 with air-conditioning, telephone, bath or shower, WC, TV, minibar; elevator. **Price** Single 180,000L, double 260,000L, suite 300,000L. **Meals** Breakfast 15,000L, served 7:00-10:00; half board and full board 180,000L (per pers.). **Restaurant** Service 12:00-14:00, 19:00-21:00; menu 40,000L, also à la carte. Specialties: Pollo in porchetta, spaghetti alla Subasio. **Credit cards** All major. **Pets** Dogs allowed. **Facilities** Parking (20,000L). **Nearby** Assisi (Basilica S. Francesco, Santa Chiara, Duomo, Ermitage Eremo delle Carceri, Basilica San Damiano, Basilica Santa Maria degli Angeli), Church Santa Maria di Rivortolo, Perugia, Abbey of San Benetto, Spello, Ellera golf course (18-hole) in Perugia. **Open** All year.

The Subasio, a historic hotel which has entertained many illustrious guests, may seem a little outdated at first, but it is being renovated. It is a very comfortble hotel in an exceptional location–near the Saint François Basilica. Perhaps you won't like the emphatic decor of the rooms, but you absolutely must have a meal in the old vaulted dining room or on the beautiful terrace covered with linden trees, overlooking the Umbrian Valley. The Subasio, mindful of Saint François, is part of the pilgrimage to Assisi.

How to get there *(Map 14): 25 km east of Perugia via S75 then S147 to Assisi; near the Basilica of San Francesco.*

Hotel Umbra

Via degli Archi, 6
06081 Assisi (Perugia)
Tel (0)75-81 22 40 - Fax (0)75-81 36 53
Sig. Laudenzi

Category ★★★ **Rooms** 25 (16 with air conditioning), with telephone, bath or shower, WC, TV, (24 with minibar). **Price** Single 95-110,000L, double 130-150,000L, suite 150-170,000L. **Meals** Breakfast 15,000L, served 8:00-10:00. **Restaurant** Service 12:30-14:00, 20:00-21:15; closed Sun.; à la carte. Specialties: Delizia di cappelletti, crespelle all' Umbra, friccò, piccione alla ghiotta, zabaione al cioccolato. **Credit cards** All major. **Pets** Dogs not allowed. **Nearby** Assisi (Basilica S. Francesco, Santa Chiara, Duomo, Ermitage Eremo delle Carceri, Basilica San Damiano, Basilica Santa Maria degli Angeli), Church Santa Maria di Rivortolo, Perugia, Abbey of San Benetto, Spello, Ellera golf course (18-hole) in Perugia. **Open** All year (except Jan. 16 – Mar. 14).

A centrally-located and yet quiet hotel in the middle of historic Assisi, with the front on the pedestrian zone of the city and the back overlooking the lower town and the valley. All the rooms are pleasant, installed like real little apartments with living area and balcony, but we would recommend the ones with the view of the valley. In summer, the restaurant serves on the terrace, under a flowered trellis. If you have succumbed to the beauty of the lovely basilica of Saint Francis, now you can discover the delights of Umbrian cooking, with local wines and specialities.

How to get there *(Map 14): 25 km east of Perugia via S75, then S147 to Assisi; in the old city.*

Le Silve di Armenzano

Armenzano 06081 Assisi (Perugia)
Tel (0)75-801 90 00
Fax (0)75-801 90 05
Sig.ra Taddia

Category ★★★★ **Rooms** 15 with telephone, bath or shower, WC, TV and minibar. **Price** Single 140,000L, double 280,000L. **Meals** Breakfast included, served 8:00-10:00; half board 180,000L. **Restaurant** Menus 50-65,000L, also à la carte. Specialties: Regional cooking. **Credit cards** All major. **Pets** Dogs not allowed. **Facilities** Swimming pool, tennis, sauna, parking. **Nearby** In Assisi: Ermitage Eremo delle Carceri, Basilica Convento San Damiano, basilica Santa Maria degli Angeli, Church Santa Maria di Rivortoto, Abbey of San Benedetto, Spello, Spoleto, Ellera golf course (18-hole) in Perugia. **Open** All year (except Oct. 20 – Apr. 1).

The quiet and solitude of the mountains await you at the Armenzano. Only seven-and-a-half miles from Assisi, this restored medieval hamlet has been transformed into a hotel. Set in a wild and grandiose landscape, the Silve has retained its rustic charm, while offering comfortable, tastefully furnished rooms, a swimming pool and tennis court. The Silve also has facilities for horseback riding and mountain motorbiking. The owners of this private estate try to outdo the professionals. A glance through the guest book will reveal all the nice things guests have written about the service and the cuisine enjoyed during their visits.

How to get there *(Map 14): 32 km east of Perugia to Assisi via S75 - when you leave Assisi, turn on the right towards Armenzano (12 km).*

Castel San Gregorio

Via San Gregorio, 16 a
San Gregorio 06081 Assisi (Perugia)
Tel (0)75-803 80 09 - Fax (0)75-803 89 04
Sig. Bianchi

Rooms 12 with telephone, bath or shower and WC. **Price** Single 75,000L, double 150,000L. **Meals** Breakfast included, served 8:00-10:00; half board 115,000L, full board 145,000L (per pers., 3 days min.). **Restaurant** Service 13:00-13:30, 20:00-21:00, closed Mon.; menu 40,000L. Specialties: Tartufo, agnello. **Credit cards** All major. **Pets** Small dogs allowed. **Facilities** Parking. **Nearby** In Assisi: Ermitage Eremo delle Carceri, Basilica Convento San Damiano, basilica Santa Maria degli Angeli, Church Santa Maria di Rivortoto, Abbey of San Benedetto, Spello, Spoleto, Ellera golf course (18-hole) in Perugia. **Open** All year (closed Mon.).

The Castel San Gregorio looks like a toy castle, with its central keep and four turrets and crenellated walls. Inside, it is not spacious, but pleasantly intimate. The rooms have low ceilings with narrow beams set in geometric patterns that, together with an indirect lighting, create a warm cozy atmosphere. The dining room, called the "magic spot," manages to exude the same warmth despite its bare stone walls. The bedrooms are comfortable and refined. A nice place in the country, halfway between Assisi and Perugia.

How to get there *(Map 14): 13 km northwest of Assisi via S147, then towards Petrignano d'Assisi.*

1998

Casa Giulia

Via S.S.Flaminia, km 140,100
06039 Bovara di Trevi (Perugia)
Tel. (0)742-78 257 - Fax (0)742-38 16 32 - Sig.ra Petrucci

Rooms 7 and 1 suite (4 pers.) with bath or shower, WC and 2 apartments. (2-4 pers.); 1 room for disabled persons. **Price** Double 160,000L, 290,000L (4 pers.); apart. 100-120,000L (per pers.). **Meals** Breakfast included, served 8:30-10:30; half board 110,000L (per pers.); evening meals. **Credit cards** Not accepted. **Pets** Dogs not allowed. **Facilities** Swimming pool, parking. **Nearby** Assisi, Perugia, Abbey of Sassovino, Montefalco, Spello, Tempietto del Clitunno, Fonti del Clitunno, Spoleto. **Open** All year.

The home of grandmother Giulia, who inherited it from her grandparents, is now a lovely guest house for visitors who want to tour Umbria. Off the main road that serves the large towns of the region, it offers travelers a quiet retreat. The old red-brick house that contains most of the rooms, now has an annex in which there are two small apartments. The rooms in the main house have kept the family furniture and those on the third floor still have traces of 17th century frescoes showing landscapes of the region. The garden is pleasantly shaded by large pines. Its finest site is occupied by the swimming pool, which has a wonderful view of the wheat fields and the village bell tower. For those who feel like lazing here all day, a snack bar is available. The countryside has a gay and smiling look, and if you're wondering what are all those large jars bordering the farms, let us inform you that the olive trees of the Trevi Hills have the largest yield of olive oil in all of Italy.

How to get there *(Map 14): On the S 75 Perugia-Spoleto, after Trevi and Campello.*

1998

Relais Il Canalicchio

Via della Piazza, 13
06050 Canalicchio di Collazzone (Perugia)
Tel. (0)75 87 07 325 - Fax (0)75 87 07 296 - Sig.Orfeo Vassallo

Rooms 35 with air-conditioning, telephone, bath or shower, WC, TV and minibar. **Price** Single 150-230,000L, double 190-270,000L, suite 290-370,000L. **Meals** Breakfast included served 8:00-10:30, half board +50,000L and full board +90,000L (per pers. 2 day min.). **Restaurant** Service 12:00-14:30, 20:00-22:30, menu 50,000L; also à la carte. Specialties: Regionale cooking. **Credit cards** Allo major. **Pets** Small dogs allowed. **Facilities** Swimming pool, sauna, mountain bikes, enclosed parking. **Nearby** Perugia, Assisi, Todi. **Open** All year.

The little fortified village of Canalicchio, not far from Assisi, has been in existence at least as far back as the 9th century. With its ancient keep and chapel within the old stone walls, it stands surrounded by woods in the middle of 50 hectares of farmland. The hotel reflects this noble rural heritage: sturdy walls of Umbrian stone, floors of terra cotta tile. The rooms bear "aristocratic" names like Contessa di Oxford or Duca di Buckingham and have the cozy charm and comfort of an English manor: wrought iron bedsteads, flower-patterned wallpaper with matching striped cotton fabrics, small armchairs in the parlor and a small writing table near the window, to enjoy the view over the green hills that are every bit as lovely as those of Tuscany. The restaurant, in one of the narrow village lanes, features local specialties and produce of the azienda. This is a pleasant, restful place to spend a holiday, for you can indulge in all the pleasures of country living - riding, fishing, hunting or just strolling through the countryside.

How to get there *(Map 14): 50 km south of Perugia. A 1 Ripabianca exit - Foligno, towards "Relais il Canalicchio".*

Hotel Tiferno

Piazza R. Sanzio, 13
06012 Città di Castello (Perugia)
Tel. (0)75 85 50 331 - Fax (0)75 85 21 196
Sig. Mauro Alcherigi - Sig. Luigi Neri

Rooms 38 with air-conditioning, telephone, bath or shower, WC, satellite TV and minibar. **Price** Single 98-115,000L, double 160-190,000L, suite 250,000L. **Meals** Breakfast included served 7:30-10:00, half board 120-155,000L and full board 150-190,000L (per pers. 3 day min.). **Restaurant** Service 12:30-14:30, 19:30-22:00, closed Mon.; menus 35-50,000L. Specialties: Regional cooking. **Credit cards** All major. **Pets** Dogs not allowed. **Facilities** Garage (25,000L). **Nearby** In Città di Castello: Duomo, Pinacoteca, Perugia, Assisi, Lake Trasimeno. **Open** All year.

This hotel is situated in the heart of the ancient and friendly little town, one of whose major claims to fame is that it was once the home of Raphael. Most of his paintings are today in other museums, but don't miss his double-faced painting, the "Creation of Eve" on one side and a "Trinity and the Saints" on the other, in the fascinating little Pinacoteca that has the second largest collection (after Perugia) of Umbrian paintings. Tiferno was the Roman name of the town, and the hotel was recently restored, in a manner that respected the original lines of the former convent, with its ribbed vaulting and large fireplaces in the common rooms. The bedrooms were redone to be both comfortable and functional. They are modern and perhaps a bit impersonal. This sober and elegant establishment is a good stopping point for a tour of Umbria. And for a dinner in town, we can suggest a very nice restaurant, the Amici miei.

How to get there *(Map 10): 50 km south of Perugia.*

Villa di Monte Solare

Colle San Paolo - Tavernelle di Panicale
Via Montali, 7
06136 Fontignano (Perugia)
Tel (0)75-83 23 76 / 83 55 818 - Fax (0)75-83 554 62
Sig. and Sig.ra Strunk

Rooms 10 and 5 suites with shower and WC. **Price** Double 1200-240,000L, suite 240-280,000L. **Meals** Breakfast included, served 8:00-10:30; half board 135-190,000L. **Restaurant** Service 13:00, 20:00; menu. **Credit cards** Diners, Visa, Eurocard and MasterCard. **Pets** Small dogs allowed. **Facilities** Swimming pools, tennis, riding, parking. **Nearby** Perugia, Assisi, Bettona, Church of Madonna dei Miracoli in Castel Rigone near by Passignano, Lake Trasimeno, Ellera golf course (18-hole) in Perugia. **Open** All year.

The road is long to Monte Solare and unpaved, but driveable, and so pretty with its Umbrian landscapes planted with vineyards and olive orchards, devoted since antiquity to the sun-god Apollo. A beautiful, 18th-century patrician house has been restored with careful attention to preserving its cachet, with original *cotto* floor, period furniture, and breakfast room frescoes. The rooms each with private bath have a lot of charm. The suites in the nearby 17th-century farmhouse are very comfortable and have salons, and are priced the same as a double room in the main house. The Italian-style garden has been replanted and a swimming pool is being built. The one-hundred-and-thirty-eight acre (56 ha) farm produces olive oil, wine, and produce that are used in the fine cuisine served here.

How to get there *(Map 13): 25 km southwest of Perugia, via SS220 towards Città delle Pieve; before Tavernelle, take the road on the right for Colle San Paolo to Monte Solare.*

Villa Montegranelli Hotel

Monteluiano
06024 Gùbbio (Perugia)
Tel (0)75-92 20 185 - Fax (0)75-92 73 372 - Sig. Mongelli

Category ★★★ **Rooms** 21 with telephone, bath or shower, WC, TV and minibar; elevator, Wheelchair access. **Price** Single 140,000L, double 175,000L, suite 250,000L. **Meals** Breakfast 12,500L, served 7:30-10:30; half board 150,000L, full board 180,000L. **Restaurant** Service 12:30-14:30, 19:00-22:30; menus 50-65,000L, also à la carte. Specialties: Caciotti fusa al coccio con tartufo, filetto con salsa ghiotta di fegatelli, tozzetti con vino santo. **Credit cards** All major. **Pets** Dogs allowed. **Facilities** Garage and parking. **Nearby** In Gùbbio: S. Francesco, Piazza della Signoria, Palazzo dei Consoli (museum), Duomo, Palazzo Ducale, Via dei Consoli; Festival of the Candles ("Ceri") every May 15.; Perugia, Spello, Spoleto, Ellera golf course (18-hole) in Perugia. **Open** All year.

A long path lined with cypress trees leads slowly up the slope to this large stone house that was, in the 18th century, the summer residence of an Italian aristocrat. From the garden, the view extends from the little village of Gobbio in the foreground all the way to the edge of the Appenines. The restoration has preserved most of the original features. The bedrooms are on the third floor, in what used to be the lofts. They are done in an attractive country style and are quite comfortable. The floor below is occupied by the suites — larger and more elegant, but less appealing. The restaurant is attractive for all its simplicity, with a vaulted ceiling and the decorative pattern of its stone walls. The menu consists of delicious local specialties that vary with the season and the market. There is a gourmet-style menu as well as country dishes, with fish as a highlight on Thursday and Friday. A good wine list is a final asset of this pleasant country stopover.

How to get there *(Map 14): 35 km northwest of Perugia, 4 km of Gùbbio.*

Hotel da Sauro

Lago Trasimeno
06060 Isola Maggiore (Perugia)
Tel (0)75-82 61 68 - Fax (0)75-82 51 30
Sig. Sauro

Category ★★★ **Rooms** 10 with telephone, bath or shower and WC. **Price** Single 60,000L, double 80-90,000L, apart. for 2-4 pers. 120-150,000L. **Meals** Breakfast included, served 7:00-10:00; half board 65-70,000L, full board 75-80,000L (per pers., 3 day min.). **Restaurant** Service 12:00-14:00, 19:00-20:30; menus 20-28,000L, also à la carte. Specialties: Regional cooking, seafood. **Credit cards** Diners, Visa, Eurocard and MasterCard. **Pets** Dogs allowed. **Nearby** In Isola Maggiore: Church of Salvatore; Perugia, Spello, Assisi, Città del Castello. **Open** All year (except Nov. 8 – 30 and Jan. 10 – Feb. 28).

If you have decided to visit Umbria, why not take the time to go all the way and explore the little islands of Lake Trasimeno. As yet undiscovered by mass tourism, they are frequented largely by the locals, which is part of their charm. The Sauro is a simple village inn, comfortable enough for a stopover of a few days. The food is good, with lots of fish, naturally, but also a variety of pasta and antipasto, like everywhere in Italy. Informality is the key word both for atmosphere and service.

How to get there *(Map 13): 20 km west of Perugia. Ferry services from Passignano and Tuoro (Navaccia) to l'Isola Maggiore (15 mn).*

Hotel Villa Pambuffetti

Via della Vittoria, 20
06036 Montefalco (Perugia)
Tel (0)742-379 417 - Fax (0)742-379 245
Sig.ra Angelucci

Category ★★★★ **Rooms** 15 with air-conditioning, telephone, bath or shower, WC, TV, safe and minibar. **Price** Single 170,000L, double 250,000L, suite 340,000L. **Meals** Breakfast included, half board 175-220,000L (per pers.). **Restaurant** Service 20:00-21:00, closed Mon.; menus 50,000L. Specialties: Regional cuisine. **Credit cards** All major. **Pets** Dogs not allowed. **Facilities** Swimming pool, parking. **Nearby** In Montefalco: Pinacoteca di San Francesco, church of S. Agostino, Palazzo Comunale (view); Bevagna, Assisi, Perugia, Bettona, Spello, Spoleto, Todi, Orvieto. **Open** All year.

The Villa Pambuffetti, a former country house now maintained as a combination private residence and guest house, has always belonged to the same family. It is in the middle of beautiful grounds which overlook the valley. The house has been reorganized to create spacious rooms each meticulously decorated with antique furniture, and all different. The most amazing one is is located in the little tower and has six windows from which create a panoramic view of the entire valley. The restaurant serves regional specialties and has an excellent wine list, including the notable Sagranito, a specialty of Montefalco. This is an elegant address in the D'Annunzio's fabled "town of silence."

***How to get there** (Map 14): 41 km southeast of Perugia to Foligno, then to Montefalco.*

La Locanda della Rocca

Viale Roma, 4
06060 Paciano
Tel. (0)75-83 02 36 - Fax (0)75-83 01 55 - Sig. and Sig.ra Buitoni

Rooms 7 and 1 suite (4 pers.) with bath or shower, WC, TV, 4 with minibar. **Price** Double 150-170 000L, suite 420-450,000L. **Meals** Breakfast included, served 8:30-10:30; half board 120,000L (per pers. in double room 3 days min.). **Restaurant** Closed Tue; also à la carte 40-70,0000L. **Credit cards** All major. **Pets** Dogs allowed.(except in restaurant). **Facilities** Parking. **Nearby** "Museo Aperto" for Castiglione del Lago, Città della Pieve, Paciano, Panicale, Lago Trasimeno. **Open** All year (except Jan. 15 - Feb.15).

Paciano is a peaceful medieval village, lovingly looked after by its residents, if we can judge by the excellent state of preservation of the fortifying walls, with seven towers and three gates, that surround the old streets and homes with flower-laden balconies. Part of the locanda is in the torrione, built in the 17th century to defend the Rastella Gate. On a level with the terrace is a beautiful vaulted dining room with arches cut into the wall that are used as a wine cellar. A mezzanine sitting room is very comfortable, with soft sofas and lots of green plants. The bedrooms are upstairs. Apart from the suite, which is in the torrione and has a balcony, the other rooms are rather small but the amenities are adequate. Most look out over the amphitheater of greenery that stretches out in front of the hotel. Paciano and the other villages around Lake Trasimeno have grouped together to offer a tour (one ticket for all the towns) that will show visitors an artistic heritage unknown to the great mass of tourists. Caterina provides a warm welcome to the hotel.

How to get there *(Map 13): On highway A1, Valdichiana exit (Firenze) or Chiusi/Chiancano Terme (Roma), towards Lago Trasimeno.*

Residenza Vecchio Molino

Via del Tempio, 34
06042 Pissignano - Campello sul Clitunno (Perugia)
Tel (0)743-52 11 22 - Fax (0)743-27 50 97
Sig.ra Rapanelli

Category ★★★★ **Rooms** 13 with air-conditioning, telephone, bath, WC and minibar. **Price** Single 142,000L, double 195,000L, suite 235,000L. **Meals** Breakfast included, served 7:30-11:30. **Restaurant** In Spoleto and Campello sul Clitunno see p. 461. **Credit cards** All major. **Pets** Dogs not allowed. **Facilities** Parking. **Nearby** Fonti del Clitunno, Tempietto del Clitunno, Ponte delle Torri, Church of S. Pietro, Basilica of S. Salvatore, Church of S. Ponziano, Monteluco and Convento of S. Francesco, Trevi, Spoleto, Spello, Orvieto, Soiano golf course (9-hole). **Open** April – Oct.

The small Christian temple just above the Vecchio Molino is a reminder of the cultural and artistic past of the cheery Clitunno Valley. This 15th-century mill is now a very pleasant hotel. Inside you can see the original equipment, and watch the river flow by. The decor is very simple, almost entirely white, which enhances the antique lines of the building. The rooms are large and superbly decorated. Each one is different, and some have a salon. On every floor are spots to read and relax. Only a few miles from Spoleto, this is one of the favorite hotels of the culture-seeking clientele which attends the Festival of Two Worlds run by Gian Carlo Menotti.

How to get there *(Map 14): 50 km southeast of Perugia via SS75 to Foligno, then S3.*

Hotel Gattapone

Via del Ponte, 6
06049 Spoleto (Perugia)
Tel (0)743-223 447 - Fax (0)743-223 448 - Sig. Hanke
E-mail: gattapone@mail.caribusiness.it - Web: http://www.caribusiness.it/gattapone

Category ★★★★ **Rooms** 16 with air-conditioning, telephone, bath or shower, WC, TV and minibar. **Price** Single 140,000L, double 170,000L, suite 270,000L. **Meals** Breakfast 15,000L, served 7:30-10:30. **Restaurant** See p. 461. **Credit cards** All major. **Pets** Dogs allowed. **Nearby** In Spoleto: Ponte delle Torrri, Duomo, Arch of Druso, Church, San Pietro, Festival of Two Worlds from mid-June to mid-July; Monteluco and the Convento di San Francesco, Fonti del Clitunno, Tempietto del Clitunno, Trevi, Spello, Soiano golf course (9-hole). **Open** All year.

Just outside the village of Spoleto, the Hotel Gattapone is the secret address of music fans who attend the celebrated festival. Built into a cliff overlooking the entire Tessino Valley, facing the Roman aqueduct beloved by Lucrecia Borgia, the duchess of Spoleto, the Gattapone is perfectly integrated into the landscape. Its interior decor is a model of comfort and harmony. The rooms are superb, modern, and have in common a panoramic view on the countryside, which gives them an atmosphere of quiet serenity. Professor Hanke, the owner, has a real sense of hospitality, and makes sure his guests feel at home.

How to get there *(Map 14): 65 km southeast of Perugia via SS3, towards Terni to Acquasparta, then S418 to Spoleto.*

Palazzo Dragoni

Via del Duomo, 13
06049 Spoleto (Perugia)
Tel (0)743-22 22 20 - Fax (0)743-22 22 25

Rooms 15 with telephone, bath or shower, WC, TV and minibar; elevator. **Price** Single and double 200,000L, suite 250,000L. **Meals** Breakfast 15,000L, served 7:30-10:30. **Restaurant** See p. 461. **Credit card** Diners. **Pets** Small dogs allowed. **Nearby** In Spoleto: Ponte delle Torrri, Duomo, Arch of Drusus, Church San Pietro, Festival of Two Worlds from mid-June to mid-July; Monteluco and the Convento di San Francesco, Fonti del Clitunno, Tempietto del Clitunno, Trevi, Spello, Soiano golf course (9-hole). **Open** All year on request.

This 15th-century *residenza d'epoca* just near the Duomo of Spoleto was once the palace of the Dragoni family. Upstairs in the bedrooms and salons you will admire the beautiful ceilings and an interior architecture that has been scrupulously preserved. The rooms are well-decorated with chairs, sofas, elegantly skirted tables and a number of nice antique pieces. The bedrooms are large and some have a real salon. There are two dining rooms: one, with arched windows that face the medieval part of town, is used as a breakfast room. The other, more intimate, with old stone walls and vaulted ceilings, is used only for private dinners. And you can rest assured that you'll be safe and snug — three green-headed dragons have been keeping watch over this house for centuries.

How to get there *(Map 14): 65 km southeast of Perugia via SS3 bis, towards Terni to Acquasparta, then S418 to Spoleto.*

Hotel Eremo delle Grazie

Monteluco
04960 Spoleto (Perugia)
Tel (0)743-49 624 - Fax (0)743-49 650
Professore Lalli

Rooms 11 with telephone, bath or shower and WC. **Price** Single 300,000L, double 350,000L, suite 450-500,000L. **Meals** Breakfast included, served 7:30-10:30. **Restaurant** On request, closed Mon.; à la carte. **Credit cards** Visa, Eurocard, MasterCard. **Pets** Dogs allowed. **Facilities** Swimming pool. **Nearby** In Spoleto: Ponte delle Torrri, Duomo, Arch of Drusus, Church San Ponziano, Festival of Two Worlds from mid-June to mid-July; Monteluco and the Convento di San Francesco, Fonti del Clitunno, Tempietto del Clitunno, Trevi, Spello, Soiano golf course (9-hole). **Open** All year.

The Eremo was a *residenza d'epoca* before it was a hotel, as the owner Pio Lalli insists on pointing out. One might add it was a *residenza historica*, built to be the mother house of the Monteluco Order, which explains why the surrounding woods became a place of refuge for many anchorites. It had its share of illustrious visitors in those days, including no less than Michelangelo and Pope Pius VI. It is also like a *residenza museo*, so filled is it with interesting souvenirs, like the library of Cardinal Cybo (who once lived here), available to anyone who likes old books. The bedrooms, once the cells, have kept their monastic atmosphere but improved their amenities. The salons are more convivial, with antique furniture and a terrace that offers an impressive view of Spoleto and the surrounding forest.

How to get there *(Map 14): 65 km southeast of Perugia via SS3 bis, towards Terni to Acquasparta, then S418 to Spoleto - 8 km southeast of Spoleto.*

Hotel Palazzo Bocci

via Cavour, 17
06038 Spello (Perugia)
Tel (0)742-30 10 21 - Fax (0)742-30 14 64 - Sig. Fabrizio Buono
E-mail: bocci@bcsnet.it

Category ★★★★ **Rooms** 23 with air-conditioning, telephone, bath or shower, WC, cable TV, safe and minibar; elevator. **Price** Single 105-130,000L, double 200-224,000L, suite 260-320,000L. **Meals** Breakfast included, served 7:30-10:00; half board +40,000L, full board +80,000L. **Restaurant** "Il Molino", service 12:30-15:00, 19:30-22:00; closed Tues.; menus: 40-60,000L, also à la carte. Specialities: Pinturicchio, tagliatelle alla molinara, oca alla fratina, funghi porcini, tartufo. **Credit cards** All major. **Pets** Dogs not allowed. **Facilities** Parking. **Nearby** In Spello: Church of Santa Maria Maggiore (cappella Baglioni), Palazzo Comunale, Ponte Venere, Belvedere, Church Tonda (2 km); Assisi, Perugia, Trevi, Bevagna, Montefalco, Spoleto, Fonti del Clitunno, Tempietto del Clitunno. **Open** All year.

Frescoes, stuccos and panoramic murals, wooden beams and stone vaults, the Palazzo Bocci offers its guests all the surroundings and atmosphere of a real little palace. The furniture is more classical and less elaborate than the decor. The rooms are large and equipped with the amenities one expects nowadays in a recently-done quality hotel (the suites have bathrooms with jacuzzis). In the summer, breakfast is served on the terrace overlooking the twisting lanes and rooftops of the old city. Just across the street is the restaurant Il Molino: known for both its cuisine and its winecellar, it brings an added plus to this hotel.

How to get there *(Map 14): 31 km southeast of Perugia.*

Hotel La Bastiglia

Piazza Vallegloria, 7
06038 Spello (Perugia)
Tel (0)742-65 12 77 - Fax (0)742-30 11 59
Sig. L. Fancelli

Category ★★★ **Rooms** 15 and 7 suites with air-conditioning, telephone, bath or shower, WC, TV and minibar. **Price** Double 140,000L, suite 180,000L. **Meals** Breakfast included, served 8:00-10:00. Half board 100-120,000L and full board 130-150,000L (per pers. 3 days min.). **Restaurant** Service 13:00-14:30, 20:00-22:00, closed Wed. and Jan.; menu: 40,000L, also à la carte. Specialties: Umbrian cooking. **Credit cards** All major. **Pets** Dogs not allowed. **Facilities** Parking. **Nearby** In Spello: Church of Santa Maria Maggiore (cappella Baglioni), Palazzo Comunale, Ponte Venere, Belvedere, Church Tonda (2 km); Assisi, Perugia, Trevi, Bevagna, Montefalco, Spoleto, Fonti del Clitunno, Tempietto del Clitunno. **Open** All year.

This charming little hotel is in the historical center of Spello, an ancient Roman town on the slopes of Mount Subasio. Formerly an old mill, it still has certain elements of its original architecture, such as the arches in the reception rooms. There is a superb terrace off of the salon with a lovely view of the olive trees and the valley. The dining room is very inviting with its white tablecloths, exposed beams and rustic furniture. The cuisine features old Umbrian specialties prepared with carefully selected regional products. The rooms are light, airy, and comfortable. Ask for the ones on the upper floors on the terrace side, which have a view of the countryside. (The suites have a private garden and a separate entry.) The service is charming, and the prices are reasonable. You just might want to prolong your visit to Umbria.

How to get there *(Map 14): 31 km southeast of Perugia.*

San Valentino Country House

Vocabolo San Valentino, 38/A
06059 Todi (Perugia)
Tel. (0)75 894 41 03 - Fax (0)75 894 41 03
Sig.ra Bastianini

Category ★★★★ **Rooms** 10 with telelephone, bath or shower, WC, satellite TV and 3 with minibar. **Price** Single 100-120,000L, double 200-250,000L, suite 300-400,000L. **Meals** Breakfast included served 8:30-11:30. **Restaurant** See p. 462. **Credit cards** All major. **Pets** Dogs allowed (10,000L). **Facilities** Swimming pool, tennis, parking at hotel. **Nearby** Todi: Church of Santa Maria Maggiore della Consolazione (1 km) towards Orvieto.Orvieto, Spoleto, Assisi, Gùbbio, ad Ellera golf (9-hole) in Perugia. **Open** Mar 15 - Oct.

This is one of the prettiest hotels in Umbria. It is set in a former 13th-century convent that has beautifully preserved its interior architecture, with its different levels and archways, with exposed beams and stone walls. The antique furniture goes with the rest. The bedrooms are spacious and elegant, sometimes with a mezzanine and a small terrace. From its location on the wooded hillside of San Valentino, the garden offers delightful shaded nooks and the terrace affords an extensive view of Todi and the valley. Marina takes charge of her guests with kindness and simplicity. This is a place you'll want to come back to. For your dinners out, you'll find at Jacopone et Umbria all the friendly atmosphere of an old osteria.

How to get there *(Map 14): 30 km south of Perugia via SS 3 Todi exit, 1 km town center.*

Hotel Fonte Cesia

Via Lorenzo Leonj, 3
06059 Todi (Perugia)
Tel (0)75-894 37 37 - Fax (0)75-894 46 77 - Sig. Felice
E-mail: f.cesia@full-service.it - Web: http://www.full-service.it

Category ★★★★ **Rooms** 32 and 5 suites with air-conditioning, telephone, bath or shower, WC, satellite TV and minibar. **Price** Single 155,000L, double 240,000L, suite 310,000L. **Meals** Breakfast included, served 8:00-10:00; half board 195-205,000L, full board 225-235,000L (per pers, 3 days min.). **Restaurant** Service 13:00-14:30, 20:00-21:30; menu, also à la carte. Specialties: Italian and umbrian cuisine. **Credit cards** All major. **Pets** Dogs not allowed on request. **Facilities** Parking. **Nearby** In Todi: Church of Santa Maria della Consolazione (1km), Orvieto, Perugia, Assisi, Spoleto, Gubbio, ad Ellera golf course (9-hole) in Perugia. **Open** All year.

The Hotel Fonte Cesia has recently opened its doors in a setting charged with history, the ancient Etruscan town of Todi, home of Jacopone da Todi, poet and author of the famous "Stabat Maler". You can still find traces of the flourishing medieval period in its small winding streets. The hotel is in a beautiful 17th century palace, a harmonious blend of tradition, elegance, and modern comfort. The well-preserved architecture is the most beautiful decorative element, notably its superb vaulted ceilings in small bricks. It is an intimate, tasteful decorated hotel with comfortable well-furnished rooms, some of which have a trompe-l'œil decor. The Umbrian delicacies served in the restaurant will convince you, if you still need convincing, that this is a great place for fine living.

How to get there *(Map 14): 45 km south of Perugia, via SS3bis, Todi exit.*

Poggio d'Asproli

06059 Todi (Perugia)
Frazione Asproli N.7
Tel. (0)75-885 33 85 - Fax (0)75-885 33 85
Sig.ra Maria Claudia Pagliari

Rooms 6 and 1 suite with telephone, shower, WC. **Price** Double 200,000L, suite 290-360,000L (2 and 4 pers.). **Meals** Breakfast included, served 8:00-10:00. **Restaurant** Service ab 20:30; menu 40,000L, also à la carte. **Credit cards** All major. **Pets** Dogs not allowed. **Facilities** Swimming pool, parking. **Nearby** Todi: Church of S. Maria della Consolazione (1 km) towards Orvieto; Orvieto, Perugia, Spoleto, Assisi, Gùbbio, Ellera golf course (18-hole) in Perugia. **Open** All year.

You can't miss the entrance to this estate - it is marked by a sculpture made by the master of the house. Several other of his works stand in the garden. The building is a beautiful old farmhouse and its architecture is suitably rustic, but inside the decor is of the most refined. There are of course some bare stone walls and archways and exposed beams in the ceiling, but the choice of fabrics, hangings and antique objects gives the whole place an elegant feel. The rooms are laid out with variations in level, creating many nooks and corners where it's nice to read or write postcards or have a quiet drink. As soon as the weather permits, meals and breakfasts are served on the terrace with its impressive view. The rooms are all attractive, the suites even more so. The swimming pool is on a par with the rest. This is not just an inn or a guest house, but in the words of the brochure, a residenza de campagna.

How to get there *(Map 14): In Todi take the road towards Orvieto and turn left towards Izzalini.*

Hotel Ristorante La Badia

La Badia
05019 Orvieto (Terni)
Tel (0)763-30 19 59/30 18 76 - Fax (0)763-30 53 96
Sig.ra Fiumi

Category ★★★★ **Rooms** 24 and 7 suites with telephone, bath or shower and WC, TV, minibar. **Price** Single 186-201,000L, double 240-270,000L, suite 394-477,000L. **Meals** Breakfast 18,000L, served 7:30-10:00; half board required in high season 223-326,000L, full board 293-396,000L (per pers.). **Restaurant** Service 12:30-14:30, 19:30-21:30; closed Wed.; menus: 70,000L, also à la carte. Specialties: Panicetti, coccinillo, scaloppe Badia. **Credit cards** Amex, Visa, Eurocard and MasterCard. **Pets** Dogs not allowed. **Facilities** Swimming pool, 2 tennis courts, parking. **Nearby** In Orvieto: Duomo, Palazzo del Popolo; Bolsena (Church Santa Cristina), Lake Bolsena, Etruscan country from San Lorenzo Nuovo to Chiusi (grotta di Castro, Pitigliano, Sorano, Sovana, Chiusi); Todi, golf course (9-hole) in Viterbo. **Open** All year (except Jan. and Feb.).

This former monastery is a wonderful stopping place in a lovely countryside. From its perch on a rock, it looks down over the town of Orvieto and the Umbrian landscape. It is a very comfortable hotel with well-appointed rooms and suites, a good restaurant, swimming pool and tennis court, all the ingredients for a perfect country inn only 5 kilometers from the historic center. And a warm, friendly welcome in addition.

How to get there *(Map 13): 86 km south of Perugia via SS3 bis to Todi exit, then S448 suivre les indications pour la plazza Duopo - In La Badia, 5 km south of Orvieto.*

Villa Ciconia

Ciconia 05019 Orvieto Scalo (Terni)
Via dei Tigli, 69
Tel. (0)763-305 582 - Fax (0)763-302 077 - Sig. Falcone

Category ★★★★ **Rooms** 10 with air conditioning on request (+20,000L), telephone, bath or shower, WC, TV, hairdryer, minibar. **Price** Single 135,000L, double 170-240,000L. **Meals** Breakfast 15,000L, served 7:30-10:30; half board +35,000L, full board +70,000L (per pers.). **Restaurant** Service 13:00-15:00, 20:00-22:00; closed Monday; menus: 45-55,000L, also à la carte; menu. **Credit cards** All major. **Pets** Dogs not allowed. **Facilities** Parking. **Nearby** Orvieto: Duomo, Palazzo del Popolo; Bolsena, Lake Bolsena, Etruscan country from San Lorenzo Nuovo to Chiusi; Todi, golf course (9-hole) in Viterbo. **Open** All year except 15 days in Feb.

Orvieto has more than one claim to fame. The first is certainly its wine. When Signorelli painted the Duomo, he asked for part of his remuneration to be paid in wine. The wines, both red and white, are excellent and there is also a regional production of *vin santo*. Stop in at the wine bar at N. 2, Piazza del Duomo, and you'll be able to taste some of the fine vintages. The other famous attraction of Orvieto is, of course, its Duomo. The Villa Ciconia is only a few kilometers away, but it's already the country, at the confluence of two streams that cross the property. It is a superb 15th-century gray stone building attributed to a student of Michelangelo. It is said he also painted the landscapes and allegorical scenes in what is today a restaurant. The rooms are large and comfortable; facing the park, they are decorated with antique furniture and traditional materials. Despite the small number of rooms, the fact that there are three restaurants shows that the Ciconia is used for meetings and receptions. You should find out what events are scheduled when making your reservation.

How to get there *(Map 13): 86 km south of Perugia via SS3 bis to Todi exit, then S448 towards Orvieto; Orvieto Scalo, drive under the motorway towards Todi-Perugia and left towards Arezzo via SS 71 to 35 km.*

Fattoria di Titignano

1998

06039 Titignano-Orvieto (Terni)
Tel. (0)763-30 83 22/75-894 76 78 - Fax (0)75-89 47 679
Famiglia Corsini

Rooms 17 with shower and WC. **Price** Double 100-120,000L. **Meals** Breakfast included, served 8:30-10:30; half board 170,000L and full board 180,000L (per pers.). **Evening meals** By reservation. **Credit cards** Not accepted. **Pets** Dogs allowed. **Facilities** Swimming pool, mountain bike, tasting of wines, parking. **Nearby** Della Piana cave, La Roccacia, Lake Corbara, Orvieto, Lake Bolsena and Etruscan country. **Open** All year.

Going to Titignano is liking traveling backwards in time. The estate, which still covers 2000 hectares, has lived through the centuries in an unchanged environment. Its buildings, still intact, form by themselves a veritable little village. Don't be surprised that you have to cross woods and fields once you have left the road - Titignano is in a way the end of the world. The main house facing the small piazza is the most comfortable place to stay and the one that has best preserved the charm of the interior architecture (the furniture has not been so fortunate). The very pleasant living room is extended by a loggia arranged for rest and recreation, and the dining room has a magnificent fireplace. The other rooms are in buildings that face both the piazza and the valley, but some have just the doorway as their only opening. Down below, overlooking the meadows and hills that border the little Lake Cobara, the swimming pool will provide some magical moments as you look out over one of the loveliest landscapes of the Umbrian countryside.

How to get there *(Map 14): On the highway A1 (Roma-Firenze), Orvieto exit. Towards Arezzo-Prodo. Take the 79 road and turn right to Titignano.*

1998

Villa La Meridiana - Cascina Reine 

Altavilla, 9
12051 Alba (Cuneo)
Tel. (0)173-44 01 12 - Fax (0)173-44 01 12 - Sig.ra Giuliana Pionzo

Rooms 5 and 2 apartments with kitchen, bath or shower, WC, (TV and telephone on request). **Price** Double 100-120,000L, apartment 130,000L (2 pers. +20,000L extra bed.). **Meals** Breakfast included, served 8:00-10:00. **Restaurant** See p. 464. **Credit cards** Not accepted. **Pets** Dogs allowed. **Facilities** Parking. **Nearby** Alba: Wine fair in April, white truffles fair in Oct., panoramic road (Langhe towards Ceva), Barbaresco and vermouth and spumante road d'Asti towards Canelli, Asti: cathedral, S.Secondo, Pallio de Asti in Sept., Sanctuary of Crea, Abbey of Vezollano, "Le Chocciole" golf course (18-hole). **Open** All year.

If you give yourself half a chance, you will be enthralled by the vine-clad hills of Piedmont that produce the famous Asti Spumante and such highly appreciated wines as Barolo and Barbaresco. Asti and Alba are charming medieval villages where life flows slowly on in the rhythm of the seasons and the work in the fields, punctuated by the traditional celebrations. Built on the heights of the town, La Meridiana is in an art nouveau style, with a modern wing recently added to provide more rooms. Some pieces of family furniture add a note of charm and the bathrooms are completely modern and comfortable. The garden is inviting, well-placed for viewing the landscape of vineyards and poplars, with the towers of the historic old town in the distance. The kitchen, where breakfast is prepared daily, can occasionally be put at your disposal, if you feel like dining in one evening. However, one should really make it a point to discover the cuisine of Piedmont, so different from what we usually think of as Italian cooking.

How to get there *(Map 7): 62 km from Torino.*

1998

La Luna e i Falo'

Regione Aie, 37
14053 Canelli (Asti)
Tel. (0)141-83 16 43 - Fax (0)141-83 16 43 - Sig.Carnero

Rooms 5 with bath or shower, WC, TV. **Price** Double 140,000L. **Meals** Breakfast included, served until 10:00. **Restaurant** (by reservation). Service 19:30; menus 45,000L and 75,000L (wine incl.). Specialties: Monferrina, lungana. **Credit cards** Not accepted. **Pets** Dogs allowed. **Facilities** Parking. **Nearby** Canelli: historical feast day in June "l'ossedio", wine fair and white truffles fair (autumn), Alba, Asti: cathedral, S.Secondo, Pallio de Asti in Sept., Monferatto, Sanctuary of Crea, Abbey of Vezollano. **Open** All year (on request).

Owner Franco Carnero is a fervent admirer of Cesare Pavese. That is why he named his house after the writer's best-known masterpiece, "La Luna e i Falo' " (The Moon and the Fires). This is Pavese country: the hills of Piedmont where every June, under a full moon, peasants light the fires that announce the start of the harvest. It is a magnificent and moving sight that you will witness from the large terrace overlooking the vineyards. The interior is inviting, though a little surprising, with its profusion of imposing furniture and its large and varied painting collection. The bedrooms have the same cozy and comfortable feel. The cooking lives up to the reputation the Carnero family had already acquired in Turin before they decided to settle here at Canelli. The region boasts a wealth of historic, cultural and gastronomic treasures that promise a wonderful vacation.

How to get there *(Map 7): 26 km from Asti. In Canelli, take the road towards "Castello Gancia".*

Villa Sassi-El Toulà

Strada Traforo del Pino, 47
10132 Torino Sassi
Tel. (0)11-89 80 556 - Fax (0)11-89 80 095
Sig.ra Aonzo

Category ★★★★ **Rooms** 17 with air-conditioning, telephone, bath or shower and WC; elevator. **Price** Single 270,000L, double 400,000L. **Meals** Breakfast 20,000L, served 7:00-10:30; half board 270-320,000L, full board 350-400,000L (per pers., 3 days min.). **Restaurant** Service 12:30-14:30, 20:00-22:30; closed Sun.; à la carte. Specialties: Local and Italian dishes. **Credit cards** All major. **Pets** Dogs not allowed. **Facilities** Parking. **Nearby** In Torino: Palazzo Madama, Museo Egizio (Egyptian Museum) and Galleria Sabauda (16th- and 17th-century Dutch and Flemish paintings), Mole Antonelliana, Sanctuario della Consolata, Galleria d'Arte Moderna; Basilica de Superga, Villa Reale in Stupinigi, Cathedral in Chieri, Church of Sant'Antonio di Ranverso, Abbey Sacra di San Michele, I Roveri golf course in La Mandria. **Open** All year.

This 17th-century villa, which stood in open country when it was first built, is now practically in the center of Turin, though it still benefits from the tranquility of the large grounds that surround it. Of the interior features, it has preserved the wooden staircase that is now in the reception area, a fine fresco on one wall and two large baroque candelabras. Each room has a personalized decoration and excellent amenities. The restaurant is of the quality of the "El-Toulà" chain and there is a lovely view of the grounds through the large modern picture windows. The farm adjoining the property guarantees the availability of fresh produce and contributes to the quality of the Piedmontese cuisine, a little different and very tasty.

How to get there *(Map 7): Torino-west exit; towards Pino Torinese or Chieri.*

Hotel Victoria

Via Nino Costa, 4
10123 Torino
Tel. (0)11-56 11 909 - Fax (0)11-56 11 806 - Sig. Vallinotto

Category ★★★ **Rooms** 100 with air-conditioning, telephone, bath or shower, WC, TV and minibar; elevator. **Price** Single 160-190,000L, double 230-260,000L, suite 300,000L. **Meals** Breakfast included (buffet), served 7:30-11:00. **Restaurant** See p. 462-463. **Credit cards** All major. **Pets** Dogs not allowed. **Nearby** In Torino: Palazzo Madama, Museo Egizio (Egyptian Museum) and Galleria Sabauda (16th- and 17th-century Dutch and Flemish paintings), Mole Antonelliana, Sanctuario della Consolata, Galleria d'Arte Moderna; Basilica de Superga, Villa Reale in Stupinigi, Cathedral in Chieri, Church of Sant'Antonio di Ranverso, Abbey Sacra di San Michele, I Roveri golf course in La Mandria. **Open** All year.

The Hotel Victoria, hidden in the middle of this secret town, is a place to experience. This recently built, modern building is in the heart of the shopping district, near the Piazza San Carlo, the Duomo, and the train station. The decor is an innovative blend of function, fantasy and humor. The rooms are all very pretty; you will have trouble choosing between the Egyptian room, the more romantic ones with their Art Nouveau prints, or the ones with a New Orleans motif. They are all very quiet, overlooking either a pedestrian street or the chamber of commerce garden. The breakfast room has all the charm of a winter garden, and the very cozy salon offers a peaceful view of a patio full of green plants. This three-star hotel offers four-star comfort. You will like the Victoria for the quiet, the nice decor, and the reasonable prices.

How to get there *(Map 8): Near Piazza San Carlo and train station.*

Castello San Giuseppe

Castello San Giuseppe
10010 Chiaverano d'Ivrea (Torino)
Tel. (0)125-42 43 70 - Fax (0)125-64 12 78
Sig. Naghiero

Category ★★★★ **Rooms** 16 with telephone, bath or shower, WC and TV. **Price** Single 135,000L, double 185,000L, suite 205,000L. **Meals** Breakfast included, served 7:30-10:00; half board 145,000L (per pers., 3 days min.). **Restaurant** Service 20:00-23:30; closed Sun.; menu: 50,000L, also à la carte. **Credit cards** All major. **Pets** Small dogs allowed. **Facilities** Parking. **Nearby** Lake Sirio de campagna, Lake S. Michele, National Park Gran Paradiso, Torino. **Open** All year.

Only 3 kilometers from the center of the village of Ivrea, the Castello di San Giuseppe stands like a watchman on a hill surrounded by the lakes of Sirio, San Michele and di Campagna. First a monastery, it served as a lovers' refuge for Arrigo Boito and Eleonora Duse before becoming a country inn. It offers guests all the charm of its well-preserved architecture and antiques or period furniture found for its redecoration. There are good quality facilities. The garden, with an exuberance of tropical species, is a wonderful place to relax between visits in the surroundings of Ivrea or while waiting to plunge into the electric atmosphere of the Carnival (February), one of the most popular in Italy, known for its "battle of the oranges."

***How to get there** (Map 7): 40 km north of Torino via A5, Ivrea exit, towards Lake Sirio.*

Il Capricorno

10050 Sauze-d'Oulx (Torino)
Le Clotes
Tel. (0)122-850 273 - Fax (0)122-850 273
Sig. and Sig.ra Sacchi

Category ★★★★ **Rooms** 7 with telephone, bath, WC and TV. **Price** Single 190,000L, double 260,000L. **Meals** Breakfast included, served 8:00-10:30; half board 200,000L (per pers., 3 days min.). **Restaurant** Service 12:30-14:30, 19:30-21:00; à la carte. Specialties: Antipasti di Mariarosa, scottata rucola e Parmigiano, tacchino su zucchini, gnocchi alla menta, ravioli alla crema di zucchini, portofoglio alla Capricorno, maltagliati al ragù di verdure. **Credit cards** Visa, Eurocard and MasterCard. **Pets** Dogs not allowed. **Facilities** Parking in summer. **Nearby** Skiing (from the hotel), Bardonecchia, Sestriere, Briançon (France), golf course (18-hole) in Sestriere. **Open** Nov. – May 1, June 8 – Sept. 15.

Sauze d'Oulx is a ski resort town located at an altitude of 4875 feet (1500 meters), near the Franco-Italian border at Clavière Montgenèvre. Il Capricorno is even higher, deep in the mountains, at 5850 feet (1800 meters). This pretty chalet has only seven rooms, all with small but very functional bathrooms. The small number of boarders allows Mariarosa, the owner, to pamper her guests. Her cuisine is absolutely delicious. Il Capricorno, in a location well adapted for both hikers and skiers, is as pleasant in summer as it is in winter, as it is only a few miles from Bardonecchia and Sestrière, and 18 miles (30 km) from Briançon. Reservations are a must.

How to get there *(Map 6): 40 km north of Briançon via the Col de Montgenève to Oulx, then towards Saure-d'Oulx. 81 km west of Torino via A70.*

Hotel Principi di Piemonte

10058 Sestriere (Torino)
Via Sauze di Cesana
Tel. (0)122-7941 - Fax (0)122-70270
Sig. Clemente

Category ★★★★ **Rooms** 94 with telephone, bath, WC, TV and minibar. **Price** On request. **Meals** Breakfast 15,000L, served 7:30-11:30. **Restaurant** Service 12:30-14:00, 19:30-21:00; menus: 45-55,000L, also à la carte. Specialties: Piedmontais cuisine. **Credit cards** All major. **Pets** Small dogs allowed. **Facilities** Sauna, beauty shops, garage (20,000L), parking. **Nearby** Skiing (from the hotel), Bardonecchia, Briançon (France), golf course (18-hole) in Sestrire. **Open** Dec. 20 – April 15 and June 17 – Aug. 23.

Surrounded by the famous towers of this ski resort, the Principi di Piemonte used to be considered the traditional grand hotel of Sestriere. The towers have now become clubs and the Principi has undergone transformations to adapt to a new clientele. The rooms are extremely comfortable and the suites are plush. In addition to the salons and dining rooms, there is a discothèque, stores, and a hairdresser. You will find everything you need to have a nice, active sports vacation and to spend enjoyable evenings here. Prices are lower in summer. Those who remember the way it was a few years ago may feel slightly nostalgic for a certain atmosphere which once reigned in this hotel inspired by Suvretta de Saint-Moritz.

How to get there *(Map 6): 32 northwest of Briançon via the Col de Montgenève to Cesana Torinese, then S 23; 93 km west of Torino via E70.*

Locanda del Sant' Uffizio

14030 Cioccaro di Penango (Asti)
Tel. (0)141-91 62 92 - Fax (0)141-91 60 68
Sig. Beppe

Category ★★★★ **Rooms** 35 and 5 in annexe, with telephone, bath or shower, WC, TV and minibar; wheelchair access. **Price** With half board 260-320,000L (per pers. in double room), 360,000L (single room). **Meals** Breakfast included, served 7:30-10:30. **Restaurant** Service 12:30-13:30, 19:30-21:00; menu: 100,000L, also à la carte. Specialties: Funghi tartufi, gnocchi de fonduta, cinghiale di bosco, lasagne con verdurini del orto, anatra stufata al miele e rhum. **Credit cards** Diners, Visa, Eurocad and MasterCard. **Pets** Small dogs allowed in rooms. **Facilities** Swimming pool, tennis, parking. **Nearby** Asti, Abbey of Vezzolano in Albrugnano, Sanctuario of Crea in Monferrato hills, golf course (18-hole) in Margara. **Open** All year (except Jan. 6 – 16, Aug. 9 – 20).

The Locanda del Sant' Uffizio is a former 15th-century convent nestled in the Monferrato hills, surrounded by vineyards. The small chapel, the marvelous and comfortable rooms, the absolute quiet, the beauty of the surrounding countryside and the red brick buildings make this, in our opinion, one of the most charming hotels in this book. Breakfast is served is a beautifully furnished room, and when the weather is warm, next to the swimming pool. The restaurant features exceptional regional cuisine accompanied by delicious wines including one produced right here. Meals are very generous. This place is not to be missed.

How to get there *(Map 7): 64 km east of Torino - 21 km north of Asti via S457 towards Moncalvo (3 km before Moncalvo).*

Albergo del Castello

Via Umberto I, 9
12060 Verduno (Cuneo)
Tel. (0)172 47 01 25 - Fax (0)172 47 02 98
Sig.ra Elisa Burlotto

Category ★★ **Rooms** 13 with shower, WC (5 with tel.). **Price** Double 160-200,000L, suite 270,000L. **Meals** Breakfast included served 8:00-11:00, half board +120,000L. **Restaurant** Service from 20:00, menus 70,000L. Specialties: Givra (stracotto di vacca), agnolotti al plin, carne di verduno, risotti albarolo, anatra con insalata, panna cotta. **Credit cards** All major. **Pets** Dogs not allowed. **Facilities** Parking at hotel. **Nearby** Torino, Asti, Bra, Alba, Abbey of Vezzolano. **Open** Feb - end Nov.

This little castle, built according to a design by the 18th-century architect Juvarra, belonged since 1847 to the Savoia family, the royal family of Italy. Located in a region known for its fine wines, barolo and barbera, the hotel still cultivates the vines on the estate and boasts an excellent wine cellar. The interior has undergone a discreet renovation, keeping the original appearance of the castle: frescoes, impressive antique furniture and some of the royal family paintings. The rooms in the main building have a monastic austerity. Those in the outbuilding, the Rose Room and the Blue Room, are more luxurious and decorated with beautiful frescoes. From the wonderful garden you can contemplate all the charms of the Piedmontese countryside.

How to get there *(Map 7): 50 km south of Torino; on A21 Asti east exit; on A 6 Marene exit.*

Hotel Pironi

Lago Maggiore
28822 Cannobio (Verbania)
Tel. (0)323-70 624/70 871 - Fax (0)323-721 84
Famiglia Albertella

Category ★★★ **Rooms** 12 with telephone, bath or shower, WC, safe and minibar; elevator. **Price** Single 115-125,000L, double 170-200,000L. **Meals** Breakfast included (buffet). **Restaurant** See p.464. **Credit cards** Amex, Visa, Eurocad and MasterCard. **Pets** Small dogs allowed on request. **Nearby** Sanctuario della Pietà, Lake Maggiore: Stresa, Borromean islands, Verbania, Villa Taranto, Ascona; Locarno (Switzerland). **Open** March – Oct.

In the old town of Cannobio, the Pironi rises like a ship's prow over the little *piazza,* at the intersection of two streets that descend toward the lake. Solidly built over an elegant portico, the hotel is made up of two adjoining palaces, which have been very ably renovated and restored in such a way as to enhance the capacity of the hotel while preserving the architectural heritage. The bedrooms are not luxurious but very comfortable. Our favorite room is number 12, which gives onto a lovely Renaissance loggia. The salon, which doubles as a breakfast room, is like a little jewel box, its walls entirely covered with frescoes from the *cinquecento.* Situated close to the Swiss border, it is a good point from which to explore the two wild and beautiful valleys of Cannobina and Vissezo.

How to get there *(Map 2): 117 km northwest of Milano via A8 (Milan-/Torino), Verbiania exit, towards Locarno.*

Hotel Ghiffa

Corso Belvedere, 88
Lago Maggiore
28052 Ghiffa (Novara)
Tel. (0)323 59 285- Fax (0)323 59 585 - Sig. Valerio Cattaneo

Category ★★★ **Rooms** 39 (32 with air-conditioning) with telephone, bath or shower, WC, satellite TV; elevator. **Price** Single 180,000L, double 255,000L. **Meals** Breakfast included, served 7:30-9:45, half board 155-190,000L and full board 175-210,000L (per pers.3 day min.). **Restaurant** Service 12:30-14:00, 19:30-21:30, menus: 50,000L. Specialties: Filetti di pesce persico alle erbe, bianco di rambo al finocchio selvatino, cannelloni alla nizarda, torta Daverina. **Credit cards** All major. **Pets** Dogs not allowed. **Facilities** Swimming pool, garage (20,000L) and parking. **Nearby** Stresa, Borromean islands, Locarno, Ascona, Pian golf course di Sole. **Open** Apr. 1 - Oct 20.

On the lush banks of Lake Maggiore, its luxuriant vegetation tamed by artistic landscape gardening, Ghiffa is a quiet and romantic resort town. The hotel, directly on the lakefront, has preserved in its salons something of its aristocratic past. The bedrooms have a rather cold, modern look, but the view of the lake and the mountains amply make up for the slight shortcoming. A swimming pool and a small private beach are attractive during the summer season. The restaurant offers a delicate cuisine and a view of the same fine panorama. A refreshing place to stop before a visit to the Borromean Islands.

How to get there *(Map 2): 102 km northwest of Milano via A 8, Gravellona Toce exit, towards Verbania/Lago Maggiore, Locarno.*

Hotel Verbano

Lago Maggiore
Isola dei Pescatori
Isole Borromee 28049 Stresa (Novara)
Tel. (0)323-30 408/32 534 - Fax (0)323-33 129 - Sig. Zacchera

Category ★★★ **Rooms** 12 with telephone, bath or shower and WC. **Price** Single 140-160,000L, double 200-230,000L. **Meals** Breakfast included; half board 160-180,000L, full board 200-230,000L (per pers.). **Restaurant** Service 12:00-14:30, 19:00-21:30; menus 45-75,000L, also à la carte. Specialties: Fish from the lake. **Credit cards** All major. **Pets** Dogs allowed. **Facilities** Boat. **Nearby** Borromean islands: Isola Bella (Palazzo Borromeo and his gardens), Isola Madre (botanical garden); Isole Borromee golf course (18-hole) in Stresa. **Open** All year (except Jan. and Feb.).

An excursion to the Borromean Islands is one of the highlights of Lake Maggiore. If you want a tour, you can catch the boat at the port of Stresa. But these wonderful little islands, with their charming villas whose lush gardens extend right up to the dock, are really worth a stay. Isola dei Pescatori is one of the smallest and the Hotel Verbano is quite small itself. Toscanini used to like to come here and work. Charming though not luxurious, the bedrooms, with their creaking wood floors, are decorated with old-fashioned family furniture and most have a splendid view of the lake. In case all this is not romantic enough, dinner in the evening is served by candlelight.

How to get there *(Map 2): Northwest of Milano via A8, towards Lake Maggiore; in Stresa or in Pallanza, ferry services for the Borromean Islands, stop at Isola dei Pescatori. Ferry service for the coast from 18:30 or bus-boat and taxi-boat.*

Hotel Villa Crespi

Lago d'Orta
28016 Orta San Giulio (Novara)
Via Generale Fava, 8
Tel. (0)322-91 19 02 - Fax (0)322-91 19 19 - Famiglia Bacchetta

Category ★★★★ **Rooms** 12 and 7 suites with air conditioning, telephone, bath, WC, TV, minibar and elevator. **Price** Single 280,000L, double 380,000L, suite 420-780,000L. **Meals** Breakfast incl, served 7:00-10:30; half board 290-330,000L, full board 330-380,000L (per pers., 3 days min.). **Restaurant** Service 12:00-14:30, 19:30-22:00; menus 90-11,000L. Specialties: Millefoglie di patate, spugnole e fegato grasso in salsa «caline», raviolini del Pun in cesto di parmigiano, carré di agnello in crosta di sale, gratin di frutta di stagione. **Credit cards** All major. **Pets** Small dogs allowed. **Facilities** Sauna (25,000L), parking. **Nearby** Orta San Giulio, Sacro Monte (view), Island of San Giulio, Fondation Calderana in Vacciago, golf course in Gignese. **Open** All year.

On the banks of the very romantic Lake Orta you will notice an unusual Moorish minaret, a luxurious homage to the Orient built by a cotton industrialist, Benigno Crespi. The villa (1880) stands in the middle of marvelous grounds shaded by pine trees. The salons and rooms are a successful blend of a somewhat heavy orientalism with more classical furniture. The rooms have a Romantic decor with imposing canopy beds and lovely velvet fabrics. The spacious marble bathrooms feature ultramodern facilities including "matrimonial" jacuzzis. This is a family-run hotel and it is the manager himself who does the cooking for the restaurant, locally famous for its traditional fine cuisine. This is a nice place in an ideal location for wandering down the narrow cobblestone streets of the peninsula.

How to get there *(Map 2): 20 km west of Stresa and of Lago Maggiore.*

Hotel San Rocco

Lago d'Orta
28016 Orta San Giulio (Novara)
Via Gippini, 11
Tel. (0)322-91 19 77 - Fax (0)322-91 19 64 - Sig. Bacchetta

Category ★★★★ **Rooms** 74 with telephone, bath, WC, TV, minibar and elevator. **Price** Single 180-250,000L, double 250-360,000L, suite 350-400,000L. **Meals** Breakfast included, served 7:00-10:00. **Restaurant** Service 12:30-14:00, 20:00; menu 72,000L. Specialties: Bacetti san Rocco, boconcini tartufati, salmone marinato al timo, code di gamberi con frutti tropicali, zabaglione al frutti di bosco. **Credit cards** All major. **Pets** Dogs not allowed. **Facilities** Sauna (26,000L), hearth center, parking, garage (15,000L). **Nearby** Orta San Giulio, Sacro Monte (view), Island of San Giulio, Fondation Calderana in Vacciago, golf course in Gignese. **Open** All year.

The Hotel San Rocco is right on the lake across from the Romanesque landscape of the island of San Giulio. Built on the foundations of a 17th century monastery, the hotel has kept its original architectural structure, enclosed shell-like on the lake and on its cloister. Inside you will find all of the efficiency of a modern hotel. The rooms all have a beautiful view and are simply decorated but very comfortable. When the weather gets warm, you can have breakfast in the garden on the lake and relax in the pool. The hotel also provides a private boat to explore all of the nooks and crannies of the island with. The restaurant features delicate variations on traditional recipes.

How to get there *(Map 2): 20 km west of Stresa and Lago Maggiore.*

Castello di San Giorgio

Via Cavalli d'Olivola, 3
15020 San Giorgio Monferrato (Alessandria)
Tel. (0)142-80 62 03 - Fax (0)142-80 65 05 - Sig. Grossi

Category ★★★★ **Rooms** 10 and 1 suite with telephone, bath, WC, TV and minibar. **Price** Single 150,000L, double 220,000L, suite 320,000L. **Meals** Breakfast 25,000L (buffet), served 8:00-10:00; half board 220,000L, full board 280,000L (per pers., 3 days min.). **Restaurant** Service 12:00-14:30, 19:30-21:30; closed Mon.; menu 85,000L, also à la carte. Specialties: Agnolotti alla monferrina, seafood, funghi, tartufi. **Credit cards** All major. **Pets** Dogs allowed. **Facilities** Parking. **Nearby** Marengo (Villa Marengo), Asti, Abbey of Vezzolano in Albugnano. **Open** All year (except Aug. 1 – 20, Dec. 27 - Jan. 10).

This hotel and remarkable restaurant are located in the outbuildings (the farmhouse and stables) of Monferrat Castle, an enormous dark brick edifice built in the 14th century for Gonzague de Mantoue. On magnificent grounds inside its original walls, the buildings have been superbly renovated and partly decorated with furnitue and old paintings from the castle. The luxurious rooms have been tastefully done, and have a very pretty view of the vast, quiet plain dotted with hills. Sig. Grossi is not only an excellent hotel director, he is also connaisseur of French cuisine. Mrs. Grossi does the cooking, and thanks to her considerable culinary talent, produces remarkable results. You will enjoy gourmet meals at San Giorgio, which, along with the setting and the service, really make it worth the detour.

How to get there *(Map 8): 26 km northwest of Alessandria via A26, Casale-Sud exit, 6 km towards Alessandria - Asti, road on the right towards San Giorgio Monferrato.*

Hotel Hermitage

Place des guides - Maquignaz, 4
11021 Breuil-Cervinia (Aosta)
Tel. (0)166-94 89 98 - Fax (0)166-94 90 32

Category ★★★★ **Rooms** 36, 4 suites and 1 apartment with telephone, bath or shower, WC, satellite TV, safe and minibar. **Price** Single 200-300,000L, double 300-400,000L, suite 500-900,000L. **Meals** Breakfast included (buffet), served 7:30-11:00; half board 200-280,000L, 400,000L in suite; full board +60,000L (per pers.). **Restaurant** Service 13:00-14:30, 20:00-22:00; menus 50-70,000L, also à la carte. Specialties: Italian and local cuisine. **Credit cards** Amex, Visa, Eurocard and MasterCard. **Pets** Dogs not allowed. **Facilities** Swimming pool, sauna, health center, parking and garage (+25,000L). **Nearby** Ski, cable car to Plateau Rosà (view), Cervino golf course (9-hole). **Open** All year.

A stay at the Hermitage combines the joys of skiing with all the well-being of a luxury hotel. You gan get your fill of thrills on the slopes of the Matterhorn at 3,000 meters or have the pleasure of skiing all the way to Zermatt on the Swiss side. Back at the hotel, you'll find excellent amenities, spacious rooms done with an Alpine flavor, both elegant and cozy, or some new attic rooms, very romantic with their sloping ceilings. In the evening, pleasant après-ski activities round the swimming pool or at the health and fitness club. And to end the day, a dinner at the hotel restaurant, known for its old family recipes, lives up to its very fine reputation. Everything here is homemade, including the Viennese pastries and the jams on the breakfast table. During certain off-season periods of December, January and April, the Hermitage offers five-day packages at affordable prices that make it possible to enjoy all the advantages of a hotel of charm in one of the finest skiing areas in Europe.

How to get there *(Map 1): 50 km northeast of Aosta via A5 Aosta-ouest exit, then RR 47.*

Les Neiges d'Antan

Frazione Cret Perrères
11021 Breuil-Cervinia (Aosta)
Tel. (0)166-94 87 75 - Fax (0)166-94 88 52
Sig. and Sig.ra Bich

Category ★★★ **Rooms** 28 with telephone, bath or shower, WC, safe and TV. **Price** Single 120,000L, double 210,000L, suite (4 pers.) 360,000L. **Meals** Breakfast included, served 7:30-10:00; half board 90,000L, full board 160,000L. **Restaurant** Service 12:30-14:00, 19:30-21:30; menu 50,000L, also à la carte. Specialties: Italian and local cuisine. **Credit cards** Visa, Eurocard and MasterCard. **Pets** Dogs allowed in rooms. **Facilities** Parking. **Nearby** Matterhorn (Monte Cervino in Italian), ski, cable car to Plateau Rosà (view), Cervino golf course (9-hole). **Open** All year (except Sept. 17 – Dec. 5, May 3 – June 29).

Isolated high up in the mountains, facing Matterhorn, the Neiges d'Antan is a charming hotel, the reflection of the soul and the passion of an entire family. The decor is simple but warm and personal. The bar has paneled walls covered with a collection of photos. You can find books, magazines and newspapers to read in the large, modern salon and music room. This is a place of simple luxury, reflected in the excellent cuisine carefully supervised by Sig.ra Bich, who also makes the jellies you will be served at breakfast, in the wine list selected by Sig. Bich and his son, the wine-waiter, and in the old, lace doily up on which you will place your wine glass. The rooms all have the same good taste and great comfort. This is a quality hotel, run by quality people.

How to get there *(Map 1): 49 km northeast of Aosta via A5, Saint-Vincent exit - Chatillon, then S406 - 4 km before Cervinia.*

Villa Anna Maria

5, rue Croues
11020 Champoluc (Aosta)
Tel. (0)125-30 71 28 - Fax (0)125-30 79 84
Sig. Miki and Sig. Origone

Category ★★★ **Rooms** 20 with telephone, TV (14 with bath or shower, WC). **Price** With half board 125,000L, full board 135,000L. (per pers., 3 days min.). **Meals** Breakfast 10,000L, served 8:15-11:00. **Restaurant** Service 12:45-14:00, 19:45-21:00; closed Sep. 16 - Dec. 1, April 20 - June 20; menus 30-40,000L, also à la carte. Specialty: Fonduta with melted Fontina. **Credit cards** Visa, Eurocard and MasterCard. **Pets** Dogs not allowed. **Facilities** Garage (6,000L). **Nearby** Skiing, Hamlets in the Valle d'Ayas: Antagnod, Perrias, Saint-Jacques; Castle of Verrès, Church in Arnad. **Open** All year.

This incontestably charming chalet is one of our favorite properties. Hidden behind spruce trees, covered with flowers in the summer and buried in snow in the winter, the Villa Anna Maria is perfect for people seeking for quiet. The dining room has a rustic, natural atmosphere with its gleaming copper pots and lovely polished wood walls. The cuisine is simple and sophisticated. The rooms have low ceilings and are a little dark, as mountain refuges often are. The hosts extend a warm and genuine welcome.

How to get there *(Map 1): 63 km east of Aosta via A5, Verrès exit, then SR 45 (Valley of Ayas) to Champoluc.*

Hotel Bellevue

Via Gran Paradiso, 22
11012 Cogne (Aosta)
Tel. (0)165-74 825 - Fax (0)165-74 91 92
Sig. and Sig.ra Jeantet and Roullet

Category ★★★★ Rooms 32, 3 chalets with telephone, bath or shower and WC, TV and minibar. **Price** Double 180-500,000. **Meals** Breakfast included, served 7:30-10:00; half board 120-280,000L, full board +30,000L (per pers., 3 days min.). **Restaurants** Service 12:30-13:30, 19:30-20:30; menus 50-80,000L, also à la carte. Specialties: Favò, carbonada con polenta, crème of Cogne. **Credit cards** All major. **Pets** Dogs not allowed. **Facilities** Swimming pool (indoor), whirlpool, turkish bath, sauna, mountain bikes, ping-pong, garage, parking. **Nearby** Alpine Garden of Valnontey, Gran Paradiso National Park. **Open** Dec. 22 – Sep. 26.

The Hotel Bellevue is located in the heart of the Gran Paradiso National Park, very near the center of Cogne, yet isolated in a field which goes on as far as the eye can see. The service is warm and the white wood and pastel decor is simple. The personnel, dressed in traditional costume, add to the charm of the place. The cuisine is exquisite and made with fine regional products; the bread, pastries, and jellies are homemade, and the hotel has its own private supplier of cheeses. The hotel owns three restaurants, two of which are at the hotel: one is for boarders, and the other small one is a place where you can dine à la carte. The third, *La Brasserie du Bon Bec,* is in the center of the village, and serves mountain specialties. The rooms, which all have a superb view, are very elegantly decorated. The hotel now has modern entertainment facilities and offers music and movie evenings.

How to get there *(Map 1): 27 km south of Aosta via S26 to Sarre, then S507.*

Hotel Herbetet

Valnontey 11012 Cogne (Aosta)
Tel. (0)165 74 180 - Fax (0)165 74 180
Sig. Carlo Cavagnet

Category ★★ **Rooms** 22 with bath or shower, WC. **Price** Single 35-40,000L, double 64-84,000L. **Meals** Breakfast 8,000L, served 7:30-9:30, half board 63-90,000L and full board 63-100,000L (per pers.). **Restaurant** Service 12:30-13:00, 19:30-20:00, closed Thu. in low season, menus 26,000L. (all incl.); also à la carte. Specialties: Fondue alla valdotena, Sosa. **Credit cards** All major. **Pets** Dogs not allowed. **Facilities** Parking at hotel. **Nearby** Alpine Garden of Valnontey, Gran Paradiso National Park. **Open** May 11 - Sep 1.

For those who love the mountains, Cogne is a strategic spot. At an altitude of 1,535 meters, you find yourself at the foot of the high mountains. Hiking in summer, cross-country skiing in winter, here you feel really close to nature. The greatest asset of the Hotel Herbetet is its view. Bedrooms, balconies and terraces face the majestic panorama of Gran Paradiso National Park. It is a little away from the village and from your room you may even catch a glimpse of the mountain goats that live protected in the park. Inside the hotel, everything is simple and comfortable, in a style some may find a bit too rustic. This is a good stop for anyone who feels like spending a few days in quiet communion with the mountains.

How to get there *(Map 1): 27 km south of Aosta via S26 to Sarre, then S 507.*

Hotel Petit Dahu

11012 Valnontey (Aosta)
Tel. (0)165 74 146 - Fax (0)165 74 146
Sig. and Sig.ra Cesare and Ivana Charruaz

Category ★★ **Rooms** 8 with telephone, shower, WC, (3 rooms with TV). **Price** 80-120,000L in half board (per pers.3 days min.). **Meals** Breakfast included served 8:00-10:00. **Restaurant** Service 19:30, menu 42,000L. Specialties: Carbonade, Fondutte, Raclette. **Credit cards** Visa, Eurocard, MasterCard. **Pets** Dogs not allowed. **Facilities** Parking at hotel. **Nearby** Alpine Garden of Valnontey, Gran Paradiso National Park. **Open** All year (except in May, Oct. and Nov.).

If you're not in the mood for the luxury of Cogne, you can lose yourself in this tiny hamlet of the Gran Paradiso National Park, as rustic as can be and consisting today only of hotels. In the heart of the village, two small houses linked by a little footbridge make up the Petit Dahu. A miniature hotel, with little rooms, a little garden and a little restaurant, it is for all its small size a place of warmth, well-kept and friendly. The owner can serve as guide if you want to hike through the valley or explore the park for marmots, deer and mountain goats, which have become quite tame in their protected environment. Excursions are proposed to Vittorio Sella, Roccia Viba or Becca di Gay, and when you return you can delight in the home cooking of Ivana, with local specialties like fondue and raclette. Once a week they organize (for a set price) a dinner by candlelight. This is a simple and convivial place.

How to get there *(Map 1): 27 km south of Aosta via S26 to Sarre, then S 507.*

La Grange

Strada La Brenva
Entrèves 11013 Courmayeur (Aosta)
Tel. (0)165-86 97 33 - Fax (0)165-86 97 44 - Sig. Berthod

Category ★★★ **Rooms** 23 with telephone, bath, WC, TV, radio and minibar. **Price** Single 100-150,000L, double 150-200,000L, suite (3-4 pers.) 300-400,000L. **Meals** Breakfast included, served 8:00-10:30. **Restaurant** See. p. 464. **Credit cards** All major. **Pets** Dogs allowed (5,000L). **Facilities** Sauna (15,000L), parking. **Nearby** Skiing, Ruitor Lake, cable car to Col du Géant and Aiguille du Midi; Val Veny and Val Ferret, Chamonix (in France), golf course (18-hole) in Chamonix, golf course (9-hole) in Plainpincieux. **Open** Dec. – end April, July – end Sept.

Despite its charm and its success, this small hotel has remained a little-known find. Hidden in what was once the depths of Val d'Aosta, at the foot of the Brenva glacier and Mont Blanc, it is today on the road of the tunnel that links Courmayeur to Chamonix. Fortunately, the village of Entreves, somewhat off the road, has not suffered from these intrusions and has remained an unspoiled mountain village. The interior of what was once an old barn has been beautifully restored and is warm and welcoming: antique furniture, old objects and engravings adorn the sitting room and the lovely breakfast room. (Breakfast, by the way, is absolutely delicious.) The rooms are comfortable, cozy and intimate. There is a possibility of a half-board arrangement with a restaurant 50 meters from the hotel (30,000 L. a meal).

How to get there *(Map 1): 20 km of Chamonix via the tunnel. 42 km west of Aosta via S26, Courmayeur, towards the Mont-Blanc tunnel.*

Hotel La Brenva

Entrèves 11013 Courmayeur (Aosta)
Tel. (0)165 869 780 - Fax (0)165 869 726
Sig. Egidio Biondi

Category ★★★ **Rooms** 14 with telephone, shower, WC, TV. **Price** Double 110-200,000L, suite 210-260,000L (4 pers.). **Meals** Breakfast included served 8:00-10:00. **Restaurant** Service 12:00-14:00, 19:30-21:00, closed Mon., menus 50-70 000L; also à la carte. Specialties: Regional cuisine. **Credit cards** All major. **Pets** Dogs allowed. **Facilities** Parking at hotel. **Nearby** Skiing, Ruitor Lake; cable car to "Col du Géant" and "Aiguille du midi"; cable car to Chécrouit; Val Veny and Val Ferret; Chamonix; 9-hole golf course in Chamonix. **Open** All year (except in May).

Located just at the base of the towering Mont Blanc, Entrèves combines the assets of a skiing resort with those of a little Alpine village. The inn has all the cozy atmosphere of a mountain chalet: thick stone walls, fireplaces, exposed beams. The rooms are paneled in wood and their balconies look out on the stunning Alpine peaks. It is rustic yet comfortable and in the evening it is an ideal retreat to rest and replenish your strength. The owner, an excellent cook, will introduce you to the local specialties, like the delicious meat dishes cooked over glowing coals. Gourmets take note.

How to get there *(Map 1): 20 km from Chamonix toward the Mont-Blanc tunnel; 42 km west of Aosta via S 26, Courmayeur, the Mont-Blanc tunnel road, Entrèves.*

Hotel Lo Scoiattolo

11020 Gressoney-la-Trinité (Aosta)
Tel. (0)125-366 313 - Fax. (0)125-366 220
Sig.ra Bethaz

Category ★★★ **Rooms** 14 with telephone, bath or shower, WC and TV. **Price** With half board 70-140,000L (per pers.). **Meals** Breakfast 15,000L, served 8:00-10:00 **Restaurant** For residents; service 13:00 and 19:30; menu, loval cooking. **Credit cards** Visa, Eurocard and MasterCard. **Pets** Dogs not allowed. **Facilities** Garage. **Nearby** Skiing, Mont Rosa. **Open** Dec. – April, June 25 – Sept.

Gressoney-la Trinité is the last in a string of villages in the Val d'Aoste at the foot of Mount Rose. Frequented mainly by Italian families and couples, this village has a very different atmosphere from the other more urbane resorts in the area, and the hotels here cater to the needs of their clientele. The nicest one is this small hotel run by Silvana and her two daughters. The rooms are large and well furnished. Every room is paneled in light wood, giving them a real mountain feel. Sig.ra Bethaz can sometimes be a little gruff, but she does see to it that everything in the hotel and the kitchen runs smoothly. This is a good hotel for an economical vacation.

How to get there *(Map 1): 100 km east of Aosta via A5, Pont-Saint-Martin exit, then S 505.*

Hotel dei Trulli

Via Cadore, 28
70011 Alberobello (Bari)
Tel. (0)80-932 35 55 - Fax (0)80-932 35 60
Sig. Farace

Category ★★★★★ **Rooms** 19 with air-conditioning, telephone, bath or shower, WC, TV and minibar. **Price** (with half board), single 170-200,000L, double 200-250,000L (per pers. 3 days min.). **Restaurant** Service 12:30-14:30, 19:30-22:30; menu 60,000L. Specialties: Orecchiette alla barese, purè di fave con cicoria, agnello Alberobellese. **Credit cards** All major. **Pets** Dogs allowed. **Facilities** Swimming pool, parking. **Nearby** Alberobello (Trulli district), Castel del Monte, Locorotondo, Martina Franca, Taranto (Museo Nazionale: Greek and Roman artifacts collection), Castellana Grotte. **Open** All year.

Alberobello is the world capital of *trulli,* cute little houses which, at first glance, might remind you of the ones the dwarves live in at Disneyland, but they are, in fact, authentic old houses, typical of the region. The hotel is entirely made up of recently built trulli, which imitate the local style; each one is freshly whitewashed and has an arbor, one or two rooms, and a small living room with a fireplace. They are all charming, comfortable, and air-conditioned. The restaurant is in the main building. The hotel swimming pool is not very attractive, but you will really appreciate it on hot summer days.

How to get there *(Map 22): 55 km southeast of Bari via S100 to Casamàssima, then S172 to Putignano and Alberobello.*

Il Melograno

Contrada Torricella, 345
70043 Monopoli (Bari)
Tel. (0)80-690 90 30 - Fax (0)80-74 79 08 - Sig. Guerra

Category ★★★★★ **Rooms** 37 with air-conditioning, telephone, bath or shower, WC, cable TV and minibar. **Price** Single 240-360,000L, double 360-600,000L, suite 670-930,000L. **Meals** Breakfast included, served 7:30-11:30; half board 240-360,000L, full board 280-400,000L. (per pers., 3 days min.). **Restaurant** Service 12:30-14:30, 20:00-22:30; menu 80,000L. Specialties: Salmone affumicato in casa, agnello al forno. **Credit cards** All major. **Pets** Dogs not allowed. **Facilities** Swimming pool, tennis, health-center with indoor swimming pool , parking. **Nearby** Ruins of Egnazia, Alberobello (Trulli district), Castel del Monte, Locorotondo, Martina Franca, Tàranto (Museo Nazionale: Greek and Roman artifacts collection), Castellana Grotte. **Open** All year (except Jan. 7 - Apr. 4).

Here, in the hot region of Apulia, is an oasis of coolness, greenery and taste. Il Melograno was originally a sharecropper's fortified farmhouse from the 16th century. It is surrounded by a maze of white buildings which blend in with bouganvilleas, and olive, lemon, and pomegranate trees. Formerly a vacation house, it has been transformed into a hotel but has kept its characteristic personal touch. The rooms are very elegant, with their antique furniture and paintings, beautiful fabrics and traditional *cotto* (ceramic tile) floors. The salons seem lost in the orange grove seen through a picture window. The dining room-veranda, where you'll dine under a white canopy next to an ancient olive tree, is on the other side of the garden. The hosts are very nice. Note that sometimes there are seminars which can disturb guests.

How to get there *(Map 22): 50 km south of Bari, 3 km from Monopoli towards Alberobello.*

Villa Cenci

(Via per Ceglie Messapica)
72014 Cisternino (Brindisi)
Tel. (0)80-71 82 08 - Fax (0)80-71 82 08
Sig.ra Bianco

Category ★★★ **Rooms** 25 with telephone, bath or shower and WC. **Price** Double 120-160,000L. **Meals** Breakfast 10,000L, served 8:30-10:30. **Restaurant** Service 13:00-14:30, 20:00-22:00; menu 30,000L. Specialties: Italian and regional cooking. **Credit cards** Visa, Eurocard and MasterCard. **Pets** Dogs allowed. **Facilities** Swimming pool, parking. **Nearby** Alberobello (Trulli district), Castel del Monte, Locorotondo, Martina Franca, Tàranto (Museo Nazionale: Greek and Roman artifacts collection), Castellana Grotte. **Open** April – Sept.

Far from the hordes of tourists in this very busy region, this agricultural estate will host you for a very modest price. The beautiful white house, isolated among the grapevines, offers its guests tranquility, which you will feel this as you walk along the paths lined with white laurels. It is surrounded by *trulli,* conic constructions typical of Apulia; those here have cool rooms with simple, tasteful decor. In the villa itself there are other more classical rooms, as well as several functional small apartments. The hotel is frequented by numerous Italian and English regulars. From the swimming pool you can have a nice view of the countryside. The fruit and vegetables served at meals are fresh from the garden, and the wine is "home made."

How to get there *(Map 22): 74 km southeast of Bari via SS16, coast to Fasano, then S172 to Laureto (towards Cisternino).*

1998

Masseria Marzalossa

C.da Pezze Vicine, 65
72015 Fasano (Brindisi)
Tel. (0)80 44 13 780 - Fax (0)80 44 13 780 - Sig.Mario Guarini

Rooms 6 and 1 suite with bath, WC, TV and fridge. **Price** Single 180-220,000L, double 260-280,000L. **Meals** Breakfast included served 8:30-9:30, half board 150-170,000L in double room, 200-250,000L in suite (per pers., 3 day min.). **Restaurant** Service 20:00-21:00; menus 50-60,000L. Specialties: Regional cooking. **Credit cards** Visa, Eurocard, MasterCard. **Pets** Dogs not allowed. **Facilities** Swimming pool, bicycles, parking. **Nearby** Ruins of Egnazia, Alberobello, Locorotondo, Martina Franca, Tàranto, Castellana Grotto. **Open** Apr. - end Sep.

An exceptional site, lost in the middle of an olive grove, not far from Ostuni and Fasano with its strange local architecture typical of Puglia. A fortified 17th-century farmhouse, it has been subtly and tastefully restored. The house is built around several patios: one planted with orange trees, one with lemon trees, and one with a swimming pool entirely surrounded by columns. The dimensions are modest and the atmosphere intimate. The masseria has only a few apartments, elegant and well-decorated with period furniture. Once owned by an ecclesiastical family, it still has traces of that past, which lend a somewhat mysterious air. You will also enjoy the wonderful local cooking based on the produce of the estate: an outstanding olive oil and delicious home-made jams for breakfast. The isolation of the place is part of its charm and you may wish to stay put and savor it. But you can easily explore the region - for a modest price, the owners can put a boat at your disposal, or another means of transport, if you wish.

How to get there *(Map 22): 60 km southwest of Bari via SS 379, Bari-North exit. Towards Brindisi, Fasano exit, 2 km towards SS 16, Ostoni exit.*

Masseria San Domenico

72010 Savelletri di Fasano (Brindisi)
Tel. (0)80 955 79 90 - Fax (0)80 955 79 78
Sig.Gianni Chervatin

Rooms 31 and 1 suite with air-conditioning, bath or shower, WC, satellite TV, minibar. **Price** Single 150-210,000L, double 320-420,000L, suite on request. **Meals** Breakfast 15,000L, served 7:30-10:30, half board +45,000L and full board +75,000L (per pers., 3 day min.). **Restaurant** Service 12:30-14:00, 19:30-22:00, closed Tue., menus 75-110,000L. Specialties: Local cooking. **Credit cards** All Major. **Pets** Dogs not allowed. **Facilities** Swimming pool, bicycles, golf, sauna (25,000L), parking. **Nearby** Ruins of Egnazia, Alberobello, Locorotondo, Martina Franca, Tàranto, Castellana Grotte; golf course (18-hole) in Riva dei Tessali, Castellaneta-Taranto. **Open** Mar. 22 - Jan. 7.

This is one of the finest examples of a fortified farmhouse in the entire Puglia region. Between the 15th and 17th centuries the landowners built these masserie a torre with surrounding walls, moats and sentry posts as protection against the pirates who used to attack this coast. The San Domenico has been wonderfully restored and furnished and the result is splendid, notably the vast room that serves as living- dining- and billiard-room all in one. Bedrooms and apartments are tasteful and comfortable. There are good recreational facilities available on the spot. As for the surroundings, various excursions are possible: The beach is 800 meters away, there are walks in the Murgia hills and cultural sightseeing in the historic hinterland.

How to get there *(Map 22): 60 km southwest of Bari via the superstrada 379, Torre Canne exit, towards Saveletti.*

Hotel Sierra Silvana

72010 Selva di Fasano (Brindisi)
Tel. (0)80-933 13 22
Fax (0)80-933 12 07

Rooms 120 with air-conditioning, telephone, bath and WC. **Price** Double 130-170,000L. **Meals** Breakfast 11,000L, served 7:00-10:00; half board 95-103,000L, full board 158-173,000L (per pers.). **Restaurant** Service 12:30-14:00, 19:30-21:00; menu 40,000L, also à la carte. Specialties: Italian and regional cooking. **Credit cards** All major. **Pets** Dogs not allowed. **Facilities** Swimming pool, parking. **Nearby** Ruins of Egnazia near by Monopoli, Alberobello (Trulli district), Castel del Monte, Locorotondo, Martina Franca, Tàranto (Museo Nazionale: Greek and Roman artifacts collection), Castellana Grotte, golf course (18-hole) in Riva dei Tessali. **Open** March 25 – Nov. 5.

The Hotel Sierra Silvana is built around an imposing old *trulli* (a conical structure common to the Apulia region). In many primitive societies, social status was reflected in the size of the dwelling. Someone important must have lived in this one, because it is enormous, with enough space for four rooms. There is a great demand for these simple and elegantly decorated rooms. The other rooms are in more modern buildings, and are quiet and comfortable; all have a balcony on the garden. The hotel is well equipped for receptions, but the staff ensures that guests are not disturbed. Located 30 miles (50 km) from Brindisi, this hotel is an interesting stopover on your way to Greece.

How to get there *(Map 22): 60 km southeast of Bari.*

1998

Grand Hotel Masseria Santa Lucia

Ostuni Marina 72017 Ostuni (Brindisi)
Tel. (0)831 33 04 18 - Fax (0)831 30 40 90
Sig. Bartolo d'Amico

Category ★★★★ **Rooms** 88 and 4 suites with air-conditioning, telelephone, bath or shower, WC, satellite TV, minibar, safe, hairdryer. **Price** Single 150-260,000L, double 190-300,000L, triple 230-370,000L. **Meals** Breakfast included, served 7:30-9:30, half board 125-215,000L and full board 140-240,000L (per pers., 7 day min.). **Restaurant** Service 12:30-15:30, 19:30-22:00; menus 50,000L; also à la carte. Specialties: Regional cooking, Fish. **Credit cards** All major. **Pets** Dogs not allowed. **Facilities** Swimming pool, tennis, archery, piano bar, parking at hotel. **Nearby** Carovigno, Martina Franca, Alberobello and Castellana cellars, Ceglie Messapico. **Open** All year.

Ostuni is undoubtedly one of the wonders of Puglia. The town, perched high on its hilltop, has preserved a vague hint of Iberia, a leftover from its period of Spanish domination. Down below, some 500 meters from the sea, the very modern Masseria Santa Lucia has tried to recover this ancient charm. Built like a small hacienda, the hotel has within its walls a swimming pool and a little Gallo-Roman theater, in which shows and concerts are held in summer. The decor is resolutely "modern design" and can be quite attractive, unless you are completely allergic to that rather bare, cold style. Each bedroom has a little terrace, protected by a hedge. Ask for a room overlooking the swimming pool and a view of the sea. Ambitious building projects are still going on, which will eventually extend the complex as far as the seafront. For the moment, the place feels rather like a building site, and the beach, which could be sumptuous, is not always as clean as one might expect.

How to get there *(Map 22): 25 km from Brindisi; 7 km from Ostuni.*

1998

Lo Spagnulo

Rosa Marina 72017 Ostuni (Brindisi)
Tel. (0)831 35 02 09 - Fax (0)831 33 37 56
Prof. Livino Massari

Rooms 35 with shower. **Price** Single 60-90,000L, double 80-140,000L, suite 120-160,000L. **Meals** Breakfast 6,000L. served 8:30-11:00; half board 65-95,000L (per pers.). **Restaurant** Service 13:00-14:30, 20:00-22:30, menus 30,000L; also à la carte. Specialties: Purè de fave e cicorie, pasta e ceci, Arrosto misto alla brace, coniglio alla cacciatora. **Credit cards** Amex, Visa, Eurocard, MasterCard. **Pets** Small dogs allowed. **Facilities** Tennis, riding (15,000L/h), archery, bicycle, parking at hotel. **Nearby** Carovigno, Ceglie Messapico. **Open** All year.

Ostuni, in the heart of Puglia, is as enchanting as it is unexpected. All the local homes are whitewashed every year, and the sparkling white facades add to the town's already Andalusian air. The Castello Lo Spagnulo, at the gates of the village, is an exceptional place. Built in 1600 by Don Savario Lopez, the governor of the region (in the name of the Spanish crown), it is a veritable little fortified castle that contains within its walls a church, a beautifully-kept garden redolent of wisteria and orange blossoms, and a noble mansion converted into a hotel. The old rustic style has been well-preserved, with bare stone walls, exposed beams, impressive fireplaces and wrought iron bedsteads. The nicest rooms are those inside the walls. One small drawback is that the owner, Livino Massari (a charming local nobleman) has chosen to make this into a popular restaurant. People from the area come and dine to the sound of traditional melodies. It's convivial, a bit noisy and the service is none too careful.

How to get there *(Map 22): 25 km from Brindisi; 4.5 km from Ostuni.*

Hotel Villa Ducale

Piazzetta Sant'Antonio
74015 Martina Franca (Taranto)
Tel. (0)80-70 50 55 - Fax (0)80-70 58 85
Sig. A. Sforza

Category ★★★★ **Rooms** 24 with telephone, bath or shower, WC and minibar. **Price** Single 95,000L, double 140,000L, suite 160,000L. **Meals** Breakfast included, served 7:30-11:30. **Restaurant** Service 12:30-14:30, 20:00-22:00; menu 40,000L, also à la carte. Specialties: Regional cooking **Credit cards** All major. **Pets** Dogs allowed. **Nearby** In Martina Franca: Piazza Roma (Palazzo Ducale), Ruins of Egnazia near by Monopoli, Alberobello (Trulli district), Castel del Monte, Locorotondo, Martina Franca, Tàranto (Museo Nazionale: Greck and Roman artifacts collection), Castellana Grotte, golf course (18-hole) in Riva dei Tessali. **Open** All year.

Like all of the hotels in town, the Villa Ducale has gone the modern road. The building itself is unappealing but wel located, close to the old town and next to a large public garden and a 16th-century convent. Once inside, however, you will forget all about the facade; the decor is very avant-garde, and the lobby, the bar and the rooms all have a designer look. The hotel is pretty incongruous but very comfortable. Ask for the corner rooms (105, 205, 305) which have two windows and are very light, though sometimes a little noisy despite the double-panes. Be sure to visit the splendid Ducal palace. The entire town has interesting architecture, though it is off the beaten tourist track and you will need to stay here awhile to appreciate it.

How to get there *(Map 22): 74 km southeast of Bari via S100, Locorotondo and Martina Franca.*

Hotel Hieracon

Isola di San Pietro
Corso Cavour, 62
09014 Carloforte (Cagliari)
Tel. (0)781-85 40 28 - Fax (0)781-85 48 93 - Sig. Ferrando

Category ★★★ **Rooms** 17 and 7 suites with air-conditioning, telephone, shower, WC, TV and minibar. **Price** Single 80,000L, double 130,000L, triple 162,000L. **Meals** Breakfast 6,000L, served 8:30-10:30; half board 105,000L, full board 130,000L. (per pers., 3 days min.). **Restaurant** Service 12:30-14:00, 19:30-21:30; menus 30,000L. Specialties: Italian and regional cuisine. **Credit cards** Amex, Visa, Eurocard, MasterCard. **Pets** Small dogs allowed. **Nearby** Beach (2 km), boat rentals. **Open** All year.

The Hotel Hieracon is located in San Pietro, a pretty little island with a rocky coastline dotted with inlets and beaches. This lovely Art Nouveau-style building is right on the port. The interior is a blend of light tile work and pastel colors. We recommend the rooms on the second floor, which have nice turn-of-the-century furniture. The ones on the other floors are darker and less comfortable. Behind the hotel there is a large terraced garden set in the shade of a tall palm tree. Four small ground floor apartments open onto the garden. The restaurant is superb with its black flagstones and its curving mezzanine which looks like the bridge of an old pre-war ocean liner. Ths cuisine is good and features typical island dishes. Dr. Ferrando will make you feel at home.

How to get there *(Map 28): 77 km west of Cagliarii via SS 130 to Portoscuro; ferry service from Porto Vesme (40 min.).*

Pensione Paola e Primo Maggio

Isola di San Pietro
Tacca Rossa
09014 Carloforte (Cagliari)
Tel. (0)781-85 00 98 - Sig. Ferraro

Category ★★ **Rooms** 21 with shower and WC. **Price** Double 60-120,000L. **Meals** Breakfast 5,500L, served 8:00-11:00; half board 65-95,000L, full board 70-110,000L. (per pers.). **Restaurant** Service 13:00-14:30, 19:00-23:00, à la carte. Specialties: Seafood. **Credit cards** Amex, Visa, Eurocard and MasterCard. **Pets** Dogs not allowed. **Nearby** Beach (2 km), boat rentals. **Open** April 16 – Oct.

The Pensione Paola, about a mile and a half from Carloforte, faces the sea and offers rooms–at very reasonable prices–which all enjoy the beautiful maritime view. In the main house, a restaurant with a large shady terrace serves fine, solid cuisine featuring many dishes typical of the island. Rooms 7, 8, and 9 are our favorites, as they are more modern and comfortable than the others. Downstairs, there are two garden-level rooms which are just as nice as the other three in a bungalow nearby.

How to get there *(Map 28): 77 km west of Cagliari via SS130 to Portoscuro; ferry services from Porto Vesme (40 min.) - 3 km north of Carloforte.*

Club Ibisco Farm

Isola di Sant'Antioco
09017 Capo Sperone (Cagliari)
Tel. (0)781-80 90 18 / (0)041-91 52 59 39 - Fax (0)781-80 90 03
Sig.ra Naef

Rooms 8 with telephone, shower, WC, TV and minibar. **Price** Single 150-230,000L, double 250-400,000L, triple 350-600,000L, apartment 450-680,000L. **Meals** Breakfast included, served 8:30-10:00; half board 150-230,000L (per pers., 7 days min.). **Restaurant** Service 20:30; menus. Specialties: Regional cuisine, seafood. **Credit cards** Visa, Eurocard and MasterCard. **Pets** Dogs not allowed. **Facilities** Tennis (25,000L at night), riding, boating, parking. **Nearby** Beach (100 m), museum and Tophet in San Antioco, Calasetta. **Open** June 19 – Sept. 18.

The Club Ibisco Farm is a nicely restored old farm on a vast 247-acre estate, overlooking the ocean. The owners, who love this unspoiled island, spend several months a year in this beautiful, wild setting. You will have a superb 17-meter wooden motor-sailboat, horses, a soccer field, and a tennis court at your disposal. The absolutely delicious dinners are made from produce and wine from the estate, and the fresh fish is caught daily. Meals are served outside around a big common table made of wood. Among the different rooms, we prefer the suite for three people and the apartment for four, which are light and spacious. The others are quite comfortable and quiet.

How to get there *(Map 28): 95 km west of Cagliari via SS136 to Sant'Antioco, then via coast towards Capo Sperone (1 km after Peonia Rosa); Cagliari airport (private bus to and from the hotel: 100,000L per pers.).*

Is Morus Hotel

09010 Santa Margherita di Pula (Cagliari)
Tel. (0)70-92 11 71 - Fax (0)70-92 15 96
Sig.ra Ketzer

Category ★★★★ **Rooms** 83 with air-conditioning, telephone, bath or shower, WC, TV and minibar. **Price** With half board 190-340,000L (per pers.). **Meals** Breakfast included, served 7:30-10:00. **Restaurant** Service 13:00-14:30, 20:00-21:30; menus: 60-80,000L. Specialties: Italian and regional cuisine, seafood. **Credit cards** All major. **Pets** Small dogs allowed. **Facilities** Swimming pool, tennis, miniature golf, private beach, parking. **Nearby** Nora (ancient city: ruins of temples, amphitheater, Roman theater, mosaic pavement); Is Molas golf course (18-hole) at S. Margherita di Pula. **Open** April – Jan.

Just like the Costa Smeralda, the coast south of Cagliari has been experiencing a boom in beach construction. The Is Morus is in Santa Margherita di Pula, right next to the golf course. It is a luxury hotel with a marvelous location, in the middle of a pine forest and on the superb turquoise-blue sea. Some of the rooms are in villas set in the cool shade of pine trees, something very rare in this part of Sardinia. The other rooms are in the main house, a low building with white walls, which looks like a large Spanish villa.

How to get there *(Map 28): 37 km southwest of Cagliari via the coast (S195) to Santa Margherita (6.5 km from Pula).*

Hotel Su Gologone

Sorgente Su Gologone
08025 Oliena (Nuoro)
Tel. (0)784-28 75 12 - Fax (0)784-28 76 68
Famiglia Palimodde

Category ★★★★ **Rooms** 65 with air-conditioning, telephone, bath or shower, WC and TV (20 with minibar). **Price** Single 105-170,000L, double 170-220,000L. **Meals** Breakfast included, served 8:00-9:30; half board 145-175,000L, full board 175-220,000L (per pers., 3 days min.). **Restaurant** Service 12:30-15:00, 20:00-23:00; menu: 60,000L, also à la carte. Specialties: Sardinian cuisine, seafood. **Credit cards** Amex, Visa, Eurocard and MasterCard. **Pets** Dogs allowed. **Facilities** Swimming pool, tennis (15,000L), riding, parking. **Nearby** Sorgente su Gologone, Chapel of San Lussurgiu at Oliena. **Open** April – Oct. and Dec.

The main attraction of Sardinia is its coast, but the beautiful inland part really deserves more than a quick detour. The Su Gologone has it all, located about 12 miles from the coast between Dorgali and Oliean, at the foot of superb rocky mountains, the Supramonten. The famous hotel restaurant, open since 1961, serves excellent regional cuisine. The architecture of the hotel, inspired by the houses in Oliena, is a great achievement. The interior has been decorated with uncommon taste, with old exposed beams complementing the beautiful antique furniture and the paintings by Biasi, a talented Sardinian painter. The rooms are all different and very pleasant. The spring-fed swimming pool is splendid. The hotel organizes numerous excursions on horseback or by Land Rover in the surrounding area. The staff is very friendly.

How to get there *(Map 28): 20 km southeast of Nuoro to Oliena, then towards Dorgali. Follow signs.*

Villa Las Tronas

07041 Alghero (Sassari)
Lungomare Valencia, 1
Tel. (0)79-98 18 18 - Fax (0)79-98 10 44

Category ★★★★ **Rooms** 29 with air-conditioning, telephone, bath or shower, WC, TV, safe and minibar; elevator. **Price** Single 200-230,000L, double 240-360,000L. **Meals** Breakfast 15-22,000L, served 7:30-9:30; half board 170-240,000L, full board 220-300,000L. **Restaurant** Service 13:00-14:30, 20:00-21:30; menus 60-70,000L, also à la carte. Specialties: Sardinian cuisine, seafood. **Credit cards** All major. **Pets** Dogs not allowed. **Facilities** Swimming pool (sea water), private beach, gym, bikes, parking. **Nearby** Cathedral in Alghero, Grotto of Neptune, heights of Capo Caccia, Porto Conte, Route 129 from Nuoro to Bosa. **Open** All year.

The Villa Las Tronas, surrounded by very well kept garden, is on a small peninsula overlooking the Gulf of Alghero. Once a vacation spot for Italian kings during their visits to Sardinia, this unusual Moorish-style building is today a hotel with a Baroque atmosphere created by vast rooms with painted ceilings and gleaming chandeliers, and numerous salons of different colors. The spacious, high-ceilinged rooms are all on the sea and have every modern comfort. Rooms 110, 112, 114, 116, 118, and 216 are the nicest ones, with a very large common terrace from which you can take in the superb panoramic view. You can enjoy the same view in the lovely dining room. There is a pretty swimming pool, with access to the sea. The style and presence of the personnel contribute to the elegant atmosphere of this hotel.

***How to get there** (Map 28): 35 km southwest of Sassari via S291 to Alghero.*

Hotel Li Capanni

Cannigione
07020 Arzachena (Sassari)
Tel. (0)789-86 041 - Fax (0)789-86 200
Sig. Pagni

Category ★★★ **Rooms** 23 and 2 suites with shower and WC. **Price** With half board 135-235,000L (per pers.). **Meals** Breakfast included. **Restaurant** For residents; service 13:00-14:00, 20:30-21:00; menus: 30-35,000L. Specialties: Sardinian and Italian cuisine. **Credit cards** Not accepted. **Pets** Dogs not allowed. **Facilities** Private beach, parking. **Nearby** Tombe di Giganti (giants' tombs) and ancient city of Li Muri, San Pantaleo, Pevero golf course (18-hole) in Porto Cervo. **Open** May 1 – Oct.

Go up a dirt road about one mile, and suddenly, as if by magic, you will find yourself far from the throngs of the Costa Smeralda (where the environment is nonetheless protected and campgrounds restricted). The Hotel Li Capanni aspires to be more of a club than a hotel, to highlight its unigueness and preserve its tranquility. It is on a very lovely site facing the archipelago of the Maddalena Islands, overlooking the sea. The small ochre houses are scattered here and there on ten-acre grounds which slope gently down to the sea and a very pretty, private beach. The rooms are simply decorated and comfortable. The dining room and salons are grouped in the main building. The dining room overlooks the bay and is very inviting with its small blue wood tables and chairs. A cozy salon looks just like the living room of a private home. For security reasons, the hotel does not accept children under 14.

How to get there *(Map 28): 32 km north of Olbia via S 125 towards Arzachena, then via the coast towards Palau to Cannigione; the hotel is 3.5 km after Cannigione.*

Hotel Don Diego

Costa Dorata
07020 Porto San Paolo (Sassari)
Tel. (0)789-40 006 - Fax (0)789-40 026

Category ★★★★ **Rooms** 50 and 6 suites with air-conditioning, telephone, bath or shower, WC and TV. **Price** Double 300-500,000L. **Meals** Breakfast 25,000L, served 8:00-10:00; half board 200-390,000L (per pers.). **Restaurant** Service 12:30-14:00, 20:00-21:30; menus 70-80,000L, also à la carte. Specialties: Sardinian cuisine, seafood. **Credit cards** All major. **Pets** Dogs not allowed. **Facilities** Swimming pool (sea water), tennis, beach, parking. **Nearby** Church San Simplicio in Olbia, Tavolara Island. **Open** All year.

Located south of Olbia, the Hotel Don Diego is a series of small villas facing the sea, scattered among beautiful bouganvilleas and pine trees. Each one has a separate entry and six to eight rooms, and there's a pleasant coolness inside. The reception area, bar, restaurant, and salons are located in the closest house to the water. You will also find a sea-water swimming pool and a sand beach here. Just across from the hotel is Tavolara Island, an impressive rocky spur jutting into the clear blue water. The Don Diego is a great place for a family vacation.

How to get there *(Map 28): 16 km southeast of Olbia via S125 until just after Porto San Paolo, then turn left towards the Costa Dorata coast.*

Hotel Cala di Volpe

Porto Cervo
07020 Cala di Volpe (Sassari)
Tel. (0)789-97 61 11 - Fax (0)789-97 66 17
Sig. Paterlini

Category ★★★★★ **Rooms** 123 with air-conditioning, telephone, bath, WC, TV, safe and minibar. **Price** With half board 300-700,000L, and full board 335-740,000L. **Restaurant** On request; service 13:00-14:30, 20:00-22:00. Specialties: Italian cuisine, seafood. **Pets** Dogs not allowed. **Facilities** Swimming pool, Fitness Centre, putting-green, private beach, private port, parking. **Nearby** Costa Smeralda, Tombe di Giganti (giants' tombs) and ancient city of Li Muri, San Pantaleo, Pevero golf course (18-hole) in Porto Cervo. **Open** All year (except Oct. 19 - Feb. 6).

Thirty years ago, Prince Karim Agha Khan and a group of international financiers decided to build luxury hotel complexes in la Gallura, this beautiful wild region of rolling hills and valleys, and called it Costa Smeralda. The buildings are a sort of cocktail of Mediterranean architectural styles–Spanish, Moorish, and Provençale. The most famous hotel in the region, the Cala di Volpe faces an enchanting bay, and was designed by a French architect, Jacques Couelle. He used a medieval village as a model, inspired by its towers and terraces, arcades and granite passageways. The interior is decorated in the same motif, but with all the modern comfort you could want. The gigantic pool, private port, and impeccable service make this a unique place.

How to get there *(Map 28): 25 km north of Olbia via S125, then towards Porto Cervo to Abbiadori and take a right towards Capriccioli to Cala di Volpe.*

Hotel Le Ginestre

07020 Porto Cervo (Sassari)
Tel. (0)789-92 030 - Fax (0)789-94 087
Sig. Costa

Category ★★★★ **Rooms** 78 with air-conditioning, telephone, bath or shower, WC, TV and minibar. **Price** With half board 175-340,000L, full board +45,000L (per pers.). **Meals** Breakfast included, served 8:00-10:30. **Restaurant** Service 13:00-14:30, 20:00-22:00. Specialties: Seafood. **Credit cards** All major. **Pets** Dogs not allowed. **Facilities** Swimming pool, tennis (35,000L), private beach, parking. **Nearby** Costa Smeralda, Tombe di Giganti (giants' tombs) and ancient city of Li Muri, San Pantaleo, Pevero golf course (18-hole) in Porto Cervo. **Open** May – Sept. or Oct. 15.

There are luxury hotels on the Costa Smeralda which are more affordable than the Ginestre, but not all of them have its charm. The rooms are in a series of small villas at the edge of a pine forest, slightly overhanging the Gulf of Pevero. It looks like a small hamlet, with its tangle of little streets on grounds with fragrant bushes and trees with brightly colored flowers typical of the Mediterrranean region. As is common in this area, the Neo-Realist architecture recalls Tuscan villages with their faded ochre facades. The rooms have pretty furniture, and most of them have balconies. A little off to one side, under a large thatched suncreen, there is a pleasant restaurant. Because of the number of rooms, the hotel loses in intimacy what it gains in atmosphere.

How to get there *(Map 28): 30 km north of Olbia via S125, towards Porto Cervo.*

Hotel Romazzino

Porto Cervo
07020 Romazzino (Sassari)
Tel. (0)789-97 71 11 - Fax (0)789-96 258

Category ★★★★★ **Rooms** 91 with air-conditioning, telephone, bath or shower, WC, TV and minibar. **Price** With half board 580-1,540,000L, full board 640-1,20,000L (2 pers., 3 days min.). **Meals** Breakfast included, served 7:30-10:30. **Restaurant** Service 13:00-14:30, 20:00-22:00; menu. Specialties: Italian and international cuisine. **Credit cards** All major. **Pets** Dogs not allowed. **Facilities** Swimming pool, tennis, private beach, parking. **Nearby** Costa Smeralda, Arcipelago di la Maddalena, Tombe di Giganti (giants' tombs) and ancient city of Li Muri, San Pantaleo, Pevero golf course (18-hole) in Porto Cervo. **Open** Apr. 23 – Oct. 12.

Next door to "Medieval village," the Romazzino, with its white walls, vaulted windows, and pink tiles, looks like an Andeluvian–if not Mexican–village. It looks magical when you see it from the road as you arrive, its superb silhouette rising in front of the sea. The Romazzino is a quiet hotel–a great place for resting and enjoying the sea. The fine sand beach is superb. A delicious barbecue awaits you at lunchtime. The interior is all curves, and gives the impression of sumptuous caverns or imaginary palaces. The bar is unique with a floor inlayed with juniper trunks. All the rooms are perfect and have private terraces. This dreamy place is all about the pleasures of the sea.

How to get there *(Map 28): 25 km north of Olbia via S125, then towards Porto Cervo to Abbiadoni, then turn right towards Capriccioli to Cala di Volpe - Romazzino is after Capriccioli.*

El Faro

Porto Conte
07041 Alghero (Sassari)
Tel. (0)79-94 20 10 - Fax (0)79-94 20 30
Sig. Sarno

Category ★★★★ **Rooms** 92 with air-conditioning, telephone, bath or shower, WC, TV and minibar. **Price** Single 150-280,000L, double 240-420,000L. **Meals** Breakfast included, served 7:30-10:00; half board 135-247,000L, full board +45,000L. (per pers., 3 days min.). **Restaurant** Service 13:00-14:00, 20:00-21:30; menu 70,000L, also à la carte. Specialties: Lobsters, seafood. **Credit cards** All major. **Pets** Dogs allowed except in restaurant and on the beach. **Facilities** Swimming pool, tennis, sauna (25,000L), parking. **Nearby** Cathedral in Alghero, Grotto of Neptune, heights of Capo Caccia, Route 129 from Nuoro to Bosa. **Open** April – Oct.

This hotel is superbly located on a small peninsula next to an old lighthouse, facing Cap Caccia with it famous Neptune caverns. The view encompasses all of the splendid Gulf with its banks almost totally unspoiled by construction. This large, ninety-two room hotel is a special place, thanks to the quality of the service and the simple, well-planned Mediterranean decor. All the rooms have a balcony and a view of the sea, with white walls brightened by engravings of nautical themes, wooden furniture, and pretty bathrooms. Down below, between several terraces, there is a superb semi-covered swimming pool overlooking the waves, and a little further beyond, a beach among the rocks. This is a luxury hotel which is still affordable.

How to get there *(Map 28): 41 km southwest of Sassari via S291 to Alghero and S127 bis to Porto Conte.*

Villa Athena

Via dei Templi
92100 Agrigento
Tel. (0)922-59 62 88 - Fax (0)922-40 21 80
Sig. Montalbano

Category ★★★★ **Rooms** 40 with air-conditioning, telephone, bath or shower, WC and TV. **Price** Single 150,000L, double 250-300,000L. **Meals** Breakfast included, served 7:30-10:00; half board 290,000L, full board 330,000L (per 2 pers., 3 days min.). **Restaurant** Service 12:30-14:30, 19:30-22:00; menu 40,000L, also à la carte. Specialties: Involtini di pesce spado, cavatelli Villa Athena, pesce fresco. **Credit cards** All major. **Pets** Dogs not allowed. **Facilities** Swimming pool, parking. **Nearby** In Agrigento: Valley of the Temples, birthhouse of Luigi Pirandello; Naro, Palma di Montechiano. **Open** All year.

Be sure to stop off at Agrigento and visit the Valley of the Temples, an epicenter of archaeology if ever there was one. Once you are there, you will see that there is only one hotel which has any charm: the Villa Athena. This old 18th-century villa used to belong to a prince and has recently been very well renovated. It enjoys an exceptional location, across from the Concord Temple; the view is best from Room 205. The rooms and bathrooms are functional and comfortable. A large salon opens onto the terrace and the temple. The swimming pool is very pleasant.

How to get there *(Map 26): 2 km south of Agrigento towards "Valle dei Templi."*

Foresteria Baglio della Luna

Contrada Maddalusa - Valle de' Templi
92100 Agrigento
Tel. (0)922 51 10 61 - Fax (0)922 59 88 02
Sig. Alfieri

Categoty ★★★★ **Rooms** 24 with air-conditioning, telephone, bath or shower, WC, TV, minibar. **Price** Single 235,000L, double 380,000L, suite 48-680,000L. **Meals** Breakfast included served 7:30-10:30; half board +60,000L and full board +90,000L (per pers., 2 day min.). **Restaurant** Service 13:00-14:30, 19:30-22:30, menus 65-70,000L, also à la carte. Specialties: Pesce. **Credit cards** Amex, Visa, Eurocard, MasterCard. **Pets** Small dogs allowed. **Facilities** Parking. **Nearby** In Agrigento: Valley of the Temples, birthhouse of Luigi Pirandello; Naro, Palma di Montechiaro. **Open** All year.

If you want to visit the Valley of the Temples without being encircled by the rather wild urban development of Agrigento, the Foresteria can offer a nice retreat. Outside of town and in the heart of an archeological site, this 13th-century tower was transformed into a country house in the 18th century. Today it is a hotel, but with its thick stone surrounding walls, it looks like an old walled inn. The rooms still have a "too new" smell from the latest renovation and the "antique" furniture is not always genuine, but the comfort is there, complete with air-conditioning, a delightful element after sightseeing in these arid valleys. From the hotel, you can see the temples on the surrounding hills, even more poetic when viewed at sunset. The restaurant does a tasty and refined interpretation of Sicilian cooking.

How to get there *(Map 26): 2 km south of Agrigento (south coast); toward "Valley dei Templi" and SS 115, towards Trapani.*

Grand Hotel Villa Igiea

Via Belmonte, 43
90142 Palermo
Tel. (0)91-54 37 44 - Fax (0)91-54 76 54 - Sig. Ternullo

Category ★★★★★ **Rooms** 115 with air-conditioning, telephone, bath, WC, TV and minibar, elevator; wheelchair access. **Price** Single 241,000L, double 367,000L, suite 800,000L. **Meals** Breakfast included, served 7:00-10:00; half board 247,000L, full board 283,000L (per pers., 3 days min.). **Restaurant** Service 12:30-14:30, 19:30-22:30; menu 80,000L, also à la carte. Specialties: Pennette alla lido, spada al forno. **Credit cards** All major. **Pets** Dogs allowed in rooms. **Facilities** Swimming pool, tennis, parking. **Nearby** In Palermo: Church of Martorana, del Gesu church, Palazzo dei Normanni (Norman Royal Palace), Church of San Giovanni degli Eremiti, S. Francesco d'Assisi, Oratorio S. Lorenzo, Regional Archeological Museum, Palazzo Abatellis (Annunciation by Antonello da Messina); Mondello, Villa Palagonia in Bagheria, Solonte, Piana degli Albanesi, Cefalù. **Open** All year.

A superb example of Art Nouveau-style, the Villa Igiea is certainly the most beautiful hotel in the west of Sicily, and its location allows it to escape from the hustle and bustle of Palermo. It's hard to find fault with this grand hotel which has kept its period furniture and decor while guaranteeing its guests almost flawless service and comfort. The bar, the winter dining room, the veranda and the rooms are so pleasant that the most sophisticated Palermians come here every night. The swimming pool and the terraced gardens overlook the bay where you can go for a swim. In summary it is impossible to pass the Villa Igiea by when you are in Palermo.

How to get there *(Map 26): Towards district of Acquasanta, by via dei Cantieri Navali.*

Centrale Palace Hotel

Corso Vittorio Emanuele, 327
90134 Palermo
Tel. (0)91-33 66 66 - Fax (0)91-33 48 81
Sig. Schifano

Category ★★★ **Rooms** 61 with air-conditioning, telephone, shower (16 with bath), WC and minibar. **Price** Single 200,000L, double 295,000L. **Meals** Breakfast included, served 7.00-11.00. Half board +50,000F. **Restaurant** Small restaurant at hotel; see p. 469. **Credit cards** All major. **Pets** Dogs not allowed. **Nearby** In Palermo: Church of Martorana, del Gesu church, Palazzo dei Normanni (Norman Royal Palace), Church of San Giovanni degli Eremiti, S. Francesco d'Assisi, Oratorio S. Lorenzo, Regional Archeological Museum, Palazzo Abatellis (Annunciation by Antonello da Messina); Mondello, Villa Palagonia in Bagheria, Solonte, Piana degli Albanesi, Cefalù. **Open** All year.

Here is just the type of "little hotel" that we needed in Palermo. Located right in the historic center of town, a recent renovation has enabled this hotel to recover its former splendor. The rooms combine modern amenities, like the very welcome air-conditioning, with traditional charm. In the summer the dining room is set up on the terrace, with a marvelous view over the rooftops of the city. An excellent place to stay to explore the mysteries of Palermo.

How to get there *(Map 26): The Corso Vittorio Emanuele begins at the piazza Independenza.*

1998

Grand Hotel et des Palmes

Via Roma, 398
90142 Palermo
Tel. (0)91 58 39 33 - Fax (0)91 33 15 45

Category ★★★★ **Rooms** 183 and 4 suites with air-conditioning, telephone, bath, WC, minibar; elevator. **Price** Single 205,000L, double 290,000L, suite +200,000L. **Meals** Breakfast included served 7:00-10:00. **Restaurant** Service 12:30-15:00, 19:30-23:00; menus 60,000L; also à la carte. **Credit cards** All major. **Pets** Dogs allowed. **Nearby** In Palermo: Martorana church, del Gesù church, Cappella palatina (Palatine Chapel), Church of San Giovanni degli Eremiti, S.Francesco d'Assisi, Oratorio S.Lorenzo, Archaeological museum, Palazzo Abatellis (Annunciation by Antonello da Messina), Duomo and Cathedral of Monreale; Mondello and Mont Pellegrino; Cefalù; Villa Palagonia in Bagheria; Solonte; Piana degli Albanesi. **Open** All year.

This grand old hotel, located in the heart of Palermo, seat of so many legends and so many rumors, has the tired charm of its bygone age. A palace first converted into a hotel in 1874, it would be hard to list all the celebrities who sojourned here: from Wagner, who came here to finish "Parsifal," to Auguste Renoir, from De Maupassant to Lucky Luciano. The salons still have the luster of their former prestige. The hall was decorated by Ernesto Basile, the great artist of Italian Art Nouveau. The other salon has a great fireplace, an ornate inlaid ceiling, frescoes, gilding and stained-glass windows. The amenities are rather more modest in the bedrooms, some of which could do with a serious renovation. The hotel restaurant, La Palmetta, serves local cuisine (pasta with fish, risotto with shrimps) in a sumptuous setting. Don't hesitate to treat yourself to a taste of this Sicilian legend, for a price that's really quite reasonable.

How to get there *(Map 26): Town center.*

Villa Lucia

96100 Siracusa
Traversa Mondello, 1 - Contrada Isola
Tel. (0)336-88 85 37 or (0)931-721 007 - Fax (0)931-61 817
Sig.ra Maria Luisa Palermo

Rooms 7 and 7 small apartments with bath or shower, WC, TV and minibar. **Price** Single 195,000L, double 290,000L, apartment (2-5 pers.) 55,000 (per pers., 2 nights min.). **Meals** Breakfast included (for the rooms), served 8:00-10:30. **Restaurant** See p. 470-471. **Credit cards** Visa, Eurocard, MasterCard. **Pets** Small dogs allowed in room (fee). **Facilities** Parking. **Nearby** In Siracusa: Archeological Museum, Ortygia island, Catacombs, Castle of Euryale, Fountain of Arethusa. **Open** All year.

The Villa Lucia is a valuable address to know, for this is not a classic hotel. The owner, Marquisa Maria Luisa Palermo, has been gradually adapting it to receive guests, but it started out as her family's country home. A path lined with pine trees leads up to the villa whose faded rosy-tinted facade gives the visitor a first taste of the charm of the place. Nothing is ostentatious: The antique furniture has been assembled over generations, there are family portraits and travel souvenirs. There is a very pleasant park with lush Mediterranean vegetation and wonderful seaside walks around the villa, with a view of the island of Ortigia. Maria Luisa can also provide information on where to find all that is most authentic in Sicily. A charming place with a charming hostess.

How to get there *(Map 27): 6 km from Siracusa. At the highway, exit Catania/Siracusa, then take SS115. When you leave the town, take the bridge on the river Ciane, first road on the left, go around the port, Contrada Isola.*

Grand Hôtel di Siracusa

Via Mazzini, 12
96100 Siracusa
Tel. (0)931 46 46 00 - Fax (0)931 46 46 11

Apartments 7 and 6 with bath or shower, WC, 5 with minibar, 3 with TV. **Price** Single 240,000L, double 350,000L; suite 400-450,000L. **Meals** Breakfast included, served 7:30-10:00. **Restaurant** Service 12:00-14:30, 20:00-22:30, menu 100,000L.; also à la carte.Specialties: Italian and Sicilian cooking. **Credit cards** Not accepted. **Pets** Small dogs allowed in rooms only (extra charge). **Facilities** Parking. **Nearby** in Siracusa: Archaeological museum and Origia island, ruins of Neapolis, catacombs; Castel of Euryale. **Open** All year.

After four long years of costly restoration, Syracuse at last has a hotel worthy of the city. The goal the architects set was to create new spaces, like the panoramic terrace-restaurant, to refurbish the entire ground floor as reception rooms, and to keep intact as many of the original features as possible. During the renovation work, the builders uncovered vestiges of Spanish fortifications from the 16th century, which are now on display in the hotel's small museum. In the two grand salons they found antique Sicilian furniture or had new pieces made by artists like Carlo Moretti, who did the Murano chandelier that hangs in the Minerva Room. The Athena Room, with its stuccos and frescoes, is in a rotunda illuminated at night and looking out over the port. A large semi-circular staircase with columns leads upstairs to the bedrooms, with luxurious comfort and a view of the sea. Every bit as stunning is the interior garden, with a panoramic elevator amid palm trees and fragrant shrubs.

How to get there *(Map 27): on Oetigia island.*

Museo Albergo L'Atelier sul Mare

Via Cesare Battisti, 4
98070 Castel di Tusa (Messina)
Tel. (0)921-34 295 - Fax (0)921-34 283 - Sig. Antonio Presti
Web: www.fiumararte.aessenet.com - www.skyolit

Rooms 40 with telephone, bath or shower and WC, elevator. **Price** Single 80-105,000L, double 120-160,000L, "chambre d'artiste" 200,000L. **Meals** Breakfast included, served 7:30-9:30; half board 95-140,000L, full board 100-165,000L (per pers., 3 days min.). **Restaurant** Service 13:00-15:00, 20:30-22:30; menu 30-40,000L, also à la carte. Specialties: Sicialian cuisine, seafood. **Credit cards** Amex, Visa, Eurocard and MasterCard. **Pets** Dogs allowed (fee). **Facilities** Swimming pool, parking. **Nearby** Halaesa, S. Stefano di Camastra (Terracotta potteries), Cefalù. **Open** April - Nov.

The Museo Albergo is a Mediterranean-style building right on the water, set on several levels with large terraces. What is really interesting is the concept which the hotel and especially the rooms are based on: art as an integral part of daily life. Each room is an "event" designed by a contemporary artist. By staying here, you will inhabit a unique work of art. In the lobby and the salon, you will find a series of paintings and sculptures, which go on right down to the beach (if the local government hasn't removed them). The art may not be to everyone's taste, but this hotel does fulfill all the criteria of a good hotel: It has comfort, good service, and a fine restaurant where you will enjoy Sicilian specialties and the hotel's fine fish dishes. Visits to the rooms are limited to hotel guests.

How to get there *(Map 27): 90 km east of Palerme; via A20 to Cefalù then along the coast towards Messina.*

San Domenico Palace Hotel

Piazza San Domenico, 5
96039 Taormina (Messina)
Tel. (0)942-23 701 - Fax (0)942-62 55 06
Sig. Anna

Category ★★★★★ **Rooms** 111 with telephone, bath, WC, satellite TV and minibar. **Price** Double 400-685,000L. **Meals** Breakfast included, served 8:00-10:00; half board 320-440,000L, full board 410-530,000L. (per pers., 3 days min.). **Restaurant** Service 12:00-14:30, 20:00-22:30, menu 100,000L, also à la carte. Specialties: Sicialian and Italian cuisine. **Credit cards** All major. **Pets** Dogs allowed in room only. **Facilities** Heated swimming pool, parking. **Nearby** In Taormina: Castello San Pancrazio, gorges of Alcantara, Castelmola (panorama from Cafe S. Giorgio), Forza d'Agro, Alcantara, Capo Schiso, Naxos, Il Picciolo Golf course (18-hole). **Open** All year.

The San Domenico Palace, formerly a monastery built in 1430, is no doubt the most beautiful hotel in Sicily. It is frequented by a rich international clientele and some top-notch tour operators. To get to the marvelous garden, meticulously kept and flowering year-round, you walk through a cloister and numerous, long hallways decorated with 17th- and 18th-century paintings, which lead to luxurious rooms resembling monk's cells from the outside. You will spend dreamlike days next to the swimming pool, from which you can enjoy the view of the Greek theater, the sea, and Mount Etna. A dinner by candlelight on the terrace will prove that the San Domenico also has the finest restaurant in Taormina.

How to get there *(Map 27): 52 km south of Messina via A18 Taormina-North exit; near the belvedere of the via Roma.*

Hotel Villa Belvedere

Via Bagnoli Croci, 79
98039 Taormina (Messina)
Tel. (0)942-237 91 - Fax (0)942-62 58 30 - Sig. Pecaut
E-mail: hotbelve@cys.it

Category ★★★ **Rooms** 51 (some with air-cond.), telephone, bath or shower, WC, TV on request. **Price** Single 81-147,000L, double 132-232,000L. **Meals** Breakfast included, served 7:00-12:00; snack from April to Oct., service 11:30-18:00. **Restaurant** See p. 421. **Credit cards** Visa, Eurocard and MasterCard. **Pets** Dogs allowed. **Facilities** Swimming pool, parking (6,000L). **Nearby** In Taormina: Greek Theater; Castello San Pancrazio, Castelmola (panorama from Cafe S. Giorgio), Forza d'Agro, Alcantara, Capo Schiso, Mazzaro beach, Messina, Il Picciolo Golf Course (18-hole). **Open** 3 week before Easter – Nov. 10 and Dec. 20 - Jan. 10.

The discreet Hotel Belvedere stands very close to the enchanting public garden of Taormina. Unlike most of the hotels of Taotmina which suffer from frenetic delusions of grandeur, the Belvedere has remained simple, comfortable and charming. It is remarkably managed by its French director, and who runs it according to three rules which have made is so popular among its clientele of artists and regulars: cleanliness, comfort, and silence. Five new very pretty rooms have been opened, with large balconies with a view of the sea. You couldn't ask for more, but the view on the Bay of Taormina and a beautiful swimming pool under the giant palm trees give it additional allure which, fortunately, you won't see in the final bill.

How to get there *(Map 27): 52 km south of Messina via A 18, Taormina-North exit - the hotel is next to the belvedere of the via Roma.*

Hotel Villa Ducale

Via Leonardo da Vinci, 60
96039 Taormina (Messina)
Tel. (0)942-28 153 - Fax (0)942-28 710 - Sig. and Sig.ra Quartucci
E-mail: villaducale@tao.it

Category ★★★ **Rooms** 10 with air-conditioning, telephone, bath or shower, WC, satellite TV, safe and minibar. **Price** Single 180-200,000L, double 240-320,000L, suite 280-300,000L. **Meals** Breakfast included, served 8:00-11:00. **Restaurant** See p. 470. **Credit cards** All major. **Pets** Small dogs allowed. **Facilities** Parking, sauna, tennis, gym. **Nearby** Greek Theater, Castello San Pancrazio, Castelmola (panorama from Cafe S. Giorgio), Forza d'Agro, Alcantara, Capo Schiso, Naxos, Mazzaro beach, Messina, Il Picciolo Golf Course (18-hole). **Open** Feb. 21 – Jan. 9.

The patrician Villa Ducale is a very comfortable and elegant hotel, built by the great grandfather of the current owners at the beginning of the century. The rooms, carefully decorated and furnished with antiques, are all different, but all have an incredible view of the sea, Etna and the valley. The ones on the third floor have a pleasant terrace with a table and lounge chairs. A very interesting library provides reading material on Sicily and its history; you can also play chess there. Don't miss the delicious breakfasts–served on the terrace–of Viennese pastries, jelly and honey from Etna, fresh fruit juice and other local products. The staff is very friendly.

How to get there *(Map 27): 52 km south of Messina via A18, Taormina-North exit.*

Hotel Villa Paradiso

Via Roma, 2
98039 Taormina (Messina)
Tel. (0)942 239 21 22 - Fax (0)942 625 800
Sig. Salvatore Martorana

Category ★★★★ **Rooms** 25 and 13 suites with air-conditioning, telephone, bath or shower, WC, minibar, satellite TV; elevator. **Price** Single 115-150,000L, double 160-250,000L; suite 280-300,000L. **Meals** Breakfast included served 7:30-10:00. **Restaurant** Service 13:00-14:00, 20:00-21:15, menu 35,000L; also à la carte. Specialties: Sicilian cooking, pesce. **Credit cards** All major. **Pets** Small dogs allowed. **Nearby** In Taormina: Greek Theater; Castello San Pancrazio; Castelmola (panorama cafe S.Giorgio); Forza d'Argo, Alcantara, Capo Schiso, Naxos, Mazzaro beach, Etna; Il Picciolo golf course (18-hole). **Open** All year.

Set between the sea and the majestic Mount Etna, Taormina is like a sampler of Sicily, all in one stunning package. The Villa Paradiso is the creation of an English adventuress of the last century who fell in love with an Italian doctor and with what was then just a little village. She built the house as a hunting lodge and it still bears the mark of its history - a blend of Sicily with far-off Albion and an air of intimacy as in a family guest house. The bedrooms have elegant painted wood furniture, the larger suites look out on the sea. The salons are a series of connecting rooms, some with a covered gallery facing the winter garden, others facing the sea. A well-appointed terrace offers a grandiose panorama of the bay. As soon as weather permits, a private bus will take you to Letojanni, where the hotel has a private beach with mattresses, swimming pool and a restaurant.

How to get there *(Map 27): 52 km south of Messina via A18, Taormina exit.*

Hotel Riis

Via Pietro Rizzo,13
98039 Taormina (Messina)
Tel. (0)942 248 74 - Fax (0)942 62 62 54
Sig. Sciglio

Category ★★★★ **Rooms** 30 with air-conditioning, telephone, bath or shower, WC, TV; elevator. **Price** Single 170,000L, double 220,000L; suite 270,000L. **Meals** Breakfast 20,000L, served 7:30-10:00. **Restaurant** L'Angelo. Service 13:00-14:00, 20:00-21:15; menu 35,000L; also à la carte. Specialties: Sicilian cooking, pesce. Credit cards All major. **Pets** Dogs allowed. **Facilities** Swimming pool, parking. **Nearby** In Taormina: Greek Theater; Castello San Pancrazio; Castelmola (panorama cafe S.Giorgio); Forza d'Argo, Alcantara, Capo Schiso, Naxos, Mazzaro beach, Etna; Il Picciolo golf course (18-hole). **Open** Mid Mar - end Oct.

Can it ever be repeated enough? Taormina is worth more than a detour. Founded by Hector's wife, the faithful Andromache, by turns Greek, Roman, Saracen and Christian, the town has kept the mark of all its conquerors. The Hotel Riis is just a few steps from the town center in a turn-of-the-century building that affords a breathtaking view of the sea and Mount Etna. The baroque decoration in the living rooms may be a bit ornate, but it does give a quaint sort of charm to this old but recently renovated hotel. Most of the rooms have a little balcony where you can take your breakfast in front of the inspiring view. There is a superb dining room extended by a terrace. And when you return from your sightseeing in the crowded town center, you can cool off in the swimming pool at the foot of the hotel.

How to get there *(Map 27): 52 km south of Messina via A 18, Toarmina exit.*

Hotel Villa Sant'Andrea

98030 Mazzaro - Taormina (Messina)
Via Nazionale, 137
Tel. (0)942 23 125 - Fax (0)942 24 838

Category ★★★★ **Rooms** 67 with air-conditioning, tel., bath or shower, WC, TV. **Price** Single 165-365,000L, double 310-530,000L, Suite +100,000L. **Meals** Breakfast included, served 7:30-10:00; half board and full board 200-310,000L, 235-345,000L (1 pers.). **Restaurant** Service 13:00-14:30 and 20:00-22:30; menu 65,000L, also à la carte. Specialties: Tagliolini con scampi e pesto alla Sant'Andrea - Spigoletta creazione "Olivero" - Parfait alle mandorle. **Credit cards** All major. **Pets** Small dogs allowed. **Facilities** Privat beach, parking (22,000L). **Nearby** In Taormina: Greek Theater; Castello on the Monte Tauro, Castelmola (terrace, panorama from Cafe S. Giorgio), Forza d'Agro, Gorges of the Alcantara, Capo Schiso, Naxos, Mazzaro beach, Trip to the Etna - Il Picciolo Golf Club (18-hole). **Open** All year.

At the Villa Sant'Andrea it is possible to enjoy the advantages of Taormina without suffering from the drawbacks. At the water's edge and away from the narrow village lanes crowded with tourists, it is only 5 minutes from town by cable car. This charming place has managed (unlike its neighbors in Mazzaro) to avoid becoming just another address for group tours. The hotel dates from the 1950s. Most of its rooms face the sea and it is very quiet. Restaurants, private beach and terrace bar are arranged with discretion and good taste. From Aug. 8 to 21, the hotel reserves the right to accept only guests staying for a minimum of one week.

How to get there *(Map 27): 52 km south of Messina via A 18, Taormina-North exit - The hotel is 5,5 km north of Taormina, along the coast.*

1998

Hotel Elimo Erice

91016 Erice (Trapani)
Via Vittorio Emanuele, 75
Tel. (0)923 86 93 77 / 86 94 86 - Fax (0)923 86 92 52
Sig. Tilotta

Rooms 21 with telephone, bath or shower, WC and TV - Elevator. **Price** Single 140,000L, double 250,000L. **Meals** Breakfast included, served 7:30-10:00; half board 140,000L, full board 180,000L (per pers., 3 days min.). **Restaurant** Service 12:30-14:30, 19:30-19:30/20:00; menu 30-60,000L, also à la carte. Specialties: Sicilian cuisine. **Credit cards** All major. **Pets** Dogs allowed. **Facilities** Parking. **Nearby** Trapani, Egadi islands and island of Pantelleria. **Open** All year.

At the western end of Sicily, Erice, which rises straight up from a rock, seems to keep watch over a peaceful and silent world. The historical center is a labyrinth of narrow little streets, Renaissance palaces and churches from the Middle Ages, all of which seem to fit together like pieces of a jigsaw puzzle. Life goes on behind these facades, in the inner courtyards which are characteristic of the houses in Erice. The hotel Elimo is in one of these old houses. Carefully restored and comfortably furnished, the hotel's decor, inspired by the colors and materials of ancient motifs, is nevertheless a bit common. This is, however, a very pleasant place to stay in this beautiful town of Erice, with its remarkable architectural heritage. Be sure to go for a walk along the fortified walls surrounding the town from which you will have stunning views of the coast. From the Castello di Venere, you can see Trapani and the islands, and on a clear day, Tunisia. Don't be surprised if you hear people speaking foreign languages–the town is the headquarters for the International Center of Scientific Culture "Ettore Majorana."

How to get there *(Map 26): 13 km north of Trapani.*

Club il Gattopardo

Isola di Lampedusa (Agrigento)
Tel. (0)922-97 00 51 - Reservation (0)11-812 40 89 - Fax 817 83 87

Rooms 11 and 2 suites with telephone, bath and WC. **Price** With full board 1,800,000-2,600,000L (per pers. for 1 week with car and boat rental included). **Restaurant** Service 13:00 and 20:30; menu, also à la carte. Specialties: Sicilian cuisine, seafood. **Credit card** Amex. **Pets** Dogs not allowed. **Nearby** Lampedusa island. **Open** June – mid-Oct.

Lampedusa, the largest of the Pelagien Islands, which are scattered between the coasts of Sicily and Tunisia, was inhabited in the Bronze Age, then deserted from antiquity until 1843. Roberto and his French wife Annette opened this hotel-club because Roberto, who loves scuba diving, wanted to become better acquainted with this still unspoiled island. Here, the word "club" takes on an intimate connotation, as Il Gattopardo has only thirteen rooms. In the purest architectural tradition of the island, the ochre stone and white domes blend perfectly with the coast and the sea nearby. The rooms are decorated in a Mediterranean style and are very comfortable. Everything is organized to take full advantage of the sea: You will have two boats (fishing and motor) at your disposal, as well as three camels, which will allow you to explore the island. In the evening, you can enjoy the chef's cuisine, and in the morning, the delicious breakfasts prepared by Annette. In May and June, sea turtles come to Lampedusa to lay their eggs on the beaches at night. The best time to visit is in September and October, when the water is warm and the sky full of birds migrating towards Africa. Children under 18 are not accepted at this hotel.

How to get there *(Map 26): From Palermo by plane (30 min.). Lampedusa Airport, tel. (39 922) 97 02 99.*

Hotel Carasco

Isole Eolie o Lipari
Porto delle Genti
98055 Lipari (Messina)
Tel. (0)90-981 16 05 - Fax (0)90-981 18 28 - Sig. Marco del Bono
E-mail: carasco@tin.it

Category ★★★ **Rooms** 98 with telephone, bath or shower and WC. **Price** With half board 85-170,000L, full board 100-185,000L (per pers.). **Meals** Breakfast included, served 7:30-9:30. **Restaurant** Service 12:30-14:00, 20:00-21:30; à la carte. Specialties: Sicilian and Italian cuisine. **Credit cards** All major. **Pets** Dogs not allowed. **Facilities** Swimming pool, parking. **Nearby** Aeolian museum in Lipari, Canneto, Acquacalda, Puntazze (view), Ovattropani, Piano Conte, Quattrocchi, Lipari island. **Open** Apr. – Oct.

The Hotel Carasco, run by an Anglo-Italian couple, offers all the comfort of a grand hotel. The rooms are very large and most of them have a terrace with a view of the sea. There is a beach right at the foot of the hotel. Lipari is the biggest and most visited island of the archipelago.

How to get there *(Map 27): Hydrofoil service from Messina all year; from Napoli, Reggio, Cefalù and Palermo June-Sept.; car ferry service from Messina, Napoli and Milazzo (50 min-2 hrs).*

Hotel Villa Augustus

Isole Eolie o Lipari
Vico Ausonia, 16
98055 Lipari (Messina)
Tel. (0)90-981 12 32 - Fax (0)90-981 22 33
Sig. D'Albora

Category ★★★ **Rooms** 35 with telephone, bath or shower and WC. **Price** Single 50-150,000L, double 70-220,000L, suite 250,000L. **Meals** Breakfast 10-20,000L, served 7:00-11:.30; half board 100-150,000L (per pers.). **Restaurant** See p. 470. **Credit cards** Visa, Eurocard, MasterCard. **Pets** Dogs allowed. **Facilities** Parking. **Nearby** Aeolian museum in Lipari, Canneto, Acquacalda, Puntazze (view), Ovattropani, Piano Conte, Quattrocchi. **Open** Mar. – Oct.

The Augustus is in an old family villa built in 1950, located on a side street in the historical center of Lipari. We like this hotel for its simplicity, its garden, and its relatively spacious and comfortable rooms. Each one has a balcony or a terrace and a view of either the sea or the Lipari castle. It is more of a boarding house than a luxury hotel, but is nonetheless one of the more pleasant hotels in town. Although there is no hotel restaurant, there are several fine restaurants in the area where you can have lunch or dinner.

How to get there *(Map 27): Hydrofoil service from Messina all year; from Napoli, Reggio, Cefalù and Palermo June-Sept.; car ferry service from Messina, Napoli and Milazzo (50 min-2 hrs); 400 m in the town center.*

Hotel Villa Meligunis

Isole Eolie o Lipari
Via Marte, 7
98055 Lipari (Messina)
Tel. (0)90-98 12 426 - Fax (0)90-98 80 149 - Sig. D'Ambra
E-mail: hmeligun@milazzo.mediaweb.it

Category ★★★★ **Rooms** 32 with air-conditioning, telephone, bath or shower, WC, satellite TV and minibar; elevator. **Price** Single 160-245,000L, double 220-340,000L, suite 70,000L. **Meals** Breakfast included, half board 145-210,000L, full board 170-240,000L (per pers.). **Restaurant** Service 12:30-14:00, 20:30-23:00; menus: 50-70,000L, also à la carte. Specialties: regional cooking, fish. **Credit cards** All major. **Pets** Small dogs allowed. **Nearby** Aeolian museum in Lipari, Canneto, Acquacalda, Puntazze (view), Ovattropani, Piano Conte, Quattrocchi. **Open** All year.

The Aeolian Islands are one of the few remaining Mediterranean paradises which are still relatively unspoiled. The director of the Villa Meligunis has opened this hotel in hopes of attracting people from northern Europe in winter. The name Meligunis is meaningful and appropriate: It is the ancient Greek name for Lipari and means "gentleness." You will find this in the climate, the wine and the color of the sea. The hotel is in an old house, to which more modern Mediterranean-style buildings have been added. There is a large terrace overlooking the sea. The rooms, which have every comfort, are spacious and simply decorated. The restaurant serves local cuisine and features mainly fish dishes.

How to get there *(Map 27): Hydrofoil service from Messina, Milazzo, all year; from Napoli, Reggio, Cefalù and Palermo June-Sept.; car ferry service from Messina, Napoli and Milazzo (50 min-2 hrs).*

Hotel Raya

Isole Eolie o Lipari
San Pietro - 98050 Isola Panarea (Messina)
Tel. (0)90-98 30 13 - Fax (0)90-98 31 03
Sig.ra Beltrami and Sig. Tilche

Category ★★★★ **Rooms** 36 with telephone, shower, WC and minibar. **Price** With half board: 170-210,000L, double 180-340,000L. **Meals** Breakfast includedL, served 8:00-11:30. **Restaurant** Service 20:30-24:00; menu 50,000L. Specialties: Mediterranean cuisinc, Sicilian pastries. **Credit cards** All major. **Pets** Dogs allowed, boat rentals, shops of the Raya. **Nearby** Bronze Age village at Capo Milazzese, Basiluzzo. **Open** Apr. 10 – Oct. 15.

It is surprising on this little Sicilian island to find a very trendy hotel–considered a local institution. It was built twenty years ago and consists of a series of pink and white bungalows which extend from the heights of the village down to the sea. Its Mediterranean architecture is ideal for its clean and modern interior decorated with beautiful, primitive art objects from Polynesia, Africa and the Orient. The lounges and all rooms overlook the sea. Each one has a terrace with a view of the windy archipelago. There is an open-air restaurant and a bar which overlook the port. The guests are mostly regulars and the hotel staff is hip. Young children are not allowed.

How to get there *(Map 27): Hydrofoil service from Milazzo and Napoli. No cars allowed on the island.*

Hotel Signum

Malfa (Messina), via Scalo, 15
Isole Eolie o Lipari - Isola Salina 98050
Tel. (0)90 98 44 222 - Fax (0)90 98 44 102

Category ★★ **Rooms** 16 with telephone, bath or shower, WC. **Price** Double 150-270,000L, single +35,000L. **Meals** Breakfast included, served 8:00-10:00, half board 115-175,000L (per pers.). **Restaurant** Closed Nov - Feb. Service 13:00-14:30, 20:30-22:00; menu 25-50,000L; also à la carte.Specialties: Pesce, Regional cuisine. **Credit cards** All major. **Pets** Dogs allowed on request. **Nearby** Santa Marina (ecomuseum), vineyard of malvoisie, Malfa; Valley of Valdichies; the volcano. **Open** All year.

We fell in love with this hotel as soon as we arrived by a narrow village lane that winds its way among the vines, oleanders and barbary fig trees. The Hotel Signum is built in the traditional style of the Aeolian Islands. From the broad terrace, the true heart of the house, there is a magical view of the Bay of Malfa, with Stromboli in the distance. The bedrooms are laid out around the terrace and each one has something special, like the rooms of an old family home. Our favorites are number 11 for its terrace, and number 16, but also those over the garden with their pergola of vines. The place owes its charm to its owners as well, Clara, always kind and helpful, and her husband, Michele, who is in charge of the cooking - refined dishes based on the local produce and the catch of the day. Clara can help you organize excursions to the other islands or boat trips to the cove of Pollara (where the film "Il Postino" was shot) or scooter rides around the local vineyards. This is the sort of place you can't leave without a twinge of sadness.

How to get there *(Map 27): Hydrofoil service from Milazzo.No cars allowed on island.*

Hotel La Sciara Residence

Isole Eolie o Lipari
98050 Isola Stromboli (Messina)
Tel. (0)90-98 60 05 / 98 61 21 - Fax (0)90-98 62 84
Famiglia d'Eufemia and Sig.ra Raffaelli

Category ★★★ **Rooms** 62 with telephone, bath or shower and WC. **Price** With half board 100-215,000L, (per pers., 7 day min. in high season). **Meals** Breakfast included, served 7:30-10:00. **Restaurant** Service 13:00-14:30, 20:00-21:30; menu: 50-75,000L, also à la carte. Specialties: Seafood, malvasia, lasagne all'eoliana. **Credit cards** All major. **Pets** Small dogs allowed. **Facilities** Swimming pool, tennis, private beach. **Nearby** The volcano, Sciara del Fuoco, Strombolicchio, Ginostra. **Open** May 18 – Sept.

Stromboli is a place to see, even if it's just for the Hotel La Sciara. The garden is splendid and filled with flowers–mostly fuchsia, pink and orange bougainvillea–which testify to the exceptional quality of the fertile volcanic soil. The rooms are spacious, comfortable and filled with antique furniture and objects of diverse origin, selected by the owner. In addition to the hotel, there are five old restored houses you can stay in, each with several rooms, one or two bathrooms, and a kitchenette. They overlook the sea and offer some hotel services.

How to get there *(Map 27): Hydrofoil service from Milazzo and Napoli. No cars allowed on island.*

1998

La Sirenetta Park Hotel

Via Marina, 33
Isole Eolie o Lipari - 98050 Isola Stromboli (Messina)
Tel. (0)90 98 60 25 - Fax (0)90 98 61 24 - Sig. Vito Russo

Category ★★★ **Rooms** 41 with telephone bath or shower, WC. **Price** Single 120-140,000L, double 160-260,000L, suite 230-330,000L. **Meals** Breakfast included served 7:30-10:00, half board 130-190,000L (per pers.) and full board 160-220,000L (per pers.). **Restaurant** Service 13:00-14:30, 20:00-21:30; menu 40-60,000L; also à la carte. Specialties: Pesce, sicilian cuisine. **Credit cards** All major. **Pets** Small dogs allowed. **Facilities** Swimming pool. **Nearby** The Volcano, Sciara del Fuoco, Strombolicchio, Ginostra. **Open** Mar - end Oct.

For many people, the name Stromboli evokes the film of Roberto Rosselini and the famous love affair with Ingrid Bergman that began right here. Domenico, the owner of the hotel, still remembers how he met Rosselini when he came scouting for locations. Desperate at the thought that there was no place on the island for the crew to stay, he rented the director his own house and worked as an aide on the production. With the money he earned he built a hotel facing the black waters of the sea and called it La Sirenetta after the sirens in the tale of Ulysses. It's a simple place with a garden, in a nice location facing the beach, and comfortable enough to satisfy all the vulcanologists who stay here when they come to study Stromboli. Choose a room with a terrace or balcony that faces the Strombolicchio. If you want to go up to the crater (an unforgettable sight) the trip takes 3 hours and you must hire a guide. The best time to do it is late afternoon, to see the sunset.

How to get there *(Map 27): Hydrofoil service from Milazzo and Napoli No cars allowed on island.*

Les Sables Noirs

Isole Eolie o Lipari
Porto Ponente - 98050 Isola Vulcano (Messina)
Tel. (0)90-98 50 - Fax (0)90-98 52 454
Sig. Elio Curatolo

Category ★★★★ **Rooms** 48 with air-conditioning, telephone, bath or shower, TV, minibar and WC. **Price** With half board 160-255,000L, full board 195-300,000L (special rates for 10 or 14 days). **Meals** Breakfast included, served 7:00-10:00. **Restaurant** Service 13:00-14:30, 20:00-22:30; menu: 65,000L, also à la carte. Specialties: Mediterranean cuisine, seafood. **Credit cards** All major. **Pets** Small dogs allowed. **Facilities** Swimming pool, tennis, bike, private beach, parking. **Nearby** Access to the volcano's crater. **Open** June – Sept.

The white houses of Porto Ponente are spread out along the black sand beaches at the foot of the Piana volcano. One of them is the Hotel La Scaria Residence. It has been recently renovated, and is now a comfortable luxury hotel with four-star service. You will find both heaven and hell on this Aeolian island dedicated to the Roman god-Vulcan and the farthest south in the Lipari archipelago. Hell is near the large 500-meter crater continually belching up ash, steam, smoke and gas. Heaven is the verdant surroundings of the volcano and the coast, with its mysterious hidden grottos, inlets, beaches and transparent turquoise water. The biggest tourist attraction is, however, the large crater, which puts on a show unique to the archipelago, the coasts of Sicily and Etna.

How to get there *(Map 27): Hydrofoil services from Milazzo and Napoli. Cars subject to restrictions.*

Albergo San Michele

Via Guelfa, 15
52044 Cortona (Arezzo)
Tel. (0)575-60 43 48 - Fax (0)575-63 01 47 - Dott. Alunno
E-mail: sanmichele@ats.it - Web: http://www.cortona.net/sanmichele

Category ★★★★ **Rooms** 40 (30 with air-conditioning) with telephone, bath or shower, WC, TV and 10 with minibar, elevator. **Price** Single 110,000L, double 170,000L, triple 200,000L (triple), 220,000L (for 4 pers.). **Meals** Breakfast included, served 7:30-9:30. **Restaurant** See p. 478. **Credit cards** All major. **Pets** Dogs not allowed. **Facilities** Swimming pool in casa Barbieri, tennis (5,000L), parking, garage (20,000L). **Nearby** Cortona (Church of Madonna del Calcinaio, Museo dell' Accademia Etrusca), Arezzo, Val di Chiana (Farneta abbey, Lucignano, Sinalunga), Trasimeno lake, Perugia. **Open** Mar. – Dec.

The fortified town of Cortona has, from time immemorial, stood watch over the valley, a bit away from the main roads down in the plain that link Arezzo to Perugia, Tuscany to Umbria. The town still has its fortress look today. You enter through gates in the medieval walls and walk around through steep, narrow lanes, often ending in stairways. There are still traces of the Etruscan epoch, and a fine collection can be seen at the Museo dell'Accademia Etrusca. The Renaissance has also left its mark, notably with the Madonna del Calcinaio church. The Albergo San Michele itself is situated in a former Renaissance palace. Simply and intelligently restored, it offers rooms with pleasant decoration and good amenities. The most charming are the attic rooms with their sloping ceilings. The largest ones have a mezzanine. The welcome is friendly but the service is not what you would expect from a 4-star hotel.

How to get there *(Map 13): 28 km south of Arezzo via SS71.*

Relais Il Falconiere

San Martino a Bolena 52044 Cortona (Arezzo)
Tel. (0)575-61 26 79 - Fax (0)575-61 29 27
Silvia and Riccardo Baracchi

Category ★★★★ **Rooms** 12 with air conditioning, telephone, bath or shower, WC, TV, minibar,safe, elevator; Room for disabled persons. **Price** Double 340,000L, suite 450,000L. **Meals** Breakfast included, served 7:00-10:30; half board 240-340,000L (per pers., 3 days min.). **Restaurant** Service 13:00-14:00, 20:00-22:00; closed Wed.; also à la carte. Specialties: Filetto cinghiale, budino di panna e formaggio con salsa de pere, tortino di cipollotti con fonduta di raviggiolo, pici alla cortenese, zuppa di fava e orzo, gnocchi alla ricottarombo con crema di asparagi, sfogliatina di mele e pinolo con cioccolato caldo. **Credit cards** All major. **Pets** Dogs not allowed. **Facilities** Swimming pool, parking. **Nearby** Cortona (Church of Madonna del Calcinaio, Museo dell' Accademia Etrusca), Arezzo, Val di Chiana (Farneta abbey, Lucignano, Sinalunga), Trasimeno lake, Perugia. **Open** All year.

This magnificent 17th century villa stands on a hill covered with olive trees and vineyards, facing Cortona. This family house, transformed into a hotel now, has kept all of the charm and polished luxury of the old days. The spacious, quiet rooms have beautiful classical furniture. Comfort and refinement pervade the hotel, creating a feeling of real well-being. We suggest, apart from the three garden-level suites (with pool-jacuzzis), the pretty little attic room from which you can see the majestic contours of the Etruscan town. And should you be inspired by "The Annunciation" by Fra' Angelico in the Diocese museum, there is a private chapel painted with frescoes at your disposal in the hotel garden.

How to get there *(Map 13): 28 km south of Arezzo via SS71. 3 km north of Cortona.*

Castello di Gargonza

Gargonza
52048 Monte San Savino (Arezzo)
Tel. (0)575-84 70 21 - Fax (0)575-84 70 54 - Sig. Fucini
E-mail: gargonza@teta.it - Web: http://www.gargonza.it

Category ★ **Rooms** 40 with telephone, bath or shower and WC. **Price** Single 140-270,000L, apartment 7703-2,520,000L (for 1 week). **Meals** Breakfast included, served 8:00-10:00; half board 120-165,000L, (per pers., 2 nights min.). **Restaurant** Service 12:30-14:30, 19:30-21:30, closed Tues.; menus: 35-50,000L. Specialties: Tuscan. **Credit cards** All major. **Pets** Dogs not allowed. **Facilities** Swimming pool. **Nearby** Monte San Savino (Loggia dei Mercanti, Church and Palazzo of Monte San Savino), Convent of San Fracesco in La Verna and La Penna (1,283 m), Arezzo. **Open** Apr. – Jan. 9.

If you are traveling with family or friends and if you want to choose a base from which to explore the region, the Castello di Gargonza may be just what you're looking for. In a completely restored and rehabilitated little village you can rent a furnished apartment in a very pretty site. When you arrive you will be given a map and the keys to your house and left to manage on your own. The interior is functional, not especially attractive, but with all the necessary amenities, and some of the units have a fireplace. There are some rooms to rent, as well, in traditional hotel style. There is also a restaurant, the Torre di Gargonza, and a swimming pool. The whole place has the family atmosphere of an apartment hotel.

How to get there *(Map 13): 29 km southwest of Arezzo via S73 to Monte San Savino, then right towards Gargonza.*

1998

Stoppiacce

52044 San Pietro a Dame (Arezzo)
Tel. (0)575-69 00 58 - Fax (0)575-69 00 58
Sig.and Sig.ra Campbell

Rooms 2 and 1 apartment with bath., WC. **Price** Doubles 180,000L, apartment 1,200,000-2,200,000L (1 week). **Meals** Breakfast included, served until 10:00. **Restaurant** (by reservation). Service 12:30, 20:00; menu 25,000L (lunch) 60,000L wine incl. **Credit cards** Not accepted. **Pets** Dogs not allowed. **Facilities** Swimming pool, parking. **Nearby** Cortona: Church of Madonna del Calcinaio, Museo dell' Accademia etrusca; Arezzo, Val di Chiana: abbey of Farneta, Lucignano, Sinalunga, Lake Trasimeno, Perugia. **Open** Feb. - Nov.

A stunning road from Cortona takes you through a wild and sun-drenched part of Tuscany, a landscape of green rolling hills reminiscent of nearby Umbria. It leads at last to an "end of the world" spot, but a very British one, indeed. For the two rooms in the superb setting of an old, meticulously-restored farmhouse are provided by an English couple. Both indoors and out, the setting is as trim as an English cottage: The garden beautifully kept, the rosebushes perfectly clipped, a chintz living room, old portraits, sumptuous bathrooms. In the dining room the table is set with great refinement, china and silver sparkle, awaiting the arrival of the guests, who are free to suggest their own menu. A wonderful choice for a complete rest and change of scene, suitable for anyone who wants to either laze about or explore this border region.

How to get there *(Map 13): 17 km from Cortona towards Citta del Castello. In Portole, phone if you have a problem for location of the hotel.*

Hotel Helvetia & Bristol

Via dei Pescioni, 2
50123 Firenze
Tel. (0)55-28 78 14 - Fax (0)55-28 83 53
Sig. Panelli

Category ★★★★★ **Rooms** 52 with air-conditioning, telephone, bath or shower, WC and satellite TV, safe; elevator. **Price** Single 346,500-390,000L, double 462-594,000L, suite 748-1,540,000L. **Meals** Breakfast 34,100-55,000L, served 7:00-10:30. **Restaurant** Service 12:30-14:30, 19:30-22:00; menus: 80-120,000L. Specialties: Mediterranean cuisine and old Tuscan recipes. **Credit cards** All major. **Pets** Dogs not allowed. **Nearby** Firenze, Fiesole, Certosa di Galluzzo, Villas and gardens around Firenze (tel. Palazzo Pitti: 055 21 48 56), Vallombrosa abbey, dell'Ugolino golf course (18-hole) in Grassina. **Open** All year.

The Helvetia & Bristol is incontestably one of the best hotels of this category in Firenze: everything here is perfect and tasteful. This large, beautiful residence, once the meeting place of the Tuscan intellegentsia, has now regained its former prestige. The main salon sets the tone, a blend of British-style comfort and Italian luxury. Pretty old Indian calico fabrics add color to the small, very elegant dining room. The bar on the veranda has the charm of a winter garden. The exquisite rooms have beautiful fabric-covered walls, comfortable beds and marble bathrooms with whirlpools. The personnel is like the hotel–high class but irresistibly friendly and Italian.

How to get there *(Map 10): Next to Piazza della Repubblica, via Strozzi, via dei Pescioni.*

Hotel Regency

50121 Firenze
Piazza Massimo d'Azeglio, 3
Tel. (0)55-24 52 47 - Fax (0)55-23 46 735
Sig. Bosi

Category ★★★★★ **Rooms** 35 with telephone, bath or shower, WC, satellite TV, safe and minibar; elevator. **Price** Single 330-400,000L, double 400-620,000L. **Meals** Breakfast included. **Restaurant** Service 12:30-14:30, 19:30-22:30, à la carte. Specialties: Tuscan and Italian cuisine. **Credit cards** All major. **Pets** Dogs allowed (fee). **Facilities** Garage. **Nearby** Firenze, Fiesole, Certosa di Galluzzo, Villas and gardens around Firenze (tel. Palazzo Pitti: 055 21 48 56), Vallombrosa abbey, dell'Ugolino golf course (18-hole) in Grassina. **Open** All year.

Modern comfort and old fashioned hospitality is the motto of the owner of the Hotel Regency, Amedo Ottaviani. On the Piazza d'Azeglio, the Regency is a villa which used to belong to Florentine nobles. The almost English comfort of the rooms and the salons characterizes this place, as does the excellent cuisine served in a paneled dining room and the large glass wall opening onto the gardens. You will find great elegance here, down to the last details. One practical note: It is easy to park on the square and the streets nearby.

How to get there *(Map 10): Next to Santa Croce by the via Borgo Pinti.*

Grand Hotel Villa Cora

Viale Machiavelli, 18-20
50125 Firenze
Tel. (0)55-22 98 451 - Fax (0)55-22 90 86
Sig. Zaccardi

Category ★★★★★ **Rooms** 48 with telephone, bath or shower, WC, TV, minibar, safe; elevator. **Price** Single 335-440,000L, double 470-820,000L, suite 820-1,320,000L. **Meals** Breakfast included, served 7:00-11:00; half board +65,000L, full board +130,000L. **Restaurant** Service 12:00-15:00, 19:30-23:00, à la carte. **Credit cards** All major. **Pets** Dogs allowed. **Facilities** Swimming pool, parking. **Nearby** Firenze, Fiesole, Certosa di Galluzzo, Villas and gardens around Firenze (tel. Palazzo Pitti: 055 21 48 56), Vallombrosa abbey, dell'Ugolino golf course (18-hole) in Grassina. **Open** All year.

Built in a pure Neo-Classical style in 1865 by Baron Oppenheim, the Villa Cora has belonged to the Empress Eugenia, and also to Baron Van Meck, Tchaikovsky's patron. It is located in a residential quarter, five minutes from the center of town, in a very pretty garden. The lobby and the salons are sumptuous, but their elegant decor shuns all heaviness. Dining under the dome of what used to be the Arab salon will give you the amusing impression of having excellent Italian food in a Morrocan palace. The rooms are tastefully furnished and very comfortable. We prefer the more modest (and less expensive) ones on the top floor, which open onto a terrace overlooking Firenze and the surrounding gardens. You can use the hotel shuttle bus to go back and forth to the center of town.

How to get there *(Map 10): Towards Forte Belvedere, Porta Romana.*

Hotel Brunelleschi

50122 Firenze
Piazza S. Elisabetta, 3
Tel. (0)55-56 20 68 - Fax (0)55-21 96 53 - Sig. Litta
E-mail: info@hotelbrunelleschi.it

Category ★★★★ **Rooms** 96 with air-conditioning, telephone, bath or shower, WC, TV and minibar; elevator. **Price** Single 320,000L, double 450,000L, suite 700,000L. **Meals** Breakfast included, served 7:00-10:00; half board +75,000L, full board +120,000L. **Restaurant** Service 12:00-14:00, 19:30-22:00, closed Sun.; menus, also à la carte. Specialties Florentine and international cuisine. **Credit cards** All major. **Pets** Dogs allowed. **Facilities** Parking (50,000L). **Nearby** Firenze, Fiesole, Certosa di Galluzzo, Villas and gardens around Firenze (tel. Palazzo Pitti: 055 21 48 56), Vallombrosa abbey, dell'Ugolino golf course (18-hole) in Grassina. **Open** All year.

The hotel was designed by Italo Gamberini, a renowned Italian architect, and set up in a 5th-century Byzantine tower and several adjoining houses, in the Duomo quarter. The decor is modern with some Art Nouveau details. There is a lot of ceruse wood, which goes nicely with the bricks in the tower and throughout the hotel. The quiet rooms all overlook pedestrian streets. The prettiest ones are on the fourth floor and have a view of the Duomo and the tower. The hotel terrace is the perfect place to watch spectacular sunsets over Firenze. This hotel, with a famous restaurant, feels like a grand hotel.

How to get there *(Map 10): Near the Duomo.*

Hotel J & J

Via di Mezzo, 20
50121 Firenze
Tel. (0)55-234 50 05 - Fax (0)55-24 02 82 - Sig. Cavagnari
E-mail: jandj@dada.it - Web: http://home.venere.it/home/firenze/jandj.htlm

Category ★★★★ **Rooms** 20 with air-conditioning, telephone, bath or shower, WC, satellite TV and minibar. **Price** Single 300,000L, double 350-400,000L, suite 500-600,000L. **Meals** Breakfast included, served 7:30-10:00. **Restaurant** See pp. 471-474. **Credit cards** All major. **Pets** Dogs not allowed. **Facilities** Public parking (35,000L). **Nearby** Firenze, Fiesole, Certosa di Galluzzo, Villas and gardens around Firenze (tel. Palazzo Pitti: 055 21 48 56), Vallombrosa abbey, dell'Ugolino golf course (18-hole) in Grassina. **Open** All year.

Nicely located in the old quarter of Santa Croce, very close to the Duomo and the center of town, this hotel is in a 16th-century palace. Vestiges of that era, such as the cloister, the vaulted ceilings, and the frescos, have been preserved and restored. The rooms have simple, contemporary decor. Some are very large and can accomodate three or four people, and all have living rooms. There can be surprises, such as the bathtub in Room 9, but the decoration is so well done that these flights of fancy do not at all detract from the atmosphere. The hotel has no elevator and the stairs to the upper floors are a bit narrow.

How to get there *(Map 10): Near Santa Croce by the via Borgo Pinti.*

Hotel Monna Lisa

Via Borgo Pinti, 27
50121 Firenze
Tel. (0)55-247 97 51 - Fax (0)55-247 97 55 - Sig. Cona
E-mail: monnalis@ats.it - Web: http://www.monnalisa.it

Category ★★★★ **Rooms** 30 with air-conditioning, telephone, bath or shower, WC, satellite TV, safe and minibar. **Price** Single 180-280,000L, double 300-450,000L. **Meals** Breakfast included (buffet), served 7:30-10:00. **Restaurant** See pp. 471-474. **Credit cards** All major. **Pets** Dogs allowed. **Facilities** Parking (20,000L). **Nearby** Firenze, Fiesole, Certosa di Galluzzo, Villas and gardens around Firenze (tel. Palazzo Pitti: 055 21 48 56), Vallombrosa abbey, dell'Ugolino golf course (18-hole) in Grassina. **Open** All year.

The atmosphere at the Monna Lisa is so warm and intimate that it feels more like some luxury *pensione* than like a four-star hotel. First of all, its little garden creates a wonderful change of scene, making you forget that you're right in the center of Florence. Secondly, the place is run by a family of artists, who seem to have real taste in antiques and decoration. Each room has its share of nice antique pieces and engravings (with, of course, many interpretations of the painting that gives the place its name). The reception room and dining room overlooking the garden are as well-appointed as the rest. The entire place is elegant and distinguished, but also inviting. We recommend you ask for a room in the main house, preferably facing the garden. The rooms in the annex are very comfortable but more impersonal.

How to get there *(Map 10): Near the Duomo and Santa Croce by the via Borgo Pinti.*

1998

Grand Hotel Minerva

Piazza Santa Maria Novella, 16
50123 Firenze
Tel. (0)55 28 45 55 - Fax (0)55 26 82 81 - Sig. Alessandro Augier
E-mail: hminerva@sole.it - Web: http://www.sole.it/hminerva

Category ★★★★ **Rooms** 94 with air conditioning, telephone, bath or shower, WC, TV, minibar, safe; elevator. **Price** Single 290-350,000L, double 390-480,000L, suite 600-1,200,000L. **Meals** Breakfast included, served 7:00-10:30, half board +60,000L (per pers.). **Restaurant** Service 12:00-14:00, 19:30-23:00, menu; also à la carte.Specialties: Florentine cuisine. **Credit cards** All major. **Pets** Dogs not allowed. **Facilities** Swimming pool. Nearby Firenze, Fiesole, Certosa di Galluzzo, Villas and gardens around Firenze (tel. Palazzo Pitti: 055 21 48 56). abbey of Vallombosa; dell'Ugolino golf course (18-hole) in Grassina. **Open** All year.

On the Piazza Santa Maria Novella you are right in the heart of Florence. Between the famous church of polychrome marble that gave its name to the piazza and the loggia San Paolo, adorned with medallions by Della Robbia, the Minerva has since the 19th century occupied a building that once belonged to a brotherhood of the nearby convent. It has recently undergone major transformations. The architects have opted for modernity, with quality materials, furniture often designed specially for the hotel and amenities for the most demanding clientele. The bedrooms are soft and cozy; the largest have a mezzanine and can sleep several people. Many have a view of the church facade or its cloister. The salon and the bar are pleasant places to relax, but the best surprise is the swimming pool on the rooftop, with the Duomo in the background - an added pleasure in the summer heat of Florence.

How to get there *(Map 10): In the town.center.*

Hotel Montebello Splendid

Via Montebello, 60
50123 Firenze
Tel. (0)55-239 80 51 - Fax (0)55-21 18 67
Sig. Lupi

Category ★★★★ **Rooms** 54 with air-conditioning, telephone, bath or shower, WC, TV, safe and minibar; elevator. **Price** Single 265-340,000L, double 340-500,000L, suite 600,000L. **Meals** Breakfast included, served 7:00-11:00; half board +50,000L, full board +100,000L (per pers., 3 days min.). **Restaurant** Service 13:00-15:00, 19:30-23:00, closed Sun. menus 50-90,000L, also à la carte. Specialties: Florentine and international cuisine. **Credit cards** All major. **Pets** Dogs allowed. **Facilities** Parking. **Nearby** Firenze, Fiesole, Certosa di Galluzzo, Villas and gardens around Firenze (tel. Palazzo Pitti: 055 21 48 56), Vallombrosa abbey, dell'Ugolino golf course (18-hole) in Grassina. **Open** All year.

This elegant hotel with refined, slightly Parisian decor is in an old 14th-century villa in the heart of Firenze. The reception area, salons and bar are imbued with a sophisticated atmosphere, with their marble mosaic columns and floors, stucco ceilings, large 1900-style couches and profusion of green plants. All the rooms are extremely comfortable and have marble bathrooms. The ones overlooking the garden are quieter. Breakfasts and meals are served in a nice garden-level greenhouse.

How to get there *(Map 10): In the village center Porta al Prato, near the teatro comunale.*

Hotel Lungarno

Borgo Sant' Jacopo, 14
50125 Firenze
Tel. (0)55-27 26 1 - Fax (0)55-26 84 37

Category ★★★★ **Rooms** 54 and 6 apartments with air-conditionig, telephone, bath or shower, WC, satellite TV, minibar and safe; elevator. **Price** 300-400,000L. **Meals** Breakfast 25,000L, served 7:00-11:00. **Restaurant** See p. 471-474. **Credit cards** All major. **Pets** Dogs not allowed. **Nearby** Fiesole, Certosa di Galluzzo - Villas and gardens around Firenze (tel. palazzo Pitti: 055 21 48 56), Vallombrosa abbey, dell'Ugolino golf course (18-hole) in Grassina. **Open** All year.

The view of the Arno from the Ponte Vecchio is one of the loveliest sights in Florence, especially at dusk when rowboats skim the waters of the river, glowing red in the setting sun. This, along with the houses on the famous bridge, is the view you will have from the salon of the Lungarno or from some of the bedrooms. Recent renovations have increased the luxury of the hotel but have still kept an elegant and contemporary atmosphere, with interesting modern paintings on the walls. Calm and comfort are its other great assets. Of course, you must book well in advance if you want to get a room facing the river. The hospitality is pleasant and professional.

How to get there *(Map 10): Beside Ponte Vecchio, near Palazzo Pitti.*

Torre di Bellosguardo

Via Roti Michelozzi, 2
50124 Firenze
Tel. (0)55-229 81 45 - Fax (0)55-22 90 08
Sig. Franchetti

Category ★★★★ **Rooms** 10 and 6 suites with telephone, bath or shower and WC, elevator. **Price** Single 290-340,000L, double 450,000L, suite 490-650,000L. **Meals** Breakfast 30-40,000L, served 7:30-10:00. **Restaurant** Lunch by the swimming pool in summer (see pp. 471-474). **Credit cards** All major. **Pets** Dogs allowed. **Facilities** Swimming pool, parking. **Nearby** Firenze, Fiesole, Certosa di Galluzzo, Villas and gardens around Firenze (tel. Palazzo Pitti: 055 21 48 56), Vallombrosa abbey, dell'Ugolino golf course (18-hole) in Grassina. **Open** All year.

Torre di Bellosguardo is on a hill just outside the center of Firenze and has an exceptional view of the city. It is an extraordinarily quiet place with a majestic palace, a 7th-century tower, a lovely harmonious garden and a beautiful swimming pool down below. Today it is an elegant and comfortable hotel, with sixteen unusually large rooms, many salons and a spectacular sun room. Each room is unique and has period furniture, extraordinary woodwork, and frescoes. In the tower, there is a suite on two floors with a marvelous view. All rooms are superb and have comfortable bathrooms. This hotel offers an elegance which today seems reserved for the happy few.

How to get there *(Map 10): Towards Forte Belvedere, Porta Romana.*

Villa Belvedere

Via Benedetto Castelli, 3
50124 Firenze
Tel. (0)55-22 25 01 - Fax (0)55-22 31 63
Sig. and Sig.ra Ceschi - Perotto

Category ★★★★ **Rooms** 26 with air-conditioning, telephone, bath or shower, WC, satellite TV, safe and minibar; elevator. **Price** Single 220-240,000L, double 290-330,000L. **Meals** Breakfast included, served 7:15-10:00. **Restaurant** Snack service for lunch and dinner (see pp. 471-474). **Credit cards** All major. **Pets** Dogs not allowed. **Facilities** Swimming pool, tennis, parking. **Nearby** Firenze, Fiesole, Certosa di Galluzzo, Villas and gardens around Firenze (tel. Palazzo Pitti: 055 21 48 56), Vallombrosa abbey, dell'Ugolino golf course (18-hole) in Grassina. **Open** Mar. – Nov.

The Villa Belvedere is in the heights of Firenze, surrounded by a large quiet garden with a swimming pool and a tennis court. You will appreciate this place if you are traveling with children. The modern veranda, which has been added to the house, detracts a bit from its charm. The rooms have been entirely renovated and are all spacious and comfortable. Most have a superb view of Firenze, the countryside or the Certosa. The ones in the front have large terraces and the nicest are on the top floor. There's no restaurant, but if you are too tired to go out, snacks are available. The Ceschi family extends the warmest of welcomes.

How to get there *(Map 10): Towards Forte Belvedere - Porta Romana. Bus (300 m) for the town center.*

Villa Carlotta

50125 Firenze
Via Michele di Lando, 3
Tel. and Fax (0)55-233 61 34
Sig. Gheri

Category ★★★★ **Rooms** 32 with air-conditioning, telephone, bath or shower, TV and minibar; elevator. **Price** Single 135-270,000L, double 190-380,000L. **Meals** Breakfast included, served 7:15-10:15; half board 160-235,000L, full board 180-265,000L. **Restaurant** Service 12:30-14:30, 19:30-21:30, closed Sun., à la carte. Specialties: Tuscan and Italian cuisine. **Credit cards** All major. **Pets** Dogs allowed. **Facilities** Parking. **Nearby** Firenze, Fiesole, Certosa di Galluzzo, Villas and gardens around Firenze (tel. Palazzo Pitti: 055 21 48 56), Vallombrosa abbey, dell'Ugolino golf course (18-hole) in Grassina. **Open** All year.

Close to the Palazzo Pitti and the Boboli Gardens, the Villa Carlotta is an old patrician villa which has retained its nice proportions and harmony. Large bow windows in the salons open onto an inviting garden. The rooms are carefully decorated–without surprises–and offer all the amenities you might want.

How to get there *(Map 10): Towards Forte Belvedere - Porta Romana.*

Hotel Hermitage

Piazza del Pesce - Vicolo Marzio, 1 (Ponte Vecchio)
50122 Firenze
Tel. (0)55-28 72 16 - Fax (0)55-21 22 08 - Sig. Scarcelli
E-mail: hermitage@italyhotel.com - Web: http://www.italyhotel.com/firenze/hermitage

Category ★★★ **Rooms** 29 with air-conditioning, telephone, bath or shower, WC and satellite TV; elevator. **Price** Single 260,000L, double 310,000L. **Meals** Breakfast included, served 7:30-9:30. **Restaurant** See pp. 471-474. **Credit cards** Visa, Eurocard, MasterCard. **Pets** Small dogs allowed. **Nearby** Firenze, Fiesole, Certosa di Galluzzo, Villas and gardens around Firenze (tel. Palazzo Pitti: 055 21 48 56), Vallombrosa abbey, dell'Ugolino golf course (18-hole) in Grassina. **Open** All year.

This small hotel takes up the entire building next to the Ponte Vecchio. The rooms are comfortable; each one is done in a slightly different antiquated style and all have double-pane windows, which makes them pretty soundproof. The quietest rooms are those on the courtyard, especially Rooms 13 and 14; but now that the area has become a pedestrian zone, you may sleep just as well on the streetside. What made us choose this hotel was its good prices and its terrace with an unforgettable view of the Ponte Vecchio and the Pitti Palace on one side and the dome of the Duomo and the rooftops of the Signoria on the other. If you are traveling alone, reserve the terrace-level room. It is hard to park, but the hotel can direct you to the nearest garage.

How to get there *(Map 10): Next to Ponte Vecchio.*

Hotel Loggiato dei Serviti

Piazza della SS. Annunziata, 3
50122 Firenze
Tel. (0)55-28 95 92 - Fax (0)55-28 95 95 - Sig. Budini Gattai
E-mail: loggiato.dei.serviti.@italyhotel.com

Category ★★★ **Rooms** 25 and 4 apartments with air-conditioning, telephone, bath or shower, WC, TV and minibar; elevator. **Price** Single 210,000L, double 310,000L, suite 340-700,000L. **Meals** Breakfast included, served 7:15-10:00. **Credit cards** All major. **Pets** Dogs allowed (fee). **Nearby** Firenze, Fiesole, Certosa di Galluzzo, Villas and gardens around Firenze (tel. Palazzo Pitti: 055 21 48 56), Vallombrosa abbey, dell'Ugolino golf course (18-hole) in Grassina. **Open** All year.

One of our favorites in Firenze, this hotel is on the Piazza della SS. Annunziata, just across from the Hospital of the Innocents. Like the hospital, it was designed by Brunelleschi, a brilliant architect of the Tuscan Rennaissance. The hotel decor is simple and elegant, respectful of the archictectural proportions of the period. The rooms are spare and charming; some open onto the square and have views of the equestrian statue of Ferdinand I of Médicis and the portico by Brunelleschi, embellished with medallions by Della Robbia. The other rooms open onto the Accademia garden and are quieter. The ones on the top floor have a nice view of the Duomo. The square has been surprisingly protected from the hustle and bustle of tourists; no café terraces or souvenir shops disturb the peace and quiet at nightfall–only the sound of swallows playing under the portico arches can be heard.

How to get there *(Map 10): Near the piazza del Duomo.*

1998

Hotel Splendor

Via San Gallo, 30
50129 Firenze
Tel. (0)55-48 34 27 - Fax (0)55-46 12 76 - Sig. and Sig.ra Masoero

Category ★★★ **Rooms** 31 (28 with air-conditioning) telephone, (25 with bath or shower, WC), satellite TV, safe. Price Single 145,000L, 160,000L (without bath), double 220,000L, triple 280,000L. **Meals** Breakfast included, served 7:30-9:30. **Restaurant** See pp. 471-474. **Credit cards** Amex, Visa, Eurocard, MasterCard. **Pets** Dogs not allowed. **Facilities** Parking (30,000L). **Nearby** Fiesole, Certosa di Galluzzo, Villas and gardens around Firenze (tel. palazzo Pitti: 055 21 48 56), Vallombrosa abbey, dell'Ugolino golf course (18-hole) in Grassina. **Open** All year.

The 19th-century building that houses the Hotel Splendor is ideally located just a few steps from the San Marco convent, famous for its frescoes by Fra Angelico. The friendly welcome makes you feel right at home in the softly-lighted and elegantly-furnished salons with their oak floors, cozy armchairs, antique Persian rugs and lovely bouquets of flowers. The breakfast room is particularly attractive with its mural paintings and large French windows opening on a flower-decked terrace where you can take your breakfast if you so desire. You can use the place as a reading room as well, and if you want to brush up on the history of Florence, the owner will offer you an interesting little volume of stories published by the hotel. The rooms are soundproofed and decorated in the same good taste. The ones most in demand (sometimes reserved from one year to the next) are those which face San Marco. A nice place for dinner nearby is the Trattoria Tito at 112 Via San Gallo.

How to get there *(Map 10): Near the piazza San Marco.*

Hotel Villa Azalee

Viale Fratelli Rosselli, 44
50123 Firenze
Tel. (0)55-21 42 42/28 43 31 - Fax (0)55-26 82 64 - Sig.ra Brizzi
E-mail: villaazalee@fi.flashnet.it

Category ★★★ **Rooms** 24 with telephone, bath or shower, WC, TV and minibar. **Price** Single 166,000L, double 250,000L, triple 336,000L. **Meals** Breakfast included, served 7:30-12:00. **Restaurant** See pp. 471-474. **Pets** Small dogs allowed. **Facilities** Parking in the street or public parking (35,000L). **Nearby** Firenze, Fiesole, Certosa di Galluzzo, Villas and gardens around Firenze (tel. Palazzo Pitti: 055 21 48 56), Vallombrosa abbey, dell'Ugolino golf course (18-hole) in Grassina. **Open** All year.

The Villa Azalee is just a few yards from the train station Santa Maria Novella, on a side lane of one of the roads that ring the city. This location may seem a bit noisy, but don't worry: the latest restorations have been done with a view to the maximum comfort of the guests. The rooms are not very large, but have modern amenities and a Tuscan-style decor that aims at recreating the atmosphere of a private villa. All the bedrooms are air-conditioned but the nicest are those that face the garden or even the ones in the small outbuilding. The dining room where breakfast is served opens right onto the garden. This hotel offers good value for the price.

How to get there *(Map 10): Near the railway station (stazione).*

Hotel Morandi Alla Crocetta

Via Laura, 50
50121 Firenze
Tel. (0)55-234 47 47 - Fax (0)55-258 09 54
Sig.ra Doyle Antuono

Category ★★★ **Rooms** 10 with air-conditioning, telephone, shower, WC, TV and minibar. **Price** Single 120,000L, double 210,000L, triple 280,000L. **Meals** Breakfast 16,000L, served 8:00-12:00. **Restaurant** See pp. 471-474. **Credit cards** All major. **Pets** Small dogs allowed. **Nearby** Firenze, Fiesole, Certosa di Galluzzo, Villas and gardens around Firenze (tel. Palazzo Pitti: 055 21 48 56), Vallombrosa abbey, dell'Ugolino golf course (18-hole) in Grassina. **Open** All year.

The small, nice Hotel Morandi Alla Crocetta is run by the equally nice Katherine Doyle who came to Firenze for the first time many years ago when she was only 12. The *pensione* occupies part of a monastery built during the Renaissance on a small street near the Piazza della SS. Annunziata. The interior is as comfortable as in British homes, and the rooms all have bathrooms and air-conditioning. The decor is very tasteful; each room has antique furniture and beautiful collector's items. Two of them have a beautiful flower-covered terrace on a countryard. The atmosphere of the hotel is quiet and serene.

How to get there *(Map 10): Near Piazza della SS. Annunziata.*

Hotel Pensione Pendini

Via Strozzi, 2
50123 Firenze
Tel. (0)55-21 11 70 - Fax (0)55-281 807 - Sig.ra Abolaffio
E-mail: pendini@dada;it - Web: http://www.tiac.net/users/pendini

Category ★★★ **Rooms** 42 with air-conditioning, telephone, bath or shower, WC and satellite TV; elevator. **Price** Single 130-160,000L, double 180-230,000L. **Meals** Breakfast included, served 7:30-10:00. **Restaurant** See pp. 471-474. **Credit cards** All major. **Pets** Small dogs allowed. **Nearby** Firenze, Fiesole, Certosa di Galluzzo, Villas and gardens around Firenze (tel. Palazzo Pitti: 055 21 48 56), Vallombrosa abbey, dell'Ugolino golf course (18-hole) in Grassina. **Open** All year.

When you cross the large Piazza della Repubblica or stop and have a drink on the terrace of the Gilli or the Giubbe Rosse, you won't be able to keep from noticing the building with the immense sign, which since 1879 has advertised the pensione within. The entrance is on a side street and an elevator will take you to the right floor. You will have an immediate impression of comfort as you walk in, and you won't be disappointed. All the rooms are large; avoid the ones on the Piazza della Republica, which is outside of the pedestrian area. This hotel is remarkable for its quality and low prices.

How to get there *(Map 10): In the town center, near Piazza della Repubblica, entrance via Strozzi.*

1998

Pensione Annalena

Via Romana, 34
50127 Firenze
Tel. (0)55-22 24 02/22 24 39 - Fax (0)55-22 24 03 - Sig. Salvestrini
E-mail: info@hotelannalena.it - Web: http://www.annalena.it

Category ★★★ **Rooms** 20 with telephone, bath or shower, WC, satellite TV and safe. **Price** Single 150-170,000, double 180-230,000L. **Meals** Breakfast 15,000L, served 8:00-10:00. **Restaurant** See pp. 471-474. **Credit cards** All major. **Pets** Dogs allowed. **Facilities** Parking (20,000L). **Nearby** Fiesole, Certosa di Galluzzo, Villas and gardens around Firenze (tel. Palazzo Pitti: 055 21 48 56), Vallombrosa abbey, dell'Ugolino golf course (18-hole) in Grassina. **Open** All year (except May).

Located a few steps from the Pitti Palace and the Boboli Gardens, the former 15th-century palace was the home of the Orlandini and Medici families before becoming the property of the beautiful Annalena who, after a tragic love story, withdrew from the world and left her palace to the Dominicans. The place is steeped in history. The former reception hall has been turned into a large entrance area where vestiges of the old frescoes are still visible, as well as several salons and a breakfast room. The rooms furnished in traditional style are not very spacious and the bathrooms are even smaller. Our favorites are those that face the gallery with a view of the old gardens, now a tree nursery (Numbers 19, 20 and 21) and those giving onto the terrace.

How to get there *(Map 10): Near the Palazzo Pitti. You can take the via Romana at Piazzale di Porta Romana.*

Hotel Tornabuoni Beacci

50123 Firenze
Via Tornabuoni, 3
Tel. (0)55-21 26 45/26 83 77 - Fax (0)55-28 35 94 - Sig. Beacci
E-mail: beacci:tornabuani@italyhotel.com

Category ★★★ **Rooms** 29 with air-conditioning, telephone, bath or shower, WC, satellite TV and minibar; elevator. **Price** Single 190,000L, double 260-300,000L. **Meals** Breakfast included, served 7:00-10:30. **Restaurant** Service 12:30-14:30, 19:30-21:30, menus, also à la carte (40,000L). **Specialties** Florentine and international cuisine. **Credit cards** All major. **Pets** Small dogs allowed (5,000L). Facilities Garage. **Nearby** Firenze, Fiesole, Certosa di Galluzzo, Villas and gardens around Firenze (tel. Palazzo Pitti: 055 21 48 56), Vallombrosa abbey, dell'Ugolino golf course (18-hole) in Grassina. **Open** All year.

This hotel, on the upper floors of a 14th-century palace, shares one of the elegant streets of Firenze with famous fashion designers and jewelers. It is one of Firenze's oldest hotels; Bismarck, himself, once stayed here. Today, many Americans like come to enjoy the excellent cuisine, the vast rooms and the old family *pensione* atmosphere. If you have a large family or if you are traveling with friends, the hotel offers discounts for reservations of ten or more.

How to get there *(Map 10): In the town center. via lungarno Guicciardini, Ponte S.Trinita and via Tornabuoni.*

1998

Hotel David

Viale Michelangelo, 1
50129 Firenze
Tel. (0)55 681 16 95 - Fax (0)55 680 602
Sig.Cecioni

Category ★★★ **Rooms** 26 with air conditioning, tel., bath or shower, WC, TV, minibar. **Price** Double 230,000L. **Meals** Breakfast included served 7:30-10:30. **Restaurant** See p. 471-474. **Credit cards** All major. **Pets** Dogs not allowed. **Facilities** Parking. **Nearby** Firenze; Fiesole; Certosa di Galluzzo; Villas and gardens around Firenze (tel. Palazzo Pitti: 055 21 48 56). abbey of Vallombosa; dell'Ugolino golf course (18-hole) in Grassina. **Open** All year.

Charm and comfort in this little villa that was enlarged when the Hotel David was created. The owner, Giovanni Cecioni, has recreated the ambience of a private house by giving each bedroom a personalized decor. Antique furniture, either belonging to the family or acquired from local dealers, contribute to the intimate feel. The same is true for the living room, which is arranged in different areas for reading, writing or playing cards. The light from a large picture window and the foliage in the little garden add to the charm. And you don't have to search for a restaurant for dinner - the hotel has arrangements with several neighborhood trattorie.

How to get there *(Map 10): Near Arno (lungarno).*

Residenza Johanna I

50129 Firenze
Via Bonifacio Lupi, 14
Tel. (0)55 48 18 96 - Fax (0)55 48 27 21
Sig.ra Gulmanelli and Sig.ra Arrighi

Rooms 11 (9 with shower or bath and WC), TV. **Price** Single 70,000 L, double 115-130,000 L, triple 150,000 L. **Meals** No breakfast. **Restaurant** See p. 471-474. **Credit cards** Not accepted. **Pets** Dogs allowed. **Facilities** Elevator, garage (22,000 L). **Nearby** Firenze; Fiesole; Certosa di Galluzzo; Villas and gardens around Firenze (tel. Palazzo Pitti: 055 21 48 56). abbey of Vallombosa; dell'Ugolino golf course (18-hole) in Grassina. **Open** All year.

In the heart of Florence, two young women had the unusual idea to transform one floor of a large building into a residential hotel. Built around two long corridors, it is like a real apartment, with a number of small bedrooms, nearly all with a private bath. There is no bar or television or breakfast room (though there is a kettle to prepare your morning tea or coffee), but it has an intimacy that no hotel can provide, and a gentle, tasteful decor that adds to the quiet comfort. You have your own keys, which makes you feel quite at home. And for Florence, the prices are exceptionally low. So why not try living like a Florentine for a few days?

How to get there *(Map 10) : in town center, 10 minutes from Duomo.*

Residenza Johanna II

Via delle cinque giornate, 12
50129 Firenze
Tel. (0)55-41 33 77 - Sig.ra Gulmanelli

Rooms 6 with telephone.(on request), shower, WC, satellite TV. **Price** Double 130,0000L. **Meals** Breakfast included. **Restaurant.** See pp. 471-474. **Credit cards** Not accepted. **Pets** Dogs allowed. **Facilities** Parking. **Nearby** Fiesole, Certosa di Galluzzo, Villas and gardens around Firenze (tel. palazzo Pitti: 055 21 48 56), Vallombrosa abbey, dell'Ugolino golf course (18-hole) in Grassina. **Open** All year.

Encouraged by the success of the Residenza Johanna, its owners have now added a second version, the Johanna II. Finding such comfortable, well-kept and well-decorated rooms (most of them are quite spacious as well) with flowered fabrics of different colors and Italian prints on the walls - and at such prices - is something of a feat in Italy (and we can't help wondering why this is?). Perhaps the trick is that the service is left up to the clients: For example, if you like, they will give you a portable phone (but only to phone within Italy), you prepare your own breakfast in your room (each room has a kettle with tea, coffee, chocolate and biscuits) and you have your own key so you are free to come and go at any hour. The nicest rooms are those on the second story, overlooking the garden (which is also used for parking, but in Florence, who can complain?) On the ground floor, there is a pleasant salon-library where you can consult a fine collection of art books on Florence and Italy.

How to get there *(Map 10): 15 minutes from the duomo.*

Villa San Michele

Via Doccia, 4
50014 Firenze - Fiesole
Tel. (0)55-59 451 - Fax (0)55-59 87 34
Sig. Saccani

Category ★★★★★ **Rooms** 41 with air-conditioning, telephone, bath, WC, satellite TV, safe and minibar. **Price** With half board: Single 720,000L, double 1,100-1,430,000L, suite 1,940-2,600,000L. **Meals** Breakfast included (buffet), served 7:00-10:30. **Restaurant** Service 13:00-14:45, 20:00-21:45; menus 105-120,000L, also à la carte. Specialties: Tuscan and Italian cuisine. **Credit cards** All major. **Pets** Small dogs allowed (except in restaurant and in swimming pool). **Facilities** Heated swimming pool, parking. **Nearby** Firenze, Fiesole, Certosa di Galluzzo, Villas and gardens around Firenze (tel. Palazzo Pitti: 055 21 48 56), Vallombrosa abbey, dell'Ugolino golf course (18-hole) in Grassina. **Open** Mar. 28 – Dec. 1.

The Villa San Michele of Fiesole, along with the Villa d'Este of Lake Como, is one of the two monuments of the Italian hotel trade. Both are luxury hotels, to be sure, but they have in addition the magic that comes from sheer beauty: the beauty of the site, for one, and then the beauty of the architecture. The former monastery that houses the San Michele is said to have been designed by Michelangelo himself. The villa with its gardens and terraces that take on a rosy glow as the sun sets over the Duomo and the rooftops of Florence is an unforgettable spectacle, as unforgettable as the elegance of the rooms, the meals and the service.

How to get there *(Map 10): 8 km north of Firenze. Bus for Firenze 200 meters from the hotel.*

Pensione Bencistà

Via Benedetto da Maiano, 4
50014 Firenze - Fiesole
Tel. (0)55-59 163 - Fax (0)55-59 163
Simone Simoni

Category ★★★ **Rooms** 44 with telephone, bath or shower and WC. **Price** With half board 115-135,000L, full board 130-150,000L. **Meals** Breakfast included, served 8:00-10:00. **Restaurant** Service 13:00-14:00, 19:30-20:30; menu. Specialties: Traditional Tuscan cuisine. **Credit cards** Not accepted. **Pets** Dogs allowed (except in restaurant). **Facilities** Parking. **Nearby** Firenze, Fiesole, Certosa di Galluzzo, Villas and gardens around Firenze (tel. Palazzo Pitti: 055 21 48 56), Vallombrosa abbey, dell'Ugolino golf course (18-hole) in Grassina. **Open** All year.

On the hills of Fiesole, this family *pensione* is a charming establishment for those who love Tuscany. It has been simply and carefully decorated with antique furniture and travel souvenirs. The library, filled with books in English, is the perfect place to spend some quiet moments. The terrace is in a natural setting, and the garden is full of flowers and trees of diverse species. The rooms, which are made more comfortable year after year, are delightful. The home-style cuisine adds to the relaxed family atmosphere. Open year-round, the Christmas and New Year's Eve are celebrated at the *pensione* according to Tuscan tradition.

How to get there *(Map 10): 8 km north of Firenze. Bus for Firenze 200 meters from the hotel.*

Hotel Villa Le Rondini

Via Bolognese Vecchia, 224
50139 Firenze - Trespiano
Tel. (0)55-40 00 81 - Fax (0)55-26 82 12
Sig.ra Reali

Category ★★★ **Rooms** 43 (some with air conditioning), telephone, bath or shower, WC, satellite TV and minibar. **Price** Single 250,000L, double 290,000L, 390,000L (suite). **Meals** Breakfast +50,000L, served 7:30-10:00; half board 1950-230,000L (per pers.), 150-180,000L (per pers. in double room). **Restaurant** Service 12:30-14:30, 19:30-21:30; menus: 45-80,000L, also à la carte. Specialties: Italian and international cuisine with farm produce's. **Credit cards** All major. **Pets** Dogs allowed (6,000L). **Facilities** Swimming pool, tennis (15,000L), sauna, parking. **Nearby** Firenze, Fiesole, Certosa di Galluzzo, Villas and gardens around Firenze (tel. Palazzo Pitti: 055 21 48 56), Vallombrosa abbey, dell'Ugolino golf course (18-hole) in Grassina. **Open** All year.

You reach the magnificent Rondini estate by driving through a vast olive grove. The hotel property spreads over 20 hectares and the guest rooms are divided into three villas. The ones in the original old house have the charm of their age and have been renovated to include modern comforts. Those in the two annexes, situated near the entrance to the estate, are less appealing but every bit as comfortable. It's a nice place, all in all, especially in summer, when the countryside is so beautiful. And there's no problem getting into Florence — the bus stop is just in front of the villa's gate.

How to get there *(Map 10): 7 km north of Firenze, towards Fortessa da Bano until the Piazza della Libertà, via Bolognese. Bus no. 25 in front of the hotel entrance.*

1998

Fattoria Il Milione

50100 Firenze - Giogoli
Via di Giogoli, 14
Tel. (0)55-20 48 713 - Fax (0)55-20 48 046 - Jessica Guscelli

6 Appartments with Kitchen, bath. **Price** Appart.: 150,000L (2 pers.), 300,000L (4 pers.). **Cradit cards** No accepted. **Pets** Dogs allowed on request. **Facilities** Swimming pool, parking. **Nearby** Firenze, Fiesole, Certosa di Galluzzo, Villas and gardens around Firenze (tel. Palazzo Pitti: 055 21 48 56), Vallombrosa abbey, dell'Ugolino golf course (18-hole) in Grassina. **Communal Meals** By reservation; menu 50,000L (Wine, Coffee, Grappa included). **Open** All year.

Il Milione di Brandimarte is a model of the art of living, and it would be a pity just to drop your luggage there and go off exploring the surroundings. Here the guests can truly share the emotions and the harmony of this unique land, "daughter of nature and of man." Life flows to the rhythm of the seasons and the work on the farm - plowing, seeding, harvesting, crop-picking. The countryside is always a visual delight - silver in the gray light of winter, splashed with bright color before the olive picking, when orange nets are spread out beneath the trees, red-hued as the sun sets over Florence. Like Brandimarte (the famous Florentine goldsmith) and Jessica and their seven children, we should also celebrate nature around their large table, where excellent *table d'hôte* meals are served. And if you're curious about the name of the place, the story is this: to open this farm, Brandimarte asked his friends for *un milione* in exchange for one of his works. "Craftwork and farmwork are genetically linked by a common root," says the man who is both artist and farmer.

How to get there *(Map 10): A 1, Florenz-Certosa exit , towards Florenz, then right towards Scandicci.*

Hotel Paggeria Medicea

Viale Papa Giovanni XXIII, 3
50040 Artimino - Carmignano (Firenze)
Tel. (0)55-871 80 81 - Fax (0)55-871 80 80
Sig. Gualtieri

Category ★★★★ **Rooms** 37 with air conditioning and ,31 apartments with telephone, bath or shower, WC, TV and minibar, wheelchair access. **Price** Single 130-150,000L, double 220-260,000L. **Meals** Breakfast included, served 7:30-10:30; half board 50,000L (per pers., 3 days min.). **Restaurant** Service 12:30-14:00, 19:30-22:00; closed Wed. and Fri. at noon; menu, also à la carte. **Credit cards** All major. **Pets** Dogs allowed. **Facilities** Swimming pool, 2 tennis, gymnasium, mountain bike, garage (50,000L). **Nearby** Artimino (church and Etruscan ancient city of Pian di Rosello, Villa dell'Artimino), Etruscan Tomb of Montefortini in Comeana, Médici Villa Gardens' in Poggio a Caiano, Prato, Pistoia, Firenze, dell'Ugolino golf course (18-hole) in Grassina. **Open** All year.

If you stay at the Paggeria Medicea, your neighbor will be the lovely "La Ferdinanda," built as a hunting lodge by the Duke Ferdinand de Medici. This undoubtedly explains the sumptuous sobriety of the "fortress-villa," flanked by bastions on the four corners, and whose only adornment is the fanciful double-curved staircase that leads to the loggia. But living in this part of the villa is only a dream, though it's a mere 30 yards away — the guest quarters are in the wing that used to house the servants. Never fear, this wing has been completely transformed into a luxury hotel that offers well-appointed rooms and suites, a restaurant where you will appreciate the products of the estate, and service that is high-style, gracious and attentive.

How to get there *(Map 10): 24 km north of Firenze via A1, Firenze-Signa exit; via A11, Prato exit.*

Residenza San Niccolo d'Olmeto 

Le Valli 50066 Incisa Valdarno (Firenze)
Tel. (0)55-24 09 51 - Fax (0)55-24 02 82
Sig.ra Valenti Cavagnari

Apartments 6 with kitchen, shower, WC, 2 with TV. **Price** 1 week 850,000L (2 pers.), 850,000L (2-3 pers.); extra bed 100-150,000L. **Credit cards** All major. **Pets** Dogs not allowed. **Facilites** Swimming pool, parking. **Nearby** Firenze, Le Valdarno between Firenze and Arezzo. **Open** Apr. - Oct.

Only 18 kilometers from Florence, after crossing a landscape that lacks the gentle charm of the best Tuscan countryside, not far from the autostrada, you will be all the more surprised to come upon the orchards and olive groves that surround the former convent of San Niccolo. Beautifully restored and very well-kept by the Cavagnari family (who earlier won distinction with the Hotel J & J in Florence), the renovation is both rustic and elegant. The apartments are in the building near the cloister and the Romanesque chapel. They are all quite comfortable with a well-equipped kitchen area, functional shower rooms and meticulous decoration: floors of terra cotta tile and modern furnishings that set off a number of well-chosen antiques. Our preference goes to those that are not near the old orange grove. When the lemon and mandarin trees are in bloom their scent is all-pervasive, further adding to the serene atmosphere of the estate.

How to get there *(Map 10): 18 km from Firenze via A1 Incisa Valdarno exit, then SS 69 to Burchio, then Le Valli.*

Salvadonica

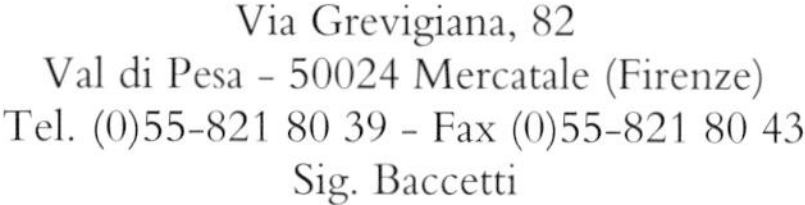

Via Grevigiana, 82
Val di Pesa - 50024 Mercatale (Firenze)
Tel. (0)55-821 80 39 - Fax (0)55-821 80 43
Sig. Baccetti

Rooms 5 and 10 apartments with telephone, bath or shower, WC and TV; Wheelchair access. **Price** Single 110,000L, double 150-170,000L, apartments (by request). **Meals** Breakfast included, served 8:00-10:00. **Restaurant** in San Casciano in Val di pesa p. 476. **Credit cards** All major. **Pets** Dogs not allowed. **Facilities** Swimming pool with whirlpool, tennis, parking. **Nearby** Firenze, Certosa di Galluzzo, Impruneta, Siena, dell'Ugolino golf course (18-hole) in Grassina. **Open** April - Nov. 16.

Two Tuscan farmhouses, dating from the 14th century, have been made into this luxurious hotel in the Tuscan countryside. Its restoration is an example of one of the more successful in the region because the rustic feeling of the original buildings has been maintained in the renovation. They used old materials and decorated the place with beautiful polished farm furniture, but also added modern conveniences. The hotel consists mostly of small apartments, which you are advised to rent by the week. The housework is done for you every day. You can have breakfast around a communal table at the hotel and dine pleasantly in San Casciano and the surrounding area in the evening. You can buy wine and olive oil produced on the farm.

How to get there *(Map 10): 20 km from Firenze via A1, Firenze-Certosa exit, then highway towards Siena, San Casciano exit; in San Casciano, go left towards Mercatale.*

Castello di Montegufoni

50020 Montagnana (Firenze)
Tel. (0)571-67.11.31 - Fax (0)571-67.15.14
Sig. Posarelli

Apartments 25 with shower, WC, public phone. **Price** For 2 pers., 160,000L (900,000L week), for 4 pers. 250,000L (1,200,000L week), for 6 pers. 300,000L (1,600,000L week). **Meals** Breakfast (fresh bread) by request. **Restaurant** By request in "La Tavena," Mon., Wed., Fri. **Credit cards** Not accepted. **Pets** Dogs not allowed. **Facilities** 2 swimming pools, parking. **Nearby** Firenze, Certosa di Galluzzo, Impruneta (Santa Maria dell'Impruneta Church; Siena, dell'Ugolino golf course (18-hole) in Grassina. **Open** 26 Mar. – Nov.

While you're in Florence, live like a Florentine — or better still, like a Florentine noble, in a castle of your own, the Castello di Montegufoni, some 15 kilometers from Florence. It is complete with lush gardens, towering cypresses and terra cotta jars overflowing with flowers, and the facades in those wonderful muted colors that are unique to Florence. The well-appointed, sometimes even sumptuous, apartments can sleep up to six people. As for the service, it is so well-organized that you can be completely independent and at the same time have fresh bread delivered every morning for your breakfast. It is also possible to have dinner in, if you wish. To make sure no one will feel crowded, there are two swimming pools. This is the sort of place that will please parents and their children as well.

How to get there *(Map 10): 15 km west of Firenze, via highway towards Livorno-Pisa, Ginestra exit; in Ginestra, follow the signs to Montespertoli, turn right, go 4 km to Baccaiano, then turn left (1 km).*

Fattoria La Loggia

Via Casciano, 40
50020 Montefiridolfi - San Casciano (Firenze)
Tel. (0)55-82 44 288 - Fax (0)55-82 44 283
Sig. Baruffaldi

Rooms 3 double and 11 apartments for 2-6 pers. with kitchen, rooms, living room, bath and WC. **Price** 150-200,000L (per 2 pers.), apart. 200-250,000L (per day per 2 pers.). **Restaurant** By request. Service 20:00-23:00; menus 45-55,000L. Specialties: Tuscan cuisine with products from the farm. **Pets** Dogs allowed. **Facilities** Swimming pool, mountain bikes, riding. **Nearby** Firenze, Le Chianti, Certosa di Galluzzo, Impruneta (Santa Maria dell'Impruneta Church), Siena, Volterra, Pisa, San Gimignano, dell'Ugolino golf course (18-hole) in Grassina. **Open** All year.

You may have to pinch yourself to make sure you're not dreaming when you cross the Tuscan countryside to one of these beautiful farmhouses perched on top of a hill among a few cypress trees with a view of the little furrowed valleys. The Fattoria is not a hotel, but a functioning agricultural estate with a carefully restored Renaissance hamlet of small private houses, which have been decorated with Tuscan-style refinement. Here, you can move at your own pace, as you would in your own country house. But everything will be ready when you arrive–from your first breakfast to the bottle of champagne to celebrate your first evening.

How to get there *(Map 10): 21 km south of Firenze via A1, Firenze-Certosa exit; then via SS Firenze-Siena, Bargino exit.*

Villa Le Barone

Via S. Leolino, 19
50020 Panzano in Chianti (Firenze)
Tel. (0)55-85 26 21 - Fax (0)55-85 22 77
Sig.ra Buonamici

Category ★★★ **Rooms** 27 with telephone, bath or shower and WC. **Price** With half board 195-225,000L (per pers.). **Meals** Breakfast included, served 8:00-10:00. **Restaurant** Service 13:00-14:00, 19:30-21:00, menu 60,000L, à la carte. Specialties: Tuscan cuisine. **Credit cards** All major. **Pets** Dogs not allowed. **Facilities** Swimming pool, tennis. **Nearby** Greve valley via S222 (vineyards of Chianti Classico from Greve to Gaiole), Firenze, Siena, dell'Ugolino golf course (18-hole) in Grassina. **Open** Apr. – Oct.

The Villa Le Barone has always belonged to famous owners, once the Della Robbia family, today the *duchesa* Visconti. The outside of the house has kept its original appearance while the inside has been remodeled into an inviting and intimate home. Nothing here reminds you that you're in a hotel; the living room with its reading nook and chimney-corner, the cheery bedrooms with their antique beds and brightly-colored spreads, all have a very homey feel. The swimming pool is wonderfully landscaped, its lawns well-shaded against the hot sun of a Florentine summer. And from the tennis court, the view extends far into the countryside, with olive groves and vineyards of *Chianti Classico.*

How to get there *(Map 10): 33 km south of Firenze via S222 to Panzano in Chianti via Greve in Chianti.*

1998

Fattoria di Petrognano

Petrognano
Pomino 50060 Rufina (Firenze)
Tel. (0)55-831 88 12/831 88 67 - Fax (0)55-242 918
Sig.ra Galeotti-Ottieri

Rooms 7 and 5 apartments (2-8 pers.) with telephone, bath or shower, WC. **Price** Double 10,000L, apart. 600,000-1,200,000L (1 week). **Meals** Breakfast included, served 8:30-10:00. **Restaurant** Service 13:00-14:00, 20:00-21:00; menu 20,000L. Specialties: farm produce. **Credit cards** Not accepted. **Pets** Dogs allowed. **Facilities** Swimming pool, tennis, parking. **Nearby** Valley of Mugello: Monastery of Santa Maria di Rosano, Vicchio, San Piero a Sieve, Scarperia, Convent of Bosco ai Frati, convent of Monte Senario in Bivigliano, Scarperia and Poppi golf course (9-hole). **Open** May - Oct.

This handsome estate once belonged to the bishops of Fiesole who were responsible for the famous vineyard as far back as the Renaissance. The main building, which once housed the convent, has kept its noble proportions, antique floors and monumental fireplace. Several farmhouses that belong to the Fattoria have been restored, including the Locanda Patricino, whose rooms are simply furnished, decorated with a few old family portraits, but they have a breathtaking view over the surrounding hills. The one up in the attic has the finest panorama of all. For long family stays the apartments are best. Meals are served in the rustic dining room where it is a pleasure to sit around the large family table and partake of the specialties of the house (including beef raised on the estate) and drink an excellent Pomino, drawn from the vat. A pleasant way to sample the hospitality of an old Tuscan family.

How to get there *(Map 10): 30 km from Firenze. Take the N 67 road via Forli to Pontassieve, Rufina and Castiglioni-Pomino.*

Villa Rucellai - Fattoria di Canneto

50047 Prato (Firenze)
Via di Canneto, 16
Tel. (0)574-46 03 92 - Fax (0)574-46 03 92
Famiglia Piqué-Rucellai

Rooms 12 with bath or shower and WC. **Price** Double 120-150,000 L. **Meals** Breakfast included, served at 8:00. **Restaurant** See p.474. **Credit cards** Not accepted. **Pets** Dogs not allowed. **Facilities** Swimming pool, parking. **Nearby** Prato: Duomo (Filippo Lippi frescoes), Palazzo Pretorio, Castello dell'Imperatore, Villa of Médici in Poggio a Caiano, Firenze. **Open** All year.

You are sure to fall in love with this wonderful Tuscan Renaissance villa, which has been in the Rucellai family of Florence since the middle of the 18th century. Your first welcome to the place is on the terrace of the Italian garden, where you will be offered a glass of wine produced on the property. Today the villa, partly turned into a hotel, is a favorite of international artists and entertainers passing through Prato for the theater or the museum of contemporary art. This is quite understandable, for the villa is beautiful and full of charm — its salons and gardens evoke the grandeur of celebrations past. The rooms are attractive, with new and modern bathrooms, and the lack of service is made up for by the kindness of the hosts. There is no restaurant, but you can partake of a family-style breakfast in the morning. One drawback is that the railroad is quite nearby, which could disturb your sleep in the summer.

How to get there *(Map 10): 15 km west of Firenze, 45 km east of Lucca. Via A11, Prato-est exit. Via A1, Prato/Calenzano exit. Then towards Prato and train station, go via Machiavelli, go left via Lambruschini; then on right "Villa S. Leonardo" and "Trattoria la Fontana," follow the railway on your left for 4 km.*

Villa Rigacci

Via Manzoni, 76
50066 Vaggio - Reggello (Firenze)
Tel. (0)55-865 67 18/865 65 62 - Fax (0)55-865 65 37
Famiglia Pierazzi

Category ★★★★ **Rooms** 25 with air-conditioning, telephone, bath or shower, WC, TV and minibar. **Price** Single 150,000L, double 200-260,000L, suite 320,000L. **Meals** Breakfast included, served 7:30-10:30; half board 160-200,000L and full board 190-230,000L. **Restaurant** Service 12:00-14:30, 20:00-22:00; menu: 60,000L, also à la carte. Specialties: French and Italian cuisine. **Credit cards** All major. **Pets** Dogs allowed. **Facilities** Swimming pool, parking. **Nearby** Vallombrosa abbey, Church of Montemignaio, Castello Pretorio in Poppi, Firenze, Siena. **Open** All year.

This old farmhouse, covered with vines and surrounded by woods, has a personality of its own. Built in the 15th century, it is now run by the Pierazzi family. Inside, a fireplace, a richly stocked library and antique furniture collected over the years make for the sort of convivial atmosphere one yearns to find on vacation. Each of the bedrooms is different, but all are furnished in bright cheery colors and equipped with all the amenities. In summer you may choose to spend a whole day between garden and swimming pool instead of going sightseeing, and in the evening you can dine at the Vieux Pressoir, where in addition to the usual Italian dishes, they serve Tuscan specialties.

How to get there *(Map 10): 30 km southeast of Firenze via A1, Incisa exit, number 24, towards Matassino and Vaggio.*

1998

La Callaiola

Strada di Magliano, 3
50021 Barberino Val d'Elsa (Firenze)
Tel. (0)55-80 76 598 - Fax (0)55-80 76 598 - Sig.ra J. Münchenbach

Rooms 2 (4 pers.) with bath and WC. **Price** 70,000L (per pers.). **Meals** Breakfast included. **Restaurant** In Colle Val d'Elsa p. 476. **Credit cards** Not accepted. **Pets** Dogs not allowed. **Facilities** Parking. **Nearby** Siena, Monteriggioni, Colle di Val d'Elsa, Firenze, San Gimignano, Certaldo, Castellina in Chianti, Volterra. **Open** All year (by reservation).

La Callaiola is a working farm run by a friendly German woman who produces organically grown products. She and her Italian husband have restored this sturdy 18th-century building, keeping intact its rustic country air. A garden lawn surrounds the house with its flower-decked facades. All around are olive trees and fields of sunflowers. The Callaiola is run like a real guest house, that is, you live in the house along with the family and share in its daily life. The house is very pleasant, perfumed by bouquets of flowers and aromatic plants set out by Jocelyne, and by the scent of hay from outside. The bedrooms are soberly but charmingly furnished, with a theatrical touch that makes them look even nicer. You reach the bedrooms through the family living room. The atmosphere is informal and living together never feels awkward.

How to get there *(Map 13): 33 km south of Firenze via A 1, Firenze-Certosa exit; towards Siena, Tavarnelle exit.*

Il Paretaio 

Srada delle Ginestre, 12
San Filippo 50021 Barberino Val d'Elsa (Firenze)
Tel. (0)55-80 59 218 - Fax (0)55-80 59 231
Sig.ra de Marchi

Rooms 6 with shower and WC. **Price** Double 120-160,000L. **Meals** Breakfast included; half board 80-120,000L (per pers., 2 days min.). **Communal meals**, service 20:00. Specialties: Traditional cuisine. **Credit cards** Not accepted. **Pets** Dogs allowed. **Facilities** Riding (25-30,000L), swimming pool, parking. **Nearby** Siena, Monteriggioni, Colle di Val d'Elsa, Firenze, San Gimignano, Certaldo, Castellina in Chianti, Volterra. **Open** All year (except Jan. 10 – Feb. 15).

What a wonderful place the Paretaio is for people who like to ride horses! This beautiful estate, in the heart of the Tuscan countryside, is surrounded by four hundred and ninety-five acres of woods, vineyards and olive trees. The young owners–excellent riders themselves–with a passion for horses, offer a series of package rates ranging from a weekend to a week, including classes to improve riding skills for children and adults, courses on breaking in and training horses, and rides in the country. The house and its decor are rustic and the rooms are large and nicely arranged. The atmosphere is very warm, especially when guests gather together in the evening around the big table for a good meal, and a great chianti. This hotel is especially aimed at riders because you have to know and love horses to understand the philosophy of the Paretaio. But if you simply enjoy conviviality and the outdoors you will also like it here.

How to get there *(Map 13): 33 km south of Firenze via A1, Firenze-Certosa exit; towards Siena, Tavarnelle exit; go past Barberino Val d'Elsa, after 2 km take road on the right towerd San Filippo.*

Fattoria Casa Sola

Cortine 50021 Barberino Val d'Elsa (Firenze)
Tel. (0)55-807 50 28 - Fax (0)55-805 91 94
Sig. Gambaro

Apartments 6 with 2-4 rooms (2-8 pers.) with kitchen, sitting room, bath, WC. **Price** 75,000-230,000L (per pers. for 1 day). **Restaurant** In Colle Val d'Elsa p. 476. **Credit cards** Visa, Eurocard and MasterCard. **Pets** Dogs not allowed. **Facilities** Swimming pool, parking. **Nearby** Siena, Monteriggioni, Colle di Val d'Elsa, Firenze, San Gimignano, Certaldo, Castellina in Chianti, Volterra.. **Open** All year.

This lovely home perched on a hilltop is impressive and of fine proportions. The garden has been left to grow wild but the swimming pool amid the olive trees is pleasant and the bench under the nut trees is an invitation to reverie. One apartment is available in this part of the estate. The others are higher up, near a cypress grove, in the old rose-covered houses that were once lived in by the peasants on the estate. They are simple and luxurious at the same time, well-appointed, sometimes in duplexes, with comfortable bathrooms, functional kitchens that makes you want to try your hand cooking the local produce, antique furniture, soft couches and refined decoration. Halfway between Florence and Siena, near the superstrada, it's a wonderful place to enjoy the Tuscan countryside.

How to get there *(Map 13): 30 km south of Firenze via A 1, Firenze-Certosa exit; towards Siena, San Donato in Poggio exit then towards Cortine.*

Villa Villoresi

Via Ciampi, 2 - Colonnata
50019 Sesto Fiorentino (Firenze)
Tel. (0)55-44 36 92 - Fax (0)55-44 20 63
Sig.ra Villoresi de Loche

Category ★★★★ **Rooms** 28 with telephone, bath and WC (10 with TV); wheelchair access. **Price** Single 170-240,000L, double 260-360,000L., suite 460,000L. **Meals** Breakfast included, served 7:00-10:30; half board +55,000 (per pers., 3 days min.). **Restaurant** Service 12:00-14:30, 20:00-22:00; closed Mon. (except for residents); menus 50-55,000L, also à la carte. Specialties: Penne al coccio, fagiano alla foglia di vite. **Credit cards** All major. **Pets** Dogs allowed. **Facilities** Swimming pool, parking. **Nearby** Sesto: Duomo and S. Maria dei Carceri, Castello dell'Imperatore in Prato, Firenze, dell'Ugolino golf course (18-hole) in Grassina. **Open** All year.

The countryside around Florence has begun to suffer from urban sprawl and this Renaissance house, which used to be a country residence, now finds itself encircled by constructions of lesser interest. The house remains appealing, however, with its fresco-painted ceilings, panoramic or allegoric murals and portraits of the ancestors on the walls. A long loggia (the longest in Tuscany) extends the length of the second floor and overlooks the garden and the swimming pool. The dining room looks out on the *cortile*. Some of the bedrooms are of truly palatial dimensions and arriving via the gallery is a most impressive sight. Signora Villoresi will be very helpful with advice on the cultural aspects of your tour. The amenities are adequate. The great asset here is authenticity.

How to get there *(Map 10): 10 km northwest of Firenze, towards Prato-Calenzano.*

Tenuta Bossi 

Via dello Stracchino, 32
50065 Pontassieve (Firenze)
Tel. (0)55-831 78 30 - Fax (0)55-836 40 08
Sig.ra Gondi

Apartments 4 with 3-5 rooms (5-10 pers.) with kitchen, sitting room, bath, WC. **Price** 780-1,450,000L (1 week). **Restaurant** In Firenze p. 471-474. **Credit cards** Not accepted. **Pets** Dogs allowed. **Facilities** Parking. **Nearby** Firenze, Valley of Mugello, Siena, dell'Ugolino golf course (18-hole). **Open** All year.

This vast estate just on the outskirts of Florence, which produces a fine white wine in addition to the famous Chianti Rufina, has been in the hands of the Gondi family since 1592. The palace, chapel and several farmhouses share 320 hectares of woods, vineyards and olive groves. The guest apartments have been installed in fully-renovated farmhouses. The furniture is comfortable, in country style. Each unit has a friendly living room with fireplace and a small private terrace. The surrounding vegetation is lush and the gardens, though rustic, are overflowing with roses and charm. The son and daughter of the Marchese are there to help the guests: The daughter provides a delightful welcome and the son, who is in charge of the vineyard, can advise you on your choice of some good bottles of wine. Besides the wines, the Tenuta also produce a quality olive oil and a vin santo, a sweet wine to be tasted with croccanti, a specialty of the region.

How to get there *(Map 10): 18 km east of Firenze.*

Villa Campestri

Via di Campestri, 19
50039 Vicchio di Mugello (Firenze)
Tel. (0)55-84 90 107 - Fax (0)55-84 90 108
Sig. Pasquali

Category ★★★ **Rooms** 15 and 6 suites with telephone, bath or shower, WC, satellite TV and minibar. **Price** Double 210-260,000L, suite 310-380,000L. **Meals** Breakfast included, served 8:00-10:00; half board +60,000 (per pers., 3 nights min.). **Restaurant** Service 20:00-21:30; menu 70,000L. **Credit cards** Amex, Visa, Eurocard and MasterCard. **Pets** Dogs allowed on request. **Facilities** Swimming pool, riding, parking. **Nearby** Firenze, Vespignano, Borgo S. Lorenzo, S. Piero a Sieve, Scarperia, convent of Bosco ai Frati, Novoli, castello del Trebbio, Pratolino, convent of Monte Senario in Bivigliano, Sesto Fiorentino and the strada panoramica (panoramic road) dei Colli Alti (13 km to the N15 towards Firenze). **Open** Apr. – Dec.

The north of Florence was the place of predilection for villas belonging to the Medici family. The Villa Campestri was one of these until it was bought by Paolo Pasquali, who also cultivates the 160-hectare estate. This lovely house overlooking the Mugello Valley has been renovated with a true respect for its past. In the villa and one of the remodeled outbuildings there are rooms as well as a number of suites suitable for families. The decoration is meticulous, the furniture consists of Florentine antiques and the bathrooms are all that one could wish. The cuisine, made with the produce of the *fattoria,* will let you appreciate the flavors of Tuscany. You can go horseriding in the country and you will never forget the Florentine light once you have seen it from the Villa Campestri.

How to get there *(Map 10): 35 km northeast of Firenze. Via A1, towards Bologna, Barberino exit di Mugello, towards Borgo San Lorenzo and Vicchio. 3 km from Vicchio.*

1998

Osteria del Vicario

Via Rivellino, 3
50052 Certaldo Alto (Firenze)
Tel. (0)571-66 82 28 - Fax (0)571-66 82 28 - Sig. Claudio Boretti

Rooms 11 with shower, WC, satellite TV. **Price** Single 80,000L, double 10,000L. **Meals** Breakfast included, served 8:00-10:30; half board 90,000L (per pers., 3 days min.). **Restaurant** Service 12:30-14:00, 19:30-21:00; closed Wed; menu 40-60,000L. Specialties: carpaccio, bisteca. **Credit cards** All major. **Pets** Dogs not allowed. **Nearby** Collegiata d'Empoli, Vinci and Anchiano (Leonardo de Vinci's birth house), Certaldo Boccace's house, church of Santi Michele e Iacopo (Boccace's tomb), palazzo Pretorio and chapel (frescoes), Castelfiorentino: church of S Verdiana Chapel of Visitation (B. Gozzoli's fresco), San Gimignano, Montelupo Fiorentino church of S.Giovanni, Abbey of Badia di San Salvatore a Settimo. **Open** All year (except in Jan.).

Don't be disappointed when you see the outskirts of Certaldo - its historic center is in the fortified medieval upper city. Here in the narrow lanes of this charming red-brick village, Boccacio, the celebrated author of "The Decameron," lived and died. (His birthplace, despite what it says in the brochure, was Paris.) The Osteria del Vicario occupies a former monastery just next to the Palazzo Pretorio. Now it is a lovely village inn that pays particular attention to its restaurant. The location is wonderful, whether you are in the cloister, under the trellis or on the terrace overlooking the wheat fields and sunflowers of Val d'Elsa. The regional cooking is carefully prepared and the owner offers a good selection of Tuscan wines. The rooms, spread over three buildings, are not very large, but full of charm. Rather than a vacation spot, El Vicario is a good place to use as a base to explore the little churches of Val d'Elsa and Val d'Arno, which often contain some little-known wonders of their own.

How to get there *(Map 13): 40 km south of Firenze.*

Park Hotel

Via di Marciano, 18
53100 Siena
Tel. (0)577-44 803 - Fax (0)577-490 20
Sig. Cadirni

Category ★★★★ **Rooms** 65 and 5 suites with air-conditioning, telephone, bath, WC, satellite TV, safe and minibar; elevator. **Price** Single 250-320,000L, double 320-430,000L, suite 650-750-900,000L. **Meals** Breakfast 26,000-40,000, served 7:30-10:30. **Restaurant** Service 12:30-14:45, 19:30-22:00; à la carte 80,000L. Specialties: Seasonal Tuscan cuisine. **Credit cards** All major. **Pets** Dogs allowed. **Facilities** Swimming pool, tennis, golf practice, parking. **Nearby** Siena, Sant'Antimo abbey, Monte Oliveto Maggiore abbey and the crestroad from Asciano to Siena, Convento dell'Osservanza, Torri abbey in Rosia, San Galgano abbey. **Open** All year.

Built on a mountain pass, the old castle of Marciano has an exceptional view of Siena and the Tuscan countryside. This massive and imposing structure built by Peruzzi is now the Park Hotel. The salons, superbly furnished in Haute Epoque style, open onto a pretty inner courtyard, a replica of the famous Piazza del Campo. The restaurant is on the Italian-style garden, as are the loggia reserved for banquets. The rooms are comfortable–our favorites are on the *premier étage*. This hotel is very good, but its prices limit its guests to primarily businessmen and top level convention-goers.

How to get there *(Map 13): 68 km south of Firenze; take the Siena-North exit; then via Fiorentina to Perticcio and right, via di Marciano (5 km northwest of the center of the town).*

Hotel Certosa di Maggiano

Strada di Certosa, 82
53100 Siena
Tel. (0)577-28 81 80 - Fax (0)577-28 81 89 - Sig.ra Grossi

Category ★★★★ **Rooms** 6, and 12 suites with air-conditioning, telephone, bath, WC, TV, safe and minibar. **Price** Single 500-700,000L, double 700-680,000L, suite 900-3,350,000L. **Meals** Breakfast included, served 7:15-11:00; half board +120,000L, full board +210,000L. **Restaurant** Service 13:00-14:30, 20:00-22:00; menus 80-140,000L, also à la carte. **Credit cards** All major. **Pets** Small dogs allowed (+50,000L) **Facilities** Heated swimming pool, tennis, parking. **Nearby** In Siena: Palio in July and Aug., Duomo, Sant'Antimo abbey, Monte Oliveto Maggiore abbey and the crestroad from Asciano to Siena, Convento dell'Osservanza, Torri abbey in Rosia, San Galgano abbey. **Open** All Year.

What could be prettier than a Carthusian monastery with its vaulted ceilings, Gothic arches, columns and capitals and the serenity of its cloister. The Certosa di Maggiano, in the hills of Siena, dates from 1316 and after a painstaking renovation, it has emerged from its ruins as a luxury hotel. In this stupendous setting there are both rooms and suites, but the suites are on the whole more attractive. The common areas of the hotel are all very beautiful. The dining room in particular has a wonderful china cabinet, painted to resemble marble, in tints to match the pottery collection it holds. The floor is done in *pietra serena*, with wicker chairs and color-coordinated tablecloths, giving an atmosphere of country elegance. The salon is more imposing, with its portraits of emperors. The swimming pool is surrounded by a lovely paving of chevron-patterned terra cotta tiles and vases of flowers, and from here you look out on a verdant landscape of 6 hectares of vineyard and the Sienese hills in the background.

***How to get there** (Map 13): 68 km south of Firenze, Siena-Sud exit, Porta Romana, on the right via Certosa.*

Grand Hotel Villa Patrizia

Via Fiorentina, 58
53100 Siena
Tel. (0)577-50 431 - Fax (0)577-50 431
Sig. Brogi

Category ★★★★ **Rooms** 33 with telephone, bath, WC, TV and minibar; elevator. **Price** Single 290,000L, double 370,000L. **Meals** Breakfast included, served 7:00-10:00, half board +50,000L, full board +75,000L. **Restaurant** Service 12:30-14:00, 19:30-21:30; menus 50,000L, also à la carte. Specialties: Ribollita, pici alla senese. **Credit cards** All major. **Pets** Dogs allowed. **Facilities** Swimming pool, tennis, parking. **Nearby** Siena: Palio, Jul. 2 and Aug. 16. Sant'Antimo abbey, Monte Oliveto Maggiore abbey and the crestroad from Asciano to Siena, Convento dell'Osservanza, Torri abbey in Rosia, San Galgano abbey. **Open** All year.

The Villa Patrizia is located outside the town walls of Siena. Most of its original architectural features have been preserved, but the interior is remodeled in a style that is modern, sober and elegant. Beneath the beamed ceilings, the walls are sparely decorated, in light colors. The living room features large leather armchairs and the dining room has white tablecloths and caned chairs. An intriguing arrangement of staircases leads to the upper stories, where the bedrooms have the same spare luxury. Some of the bathrooms are a bit small but all are perfectly well-equipped. The garden is well-tended, with flowers and trees, swimming pool and tennis court. Along with the other qualities of a good hotel, the service is attentive and courteous.

How to get there *(Map 13): 68 km south of Firenze, Siena-North exit; then via Fiorentina to the intersection between viale Cavon and via Achille Sclavo; 5 km northwest of the city center.*

Hotel Villa Scacciapensieri

Via di Scacciapensieri, 10
53100 Siena
Tel. (0)577-41 441 - Fax (0)577-27 08 54
Famiglia Nardi

Category ★★★★ **Rooms** 32 with air-conditioning, telephone, bath, WC, satellite TV and minibar; elevator. **Price** Single 170-210,000L, double 270-360,000L, suite 380-400,000L. **Meals** Breakfast included, served 7:30-10:00; half board 230,000L, full board 380,000L (per pers. 3 days min.). **Restaurant** Service 12:30-14:00, 19:30-21:00; closed Wed.; menus 50-70,000L, also à la carte. Specialties: Tuscan cuisine, pici alla senese. **Credit cards** All major. **Pets** Dogs allowed. **Facilities** Swimming pool, tennis, bus to Siena, parking. **Nearby** Siena: Palio, Juli 2 and August 12. Sant'Antimo abbey, Monte Oliveto Maggiore abbey and the crestroad from Asciano to Siena, Convento dell'Osservanza, Torri abbey in Rosia, San Galgano abbey. **Open** Mar. 15 – Jan. 6.

A few kilometers from Siena, this old inn has been lovingly run by the same family for many years. The long ochre facade of the building is surrounded by an Italian garden with box hedges and masses of flowers. The old-fashioned charm of the comfortable rooms combines with the charm of the old traditional hospitality. A fine old house that seems to come from another time — an idea echoed in the name of the restaurant, Altri Tempi, a name that seems to sum up the atmosphere of the Villa Scacciapensieri.

How to get there *(Map 13): 68 km south of Firenze-Siena, Siena North exit; stazione ferroviara (rail station) 3 km north of the city center.*

Hotel Antica Torre

53100 Siena
Via di Fieravecchia, 7
Tel. and Fax (0)577-22 22 55
Sig.ra Landolfo

Rooms 8 with telephone, shower and WC (2 with TV). **Price** Single 130,000L, double 160,000L. **Meals** Breakfast 12,000L, served 8:00-10:30. **Restaurant** See p. 474-475. **Credit cards** All major. **Pets** Dogs not allowed. **Nearby** Siena: Palio, Juli 2 and August 16, Abbey Sant'Antimo, Abbey Monte Oliveto Maggiore, Convento dell'Osservanza, Abbey Torri in Rosia, Abbey San Galgano. **Open** All year.

Just outside of Siena you will find one of the best hotels in Tuscany. This charming, affordable hotel in the center of town is so small and so discreet that we really had to dig it up. And what a find! It is a typical 16th century *casa torre,* on one of the quietest streets in Siena. A small central stairway (with beautiful 19th century portraits) leads to two rooms on every floor. They have travertine floors, wrought iron beds, antique furniture, engravings, and small, but well-equipped, bathrooms with showers. A former pottery store in the basement, serves as the breakfast room.

How to get there *(Map 13): SS Firneze-Siena, Siena-sud exit; then towards town center (Porta Romana).*

Hotel Santa Caterina

Via Enea Silvio Piccolomini, 7
53100 Siena
Tel. (0)577-22 11 05 - Fax (0)577-27 10 87
Sig.ra Minuti Stasi

Category ★★★ **Rooms** 19 with air-conditioning, telephone, bath, WC and minibar. **Price** (Low season : Nov. 3 - Dec. 22.); Single 120-160,000L, double 160-220,000L, triple 220-270,000L, for 4 pers. 250-300,000L. **Meals** Breakfast included, served 8:00-10:00 (self-service). **Restaurant** See p. 474-475. **Credit cards** All major. **Pets** Dogs allowed. **Facilities** Parking (15,000L). **Nearby** Siena: Palio, Juli 2 and August16; Sant'Antimo abbey, Monte Oliveto Maggiore abbey and the crestroad from Asciano to Siena, Convento dell'Osservanza, Torri abbey in Rosia, San Galgano abbey. **Open** All year.

The Hotel Santa Caterina is in a former private home in the center of Siena, a few yards from the Porta Romana. The facade is plain and the street corner location is not wonderful, but the double pane windows make the rooms fairly soundproof. All of the rooms are comfortably furnished and have modern bathrooms. Ask for a room off the marvelous flower garden, which overlooks the valley and the red rooftops of Siena. This view is the most charming aspect of this hotel.

How to get there *(Map 13): SS Firenze-Siena, Siena-South exit; then towards town center to Porta Romana via E.S. Piccolomini.*

1998

Palazzo Squarcialupi

Via Ferruccio, 26
53011 Castellina in Chianti (Siena)
Tel. (0)577-74 11 86 - Fax (0)577-74 03 86 - Sig.ra Targioni
E-mail: h.squarcialupi@agora.stm.it - Web: http://chiantinews.it/market/hotsqua.htm

Category ★★★ **Rooms** 15 and 2 suites with air-conditioning, bath or shower, WC, satellite TV and minibar, elevator. **Price** Doubles 170-220,000L, suite 270,000L. **Meals** Breakfast (buffet) included, served 7:30-10:30. **Restaurant** See p. 476. **Credit cards** Visa, Eurocard, MasterCard. **Pets** Small dogs allowed. **Facilities** Swimming pool. **Nearby** Castellina: Wine fair (May), Firenze, Vineyards of Chianti Classico (S 222), Castello di Meleto, Castello di Brolio (Cappella S. Jacopo and Palazzo Padronale), Siena. **Open** All year.

In the main street of the medieval village of Castellina, the imposing Renaissance palace of Squarcialupi has just undergone a complete restoration of its upper floors and now houses a charming hotel. Part of the ground floor is occupied by the cantina enoteca. Castellina still produces Chianti, whose different vintages can be sampled in the pleasant and inviting bar. The rooms have been appointed in a sober and elegant manner. Beams and woodwork, panoramic murals and antique furniture mingle with modern paintings and pretty flower arrangements. The bedrooms, all brand new, are very comfortable. From the hotel terrace and from some of the rooms, one can admire the beauty of the Tuscan skyline, the colors and light of this lovely countryside whose praises have been sung for so many centuries. The Squarcialupi has all the charm of its roots.

How to get there *(Map 13): 21 km north of Siena via S 222.*

Hotel Salivolpi

Via Fiorentina, 13
53011 Castellina in Chianti (Siena)
Tel. (0)577-74 04 84
Fax (0)577-74 09 98

Category ★★★ **Rooms** 19 with telephone, bath or shower and WC. **Price** Double 125,000L. **Meals** Breakfast included, served 8:00-10:00; half board 40,000L, full board 750,000L. **Restaurant** See p. 473. **Credit card** Amex. **Pets** Dogs not allowed. **Facilities** Swimming pool, parking. **Nearby** Firenze, Vineyards Chianti Classico (S 222) from Impruneta to Siena, Castello di Meleto, Castello di Brolio (Cappella S. Jacopo and Palazzo padronale), Siena. **Open** All year.

The Hotel Salivolpi consists of two old houses and a more modern annex, reconverted some years ago into an inn. Although it is on the small road from Castellina to San Donato, it is nevertheless quiet and peaceful. From the garden or the terrace, there is a lovely view of the vineyards that produce the famous Gallo Nero wine. In the old part, the rooms are delightful, with sloping ceilings and antique regional furniture. The new part, once lacking in charm, has been much improved by new amenities and decorations. Good facilities, a friendly welcome, a swimming pool (a godsend in the summer) and very advantageous prices make the Hotel Salivolpi an excellent base from which to explore the Chianti region.

How to get there *(Map 13): 21 km north of Siena via S222, exit northwest of the town.*

Tenuta di Ricavo

53011 Ricavo Ricavo - Castellina in Chianti (Siena)
Tel. (0)577-74 02 21 - Fax (0)577-74 10 14 - Famiglia Lobrano
E-mail: ricavo@chiantinet.it

Category ★★★★ **Rooms** 23 with telephone, bath, WC, satellite TV, minibar and safe. **Price** Double 320-405,000L, suite with terrace 450,000L. **Meals** Breakfast included, served 7:15-10:00. **Restaurant** «La Pecora Nera», by reservation. Service 19:30-20:00, 21:45-22:00, closed Tues. and Wed., à la carte 60-90,000L, Specialties: Tuscan cuisine and very good Tuscan wines. **Credit cards** Visa, Eurocard and MasterCard. **Pets** Dogs not allowed. **Facilities** 2 swimming pools, ping-pong, palestre, gymnase, parking (12,000L). **Nearby** Firenze, Vineyards Chianti Classico (S 222) from Impruneta to Siena, Castello di Meleto, Castello di Brolio (Cappella S. Jacopo and Palazzo padronale), Siena. **Open** Mars. 15 – Nov. 15.

The Tenuta di Ricavo is one of the nicest restorations carried out in all of Chianti. On this estate they have recreated a sort of village where the farmhouses and barns now hold living rooms, a dining room and delightful bedrooms. The windows of the bungalows are hung with pots of geraniums. Everything has been done to enhance the surroundings so that guests can get full enjoyment from their stay. The cooking is delicious — you have a choice between full- and half-board. The swimming pool is heated in winter. With all of Tuscany at your doorstep, the scent of the pine forest and the chirping of the cicadas in summer will make you realize why this region has been an inspiration to so many.

How to get there *(Map 13): 25 km north of Siena, San Donato in Poggio exit, then towards Castellina in Chianti, before 8 km, take small road to the left and 1 km.*

Hotel Villa Casalecchi

53011 Castellina in Chianti (Siena)
Tel. (0)577-74 02 40 - Fax (0)577-74 11 11
Sig.ra Lecchini-Giovannoni

Category ★★★★ **Rooms** 19 with telephone, bath and WC. **Price** Double 300-380,000L. **Meals** Breakfast included, served 8:00-10:30; half board 230-270,000L (per pers.). **Restaurant** Service 12:30-14:30, 19:30-21:30; menus 65-85,000L. Specialties: Tuscan cuisine. **Credit cards** All major. **Pets** Dogs allowed. **Facilities** Swimming pool, tennis, parking. **Nearby** Firenze, Vineyards Chianti Classico (S 222) from Impruneta to Siena, Castello di Meleto, Castello di Brolio (Cappella S. Jacopo and Palazzo padronale), Siena. **Open** Apr. – Oct.

This is the heart of that noble Tuscan vintage, Chianti Classico. The Villa Casalecchi is one of those places that offer real old-fashioned hospitality in the middle of beautiful rural surroundings. The atmosphere is serene, perhaps in part because of the very small number of rooms. There is a feeling of well-being, good food and, for those gentle country evenings, a large and wonderfully fragrant garden. This is a fine hotel that has kept its good reputation for many years.

How to get there *(Map 13): 21 km north of Siena via S222, exit northwest of the town.*

Albergo Fattoria Casafrassi

Via Chiantigiana, 40
Casafrassi 53011 Castellina in Chianti (Siena)
Tel. (0)577-74 06 21 - Fax (0)577-74 08 05
Sig. Kehren and Sig. Vidali

Category ★★★★ **Rooms** 22 with air-conditioning, telephone, bath or shower, WC; elevator. **Price** Single 160-180,000L, double 240-300,000L. **Meals** Breakfast included, served 8:00-10:00. **Restaurant** Service 13:30-14:30, 19:30-21:00; menu 45,000L, also à la carte. Specialties: Tuscan cuisine. **Credit cards** All major. **Pets** Dogs allowed (8,000L). **Facilities** Swimming pool, tennis, parking (10,000L). **Nearby** Firenze, Vineyards Chianti Classico (S222) from Impruneta to Siena, Castello di Meleto, Castello di Brolio (Cappella S. Jacopo and Palazzo padronale), Siena. **Open** Apr. – Nov. 3.

Casafrassi is an 18th-century villa on a beautiful road which crosses the Chianti Classico vineyards called "The Chiantigiana." It has been carefully restored to the original spirit of the house. Almost all of the rooms are in the villa; they are comfortable, spacious, and filled with antique furniture. The restaurant serves fine regional specialties. At the edge of the grounds there is a swimming pool and a tennis court. This is a good place to come for a lengthy stay. The Albergo will be coming under new management, so we cannot say what changes this may incur.

How to get there *(Map 13): 10 km north of Siena via S222, exit northwest of the town. Casafrassi is south of Castellina.*

Hotel Belvedere di San Leonino

San Leonino - 53011 Castellina in Chianti (Siena)
Tel. (0)577-74 08 87 - Fax (0)577-74 09 24
Sig.ra Orlandi

Category ★★★ **Rooms** 28 with telephone, bath or shower and WC. **Price** Double 165-170,000L. **Meals** Breakfast included, served 8:00-10:00. **Restaurant** Service 19:30; menu 28-35,000L, also à la carte. Specialties: Bruschette toscane, farfallette confiori di zucca, lombo di miale al forno con fonduta di gorgonzola pecorino e funghi, semi freddo di ricotta e frutti di bosco. **Credit cards** Amex, Visa, Eurocard, MasterCard. **Pets** Dogs not allowed. **Facilities** Swimming pool, parking. **Nearby** Firenze, Vineyards Chianti Classico (S222) from Impruneta to Siena, Castello di Meleto, Castello di Brolio (Cappella S. Jacopo and Palazzo padronale), Siena. **Open** All year.

The Hotel San Leonino is surrowded by the beautiful countryside. The rooms are in several buildings; they are spacious, simply furnished and impeccably clean. The salon and the dining room on the ground floor have been modernized. The swimming pool at the end of the garden has a panoramic view of the valley. Staying here is a good way to get to know Tuscany, away from the hordes of tourists who periodically overrun Firenze and Siena.

How to get there *(Map 13): 10 km north of Siena via S222, Badesse exit; 8 km south of Castellina, in Quercegrossa go left towards San Leonino.*

Castello di Spaltenna

53013 Gaiole in Chianti (Siena)
Tel. (0)577-74 94 83 - Fax (0)577-74 92 69 - Sig. Bartoli
E mail: castellospalternna@chiantinet.it - Web: http://www.chiantinet.it/castellospalternna

Category ★★★★ **Rooms** 26 with air-conditiong, telephone, bath, WC, TV and minibar. **Price** Single 265,000L, double 310-395,000L, suite 455,000L. **Meals** Breakfast included **Restaurant** Service 12:30-14:30, 19:30-21:30, closed Mon.; also à la carte. Specialties: Tortelli di zucca in salsa al tartuffo, rosa di manzo in salsa al vino rosso, torta di ricotta e pinolli. **Credit cards** All major. **Pets** Dogs allowed (10,000L). **Facilities** 2 swimming pools (1 heated and covered), parking. **Nearby** Firenze, vineyards Chianti Classico (S222) from Impruneta to Siena, Castello di Meleto, Castello di Brolio (Cappella S. Jacopo and Palazzo padronale), Siena. **Open** Mar. 20 – Nov. 20.

This former monastery, built between the 10th and 13th centuries, is now under new management. The renovation and conversion to a hotel have successfully preserved all its ancient majesty. Since one of the foremost assets of the place is its marvelous location, it was decided to have as many of the rooms as possible benefit from the panoramic view of the woods and vineyards of Chianti. The impressive interior architecture, always turned outward on the natural surroundings, has also been well-preserved. As for the cooking, it is in the able hands of Sabina Busch, who for a long time ran one of the finest restaurants in Florence. Calm, comfort and gastronomy are the key words here — all guarantees of an enjoyable stay at the Castello di Spaltenna.

How to get there *(Map 13): 28 km northeast of Siena via S408.*

1998

Castello di Tornano

Tornano 53013 Gaiole in Chiati (Siena)
Tel. (0)577-74 60 67 - (0)55 80 918 - Fax (0)577-74 60 94
Mmes Selvolini

Apartments 10 (2-7 pers.) with rooms, kitchen, bath or shower, WC. **Price** For 1 week (1 room) 750-1,200,000L, (2 rooms) 1,150-2,300,000L, Torre (2 rooms) 1,950-3,700,000L. **Meals** Breakfast 10,000L, served from 9:00. **Restaurant** Service 12:00-19:00; closed Tue. and Wed. (lunch); menu 30,000L. Specialties: Property produce. **Credit cards** Amex, Visa, Eurocard, MasterCard. **Pets** Small dogs allowed (on request). **Facilities** Swimming pool, tennis (10,000L), riding (25,000L), parking. **Nearby** Monteriggioni, Firenze, Siena, San Gimignano, Arezzo. **Open** May - Oct.

Castello di Tornano is a 12th century castle today officially designated as a landmark. Beautifully set on a hilltop covered with vineyards and oak trees, it towers over the surroundings. The farm is now run by two charming sisters, who have also fitted out the tower as a very comfortable apartment, whose spacious, narrow-windowed rooms are served by a spiral staircase going up three levels to a panoramic terrace. Rooms of more modest proportions are situated in other farm buildings. Around the castle extends a large lawn filled with flowers and bordered by cypresses with a swimming pool set cleverly into the former moat. At a restaurant some 500 meters away you can taste the products of the estate.

How to get there *(Map 13): 19 km of Siena. On Highway A1, Valdarno exit, then SS 408 towards Siena. From Siena take the road towards Gaiole in Chianti to Lecchi. In Lecchi towards Tornano-Ristorante Guarnelotto.*

Residence San Sano

San Sano
(53010) Lecchi in Chianti (Siena)
Tel. (0)577-74 61 30 - Fax (0)577-74 61 56
Sig. and Sig.ra Matarazzo

Category ★★★★ **Rooms** 14 with telephone, shower, WC, TV and minibar. **Price** Double 170-190,000L. **Meals** Breakfast included, served 8:00-10:00. **Restaurant** Service 19:30; closed Sun.; menus 30,000L. Specialties: Tuscan cuisine. **Credit cards** All major. **Pets** Dogs allowed by request. **Facilities** Swimming pool, parking. **Nearby** Monteriggioni, Abbadia Isola, Colle di Val d'Elsa (colle Alta), Firenze, Siena, San Gimignano, Arezzo. Open Mar. 15 – Nov. 3.

Foreigners who fall in love with a country, a region or a house are sometimes those who best know how to respect and preserve the soul of the place. That is the case of the Italian/German couple who settled in Tuscany and who welcome you today to this old stone farmhouse that combines the charm and warm hospitality of a guest house with the independence and service of a hotel. The rooms are each done with a particular theme; each is appealing and very comfortable. The cooking emphasizes regional specialties. Only 20 kilometers from Siena, you can enjoy the lovely countryside as you visit Tuscany.

How to get there *(Map 13): 20 km north of Siena via S408; then left towards Lecchi, then San Sano.*

1998

Castello di Uzzano

Via Uzzano, 5
50022 Greve in Chianti (Firenze)
Tel. (0)55-85 40 32 / 33 - Fax (0)55 85 43 75 - Sig.ra de Jacobert

Apartments 6 with telephone, bath or shower, WC, TV, kitchen. **Price** 500-2,500,000L (for 1 week). **Meals** Breakfast 18,000L, served 8:30-10:30. **Restaurant** See p. 475. **Credit cards** All major. **Pets** Dogs allowed. **Facilities** Mountain bikes, parking. **Nearby** Firenze, Vineyards of chianti Classico (S222). **Open** All year. (except Sunday in low seaon).

The Castello di Uzzano is on a 1,235-acre estate; 150 acres of this is a vineyard. The castle was built around the year 1000 on an Etrusco-Roman site. It was redesigned by Orcagna and enlarged during the Renaissance; between the 16th and 17th centuries it was transformed into a villa. The present owners restored the Castle to full splendor. The comfortable, charming apartments are on the courtyard. The furniture, paintings, old engravings and fireplaces make the atmosphere very warm. The grounds and the maze in the garden, in the 18th-century style, are open to guests (except Sundays). For a souvenir, you can buy items produced on the estate, such as wine, olive oil and brandy. A visit to the castle with a wine tasting are a good idea even if you don't stay here.

How to get there *(Map 10): 22 km south of Firenze via A 1 Roma/Firenze, Incisa-Valdarno exit; via A 1 Milano/Bologna, Firenze-Certosa exit.*

Hotel Monteriggioni

53035 Monteriggioni (Sienna)
Tel. (0)577-30 50 09 - Fax (0)577-30 50 11
Sig.ra Gozzi

Category ★★★★ **Rooms** 12 with air conditioning, telephone, bath, WC, TV and minibar, elevator. **Price** Single 200,000L, double 310,000L. **Meals** Breakfast included, served 8:00-10:00. **Credit cards** Amex, Visa, Eurocard and MasterCard. **Pets** Dogs not allowed. **Nearby** Siena, Abbadia Isola, Colle Val d'Elsa, Basilica dell' Osservanza and chartreuse de Pontignano, San Gimignano; Volterra **Open** All year (except Jan. 16 – Feb. 14.).

The towers of Monteriggioni rise like a mirage on the highway connecting Firenze and Siena. The beauty of the decapitated walls and towers, especially at sunset, will make you want get off the highway for a closer look. This small village is made up of what originally were old military buildings dating back to the time when Montérriggioni was still a Sienian garrison (the 8th century). The hotel, in the village, discreet is luxuly now. The rooms are all different and are very comfortable. We prefer the ones on the garden where breakfast is served in summer. Just across the street is one of the best restaurants in the region, Il Pozzo, which more than makes up for the lack of a restaurant in the hotel.

How to get there *(Map 13): 12 km north of Siena, on 4 Corsie, Colle di Val d'Elsa-Monteriggioni exit.*

La Chiusa

Via della Madonnina, 88
53040 Montefollonico (Siena)
Tel. (0)577-66 96 68 - Fax (0)577-66 95 93
Sig.ra Masotti and Sig. Lucherini

Rooms 6 and 6 apartments with telephone, bath, WC, TV and minibar. **Price** Double 300,000L, suite 490-630,000L. **Meals** Breakfast 25,000L, served 8:30-10:30. **Restaurant** Service 12:30-15:00, 20:00-22:00; closed Tues.; menus 130,000L, also à la carte. Specialties: Collo d'oca ripieno, pappardelle Dania, coniglio marinato al romarino, piccione al vinsanto. **Credit cards** All major. **Pets** Dogs allowed. **Nearby** Montepulciano, Monticchiello, Montalcino, Terme in Bagno Vignoli, Val d'Orcia villages (Castiglione d'Orcia, Rocca d'Orcia, Ripa d'Orcia, Campiglia d'Orcia), Pienza, Collegiale San Quirico d'Orcia, Museo Nazionale Etrusco in Siusi, Chianciano Terme, Siena. **Open** Mar. 20 – Nov. 10 and Dec. 28 – Jan. 10.

La Chiusa is more than just a famous restaurant and inn–it's the house of Dania, a gracious young woman whose charm plays an important role in the reputation of this magical place. She passionately loves her work and takes pleasure in receiving her guests as if they were good friends. The delicious meals are always prepared with fresh products from the farm. The rooms and the apartments are very comfortable and very well kept. The breakfasts, of homemade jellies and brioches and fresh fruit juices are generous. When you watch the sun set over the Val di Chiana and the Val d'Orcia, you will start planning your next trip back.

How to get there *(Map 13): 60 km south of Siena via A1, Valdichiana exit - Bettole, Torrita di Siena Montefollonico.*

La Saracina

Strada Statale, 146 (km 29,7)
53026 Pienza (Siena)
Tel. (0)578-74 80 22 - Fax (0)578-74 80 18
Sig.ra Vessi Chelli

Rooms 2, 3 suites and 1 apartment with telephone, bath, WC and TV. **Price** Double 300,000L, apartment 330,000L, suite 350,000L. **Meals** Breakfast included. **Restaurant** See p.478. **Credit cards** All major. **Pets** Dogs not allowed. **Facilities** Swimming pool, tennis, parking. **Nearby** Pienza (Duomo, Palazzo Piccolomini), Montepulciano, Monticchiello, Montalcino, Terme in Bagno Vignoni, villages in Val d'Orcia (Collegiale San Quirico d'Orcia, Castiglione d'Orcia, Rocca d'Orcia, Ripa d'Orcia, Campiglia d'Orcia), Sant'Anna Camprena abbey (frescoes of Sodoma), Spedaletto, Chiusi, Cetona, Chianciano. **Open** All year.

The Saracina is in an old farmhouse on a small hill, which has a view of Pienza, Monticchiello and Montefollonico. The rooms are very beautiful; they are decorated with antique furniture and have large bathrooms and very comfortable salons. Everything has been done with exquisite taste. A savory breakfast is served in the shade of the pretty garden or on the terrace. Be sure to spend some time visiting the enchanting town of Pienza, which has remained intact since the Renaissance and is not a tourist trap. It was the work of Pope Pius II of Piccolomini, who wanted, with the help of architect B. Rossellino, to create the ideal town. Several palaces and the cathedral were built before the work was interrupted by the sudden death of the two sponsors. Fortunately, no one has disturbed the harmony of this small town which served as the set of Zefferelli's *Romeo and Juliet.*

How to get there *(Map 13): 52 km southeast of Siena via S2 to San Quirico then Pienza.*

Relais Il Chiostro di Pienza

Corso Rossellino, 26
53026 Pienza (Siena)
Tel. (0)578-74 84 00/42 - Fax (0)578-74 84 40
Sig.ra Codogno

Category ★★★ **Rooms** 37 with telephone, bath or shower, WC, TV and minibar; 2 rooms for disabled persons. **Price** Single 160,000L, double 220,000L, suite 280,000L. **Meals** Breakfast included **Restaurant** Service 13:00-14:30, 19:00-21:00, closed Mon.; menu, also à la carte. Specialties: regional cooking. **Credit cards** All major. **Pets** Dogs not allowed. **Facilities** Swimming pool. **Nearby** Pienza (Duomo, Palazzo Piccolomini), Montepulciano, Monticchiello, Montalcino, Terme in Bagno Vignoni, villages in Val d'Orcia (Collegiale San Quirico d'Orcia, Castiglione d'Orcia, Rocca d'Orcia, Ripa d'Orcia, Campiglia d'Orcia), Sant'Anna Camprena abbey (frescoes of Sodoma), Spedaletto, Chiusi, Cetona, Chianciano. **Open** All year.

Pienza, which long deserved to have a hotel of charm, has now found one in the Relais Il Chiostro di Pienza, set in a former 15th-century monastery in the center of the historic old town. The building has been beautifully restored: We see arches, beams and frescoes and, of course, the old cloister of the convent. The rooms are large, soberly furnished and decorated. The whole place has a great calm and serenity. An excellent spot from which to discover the wonderful little Renaissance town of Pienza, as well as the medieval and Roman/Etruscan sites nearby.

How to get there *(Map 13): 52 km southeast of Siena. Motorway A 1, Valdichiana or Chiusi-Chianciano exit.*

1998

L'Olmo

53020 Monticchiello di Pienza (Siena)
Tel. (0)578-755 133 - Fax (0)578-755 124 - Sig.ra Lindo
Web: http://www.nautilus.mp.com/olmo

Suites 5 and 1 room (single) with telephone, bath, WC, TV, minibar and safe. **Price** Single 200-240,0000L, suite 320,000L. **Meals** Breakfast included, served 8:30-10:30; half board +55,000L (per pers.). **Restaurant** For residents; menu 55,000L. **Credit cards** Visa, Eurocard, MasterCard. **Pets** Dogs not allowed. **Facilities** Heated swimming pool, parking. **Nearby** Pienza, Montepulciano, Montalcino, Terme de Bagno Vignoni, Villages of Val d'Orcia (Collegiale San Quirico d'Orcia, Castiglione d'Orcia, Rocca d'Orcia, Ripa d'Orcia, Campiglia d'Orcia), Abbey of Sant'Anna Camprena (fresco of Sodoma), Spedaletto, Chiusi, Cetona, Chianciano. **Open** March - Oct.

The Olmo is an elegant country inn which has only suites and where the service is attentive without being effusive. Thanks to a respectful restoration, the house has regained its noble appearance in keeping with its old stones. Inside, there are exposed beams in the ceilings, but for the rest, the spaces have been treated in a more contemporary way. The entire installation has a refined look, mingling antique furniture, hand-crafted objects, fine fabrics and traditional floors. Each lodging is different in size and style. Two suites open directly onto the garden and a private terrace. Of those upstairs, the largest has two rooms and can sleep three, others have a fireplace (pleasant when the weather is cool), and one offers a panoramic view of the Val d'Orcia. The public areas have the same tasteful luxury. With notice in advance, you can dine by candlelight. The same careful attention has been given to the garden and swimming pool, which blend beautifully with the surroundings.

How to get there *(Map 13): 52 km southeast of Siena. On highway A 1 Valdichiana exit, towards Torina di Siena, Pienza e monticchiello 110.*

Castello di Ripa d'Orcia

Ripa d'Orcia 53023 San Quirico d'Orcia (Siena)
Tel. (0)577-89 73 76 - Fax (0)577-89 80 38 - Famiglia Aluffi Rossi
E-mail: ripa.dorcia@comune.siena.it - Web: http://www.nautilus-mp.com:ripa

Category ★★★ **Rooms** 6 and 7 apartments with bath or shower and WC. **Price** Double 140-160,000L, breakfast included; apart. 750-850,000L (2 pers., 1 week), 1,200-1,270,000L (4 pers., 1 week). **Restaurant** Service 19:30-20:30; closed Mon., also à la carte 35-50,000L. Specialties: Tuscan cuisine.**Credit cards** All major. **Pets** Dogs not allowed. **Facilities** Parking. **Nearby** Val d'Orcia: Peinza, Montepulciano, Monticchiello, Montalcino and Sant' Antimo abbey, Terme de Bagno Vignoni, villages of the Val d'Orcia (Collegiale San Quirico d'Orcia, Castiglione d'Orcia, Rocca (d'Orcia, Ripa d'Orcia, Campiglia d'Orcia), Sant'Anna Camprena abbey, Spedaletto, Chuisi, Cetona, Chianciano. **Open** All year (except Jan. 7 - Mar.).

Ripa d'Orcia is one of those wonderful little medieval hamlets that have remained just as they were in the Middle Ages. To get there, you must leave the road at San Quirico and drive into the countryside for about 5 kilometers. Don't be impatient — the road may not be very well-kept, but the *castello* makes it all worth it when you see it rising up from behind a wall of cypresses. An intelligent restoration has given new life to some old houses in a village deserted by its inhabitants. There are a variety of rooms and apartments with facilities to enable independent living: a reading or television room, a restaurant and a marvelous meeting room. The bedrooms are attractive and comfortable; the apartments are more rustic in style, but some recent renovations should make them just as inviting as the rest. In the heart of a protected natural setting, Ripa d'Orcia is well worth a tour.

How to get there *(Map 13): 45 km south of Siena (towards lago di Bolsena and Viterbo) via S2 to San Quirico and Ripa d'Orcia. A1, Val di Chiana or Chiusi-Chanciano exit and towards Pienza.*

Cantina Il Borgo

Rocca d'Orcia 53023 Castiglione d'Orcia (Siena)
Tel. and Fax (0)577-88 72 80
Sig. Tanganelli

Rooms 3 with air-conditioning, shower, WC and TV. Wheelchair access. **Price** 110-130,000L. **Meals** Breakfast included, served 8:30-10:00. **Restaurant** Service 12:30-14:30, 19:00-21:30; closed Mon., à la carte 40,000L. **Credit cards** Amex, Visa, Eurocard, MasterCard. **Pets** Dogs allowed. **Nearby** Val d'Orcia, Peinza, Montepulciano, Monticchiello, Montalcino and Sant' Antimo abbey, Terme de Bagno Vignoni, villages of the Val d'Orcia (Collegiale San Quirico d'Orcia, Castiglione d'Orcia, Rocca (d'Orcia, Ripa d'Orcia, Campiglia d'Orcia), Sant'Anna Camprena abbey, Spedaletto, Chuisi, Cetona, Chianciano. **Open** All year (except Jan. 16 – Feb. 14).

You can see the Rocca di Tentennano, the imposing military fortress, towering above the Val d'Orcia from a distance. The old Medieval town is discreetly set back, down below, as if to protect itself from a few curious tourists. The village looks like it has been asleep for centuries. The telephone booth (from which you can easily call long distance) is the only reminder of the present. The restaurant, the Cantina Il Borgo, is in one of the austere houses on the site–a refurbished coach house–across from a superb octagonal, cited in texts since the 12th century. The owner will welcome you simply, but he's more than willing to share what he loves in this region with you: its wine, cuisine, and the numerous trails which criss-cross the Val d'Orcia. The three carefully prepared rooms have whitewashed walls, wrought iron beds, antique furniture, and an array of fabrics combining stripes and gingham, for a modern touch. The shower rooms are comfortably equipped. This place is surprisingly nice.

How to get there *(Map 13): 50 km south of Siena (towards lago di Bolsena and Viterbo) via S2, towards Castiglione d'Orcia and Rocca. A1, Val di Chiana or Chiusi-Chanciano exit towards Pienza.*

Castello di Modanella 

Modanella 53040 Serre di Rapolano (Siena)
Tel. (0)577-70 46 04 - Fax (0)577-70 47 40
Sig.ra Cerretti

Apartments 32 with bath, WC, TV. **Price** For 1 week 710-1,095,000L(with 2 rooms), 945-1,480,000L (3 rooms), 1,275-1,990,000L (4 rooms), 1,445-2,235,000L (5 rooms). **Restaurant** In Aciano and in Montalcino, see p. 477. **Credit cards** All major. **Pets** Dogs allowed. **Facilities** 2 swimming pools, tennis, ping-pong, parking. Nearby Rapalano Terme, Bagno Vignoni, Petriolo, the crestroad from Asciano to Siena, Monte Oliveto Maggiore abbey, Sant'Antimo abbey, Montalcino, Pienza, Lucignano, Arezz. **Open** All year.

Leave behind the marble and travertine quarries of the industrial zone of Serre di Rapolano and make your way confidently, for as soon as you cross the railroad tracks you will catch sight of the castle of Modanella and its farm buildings scattered over a large wine-growing estate. To provide such a large number of apartments, they have transformed all the stables, barns, granges, silos and even the old schoolhouse. All designed with taste and simplicity, they charmingly combine rusticity and comfort: white walls, blond wood furniture, comfortable bedding, a well-equipped kitchen and handsome bathrooms (all done in tavertine stone, of course). There are no rooms in the castle itself, as it is still being restored. All in all, a beautiful place. Better take advantage of it while you can, as further development projects (the addition of more apartments, a restaurant and a new swimming pool) may very well turn it into a sort of holiday club.

How to get there *(Map 13): 35 km from Siena; 30 km from Arezzo; in Siena take road E78 326 to Rapolano terme, and before Serre take a right towards Modanella*

Relais La Suvera

La Suvera
53030 Pievescola di Casole d'Elsa (Siena)
Tel. (0)577-96 03 00/1/2/3 - Fax (0)577-96 02 20
Sig. Buso

Category ★★★★ **Rooms** 16, and 19 suites, with telephone, bath, WC and satellite TV. **Price** Double 370-500,000L, suite 470-700,000L. **Meals** Breakfast included; half board +80,000L. **Restaurant** Service 13:00-16:00 and 19:00-23:00; also à la carte 70-80,000L. Specialties: Regional cuisine. **Credit cards** All major. **Pets** Dogs allowed. **Facilities** Swimming pool, sauna, tennis, parking. **Nearby** Colle di Val d'Elsa, Abbadia Isola, Monteriggioni, Firenze, San Gimignano, Siena, dell'Ugolino golf course (18-hole) in Grassina. **Open** Apr. 1 – Oct.

There is no way to describe La Suvera without using superlatives. This papal villa, built in the 18th century, first belonged to an important Italian family, the Borgeses, then was bought several decades ago by Lucchinio Visconti, who passed it on to the Marquis de Ricci, the current owner. Today, La Suvera is both a luxury hotel and the sumptuous residence of a collector with a passion. The hotel consists of three buildings: The Oliviera and the Scederies have beautiful, very plush rooms, and the papal villa has suites, created by the marquis and his wife, which are perfect reconstitutions of a historical period or character; they are a collector's dream and a traveler's delight. The service at La Suvera is perfect, the cuisine excellent, and the gardens admirable.

How to get there *(Map 13): 61 km south of Firenze via SS Firenze-Siena, Colle di Val d'Elsa-sud exit, then via Grosseto; after 15 km, Pievescola.*

Hotel Villa San Lucchese

50036 Poggibonsi (Siena)
Via S. Lucchese, 5
Tel. (0)577-93 42 31 - Fax (0)577-93 47 29 - Sig. Ninci
E-mail: villasalucchese@etr.it - Web: http://www.etr.it.hotel-villa-san-lucchese

Category ★★★★ **Rooms** 36 with air-conditioning, telephone, bath or shower, WC, TV, minibar and elevator. **Price** Single 100-180,000L, double 200-300,000L, suite 250-300,000L. **Meals** Breakfast included, served 7:30-10:00; half board +40,000L, full board +80,000L (per pers.). **Restaurant** Service 12:30-14:00, 19:30-22:00; closed Tues.; menu 50,000L, à la carte. Specialties: Tuscan cuisine. **Credit cards** All major. **Pets** Dogs not allowed. **Facilities** Swimming pool, tennis, parking. **Nearby** Firenze, Sienna, Colle Val d'Elsa, San Gimignano, Volterra, Monterrigioni Chianti Route. **Open** All year.

The hotel is ideally located in Poggibonsi, at the crossroads of the main cities of Tuscany, Florence and Siena. It is next to the San Lucchese monastery, overlooking the town and all of its commotion. This 15th century noble villa, has vast, light rooms and a pleasant classical decor. On the ground floor the restaurant opens onto a very large terrace, which looks out over the Val d'Elsa plain. In the garden, next to a grove of superb centenarian trees, there is a large pool. The hotel is well equipped for receptions.

How to get there *(Map 13): 19 km north of Siena. Superstrada «4 Corsie,» Poggibonsa exit. A1, Firenze Certosa exit.*

Hotel Borgo Pretale

Borgo Pretale
53018 Sovicille (Siena)
Tel. (0)577-34 54 01 - Fax (0)577-34 56 25
Sig. Ricardini

Category ★★★★ **Rooms** 35 with telephone, bath, WC, TV and minibar. **Price** 160-175,000L (per pers. in double room), suite +32,000L (per pers.). **Meals** Breakfast included, served 7:30-10:00; half board 65,000L (par pers., 3 days min.). **Restaurant** Service 19:30-21:30; menu: 60,000L, also à la carte. Specialties: Tuscan and Italian cuisine. **Credit cards** All major. **Pets** Dogs not allowed. **Facilities** Swimming pool, tennis, fitness center with sauna, mountain bikes, golf practice, parking. **Nearby** Villa Cetinale in Sovicille, Torri abbey in Rosia, abbey of Torri in Rosia, San Galgano abbey, Siena. **Open** Apr. – Nov. 1.

Eighteen kilometers from Siena, in a village that has kept its Tuscan colors and all its authenticity, the Torre Borgo Pretale has been transformed into a hotel. There are eight marvelous rooms in the tower itself; the others and several apartments are located in cottages at garden level. The interior amenities are very comfortable and in excellent taste. The service is most attentive. From June to September, a buffet lunch is served at the swimming pool. The availability of swimming, tennis and other recreations are a plus, even for those who have come primarily on a pilgrimage of the Quattrocento, as Borgo Pretale is located in the heart of historic Tuscany.

How to get there *(Map 13): 18 km southeast of Siena via S73 towards Rosia. Follow signs.*

Azienda Agricola Montestigliano 

53010 Rosia (Siena)
Tel. (0)577-34 21 89 - Fax (0)577-34 21 00
Sig. Donati

Apartments 10 (2-8 pers.) and 1 villa (12 pers.) with kitchen, shower, WC, telephone. **Price** For 1 week 630-1,351,000L (2-3 pers.), 966-1,890,000L (6-8 pers.), 1,778-3,892,000L (12 pers.). **Meals** Breakfast 12,000L, served 8:30-10:00. **Evening meals** (For residents, on request). Service 20:00; menu 40,000L. Specialties: Tuscan cuisine. **Credit cards** Not accepted. **Pets** Small dogs allowed. **Facilities** 2 swimming pools, parking. **Nearby** La Montagnala: Church of S. Giovanni in Rosia, abbey of Torri, abbey of San Galgano, Monteriggioni, Abbadia Isola, Siena. **Open** All year.

Only 16 kilometers from Siena, discover the property of Montestigliano, which has been in the Donati family for over 50 years. The various farm buildings form a veritable village overlooking fields of olive trees that cover the broad plain of the Merse River. The farmhouses and noble estates have all been restored in traditional style and furnished in a pleasant country manner. They are all comfortable: The kitchens are well-equipped (they all have washing machines and the villa also has a dishwasher) and each one has a terrace or a private garden. If you wish, you can have your breakfast and dinner in a wing of the main house, which also contains the offices of the cereal farm, or better still, on the well-shaded terrace of the owners' stately home. For the greater comfort of the guests, there are two swimming pools. The warm welcome is both Italian and English - Susan Pennington will advise you on all the possible walks to be done in the Montagnola area.

How to get there *(Map 13): 15 km south of Siena via SS 73 to Rosia. L'Azienda is 5 km after Torri, Stigliano and Montestigliano*

Relais Fattoria Vignale

Via Pianigiani, 9
53017 Radda in Chianti (Siena)
Tel. (0)577-73 83 00 - Fax (0)577-73 85 92
Sig.ra Kummer

Category ★★★★ **Rooms** 34 with air-conditioning, telephone, bath, WC, TV and minibar. **Price** Single 180-200,000L, double 270-350,000L. **Meals** Breakfast included (buffet), served 7:30-10:30. **Restaurant** Service 13:00-14:30, 19:30-21:00; closed Nov. 10 – Mar. 20; menus: 60-90,000L, also à la carte. Specialties: Seasonal and Tuscan cuisine. **Credit cards** All major. **Pets** Dogs not allowed. **Facilities** Swimming pool, parking. **Nearby** Siena, vineyard Chianti Classico (N 222), Impruneta, Firenze, dell'Ugolino golf course (18-hole) in Grassina. **Open** (All year except Jan. 5 - Mar. 22).

Formerly the home of wealthy landowners, it was bought and entirely renovated in 1983. The decoration is discreet and consistent, perfectly in tune with the surroundings, and one feels the constant fidelity to the past: the vaulted cellar that serves as a breakfast room, the wall paintings in the library, the austerity with which all the bedrooms have been furnished. Aside from the traditional restaurant, there is also the Taverna, which is open from 5 p.m. to midnight. Anyone interested in wine should make it a point to stop here. The estate produces an excellent wine and offers its clients an *onoteca* as well as a fine collection of books on wine for connoisseurs.

How to get there *(Map 13): 30 km north of Siena via S222 to Castellina in Chianti, then S429.*

Podere Terreno 

Volpaia - 53 017 Radda in Chianti (Siena)
Tel. (0)577-73 83 12 / 73 84 00 - Fax (0)577-73 83 12 / 73 84 00
Sig.ra Haniez-Melosi
E-mail: podereterreno@chiantinet.it

Rooms 7 with shower and WC. **Price** With half board 140-150,000L (per pers., 2 nights min. in high season). **Meals** Breakfast included, served 8:30-10:30. **Restaurant** Service 20:00; menu. Specialties: Tuscan and Mediterranean cuisine. **Credit cards** Amex, Visa, Eurocard, MasterCard. **Pets** Dogs allowed. **Facilities** Parking. **Nearby** Lake, Siena, Vineyard Chianti Classico (N 222), Impruneta, San Gimignano, Firenze, dell'Ugolino golf course (18-hole) in Grassina. **Open** All year.

This beautiful stone farmhouse is in the middle of a large estate of more than one hundred and twenty four acres with oak and chestnut trees, olive orchards and a vineyard, which produces quality wine and excellent olive oil. The old traditional Tuscan kitchen has been converted into a salon. The large couch in front of the fireplace, the rustic antique furniture and Marie-Sylvie's and Roberto's collections, all add to the decor. The very charming rooms are comfortable and decorated with taste and simplicity. Marie-Sylvie makes the jellies she serves for breakfast and Roberto supervises the kitchen. Meals are served around a large common table, accompanied by wine from the estate vineyards. The billiards room and library in the cellar are good places to spend a quiet moment alone, as is the arbor in the garden.

How to get there *(Map 13): 30 km north of Siena via S222 to Panzano in Chianti, towards Radda in Chianti. Before Radda, left towards Volpaia and Podere Terreno.*

Albergo Vescine

Vescine - 53017 Radda in Chianti (Siena)
Tel. (0)577-74 11 44 - Fax (0)577-74 02 63 - Sig.ra Fleig
E-mail: vescine@chiantinet.it

Rooms 25 with telephone, bath or shower, WC, TV, minibar. **Price** Double 260-270,000L (per 1 pers.), suite 350-370,000L. **Meals** Breakfast included, served 8:00-10:30. **Credit cards** Amex, Visa, Eurocard, MasterCard. Pets Dogs allowed (10,000L). **Facilities** Swimming pool, tennis, parking. **Nearby** Siena, Vineyard Chianti Classico (N 222), Impruneta, San Gimignano, Firenze, dell'Ugolino golf course (18-hole) in Grassina. **Open** All year.

If it's calm and solitude you're seeking, don't hesitate — Vescine is the place for you. In the heart of Chianti, this little hamlet surrounded by 75 hectares of land has been reconverted into a country inn and offers a unique setting for a stay in Tuscany. Completely restored and renovated, the various buildings are connected by pretty cobbled paths lined with masses of flowers. The young woman who runs the place has managed to combine a gentle Tuscan atmosphere with very functional facilities. The rooms are sober and functional as well. Many recreational possibilities, from a swimming pool to an *onoteca* offering many regional vintages. The welcome is rather impersonal. You can have your meals in a restaurant, La Cantoniera di Vescine, located about 700 meters away and also run by the hotel.

How to get there *(Map 13): 54 km south of Firenze. A1 Firenze-Certosa exit, then take superstrada for Siena, San Donato exit in Poggio to Catellina in Chianti. The hotel is on the road n°429 between Castellina and Radda in Chianti.*

Castello di Montalto

1998

Montalto 53019 Castelnuovo Berardenga (Siena)
Tel. (0)577-35 56 75 - Fax (0)577-35 56 82 - Sig.ra Coda-Nunziante
E-mail: montaldo@iol.it

Apartments 7 (2-6 pers.) with 1-3 rooms, kitchen, sitting room, bath, WC (4 apart. with telephone, 1 apart with TV.). **Price** For 1 week 2,800-3,300,000L (in the Castle), 770-2,100,000L (in village), 850-1,000,000L (in farm, 2 km). **Restaurant** See p. 476. **Credit cards** Visa, Eurocard, MasterCard. **Pets** Dogs not allowed. **Facilities** Swimming pool, tennis, bikes, parking. **Nearby** Castello delle quattro torri near Due Ponti, Castello di Brolio and vineyards of Chianti (Meleto), Gaiole, Badia a Coltibu ono, Radda and Castellina in Chianti. **Open** Dec. 28 - Jan. 6 and March 15 - Nov. 6.

The Castello di Montalto is in itself a small fortified village with a well-preserved tower and crenellated facades of genuine beauty and nobility. It is owned by an Italian Count and run by his American wife. The outbuildings of the estate have been transformed into comfortable apartments and the atmosphere is distinguished. You may also be able to live in the castello itself, where the largest apartment is situated, with access to the tower's rooftop terrace. It is possible, too, to rent an independent farmhouse, more rustic, 2 kilometers from the castle, but provided with phone and garage for anyone who might otherwise feel too far away. The decoration varies from house to house but is always nice even when quite simple. Most of them have a fireplace and a garden where you can have lunch outdoors. An added pleasure is going to the farm to buy oil, honey, eggs and fresh vegetables. The welcome is warm and discreet. Nature lovers will be right in their element.

How to get there *(Map 13): 20 km southeast of Siena via SS Siena-Perugia towards Arezzo. At the junction for Arezzo, take the road towards Bucine/Ambra; then after 3 km the road on the left towards Montalto (3 km).*

Hotel Villa Arceno

53010 San Gusmé - Castelnuovo Berardenga (Siena)
Tel. (0)577-35 92 92 - Fax (0)577-35 92 76
Sig. Mancini

Category ★★★★ **Rooms** 16 with telephone, bath, WC, TV and minibar. **Price** Single 250,000L, double 400,000L, suite 508,000L. **Meals** Breakfast included, served 7:30-10:30; half board 290-345L (per pers.). **Restaurant** Service 13:00-14:30, 20:00-22:00; menus about 85,000L, also à la carte. Specialties: Italian and Tuscan cuisine. Credit cards All major. **Pets** Dogs not allowed. **Facilities** Swimming pool, practice golf course, tennis, parking. **Nearby** Siena, Arezzo, Monte San Savino, Monte Oliveto abbey, crest road from Asciano to Siena. **Open** Mar. – Oct.

Getting to Castelnuovo Berardenga from Siena is no problem, and along the way you will enjoy the marvelous landscape and light that inspired Sienese painters. Finding the small hamlet of San Gusmé, once outside of the village, is doable, but finding the Villa Arceno is impossible without some help. When you are on the road, look for a big arch with "Arceno" written on it. Drive through the gate, follow the road through the woods, vineyards and olive trees, and if, at this point, you haven't turned around and gone back thinking you are lost, you will arrive at the villa. This beautiful 17th-century country house is on a 24,700-acre estate; it is an old hunting lodge which belonged to a rich Italian family until recently when it was transformed into a very nice hotel. The 19 farms on the estate were also carefully restored. The hotel is decorated with beautiful fabrics. The rooms are spacious and comfortable, and the staff is very welcoming.

How to get there *(Map 13): 25 km east of Siena via A1; Valdichiana or Monte San Savino exit towards Monte San Savino, to Castelnuovo Berardenga, San Gusmé.*

Hotel Relais Borgo San Felice

San Felice
53019 Castelnuovo Berardenga (Siena)
Tel. (0)577-35 92 60 - Fax (0)577-35 90 89
Sig. Righi

Category ★★★★ **Rooms** 50 and 12 suites with telephone, bath, WC, TV and minibar. **Price** Single 305,000L, double 450,000L, suite 650,000L. **Meals** Breakfast included, served 7:30-10:30; half board 340-440,000L, full board 510-530,000L (per pers.). **Restaurant** Service 12:30-14:00, 19:30-21:30; menus 80-150,000L. Specialties: Tuscan and Italian cuisine. **Credit cards** All major. **Pets** Dogs not allowed. **Facilities** Swimming pool, tennis, parking. **Nearby** Castello delle quattro torri near by de Due Ponti, Castello di Brolio and Chianti vineyard via Meleto, Gaiole, Badia Coltibuono, Radda and Castellina in Chianti. **Open** Mar. – Oct.

A little square in front of a postcard chapel, small cobblestone streets lined with houses covered with flowers, cute gardens, stone stairways, beautiful Virginia creeper-covered facades–you will find all this and more in Borgo San Felice, a Medieval Tuscan village. It feels like a village which has continued its agricultural activity of producing wine and olive oil. The houses are very tastefully decorated, with nice open spaces, shades of ochre and pretty furniture. A beautiful swimming pool, very professional service and an excellent restaurant make Borgo San Felice a hotel which we heartily recommend.

How to get there *(Map 13): 17 km east of Siena; in Siena, SS Siena-Perugia towards Arezzo, then 7 km to Montaperti.*

Hotel l'Antico Pozzo

Via San Matteo, 87
53037 San Gimignano (Siena)
Tel. (0)577-94 20 14 - Fax (0)577-94 21 17 - Sig. Marro and Sig. Caponi
E-mail: antpozzo@tin.it - Web: http://web.tin.it/antozzo

Rooms 18 with air-conditioning, telephone, bath or shower, satellite TV, safe and minibar. **Price** Single 145,000L, double 190,000L, suite 240,000L. **Meals** Breakfast included. **Restaurant** See p.478. **Credit cards** All major. **Pets** Dogs not allowed. **Nearby** San Gimignano (Church of sant'Agostino), piazza del Duomo, piazza della Cisterna; Etruscan ancient city of Pieve di Cellole, Convent of S. Vivaldo, Certaldo, Pinacoteca and Visitation chapel (frescoes of Benozzo Gozzoli) in Castelfiorentino, Firenze, Siena, Volterra, Castelfalfi golf course (18-hole). **Open** All year.

Two talented young people with impeccable taste have restored this very beautiful 15th-century residence in the heart of San Gimignano. The house still has its original architecture and frescos. There is an old well inside the house, which is why the hotel has this name. Pretty, antique furniture and beautiful fabrics add to the atmosphere of elegance. If you ask for the fresco room, beware, it is unfortunately on the fire escape. The salon and breakfast room are very pleasant.

How to get there *(Map 13): 38 km northeast of Siena, in town center. Parking: Porta San Matteo (100 m).*

Hotel La Cisterna

Piazza della Cisterna, 24
53037 San Gimignano (Siena)
Tel. (0)577-94 03 28 - Fax (0)577-94 20 80 - Sig. Salvestrini
E-mail: lacisterna@id.it

Category ★★★ **Rooms** 49 and 2 suites with telephone, bath or shower, WC, satellite TV and safe. **Price** Single 113,000L, double 1461-186,000L, suite 211,000L. **Meals** Breakfast included, served 7:30-10:00; half board 115,000-135,000L, full board 150,000-1670,000L (per pers.). **Restaurant** Service 12:30-14:30, 19:30-21:30; closed Tues. and Wed. at noon; menus 55-75,000L. Specialties: Intercosta scaloppata al chianti, specialita' ai funghi e ai tartufi, pasta fatta in casa, dolci freschiescechi. **Credit cards** All major. **Pets** Dogs not allowed. **Facilities** Parking (15,000L). **Nearby** San Gimignano (church of Sant'Agostino, piazza della Cisterna, piazza della Duomo), Etruscan ancient city of Pieve di Cellole, Monastery of S. Vivaldo, Certaldo, Pinacoteca and Visitation chapel (frescoes of Benozzo Gozzoli) in Castelfiorentino, Firenze, Siena, Volterra, Castelfalfi golf course (18-hole). **Open** All year (except Jan. 11 – Mar. 9).

Situated on the main *piazza* in the very heart of San Gimignano, La Cisterna (named after the well which is, along with the famous towers, one of the attractions of San Gimignano) is a beautiful old hotel. Once a palace, it still has many vestiges of the past, like the stunning salon whose architecture is an attraction in itself. Well-chosen Florentine furniture of great refinement creates an atmosphere of elegance and comfort throughout the hotel. Worth special mention is La Terrasse, the restaurant known not only for its cuisine but also for its panoramic view over all the valley. In short, a quality hotel in this miniature city that seems to contain more than its share of the best addresses in Tuscany.

How to get there *(Map 13): 38 km northeast of Siena, in town center. Parking: Porta San Matteo (200 meters).*

Hotel Bel Soggiorno

Via San Giovanni, 91
53037 San Gimignano (Siena)
Tel. (0)577-94 03 75/94 31 49 - Fax (0)577-94 03 75/94 31 49 - Sig. Gigli
E-mail: pescille@iol.it - Web: http://web.tin.it.san-gimignano

Category ★★★ **Rooms** 21 with air-conditioning, telephone, bath, WC, TV and (6 with minibar), elevator. **Price** Double 150,000L, suite 200,000L. **Meals** Breakfast 12,500L, served 8:00-10:00, half board about 115,000L, full board about 150,000L (per pers.). **Restaurant** With air-conditioning. Service 12:15-14:30, 19:30-21:30; closed Jan. 10 – Feb. 10; menu about 45-80,000L, à la carte. Specialties: Traditional cuisine. **Credit cards** All major. **Pets** Dogs not allowed. **Facilities** Parking and garage (15,000L). **Nearby** San Gimignano (church of Sant'Agostino, piazza della Cisterna, piazza della Duomo), Etruscan ancient city of Pieve di Cellole, Monastery of S. Vivaldo, Certaldo, Pinacoteca and Visitation chapel (frescoes of Benozzo Gozzoli) in Castelfiorentino, Firenze, Siena, Volterra, Castelfalfi golf course (18-hole). **Open** All year (except Jan. 11 - Feb. 9).

This very beautiful 13th-century house, in the center of San Gimignano, has belonged to the family that also runs Le Pescille, for five generations. A warm welcome awaits you here. The rooms are unevenly charming: some are on the street and others have a magnificent balcony overlooking the countryside (Rooms 1, 2, and 6). The two suites (11 and 21) are the most beautiful; they have small terraces overlooking the valley. The restaurant also has an extraordinary view, and you can enjoy excellent traditional cuisine, which has been the cause of Bel Soggiorno's good reputation for several generations.

How to get there *(Map 13): 38 km northeast of Siena, in town center.*

La Collegiata

Strada 27 - 53037 San Gimignano (Siena)
Tel. (0577) 94 32 01 - Fax (0577) 94 05 66
Sig. Bonomi

Rooms 22, with air-conditioning, Tel., bath or shower, satellite TV, minibar, safe - Elevator. **Price** Double 550-650,000L, suite 670-750,000L. **Meals** Breakfast included, served 7:30-10:30. **Restaurant** Service 12:30-14:00, 19:30-22:00; menu and also à la carte. Specialties: Regional cooking. **Credit cards** All major. **Pets** Small dogs allowed. **Facilities** Swimming pool, parking. **Nearby** San Gimignano (church of Sant'Agostino, piazza della Cisterna, piazza della Duomo), Etruscan ancient city of Pieve di Cellole, Monastery of S. Vivaldo, Certaldo, Pinacoteca and Visitation chapel (frescoes of Benozzo Gozzoli) in Castelfiorentino, Firenze, Siena, Volterra, Castelfalfi golf course (18-hole). **Open** All year except in January.

This former Franciscan convent, built in 1587 at the request of the inhabitants of San Gimignano, is a beautiful composition of red brick and *pietra serena*, standing against a backdrop of tall cypress trees. Around the buildings are an Italian-style garden and a large swimming pool amid green lawns, which invite the visitor to enjoy the delights of the surrounding countryside. The view from the property stretches as far as the famous towers. Inside, carefully chosen fabrics and furnishings give great elegance to the hall and the salons, situated near the cloister. The restuarant has been installed in what was once the chapel, which lends it an air of nearly religious reverence. Meals are based on local specialties that change with the season and the inspiration of the market. In the tower is a suite with a view 180° around, but this is not our favorite room because of the enormous jacuzzi that takes up a good part of it. The other rooms are large, comfortable and attractive, and far less ostentatious, and the service is uniformly good.

How to get there *(Map 13): 38 km northeast of Siena, in town center. Parking at Porta San Matteo, 100 m.*

Villa San Paolo

53037 San Gimignano (Siena)
Tel. (0)577-95 51 00 - Fax (0)577-95 51 13
Sig.ra Sabatini-Volpini and Sig. Squarcia
E-mail: sanpaolo@vol.it - Web: http://web;tin.it/san-gimignano

Category ★★★★ **Rooms** 18 with air-conditioning, telephone, bath, WC, satellite TV and minibar, elevator; wheelchair access. **Price** Single 100-185,000L, double 140-265,000L. **Meals** Breakfast included, served 7:30-10:30; half board 275-330,000L, full board 335-390,000L. **Restaurant** "Leonetto" in Hotel Le Renaie (see p. 478). **Credit cards** All major. **Pets** Dogs allowed. **Facilities** Swimming pool, tennis. **Nearby** San Gimignano (Church of sant'Agostino), piazza del Duomo, piazza della Cisterna, Palazzo del Popolo; etruscan ancient city of Pieve di Cellole, Monastery of S. Vivaldo, Certaldo, Pinacoteca and Visitation chapel (frescoes of Benozzo Gozzoli) in Castelfiorentino, Firenze, Siena, Volterra, Castelfalfi golf course (18-hole). **Open** All year (except Jan. 10 – Feb. 10).

This small hotel in a beautiful villa is in the San Gimignano countryside on large grounds full of pine and olive trees. The owners also have a hotel next door, Le Renaie. There are only a few rooms; all are air-conditioned and extremely comfortable. The "winter-garden" decor is cheery and warm. There is a superb pool with snack service and an unforgettable view of the countryside around San Gimignano. There is no restaurant, but you can always go the "Leonetto" next door. In the local area, there are historical sites to visit and numerous trails for hiking or horseback riding (there is a club a few miles away).

How to get there *(Map 13): 38 km northeast of Siena; 5 km north of San Gimignano towards Certaldo.*

Hotel Le Renaie

53037 San Gimignano
Pancole (Siena)
Tel. (0)577-95 50 44 - Fax (0)577-95 51 26
Sig. Sabatini

Category ★★★ **Rooms** 25 with telephone, bath, WC, satellite TV, minibar, safe. **Price** Single 100,000L, double 130-180,000L. **Meals** Breakfast 15,000L, served 8:00-10:00; half board 125-140,000L (per pers., 3 days min.). **Restaurant** Service 12:30-14:30, 19:30-22:00; closed Tues.; menus 30-60,000L, also à la carte. Specialties: Coniglio alla vernaccia, piatti al tartufi, piatti agli asparagi e ai funghi. **Credit cards** All major. **Pets** Dogs allowed. **Facilities** Swimming pool, tennis, parking. **Nearby** San Gimignano (Church of sant'Agostino), piazza del Duomo, piazza della Cisterna, Palazzo del Popolo; etruscan ancient city of Pieve di Cellole, Monastery of S. Vivaldo, Certaldo, Pinacoteca and Visitation chapel (frescoes of Benozzo Gozzoli) in Castelfiorentino, Firenze, Siena, Volterra, Castelfalfi golf course (18-hole). **Open** All year (except Nov. 5 – Dec. 5).

Le Renaie is in the countryside near San Gimignano. Recently constructed, it respects the traditional Tuscan materials and colors. Tiles, bricks, terra cotta and wood form a harmonious blend of textures and colors: pale pink and off-white colors predominate. The contemporary salon, with its large fireplace and a pretty little bar open onto a gallery surrounded by plants and flowers, particularly pleasant for having breakfast or a drink. The rooms are all comfortable and pleasant, but try to get the ones with a terrace overlooking the countryside.

How to get there *(Map 13): 38 km northeast of Siena; 6 km northwest of San Gimignano to Pieve di Cellole, then Pancole.*

Il Casale del Cotone 

Il Cotone 53037 San Gimignano (Siena)
Tel. (0)577 94 32 36 - Fax (0)577 94 32 36

Rooms 4 and 3 apartments with shower, WC, satellite TV and minibar. **Price** Single 120,000L, double 140,000L, suite 160,000L. **Meals** Breakfast 10,000L, served 8:00-10:30, half board 210-260,000L. **Restaurant** See p. 478. **Credit cards** Amex, Visa, Eurocard, MasterCard. **Pets** Dogs allowed. **Facilities** Mountain bikes, parking at hotel. **Nearby** In San Gimignano: Etruscan ancient city of Pieve di Cellole, Convent of S.Vivaldo, Certaldo, Pinacotecaand visitation chapel (frescoes of Benozzo.Gozzoli) in Castelfiorentino, Firenze, Siena, Volterra, Castelfalfi golf course (18-hole). **Open** All year.

Beautiful little San Gimignano, situated between Siena, Florence and Pisa, is an excellent base from which to tour the region, and it abounds in nice hotels. But that's no reason to exclude another one, which is both nice and reasonably-priced. It is an 18th-century farmhouse surrounded by 30 hectares of vineyards and olive trees. The owners recently set up several rooms sleeping two or three persons and two mini-apartments, with their own separate entrance, suitable for families. Country-style decor, with some antique furniture. Brand new and very comfortable shower rooms. Breakfast is served in the hunting room or the garden, depending on the season. The owners take great pains to give guests a good welcome - there is bar service at all times and they will even prepare a light meal at your request. But San Gimignano is only 2 kilometers away and the evening is really the best time to discover this historic city.

How to get there *(Map 13): 2 km from San Gimignano, towards Certaldo.*

Il Casolare di Libbiano 

Libbiano 53037 San Gimignano (Siena)
Tel. and Fax (0)577-94 60 02
Sig. Bucciarelli and Sig.ra Mateos

Rooms 5 with shower, WC and 1 suite with bath, WC, lounge, terrace. **Price** Double 220,000L, suite 290,000L. **Meals** Breakfast included, served 8:30-10:00; half board 270,000L (in double room), 340,000L in suite. **Restaurant** Service 20:00. Specialties: Traditional Tuscan cuisine. **Credit cards** Visa, Eurocard, MasterCard. **Pets** Dogs allowed. **Facilities** Swimming pool, mountain bikes, parking. **Nearby** San Gimignano (Sommer of San Gimignano); etruscan ancient city of Pieve di Cellole, Monastery of S. Vivaldo, Certaldo, Pinacoteca and Visitation chapel (frescoes of Benozzo Gozzoli) in Castelfiorentino, Firenze, Siena, Volterra, Castelfalfi golf course (18-hole). **Open** Mar. – Oct.

Leaving San Gimignano on the road to Certaldo, you drive into the countryside of Val d'Elsa until you catch sight of a small hill on which stands the church of Cellole. A few kilometers farther on you come to Libbiano and the Casolare. A dynamic couple have completely transformed this old farmhouse into a warm and inviting holiday home that is comfortable and authentic. The hospitability is particularly attentive and your hosts are eager to tell you about their region and let you share in its varied riches — be it the cuisine, the wine or the culture. Be sure you go and see the beautiful abbeys of Sant'Antimo and San Galgano, which you can visit in complete tranquility as they are still a bit off the main tourist paths.

How to get there *(Map 13): 8 km from San Gimignano, towards Gambassi, left to Libbiano.*

1998

Hotel Pescille

Pescille 53037 San Gimignano (Siena)
Tel. (0)577 94 01 86- Fax (0)577 94 31 65 - Fratères Gigli
E-mail: pescille@iol.it - Web: http://web.tin.it/san-gimignano

Category ★★★ **Rooms** 40 with tel., bath, WC., 7 with TV and minibar. **Price** Simple 110,000L, double 145,000L, suite 190,000L. **Meals** Breakfast 15,000L, served 8:00-9:30. **Restaurant** See p. 478. **Credit cards** All major. **Pets** Dogs not allowed. **Facilities** Swimming pool, tennis (10,000L), parking. **Nearby** In San Gimignano, piazza della Cisterna; carnaval, San Gimignano, Etruscan ancient city of Pieve di Cellole, Convent of S.Vivaldo, Certaldo, Pinacoteca and visitation chapel (frescoes of Benozzo.Gozzoli) in Castelfiorentino, Firenze, Siena, Volterra, Castelfalfi golf course (18-hole). **Open** All year (except Jan. and Feb.).

The towers of San Gimignano are among the great tourist attractions of Tuscany. The Hotel Pescille, a sturdy and rustic old farmhouse converted into a hotel some years ago, is located outside of town. It was recently renovated and has all the facilities that a hotel in the city lacks: garden, tennis, swimming pool. The spot is pleasant and restful. You can relax after a hard day's sightseeing in the maze of little gardens around the hotel. The bedrooms have all the necessary amenities, in a sober decor that blends old and contemporary. All in all, a nice country inn.

How to get there *(Map 13): 38 km northeast of Siena; 6 km from San Gimignano towards Castel San Gimignano-Volterra after 3.5 km.*

Casanova di Pescille 

Pescille 53037 San Gimignano (Siena)
Tel. (0)577-94 19 02 - Fax (0)577-94 19 02
Sig.ra Cappellini - Sig. Fianciullini

Rooms 8 and 1 apartment. (2 pers. with kitchen) with shower and satellite TV. **Price** Double 110,000L, apartment 150,000L. **Meals** Breakfast included. **Restaurant** See p. 478. **Credit cards** Visa, Eurocard, MasterCard. **Pets** Dogs allowed. **Facilities** Parking. **Nearby** San Gimignano: collegiata, piazza del Duomo, piazza della Cisterna; Annual carnival, San Gimignano, Convent of S.Vivaldo, Certaldo, Pinacoteca, Visitation chapel (frescoes by B. Gozzoli) in Castelfiorentino, Firenze, Siena, Volterra, Castelfalfi golf course, (18-hole). **Open** All year.

For young people or others of limited means, or if you plan on a long stay, here is an address that will give you a base two kilometers from San Gimignano for far less money than you would pay in town. The owners of this estate, which produces the local white wine, Vernaccia, and also a good olive oil, have set up several rooms to receive guests. The house is simple but has a pleasant, well-kept garden, adorned with enormous pots of hydrangeas. Though the ground floor decor is really not to our taste, the bedrooms are nicely, if simply, decorated. They are not very large, but quite comfortable. The individual little house with its kitchenette gives a guest greater independence. One strong point: the breathtaking view from the bedrooms of the 13 towers of San Gimignano, and even better, the view from the pleasant terrace, which is open to all who want to taste the wine of the estate.

How to get there *(Map 13): 38 km northeast of Siena; 5 km north of San Gimignano, on the road to Volterra 2 km on the left.*

Azienda Piccolomini Bandini 

1998

Lucignanello Bandini 53020 SanGiovanni d'Asso (Siena)
Tel. (0)577-82 30 68 - Fax (0)577-82 30 82

Houses 5 with kitchen, sitting room, 2-4 rooms, bath and TV. **Price** For 1 week "Casa Severino" (2-4 pers.) 1,400,000-1,600,000L; "Amadeo" (4-6 pers.); "Clementina" (2-4 pers.); "Remo" (2-4 pers.) 1,800-2,000,000L; "Sarageto" (7 pers.) 4,500-5,000,000L. **Credit cards** Diners, Visa, Eurocard, MasterCard. **Pets** Dogs allowed. **Nearby** Val d'Orcia: Pienza, Montepulciano, Monticchiello, Montalcino (Brunello's cellars) and Abbey of Sant'Antimo, Terme of Bagno Vignoni, Collegiata San Quirico d'Orcia, Castiglione d'Orcia, Rocca d'Orcia, Campiglia d'Orcia, Abbey of Sant'Anna Camprena, Abbey of Monte Oliveto Maggiore. **Open** All year.

If you dream of houses in Tuscany, of the light and the landscape of the Sienese masters, treat yourself to a stay in the hamlet of Lucignano d'Asso where the lovely Lippi sisters have refurbished five of the village houses, with excellent taste and a real flair for decoration. They are all equally equipped with household and sanitary facilities of the highest quality. Each one has its own charm. Signora Lippi likes to tell the story of the Frenchman who came to spend a few days at the Casa Severino (the smallest but with the nicest view) and wound up staying nine years. The Casa Sarageto, the largest, is quite spectacular with its grand salon and its trophy-cases, its superb bedrooms, a garden and a private swimming pool. Nearby, you will find a typical little grocer's shop, well-stocked with local products, where you can even go to have lunch. In such marvelous surroundings, you can give free range to the emotions produced by art and nature in the heart of Tuscany.

How to get there *(Map 13): 35 km south of Siena, towards Montalcino-S. Quirico d'orcia. In Torrenieri, towards S. Giovanni d'Asso. Halfway take the road on the right for Lucignano d'Asso and Lucignanello Bandini.*

Locanda dell'Amorosa

L'Amorosa
53048 Sinalunga (Siena)
Tel. (0)577-67 94 97 - Fax (0)577-63 20 01
Sig. Citterio

Category ★★★★ **Rooms** 12 and 5 suites with air-conditioning, telephone, bath, WC, TV and minibar. **Price** Standard 360,000L, superior 420,000L, luxury 490,000L, suite 540,000L. **Meals** Breakfast included, served 7:30-10:30. **Restaurant** Service 12:30-14:30, 20:00-21:30; closed Mon. and Tues. at noon; à la carte. Specialties: New regional cuisine, very good Italian wines. **Credit cards** All major. **Pets** Dogs allowed in room. **Facilities** Parking. **Nearby** Collegiata di San Martino and church of S. Croce de Sinalunga, Museo Civico, Palazzo Comunale, Church Madonna delle Averce in Lucignano, Monte San Savino (loggia), Pienza, Montepulciano, Perugia, Savino (loggia), Arezzo, Siena. **Open** All year (except Jan. 7 - Mar. 5).

After crossing the plain where Piero della Francesca was born, a long cypress-lined path will lead you to the entrance of the Locanda. Once you have gone through the vaulted archway, you will find enchanting old buildings built out of a mixture of stone, brick and the pink terra cotta of Siena. Quiet confort and good taste are the great luxuries of this inn, one of the most beautiful in Italy. The cuisine, made from numerous products from the farm, is excellent. The selection of wines from the region is also nice. Don't miss this place if you can afford it.

How to get there *(Map 13): 50 km southeast of Siena via S326; via A1, Val di Chiana exit; 2 km south of Sinalunga to L'Amorosa.*

La Frateria

53040 Cetona (Siena)
Convento San Francesco
Tel. (0)578-23 80 15 - Fax (0)578-23 92 20

Category ★★★★ **Rooms** 7 with bath and WC. **Price** Single 230,000L, double 320,000L, suite 420-000L. **Meals** Breakfast included, served 7:30-10:00. **Restaurant** Service 13:00, 20:00; closed Tues. except on request; menu: 120,000L. Specialties: New traditional cuisine. **Credit cards** Amex in the restaurant only, Visa, Eurocard, MasterCard. **Pets** Dogs not allowed. **Facilities** Parking. **Nearby** Montepulciano, Monticchiello, Montalcino, Terme de Bagno Vignoli, Val d'Orcia villages (Castiglione d'Orcia, Rocca d'Orcia, Ripa d'Orcia, Campiglia d'Orcia), Pienza, Collegiale San Quirico d'Orcia, Museo Nazionale Etrusco in Siusi, Chianciano Terme, Siena. **Open** All year (except Feb. by request).

A young Franciscan priest decided to restore an abandoned convent with the help of a community of troubled youth called "Mondo X." The result is nothing short of extraordinary. After a considerable amount of restoration, the convent once again has its chapels, cloisters with laurel flowers, meditation room, and very recently, dining hall. The garden is overloaded with clematis, camellias and azalies. In summer, the rose bushes and kiwi trees take over. The feeling here is harmony with nature. The cuisine in the restaurant consists of Tuscan specialties made exclusively with products from La Frateria's farm. The rooms are very nicely decorated and have a slightly monastic feel to them. If you didn't know that the founder of the order, Saint Francis of Assissi, had a taste for nice things, you might be surprised by so much elegance.

How to get there *(Map 13): 89 km of Siena, via A1, Chiusi exit; Chianciano Terme and S428 to Sarteano, towards Cetona.*

La Palazzina

Le Vigne 53040 Radicofani (Siena)
Tel. and Fax (0)578-55 771
Sig.ra Innocenti

Rooms 10 with bath and WC. **Price** With half board 98-112,000L, full board 120-140,000L (per pers., 3 days min.). **Meals** Breakfast included, served 8:00-10:00. **Restaurant** Service 12:45-13:30, 20:00-20:30; menus: 38-48,000L. Specialties: Zuppe e vellutate di stagioni, pici, gnochetti agli aromi, tagliolini d'ortica arrosto alla cannella o alla mentta, mousse al limone, bianco mangiare alle mandorle. **Credit cards** Amex, Visa, Eurocard, MasterCard. **Pets** Dogs allowed (15,000L). **Facilities** Swimming pool, parking. **Nearby** Montepulciano, Monticchiello, Montalcino, Terme de Bagno Vignoli, Val d'Orcia villages (Castiglione d'Orcia, Rocca d'Orcia, Ripa d'Orcia, Campiglia d'Orcia), Pienza, Collegiale San Quirico d'Orcia, Museo Nazionale Etrusco in Siusi, Chianciano Terme, Siena. **Open** All year (except 2nd week in Nov. and third week in Mar.).

Here in this little corner of Tuscany we have found what may well be a paradise on earth: a verdant landscape of gently rolling hills, bathed in a soft light. On the hilltops, signs of man-made beauty, old farmhouses, or villas like the Palazzina, surrounded by walls of tall dark cypress trees. Life in this handsome *fattoria* is essentially run by two women, Bianca and Nicoletta, mother and daughter, and each of the rooms (all prettily arranged) bears a woman's name. In an atmosphere of great refinement, you will nevertheless be close to nature. With baroque music in the background, you can taste dishes that are simple but delicious, all with home-made products, including the excellent wine that the owner can tell you so much about. All this in surroundings that resemble a Lorenzetti or Simone Martini or some such landscape of the Sienese school.

How to get there *(Map 13): 80 km south of Siena via A1, Chiusi-Chianciano Terme exit, to Sarteano. Turn on the left for Radicofani. Before 14th km turn on left towards Celle sul Rigo. 1.5km, on right.*

California Park Hotel

Via Colombo, 32
55042 Forte dei Marmi (Lucca)
Tel. (0)584 78 71 21 - Fax (0)584 78 72 68
Sig. Mario Viacava

Category ★★★★ **Rooms** 44 with air conditioning, telephone, bath or shower, WC, satellite TV, safe; elevator. **Price** Double 280-520,000L, suite 450-8650,000L. **Meals** Breakfast included, served 8:00-10:00, half board 180-290,000L, full board 190-300,000L (per pers., 3 day min.). **Restaurant** (For residents) Served 12:30-14:00, 20:00-21:30; menu; also à la carte. **Credit cards** All major. **Pets** Dogs not allowed. **Facilities** Swimming pool, parking. **Nearby** Duomo de Carrara; Carrières de marbres; cave di marmo di Colonnata, cava dei Fantiscritti; Lucca; Pisa; Viareggio; Versilia Golf club (18 holes). **Open** All year. (except Oct.).

In the residential quarter of this seaside resort and only 300 meters from the beaches, a park full of luxuriant trees and flowers protects the three villas that make up the California Park Hotel. They are large modern buildings in Mediterranean style, built around a swimming pool. The bedrooms are bright, the furnishings functional but pleasant. Many of them have a balcony or terrace, or are directly on the garden. Well-prepared traditional cooking, served in a dining room that opens onto the park. The park, with tables and beach chairs, is indeed a wonderful and quiet place to sit if the swimming pool gets too hectic for you. The service and welcome are professional.

How to get there *(Map 9): 35 km from Pisa via A 12 (Genova-Livorno), Versilia exit - Forte dei Marmi.*

Hotel Byron

Viale Morin, 46
55042 Forte dei Marmi (Lucca)
Tel. (0)584 78 70 52 - Fax (0)584 78 71 52
Sig.Franco Nardini

Category ★★★★★ **Rooms** 24 and 6 suites with air conditioning, telephone, bath or shower, WC, satellite TV, minibar; elevator. **Price** Single 190-420,000L, double 295-570,000L, suite 505-990,000L. **Meals** Breakfast 40 000L, served 7:30-12:00, half board 275-465,000L, full board 315-495,000L (per pers., 3 day min.). **Restaurant** Service 13:00-14:30, 20:00-21:30; menus 80,000L; also à la carte.Specialties: Scampi in passatina di cannellini, crêpes alla crema di asparagi, risotto con zafferno, scampi e zucchine, pesce misto all'acqua pazza, torta al limone. **Credit cards** All major. **Pets** Dogs not allowed. **Facilities** Swimming pool, billards, parking. **Nearby** Duomo de Carrara; Carrières de marbres; caves di marmo di Colonnata, cava dei Fantiscritt, Lucca, Pisa, Viareggio,Versilia Golf club (18 holes). **Open** All year.

A few meters from the sea, which you can contemplate from the terraces, the Hotel Byron is composed up two villas dating from the turn of the century. In the most residential area of Forte dei Marmi, protected from the outside world by a verdant rampart of foliage, it is a haven of peace and comfort on this rather frenetic coast. The whole place has the calm and serene feeling of a colonial mansion. Salons and bedrooms have kept their elegance despite a few modern notes introduced during recent renovations. The balconies face either the sea or a vast garden that contains a large swimming pool. A pleasant luxury vacation.

How to get there *(Map 9): 35 km from Pisa via A 12 (Genova-Livorno), Versilia exit - Forte dei Marmi.*

Hotel Tirreno

Viale Morin, 7
55042 Forte dei Marmi (Lucca)
Tel. (0)584-78 74 44 - Fax (0)584-787 137
Sig.ra Daddi Baralla

Category ★★★ **Rooms** 59 with telephone, bath or shower and WC. **Price** Single 105,000L, double 175,000L. **Meals** Breakfast 16,000L, served 7:30-11:00; half board 145-190,000L, full board 160-200,000L. **Restaurant** Service 13:00-14:00, 20:00-21:00; menus 50-70,000L, also à la carte. Specialties Tuscan cuisine. **Credit cards** All major. **Pets** Dogs not allowed. **Nearby** Duomo de Carrara, Cave di marmo di Colonnata, cava dei Fantiscritti, Lucca, Pisa. **Open** Apr. – Sept.

The part of the hotel which is visible from the street is a little disconcerting–it is 70s' style–but there is a surprise deep in the garden: the outbuilding, an old 19th-century summer house. Don't plan to stay anywhere in Tirreno but here, in one of the rooms on the pretty garden (57, 58, and 60) or on the sea. The hotel is both centrally located in Tirreno and close to the beach. The service is meticulous and the Tuscan cuisine is great.

***How to get there** (Map 9): 35 km north of Pisa via A12 (Genova-Livorno); Versilia exit, Forte dei Marmi.*

Hotel Plaza e de Russie

Piazza d'Azeglio, 1
55049 Viareggio (Lucca)
Tel. (0)584 44 449 - Fax (0)584 44 031
Sig.Gian Piero Guarnori

Category ★★★★ **Rooms** 52 with air conditioning, telelephone, bath or shower, WC, satellite TV, minibar; elevator. **Price** Single 160-240,000L, double 240-360,000L, suite 380-390,000L. **Meals** Breakfast 15,000L, served 7:00-11:00, half board 160-235,000L, full board 190-275,000L (per pers., 3 day min.). **Restaurant** Service 12:30-14:30, 19:00-22:30, menus 60-75,000L; also à la carte.Specialties: Sparnocchi in pllata di finochio, stracci neri ai frutti di mare, filetto di branzino al limone candito. **Credit cards** All major. **Pets** Dogs not allowed. **Facilities** Parking. **Nearby** Duomo de Carrara; cave di marmo di Colonnata, cava dei Fantiscritti; Lucca; Pisa; Viareggio; Versilia Golf club (18 holes). **Open** All year.

Built in 1871, this was the first hotel in Viareggio, a little resort town that has still managed, despite a flourishing tourism industry, to preserve some of the charm it had at the turn of the century. Located just a few steps from the sea and the beaches, it has been completely renovated and at the same time enhanced by the addition of marble and chandeliers. Still, the bedrooms are sober and elegant, and have kept their original parquet floors. If possible, avoid the bedrooms on the first floor, as they face a promenade that remains rather noisy till late into the night. The restaurant, featuring all the products of the sea, has a terrace with an outstanding view of the sea and the town. This can serve as an excellent base for anyone who wants to visit Pisa, Lucca and the region, without giving up the pleasures of a holiday by the sea.

How to get there *(Map 9): 25 km from Pisa via A 12 (Genova-Livorno), Viareggio exit.*

Azienda Costa d'Orsola 

Orsola 54027 Pontremoli (Massa Carrara)
Tel. and Fax (0)187-83 33 32
Sig.ra Bezzi

Rooms 14 with telephone and shower. **Price** Double 110-130,000L. **Meals** Breakfast included; half board 85-105,000L (per pers., 2 days min.). **Restaurant** Service 20:00-21:00; closed for lunch execpt Sun., menus 40-50,000L, à la carte. Specialties: Tuscan cuisine. **Credit cards** Diners, Visa, Eurocard and MasterCard. **Pets** Small dogs allowed. **Facilities** Swimming pool, tennis, parking. **Nearby** La Spezia, Cinqueterre, Val Lunigiana (Aula, Villafranca in Lunigiana), Appenin parmesan (Berceto, Cassio, Bardone, Fornovo di Taro Collechio, Parme). **Open** Mar. 16 - Nov. 2.

On the road from Tuscany to Liguria (from Parma to Spezia), don't hesitate to stop off and enjoy the hospitality of this little hamlet perched above Pontremoli. The Costa d'Orsola is a vast old farm recently transformed into an inn. The buildings are connected by a maze of stairways. The pleasant rooms, simply but prettily decorated, have a superb view of the Appenin Parmesan and the Val Lunigiana. The home-style cuisine is made from fresh ingredients from the farm and regional specialties such as "Testaroli," a delicious pasta dish. This is a great place for hikers and nature-lovers.

***How to get there** (Map 9): 35 km of La Spezia. Via A15 (La Spezia/Parma) Pontremoli exit; after the tollgate on the right and on left towards Costa d'Orsola.*

Il Frassinello 

56040 Montecatini Val di Cecina (Pisa)
Tel. and Fax (0)588-300 80
Sig.ra Sclubach Giudici

Rooms 4 and 4 apartments with bath or shower. **Price** 140,000L (per 2 pers.). **Meals** Breakfast 10,000L, served about 8:00-10:00. **Restaurant** In Hotel Buriano or in Volterra (see p. 429). **Credit cards** Not accepted. **Pets** Dogs allowed. **Facilities** Parking. **Nearby** Volterra, San Gimignano, Siena, Lucignano, Marina di Cecina (beach), Pisa. **Open** Easter – late Sept.

This is an old farmhouse turned into an appealing little guest house, located in a region where few tourists venture. You will discover a more genuine Tuscany (even though your hostess is of German origin) only 50 kilometers from the world-famous sites. Il Frassinello is rather isolated and not so easy to reach — the last 4 kilometers are on a dirt road. But you will have the added surprise of seeing the Elga deer farm, the largest in Europe. You will be in the heart of a grandiose and unspoiled natural site, better suited to a longer stay than just a stopover. The ambience in the rooms and small apartments is pleasantly rustic but not lacking in comfort. Civilization is not so far away, and your hostess is happy to suggest restaurants for a dinner out: the *Locanda del Sole* at Querceto, the *Vecchio Molino* at Saline di Volterra, the *Scaccipensieri* in Cecina or the *Biscandola da Nicola* in Volterra. If you prefer to dine in, however, you can have a meal prepared for you on simple request.

How to get there *(Map 12): 60 km northwest of Siena (towards Firenze); Colle di Val d'Elsa-South exit, towards Volterra and Monticatini Val di Cecina.*

Casetta delle Selve

56 010 Pugnano
San Giuliano Terme (Pisa)
Tel. and Fax (0)50-85 03 59
Sig.ra Nicla Menchi

Rooms 6 with bath or shower and WC. **Price** Double 105-114,000L. **Meals** Breakfast 13,000L, served about 9:00. **Restaurant** See p. 479. **Credit cards** Eurochèques. **Pets** Dogs allowed. **Facilities** Parking. **Nearby** Certosa di Calci, Pisa, Lucca, beach and sea. **Open** Apr. - Oct.

The enchantment will start as soon as you leave the road to take the scented path that leads up to the casetta. Flooded with light, surrounded by chestnut and olive trees, the house offers a stunning view of the Tuscan hills with, in the background, the sea and the islands of Corsica and Gorgona. It is a simple, pleasant place and Nicla provides a warm and friendly welcome. She has artistically seen to the comfort and decoration of each room, to the point of adding her own handmade rugs and pillow cases, not to mention her paintings that adorn the walls. At breakfast, you can appreciate her homemade jams as you enjoy the view from the delightful terrace. A good base for visiting Pisa and Lucca, both close by.

How to get there *(Map 9): 10 km south of Lucca, via A11 Lucca exit; then SS12 and SS12bis towards San Giuliano Terme; in Pugnano follow the small partly unpaved road.*

Hotel Villa di Corliano

Rigoli 56010 San Giuliano Terme (Pisa)
Via Statale, 50
Tel. (0)50-81 81 93 - Fax (0)50-81 88 97
Sig. Agostini della Seta

Category ★★★ **Rooms** 18 with telephone (8 with bath, WC). **Price** Double 107-160,000L, suite for 4 pers. 267,000L. **Meals** Breakfast 18,000L, served 8:00-10:00. **Restaurant** On the property. Specialties: Seafood. **Credit cards** Visa, Eurocard and MasterCard. **Pets** Dogs allowed. **Nearby** Santa Maria del Giudice, Pisa, Lucca. **Open** All year.

The Villa di Corliano is, like a jewel, its own lovely jewel box. A jewel of measured and elegant architecture amid extensive grounds that have been allowed to remain natural. In front of the house, a large prairie stretches toward a background of wooded hills. The interior has kept its original appearance with chandeliers, gilded wood and antique furniture. Unfortunately, all this splendor is just a decor and not accessible to guests. The bedrooms are more modest and the owner not always very affable. Still, the spot is unique and the prices reasonable for the facilities offered. So perhaps it's worth taking advantage of before it is restored and redecorated, with who knows what result. A good restaurant on the property is also worth mentioning.

How to get there *(Map 9): 8 km north of Pisa via SS12bis to San Giuliano Terme, then northwest S12 towards Rigoli.*

Albergo Villa Nencini

Borgo San Stefano, 55
56048 Volterra (Pisa)
Tel. (0)588-86 386 - Fax (0)588-80 601
Sig. Nencini

Rooms 34: 11 with shower, WC and TV on request), 21 with Tel, bath, WC, satellite TV and 1 suite; wheelchair access. **Price** Single 90,000L, double 120,000. **Meals** Breakfast 10,000L, served 7:00-11:00. **Restaurant** See p.479. **Credit cards** Visa, Eurocard, MasterCard. **Pets** Dogs allowed. **Facilities** Swimming pool. **Nearby** Volterra: piazza dei Priori, Duomo, Museo Etrusco Guarnacci, Les Balze - San Gimignano, Lucignano, Siena, Firenze, Piza. **Open** All year.

The Villa Nencini is just outside the walls of Volterra, an ancient Etruscan, Roman and medieval town, with "one of the most beautiful medieval squares in Italy," the Piazza dei Priori. On the edge of town, it has a great view of the valley. The house is very old; the interior is unpretentious and friendly. A wing has been added onto the house; the rooms there are more modern and more comfortable but the ones in the villa are more traditional and authentic. The very pretty garden and swimming pool overhanging the valley are good places to take in the marvelous panorama.

How to get there *(Map 12): 60 km northwest of Siena, via SS or A1; Colle di Val d'Elsa exit.*

Hotel Grotta Giusti

Via Grotta Giusti, 17
51015 Monsummano Terme (Pistoia)
Tel. (0)572-51 165/6 - Fax (0)572-51 269
Sig. Giovanetti

Category ★★★★ **Rooms** 70 with air-conditioning, telephone, bath, WC and TV; elevator. **Price** Single 150-170,000L, double 250-270,000L. **Meals** Breakfast included, served 7:30-10:00; half board 205-225,000L, 160-180,000L (per pers., in double room), full board, 215-235,000L, 170-190,000L (per pers in double room, 3 days min.). **Restaurant** Service 12:30-14:00, 19:30-21:00; menu 55,000L, also à la carte. Specialties: Tuscan and international cuisine. **Credit cards** All major. **Pets** Small dogs allowed. **Facilities** Swimming pool, tennis, sauna, health center (thermal swimming pool). **Nearby** Montecatini, Serra Pistoiese, Pistoia, Villa Mansi near Segromigno Monte, Lucca, golf course (18-hole) in Pievaccia and in Monsummano. **Open** Mar. – Nov.

This former residence of the rich poet Giusti is built around an amazing grotto with a stream of hot blue water. Giuseppe Verdi was often a guest at this house. You can still see some of the splendor of the original decor in the reception area. The rooms are functional, but the ones in the old building, which look out over the park, are by far the nicest. They all have hot running spring water, so ask for one with a bathtub. In addition, beautiful grounds with a spring water swimming pool, a tennis court and running trail make this hotel an ideal place for a relaxing stay.

How to get there *(Map 9): 37 km northwest of Firenze; 13 km west of Pistoia via A11, Montecatini exit; then S435 to Monsummano Terme.*

Grand Hotel e La Pace

Viale della Toretta, 1
51016 Montecatini Terme (Pistoia)
Tel. (0)572-758 01 - Fax (0)572-784 51
Sig. Tongiorgi

Category ★★★★★ **Rooms** 136 and 14 apartments with telephone, bath, WC, TV and minibar; elevator. **Price** Single 280-320,000L, double 450-490,000L. **Meals** Breakfast 30,000L, served 7:30-10:30. **Restaurant** Service 12:30-14:00, 20:00-21:30, also à la carte. Specialties: Tuscan cuisine. **Credit cards** All major. **Pets** Dogs allowed (fee). **Facilities** Heated swimming pool, sauna, tennis, health center, parking. **Nearby** Pescia, church in Castelvecchio, Collodi, Lucca, Pistoia, Firenze, Pisa, golf course (18-hole) in Pievaccia and in Monsummano Terme. **Open** Apr. – Oct.

All of the traditional splendor of this 1870 palace is completely intact. The hotel's sumptuous, thick carpeted salons, first-class dining room with a baywindow and very comfortable rooms, decorated in harmonious pastel colors, make the atmosphere warm. On the superb five-acre grounds there is a large heated swimming pool, a tennis court and a spa for medically supervised mud baths, saunas, massages, ozone baths and algae beauty treatments.

How to get there *(Map 9): 49 km northwest of Firenze; 15 km west Pistoia via A11, Montecatini exit.*

Villa Lucia

Via dei Bronzoli, 144
51010 Montevettolini (Pistoia)
Tel. (0)572-61 77 90 - Fax (0)572-62 8817
Sig.ra Vallera

Rooms 7 (1 with bath, 6 with shower, 6 with WC, 3 with TV). **Price** (2 days min.): Single 150,000L, double 225,000L, suite 320,000L (1 week min.). **Meals** Breakfast included **Restaurant** For residents only, by reservation. Service 20:30; menu 30,000L. **Credit cards** Not accepted. **Pets** Dogs not allowed. **Facilities** Small swimming pool. **Nearby** Firenze, Montecatini, Serra Pistoiese, Pistoia, Villa Mansi near Segromigno Monte, Lucca, golf course (18-hole) in Pievaccia and in Monsumanno. **Open** Apr. 15 – Nov. 15.

The Villa Lucia is part bed and breakfast and part Tuscan inn. Everything is pretty and authentically Tuscan, though there is a hint of California as well. This is no accident: it is run by a charming lady who caters to the many Americans who come here for the warm convivial atmosphere, the pretty copper beds, the regional furniture and a nice glass of *vinsanto* (fortified dessert wine) and *cantuccini* (almond biscuits). Her savory cuisine is based on house recipes. On summer evenings there are parties on the lawn. You may not make much progress with your Italian while you are here, but you are sure to have a great time.

How to get there *(Map 9): 40 km of Firenze; 13 km west Pistoia via A11, Montecatini exit; then S435 to Monsummano Terme and little road for Montevettolini.*

Il Convento

Via San Quirico, 33
51030 Pontenuovo (Pistoia)
Tel. (0)573-45 26 51/2 - Fax (0)573-45 35 78
Sig. Petrini

Rooms 24 with telephone, bath, WC and TV. **Price** Single 120,000L, double 150,000L. **Meals** Breakfast 13,000L, served 7:30-9:30; half board 120,000L; full board 140,000L (per pers., 3 days min.). **Restaurant** Service 12:30-14:30, 19:30-22:00; closed Mon. in Jan. – Easter; menus 45-55,000L, also à la carte. Specialties: Tuscan cuisine. **Credit cards** Visa, Eurocard and MasterCard. **Pets** Dogs not allowed. **Facilities** Swimming pool, parking. **Nearby** Pistoia, De Maresca, Lake of Scaffaiolo, Corno alle Scale (1 945 m), Firenze, Lucca, dell'Ugolino golf course (18-hole) in Grassina. **Open** All year.

This old Franciscan monastery, in keeping with its name, still has a small chapel and a tranquil atmosphere. Surrounded by a vast flower garden overlooking the plain, this charming hotel is a little old and could use some modernizing. But it is a pleasant place from which to visit Pistoia and the northern part of Tuscany. A pool above the garden is at your disposal. The restaurant serves very good, traditional Tuscan cuisine.

How to get there *(Map 9): 40 km of Firenze; 5 km east of Pistoia towards Montale then to Pontenuovo.*

Rifugio Prategiano

Via Prategiano, 45
58026 Montieri (Grosseto)
Tel. (0)566-99 77 03 - Fax (0)566-99 78 91
Sig. Paradisi

Category ★★★ **Rooms** 24 with telephone, bath, WC and TV. **Price** Single 88-150,000L, double 140-214,000L. **Meals** Breakfast included; half board 90-129,000L (per pers.,3 days min.). **Restaurant** Service 13:00, 20:00; menus. Specialties: Tortelloni, cinghiale, acqua Cotta. **Credit cards** All major. **Pets** Dogs allowed. **Facilities** Swimming pool, tennis, riding, parking. **Nearby** Roman and Etruscan ruins of Roselle, Vetulonia, Montepescali, National Park of Maremma, Volterra. **Open** All year.

The Prategiano is on Montieri Hill, an old Medieval citadel deep in the High Maremma part of the little-known Métallifère Forest in Tuscany. The ambience is that of a mountain inn. The decor is very simple and rustic, as most of the hotel guests are horseback riders. There are riding lessons and daytime excursions for children and beginners, while more experienced riders can gallop through the Tuscan hills, crossing woods and forests to the deserted beaches of Punta Ala to get to Volterra. The setting is perfect and the owner is friendly and very careful about the security of his guests. This is the perfect address for those seeking a small adventure.

How to get there *(Map 13): 50 km southwest of Siena via S73 to Bivio del Madonnino, then S441 (15km); on the right towards Montieri.*

Hotel Il Pellicano

Lo Sbarcatello 58018 Porto Ercole (Grosseto)
Tel. (0)564-83 38 01 - Fax (0)564-83 34 18 - Sig. Fanciulli
E-mail: pellicano@ouverture.it. - Web: http://www.ouverture.it./pellicano

Category ★★★★ **Rooms** 41 with telephone, bath, WC, TV and minibar. **Price** Double 315-920,000L, suite 672-1,845,000L. **Meals** Breakfast included, served 7:30-10:30. **Restaurant** Service 13:00-14:30, 20:00-22:00; menus 110-140,000L, also à la carte. Specialties: Risotto al , fettuccine con scampi e zucchine, spaghetti al Pellicano. **Credit cards** All major. **Pets** Dogs not allowed. **Facilities** Sea-water swimming pool, health center, tennis, private beach, windsurfing, parking. **Nearby** Giannutri and Giglio islands, Tombolo di Feniglia, Sovona, Sorano, Pitigliano. **Open** Apr. 3 – Nov. 1.

The guest book of the Pelicano is full of prestigious names. Inaugurated in 1975 in the presence of Charlie Chaplin, it has been visited by celebrities ever since. Nestled in a little valley of cypress trees overlooking the gulf of Argentaro, the hotel consists of a number of villas, contiguous but independent. It is a luxury establishment with the atmosphere of a private home. The sitting rooms are arranged around the fireplace or the library. In the summer the restaurant serves on the terrace, from which you have a view of the sea through the branches of pine trees. A large swimming pool has been cut directly into the rock face of the cliff. It is reached by an elevator. The quality service comes up to the standards of its demanding clientele.

How to get there *(Map 13): 55 km south of Grosseto via SS51, then along the coast to Porto Ercole; then strada panoramica to Lo Sbarcatello.*

Hotel Cala del Porto

Via Cala del Pozzo
58040 Punta Ala (Grosseto)
Tel. (0)564-92 24 55 - Fax (0)564-92 07 16
E-mail: cala.puntaala@bcedit.it

Category ★★★★ **Rooms** 36 and 5 apartments with air-conditioning, telephone, bath, WC, TV and minibar. **Price** Single 245-496,000L, double 400-800,000L, apartment 480-1,000,000L. **Meals** Breakfast 30,000L, served 7:30-10:30; half board 205-440,000L, 255-490,000L (per pers.,3 days min.). **Restaurant** Service 13:00-15:00, 19:30-21:30; menus 45-80,000L, also à la carte. Specialties: Mediterranean cuisine, seafood. **Credit cards** All major. **Pets** Dogs not allowed. **Facilities** Swimming pool, tennis (35,000L), private beach, parking. **Nearby** Tombolo, Massa Maritima, Volterra, National Park of Maremma, Punta Ala golf course (18-hole). **Open** May – Sept.

Punta Ala is the chic beach resort of Grossetto, which is at the tip of the Gulf of Follonica across from the Island of Elba. The Cala del Porto is a comfortable modern hotel with a beautiful flower garden. The rooms are elegantly furnished and have balconies with views of the historical island. Pleasant Tuscan-inspired cuisine is served on the beautiful terrace.

How to get there *(Map 12): 41 km west of Grosseto via S327, along the coast to Punta Ala.*

Piccolo Hotel Alleluja

Via del Porto
58040 Punta Ala (Grosseto)
Tel. (0)564-92 20 50 - Fax (0)564-92 07 34
E-mail: alleluja.puntaala@bcedit.it

Category ★★★★ **Rooms** 38 with air-conditioning, telephone, bath, WC, safe and minibar, elevator. **Price** Single 260-600,000L, double 340-8400,000L. **Meals** Breakfast 30,000L, served 7:30-10:30; half board 220-470,000L, 270-520,000L (per pers.,3 days min., oblig. in July – Aug.). **Restaurant** Service 13:00-14:30, 19:30-21:30; menus 75-85,000L, also à la carte. Specialties: Regional and international cuisine, seafood. **Credit cards** All major. **Pets** Dogs not allowed. **Facilities** Swimming pool, beach, tennis, parking. **Nearby** Tombolo, Massa Maritima, Volterra, National Park of Maremma, Punta Ala golf course (18-hole). **Open** All year.

The pink roughcast walls, tile roofs and exposed beams of this recently built hotel reflect the architect's respect for the region. An airy space opens onto the impeccably maintained lawns. The hotel is decorated with simple unpretentious furniture. The rooms open onto either an Italian-style terrace or a small garden on the lake. The numerous advantages of this hotel include a private beach, tennis courts and a nearby golf course.

How to get there *(Map 12): 41 km west of Grosseto via S327, along the coast to Punta Ala.*

Hotel Terme di Saturnia

58050 Saturnia (Grosseto)
Provinciale della Follonata
Tel. (0)564-60 10 61 - Fax (0)564-60 12 66
Sig. San Giovanni

Category ★★★★ **Rooms** 80 and 10 suites with air-conditioning, telephone, bath or shower, WC, satellite TV, safe, minibar and elevator. **Price** Double 540-640,000L, suite 890,000L. **Meals** Breakfast included, served 7:30-10:00. **Restaurant** Service 12:45-14:00, 20:00-21:15; closed Mon.; menus 75,000L, also à la carte. Specialties: Regional cuisine. **Credit cards** All major. **Pets** Dogs not allowed. **Facilities** Swimming pool, tennis, thermal baths, parking. **Nearby** Tombolo, Massa Maritima, Volterra, National Park of Maremma, Punta Ala golf course (18-hole). **Open** All year.

The Hotel Terme di Saturnia is located in the historical Saturnia woods, where legend has it that you can still hear the Etruscans, whose brilliant and mysterious civilization and language we know so little about. Tuscanny is named after the "Tusci", as the Etruscans were called, its first known inhabitants. Saturnia is also famous for its Renaissance heritage, and is surrounded by interesting vestiges such as Pitigliano, Sovana, and Sorano. The hotel is profoundly attached to this historical context, as well as the spring water which has flowed here from deep in the ground for thousands of years, beneficial for both body and mind. This is why the entire hotel is laid out around an immense pool, the centerpiece of a modern health and beauty complex. If you prefer, you can enjoy all of the comfort of the hotel, the garden, and the fine cuisine without doing a treatment. The staff, most of whom have worked there for more than 10 years, are very friendly and attentive.

How to get there *(Map 13): 57 km southeast of Grosseto via A1 (towards Roma) Manciano exit, then Montemerano, towards Saturnia.*

1998

Hotel Villa Clodia

Via Italia, 43
58050 Saturnia (Grosetto)
Tel. (0)564-60 12 12 - Fax (0)564-60 12 12 - Sig. Giancarlo Ghezzi

Category ★★★ **Rooms** 8 and 2 suites with telephone, shower, WC, satellite TV. **Price** Single 90,000L, double 140,000L, suite 180 000L. **Meals** Breakfast included, served 8:00-10:30. **Restaurant** See p. 480. **Credit cards** Visa, Eurocard, MasterCard. **Pets** Dogs not allowed. **Facilites** Swimming pool. **Nearby** Tombolo, Massa Marittima,Voltera, National Park of Maremma, Punta Ala golf course (18-hole). **Open** All year (except Dec.).

Saturnia is a spa town where many people come to take the cure. It can also be a stop on the way to Rome and the south or a base for those who want to visit the Etruscan sites of Tuscany and Latium. The Villa Clodia is a jewel of a small hotel, lovingly looked after by its owners. The house is built right up against the mountain and after extensive remodeling of the interior, the rooms are laid out on different levels all the way down to the garden. The decor is simple and in the finest taste. The color scheme is blue and white, in harmony with the thermal waters and the well-being they have produced for centuries. All the rooms but one have a panoramic view of the valley. Both suites are really spacious and have a terrace as well. In the little garden lawn that seems to be suspended in its natural setting, the blue waters of the star-shaped swimming pool add a final decorative touch to this adorable house.

How to get there *(Map 13): 57 km southeast of Grosseto via A 1 (via Roma) Manciano exit, then Montemerano, towards Saturnia.*

Saturnia Country Club

58050 Pomonte Scansano (Grosseto)
Tel. (0)564-59 91 88 - Fax (0)564-59 92 14
Sig. Grifoni

Rooms 18 with telephone, bath, WC, TV, minibar. **Price** Single 130,000L, double 190,000L. **Meals** Breakfast 14,000L, served 8:00-10:00. **Restaurant** Service 13:00-14:30, 20:00-21:30, menu 40,000L. Specialties: Regional cooking; game in season. **Credit cards** All major. **Pets** Dogs allowed. **Facilities** Swimming pool, fishing, hunting, riding (25,000L), thermal baths, parking. **Nearby** Tombolo, Massa Maritima, Volterra, National Park of Maremma, Punta Ala golf course (18-hole). **Open** All year.

The Terme di Saturnia hotel group also has another place to stay: the *Azienda,* a beautiful working farm, several miles away. In addition to the usual accommodations, the Fattoria offers packages with daily excursions including horseback riding, hunting (wild boar, deer) and fishing (trout, eel and other fresh water fish), to help you get to know this ancient land. You can also go to the thermal baths. Whatever you choose, ask for the "Itinerari et Passagiate Ecologiche" brochure at the hotel, which lists a wealth of information on the artistic and ecological heritage of the region.

How to get there *(Map 13): 40 km southeast of Grosseto via A1 (towards Roma) Manciano exit, Montemerano, towards Scansano.*

Park Hotel Napoleone

Isola d'Elba
57037 San Martino di Portoferraio (Livorno)
Tel. (0)565-91 85 02 / (0)565-91 11 11 - Fax (0)565-91 78 36
Sig. de Ferrari

Category ★★★★ **Rooms** 64 with air-conditioning, telephone, bath, WC, TV and minibar. **Price** Single 120-205,000L, double 170-410,000L. **Meals** Breakfast included, served 8:00-10:00; half board 155-252,000L (per pers., 3 days min.). **Restaurant** Open Apr. – Oct.; service 12:30-14:00, 20:00-21:30; menu 60,000L. Specialties: Italian and international cuisine. **Credit cards** All major. **Pets** Small dogs allowed (except in restaurant and on the beach (40,000L). **Facilities** Swimming pool, private beach (30,000L), 2 tennis (27,000L), riding, miniature golf (7,000L), parking. **Nearby** Portoferraio (Napoleon House), Villa Napoleone in San Martino, Madonna del Monte in Marciana, dell'Acquabona golf course (9-hole). **Open** Apr. 3 – Sep. 27.

The Park Hotel Napoleone is close to the Emperor's villa, which you can see from certain windows. The hotel itself has historical significance: it was built at the end of the last century by a famous aristocratic Roman family. It is surrounded by a lush garden dotted with white canvas chairs. The rooms are tastefully furnished. The hotel has a beautiful swimming pool, several horses and a private beach a few miles away. Being near the Imperial Villa has several drawbacks, however. The path is lined with small souvenir shops, but they disappear at nightfall.

How to get there *(Map 12): Ferry services from Livorno (2 hrs. 50 min.) or Piombino (1 hr.); the hotel is 6 km southwest of Portoferraio.*

1998

Hotel Hermitage

Piazza del Pesce - Vicolo Marzio, 1 (Ponte Vecchio)
50122 Firenze
Tel. (0)55 28 72 16 - Fax (0)55 21 22 08 - Sig. Scarcelli
E-mail: hermitage@italyhotel.com - Web: htt://www.italyhotel.com/firenze/hermitage

Category ★★★ **Rooms** 130 with air-conditioning, telephone, bath, WC, TV, minibar, safe. **Price** Simple and double 100-600,000L. **Meals** Breakfast 25,000L, served 7:30-10:00, half board 159-364,000L, full board +29,000L (per pers., 3 days min.). **Restaurant** Service 12:30-14:00, 19:30-21:00; menus 60-70,000L. Specialties: Italian and regional cooking.. **Credit cards** All major. **Pets** Dogs allowed.(+35-45,000L). **Facilities** Swimming pool, tennis (25,000L), private beach, parking. **Nearby** Portoferraio (Napoleon House), Villa Napoleone in San Martino, Madonna del Monte in Marciana, dell'Acquabona golf course (9 holes). **Open** May - end Sep.

The lovely isle of Elba often seems to have much in common with its neighbor Corsica, which is visible in clear weather. Both are linked to the name of Napoleon who, after his abdication in 1814, became its governor until 1815 and left numerous traces of his passage. Sheltered in a charming bay, the Hermitage is hidden, like all the houses here, in a forest of pines. Discreet and luxurious, it is in the wealthiest part of the island. A beautiful private beach, three sea water swimming pools, tennis and miniature golf - a host of advantages to win favor with the guests. The bedrooms are simply decorated but all have a balcony with view of the sea. A large staff and attentive service. Need it be mentioned, however, that in August the whole town of Biodola is taken by storm.

How to get there *(Map 12): Ferry services from Livorno (2 hrs. 50 min) ourPiombino (1 hr.); the hotel is 7 km east of Portoferraio.*

Hotel da Giacomino

Isola d'Elba
Capo Sant'Andrea 57030 Marciana (Livorno)
Tel. (0)565 90 80 10 - Fax (0)565 90 82 94
Sig. Giacomino Costa

Category ★★★ **Rooms** 33 with telephone, shower, WC. **Price** Single 35-75,000L, double 60-125,000L. **Meals** Breakfast 20,000L, served 8:00-9:30, half board 65-135,000L and full board 78-150,000L (per pers.). **Restaurant** Service 13:00-14:00, 20:00-21:00; menus 45,000L. Specialties: Familial and regional cuisine. **Credit cards** All major. **Pets** Dogs allowed. **Facilities** Swimming pool, beach, parking at hotel. **Nearby** Portoferraio (Napoleon House), Villa Napoleone in San Martino, Madonna del Monte in Marciana, dell'Acquabona golf course (9 holes). **Open** Apr. - Oct.

On a little promontory that separates it from the very touristy Bay of Sant'Andrea, the Hotel da Giacomino is perfectly suited to anyone who wants a quiet spot by the sea. Its shaded gardens go right down to the water. There is no beach but a jagged rocky shoreline with lots of private little nooks for swimming. However, you may prefer the swimming pool with a panoramic view of the little bay. The nice family-style service, run by the owner, Signor Giacomino, will help you forget (as much as possible) the rather unfortunate decor. The comfort of the bedrooms is adequate, but the decoration is minimal and the pastel colors a bit strident. Some of the bungalows have kitchen facilities, so you can isolate yourself even more from the seasonal hyperactivity. This is an unpretentious hotel offering unbeatable value for price in an island known to be very expensive.

How to get there *(Map 12): Ferry services from Livorno (2 hrs. 50 min) or Piombino (1 hr.); the hotel is 33 km from Portoferraio.*

Hotel Castel Labers

Via Labers, 25
39012 Merano (Bolzano)
Tel. (0)473-23 44 84 - Fax (0)473-234 146
Sig. G. Stapf-Neubert

Category ★★★ **Rooms** 32 with telephone, bath or shower and WC (TV and minibar on request). **Price** 100-150,000L (per pers.). **Meals** Breakfast included, served 7:30-10:00; half board 120-175,000L (per pers., 3 days min.). **Restaurant** Service 12:00-14:00, 19:30-21:00; menus 35-70,000L, also à la carte. Specialties: Italian and Tyrolese cuisine. **Credit cards** Amex, Visa, Eurocard, MasterCard. **Pets** Dogs allowed (15,000L). **Facilities** Heated swimming pool, tennis (15,000L), parking, garage. **Nearby** Castel Tirolo, Castel Scena, Castel Coira in Sluderno, Glorenza, Monte Maria abbey near Malles Venosta, golf in Lana, Petersberg golf course in Karersee. **Open** Apr. 5 – Nov. 4

On a perfectly quiet site surrounded by vineyards, is Castel Labers, a pretty Dolomite castle. An intimate atmosphere and an unusually warm welcome await the traveler here. Antique furniture and paintings decorate the salons and the foyer. You can get to the rooms either by a charming stairway or a pretty elevator. The rooms are comfortable and have old fashioned charm–and they open onto a dazzling panorama. The service is attentive and efficient. The owners are true art and music lovers and they sometimes organize concerts for hotel guests.

How to get there *(Map 3): 28 km northwest of Bolzano via A22, Bolzano-South exit; then S38 to Merano. Sinigo, towards Scena, then via Labers (5 km).*

Hotel Oberwirt

Casa di Salute Raphael
39020 Merano - Marling (Bolzano)
Tel. (0)473-47 111 - Fax (0)473-47 130 - Sig. Joseph Waldner
E-mail: oberwit@dnet.it

Category ★★★★ **Rooms** 40 with telephone, bath or shower, WC, TV and minibar. **Price** With half board 145-162,000L (in single and in double), 177-207,000L (in suite, per pers., 3 days min.). **Meals** Breakfast 15,000L, served 7:00-10:00. **Restaurant** Menus 50-72,000L, also à la carte. **Credit cards** All major. **Pets** Dogs allowed (14,000L). **Facilities** Indoor and outdoour swimming pool, sauna, tennis, riding, golf course (9-hole), parking. **Nearby** Castel Tirolo, Castel Scena, Castel Coira in Sluderno, Glorenza, Monte Maria abbey near Malles Venosta, Petersberg golf course in Karersee. **Open** Mar. 15 – Nov. 11.

The Hotel Oberwirt is in Marling, a village on the outskirts of Merano, near the racetrack in the hills of the town. It has been run by the same family for two centuries, so there is no lack of professionalism. The hotel only has about forty rooms, all comfortably furnished in traditional and more modern styles. Our favorite is the one in the tower. The traditional *Stube* and the salons have the warmth of Tyrolean style. The Franz Liszt salon was the workplace of the famous musician during the summer of 1874. The hotel has two covered, heated swimming pools and a farm where you can go horseback riding; you can also do a week-long tennis clinic on the grounds (around $675 for half board per person per week). The region offers wonderful possibilities for hikes in the woods.

How to get there *(Map 3): 28 km northwest of Bolzano via A22, Bolzano-South exit; then Superstrada to Merano. Marlengo is 4 km south of Merano, next to the hippodrome.*

Hotel Schloss Korb

Missiano
39050 San Paolo Appiano (Bolzano)
Tel. (0)471-63 60 00 - Fax (0)471-63 60 33
Famiglia Dellago

Category ★★★★ **Rooms** 56 with telephone, bath, WC and TV; elevator. **Price** Double 200-280,000L. **Meals** Breakfast included, served 7:30-10:00; half board 140-230,000L, full board 170-260,000L (per pers.). **Restaurant** Service 12:00-14:00, 19:00-21:30; menu 60,000L, also à la carte. Specialties: Regional and Italian cuisine. **Credit cards** Not accepted. **Pets** Dogs allowed. **Facilities** 2 Swimming pool, parking and garage (15,000L). **Nearby** Wine road (N 42) from Appiano to the Caldaro Lake, Bolzano. **Open** Apr. 4 – Nov. 2.

On top of a hill, the Schloss Korb is an old castle which has a superb view and is surrounded by vineyards, which make it absolutely quiet. It is decorated in a Baroque style reminiscent of the Tyrol. Colors, hand crafted objects, a profusion of gilded wood and bouquets of flowers give the place a look of comfortable luxury. You can go for a pleasant walk to the ruins of a neighboring castle where a picnic is served with wine from the property, in a small shelter set up for hotel guests.

How to get there *(Map 4): 13 km west via S42 to San Paolo, then towards Missiano.*

Schloss Freudenstein 

Via Masaccio, 6
39057 Appiano (Bolzano)
Tel. (0)471-66 06 38 - Fax (0)471-66 01 22

Rooms 15 with telephone, bath and WC. **Price** With half board 160-180,000L (per pers.). **Meals** Breakfast included. **Restaurant** For residents only. Service 19:30-22:00; menus. Specialties: Regional cuisine. **Credit cards** Not accepted. **Pets** Dogs not allowed. **Facilities** Swimming pool, parking. **Nearby** Wine road (N 42) from Appiano to the Caldaro Lake, Bolzano, Santa Giustina Lake, Santuario de San Romedio and lake of Tavon. **Open** Apr. 1 – Nov. 10.

The back country of Bolzano is a very beautiful region of vineyard-covered hills along Caldaro Lake. The castle overlooks this beautiful southern Tyrolean landscape. The arches, columns and loggias of the castle create elegant spaces around the small cobblestone courtyard. Inside, the simplicity of the decor preserves the original spirit of the castle. The rooms and bathrooms are very comfortable. There is a swimming pool in the garden. You will find traditional breakfasts, dinners and regional wines at incomparable prices here.

How to get there *(Map 4): 10 km southwest of Bolzano.*

Pensione Leuchtenburg

Klughammer, 100
39052 Caldaro sulla Strada del Vino (Bolzano)
Tel. and Fax (0)471-96 00 93
Sig. Sparer

Category ★★ **Rooms** 17 and 1 suite with shower and WC. **Price** Double 110,000L, suite 220,000L. **Meals** Breakfast included; half board 18,000L (per pers.). **Restaurant** For residents. **Credit cards** Visa, Eurocard, MasterCard. **Pets** Dogs allowed. **Facilities** Private beach, windsurfing, mountain biking, parking. **Nearby** Wine road (N 42) from Appiano to the Caldaro Lake, Appiano, Merano, Petersberg golf course. **Open** Mar. – Nov. (closed Wed.).

The *pensione* is in the outbuildings of the Leuchtenberg castle. It is a very pleasant house with pretty arbor-covered courtyards and a large terrace, filled with flowers, on the lake. The interior is simple but charming. The tavern is typical of the region and the rooms are decorated with pretty painted wood furniture. A private beach, sailboards and mountain bikes are at the disposal of hotel guests at no charge. This is a good place for a nice vacation at a low price.

How to get there*: (Map 4) 25 km south of Merano, via A22, Ora-Lago Caldaro exit (Kaltern); on the left bank of the lake.*

Berghotel Zirmerhof

39040 Redagno (Bolzano)
Oberradein, 59
Tel. (0)471-88 72 15 - Fax (0)471-88 72 25 - Sig. Perwanger
E-mail: zh.sepp@dnet.it

Rooms 32 with bath or shower and WC. **Price** With half board 101-145,000L, 140-180,000L (suite), full board 20,000L (per pers., 3 days min.). **Meals** Breakfast 27,000L, served 8:00-10:00. **Restaurant** Service 12:00 and 19:30 (for residents only); closed Mon., menus 40-60,000L. Specialties: Sella di vitello, carne, verdure e vini del proprio maso. **Credit cards** Not accepted. **Pets** Dogs allowed. **Facilities** Parking. **Nearby** Wine road (N 42) from Appiano to the Caldaro Lake, Appiano, Merano, Petersberg golf course. **Open** Dec 26 – Mar. 29 and Mai 21 – Nov. 4.

Away from the hordes of tourists, the Redagno region and the Monte Corno Reserve have not lost any of their traditional, natural beauty. This inn, which opened in 1890, was a popular vacation spot for the aristocracy and upper classes of Vienna and Berlin and a place where intellectuals came for inspiration. The rooms are cosy and comfortable, the *stube* and the family library still have that "Magic Mountain" atmosphere, and the great "Sala Grimm" the work of Ignaz Sthol, has kept its beautiful frescos. The fine cuisine of the house restaurant is still influenced by the recipes of the *nonna* Hanna Perwanger, of German origin, who loved the Upper Adige very much. Friendly service is a priority here, as is the happiness of the guests.

How to get there *(Map 4): 40 km south of Bolzano via A22, Egna Ora exit towards Cavalese to Kaltenbruno; after on your left towerds Redagno.*

Park Hotel Laurin

Via Laurin, 4
39100 Bolzano
Tel. (0)471-31 10 00 - Fax (0)471-31 11 48 - Sig. Havlik
E-mail: info@laurin.it - Web: http://www.laurin.it

Category ★★★★ **Rooms** 96 with air-conditioning, telephone, bath or shower, WC, cable TV, minibar, fax and PC outlets. **Price** Single 190-275,000L, double 285-495,000L. **Meals** Breakfast included, served 7:30-10:30. **Restaurant** Service 12:00-14:00, 19:00-22:00; menus 38-56,000L, also à la carte. Specialties: Regional and Italian cuisine. **Credit cards** Amex, Visa, Eurocard, MasterCard. **Pets** Dogs allowed (20,000L). **Facilities** Heated swimming pool, parking. **Nearby** Wine road (N 42) from Appiano to Caldaro Lake, Bolzano, Castel Roncolo and Sarentina valley to Vitipeno. **Open** All year.

This old palace in the center of Bolzano, six hundred and fifty feet (200 meters) from the train station, remains an important address for a clientele of businessmen and upper-class families. The dining room, salons and guest rooms are large and "international palace" style. The hotel has every modern convenience and a very attentive personnel. *La Belle Epoque* is one of the best known restaurants in the region. The rooms look out onto the grounds and are all decorated with contemporary paintings from the hotel's own collection. The swimming pool, hidden in a box of greenery and coolness, is very pleasant. This establishment confirms the advantages of tradition.

How to get there *(Map 4): 140 km north of Verona via A22, Bolzano-South or North exit toward the stazione (railway station).*

1998

Albergo Monte San Vigilio

Monte San Vigilio
39011 Lana (Bolzano)
Tel. (0)473-561 236 - Fax (0)473-561 410 - Sig. Gapp

Category ★★★ **Rooms** 40 with telephone, bath or shower, WC. **Price** With half board 80-120,000L (per pers., 3 days min.). **Meals** Breakfast included, served 8:00-10:00. **Restaurant** Service 12:00-14:00, 19:00-20:30; menus 30-40,000L. **Credit cards** Not accepted. **Pets** Dogs not allowed. **Facilities** Heated swimming pool, riding, Boccia, garage (7,000L). **Nearby** Skiing, Castel Tirolo, Castel Scena, Castel Coira in Sluderno, Glorenza, Monte Maria abbey near Malles Venosta, Petersberg golf course in Karersee. **Open** Dec. 20 - Nov. 8.

This chalet is the perfect place for mountain lovers. The obligatory access by cable car will satisfy even the most demanding aficionados of rest and fresh air. Decorated with naive paintings, this chalet is undoubtedly one of the most charming places in this guide. There is a nice family atmosphere, warmly fostered by the manager, who willingly acts as a guide for guests who want to explore one of the many hiking trails in the area. The lifts work during the summer too, so you can get to beautiful natural sites and shelters where it is pleasant to stop and rest for awhile. The rooms all have a superb panoramic view. The cuisine is simple and good. This place is ideal for a family vacation.

How to get there *(Map 3): 30 km northwest of Bolzano via S38, towards Merano to Portal, then Lana; in Lana take the funicular (summer 8:00-19:00, winter 8:00-18:00).*

Hotel Turm

39050 Fié Allo Sciliar (Bolzano)
Tel. (0)471-72 50 14 - Fax (0)471-72 54 74
Sig. Pramstrahler

Category ★★★★ **Rooms** 23 with telephone, bath, WC and TV. **Price** Single 90-137,000L, double 180-294,000L, suite 220-314,000L. **Meals** Breakfast included, served 8:00-10:00; half board 113-170,000L, full board 138-198,000L (per pers.). **Restaurant** Service 12:00-14:00, 19:00-21:00; closed Thu.; menus 38-60,000L, also à la carte. Specialties: Soupe d'orties, Chevreuil, Parfait à la rose. **Credit cards** Amex, Visa, Eurocard and MasterCard. **Pets** Dogs allowed (10,000L). **Facilities** Swimming pool, sauna, garage (7,000L). **Nearby** Alpe di Siusi (16 km), Bolzano. **Open** Dec. 20 – Nov. 5.

This hotel is in Fié, a small village in Val Gardena, a superb region just below the spectacular and impressive Mount Sciliar. It is in the old town hall, right in the middle of Fié and has been run by the same family for three generations. Very comfortable and nicely decorated interior, it has antique furniture and a large collection of paintings. Most of the rooms are cozy and tastefully furnished and have a superb view of the mountains. Stefano, the owner's son and manager of the restaurant, is also an excellent cook: his fine inventive cuisine skillfully blends the particularities of regional cuisine with the sophistication of recipes of the great French chefs. In the summer, this is a marvelous place for hiking around the lake and in the winter, you can go cross-country skiing, skating and downhill skiing at Alpe di Suisi, only twenty minutes away.

How to get there *(Map 4): 16 km east of Bolzano (via A22 Bolzano-North exit) via S49 to Prato all'Isarco, then Fié.*

Hotel Cavallino d'Oro

Piazza Kraus
39040 Castelrotto (Bolzano)
Tel. (0)471-706 337 - Fax (0)471-707 172
Sig. and Sig.ra Urthaler

Category ★★★★ **Rooms** 20 with telephone, bath or shower, WC, TV and safe. **Price** Single 55-80,000L, double 80-120,000L. **Meals** Breakfast included, served 7:30-11:00; half board 70-110,000L, full board 90-135,000L. **Restaurant** Service 11:30-14:00, 18:00-21:00; closed Sun. dinner; menus 25-50,000L, also à la carte. Specialties: Italian and regional cuisine. **Credit cards** All major **Pets** Dogs allowed (fee). **Nearby** Skiing, Alpe de Siusi, Val Gardena, Ortisei. **Open** All year (closed Tues.).

The Cavallino d'Oro is a traditional inn typical of Southern Tyrol. It is in Castelrotto, a village in the Val Gardena where Ladin is still spoken and where the inhabitants still dress in traditional costume and live in houses with painted facades. The *stube* (locale) is friendly and the restaurant features local specialties. The rooms are very well kept. In the summer, a small terrace is set up on the square, the prettiest spot in the village. This still relatively unvisited region is worth exploring, especially at these prices.

How to get there *(Map 4): 26 km northeast of Bolzano via S12 to Ponte Gardena, then towards Castelrotto.*

Hotel Adler

Via Rezia, 7
39046 Ortisei (Bolzano)
Tel. (0)471-79 62 03 - Fax (0)471-79 62 10
Famiglia Sanoner

Category ★★★★ **Rooms** 100 with telephone, bath, WC, TV, minibar, safe; elevator. **Price** With half board and full board 258-266,000L (single), 139-247,000L (per pers. Double room). **Meals** Breakfast included, served 7:00-10:00; 21,000L, 42,000L (per pers.). **Restaurant** Service 12:00-14:00, 19:00-21:30; menus 30-49,000L, also à la carte. Specialties: Tyrolese cuisine. **Credit cards** Amex, Visa, Eurocard, MasterCard **Pets** Dogs allowed. **Facilities** Heated indoor swimming pool, tennis (16,000L), sauna, health center, garage, parking. **Nearby** Alpe di Siusi (1996 m) and Seceda (2500 m) by cabble car, Castelrotto, Val Gardena, Bolzano. **Open** May 15 – Oct. 20, Dec. 15 – Apr. 15.

In the center of Ortisei, this hotel, born from the fusion of two buildings with very different architectural styles, is an island of greenery and quiet. It is also the meeting place for German tourists staying in the region. In summer and winter it is frequented by a clientele of regulars for whom solitude and proximity to the slopes are not priorities; they enjoy the animated ambience of the little village of Ortisei. All of the rooms have been redone.

How to get there *(Map 4): 35 km east of Bolzano via A22; Chiusa exit (or S12 to Ponte Gardena), then S242 to Ortisei.*

Uhrerhof Deur

Bulla 39046 Ortisei
Tel. (0)471-79 73 35 - Fax (0)471-79 74 57 -
Famiglia Zemmer

Rooms 10 suites (no smoking) with telephone, bath or shower, WC, TV. **Price** Double 200-300,000L. **Meals** Breakfast included, served 8:00-10:00; half board 120-150,000L (per pers., 3 day min.). **Restaurant** (by reservation). Service 19:00; menus 40-60,000L. **Credit cards** Visa, Eurocard, MasterCard. **Pets** Dogs not allowed. **Facilities** Sauna, steam bath, solarium (20,000L), whirlpool, parking. **Nearby** Alpe di Siusi (1 996 m) and Seceda (2 500 m) by cable car, Castelrotto, Val Gardena, Bolzano. **Open** All year.

Ortisei is a large resort in Val Gardena where all those who love the mountains can enjoy skiing or hiking in the forests of Rasciesca or on the slopes of Alpe di Siusi. Its charm lies also in its people's attachment to local tradition, which lends a picturesque quality to village life. The Uhrerhof Deur is faithful to this spirit. Located just a few kilometers from the village, it has the feel of a guest house and you are welcomed like a friend. The atmosphere is warm, the site grandiose and the cooking excellent, but we would emphasize (in case you missed it above) that the house is completely non-smoking - a good way for smokers to test the degree of their dependence.

How to get there *(Map 4): 35 km east of Bolzano via A 22, Chiusa or Bolzano-north exit (or S 12 to Ponte Gardena), then S 242 to Ortisei. Bulla is 5 km from Ortisei.*

Hotel Elephant

39042 Bressanone (Bolzano)
Via Rio Bianco, 4
Tel. (0)472-83 2750 - Fax (0)472-83 65 79 - Famiglia Heiss-Falk
E-mail: elephant.brixer@acs.it

Category ★★★★ **Rooms** 44 with telephone, bath, WC and TV. **Price** Single 108-116,000L, double 216-232,000L. **Meals** Breakfast 24,000L; half board 194,000L, full board 230,000L (per pers., 3 days min.). **Restaurant** Service 12:00-14:15, 19:00-21:15; closed Mon.; menus 65,000L. Specialty: Piatto Elephante **Credit cards** All major. **Pets** Dogs allowed in room (11,000L). **Facilities** Heated swimming pool, tennis, parking (11-15,000L). **Nearby** Plose (2504 m), Convent of Novacella, Val Gardena (castle of Velturno, Chiusa, Ortisei). **Open** Mar. – Nov. 10, Dec. 25 – Jan. 7.

The many Episcopal monasteries and castles around Bressanone testify to the artistic, cultural and spiritual influence this town had on the region during the 18th-century. The Hotel Elephant is the ideal base for exploring the area. The paneled reception rooms are decorated with antique furniture, tapestries and rugs. The rooms are all very comfortable and most of them look out onto the swimming pool or the mountains (only certain rooms face north). The cuisine is remarkable and the personnel is excellent. The hotel has consistently lived up to its reputation since 1550 when a convoy with an elephant, given to the Emperor Ferdinand of Habsbourgby the King of Portugal, stayed here.

How to get there *(Map 4): 40 km northeast of Bolzano via A22; Bressanone exit. The hotel is northwest of town center: from via Roma, via Fichini, then via Rio Bianco.*

Hotel La Perla

Via Centro, 44
39033 Corvara in Badia (Bolzano)
Tel. (0)471-83 61 32/33 - Fax (0)471-83 65 68
Famiglia Costa

Category ★★★★ **Rooms** 52 with telephone, bath, WC and TV. **Prices** Single 170-320,000L, double 300-600,000L, suite 360-700,000L. **Meals** Breakfast included, served 7:30-11:00; half board 168-318,000L (per pers., 3 days min.). **Restaurant** "La Stüa de Michil" Service 12:00-14:00, 19:00-22:00; menus 58-85,000L. Specialties: Carpaccio di verdure crude con caprio fresco e basilico, guancio di vitello al forno co porri e finferli, strudel caldo di cioccolato con ciliegie al porto e gelato alla cannella. **Credit cards** Amex, Visa, Eurocard and MasterCard **Pets** Small dogs allowed. **Facilities** Heated swimming pool, massage, sauna, fitness, garage, parking. **Nearby** Skiing, Val Badia, great road of Dolomites (N 48), Ortisei. **Open** Dec. 4 – Apr. 12, Juny 20 – Oct. 5.

The Hotel La Perla is a real gem. A beautiful chalet in a quiet part of the center of Corvara, it is perfect in every way. It is more elegant than rustic, and it manages to maintain a certain intimacy despite the numerous services worthy of a grand hotel (sauna, hairdresser, wine cellar, heated pool). Just twenty seven miles (45 km) from Cortina d'Ampezzo, this place is great all year round.

How to get there *(Map 4): 65 km east of Bolzano via A22; Chiusa exit (or S12 to Ponte Gardena), then S242 to Corvara via Ortisei.*

Hotel Armentarola

Via Prè de Vi, 78
39030 San Cassiano (Bolzano)
Tel. (0)471-84 95 22 - Fax (0)471-84 93 89
Famiglia Wieser

Category ★★★★ **Rooms** 50 with telephone, bath or shower, WC, safe, TV and minibar. **Price** With half board single 140-225,000L, double 120-225,000L (per pers.), suite 180-260,000L (per pers.). **Meals** Breakfast included, served 7:30-11:00. **Restaurant** Service 11:00-18:00, 19:00-21:00; menus 45-70,000L. Specialty: Regional cuisine. **Credit cards** Not accepted **Pets** Dogs allowed (20,000L). **Facilities** Indoor swimming pool, tennis, riding, sauna, solarium, garage (10,000L). **Nearby** Skiing, Cortina d'Ampezzo, great road of Dolomites (N 48), Ortisei. **Open** Dec. 8 – Apr. 14, July 14 – Oct. 8.

The story of the Armentarola began with the Wieser family in 1938, when Paolo and Emma transformed the family chalet into an inn. It is isolated at an altitude of 5,200 feet (1,600 meters), in an enchanting landscape of pastures and woods with the Dolomites in the background, but the Armentarola has continually adapted to the changing standards of modern comfort, while keeping all of its original charm intact. There are plenty of well-organized leisure activites here all year round. In summer, you can play tennis and go horseback riding, and in winter, you can swim in the covered swimming pool or take the ski lift from the hotel, which is linked to the large ski *caroussel* of the upper Badia Valley. Enjoy the grandeur of nature at this hotel, only a few kilometers from Cortina d'Ampezzo.

How to get there *(Map 4): 75 km east of Bolzano via S12, S242d and S242 towards Selva di Valgardena; then S243 to Corvara and S244.*

Parkhotel Sole Paradiso

Via Sesto, 13
39038 San Candido - Innichen (Bolzano)
Tel. (0)474-913 120 - Fax (0)474-913 193
Famiglia Ortner

Category ★★★★ **Rooms** 39 and 4 suites with telephone, bath or shower, WC and TV. **Price** Single 130-175,000L, double 220-250,000L. **Meals** Breakfast included (buffet), served 8:00-10:30; half board 120-195,000L, full board 150-225,000L (per pers., 3 days min.). **Restaurant** Service 12:30-13:30, 19:00-20:30; menus 45-70,000L. Specialtie: Schlutzkrapfen, maccheroni alla boscaiola, trota del vivaio Kaiserschmarrn. **Credit cards** All major. **Pets** Dogs not allowed. **Facilities** Indoor swimming pool, tennis (15,000L), sauna, garage (15,000L). **Nearby** Lago di Braies, lago di Misurina, Croda Rossa, Tre cime di Lavaredo, Cortina d'Ampezzo. **Open** Dec. 22 – Apr. 10, June 14 – Oct. 6.

The architecture and the red and yellow colors of this large chalet will remind you, if you need to be reminded, that you are only a few miles from the Austrian border. The warm cozy atmosphere of a mountain home pervades the hotel. The walls are covered with blond wood and the ceiling and table lamps are made of very beautiful sculpted wood. The rooms have large canopy beds, heavy drapes and pretty flower-covered balconies with nice views of the Val Pusteria. The hotel is very wellequipped for leisure activities: There is a tennis court, a heated swimming pool open year round, cross-country ski trails and a ski shuttle bus which stops just in front of the hotel.

How to get there *(Map 4): 110 km northeast of Bolzano via A22, Bressanone exit; then S49 to San Candido. 200 m North of Venice.*

Albergo Accademia

Vicolo Colico, 4-6
38100 Trento
Tel. (0)461-23 36 00 - Fax (0)461-23 01 74
Sig.ra Fambri

Category ★★★★ **Rooms** 43 with air-conditioning, telephone, bath or shower, WC, satellite TV and minibar, elevator. **Price** Single 180,000L, double 250,000L. **Meals** Breakfast included, served 7:30-10:30; half board 18,000L, full board 32,000L (per pers., 3 days min.). **Restaurant** Service 12:30-14:30, 19:30-22:30; closed Sun.; menus 45-55,000L, also à la carte. Specialties: Storione affumicato con finferli crudi, ravioli fatti in casa, carrello dei bolliti, panna cotta al caffè. **Credit cards** All major. **Pets** Dogs allowed. **Nearby** Trento, Lake Garda, Brenta Dolomites, Lake Toblino, La Paganella, the "Ormeri" di Segonzaro. **Open** All year (except Dec. 24 - Jan. 06).

The Albergo Accademia is in an old house from the Middle Ages on a small square in this pretty neighborhood of this medieval town. The decor is resolutely modern, but highlights what remains of the original architecture and a few antique pieces. The rooms are large, light, quiet and very comfortable. The hotel restaurant is renowned for its innovative cuisine, including local specialties. The old inner courtyard is now a garden where breakfast is served and the terrace is a nice place from which to enjoy the view of the rooftops, the towers and the bell-towers of Trento. This is a charming address in a town that is really worth the trip.

How to get there *(Map 3 and 4): 101 km north of Verona via A22, Trento exit; the hotel is located in the town center.*

1998

Castello Pergine

38057 Pergine Valsugana (Trento)
Tel. (0)461-53 11 58 - Fax (0)461-53 13 29
Sig. and Sig.ra Schneider-Neff

Rooms 21 with telephone, bath or shower, WC, TV. **Price** With half board: single 100,000L, double 200,000L (2 pers.). **Meals** Breakfast included, served 8:00-9:30. **Restaurant** Service 12:30-14:00,19:30-21:30; closed Mon. lunchtime; carte 50,000L. Specialties: strangola con su salsa formaggiconiglio disossaso farciso con la verza, Carpaccio di carne salada. **Credit cards** Amex, Visa, Eurocard, MasterCard. **Pets** Dogs allowed in rooms. **Facilities** Parking. **Nearby** Caldonazzo Lake (San Cristoforo al Lago), Canal of the Brentaby (N47) after Primolano, Trento. **Open** Easter - Oct.

On the border between Latin and German civilization, Trento is an interesting town, its Duomo and Castello del Buonconsiglio well worth a visit. The mountainous back country is also pleasant, with small rural villages like Pergine Valsugana. The hotel is in a medieval castle. Known primarily for its good restaurant, serving regional specialties, the building has undergone alterations that have made the rooms more comfortable. The location and the green surroundings create an atmosphere of serenity. An appealing place.

How to get there *(Map 4): 11 km east of Trento via S 47; 2.5 km from the town.*

Lido Palace Hotel

Lago di Garda
Viale Carducci, 10
Riva del Garda (Trento)
Tel. (0)464-55 26 64 - Fax (0)464-55 19 57
Sig. Genetin

Category ★★★★ **Rooms** 62 with telephone, bath or shower, WC and TV, elevator. **Price** Double 220-290,000L. **Meals** Breakfast included, served 7:30-10:00; half board 135-175,000L, full board 165-200,500L (per pers., 3 days min.). **Restaurant** Service 12:30-14:00, 19:30-21:00; menu 40,000L. Specialties: International and Italian cuisine. **Credit cards** All major. **Pets** Small dogs allowed (15,000L). **Facilities** Swimming pool, tennis, parking. **Nearby** Cascade of Varone, Lake of Tenno, Trento. **Open** Apr. – Oct. 31.

The main attraction of the Lido is its proximity to the small port of Riva del Garda. The grounds are next to the public garden and the lakeside docks where you will find a quaint 19th-century spa atmosphere. The building is from the same period and has been very tastefully renovated. The rooms are bright and simple; from them you can see the lake through the foliage of cedar trees. A family atmosphere pervades the hotel despite its conventional, classic appearance.

How to get there *(Map 3): 50 km southwest of Trento; 87 km north of Verona via A22; Rovereto South exit, then S240.*

Palace Hotel

Casa di Salute Raphael
38050 Roncegno (Trento)
Tel. (0)461-76 40 12 - Fax (0)461-76 45 00
Sig.ra Noacco

Category ★★★★ **Rooms** 85 with telephone, bath or shower, WC and TV; elevator. **Price** Single 130,000L, double 220,000L. **Meals** Breakfast included, served 7:30-10:00; half board 145,000L, full board 160,000L (per pers., 3 days min.). **Restaurant** Service 12:30-14:00, 19:30-21:30; menus 40-50,000L, also à la carte. Specialties: Tronco de pontesel, cumel alla paesana. **Credit cards** Amex, Visa, Eurocard, MasterCard. **Pets** Dogs not allowed. **Facilities** Indoor swimming pool, tennis, squash, health center, parking. **Nearby** Ruins of the castles of Borgo Valsugana, Canal of the Brenta (N47) after Primolano, Trento. **Open** Apr. – Oct.

Built at the beginning of the century on twelve and a half acres, the Palace Hotel still has all of the elegance and the picturesque quality of that time. It has long been the summer meeting place for the Italian aristocracy. The salons and the dining room testify to its past. It has been completely renovated and has all the requisite amenities of a four-star hotel, including a squash court, a health center with an indoor pool and a sauna. This blend of old-fashioned elegance and modern efficiency is the main appeal of this hotel.

How to get there *(Map 4): 33 km east of Trento via S47.*

Hotel Cipriani - Palazzo Vendramin

Isola della Giudecca, 10
30133 Venezia
Tel. (0)41-520 77 44 - Fax (0)41-520 39 30/77 45 - Sig. Rusconi

Category ★★★★ **Rooms** 104 with air-conditioning, telephone, bath, WC, TV and minibar; elevator. **Price** Single 680-950,000L, double 950-1,400,000L. **Meals** Breakfast included, served 7:00-10:30. **Restaurant** Service 12:30-15:00, 20:00-22:30; à la carte. Specialties: Vitello Cipriani, scampi "Carlina." **Credit cards** All major. **Pets** Small dogs allowed. **Facilities** Swimming pool, tennis (40,000L), sauna (25,000L), turkish bath, private port. **Nearby** Events: Carnival of Venice, the Regata Storica (Sept.), the Mostra of Venice (Aug.-Sept.), Venice Biennale. Murano, Torcello (S. M. Assunta, S. Fosca), Villa Foscari in Fusina, Venetian villas (cruise along the Brenta Canal with the boat "Il Burchiello"), al Lido Alberoni golf course (18-hole). **Open** All year.

On the floating docks that border the Piazza San Marco, the Cipriani is the only hotel that has a spot for its own private craft — luxurious small boats of varnished wood, which assure the hotel's own shuttle service. Everything here is exceptional, for the name Cipriani has come to mean high quality and luxury. Giuseppe Cipriani also founded Harry's Bar, world famous for its cuisine as well as for its famous cocktail, the Bellini. Located at one end of the island of Giudecca, the hotel offers its guests many other luxuries: an Olympic swimming pool, a private yacht club, salons and bedrooms with great refinement and superb views of the lagoon with San Giorgio Maggiore and the Palladian domes of the Redentore and Zitelle. The service is personal but not obsequious. As for the Palazzo Vendramin, the luxurious annex of the Cipriani, what can we say except that we prefer the original?

How to get there *(Map 4): On Isola della Giudecca.*

Bauer Grünwald et Grand Hotel

Campo San Moise, 1459
30124 Venezia
Tel. (0)41-520 70 22 - Fax (0)41-520 75 57
Sig. D'Este

Category ★★★★★ **Rooms** 214 with air-conditioning, telephone, bath or shower, WC, TV and minibar. **Price** Single 250-440,000L, double 360-850,000L. **Meals** Breakfast included, served 7:00-10:30. **Restaurant** Service 12:30-14:30, 19:00-22:30; menu: 90,000L, also à la carte. Specialties: Risotto alla torcellana, fegato alla veneziana. **Credit cards** All major. **Pets** Dogs allowed (60,000L). **Nearby** Events: Carnival of Venice, the Regata Storica (Sept.), the Mostra of Venice (Aug.-Sept.), Venice Biennale. Murano, Torcello (S. M. Assunta, S. Fosca), Villa Foscari in Fusina, Venetian villas (cruise along the Brenta Canal with the boat "Il Burchiello"), al Lido Alberoni golf course (18-hole). **Open** All year.

The Bauer Grünwald was born out of Italian unity: a young Venetian man, Jules Grünwald, married Miss Bauer. First they opened a tavern, which was a great success, and then they built the Grand Hotel. The difference between the Bauer and other palaces in Venice is its "class": An atmosphere of quiet luxury reigns here. Only a few steps from Piazza San Marco, it also has the advantage of having a terrace on the Grand Canal, where you can dine by candlelight facing the Salute and the island of San Giorgio.

How to get there *(Map 4): Near Piazza San Marco, along the Grand Canal, between Chuch of Salute and San Giorgio island.*

Gritti Palace Hotel

30124 Venezia
Campo Santa Maria del Giglio, 2467
Tel. (0)41-79 46 11 - Fax (0)41-520 09 42
Sig. Feriani

Category ★★★★★ **Rooms** 87 and 6 suites with air-conditioning, telephone, bath or shower, WC, safe, TV and minibar, elevator. **Price** Single 500-570,000L, double 770-850-1,000,000L, suite 1,900,000L, apartment 2,400,000-3,800,000L. **Meals** Breakfast 35-60,000L, served 7:00-11:00 or at any time in room. **Restaurant** Service 12:30-15:00, 19:30-22:30; menu: 100-140,000L, also à la carte. Specialties: Bresaola Gritti Palace, i risotti del Gritti, scampi fritti in erbaria. **Credit cards** All major. **Pets** Small dogs allowed (except in restaurant). **Nearby** Events: Carnival of Venice, the Regata Storica (Sept.), the Mostra of Venice (Aug.-Sept.), Venice Biennale. Murano, Torcello (S. M. Assunta, S. Fosca), Villa Foscari in Fusina, Venetian villas (cruise along the Brenta Canal with the boat "Il Burchiello"), al Lido Alberoni golf course (18-hole). **Open** All year.

Ernest Hemingway wrote of this 15th-century palace built by Andrea Gritti, "The best hotel in Venice, which is a town made of grand hotels." Its splendid and famous terrace on the Grand Canal is a magic place. Everything here, from the rooms and suites to the salons and dining rooms, emanates luxury and refinement. The restaurant is also one of the best in Venice. If you are planning to stay at the Gritti, try to get a room on the Grand Canal so you can enjoy the show for longer.

How to get there *(Map 4): Near San Marco, on the Grand Canal.*

Hotel Monaco e Grand Canal

San Marco - Calle Vallaresso, 1325
30124 Venezia
Tel. (0)41-520 02 11 - Fax (0)41-520 05 01 - Sig. Zambon
E-mail: hmonaco@tin.it

Category ★★★★ **Rooms** 72 with air-conditioning, telephone, bath or shower, WC, TV and minibar elevator. **Price** Single 370-450,000L, double 590-680,000L, suite 790-990,000L. **Meals** Breakfast included, served 7:00-11:00 in room, 8:00-10:30 in restaurant. **Restaurant** Service 12:30-15:00, 19:30-22:00; à la carte. Specialties: "Cape sante" gratinate, ravioli di magro al burro e salvia, scampi Ca' d'Oro e riso pilaf, fegato alla veneziana con polenta, zabaglione con amaretti. **Credit cards** All major. **Pets** Small dogs allowed. **Nearby** Events: Carnival of Venice, the Regata Storica (Sept.), the Mostra of Venice (Aug.-Sept.), Venice Biennale. Murano, Torcello (S. M. Assunta, S. Fosca), Villa Foscari in Fusina, Venetian villas (cruise along the Brenta Canal with the boat "Il Burchiello"), al Lido Alberoni golf course (18-hole). **Open** All year.

The elegant atmosphere, plush salons, flowering patio and small but very well-decorated rooms make this one of the great hotels of Venice. It also has a superb terrace on the Grand Canal, where you can have lunch and dinner. The restaurant is excellent, but very expensive. In the summer, it is nicer to have a room on the interior patio. If you really want to have a view of the Grand Canal, try to get room farthest from the *vaporetto* station at the foot of the hotel. Our favorite is Room 308. Prices are reasonable, especially off-season.

How to get there *(Map 4): Near Piazza San Marco.*

Hotel Londra Palace

San Marco - Riva degli Schiavoni, 4171
30124 Venezia
Tel. (0)41-520 05 33 - Fax (0)41-522 50 32
Sig. Samueli

Category ★★★★ **Rooms** 53 with air-conditioning, telephone, bath, WC, safe, satellite TV, whirl pool, hairdryer and minibar. **Price** Double 375-680,000L, suite 520-950,000L. **Meals** Breakfast included, served 7:00-11:00. **Restaurant** Service 11:30-16:00, 19:00-24:00; menus: 70-93,000L, also à la carte. Specialties: Italian and Venitian cuisine. **Credit cards** All major. **Pets** Dogs allowed. **Nearby** Events: Carnival of Venice, the Regata Storica (Sept.), the Mostra of Venice (Aug.-Sept.), Venice Biennale. Murano, Torcello (S. M. Assunta, S. Fosca), Villa Foscari in Fusina, Venetian villas (cruise along the Brenta Canal with the boat "Il Burchiello"), al Lido Alberoni golf course (18-hole). . **Open** All year.

Standing at the edge of the San Marco basin near several other de luxe establishments, this neo-gothic palace built in the second half of the 19th century once played host to D'Annunzio and Tchaikovsky. The latest renovation gave it back its charm and also its rightful place among the great hotels of Venice. All the rooms have been furnished with Bidermeier furniture and Venetian-style objects, and of course, the amenities are commensurate with the class of the hotel. We would strongly recommend the rooms over the lagoon, facing the island of San Giorgio Maggiore and the good restaurant Da Leoni (a reference to Molière and Goldoni). Considering all its advantages, the prices are still reasonable.

How to get there *(Map 4): Near Piazza San Marco.*

Hotel Gabrielli Sandwirth

San Marco - Riva degli Schiavoni, 4110
30122 Venezia
Tel. (0)41-523 15 80 - Fax (0)41-520 94 55 - Sig. Perkhofer

Category ★★★★ **Rooms** 110 with telephone, bath or shower, WC and TV. **Price** Single 370,000L, double 590,000L. **Meals** Breakfast included, served 7:00-12:00; half board 620,000L, full board 680,000L. **Restaurant** "Trattoria al Buffet" Service 12:00-14:30, 19:00-21:30. Specialties: Buffet of Italian and Venetian cuisine; 44,000L. **Credit cards** All major. **Pets** Dogs allowed. **Nearby** Events: Carnival of Venice, the Regata Storica (Sept.), the Mostra of Venice (Aug.-Sept.), Venice Biennale. Murano, Torcello (S. M. Assunta, S. Fosca), Villa Foscari in Fusina, Venetian villas (cruise along the Brenta Canal with the boat "Il Burchiello"), al Lido Alberoni golf course (18-hole). **Open** Feb. – Nov.

This old 13th-century Veneto-Gothic palace is on the Riva degli Schiavoni, among some of the most luxurious hotels in Venice. It has been expanded to incorporate two other medieval houses and the interior is now a real maze. The rooms are decorated in a classical style and are very comfortable. The ideal is to get one with a loggia on the San Marco Basin, facing the San Giorgio Church. There is no trace of the old palace left in the modern decor of the bar, but this hotel is the only one on the Riva degli Schiavoni with an inner courtyard and a palm tree-shaded rose garden where you can dine by candlelight and Venetian lanterns. There is also a terrace on the roof with a view of the Grand Canal and the lagoon.

How to get there *(Map 4): Near Piazza San Marco.*

Hotel Metropole

San Marco - Riva degli Schiavoni, 4149
30122 Venezia
Tel. (0)41-520 50 44 - Fax (0)41-522 36 79 - Sig. Beggiato
E-mail: hotel.metropole@venere.it - Web: http://www.venere.it/venezia/metropole

Category ★★★★ **Rooms** 73 with air-conditioning, telephone, bath or shower, WC, safe, TV and minibar. **Price** Single 210-410,000L, double 320-630,000L, suite 500-700,000L. **Meals** Breakfast included, served 7:00-10:30; half board 59,000L, full board 118,000L. **Restaurant** Service 12:30-15:00, 19:00-22:00; buffet: 59,000L. Specialties: Italian and Venetian cuisine. **Credit cards** All major. **Pets** Small dogs allowed. **Nearby**Events: Carnival of Venice, the Regata Storica (Sept.), the Mostra of Venice (Aug.-Sept.), Venice Biennale. Murano, Torcello (S. M. Assunta, S. Fosca), Villa Foscari in Fusina, Venetian villas (cruise along the Brenta Canal with the boat "Il Burchiello"), al Lido Alberoni golf course (18-hole). **Open** Feb. – Nov.

We will say this up front: this hotel, in one of the most busy parts of Venice, is more pleasant off-season. Behind its slightly banal facade you will find it deliciously quaint. The salon is vast and pleasant and the breakfast room on the canal is exquisite. In the hallways you will find pretty collections of objects, mirrors and Venetian paintings. The rooms are fairly spacious and look like the rest of the hotel. The ones on the top floor have small terraces with a phenomenal view of the rooftops of Venice.

How to get there *(Map 4): On the laguna, near Piazza San Marco, entrance by the Riva degli Schiavoni and by the Canale di San Marco.*

Pensione Accademia - Villa Maravegie

Dorsoduro - Fondamenta 1058
30123 Venezia
Tel. (0)41-521 01 88 or (0)41-523 78 46 - Fax (0)41-523 91 52
Sig. Dinato

Rooms 27 with telephone, bath or shower and TV. **Price** Single 120-1745,000L, double 190-330,000L. **Meals** Breakfast included, served 7:15-10:30. **Restaurant** See p. 483-487. **Credit cards** All major. **Pets** Dogs not allowed. **Nearby** Events: Carnival of Venice, the Regata Storica (Sept.), the Mostra of Venice (Aug.-Sept.), Venice Biennale. Murano, Torcello (S. M. Assunta, S. Fosca), Villa Foscari in Fusina, Venetian villas (cruise along the Brenta Canal with the boat "Il Burchiello"), al Lido Alberoni golf course (18-hole). **Open** All year.

This charming *pensione* whose popularity never wavers is located just near the Accademia and the Guggenheim Foundation, at the end of a small canal and surrounded by a romantic garden. The interior is just as beguiling, with poetic little sitting rooms offering antique furniture and nicely-decorated bedrooms, no two alike. Some are in the villa, others in an adjacent house which has been cleverly joined together to form one ensemble. Family furniture and souvenirs collected over the years create the climate of a real private home. You can choose a view on the canal or on the garden — both are attractive. It's the sort of place where you feel like a privileged guest — and many return again and again. This also means that if you are interested, you'd best make your arrangements well in advance.

How to get there *(Map 4): Vaporetto No.1 to Accademia stop, No.2 to Zattere stop.*

Hotel Flora

Via xxii Marzo, 2283 a
30124 Venezia
Tel. (0)41-520 58 44 - Fax (0)41-522 82 17 - Sig. Romanelli

Category ★★★ **Rooms** 44 with air-conditioning, telephone, bath or shower and WC; elevator. **Price** Single 230,000L, double 320,000L. **Meals** Breakfast included. **Restaurant** See p. 483-487. **Credit cards** All major. **Pets** Dogs allowed. **Nearby** Events: Carnival of Venice, the Regata Storica (Sept.), the Mostra of Venice (Aug.-Sept.), Venice Biennale. Murano, Torcello (S. M. Assunta, S. Fosca), Villa Foscari in Fusina, Venetian villas (cruise along the Brenta Canal with the boat "Il Burchiello"), al Lido Alberoni golf course (18-hole). **Open** All year.

At the end of a small hidden street not far from the Piazza San Marco you will find the Hotel Flora, a true oasis of cool, quiet greenery. The decor is of mostly English inspiration, a vestige of the time when the clientele was primarily British. If you make your reservation early enough, you might be able to have a room on the garden. All the bathrooms are tiny. The salon and the dining room are delightful but there is nothing like breakfast in the verdant garden around the fountain. The Saint Moses Church near the hotel has many 17th- and 18th-century paintings, including a Tintoretto and a "Cène" by Palma the Younger.

How to get there *(Map 4): Vaporetto, San Marco stop, behind the Museo Correr.*

1998

Hotel Torino

Calle delle Ostreghe, 2356
30124 Venezia
Tel. (0)41-520 52 22 - Fax (0)41-522 82 27 - Sig.Claudio Vecchiato

Category ★★★ **Rooms** 20 with air-conditioning, telephone, shower, WC, satellite TV, minibar and safe. **Price** Single 150-230,000L, double 200-320,000L. **Meals** Breakfast included, served 7:30-10:00. **Restaurant** See pp. 483-487. **Credit cards** All major. **Pets** Dogs allowed. **Nearby** Events: Carnival of Venice, the Regata Storica (Sept.), Mostra of Venice (Aug.-Sept.), Venice Biennale, Torcello (S. M. Assunta, S. Fosca), Burano, Villa Foscari in Fusina, Venetian Villas, cruise along the Brenta Canal the "Il Burchiello", al Lido Alberoni golf course (18-hole). **Open** All year.

Behind the Piazza San Marco, near the Corer Museum, is a street called Larga XXII Marzo, one of the main shopping streets in Venice. This street has an extension toward San Giglio and this is where the Hotel Torino is located. The entrance is quiet and intimate. A staircase leads to the upper floors, where you will find a small salon and a breakfast room filled with lovely bouquets of fresh flowers. The rooms are well-kept and decorated in antique style. The shower rooms are small, as is this whole miniature palace. Better ask for a room facing the rear if you're sensitive to noise and choose a higher floor if you want more light. But you won't have much choice unless you book well in advance, for an address of this quality is very sought after and the place fills up early.

How to get there *(Map 4): Vaporetto n°1 stazione Santa Maria del Giglio then towards piazza San Marco or n° 82 stazione San Marco then via XXII Marzo and calle delle Ostreghe.*

Hotel Bel Sito & Berlino

San Marco - Campo Santa Maria del Giglio, 2517
30124 Venezia
Tel. (0)41-522 33 65 - Fax (0)41-520 40 83
Sig. Serafini

Category ★★★ **Rooms** 38 with air-conditioning, telephone, bath or shower and WC (30 with minibar). **Price** Single 158,000L, double 242,000L, triple 3110,000L. **Meals** Breakfast included, served 8:00-10:00. **Restaurant** See p. 483-487. **Credit cards** Amex, Visa, Eurocard, MasterCard. **Pets** Dogs allowed. **Nearby** Piazza San Marco, Grand Canal, Gallery of the Academy, Ca' d'Oro, Guggenheim collection, scuola di San Rocco, scuola di San Giorgio degli schiavoni, the Ghetto, the Lido and lagoon, Murano (venetian glass), Burano (center of lacemaking), Torcello (S. M. Assunta, S. Fosca), Venetian villas (cruise along the Brenta Canal the "Il Burchiello" or by rented car: Amex), events: Carnival of Venice, the Regata Storica (Sept.), the Mostra of Venice (Aug.-Sept.), Venice Biennale; al Lido Alberoni golf course (18-hole). **Open** All year.

The Hotel Bel Sito is in San Marco near Gritti. The rooms are furnished in Venetian style and are comfortable, air-conditioned and quiet, especially the ones on the canal. Our favorite ones are in the front, however: notably, Rooms 30 and 40, which are sunny and have flowering balconies and a view of the Baroque sculptures of the church of Santa Maria del Giglio. Breakfast and bar service on the terrace will allow you to enjoy the magic atmosphere unique to Venice. The hotel has an extra room used only when the hotel is fully booked, so if you agree to take it you should know that you will be charged the regular price.

How to get there *(Map 4): Vaporetto No. 1, Santa Maria del Giglio stop.*

Hotel La Fenice et des Artistes

San Marco - Campielo de la Fenice, 1936
30124 Venezia
Tel. (0)41-523 23 33 - Fax (0)41-520 37 21
Sig. Appollonio

Category ★★★ **Rooms** 68 with air-conditioning, telephone, bath or shower, WC and satellite TV, elevator. **Price** Single 200,000L, double 330,000L, suite 340-460,000L. **Meals** Breakfast included, served 7:30-10:30. **Restaurant** "Taverna La Fenice", see p.483-487. **Credit cards** All major. **Pets** Dogs allowed. **Nearby** Events: Carnival of Venice, the Regata Storica (Sept.), the Mostra of Venice (Aug.-Sept.), Venice Biennale. Murano, Torcello (S. M. Assunta, S. Fosca), Villa Foscari in Fusina, Venetian villas (cruise along the Brenta Canal with the boat "Il Burchiello"), al Lido Alberoni golf course (18-hole). **Open** All year.

The hotel is on a quiet little square, behind the Fenice Theatre. It consists of two pretty houses connected by a patio where you can have a nice breakfast or unwind after hours of running around Venice. The rooms are all comfortable, but ask for one of the three rooms with terraces, which are also the most pleasant ones: Rooms 354, 355, and 406. The hotel has no restaurant, but it is next door to the famous *Taverna La Fenice*, a Venice classic.

How to get there *(Map 4): Near La Fenice.*

Hotel Do Pozzi

Via XXII Marzo, 2373 - Calle do Pozzi
30124 Venezia
Tel. (0)41-520 78 55 - Fax. (0)41-522 94 13
Sig.ra Salmaso

Category ★★★ **Rooms** 35 with telephone, bath or shower, TV and minibar. **Price** Single 115-160,000L, double 160-240,000L. **Meals** Breakfast included, served 7:00-10:30; half board 35,000L, full board 70,000L (per pers.). **Restaurant** Service 12:00-15:00, 18:45-22:30; closed Fri., Dec., Jan.; menu: 35,000L, also à la carte. Specialties: Venetian and Italian cuisine. **Credit cards** All major. **Pets** Dogs allowed. **Nearby** Piazza San Marco, Grand Canal, Gallery of the Academy, Ca' d'Oro, Guggenheim collection, scuola di San Rocco, scuola di San Giorgio degli schiavoni, the Ghetto, the Lido and lagoon, Murano (venetian glass), Burano (center of lacemaking), Torcello (S. M. Assunta, S. Fosca), Venetian villas (cruise along the Brenta Canal the "Il Burchiello" or by rented car: Amex), events: Carnival of Venice, the Regata Storica (Sept.), the Mostra of Venice (Aug.-Sept.), Venice Biennale, al Lido Alberoni golf course (18-hole). **Open** All year (except Jan.).

After plowing your way through the crowds on the small commercial streets of the San Marco quarter, it is easy to miss the little cul de sac which leads to the Hotel Do Pozzi. Hidden in one of those tiny squares so typical of Venice, the hotel is sheltered from the crowds. The rooms and bathrooms are small, modern and well equipped. The *campullo* full of flowers makes the hotel feel like an inn, there is also a restaurant, *Da Raffaele*. In summer, you can dine next to the canal and in winter, in a large picturesque room with a fireplace, decorated with old weapons and copper.

How to get there *(Map 4): Vaporetto, San Marco stop. In the via XXII Marzo, behind the Museo Correr, on a very small street.*

Hotel Panada

30124 Venezia
Calle dei Specchieri, 646
Tel. (0)41-520 90 88 - Fax (0)41-520 96 19
E-mail: htlpanne@gpnet.it

Category ★★★ **Rooms** 48 with air-conditioning, telephone, bath, WC; elevator. **Price** Single 180-280,000L, double 220-380,000L, triple 270-450,000L, 320-520,00L (4 pers.). **Meals** Breakfast included, served 7:00-11:00. **Restaurant** See p. 483-487. **Credit cards** All major. **Pets** Dogs allowed. **Nearby** Events: Carnival of Venice, the Regata Storica (Sept.), the Mostra of Venice (Aug.-Sept.), Venice Biennale. Murano, Torcello (S. M. Assunta, S. Fosca), Villa Foscari in Fusina, Venetian villas (cruise along the Brenta Canal with the boat "Il Burchiello"), al Lido Alberoni golf course (18-hole). . **Open** All year.

The hotel is on the hard to find calle dei Specchieri, just a few yards from the Basilica of San Marco (northeast of the Torre dell'Orologio). It is worth the effort, though, because it would be hard to find anything better (at this price) right in the heart of Venice. As soon as you walk in, the noise and the crowds fade in the distance. The hotel is quiet and comfortable. The rooms are cozy and have Venetian-style furniture in different pastel shades. All have comfortable bathrooms. There is no restaurant, but there is a bar, "Ai Speci," which is very popular with locals. This is a good place to relax, to meet friends for a drink or to have a light meal.

How to get there *(Map 4): Vaporetto No. 1 and 82, 52, San Marco stop. Behind Basilica of San Marco.*

Hotel Ai due Fanali

30120 Venezia
S. Croce, 946
Tel. (0)41-71 84 90 - Fax (0)41-78 83 44
Sig.ra Ferron

Category ★★★ **Rooms** 16 with telephone, bath or shower, WC, TV, safe and minibar. **Price** Single 120-240,000L, double 150-300,000L, triple 250-350,000L, apart. 250-500,000L. **Meals** Breakfast included, served 8:00-10:30. **Restaurant** See p. 483-487. **Credit cards** Amex, Visa, Eurocard and MasterCard. **Pets** Dogs not allowed. **Nearby** Events: Carnival of Venice, the Regata Storica (Sept.), the Mostra of Venice (Aug.-Sept.), Venice Biennale. Murano, Torcello (S. M. Assunta, S. Fosca), Villa Foscari in Fusina, Venetian villas (cruise along the Brenta Canal with the boat "Il Burchiello"), al Lido Alberoni golf course (18-hole). **Open** All year (except Jan. 10 - Jan. 30.).

In the *sestiere* of Santa Croce, just near the Santa Lucia railroad station, a nice little hotel has opened in what was once the school of the church San Simeon Grando. The dimensions of the building have made it possible to create a reception area furnished in antique style, extending into a salon. Breakfast is served in the dining room on the third floor or if the weather is fine, on the terrace. The bedrooms, done in Venetian style, are sober and elegant, not very large but with good amenities. There are also two apartments on the Riva degli Schiavoni with a view on the San Marco basin and the isle of San Giorgio.

How to get there *(Map 4): Vaporetto No. 1 Riva di Biario stop.*

1998

Hotel La Residenza

Castello 3608 Campo Bandiera e Moro
30122 Venezia
Tel. (0)41-52 85 315 - Fax (0)41-52 38 859 - Sig. Giovanni Ballestra

Category ★★ **Rooms** 15 with air-conditioning, telephone, bath or shower, WC, TV and minibar. **Price** Single 100-150,000L, double 180-220,000L. **Meals** Breakfast included, served 730-9:30. **Restaurant** See p. 483-487. **Credit cards** All major. **Pets** Dogs not allowed. **Nearby** Events: Carnival of Venice, the Regata Storica (Sept.), Mostra of Venice (Aug.-Sept.), Venice Biennale, Burano, Torcello (S. M. Assunta, S. Fosca), Villa Foscari in Fusina, Venetian Villas, cruise along the Brenta Canal the "Il Burchiello", al Lido Alberoni golf course (18-hole). **Open** All year.

La Residenza is on the Campo Bandiera e Moro, a quiet square near the quays of the Arsenal and the church of San Giovanni in Bragora (where you can see a fine painting by Cima da Conegliano). The building, which once belonged to the Gritti family, has preserved the charm of an old palazzo, with a gothic facade, 18th-century frescoes, stuccos and dazzling chandeliers of Murano glass - like something you dream about when you think of the city of the Doges. The salon is particularly regal, but be forewarned that the bedrooms are not quite the same - much smaller and simpler, in Venetian laccato style, with bathrooms dating from the 1950s, said to be identical to those in many patrician homes (unchangeable because of strict "landmark protection" regulations). Aside from this, you can appreciate this hotel for its quiet and its "invitation to the palace" ambience.

How to get there *(Map 4): Vaporetto Arsenale stop. On the quay, turn on left, after the bridge 1st alley on right, the place is at the end of the alley on left.*

Locanda Ai Santi Apostoli

Strada Nova, 4391
30131 Venezia
Tel. (0)41 521 26 12 - Fax (0)41 521 26 11
Sig. Stefano Bianchi Michiel

Category ★★★ **Rooms** 11 with air-conditioning, telephone, bath or shower, WC, TV, minibar; elevator. **Price** Single 220-300,000L, double 290-440,000L, 500,000L (4 pers.with 1 bath). **Meals** Breakfast included, served 7:40-11:40. **Restaurant** See pp. 483-487. **Credit cards** All major. **Pets** Dogs allowed. **Nearby** Events: Carnival of Venice, the Regata Storica (Sept.), the Mostra of Venice (Aug; - Sept.), Venice Biennale, Murano, Torcello (S.M. Assunta, S.Fosca); Burano, villa Foscari in Fusina, venetian villas, Cruise along the Brenta Canal the"Il Burchiello", al Lido Alberoni golf course (18 holes). **Open** All year (except Aug.10 - Aug. 24 and in festival).

On the Grand Canal, just near the Rialto, the Locanda Ai Santi Apostoli, on the third floor of an old palazzo, offers the atmosphere and hospitality of a patrician home of bygone times. The owners have the knack of receiving guests with warmth, attention and discretion, and the ambience, glamourous and cozy at the same time, make this a very good place to know. The bedrooms, all recently restored, are elegantly decorated with pieces of family furniture. Two of them face the Grand Canal, a spectacle you shouldn't miss: You can see the famous Rialto Bridge and the fish market and hear the serenades of the gondoliers. These rooms are much in demand, of course, and if they are not available, don't hesitate to accept another room, for you can always enjoy the same view from the very pleasant living room. Also in the neighborhood (Rialto and San Polo) are some of the nicest restaurants, both large and small, in Venice.

How to get there *(Map 4): vaporetto n°1, Ca'd'Oro stop.*

Hotel Agli Alboretti

Dorsoduro - Rio Terrà Foscatini, 884
30123 Venezia
Tel. (0)41-523 00 58 - Fax (0)41-521 01 58 - Sig.ra Linguerri

Category ★★ **Rooms** 20 with air-conditioning, telephone, bath or shower, WC and TV. **Price** Single 150,000L, double 230,000L. **Meals** Breakfast included, served 7:30-9:30. **Restaurant** Closed Wed., 3 weeks between July and Aug., Jan.; menus: 45-65,000L, also à la carte. Specialties: Venetian cuisine, very good Italian wines. **Credit cards** All major. **Pets** Dogs allowed. **Nearby** Events: Carnival of Venice, the Regata Storica (Sept.), the Mostra of Venice (Aug.-Sept.), Venice Biennale. Murano, Torcello (S. M. Assunta, S. Fosca), Villa Foscari in Fusina, Venetian villas (cruise along the Brenta Canal with the boat "Il Burchiello"), al Lido Alberoni golf course (18-hole). **Open** All year.

The entrance to the Hotel Agli Alboretti has a blond wood parquet floor and an atmosphere, which is as warm as the welcome Isabella and Federica Linguerri will give you. The rooms are all pleasant, though some are larger than others. The most charming ones are on the interior gardens, such as Room 18, and especially Room 15, which has a balcony big enough to have breakfast on. The owner's, daughter Anna, is a certified wine-waitress and runs the restaurant with a talented chef. She will help you select the right wine, which you can order by the glass, to accompany dishes. The dining room is pleasant, but the interior terraces and the *pergola* are really charming. This hotel is the best value in Venice.

How to get there *(Map 4): Vaporetto No. 1 and 82, Accademia stop.*

Hotel Santo Stefano

San Marco - Campo San Stefano, 2957
30124 Venezia
Tel. (0)41-520 01 66 - Fax (0)41-522 44 60
Sig. Roberto Quatrini

Category ★★ **Rooms** 11 with telephone, bath, WC, TV, safe and minibar (air-conditioning on request); elevator. **Price** Single 210-250,000L, double 270-300,000L, triple 330-390,000L. **Meals** Breakfast included, served 8:30-10:00. **Restaurant** See p. 483-487. **Credit cards** Amex, Visa, Eurocard, MasterCard. **Pets** Small dogs allowed. **Nearby** Events: Carnival of Venice, the Regata Storica (Sept.), the Mostra of Venice (Aug.-Sept.), Venice Biennale. Murano, Torcello (S. M. Assunta, S. Fosca), Villa Foscari in Fusina, Venetian villas (cruise along the Brenta Canal with the boat "Il Burchiello"), al Lido Alberoni golf course (18-hole). **Open** All year .

The Santo Stefano stands on the large *Campo* that is the main point of passage between the Piazza San Marco and the Accademia. The hotel occupies a small *palazzo,* six stories high but with only two rooms per floor. The rooms have all the amenities, including air-conditioning and well-equipped bathrooms. The modern Venetian decor sometimes borders on *kitsch,* but it is never in poor taste. Everything is miniature here — the reception area, the breakfast room, the patio and the terrace facing the open square, where you look out on the church of San Stefano. Its campanile, lovely but distinctly out of plumb, makes you realize that it's not only in Pisa that old towers tend to lean.

How to get there *(Map 4): Vaporetto No. 82 San Samuele stop - No. 1, Accademia stop.*

Pensione Seguso

Dorsoduro-Zattere, 779
30123 Venezia
Tel. and Fax (0)41-522 23 40
Sig. Seguso

Category ★★ **Rooms** 36 with telephone (16 with bath or shower, 10 with WC), elevator, wheelchair access. **Price** With half board for 1 pers.: 190-200,000L (without bath), 210-220,000L (with bath); for 2 pers.: 310-320,000L (without bath); 330-340,000L (with bath). **Meals** Breakfast included, served 8:00-10:00. **Restaurant** Service 13:00-14:00, 19:30-20:30; closed Wed.; menu: 40,000L. Specialties: Home Venetian cooking. **Credit cards** All major. **Pets** Dogs allowed. **Nearby** Events: Carnival of Venice, the Regata Storica (Sept.), the Mostra of Venice (Aug.-Sept.), Venice Biennale. Murano, Torcello (S. M. Assunta, S. Fosca), Villa Foscari in Fusina, Venetian villas (cruise along the Brenta Canal with the boat "Il Burchiello"), al Lido Alberoni golf course (18-hole). **Open** Mar. – Nov.

The Zattere quarter is a rather quiet area, a residential part of Venice. It is bordered by the Giudecca Canal, where you can watch the ceaseless ballet of the large ships sailing back and forth to the Lido and the *vaporetti* crossing the canal. From the terrace of the Pensione Seguso you can sit and watch the sun set over the island and church of San Giorgio — an unforgettable spectacle. This little building, slightly set back off the street, has been run for years by the same family, carrying on the tradition of the family pension, with dinner at the hotel (except July and August) served in the cozy dining room by a Venetian *mamma*. The rooms are old-fashioned but very well kept, with fine 19th-century furniture. It is another one of those places that it's a good idea to get to before it is "updated" to conform with European standards.

How to get there *(Map 4): Vaporetto No. 52 and 82, Zattere Gesuati stop.*

Pensione La Calcina

Dorsoduro-Zattere, 780
30123 Venezia
Tel. (0)41 520 64 66 - Fax (0)41 522 70 45
Sig. Alessandro Szemere

Category ★★ **Rooms** 29 with telephone, bath or shower. **Price** Single 105,000, double 180,000. **Meals** Breakfast included, served 7:30-10:00. **Restaurant** See pp. 483-487. **Credit cards** All major. **Pets** Dogs not allowed. **Nearby** Events: Carnival of Venice, the Regata Storica (Sept.), the Mostra of Venice (Aug; - Sept.), Venice Biennale, Murano, Torcello (S.M. Assunta, S.Fosca); Burano, villa Foscari in Fusina, venetian villas, Cruise along the Brenta Canal on the "Il Burchiello", al Lido Alberoni golf course (18 holes). **Open** All year.

This pensione is situated on the Zattere (meaning "the rafts"), one of the favorite spots of real Venetians who appreciate its calm and the long promenade along the waterfront, with the floating docks, where people come to sun themselves. From here the view of the canal, at any hour of the day or night, is one of the finest you can have in Venice. La Calcina is a good address for its location and moderate prices. It was here than John Ruskin chose to live during his stay in Venice. The entrance hall, living and dining rooms, all facing the quay are pleasant and inviting, as is the large waterside terrace. The bedrooms are nicely decorated, but of course the ones we recommend are those that face the Giudecca Canal. Our favorites are numbers 2, 4, 22 and 32. Be careful, only 11 rooms have a view and their prices vary depending on whether they are on the front, side or corner. Numbers 37, 38 and 39 have no view, but they do have a balcony.

How to get there *(Map 4): vaporetto n°52 and 82, Zattere Gesuati stop; n ° 1, 82, Accademia stop.*

Pensione Alla Salute Da Cici

Fondamenta Cà Balla, 222
30123 Venezia
Tel. (0)41-523 54 04 - Fax. (0)41-522 22 71
Sig. Cici

Rooms 38 with telephone, shower and WC. **Price** Single 100-140,000L, double 130-190,000L, triple 190-250,000L. **Meals** Breakfast included, served 7:30-10:00. **Restaurant** See p. 483-487. **Credit cards** Not accepted. **Pets** Dogs not allowed. **Nearby** Events: Carnival of Venice, the Regata Storica (Sept.), the Mostra of Venice (Aug.-Sept.), Venice Biennale. Murano, Torcello (S. M. Assunta, S. Fosca), Villa Foscari in Fusina, Venetian villas (cruise along the Brenta Canal with the boat "Il Burchiello"), al Lido Alberoni golf course (18-hole). **Open** Carnival – Nov. 7, 2 weeks at Christmas.

Alla Salute "da Cici" is one of the old *pensiones* of Venice, in one of the most poetic places in the town–on a canal behind the Salute. Though the house has lost some of its traditional appearance, the old family furniture is still in the large rooms. The rooms don't all have bathrooms, but they are impeccably well kept. Ask for the ones on the canal; the neighborhood is very quiet. Despite a kitchen just waiting to be used and an inner courtyard, the restaurant remains closed. But the bar service in the small adjoining garden is great.

How to get there *(Map 4): Vaporetto No. 1, La Salute stop (at the exit take the bridge in wood, walk to the next bridge; take on left the Fondamenta Cà Balla); take No. 52, Zattere stop. Take No., 82 Accademia stop.*

Hotel Pausania

Dorsoduro, 2824
30123 Venezia
Tel. (0)41-522 20 83 - Fax (0)41-522 22 989
Sig. Gatto

Category ★★★ **Rooms** 26 with air conditioning, telephone, bath or shower, WC, TV and minibar. **Price** Single 90-200,000L, double 150-295,000L. **Meals** Breakfast included, served 7:30-10:30. **Restaurant** See p. 483-487. **Credit cards** Amex, Visa, Eurocard and MasterCard. **Pets** Small dogs allowed. **Nearby** Piazza San Marco, Grand Canal, Gallery of the Academy, Ca' d'Oro, Guggenheim collection, scuola di San Rocco, scuola di San Giorgio degli schiavoni, the Ghetto, the Lido and lagoon, Murano (venetian glass), Burano (center of lacemaking), Torcello (S. M. Assunta, S. Fosca), Venetian villas (cruise along the Brenta Canal the "Il Burchiello" or by rented car: Amex), events: Carnival of Venice, the Regata Storica (Sept.), the Mostra of Venice (Aug.-Sept.), Venice Biennale, al Lido Alberoni golf course (18-hole). **Open** All year.

The Hotel Pausania is in the quarter of Dorsoduro, just near the *sestiere* of San Polo, a real working class district where you will at last be able to see the people of Venice at work, the children going to school and even the yapping little Venetian dogs, a species of lap dog that you can see depicted in the old paintings. It's also just near the Ca' Rezzonico palace and the two marvels — the Scuola Grande del Carmine, with its superb Tiepolo ceilings, and the Gothic church of Santa Maria del Carmelo. All this has decidedly more charm than the hotel itself, but it is a good address nonetheless — quiet, comfortable and friendly.

How to get there *(Map 4): Vaporetto No. 1, Ca' Rezzonico stop.*

Palazetto da Schio 

30123 Venezia
Dorsoduro 316/B - Fondamenta Soranzo
Tel. and Fax (0)41-523 79 37 - Contesse da Schio
E-mail: avenezia@tin.it - Web: http://web.tin.it/rent&receptionvenice

Apartments 3 with 1 or 2 rooms, lounge, kitchen, bath, telephone and TV. **Price** 930-1,180,000L (1 week), 1,200-1,400,000L (during the carnival). **Restaurant** See p. 483-487. **Credit cards** Not accepted. **Pets** Dogs not allowed. **Nearby** Events: Carnival of Venice, the Regata Storica (Sept.), the Mostra of Venice (Aug.-Sept.), Venice Biennale. Murano, Torcello (S. M. Assunta, S. Fosca), Villa Foscari in Fusina, Venetian villas (cruise along the Brenta Canal with the boat "Il Burchiello"), al Lido Alberoni golf course (18-hole). **Open** All year.

If you are traveling with your family and plan to spend more than two nights in Venice, a pleasant apartment in the center of town is undoubtedly the most economical option. The small but charming Palazetto da Schio is in a palace, close to the Academy. It is a good place to relax after a day of sightseeing. There are two light, spacious apartments. The antique family furniture creates an atmosphere which is both Romanesque and intimate. The owners are very nice and live downstairs on the "noble floor" of the house. Staying here will allow you to live like a Venetian for a while (without having to go to the Rialto market as a tourist). You will also enjoy both the intimacy of a home and the comfort of a hotel (maid service is available for all of your household needs). A deposit and references are required.

How to get there *(Map 4): Vaporetto No. 1 La Salute stop, (at the exit take the bridge in wood, go to the first bridge after the canal; take immediately on your left la Fondamenta (the river Cà Balla); take No. 52, Zattere stop. Take No. 82 Accademia stop.*

Hôtel des Bains

Lido - Lungomare Marconi, 17
30126 Venezia
Tel. (0)41 526 59 21 - Fax (0)41 526 01 13

Category ★★★★ **Rooms** 191 with tel., bath, TV, minibar; elevator. **Price** Single 297-392 000L, double 480-621,000L, suite 1,234,000L. **Meals** Breakfast included., served 7:00-10:30. Half board and full board: +93,500L and +197,000L (per pers.). **Restaurant** Service 13:00-15:00, 19:30-22:30; menus 120,000L; also à la carte.Specialties: Pesce. **Credit cards** All major. **Pets** Small dogs allowed. **Facilities** Swimming pool, tennis, fitness room, private beach, sauna, parking. **Nearby** Events: Carnival of Venice, the Regata Storica (Sept.), the Mostra of Venice (Aug; - Sept.), Venice Biennale, Murano, Torcello (S.M. Assunta, S.Fosca); Burano, villa Foscari in Fusina, venetian villas, Cruise along the Brenta Canal in the "Il Burchiello", al Lido Alberoni golf course (18 holes). **Open** Mar. 16 - 10 Nov.

The Hotel des Bains has been forever immortalized by Visconti's film "Death in Venice." Though not quite as sumptuous as the film version, it still preserves much of the charm the Lido beaches must have had at the turn of the century when they were frequented by Thomas Mann and other illustrious visitors of that elegant era. Grand salons filled with nostalgia for the past, comfortable bedrooms (we prefer those facing the famous boardwalk and cabins of the Lido), a large dining room, terraces, gardens and, above all, that "Grand Hotel" atmosphere that only such a palatial establishment can provide.

How to get there *(Map 4): vaporetto via the Lido from piazza San Marco.*

Albergo Quattro Fontane

Lido - Via delle Quattro Fontane, 16
30126 Venezia
Tel. (0)41-526 02 27 - Fax (0)41-526 07 26 - Famiglia Friborg-Bevilacqua
E-mail: quafonue@tin.it

Category ★★★★ **Rooms** 61 with air-conditioning, telephone, bath and TV. **Price** (except during the Cinema's Festival) : Single 260-310,000L, double 370-410,000L. **Meals** Breakfast included, served 7:00-10:30; half board 230-305,000L, full board 290-360,000L (per pers. 3 days min.). **Restaurant** Service 13:00-14:30, 19:45-22:30; menus: 80-90,000L, also à la carte. Specialties: Seafood. **Credit cards** All major. **Pets** Dogs allowed. **Nearby** Events: Carnival of Venice, the Regata Storica (Sept.), the Mostra of Venice (Aug.-Sept.), Venice Biennale. Murano, Torcello (S. M. Assunta, S. Fosca), Villa Foscari in Fusina, Venetian villas (cruise along the Brenta Canal with the boat "Il Burchiello"), al Lido Alberoni golf course (18-hole). **Open** Apr. 20 – Oct. 20.

For those who would like to see a different Venice, the Albergo Quattro Fontaine is a fabulous villa in the Lido run by two very friendly sisters, heiresses of great Venetian voyagers, one with a passion for Africa and the other for South America. A fabulous collection of memorabilia from their travels decorates the salons of the villa. Everything is perfectly elegant and comfortable here: the well-kept gardens, the shaded flagstone terraces with wicker furniture, the personalized rooms on the garden and the impeccably served Venetian cuisine. The annex built in the style typical of the islands of the lagoon, has newer and even more comfortable rooms.

How to get there *(Map 4): Vaporetto via the Lido from Piazza San Marco.*

Hotel Villa Mabapa

Lido - Riviera San Nicolo, 16
30126 Venezia
Tel. (0)41-526 05 90 - Fax (0)41-526 94 41 - Sig. Vianello
E-mail: mabapa@mbox.vol.it - Web: http://www.venicehotel.com/hotelmabapa

Category ★★★★ **Rooms** 60 with air-conditioning, telephone, bath, WC, hairdryer, safe, and TV; elevator. **Price** Single 105-290,000L, double 200-450,000L. **Meals** Breakfast included (buffet), served 7:30-10:00; half board +37-47,000L, full board +73-90,000L (per pers., 3 days min.). **Restaurant** Service 12:30-14:00, 19:30-21:30; menu: 50-55,000L, also à la carte. Specialties: Venetian cuisine, seafood. **Credit cards** All major. **Pets** Small dogs allowed in room. **Facilities** Parking. **Nearby** Events: Carnival of Venice, the Regata Storica (Sept.), the Mostra of Venice (Aug.-Sept.), Venice Biennale. Murano, Torcello (S. M. Assunta, S. Fosca), Villa Foscari in Fusina, Venetian villas (cruise along the Brenta Canal with the boat "Il Burchiello"), al Lido Alberoni golf course (18-hole). **Open** All year.

It is possible to find a bit of quiet country in Venice, even in the middle of August. These are the two major attractions of this property, built in the Lido in 1930 and subsequently transformed into a hotel. It is still run by the same family; the name Mabapa comes from the first syllables of "mama, bambini, papa." The interior of the villa still looks like a private house. The most charming rooms are the ones on the second floor of the main house. In the summer you can have your meals in the garden on the lagoon. A bit far from the center of town, but close to the Lido beach and convenient *vaporetto* (ferry) service, the Mabapa is a nice refuge for those who fear the tourist frenzy of Venice in the summer.

How to get there *(Map 4): from the rail station, Vaporetto 1, 52, 82 (in summer). By car, from Tronchetto ferry-boat ligne Nr. 17 (30 mn). From the airport, boat "Cooperativa S. Marco" (40 mn).*

Locanda Cipriani

Isola Torcello - Piazza Santa Fosca, 29
30012 Venezia
Tel. (0)41-73 01 50 - Fax (0)41-73 54 33 - Sig. Brass

Category ★★★ **Rooms** 6 with air-conditioning, telephone, bath, WC and TV. **Price** With half board 260,000L, full board 350,000L (per pers.). **Meals** Breakfast included, served 7:00-12:00. **Restaurant** Service 12:00-15:00, 19:00-22:00; menus: 60-80,000L, also à la carte. Specialties: Risotto alla torcellana, zuppa di pesce. **Credit cards** Amex, Visa, Eurocard, MasterCard. **Pets** Dogs not allowed. **Nearby** Events: Carnival of Venice, the Regata Storica (Sept.), the Mostra of Venice (Aug.-Sept.), Venice Biennale. Murano, Torcello (S. M. Assunta, S. Fosca), Villa Foscari in Fusina, Venetian villas (cruise along the Brenta Canal with the boat "Il Burchiello"), al Lido Alberoni golf course (18-hole). **Open** All year (except Jan. 5 - Feb. 5, closed Tues.).

Giuseppe Cipriani discovered this old inn on the island of Torcello while driving a visiting couple around the lagoon. It was love at first sight and he ended up buying it. The Locanda has four rooms and is known for its fine cuisine, notably the fish specialties. The exterior has kept its rustic flavor, but the salons and rooms are elegantly decorated. Meals are served in the garden or in the gallery with arcades. It is hard to stay very long in Torcello, where there's only the Santa Fosca Church and the superb Veneto-Byzantine Santa Maria Assunta Cathedral, but this old inn's isolation and charm make it well worth spending at least one evening here. Reservations are a must.

How to get there *(Map 4): From San Marco, boat via Torcello (30-45min.).*

Villa Ducale

Riviera Martiri della Libertà, 75
30031 Dolo (Venezia)
Tel. (0)41-56 080 20 - Fax (0)41-56 080 04

Category ★★★ **Rooms** 11 with air-conditioning and soundproofing, telephone, bath or shower, WC, satellite TV, safe and minibar. **Price** Single 120-160,000L, double 160-280,000L. **Meals** Breakfast included (buffet), served 7:00-10:00; half board 60,000L, full board 120,000L (per pers.). **Restaurant** Closed Tue.; menu, also à la carte. Specialties: Seafood. **Credit cards** Amex, Visa, Eurocard, MasterCard. **Pets** Small dogs allowed. **Facilities** Parking. **Nearby** Riviera del Brenta and Palladian Villas (S11) between Padua and Venice (Villas Ferretti-Angeli in Dolo, Villa Venier-Contarini-Zen in Mira Vecchia, Palais Foscarini in Mira, Villa Widmann, Villa Piscani in Srada, Villa Malcontenta in Malcontenta), Ca' della Nave golf course (18-hole) in Martellago. **Open** All year.

The Villa Ducale is, alas, next to a rather noisy road. But the building is magestic. The lobby has marvelous decorated ceilings and is very elegant. The rooms have beautiful period furnitureare very comfortable and they are air-conditioned and soundproofed, so traffic noise from the road is not a problem. The hotel provides quality round-the-clock service and has a fine restaurant. In this sublime setting you will feel like you are in a waking dream, especially if you are lucky and have a room with a terrace facing the grounds.

How to get there *(Map 4): 22 km west of Venezia via A4, Dolo-Mirano exit then towards Dolo; 2 km east of town center via S11, towards Venezia.*

Hotel Villa Margherita

Via Nazionale, 416/417
30030 Mira Porte (Venezia)
Tel. (0)41-426 58 00 - Fax (0)41-426 58 38
Famiglia Dal Corso

Category ★★★★ **Rooms** 19 with telephone, bath or shower, WC, TV and minibar. **Price** Single 155-185,000L, double 220-300,000L. **Meals** Breakfast included, served 7:30-10:30; half board 185-210,000L (per pers.) **Restaurant** Service 12:00-14:30, 19:00-22:00; closed Tues. dinner, Wed.; à la carte. Specialties: Seafood, Venetian cuisine. **Credit cards** All major. **Pets** Small dogs allowed. **Facilities** Parking. **Nearby** Riviera del Brenta and Palladian Villas, Venezia, Padova. **Open** All year.

This old 17th-century patrician villa is ideally on the tourist circuit of villas which rich Venetians built on the banks of the Brenta. It is luxuriously decorated; and particular attention has been paid to architectural details such as the quality of materials used, the studied mixture of antique and contemporary furniture, the richness of the decor with frescos, the *trompe l'œil,* the drapes and the fabrics. The surrounding fields and the small number of rooms, make this hotel a very quiet place. The personnel is charming and discreet and the price is justified.

How to get there *(Map 4): 15 km west of Venezia via A4, Dolo-Mirano exit; then S11 towards Dolo/Venezia.*

Villa Conestabile

Via Roma, 1
30037 Scorzé (Venezia)
Tel. (0)41-44 50 27 - Fax (0)41-584 00 88
Sig.ra Martinelli

Category ★★★ **Rooms** 19 with telephone, bath or shower, WC, TV and minibar. **Price** Single 100,000L, double 150,000L. **Meals** Breakfast included, served 7:00-10:00, half board 110-130,000L (per pers.). **Restaurant** Service 12:30-14:00, 19:30-22:00; closed Sun.; menu: 38,000L, also à la carte. Specialties: Venetian cuisine. **Credit cards** Amex, Visa, Eurocard, MasterCard. **Pets** Dogs allowed. **Facilities** Parking. **Nearby** Riviera del Brenta and Palladian Villas (S11) between Padua and Venice (Villas Ferretti-Angeli in Dolo, Villa Venier-Contarini-Zen in Mira Vecchia, Palais Foscarini in Mira, Villa Widmann), Ca' della Nave golf course (18-hole) in Martellago. **Open** All year.

This villa, a vacation house for a noble Venetian family since the 15th century, was badly damaged during WWII. In 1960 it was restored into a hotel. The rooms are furnished in a slightly provincial way, but they are large and quiet. Here you will find all of the charm of a country hotel, only 12 miles (20km) from Venice and 18 miles (30km) from Padua.

How to get there *(Map 4): 28 km northeast of Padova by A4, Padova-East exit towards Treviso.*

Hotel Bellevue

Corso Italia, 197
32043 Cortina d'Ampezzo (Belluno)
Tel. (0)436-88 34 00 - Fax (0)436-86 75 10
Famiglia Fabiani

Category ★★★★ **Rooms** and apartments 20 with telephone, bath or shower, WC, satellite TV, safe and minibar, elevator. **Price** Double 290-520,000L. **Meals** Breakfast included; half board 185-300,000L (per pers.). **Restaurant** "L'Incontro al Bellevue", service 12:30-14:00, 19:30-21:00; menus: 40-70,000L, also à la carte. Specialties: Italian cuisine. **Credit cards** All major. **Pets** Dogs not allowed. **Facilities** Garage. **Nearby** Skiing, excursions by cable car to the Tofana (10,543 feet) and to the Cristallo, Ghedina lake, Misurina lake, Tiziano's house in Pieve di Cadore. **Open** Dec. - Apr. and jul. - Sep.

The historical Hotel Bellevue has been one of the most popular inns in Cortina with celebrities since the beginning of the century. It is the jewel of this famous resort. Wood–used as the main decorative element in the hotel–is paneled, painted, parqueted and sculpted, and the result is magnificent. Most of the work has been done by hand using traditional techniques, which gives the entire hotel an atmosphere of elegant warmth. Beautiful fabrics by Pierre Frey and Rubelli complement the regional antique furniture. You will find the same atmosphere in the restaurant, which as excellent cuisine. This hotel is a model of simplicity and good taste–the essential ingredients of what we call "class."

How to get there *(Map 4): 168 km north of Venezia via A27 to Alemagna, then S51 to Cortina d'Ampezzo.*

Hôtel de la Poste

Piazza Roma, 14
32043 Cortina d'Ampezzo (Belluno)
Tel. (0)436 42 71 - Fax (0)436 86 84 35
Sig.Renato Manaigo

Category ★★★★ **Rooms** 81 with telephone, bath or shower, WC, satellite TV, safe, minibar; elevator. **Price** Single 155-295,000L, double 250-480,000L. **Meals** Breakfast 27,000L; half board 160-380,000L, full board 180-410,000L (per pers.). **Restaurant** Service 12:30-14:30, 19:30-21:30; menus; also à la carte 70,000L. Specialties: Italian cuisine. **Credit cards** All major. **Pets** Dogs not allowed. **Facilities** Garage (+25 000L). **Nearby** Skiing, excursions by cable car to the Tofana, Ghedina lake, Misurina lake; Tiziano's house in Pieve di Cadore. **Open** Dec. - Mar. and Jun - Sep.

The pearl of the Dolomites has its historic hotel - the Hotel de la Poste, around which the life of sophisticated Cortina revolves. You will find here, of course, all the usual assets of a mountain inn. Situated in the center, in a sunny spot, peaceful, with its popular bar (don't forget that the local cocktail is called the Dolomite), beautifully-prepared cuisine and attentive service. Despite the drawbacks caused by its fame, it is still one of the nicest places in the region. The bedrooms are inviting, comfortable and quiet. This is recommended to all those who like the mountains but who don't want to give up the pleasures of shopping and meeting people.

How to get there *(Map 4): 168 km north of Venezia via A 27 to Alemagna, then S51 to Cortina d'Ampezzo.*

Hotel Ancora

Corso Italia, 62
32043 Cortina d'Ampezzo (Belluno)
Tel. (0)436 32 61 - Fax (0)436 32 65
Sig.ra Flavia Sartor

Category ★★★★ **Rooms** 50 and 10 suites with telelephone, bath or shower, WC, satellite TV, safe, minibar; elevator. **Price** Single 175-270,000L, double 270-460,000L, suite +100-200,000L. **Meals** Breakfast included, served 8:00-10:00, half board 175-270,000L +40,000L, and full board 483,000L for Christmas (per pers, 7-10 days min.). **Restaurant** Service 12:30-14:00, 19:00-21:00; menus 40-60,000L; also à la carte. Specialties: Italian cuisine. **Credit cards** All major. **Pets** Dogs allowed (+30,000L). **Nearby** Skiing, excursions by cable car to the Tofana, Ghedina lake, Misurina lake; Tiziano's house in Pieve di Cadore. **Open** Jan. - Mar. and Aug. - Oct.

This wonderful place owes a lot to its owner, Flavia, an expert in antiques and decoration, who has given this pretty hotel a lot of personality. Behind the traditional facade of a simple chalet lies a hidden elegance and refinement, quiet comfort in the salons and bedrooms, and a restaurant, La Petite Fleur, which serves a creative cuisine of Italian inspiration. The Terrazza Viennese is the meeting place for all those who flock here after the day's skiing to enjoy a sachertorte or a drink at the piano bar. In a perfect location - this is the "in" to be in Cortina.

How to get there *(Map 4):168 km north of Venezia via A 27 to Alemagna, then S51 to Cortina d'Ampezzo.*

Hotel Pensione Menardi

Via Majon, 110
32043 Cortina d'Ampezzo (Belluno)
Tel. (0)436-24 00 - Fax (0)436-86 21 83 - Famiglia Menardi
E-mail: hmenardi@sunrise.it - Web: http://www.sunrise.it/cortina/alberghi/menardi

Category ★★★ **Rooms** 51 with telephone, bath or shower, WC and satellite TV. **Price** Single 70-150,000L, double 120-280,000L. **Meals** Breakfast 10,000L, served 7:30-10:00; half board 115-205,000L, full board 125-220,000L (per pers.). **Restaurant** Service 12:30-14:00, 19:30-21:00, menu: 35,000L. Specialties: Italian cuisine. **Credit cards** Visa, Eurocard, MasterCard. **Pets** Dogs not allowed. **Facilities** Garage. **Nearby** Skiing, excursions by the cable car to the Tofana (10,543 feet) and to the Cristallo, Ghedina lake, Misurina lake, Tiziano's house in Pieve di Cadore. **Open** Dec. 22 – Apr., June 17 – Sept. 18.

The Hotel Menardi is an old postal inn. It is charming: as soon as you enter the village you can't help noticing this pretty building with light green wood balconies covered with flowers in the summer. You will find the same charm and warmth inside the house is wood with regional decor. Don't get the wrong idea from its location next to the road; the hotel has large grounds in the back. The quietest rooms are on the garden and have a nice view of the Dolomites. The kindness of the Menardi family and their dedication to running their hotel well has earned them a clientele of regulars. The prices are also particularly good, considering the quality of the service.

How to get there *(Map 4): 168 km north of Venezia via A27 to Alemagna, then S51 to Cortina d'Ampezzo.*

Franceschi Park Hotel

Via Cesare Battisti, 86
32043 Cortina d'Ampezzo (Belluno)
Tel. (0)436-86 70 41 - Fax (0)436-2909
Famiglia Franceschi

Category ★★★ **Rooms** 49 with telephone, bath, WC and TV; elevator. **Price** (rooms and suites): 60-400,000L, 288-780,000L. **Meals** Breakfast included, served 7:40-10:15. **Restaurant** Service 12:30-13:45, 19:30-20:45; menus: 42-75,000L. Specialties: Italian cuisine. **Credit cards** All major. **Pets** Dogs not allowed. **Facilities** Tennis, sauna, turkish bath, beauty, parking. **Nearby** Skiing, excursions by the cable car to the Tofana (10,543 feet) and to the Cristallo, Ghedina lake, Misurina lake, Tiziano's house in Pieve di Cadore. **Open** Dec. 20 – Easter, June 21 – Sept. 22.

This pretty turn-of-the-century building has housed the Franceschi family hotel for three generations. It is on large grounds with a pretty garden, near the center of town. The hotel has kept its old-time flavor. Woodwork, parquet floors and blond wood exposed beams make the atmosphere very warm, as does the furniture and the large Austrian stove. The cozy, comfortable rooms have the same decor. This hotel is ideal for a family vacation.

How to get there *(Map 4): 168 km north of Venezia via A27 to Alemagna, then S51 to Cortina d'Ampezzo.*

Baita Fraina

Fraina 32043 Cortina d'Ampezzo (Belluno)
Tel. (0)436 36 34 - Fax (0)436 86 37 61
Famiglia Menardi

Category ★★ **Rooms** 6 with telephone, bath or shower, WC and TV. **Price** Double 130-158,000L. **Meals** Breakfast included, served 7:00-9:00, half board 105-115,000L (per pers.). **Restaurant** Service 12:30-13:45, 19:30-20:45; closed Mon. in low season; menus 46-75,000L. Specialties: Capriolo con polenta. **Credit cards** All major. **Pets** Dogs not allowed. **Facilities** Sauna. **Nearby** Skiing, excursions by cable car to the Tofana, Ghedina lake, Misurina lake; Tiziano's house in Pieve di Cadore. **Open** Dec. 15 - Apr. 19 and Jun 16 - Oct. 15.

A little away from the chic effervescence of Cortina, here you will appreciate the beauty of the site without getting caught up in the whirlwind of tourism. In winter as in summer, it is completely immersed in nature, only one kilometer from the center. The hotel has only six rooms, modest but comfortable. The place is run in family style, which only enhances the intimacy and simplicity, two aspects to be appreciated. A good address to know at reasonable prices in Italy's most upscale ski resort.

How to get there *(Map 4): 168 km north of Venezia via A 27 to Alemagna, then S51 to Cortina d'Ampezzo.*

Villa Marinotti

Via Manzago, 21
32040 Tai di Cadore (Belluno)
Tel. (0)435-322 31 - Fax (0)435-333 35
Sig. and Sig.ra Giacobbi de Martin

Suites 5 and 2 bungalows, with telephone, bath and WC. **Price** Suite 110-130,000L (per 1 pers.), 150-180,000L (per 2 pers.), bungalow 250-795,000L. **Meals** Breakfast included, served until 10:00. **Restaurant** Open in summer only. Service 19:30-21:00; menu. Specialties: Home cooking. **Credit card** Amex. **Pets** Small dogs allowed. **Facilities** Tennis (15,000L), sauna (20,000L), parking. **Nearby** Skiing in Pieve di Cadore (2 km) and in Cortina d'Ampezzo (25 km), Tiziano's house in Pieve di Cadore, the Great Dolomite Road. **Open** All year.

The owners of this house had the fortunate idea of transforming the family chalet into a small hotel, which is still a precious secret. The house has only five rooms, or rather five suites, as each one has a small, private salon. Simplicity and good taste pervade the decor (the "Rosa" suite is the nicest one). The house is surrounded by large grounds, which have a tennis court and a sauna. Breakfasts are excellent. You can now have dinner at the restaurant at the chalet. You can expect a warm welcome here.

How to get there *(Map 4): 34 km north of Belluno via S51.*

Golf Hotel

Via Oslavia, 2
34070 San Floriano del Collio (Gorizia)
Tel. (0)481-88 40 51 - Fax (0)481-88 40 52
Comtesse Formentini

Category ★★★★ **Rooms** 14 and 1 apartment (some with air-conditioning) with telephone, bath or shower, WC and TV. **Price** Single 180,000L, double 315,000L, apart. 440,000L. **Meals** Breakfast included **Restaurant** Service 12:00-14:00, 20:00-21:30; closed Mon. and Tues. lunch; menus 70-80,000L, also à la carte. Specialties: Regional cuisine. **Credit cards** All major. **Pets** Dogs allowed. **Facilities** Swimming pool, tennis, golf (9 holes), parking. **Nearby** Fortress of Gradisca d'Isonzo, Gorizia castle, Trieste,Monastery of Kostanjevica, Cividale (medieval city), Cathedral of Grado and of Aquileja. **Open** Mar. – Nov. 15.

Two houses of the San Floriano castle make up this hotel. Each of the rooms bears the name of one of the famous of regional wines. They are all furnished in a blend of styles, from 17th-century to Biedermeier, like in old family houses where each generation has left its mark. The hotel has a nine-hole golf course with a practice and putting green. The restaurant Castello Formentini is next to the castle and is one of the region's finest.

How to get there *(Map 5): 47 km northwest of Trieste via A4, Villesse-Gorizia and San Floriano exit.*

Haus Michaela

32047 Sappada (Belluno)
Borgata Fonta, 40
Tel. (0)435-46 93 77 - Fax (0)435-46 93 77
Sig. Piller Roner

Category ★★★ **Rooms** 20 with telephone, shower and 1 with bath, WC, satellite TV. **Price** Double 100-150,000L, suite 170-210,000L. **Meals** Breakfast 12,000L, served 8:00-10:00; half board 75-135,000L, full board 85-150,000L (per pers. 3 days min.). **Restaurant** Service 12:30-13:30, 19:30-20:30; menus 35,000L. Specialties: sappadina and regional cooking. **Credit cards** Visa, Eurocard, MasterCard. **Pets** Dogs not allowed. **Facilities** Swimming pool, sauna, parking. **Nearby** Skiing, Cortina d'Ampezzo, Titien house in Pieve di Cadore. **Open** Dec. 5 - end Mar. and Apr. 1 - Sep. 26.

Haus Michaela is located in Sappada, a beautiful town on the outskirts of Venetia, where you can already feel the charms of Austria (just 5 km away). It extends down to the floor of a valley dominated by the majestic furrowed summits and sharp peaks of the Dolomites. You can enjoy the mountains to the fullest here year round: it is a fine ski resort in the winter and a marvelous vacation spot in summer. Among the many hiking trails don't miss the one going up to the sources of the Piave, the legendary river which is the main supplier of the lagoon of Venice and flows through all of Venetia.The hotel offers simply decorated but highly comfortable rooms, and three large studios ideal for family vacations. Hotel facilities include a heated pool, a complete health care complex with Turkish baths, and a restaurant featuring local and Tyrolian specialties, notably a wide variety of deer dishes.

How to get there *(Map 5): 169 km north of Venezia. A27, Vittorio Veneto exit, then towards Cortina, then towards Sappada.*

Albergo Leon Bianco

Piazzetta Pedrocchi, 12
35122 Padova
Tel. (0)49-65 72 25 - Fax (0)49-875 61 84 - Sig. Morosi
E-mail: leonbianco@:writeme.com

Category ★★★ **Rooms** 22 with air-conditioning, telephone, bath or shower, WC, TV and minibar; elevator. **Price** Single 101-125,000L, double 149-161,000L. **Meals** Breakfast 15,000L, served 7:30-10:30. **Restaurant** See p. 489-490. **Credit cards** All major. **Pets** Dogs allowed (+12,000L). **Facilities** Garage (25,000L). **Nearby** Padova: Piazza delle Erbe and Palazzo della Ragione, Basilica di San Antonio, Chiesa degli Eremitani, Cappella degli Scrovegni (frescoes of Giotto); Pallandian villas: tour in car from Padua to Venice via the Brenta Riviera-N 11 (Villa Pisani, Villa "La Barbariga," villa Foscari) by boat *Il Burchiello*; Villa Simes in Piazzola sul Brenta; Villa Barbarigo in Valsanzibio; Praglia abbey; Pétrarque's house in Arqua Petrarca; Valsanzibio and Frassanelle golf course (18-hole). **Open** All year.

When Théophile Gautier visited Padua, he was struck by two sights (described in his *"Italia"*): the café Pedrocchi, which is still there, "monumentally classic, with pillars and columns... all very large and all very marble...," and the Scrovegni chapel, with its frescoes by Giotto. Aside from these, though, the lively university city of Padua has many more attractions worth visiting. The Albergo Leon Bianco is right in the center of town. It is a small hotel that constantly endeavors to improve its comfort, service and hospitality. Though the decoration in the bedrooms is standardized, it is nevertheless a nice place for a stopover in Padua.

How to get there *(Map 4): 37 km east of Venezia via A4, Padova-East exit; then towards town center, Palazzo della Ragione.*

Hotel Villa Regina Margherita

Viale Regina Margherita, 6
45100 Rovigo
Tel. (0)425-36 15 40 - Fax (0)425-313 01
Sig. Calore

Category ★★★★ **Rooms** 22 with telephone, bath or shower, WC, TV and minibar; elevator. **Price** Single 130,000L, double 160,000L, triple 180,000L suite 220,000L. **Meals** Breakfast 12,000L (buffet), served 7:30-9:30; half board 150,000L and full board 180,000L (per pers. 3 days min.). **Restaurant** Service 12:30-14:00, 19:30-22:00; menus 35-50,000L, also à la carte. Specialties:Pesce spada all'aceto balsamico, risotto. **Credit cards** All major. **Pets** Dogs allowed. **Facilities** Piano-bar, parking. **Nearby** Villa Badoer (Palladio), Villa Bragadin, Villa Molin in Fratta Polesine, Abbey of the Vangadizza in Badia Polesino, Padua, Ferrara. **Open** All year.

This charming hotel and its excellent restaurant are in a very pretty Art Deco villa. In the center of the little town of Rovigo, on a beautiful and slightly old-fashioned residential avenue, the Hotel Regina Margherita has recently been tastefully renovated. The stained glass, in vogue in the 1930s, has been preserved, along with some beautiful pieces of furniture which, combined with pretty, warm colors, make the salons and the lobby particular charming. The rooms, some of which are on the garden, are pleasant, comfortable and particularly well kept. The hotel restaurant deserves special mention for its remarkable setting, service and cuisine.

How to get there *(Map 10): 45 km south of Padova via A13, Boara exit.*

Hotel Villa Cipriani

Via Canova, 298
31011 Asolo (Treviso)
Tel. (0)423-95 21 66 - Fax (0)423-95 20 95
Sig. Burattin

Category ★★★★ **Rooms** 31 with air-conditioning, telephone. **Price** Double (with terrace) 627,000L. **Meals** Breakfast 29,700-51,700L, served 7:00-10:00; half board 132,000L (per pers.). **Restaurant** Service 12:30-14:30, 20:00-22:00, also à la carte. Specialties: Risotto Asolo, pasta, seafood. **Credit cards** All major. **Pets** Dogs allowed. **Facilities** Parking. **Nearby** Possagno (casa and tempio del Canova d'Antonio Canova), Villa Barbaro in Maser, Villa Rinaldi-Barbini, Villa Emo in Panzolo, Golf (7 km). **Open** All year.

Asolo is a must during any visit to Venetia. Don't worry if you have to drive through some industrial zones to get there — it will seem all the more beautiful once you reach it, perched on its hill in the middle of the countryside, a little medieval village with the castle as its crown. The lovely Villa Cipriani is a must in itself. It offers you elegant rooms, a lovely garden scented with rose trellises, a beautiful vista of the distant landscape and in the evening before dinner, a singer of charm murmuring those irresistible Italian melodies.

How to get there *(Map 4): 65 km northwest of Venezia; 35 km northwest of Treviso via S348 to Montebelluna, then S248 to Asolo; towards Bassano, D/Grappa.*

1998

Villa Emo

Via Stazione, 5
31050 Fanzolo (Treviso)
Tel. (0)423-47 64 13/423 47 64 14 - Fax (0)423-48 70 43
Sig.Leonardo Emo Capodilista

Category ★★★★ **Rooms** 8 and 3 suites with air-conditioning, telephone, bath, WC, minibar. **Price** Single 240,000L, double 300,000L, suite 600,000L. **Meals** Breakfast included, served 7:00-10:30. **Restaurant** Service 12:30-14:30, 19:30-22:00; closed Mon. and Tue. (lunch). Specialties: Venetian cuisine. **Credit cards** All major. **Pets** Dogs not allowed. **Facilities** Parking. **Nearby** Castelfranco, Conegliano: White wine road (Spumante Fair in Sept.), Palladian Villas road (villa Maser), Treviso, Venezia, Asolo, Vicenza; Golf course in Ca' Amata. **Open** All year.

Andrea Palladio is undoubtedly the most original Italian architect of the very rich 16th century. It was he who was commissioned to build this villa for the patrician Lunardo Emo in 1536. Today it still belongs to the Emo family, but the building is divided into a museum, with frescoes by Giovanni Zelotti, a restaurant, and very recently a hotel. Obliged to respect the architecture of the palace, the bedrooms have kept their original dimensions, which adds a certain charm. They all have painted furniture, with patterns echoing those of the frescoes and enormous bathrooms. If the beauty of the decor does not distract you from other pleasures, you must absolutely taste the delicate cuisine served in the restaurant. In the summer, you can eat outdoors under the graceful arcades facing the garden. A precious place to know in the very heart of Venetian art history.

How to get there *(Map 4): 20 km norh of Treviso.*

Hotel Abbazia

Via Martiri della Libertà
31051 Follina (Treviso)
Tel. (0)438-97 12 77 - Fax (0)438-97 00 01
Sig.ra Zanon de Marchi

Category ★★★ **Rooms** 17 and 7 suites with air-conditioning, telephone, bath or shower, WC, satellite TV and minibar. **Price** Single 130,000L, double 200-220,000L, suite 280,000L. **Meals** Breakfast included, served 7:00-12:00. **Restaurant** In Miane see p. 491 or Lino in Solighetto see p. 424. **Credit cards** All major. **Pets** Dogs not allowed. **Facilities** Parking. **Nearby** Abbey of Follina, from Conegliano (white wine road to Valdobbiadene (Spumante), Palladian villas tour, Treviso, Venice, Asolo, Pian del Cansiglio golf course (9-hole) in Vittorio Veneto. **Open** All year.

The Hotel Abbazia is a pretty, 17th-century house in the soft green Venetian Pre-Alps, facing a splendid Cistercien abbey. It is a small, luxurious hotel that offers everything you can imagine in terms of comfort, service and elegance. The rooms, some of which have pretty flower-filled terraces, are vast and each one is differently with antique furniture, pretty engravings decorated and soft, quiet colors. This dream house does not have a garden, but Follina is in the heart of the marvelous province of Trévise, which is filled with often undiscovered villas and Paladian farms. If you stay four nights in July and August you'll get one night free.

How to get there *(Map 4): 40 km north of Treviso. Via A4, A27 Vittorio Veneto exit towards Lago Revine; Follina is located at 15 km.*

Villa Stucky

Via Don Bosco, 47
31021 Mogliano Veneto (Treviso)
Tel. (0)41-590 45 28 - Fax (0)41-590 45 66
Sig. Pianura

Category ★★★★ **Rooms** 20 with air-conditioning, telephone, bath, fax, bath or shower (7 with whirpool), WC, TV, video, safe and minibar, elevator. **Price** Single 170,000L, double 270,000L, suite 330,000L. **Meals** Breakfast 15,000L, served 7:30-10:30. **Restaurant** Service 19:30-14:30, 19:30-22:30, à la carte. **Credit cards** All major. **Pets** Dog not allowed. **Facilities** Parking. **Nearby** Venice, Treviso, Villa Condulmer golf course (18-hole). **Open** All year.

Villa Stucky is an 18th-century Venetian villa built by the Countess Seymour. It had become pretty run down until major renovations were undertaken to transform it into the luxury hotel it is today. It has twenty rooms, which all took out onto the grounds, but are all different. Each one has decor that corresponds to the name it bears. "Princess Sissi" is precious with pastel colors; others are simpler and more elegant. In the ones on the top floor you can sleep in the moonlight, thanks to a skylight which you can open.

How to get there *(Map 4): 12 km south of Treviso via S13.*

Villa Giustinian

Via Giustiniani, 11
31019 Portobuffolé (Treviso)
Tel. (0)422-85 02 44 - Fax (0)422-85 02 60

Category ★★★★ **Rooms** 40 with air-conditioning and 8 suites, with telephone, bath or shower , WC, TV, radio and minibar. **Price** Single 120-140,000L, double 220-250,000L, suite 400-550,000L. **Meals** Breakfast 15,000L, served 7:30-10:30. **Restaurant** Service 12:30-14:30, 19:30-22:30, à la carte. **Credit cards** All major. **Pets** Dogs not allowed. **Facilities** Parking. **Nearby** Venice, from Conegliano (White Wine Road to Valdobbiadene (Spumante), Red Wine Road to Roncade), Treviso. **Open** All year.

The Villa Giustinian is in Portobuffolé, a beautiful Medieval village on the border between Venetia and Frioul. Around 1700, a noble Venetian family built this magnificent villa in a classical architectural style on a large piece of land. The interior is sumptuously Baroque, with stucco, frescos of the Veronese school and trompe l'œil. In this grandiose decor you will nonetheless find an intimate atmosphere. A superb stairway leads up to the comfortable rooms of different sizes; they are tastefully decorated. The suites are as big as ballrooms and have Venetian furniture. The presidential suite, which has a bed in a sculpted alcove, is amazing. You will really like the restaurant and its excellent wine list.

How to get there *(Map 5): 40 km northeast of Treviso, towards Oderzo, Mansué and Portobuffolé.*

Locanda Da Lino

31050 Solighetto (Treviso)
Tel. (0)438-84 23 77 - Fax. (0)438-98 05 77
Sig. Lino Toffolin

Category ★★★ **Rooms** 17 with telephone, bath, WC, TV and minibar. **Price** Single 100,000L, double 130,000L, suite 150,000L. **Meals** Breakfast 15,000L, served 8:00-11:00. **Restaurant** Service 12:00-15:00, 19:00-22:00; closed Mon. and Christmas; menus: 50-60,000L, also à la carte. Specialties: Tagliolini alla Lino, spiedo, faraona con salsa peverada, dolci della casa. **Credit cards** All major. **Pets** Dogs allowed. **Facilities** Parking. **Nearby** Venice, Villa Lattes in Istrana, Villa Barbaro Maser, Villa Emo Fanzolo di Vedelago, Conegliano (White Wine Road to Valdobbiadene (Spumante), Red Wine Road to Roncade), Treviso, Villa Condulmer golf course (18-hole). **Open** All year (except July and Monday).

Da Lino is, a character who regularly makes news in his village of Solighetto. He started by opening a restaurant, which quickly put the town, in the beautiful countryside of Montello and at the foothills of the Pre-Alps, between Venice and Cortina, famous for its Prosecco and its Marzemino sung by Don Juan, on the map. His painter, novelist and poet friends, among whom Zanzotto is the most faithful, have an open table and it is here that the great singer Toti del Monte came to spend her last days. In her memory, Lino has created the *Premio Simpatia,* a cultural event. Marcello Mastroainni, on the back cover of the book «Que Bonta» dedicated to Lino, boasts the atmosphere of well being of the house. The rooms bear the names of regulars and friends: "Marcello" (Mastroainni) and "Marta Marzotto" are comfortable and decorated with originality. In the restaurant, there are two rooms frequented by regulars; one is bigger and more touristy.

How to get there *(Map 4): 33 km northwest of Treviso.*

Hotel Villa Condulmer

Via Zermanese
31020 Zerman Mogliano Veneto (Treviso)
Tel. (0)41-45 71 00 - Fax (0)41-45 71 34
Sig. Zuindavide

Category ★★★★★ **Rooms** 49 with air-conditioning, telephone, bath, WC, TV. **Price** Single 200,000L, double 300,000L, suite 360,000L. **Meals** Breakfast included, served 7:00-10:30. **Restaurant** Service 12:30-14:30, 19:30-22:00; menus: 80-100,000L, also à la carte. Specialties: Regional cuisine. **Credit cards** All major. **Pets** Dogs not allowed. **Facilities** Swimming pool, tennis, golf (27 holes), riding, parking. **Nearby** Venice, Treviso. **Open** All year.

The Venetian villas flourished in the 18th century, when the wealthy merchants who traded with the Orient decided to convert their fortunes into real estate. This was the birth of a new architectural style consisting of a central, often sumptuous, building, where the family lived, flanked by two wings called *barchesse,* that were used as storage space. At the Villa Condulmer the reception rooms are still very well preserved and one can still admire the ceiling with ornate stuccos and large Venetian chandeliers, painted medallions that adorn the walls and a floor of terra cotta tile. The nicest rooms are those in the villa, though the others have more modern amenities. To be able to live in the country, with a large swimming pool and just near a golf course, is really a blessing during the summer months — and it's only 20 kilometers from Venice.

How to get there *(Map 4): 18 km north of Venezia via A4, Mogliano Veneto exit; then towards Zerman.*

Locanda al Castello

Via del Castello, 20
33043 Cividale del Friuli (Udine)
Tel. (0)432-73 32 42/73 40 15 - Fax (0)432-70 09 01
Sig. Balloch

Category ★★★ **Rooms** 17 with telephone, bath or shower, WC and TV; elevator; wheelchair access and rooms for disabled persons. **Price** Single 95,000L, double 135,000L. **Meals** Breakfast 12,000L; half board 110,000L, full board 140,000L (per pers, 3 days min.) **Restaurant** Service 12:00-14:30, 19:00-22:00; closed Wed.; menu: 45,000L, also à la carte. Specialties: Antipasti misti di pesce e di selvagigina, pesce e carne ai ferri. **Credit cards** All major. **Pets** Dogs allowed. **Facilities** Parking. **Nearby** Tempietto, Duomo and Archeological Museum; Udine; Villa Manin in Passariano, golf course (9-hole) in Lignano, golf course (9-hole) in Tarvisio. **Open** All year (Nov. 1 - Nov. 15).

For the curious traveler who wants to venture deeper into Italy, Friuli offers its smiling countryside and some interesting towns. Cividale del Friuli has a museum of architecture with some fine pieces from the early Middle Ages, and the Duomo (16th century) contains paintings by Palma the Younger and a wonderful altarpiece of pure silver. The Locanda Al Castello is in an unpretentious but pleasant stopping place. It is a typical provincial small town inn, with rooms that exude a prosperous comfort, a restaurant that serves generous meals and a hospitality that is simple and natural.

How to get there *(Map 5): 17 km east of Udine via A23, Udine exit; then towards Cividale (1.5 km from Cividale).*

Hotel Gabbia d'Oro

Corso Porta Borsari, 4a
37121 Verona
Tel. (0)45-800 30 60 - Fax (0)45-59 02 93
Sig.ra Balzarro

Category ★★★★★ **Rooms** 5 and 22 suites with air-conditioning, telephone, bath, WC, TV and minibar; elevator. **Price** Double 250-550,000L, suite 410-1,200,000L. **Meals** Breakfast 40,000L, served 7:00-11:00. **Restaurant** See pp. 488-489. **Credit cards** All major. **Pets** Small dogs allowed. **Facilities** Parking (50,000L). **Nearby** In Verona: Piazza delle Erbe, Piazza dei Signori, the Arena, Juliet's House, Arche Scaligere, Church of San Zeno, Castelvecchio. Tradition: Festival of Verona in the Arena mi-July–mi-Aug. Villa Boccoli-Serego in Pedemonte, Villa della Torre in Fumane, Soave, Castle Villafranca di Verona; golf course (18-hole) in Sommacampagna. **Open** All year.

The luxurious Hotel Gabbia d'Oro is a discreet 14th-century palace. At first glance it seems like a secret place. The entrance is barely distinguishable from the street. There are two small salons with superb exposed beams, very beautiful period furniture and nice armchairs around an old fireplace. The courtyard, with pretty flowers, is surrounded by rooms which are not very large, but are very luxurious. On the top floor there is a peaceful terrace from which you can see the rooftops of the old town. The service is as nice as the setting. Alas, nothing is perfect–the prices are high, but justifiably so. The hotel is in a historical pedestrian area. If you come by car, a taxi (at the hotel's expense) will accompany you to the nearest garage–one less thing to worry about.

How to get there *(Map 3): Via A4, Verona-South exit. Via A22, Verona-West exit. The hotel is in front of Piazza delle Erbe.*

Albergo Aurora

37121 Verona
Piazza Erbe, 2
Tel. (0)45-59 47 17 - Fax (0)45-801 08 60
Sig.ra Rossi

Rooms 19 with air-conditioning, telephone, bath or shower, WC, satellite TV; elevator. **Price** Single 110-155,000L, double 130-180,000L, apartment with 2 double rooms and 1 bath 220-330,000L. **Meals** Breakfast included, served 7:30-10:00. **Restaurant** See pp. 488-489. **Credit cards** All major. **Pets** Dogs allowed. **Nearby** In Verona: Piazza delle Erbe, Piazza dei Signori, the Arena, Juliet's House, Arche Scaligere, Church of San Zeno, Castelvecchio. Events: Festival of Verona in the Arena mi-July–mi-Aug. Villa Boccoli-Serego in Pedemonte, Villa della Torre in Fumane, Soave, Castle Villafranca di Verona, golf course (18-hole) in Sommacampagna. **Open** All year.

The Albergo Aurora is on the Piazza dell'Erbe in the heart of the town (a pedestrian area). It is very well kept and very comfortable (air-conditioning and well-equipped shower room). The service is discreet and charming and the prices are very competitive. There is one sour note, however, the decor and the lighting are reminiscent of a train station. So, should you decide to come here, choose the front rooms with a view of the piazza (they are the smallest but there are plans to enlarge them). The terrace, which looks out on those famous sun umbrellas, is a wonderful place to sit back and relax.

How to get there *(Map 3): A4, Verona-sud exit; A22, Verona-north exit. (Parking, Cittadella, piazza Arsenale, here you can phone a taxi for the center).*

Hotel Villa del Quar

Via Quar, 12
37020 Pedemonte (Verona)
Tel. (0)45-680 06 81 - Fax (0)45-680 06 04
Sig.ra Acampora Montresor

Category ★★★★ **Rooms** 22 with telephone, bath or shower, WC, TV and minibar. **Price** Double 380-430,000L, suite 540-600,000L. **Meals** Breakfast included, served 7:30-10:00. **Restaurant** Service 12:30-14:00, 19:30-22:00; menus: 120,000L. Specialties: Zuppa di funghi con scampi, frittura del mare e dell'orto, coulins di fichi in salsa di amarone. **Credit cards** All major. **Pets** Dogs allowed. **Facilities** Swimming pool, parking **Nearby** Villa Boccoli-Serègo in Pedemonte, Verona, villa della Torre in Fumane, Soave, Castle Villafranca di Verona, Lago di Garda, Mantova, Venise. Tradition: Festival of Verona in the Arena mi-July–mi-Aug. Golf course (18-hole) in Sommacampagna and in Garde. **Open** All year.

The younger generation of owners of the Villa del Quar have transformed the family estate into a luxury hotel, continuing to cultivate the hectares of vineyards that surround the villa. The building is typical of the region, with three wings around a central garden. There are beautiful salons and bedrooms, each differently furnished, that combine a refined setting and good amenities. Elegance is the key word here, even if you're way out in the country. And what a joy it is to stroll through the vineyard in the morning, knowing you're only a few kilometers from Verona.

How to get there *(Map 3): 5 km northeast of Verona, via Trento; before Parona take the Valpolicella road towards Pedemonte. Via A4, Verona-North exit, highway towards S. Pietro in Cariano, right (towards Verona) to Pedemonte.*

Foresteria Serègo Alghieri

37020 Gargagnano di Valpolicella (Verona)
Tel. (0)45-770 36 22 - Fax (0)45-770 35 23
Sig. Pieralvise Serègo Alighieri

Apartments 8 with air-conditioning, telephone, bath, 7 with WC, 7 with TV and minibar. **Price** 2-4 pers. 210-490,000L (1 night), 130-350,000L (1 night during 1 week). **Meals** Breakfast 15,000L, served 8:00-10:00. **Restaurant** In Verona. See p. 488-489. **Credit cards** All major. **Pets** Dogs allowed. **Facilities** Parking. Nearby Verona, Tradition: Festival of Verona in the Arena mi-July–mi-Aug. Vineyards of Valpolicella (Villa Boccoli-Serego, Villa della Torre, Fumane, S. Floriano, San Giorgio, Volargne and the Villa del Bene), Soave, golf course (18-hole) in Sommacampagna. **Open** All year (except Jan.).

Go up the long path lined with majestic cypress trees and you will soon see a massive residence with a large enclosed courtyard of flagstones in the middle of the Valplolicella vineyards. Dante used to come here on vacation when he lived in Verona. The Casal dei Ronchi was bought in 1353 by his eldest son, Pietro, and has been the home of the poet‘s descendants ever since. Today it is a prosperous estate with a working farm with wine and oil you can taste during your stay here. Eight elegantly decorated apartments are available (for 2 to 4 people). Between Lake Garda and Verona, and Venice less than 60 miles away, this villa is a magical, rare delight.

How to get there *(Map 3): 20 km of Verona via A22, Verona-north exit; then towards S. Ambrogio di Valpolicella.*

Relais Villabella

Villabella 37047 San Bonifacio (Verona)
Tel. (0)45-61 01 777 - Fax (0)45-61 01 799
Sig. Cherubin

Category ★★★ **Rooms** 9 with telephone, bath or shower, WC, TV and minibar. **Price** Single 160,000L, double 250,000L, suite 290,000L. **Meals** Breakfast included; half board 190,000L and full board 225,000L (per pers., 3 days min.). **Restaurant** Closed Sunday and Monday. Service 12:00-14:00, 20:00-22:00; also à la carte 70-100,000L. **Credit cards** All major. **Pets** Dogs allowed. **Facilities** Swimming pool, parking. **Nearby** In San Bonifacio: Churche of S. Abbondio, Abbey of S. Pietro Apostole; Verona, Soave, Vicenza; tradition: Wein Feast in Soave, Festival of Verona in the Arena mid-July–mid-Aug., golf course (18-hole) in Sommacampagna. **Open** All year.

The most famous town in the Alpone Valley is the fortified medieval village of Soave, known for its wine. Just a few kilometers away is Villabella, with the hotel of the same name, a traditional villa of the region now converted into a comfortable country inn. The excellent decoration of the bedrooms and the great attention paid to the cooking attract both a regional clientele, who want to spend a weekend in the country, and tourists who are looking for a quiet country hideaway after their day's touring. And quiet though it is, the Villabella is easy to reach, located just off the autostrada.

How to get there *(Map 4): 20 km west of Vierona, via A4, Soave exit; Villabella is located near the highway.*

1998

Coop. 8 Marzo - Ca` Verde

Ca`Verde 30021 Sant' Ambrogio di Valpolicella (Verona)
Tel. (0)45-686 17 60 - Fax (0)45-686 12 45
Sig.ra Vilma Zamboni

Rooms 10 (4 with bath, WC). **Price** Single 28-45,000L, double 50-70,000L. **Meals** Breakfast 8,000L, served 8:30-10:00. **Restaurant** Service 12:30-14:00, 19:30-21:30; closed Mon; menu 35,000L.Specialties: pasta fatta in casa, Gnocchi di ricotta, Carni alla griglia, piatti vegetariani. **Credit cards** Visa, Eurocard, MasterCard. **Pets** Dogs not allowed. **Facilities** Parking. **Nearby** Verona, Villa Boccoli-Serègo in Pedemonte, Villa della Torre in Fumane, Soave, Castel of Villafranca di Verona, Lake Garda. **Open** All year (except Jan. and Feb.).

A rustic site, it officially became an agricultural cooperative some ten years ago after its owners had occupied unused land. Today it functions as a cooperative, with a team that have divided up the tasks, both the farming and the commercial work, with the aim of distributing their products directly. They have opened a latteria where dairy products (milk, yogurt and cheese) and honey, all organically produced on the farm, are sold to the public, and have also created facilities to enable them to receive guests. There are two kinds of lodgings. In one wing are the recently-built, more comfortable rooms. In the other there are dormitories, as well as several large rooms suitable for families, but with showers outside. There are several large picnic tables on the property, but the restaurant prices are low enough to tempt anyone to sample the cooking, which is family-style and based on home-made products. Ca`Verde is not easy to get to. Once you have left the road you have to drive 2 kilometers further on a dirt track before you catch a glimpse of it, standing there completely surrounded by farmland.

How to get there *(Map 3): 20 km from Verona, Verona North exit to S. Ambrogio. In the village, towards Monte; 3nd turning point, take road on the left after 2 km.*

Hotel Gardesana

Lago di Garda
Piazza Calderini, 20
37010 Torri del Benaco (Verona)
Tel. (0)45-722 54 11 - Fax (0)45-722 57 71 - Sig. Lorenzini
E-mail: gardesana@easynet.it

Category ★★★ **Rooms** 34 with air-conditioning (in July and Aug.), telephone, bath or shower, WC and TV; elevator. **Price** Single 65-90,000L, double 90-160,000L. **Meals** Breakfast 20,000L, served 7:00-11:00. **Restaurant** Service 19:00-23:00; menus: 45-85,000L, also à la carte. Specialties: Zuppetta di pesci del Garda, Seafood. **Credit cards** All major. **Pets** Dogs not allowed. **Facilities** Parking. **Nearby** Cap San Vigilio (Villa Guarienti), Verona, golf course (18-hole) in Marciaga. **Open** Mar. – Oct. 25, Dec. 26 – Jan. 15.

This 15th-century harbormaster's office faces the ruins of the Scalinger castle built on the other side of the port. From the terrace, where breakfast and dinner are served, you can look down onto the small port on Garde Lake. The rooms all have identical decor; ask for one on the third floor overlooking the lake–it is quieter. The famous restaurant attracts clientele from outside of the hotel and on certain evenings it celebrities from the world of art, literature, show business and sports host the dinner. Torri del Benaco is one of the most charming places on the lake. André Gide enjoyed his stay here and Room 23 bears his name. The owner and his family will make you feel at home too.

How to get there *(Map 3): 39 km northwest of Verona via A4, Peschiera exit; Via A22, Affi-Lago di Garda exit.*

1998

Il Castello

Via Castello, 6
36021 Barbarano Vicentino (Vicenza)
Tel. (0)444-88 60 55 - Fax (0)444-88 60 55 - Sig.ra Elda Marinoni

Apartment with kitchen, bath, WC. **Price** 35,000L (per pers., 3-7 days min.) +15,000L for heating in low season. **Restaurant** In Vicenza p. 490. **Credit cards** Not accepted. **Pets** Dogs allowed. **Facilities** Parking. **Nearby** Vicenza, Venetian villas road: villas Guiccioli, Valmarana, La Rotonda; in Arcugnano, villa Franceschini or Canera di Salasco; in Costoza di Longare villa Trento-Carli and Villa Garzadori-Da Schio; in Montegalda La Deliziosa; in Barbano di Grisignano villa Ferramosca-Beggiato, in Vancimuglio villa Trissino-Muttoni; in Bretisina da Vicenza villa Ghislanzoni-Curti and villa Marcello-Curti. **Open** All year.

When people mention Venetian villas, we think immediately of those that line the Brenta Canal. In fact, over a period of three centuries, more than 2,000 villas were built on all the hills of the little towns near Venice. The Castello is in the Berici Mountains and will give you the opportunity to explore the villas of this region. Standing on the heights of the old village, it is the home of Elda Marinoni and her two charming daughters. The entranceway leads through the building directly into the garden. The large farmhouse and one of the outbuildings have been made over into apartments for rent. A pleasant entrance is hung with old photos that depict the life in Barbarano at the turn of the century. The apartments are functional and comfortable. One can enjoy the large meadow that overlooks the little valley. There is also a romantic Italian-style garden just below, planted with orange trees. The welcome is not effusive but very kind.

How to get there *(Map 4): 25 km southeast of Vicenza. On highway A4 Vicenza-east exit towards Ponte di Barbarano or Montebello exit towards Orgiano and Ponte di Barbarano.*

Relais Ca' Massieri

Masieri 36070 Trissino (Vicenza)
Tel. (0)445-490 122 - Fax (0)445-490 455
Sig. Vassena

Rooms 8 (5 with air-conditioning), telephone, bath, WC, TV, minibar. **Price** Single 100,000L, double 145,000L, apartment 180,000L. **Meals** Breakfast 12,000L, served 7:30-11:00. **Credit cards** Amex, Visa, Eurocard, MasterCard. **Pets** Dogs allowed. **Facilities** Covered swimming pool, parking. **Nearby** in Trissino: Park of the villa Marzotto, from Montecchio Maggiore, castellodi (panorama), Bellaguardia and castello della Villa, Romeo and Juliet's castle, Villa Cordellina-Lombard, Vicenza. Restaurant Service 12:30-14:00, 19:30-22:00; menus 70-90,000L; Specialties: insalata di capresante, Bigoli al torchio, Filetto bollito. **Open** All year (except end Jan. - beg. Feb.).

A beautiful inn in the Venetian countryside, known and appreciated primarily for its cooking and its wines. It will also make a pleasant stopover in your explorations of this region of Palladian art. The surroundings are calm, with soft rolling hills. Inside, it is very comfortable. The rooms are large with decor to suit every taste. The apartment is even larger and has its own terrace. Adjoining the hotel is an attractive restaurant where you can have delicious meals. The hospitality is friendly and the whole place is most professional.

How to get there *(Map 4): 20 km northwest of Vicenza. On highway A4 Montecchio Maggiore exit, 15 km towards Valdagno.*

Grand Hotel Duchi d'Aosta

Piazza Unità d'Italia, 2
34121 Trieste
Tel. (0)40-76 000 11 - Fax (0)40-36 60 92
Sig.ra Hedy Benvenuti

Category ★★★★ **Rooms** 48 with air-conditioning and 2 suites with telephone, bath or shower, WC, TV and minibar; elevator. **Price** Single 248-260,000L, double 330,000L, suite 525-548,000L. **Meals** Breakfast included, served 7:00-10:30. **Restaurant** Service 12:30-14:30, 19:30-22:30; menus: 50-70,000L, also à la carte. Specialties: Seafood. **Credit cards** All major. **Pets** Dogs allowed. **Facilities** Garage (37,000L), parking. **Nearby** Trieste (Piazza dell'Unita, Roman theater, Cathedral of S. Giusto, the port), Castello di Miramare, Grotta Gigante, Church of Monrupino. Extention vers la Yougoslavie : haras de Lipizza, basilique de Porec, caves of Postojna. **Open** All year.

Like the rest of the town of Trieste, the Hotel Duchi d'Aosta has the nostalgic charm of one of those places with a fabulous history, which is now overlooked. It is a palace from another century, where you might expect to see some rich Austro-Hungarian family with its entourage, stopping off for an evening on the way to Venice, enter one of the plush salons. It is an excellent hotel with vast, pleasant rooms, equipped with every modern convenience. The service is in the fine and all too rare tradition of the international hotels of yesteryear. The trilingual personnel is omnipresent, attentive, friendly, discreet and efficient. The restaurant is also excellent. The hotel is right in the center of the old part of Trieste, only a few minutes away from the fort.

How to get there *(Map 5): Via A4, Trieste-Costieza exit.*

RESTAURANTS

RESTAURANTS

BASILICATA CALABRE

Maratea

Taverna Rovita, via Rovita 13, tel. (0973) 876 588 – Closed November-March 15 – 35-50,000L. A pretty

restaurant on a narrow street in the historical center of Maratea. It serves regional cuisine, has a good wine cellar – **Za' Mariuccia**, on the port, tel (0973) 876 163 – Closed Thursday except in the summer and from December to February – 50-80,000L. Wide variety of fish specialties.

Fiumicello

5km from Maratea

La Quercia, tel. (0973) 876 907 – Closed October-Easter – 30-40,000L. It Serves seafood and traditional regional Italian cuisine in a romantic atmosphere. Meals are served in a rustic but elegant dining room, or in the garden in the shade of the big oak tree.

Matera

Il Terrazzino, Bocconcino II, vico San Giuseppe 7, tel. (0835) 332 503 – Closed Tuesday – 40,000L. The town's amazing vestiges of the Troglodyte period are worth seeing. Terrazzino is a great place to stop in for a family meal. Matera has some of the best bread in Italy.

LOCAL SPECIALTIES

Il Buongustaio, piazza Vittorio Veneto 1 – It features smoked ham from Lauria, Picerno, and Palazzo San Gervasio, and the *Aglianico* wine.

Potenza

Taverna Oraziana, via Orazio Flacco 2, tel. (0971) 21 851 – Closed Sunday, August – 40-50,000L. This classic restaurant has long been the haunt of town notables who come for rich hearty regional cuisine. *Aglianico dei Vulture* is a good local wine.

Altomonte

Barbieri, via San Nicolas 32, tel. (0981) 948 072 – A famous restaurant, regional cooking.

LOCAL SPECIALTIES

Bottega di Casa Barbieri, has a very good selection of regional products such as the *Ciro classico*, one of the best wines of Calabria.

Cosenza

Da Giocondo, via Piave 53, tel. (0984) 29 810 – Closed Sunday, August – 30,000 L. It is very small, so reservations are a must.

Castrovillari

La Locanda di Alia, via Jetticelle 69, tel. (0981) 46 370 – Closed Sunday – 50-70,000L. It is located a few miles from the ancient Greek town of Sibari, and serves traditional Calabrian cuisine in a very lovely decor.

Reggio di Calabria

Bonaccorso, via Nino Bixio 5, tel. (0965) 896 048 – Closed Monday, August 45-50,000L. Italian and French cuisine with some Calabrian specialties, *fettucine, cinzia, semifreddi* – **Conti**, via Giulia 2, tel (0965) 29 043 - Closed Monday - 45-60,000L. It has 2 rooms, one is elegant, the other more casual with a piano bar.

Gallina

2km from Reggio di Calabria

La Collina dello Scoiattolo, via Provinciale 34, tel. (0965) 682 255 – Closed Wednesday, November - 40,000L. There is an avalanche of *antipasti,penne all'imbriacata* and very good desserts, in pleasant surroundings, but it is always overcrowded.

Soverato

Il Palazzo, Corso Umberto I 40, tel. (0967) 25 336 – Closed Monday, November – 40,000L. Old very well restored and tastefully decorated palace and features regional cuisine. In the summer, meals are served in the garden.

Catanzaro Lido

La Brace, 102 via Melito di Porto Salvo, tel. (0961) 31 340 – Closed Monday, July – 40-60,000L. A pretty restaurant with a panoramic view on the Gulf of Squillace, fine cuisine (spaghetti with zucchini flowers, octopus ravioli, homemade pie) and a good selection of Calabrian wine.

CAMPANIE

Napoli / Naples

La Cantinella, via Cuma 42, tel. (081) 764 86 84 – Closed Monday,

August – 70-120,000L. It has a nice view on Vesuvius and serves elegant cuisine in the great Neopolitan tradition – **La Sacrestia**, via Orazio 116, tel. (081) 7611051 – Closed Monday, August – 70-100 000L. People come here religiously for its elegant simplicity, very good cuisine, and great Campanian wines – **Amici Miei**, via Monte di Dio 78, tel. (081) 764 60 63 Closed Monday, August –

40,000L. Has good traditional family-style cuisine and a friendly atmosphere – **Ciro a Santa Brigida**, via Santa Brigida 71, tel. (081) 552 40 72 – Closed Sunday, Christmas, August – 60,000L. People come here

to enjoy simple authentic Neopolitan cuisine – **Bellini**, via Santa Maria di Costantinopoli 80, tel. (081) 459 774 – Closed Wednesday, August – 45,000L. Has good pizza and other Neopolitan specialties – **Don Salvatore**, via Mergellina 5, tel. (081) 681 817 - Closed Wednesday,

June – 50,000 L. Neopolitan pizzeria, fish – **Ciro a Mergellina**, via Mergellina, 21, Find the pushcart vender wandering on the boardwalk, and try his *Ostrecaro Ficico* and other seafood specialties – **I Primi,** via Mergellina 1, tel. (081) 761 61 08 – Closed Sunday, May – 45,000 L. Mediteranean cooking – **Giuseppone a Mare**, via F. Russo 13, tel. (081) 575 60 02. Typically Neopolitan restaurant in an inlet in Posilippe which serves seafood specialties – **Dante et Beatrice**, piazza Dante 44, tel. (081) 549 94 38. Typical Neopolitan trattoria – **Bersagliera**, Borgo Marino, tel. (081) 764 60 16, faces the Castel dell'Ovo, on the small port of Santa Lucia. It is is famous, so you must reserve – **Al Poeta**, piazza Giacomo, 134, is the in restaurant for young Neopolitans.

CAFFE' – BARS

Scaturchio, piazza San Domenico Maggiore – Closed Thursday. The best place to try real traditional rum cake and *brevettata* (chocolate cake) **Bar Marino**, via dei Mille, 57 – **Caffe' Latino**, Gradini di Chiesa, 57, the best *espresso* – **Bilancione**, via

Posillipo, 238, Closed Wednesday, the best ice creams in Naples – **Gambrinus,** via Chiaia 1, is an old Neopolitan cafe, once closed down by the fascist regime and transformed into a bank, now restored in the finest tradition.

LOCAL SPECIALTIES, CRAFTS

Pintauro, via S. M. di Constantinopoli and vico d'Affuto, has made *sfogliatelle,* a specialty of the house since 1848 – **Light**, via Chiaia, 275, is a coral boutique – **Marinella**, via Chiaia, 287 is where you can find the same silk ties as Don Corleone!

Pompeii

Il Principe, piazza B. Longo 8, tel. (081) 850 55 66 – Closed Monday, August 1–15 – 60,000L. You will find only the best, the most elegant, and the most expensive here - **Zi Caterina**, via Roma – Closed Tuesday, June 28-July, more traditional and less expensive.

Caserta

Antica Locanda-Massa 1848, via Mazzini, 55, tel. (0823) 321 268 – serves regional specialties, with service in the garden in the summer. It is only about thirty kilometers from Naples. Don't miss the Palazzo Reale and the Parco-Giardino in Caserta.

CASERTA VECCHIA (10 km away) **La Castellana**, Closed Thursday - 20-50,000L – It is rustic, regional, and has a cool terrace in the summer.

Capri

CAPRI:

La Capannina, via Le Botteghe 12 b, tel. (081) 8370 732 – Closed Wednesday, November 7-March 15 – 50-75,000L. It is elegant and serves very good fish from Capri – **La Pigna**, via Roma 30, tel. (081) 837 0280 – Closed Tuesday October 15-Easter – 50-60,000L. It has been a wine bar since 1876, and is today one of the most popular restaurants on the island. It has an elegant room, a beautiful garden with lemon trees, and a view on the Bay of Naples – **Luigi**, ai Faraglioni, tel. (081) 837 0591 – Closed October-Easter – 60-80,000L. It has good cuisine, a flower-covered terrace, and a great view. Take a walk to the Faraglioni, the famous rocks across from Capri, a half an hour away on foot, or go there by boat from Marina Piccola **Pizzeria Aurora**, via Fuorlovado 18, tel. (081) 837 0181 – Closed Tuesday, December 10-March 10 – 40-50,000L. Excellent cuisine by Peppino.

ANACAPRI

Da Gelsomina, à Migliara 72, tel. (081) 837 14 99 Closed Tuesday, February 1-15. You can see the sea and the gulf from the terrace through the vineyards and the olive trees.

CRAFTS

Capri Flor, via Tragara, is a nursery. Capri will make you start dreaming about gardens, and Carthusia **Carthusia**, via Matteotti 2, will about perfumes – **Massimo Godericci** offers a large selection of pottery and fine Italian china.

Ischia

ISCHIA PONTE

Giardini Eden, via Nuova Portaromana, tel. (081) 993 9091 Closed the evening, October-April – 45,000L. Away from the hordes of tourists, come have a quiet lunch and enjoy good southern Italian cuisine in this garden full of exotic flowers – **Gennaro**, via Porto, tel 992 917, has a convivial, typical atmosphere.

ISCHIA-FORIO

La Romantica, via Marina 46, tel. 997 345 Closed Wednesday, January 40,000L. It serves seafood cuisine in an elegant classical setting.

BAGNO-LIDO PORTO-D'ISCHIA

Alberto tel. 981 259 – Closed Monday evening, November–March 40, 000L. This friendly trattoria has a veranda on the beach, regional cuisine, and good house wine by the pitcher.

Ravello

Garden, via Boccaccio 4, tel. (089) 857 226 – Closed Tuesday in the winter – 40,000L. In the summer, you can dine on the picturesque terrace with a view on the gulf.

Sorrento

O Parrucchiano Corso Italia 71, tel. (081) 878 13 21, Closed Wednesday in

the winter - 35-50,000L. It has been the "must-see" of Sorrento for more than a century now. Be sure to end your meal with a *limoncello*, the liquor of the house – **Il Glicine**, via Sant'Antonio 2, tel. (081) 877 2519 – Closed Wednesday off season, January 15 - March 1– 30-50,000L. Elegant, friendly, reservations necessary – **La Pentolaccia**, via Fuorimura 25, tel. (081) 878 5077 Closed Thursday – 35,000L. A classic restaurant in the heart of town serving traditional cuisine.

CRAFTS

Handkerchiefs, via Luigi di Maio 28 sells beautiful handkerchiefs, one of the specialties of Sorrento, monogrammed to your specifications.

Sant'Agata Sui Due Golfi

9 km from Sorrento

Don Alfonso 1890, piazza Sant'Agata, tel. (081) 878 0026 – Closed Monday off season., Tuesday, January 10–February 25 – 70-95,000L. It is the best restaurant in Campania, and in Italy, superbly located on a little hill between Sorrento and Amalfi, featuring traditional cuisine made with produce fresh from the market.

Vico Equense

Pizza A Metro Da Gigino, via Nicotera 10, tel. (081) 879 8426 – 35,000L, has a wide selection of delicious pizzas and local specialties – **San Vicenzo** in Montechiaro (3km), tel 802 8001 – Closed Wednesday in the winter.

Salerno

Vicolo della Neve, Vicolo della Neve 24, tel. (089) 225 705 – Closed Wednesday, Christmas – 30,000 L. Despite its name, it is not a pizzaria, and serves fine local traditional cuisine made with fresh produce from the grounds – **Al Fusto d'Oro**, via Fieravecchia 29, unpretentious pizzeria and seafood dishes – **La Brace**, lungomare Trieste 11, tel. 225 159 - Closed Wednesday and from 20. to 31 December.

Paestum

Nettuno, closed in the evening, Monday except July, August, Christmas – 30-50,000L. It is on the archaeological site and has a lovely dining room and terrace with a view on the temples. It is closed Mondays and Christmas.

Palinoro

Da Carmelo, in Iscia, tel. (0974) 931 138 – Closed Monday off season, October, November – 30-35,000L. It has a rustic dining room, a pretty verdant garden, and traditional cuisine with seafood specialties.

Positano

San Pietro, via Laurito 2, 2km from Positano, tel. (089) 875 455 – Dinner on the terrace perched on a rocky crag is magic. The view is sublime and the cuisine delicious – **Chez Black**, via Brigantino 19, tel. (089) 875 036 – Closed November-January – 30-45,000L is a charming place near the beach, serving pizzas, grilled fish, and spaghetti – **Da Constantino**, via Corvo 95, tel. (089) 875 738 – Closed November- December – 20,000L is 5 km from Positano, and has a marvelous view on the sea. A minibus will take you to the restaurant. Reservations are a must in the summer.

Praiano

9km from Positano

La Brace, via G. Capriglione, tel. (089) 874226 – Closed October 15-March 15, Wednesday off season. You can enjoy a superb view of Posiatno and the *faraglioni* of Capri from the terrace.

Amalfi

Il Tari', via Capuano, tel. (089) 871 832 – Closed Tuesday, Nov. – 20,000L. Good seafood specialties – **Da Gemma**, via Cavalieri di Malta, tel. (089) 871 345 – Closed Tuesday,

Jan. 15–Feb. 15 – 35-45,000L. An old restaurant where you can have deli-

cious Neopolitan specialties such as *genovese*, along with good regional wines – **La Caravella**, via M. Camera, tel/. (089) 871 029, Closed Tuesday and Nov. Here is another classic Amalfi address. Reservations are required.

EMILIA ROMAGNA

Bologna

I Carracci, via Manzoni 2, tel. (051) 270 815 – Closed Sunday, August – 60-80,000L. It features fine cuisine for elegant suppers – **Il Battibecco**, via Battibecco 4, tel. (051) 223 298 – Closed Sunday between Christmas and New Year's Day, August 10-20 – 60-90,000L. It has delicious risottos, spaghetti with clams, and roast beef pie – **Il Bitone**, via Emilia Levante 111, tel. (051) 546 110 – Closed Monday, Tuesday, August – 55,000L. The favorite restaurant of the Bolognese. There is a large garden where you can have tea in the summer – **Diana**, via Indipendenza 24, tel. (051) 231 302 – Closed Monday, August – 50,000 L. A traditional restaurant with classic cuisine – **Rodrigo**, via della Zecca 2-h tel 220 445 – Closed Sunday, August 4–24. Excelent – **Rosteria Da Luciano**, via Nazario Sauro 19, tel. (051) 231 249. Closed Tuesday evening, Wednesday, August, Christmas and New Year – 35-80,000 L. One of the best restaurants in Bologna, reservation – **Torre de' Galluzzi'**, corte de' Galluzzi 5-A, tel. (051) 267 638. Located inside the old tower, fine meat and fish dishes.

Anna Maria, via delle Belle Arti 17, tel. (051) 266 894 Closed Monday in

August - 45 000 L **Rostaria Antico Brunetti**, via Caduti di Cefalonia 5, tel. (051) 234 441 – 40,000L. A very old restaurant with delicious pasta, and good *lambrusco* – **Antica Trattoria del Cacciatore**, Casteldebole, tel. (051) 564 203 Closed Monday, August, January – 50,000 L. Located

7km west of Bologna, it is a rustic but very chic trattoria, with fine cuisine.

LOCAL SPECIALTIES

Bottega del vino Olindo Faccioli, large selection of wines. Among Emilian wines, try the young and bubbly *Lambrusco,* and the *Sangiovese* – **Brini**, via Ugo Bassi, 19-C, is great for its wide selection of cheeses, and of course the famous *parmigano regiano* - **Salsamenteria Tamburini**, via Caprarie 1, features ham from Parma, *mortadelle* and *culatello*, reputed to be the best Italian salami – **Casa della Sfoglia**, via Rialto 4. Here they make traditional Bolognese pasta and tagliatelles, invented, legend has it, for the wedding of Lucrecia Borgia and the Duke of Ferrara in 1487.

Imola

30km from Bologna

San Domenico, via Sacchi 1, tel. (0542) 29 000 – Closed Monday, January 1-13, July, August 1–22 – 90-130,000L. Gourmets from all over the world come here for the San Domenico pilgrimage as well as for this restaurant's ingenious interpretation of regional Italian cuisine.

Brisighella

La Grotta, via Metelli 1, tel. (0546) 81 829 – Closed Tuesday, January, June 1–15 – 30-55,000L. La Grotta shares the gastronomic honors of this very pretty little town with **Gigiolé**, piazza Carducci 5, tel. (0546) 81 209, Closed February, July 1–15. Several gest rooms.

Ferrara

Grotta Azzurra, piazza Sacrati 43, tel. (0532) 209 152 – Closed Wednesday, Sunday evenings, January 2-10, August 1-15 – 40,000L. The decor is Mediterranean, but the cuisine is traditional northern Italian, with some Emilian specialties – **Vecchia Chitarra**, via Ravenna 13, tel. (0532) 62 204 – Closed Tuesday, August 1–15 – 30,000L. Regional specialties and home made pasta – **La Provvidenza**, corso Ercole I d'Este 92, tel. (0532) 205 187 – Closed Monday, August – 40-60,000L. The interior resembles a farmhouse with a little garden full of regular customers. You will need a reservation.

Quel Fantastico Giovedi, via Castelnuovo 9, tel. (0532) 76 05 70. Closed Wednesday, June20-July 20 and 10 days on January - Menu : 25 000 L (lunch), 45 000 L (diner), reservation

Enoteca Al Brindisi, via degli Adelardi II. The Guinness Book of World Records says this is the oldest tavern in the world. Benvenuto Cellini, the Titien was said to have frequented this "Hostaria del Chinchiolino". There are wine tastings and wine is also sold here.

Argenta

34km from Ferrara

Il Trigabolo, piazza Garibaldi 4, tel. (0532) 804 121 – Closed Sunday evening, Monday – 100-130,000L. A good place to enjoy fine cuisine in Emilia-Romagna.

Modena

Fini, rua Frati Minori 54, tel. (059) 223 314 – Closed Monday, Tuesday, August, Christmas – 60-75,000L. Fini's *tortellini* and *zamponi* are almost as famous as the Ferraris of Modena.

Bianca, via Spaccini 24, tel.(059) 311 524 – Closed Saturday at noon, Sunday, August, Christmas holidays – 45-65,000L. You will like this trattoria and the authentic cuisine served here.

Hostaria Giusti, vivolo Squallore 46, tel (059) 222 553 – Open only at noon, diner only on request – Closed Sunday, Monday, November, December, August – 50,000 L. A famous salumeria, Emilian specialties.

Ravenna

Tre Spade, via Faentina 136, tel. (0544) 500 5222 – Closed Sunday nights, Monday – 55,000L. It features Italian cuisine from different provinces in a pretty decor – **Al Gallo**, via Maggiore 87 tel 213 775 - Closed Monday nights, Tuesday, Christmas, Easter. Reservation.

La Gardèla, via Ponte Marino 3, tel. (0544) 217 147 – Closed Thursday, August 10-25. It serves savory cuisine **Enoteca Ca' de Ven**, via Ricci 24 – Closed Monday. This wine bar in an old palace offers wine tasting and sales, and light meals.

Parma

Il Cortile, borgo Paglia 3, tel. 285 779. Closed Sunday, Monday noon, August 1–22 – 30-40,000L. Reservations are recommended – **Gallo d'Oro**, Borgo della Salina 3, tel. (0521) 208 846. Closed Sunday A tavern. Try their famous *culatello de Parme, maltaglioti,* and *tortellini.* **La Greppia**, via Garibaldi 39, tel. (0521) 233 686 – Closed Monday, Tuesday, July – 50-70,000 L. Near the Opera, and has very good Italian cuisine and a cheery decor. Reservations are recommended –

L'Angiol d'Or, vicolo Scutellari 1, tel. (0521) 282 632 – Closed Sunday,

Christmas, August 14-15, January 10–20. At the corner of the piazza del Duomo – You can enjoy savory cuisine and the illuminated baptistry at night in this elegant restaurant – 65,000L – **Croce di Malta**, Borgo Palmia, tel. 235 643. A small

restaurant with innovative cuisine and a terrace in the summer – **Vecchio Molinetto,** viale Milazzo 39, tel 526 72. Traditional trattoria - **La Filoma**, via XX Marzo 15, tel. (0521) 234 269 – Closed Sunday, August – 40-50,000L. One of our favorites with an intimate atmosphe-

re and personalized regional cuisine

AROUND PARMA

Sacca di Colorno, 15km from Parma **Le Stendhal**, tel. (0521) 815 493 - Closed Tuesday, January 1-15, July 20-August 10. If you are following the footsteps of Fabrice del Dongo, try the Stendhal.

Noceto, 14km from Parma : **Aquila Romana**, via Gramsci 6, tel. (0521)

62 398, Closed Monday, Tuesday, 15 July 15-August 15, 30-50,000L. An old postal inn, famous for its regional specialties inspired by old recipes.

Busseto, 35km from Parma, **Ugo** via Mozart 3. Country atmosphere.

Polesine Parmense, Santa Franca 6km from Busseto**: Da Colombo**, tel. (0524) 98 114 – Closed Monday evening, Tuesday, January, July 20–August 10 - 40,000 L. It is famous, so you'd better reserve.

Zibello, 10km from Busseto: **Trattoria La Buca**, tel. (0524) 99 214, Closed Monday evening, Tuesday, July 1-15 45,000 L. It is very popular, so you will need a reservation.

Berceto, 50km from Parma **Da Rino**, piazza Micheli 11 tel. (525) 64 306 – Closed Monday, December 20-February 15 – 30-60,000L. The masters of the mushroom in season, and of ravioli of all sorts year round.

Reggio nell'Emilia

5 Pini-da-Pelati, viale Martiri di Cervarolo 46, tel. (0522) 5536 63 – Closed Tuesday evening, Wednesday, August 1-20 – 45-70,000L – **La Zucca**, piazza Fontanesi 1/L, tel. 437 222 – Closed Sunday, January 5-12, August – **Enoteca Il Pozzo**, viale Allegri 6/A. It has wine tasting and sales, and a restaurant with garden.

Sant'Arcangelo di Romagna, **Zaghini**, piazza Gramsci – Closed Monday, 30,000L.

LATIUM ABRUZZI

Roma / Rome

near Villa Borghèse

Il Caminetto, viale Parioli 89, tel. (06) 808 3946 – Closed Thursday, August – 50,000L. Success has not spoiled the quality of this restaurant.

near Pantheon

La Campana, vicolo della Campana 18, tel. (06) 686 7820 – Closed Monday, August – 45-55,000 L. One of the oldest, if not the oldest trattoria of the capital, with good Roman cuisine and good house wine – **Il Bacaro**, via degli Spagnoli 27. Près du Panthéon, tel. (06) 686 4110 – Closed Sunday – 60,000L. near the Pantheon and has an elegant bistro decor – **L'Eau Vive**, via Monterone 85, tel. (06) 688 01 095 Closed Sunday, August 10-20 – 50-70,000L. Missionary sisters serve their specialties every day (near the Pantheon) – **La Rosetta**, via della Rosetta 9, tel. (06) 686 1002 – Closed Saturday noon, Sunday, August – 80-100,000L (near the Pantheon) is well known for its fish specialties – **Papa' Giovanni**, via dei Sediari 4, tel. (06) 686 1002 – Closed Sunday, August – 80,000 L. Near Palazzo Madama and Pantheon.

«Nouvelle cuisine» – **Trattoria al Panthéon,** vial del Panthéon 55, tél. (06) 679 27 88.

Near Piazza di Spagna

Nino, via Borgognona 11, tel. (06) 679 5676 – Closed Sunday – 50,000L. Near the stairs of the Piazza di Spagna, it is frequented by local artists and writers who come here for Tuscan specialties and the "Mont Blanc", a house dessert. – **Osteria Margutta**, via Margutta 82, tel. (06) 679 8190 – Closed Sunday – 40,000L. Friendly trattoria with a nice atmosphere, very close to the Piazza di Spagnanice, closed Sundays. There are many galleries and antique shops on this street where Fellini used to live – **Da Mario**, via delle Vite, tel. (06) 678 38 18 – Closed Sunday and August - 50,000 L - Tuscany cooking – **Alfredo l'Originale**, piazza Augusto Imperatore 30, tel. (06) 678 10 72. Typical, reservation.

Near Piazza Navona

Pino e Dino, piazza di Montevecchio 22, tel. (06) 686 1319 Closed Monday, August – 70,000L. Is an intimate place near the Piazza Navona, hidden behind heavy curtains on this Renaissance square so dear to Raphael and Bramante, where Lucrecia Borgia fomented numerous intrigues. Reservations are necessary **Majella**, 45 piazza Sant'Appolinare 45, tel. (06) 65 64 174, Closed Sunday. The restaurant is in a beautiful old house, and features – **Tre Scalini**, Close to the Piazza Navona and facing the Bernin fountain, it is a great place for breakfast, with delicious *tartuffo,* a typically Italian atmosphere and family-style cuisine.

Near Piazza di Trevi

Al Moro, vic. delle Bollette 13, tel. (06) 67 83 495 – Typically Italian trattoria. Reservation.

Near Piazza del Campidoglio and Teatro di Marcello

Vecchia Roma, Via della tribuna di Campitelli, tel. (06) 686 46 04 – Closed Wednesday, August 10-25 – 50-60,000 L. Roman specialties and fish – **Da Giggetto**, via del Portico d'Ottavia 21/a, tel. (06) 686 11 05. Typical - Patio.

Neat Terme di Caracalla

Checcino dal 1887, Via Monte Testaccio 30, tel. (06) 574 38 16 – Closed Sunday evening, Monday,

August, Christmas - 60-80,000 L. Specialtie: *coda alla vacinara.*,

Near Janicule

Antica Pesa via Garibaldi 8, tel. (06) 58 09 236 - Closed Sunday –

Specialtie: *rittico di pastasciutta.*

Near Piazza Barberini

I Giardino, 29 via Zucchelli, Closed Monday. near the Piazza Barberini is one of the best trattorias in town, with low prices – **La Carbonara**, piazza Campo dei Fiori, tel. (06) 68 64 783, Closed Tuesday. One of the most beautiful market places in Rome, featuring fish specialties – **El Tartufo**, vicolo Sciarra, tel. (06) 678 02 26 – Closed Sunday. An authentic place. The *Navone* meal is a true delight.

Dinners in the Trastevere

Romolo, via di Porta Settimania, tel. (06) 581 8284 – Closed Monday, August. Dine by candlelight in the garden Raphael used to visit. The interior is also has charm and atmosphere – **Sabatini I**, piazza Santa Maria in Trastevere 10, tel. (06) 581 2026 – Closed Wednesday and two-weeks in August – 60,000L. It is the most famous and popular restaurant in the Trastevere. If it is full, you can always try the **Sabatini II**, vicolo di Santa Maria in Trastevere 18, tel. (06) 581 8307 – **Checco er Carettiere**, via Benedetta 10, tel. (06) 581 70 18 – Closed Sunday evening, Monday, August, Christmas – 50-75,000 L – An osteria typical of the Trastevere with a decor reminiscent of the time when the *carettieri* came here, and very good Roman cuisine with old recipes – **La Tana de Noiantri**, via della Paglia 13, Closed Tuesday. friendly and inexpensive, with simple cuisine and tables on the sidewalk in the summer – **Alberto Ciarla**, piazza San Cosimato, tel (06) 581 86 68 – Closed at noon, Sunday, 1-15 August, 1-13 January – 50-95,000L. Reservation

PIZZERIAS

Pizzeria Berninetta, via Pietro Cavallini 14, tel. (06) 360 3895 – Closed Monday, August, open only in the evening – 25,000L is also very popular, a good place for pizza, *crostini,* and pasta – **Pizzeria Da Fieramosca ar Fosso**, piazza de Mercanti 3, tel. (06) 589 0289 – Closed Sunday – open only in the evening – 20-30,000L. The best pizzeria in the Trastevere – **Pizzeria San Marco**, via Taano 29, tel. (06) 687 8494 – Closed Wednesday, August – 20,000L. It has fine, crisp Roman pizza and a clientele of Roman yuppies who won't think twice about having champagne with their pizza. There is a good selection of wines too – **Ivo a Trastevere**, via di San Francesco a Ripa 150. Delicious pizzas in a tiny room.

CAFFE' – BARS

near the piazza Navona

Tre Scalini, piazza Navona, is across from the Bernin fountain, and has the

best *granita di caffe* and *tartufo*. **Antico Caffe' della Pace**, via della Pace 6, has a turn of the century artistic atmosphere, and is frequented in the evening by a hip intellectual crowd – **Enoteca Navona**, piazza Navona offers wine tasting and *crostini*.

near the via Veneto : **Gran Caffe' Doney**, via Veneto 39, was born in Florence in 1822, moved to Rome in 1884 and to the Via Veneto in 1946. Coctails, salads, and pastries are served here – **Harry's Bar**, via Veneto 148. Like its brothers, it is chic and elegant.

near the piazza del Popolo : **Casina Valadier**, Pincio, Villa Borghese. The chic terrace restaurant is a great place to enjoy a superb view at sunset, good cocktails and fine ice cream when the weather gets warm – **Caffe' Rosati**, piazza del Popolo, serves sandwiches and pastries. The large terrace has been completely overrun.

near the piazza di Spagna

Caffe' Greco, via Conditi 86. Casanova mentioned this place in his memoirs, and Stendhal, Goethe, and D'Annunzio have all been here. You can have small sandwhiches in a nice Napolean III-style decor. Try the *paradiso,* a house specialty – **Babington**, on the Piazza di Spagna, this is a something of a local institution for having English tea – **Le Cornacchie**, piazza Rondanini. This place has style, an upbeat friendly atmosphere, and family-style cuisine.

THE BEST CAPPUCCINO: **Caffe' San Eustachio**, piazza San Eustachio **La Tazza d'Oro**, via degli Orfani, near the piazza del Pantheon.

THE BEST GELATI: **Giolitti**, Offici del Vicario 40.

THE OLDEST BAKERY IN ROME: **Valzani**, via del Moro 37.

SHOPPING

Gamarelli, via Santa Chiara 34 - Closed Saturday, sells religious accessories. Lay people come here to buy their famous socks, violet for bishops, and red for cardinals – **La Stelletta**, via delle Stelletta 4, is great for costme jewelry – **Aldo Fefe**, via delle Stelleta 20b. Closed Saturday, sells beautiful cardboard boxes – **Papirus**, via Capo le case, has a large selection of elegant stationery – **Libreria antiquaria Cascianelli**, largo Febo 14, is specialized in old and modern works on Rome, across from the Hotel Raphaël **Limentani**, via Portico d'Ottavia 25 is in the old ghetto, in a basement, and offers a wide selection of household linens.– **Ai Monasteri**, corso Rinascimento 72, sells liquors, elixirs, and other products produced by monastic orders, in a beautiful Neo-Gothic decor – **Trimani Wine Bar,** via Cernaia 37-B is a good place for tasting and buying fine Italian food products.

Antique Shops via del Babbuino, via dei Coronari, in the Corso Emanuele distric.

NEARBY ROMA

Le Cinque Statue, via Quintilio Varo 1, tel. (0774) 20 366 – Stop in while visiting the Villa d'Este gardens in Tivoli – **Sibella**, via della Sibella 50, tel. (0774) 20281 – 45,000L. has the same beautiful interior and garden which Chateaubriand admired in 1803.

Villa Adriana

Albergo Ristorante Adriano, , tel. (0774) 382 235 – Closed Sunday evening –has terra cotta walls, Corinthian columns decorating the interior, and a beautiful shady garden in the summer, a nice place to relax after visiting Hadrian's villa.

Frascati, 22km from Roma

Cacciani, via Armando Diaz 13, tel. (06) 9420 378 – Closed Monday, January 7-17, August 17-27– 50,000L. Thirty years of great Roman cooking, delicious house wine and a beautiful terrace in the summer make this place well worth the trip – **Cantina Comandini**, via E. Filiberto – Closed Sunday. A good place to buy wine and has a nice wine bar – **Pasticceria Renato Purificato**, piazza del Mercato or **Bar degli Specchi** , via Battisti 3, Try the lady-shaped *biscottini*. – **Villa Simone**, via Toricella 2 at Monteporzio Catone. You will find the best *Frascati* of the region and very good olive oil here.

Castel Gandolfo, 22km from Roma

Sor Campana, corso della Repubblica – Closed Monday, is one of the oldest restaurants of the region

Anagni

Del Gallo, Via V. Emanuele 164, tel. (0775) 727 309, has a long family tradition of fine regional cuisine.

L'Aquila

Tre Marie, via Tre Marie, tel. (0862) 413 191 – Closed Sunday evening, Monday. This historical monument has a superb decor, very good cuisine, and a delicious dessert "Tre

Marie". **Ernesto,** (Ai benefattori del Grillo), piazza palazzo 22, tel. (0862) 2 10 94, closed Sunday and Monday, August; After having *Sagnarelle alla pastora, pastasciutta,* or *bigolo al torchio*, be sure to visit the two "botti a camera", superb rooms whe re wine is stored.

Isola di Ponza

Da Mimi, Terrazza Mari, via dietro la Chiesa, tel. (0771) 80 338 – 50,000L, is one of the best restaurants on the island – **Eéa**, via Umberto 1 and **La Kambusa**, via Banchina Nuova 15, serve regional cuisine.

Viterbo

Il Grottino, via della Cava 7, tel. (0761) 308 188 – Closed Tuesday, June 20-July 10 – 50,000L.– **Aquilanti**, La Quercia, 3km, tel.

(0761) 341 701 - Closed Sunday evening, Tuesday, August 1-20 – 50,000L. You will need a reservation for this classic regional restaurant with a beautiful "Etruscan room" among the other more modern ones.

L I G U R I A

San Remo

Da Giannino, lungomare Trento e Trieste 23, tel. (0184) 504 014 – Closed Sunday evening, Monday, May 15-31 – 80-90,000L. This is the chic gourmet restaurant of the town – Pao**lo e Barbara**, via Roma, 47, tel. (0184) 53 16 53 - Closed Wednesday, December-15-January-6, 10 days in June and in July - 80-100 000 L – **Pesce d'oro**, corso Cavalotti 300, tel. (0184) 576 332 – Closed February 15-March 15, Monday – 65,000L. It has some of the best food on the Italian Riviera – **Osteria del Marinaio da Carluccio**, via Gaudio 28, tel. (0184) 501 919 – Closed Monday, October, December – 70-90,000L. This very small osteria serves excellent seafood cuisine to a distinguished clientele. Reservations are a must.

Cervo

35km from San Remo

San Giorgio, via Volta 19, tel. (0183) 400 175 – Closed Tuesday, Christmas vacation – 50-60,000L. This adorable little restaurant serves seafood *antipasti* , excellent cuts of meat, and *zabaione*.

Savona

Vino e Farinata, Via Pia 15 R. 20 000 L - Popular, typical, friendly.

Genova

Genova / Genoa

Gran Gotto, via Fiume 11r, tel. (010) 564 344 – Closed Saturday noon, Sunday, August – 60-80,000L. This is the chic restaurant of the town with an elegant decor and very good classic Ligurian cuisine – **Giacomo**, Corso Italia, tel. (010) 369 67 – Closed Sunday, August – 65-80,000L. It is an elegant place with a beautiful view on the sea – **Il Cucciolo**, viale Sauli 33, tel. (010) 546 470 – Closed Monday, August – 40-50,000L, has great Tucsan cuisine. If you don't know your way around town, you'd better come by taxi.

Da Walter, vico Colasanto 2 rosso,

tel. (010) 290 524 - ouvert at noon every day and all the Saturday night – Closed Sunday, Christhmas, August - 40 000 L.

Antica Osteria el Bai, via Quarto 12, Quarto dei Mille, tel. (010)387 478 - Closed Monday, January 10-20, August 1-20 - 55-90 000 L.

SAN CIPRIANO

Ferrando, in on the hill tel. (010) 75 19 25 – Closed Sunday, Monday and Wednesday evening. Specialties: mushroom dishes.

San Desiderio

Bruxaboschi, via Mignone 8 - Sundat night, Monday, Christmas, August - 50 000 L.
Specialties: *picaggia al pesto antico, frito misto, cuculli.*

CAFFE' IN GENOVA

Caffe' Mangina, via Roma 91, Closed Monday. You can admire the equestrian statue of Victor Emmanuel II on Corvetto Square from this elegant cafe – **Caffe' Klainguti**, piazza Soziglia 98. This is one of Italy's historical cafés.

Finale Ligure

Osteria della Briga, altipiano delle Marie, tel. (019) 698 579 – Closed Tuesday, Wednesday – 20-25,000L. It has a rustic family atmosphere, and memorable *lasagne alle ortiche* and *grappe "al latte"* .

Rapallo

Da Monique, lungomare Vittorio Veneto 6, tel. (0185) 50 541 – Closed Tuesday, February – 45-50,000L. It is the most famous seafood restaurant of the port – **U Giancu**, in San Massimo 3km, tel. (0185) 260 505 – Closed Wednesday, Thursday noon, October 4-13, November 13-December 6 – 30,000L. Nice country atmosphere, and service on the terrace in the summer.

Santa Margherita Ligure

Trattoria Cesarina, via Mameli 2, tel. (0185) 286 059 – Closed Wednesday, December – 85,000L, is one of the better restaurants on the Ligurian coast, with excellent service **Trattoria l'Ancora**, via Maragliano 7, tel. (0185) 280 559 – Closed Monday, January, February. serves a mostly local clientele. Marinated spaghetti is a house specialty.

Portofino

Il Pistoforo, Molo Umberto 1, tel. (0185) 269 037 – Closed Tuesday, Wednesday noon, January, February – 70-100,000L. It serves fish soup, fish stew, and grilled fish in the shade of the centuries-old *pistoforum.* - **Puny**, piazza M. Olivetta 7, tel. (0185) 269 037 – Closed

Thursday – 45-70,000L. It is a classic Portofino restaurant, with a nautical decor and a beautiful view of the port **Delfino**, piazza M. dell' Olivetta 40, tel. (0185) 269 081 – Closed Thursday, November, December 75 000L. One of the most stylish restaurants of this port town - **Da Ü Batti**, vico Nuovo 17, tel. (0185) 269 379, is a small fish trattoria. Reservations are a must – **Splendido Restaurant,** tel. (0185) 269 551 closed from November to April. Fine Italian cuisine on an enchanting site with a superb view – **Tripoli,** piazza M. Olivetta 1 - Typical trattoria.

CAFFE' – BARS

Bar Sole, piazza Olivetta. People come here for sandwiches, cocktails, to see and be seen – **Caffe' Excelsior**, piazza M. Olivetta. A good place to drink expresso and read the morning paper.

Sestri Levante

El Pescador, via Pilade Queirolo 1, tel. (0185) 41 491 - Closed Tuesday, frm December 15 to March 1st– Specialties: fish – **San Marco**, port, tel. (0185) 41 459 - Closed Wednesday except August, February 1st-15 November - 40-60 000 L. Fish – **Fiammenghilla Fieschi**, at Erigox, Riva Trigoso 2 km via Pestella 6, tel. (0185) 481 041 – Closed Monday at noon off season – 50-85,000L. It has very good traditional cuisine and a pretty garden

Portovenere

La Taverna del Corsaro, lungomare Doria 102, tel. (0187) 790 622 – Closed Tuesday, November, June 1-22 – 60,000L. There is a very nice view of the island of Palmaria from the dining room. The cusisne is based on fish fresh and produce from the market as well as local specialties.

LOMBARDY

Milano / Milan

Historical center

Peck, via Victor Hugo 4, tel. (02) 876 774 Closed Sunday, January 1-10, July 1-10- 60,000L .It features traditional and creative cuisine, with a snack bar at street level, and the restaurant in the basement – **Trattoria Milanese**, via Santa Marta 11 tel. (02) 864 519 91 – Closed

Tuesday, it is true to tradition – **Trattoria Bagutta**, via Bagutta 14, tel. (02) 7600 27 67 – Closed Sunday, August, Christmas holidays 60-100,000L. The sequential rooms are decorated with characatures. This is undoubtedly the most famous trattoria in town (a litterary award is given here every year). Although the cuisine is nothing to write home about, the decor is nonetheless attractive.– **Papper Moon,** via Bagutta 1, (near Via Spiga et Montenapo-leone), tél. (02) 76 02 22 97. A very good adress – 45 000 L and **Moon Fish** via Bagutta 1, tel. (02) 76 00 57 80 –Closed Sunday - **Don Lisander,** via Manzoni 12, tel. (02) 7602 0130 – 68-105 000L – Closed Saturday evening and Sunday. The restaurant is especially nice in the summer, as it serves fine cuisine to its upscale clientele on a very pleasant canvas-covered terrace with an Italian-style decor and flowering plants. You will need a reservation – **Franco il Contadino**, via Fiori Chiari 20, tel. (02) 8646 3446 – Closed Tuesday, Wednesday at noon, July – 45-60,000L. It has a nice atmosphere and is frequented by artists. It is open Sundays – **Boeucc**, piazza Belgioioso 2, tel. (02) 760 20224, Closed Saturday, Sunday at noon, Christmas holidays, August. 60-80,000L. Reservations are necessary for this chic restaurant, where you can dine on the terrace as soon as the weather permits.

DOPO SCALA

Le Santa Lucia, via San Pietro

all'orto 3, tel. (02) 760 23155. – **Biffi Scala,** piazza della Scala, tel. (02) 86 66 51, closed Sunday and Chrismas, 10.-20 August. - **Don Carlos,** Don Carlos is the restaurant at the superb Grand Hotel et de Milan where Verdi spent his last days. The atmosphere is

appropriately theatrical.

Porta Romana, Corso Vittoria

Giannino, via Amatore Sciesa 8, tel. (02) 551 955 82 – Closed Sunday, August – 60-100,000L. You will enjoy some of the finest gourmet cuisine in Lombardy here in this classic chic Milanese restaurant – **Masuelli San Marco,** viale Umbria, tel. 551 841 38, Closed Sunday, Monday noon, Christmas holidays, August 15-September 15 – 50 000 L

Near centro direzionale

Rigolo, largo Treves angle via Solferino, tel. (02) 8646 3220 – Closed Monday, August 30-50,000L. It is in the Brera quarter, and is frequented by a stylish crowd of regulars. Another plus, it is open Sundays – **Trattoria della Pesa**, via Pasubio, tel. (02) 65 55 74. Closed Sunday, August, 70;000L. The four

G. Armani's best adresses to taste the *risotto all'osso buco*

Alla Cucina delle Langhe, corso Como, 6, tel. (02) 6 55 42 79. Closed Sunday, three weeks in July,

Christmas - 60,000 L. Typical Piemontian cuisine – **La Tana del Lupo**, viale Vittorio Veneto, 30, tel. (02) 6 59 90 06 - Open only for the dinner, closed Sunday, August - 40-65 000 L. Specialties from Trentino

and Veneto country.

Navigli

Osteria del Binari, via Tortona 1, tel. (02) 8940 9428 – Closed at noon, Sunday, August 10-20 – 50 000L. This is an atmosphere restaurant, with a very convivial dining room, a very shady garden, and somewhat traditional cuisine

Fiera -Sempione

Alfredo Gran San Bernardo via Borghese 14 tel. (02) 331 90 00, closed Christmas, August, Sunday, Saturday in June and July - 65-99,000L – **Torre di Pisa**, via Fiori Chiari 21, tel. (02) 874 877 – Closed Sunday – 40-50,000L. It is a Tuscan restaurant frequented by designers and people from the fashion industry.

CAFFE' – BARS

Cova, via Montenapoleone 8, is the most elegant café in Milan, and serves teas, coffee, pastries, champagne, and cocktails – **Pozzi**, piazza Cantore 4, glacier. features a wide assortment of ice cream and sherbert – **Pasticceria Marchesi**, via santa Maria alla Porta, 1. This is a good place for a coffee and an Italian croissant with jelly. They have made the best holiday pastries, (Panattone at Chrismas and Colombe at Easter) since 1824.- **Bar del Comparino**, the original Frescos and Liberty-style mosaics have recently been restored in this historical landmark, the former haunt of Toscanini, Verdi, and Carrà – **Peck,** via Spadari 9 – **Sant Ambrœus**, corso Matteoti 7, spécialité l'Ambrogitto, is the most elegant tearoom in Milan, but there is also **Biffi**, corso Magenta 87, **Taveggia**, via Visconti di Modrone 2, **Galli**, corso di Porta Romana 2 which has delicious candied chestnuts.

SHOPPING

Casa del formaggio, via Speronari 3, has a wide asssortment of cheeses from all over Italy – **Peck**, via Spadari 9, is still the finest gourmet food store in Milano – **La Fungheria di Bernardi**, viale Abruzzi 93, has a wonderful variety of fresh and canned mushrooms – **Enoteca Cotti**, via Solferino 32 – **Memphis Design** for Ettore Sottsass' creations – **De Padova** corso Venezia 14, modern furniture by Vico Magistretti and Gae Aulenti – **High Tech**, piazza 25 Aprile 14 - **Pratesi**, via Montenapoleone 27, supplies the finest house linen – **Libreria Rizzoli,** galleria Vittorio Emanuele 79, has rare French publications and art books - **Libreria Hoepli**, via Hoepli 5, has modern works, manuscripts, and authentic signatured drawings.

Bergamo

Lio Pellegrini, via San Tomaso 47, tel. (035) 247 813 – Closed Monday, Tuesday at noon, January 4-11, August 2-24 – 50-90,000L. Resevation advised – **Taverna del Colleoni**, piazza Vecchia 7, tel. (035) 232 596 – Closed Monday, August – 50-70,000L. It serves regional cuisine in a Renaissance decor. The *tagliatelle* and the *filetto alla Colleoni* are house specialties. There is also **Il Gourmet**, via San Vigilio, 1 tel. (035) 437 30 04 - Closed Tuesday, January 1-6 – 40-60,000L.- **La Marianna**, largo Colle Aperto 2/4, tel. (035) 237 027 - closed Monday, from January 1 to 14. You can dine on a beautiful flower-covered terrace when the weather is nice.

Brescia

La Sosta, via San Martino della Battaglia 20, tel. (030) 295 603 – Closed Monday, August – 50-80,000L. The handsome 17th century building and fine cuisine make it worth stopping off here for a meal.

Cremona

Ceresole, via Ceresole 4, tel. (0372) 23 322 – Closed Sunday evening, Monday, January, August – 60-80,000L. It is considered to be something of an institution in this town famous for its violins. If you are interested, you can visit the Antonio Strativari Museum – **Antica Trattoria del Cigno**, via del Cigno 7, tel. (0372) 21 361 – Closed Sunday, January, July 20- October 4 30,000L. In the shadow of the Torrazzo, this old trattoria is the favorite of the inhabitants of Cremona .

Mantova / Mantua

San Gervasio, via San Gervasio 13, tel. (0376) 323 873 - Closed Wednesday, August 12-31 – 40-70,000L - **Cento Rampini**, piazza .delle Erbe, tel. (0376) 366 349. It is nicely located under the portico of the Palazzo Comunale, and has service on the terrace – **L'Aquila Nigra**, vicolo Bonacolsi 4, tel. (0376) 327 180. Closed Sunday, Monday, Christmas, August, 45,000L. It is famous for its cuisine, which you will enjoy in a beautiful decor of frescos in a former monastery

CAFFE'

Caravatti, from 1865 in the piazza delle Erbe. Specialties: la *Sbrizolona*.

Pavia

Antica Trattoria Ferrari da Tino, via del Mille 111, tel. (0382) 310 33 – Closed Sunday evening, Monday, August – 35-70,000L. This traditional country trattoria serves savory cuisine.

Certosa di Pavia

Vecchio Mulino, via al Monumento 5, tel. (0382) 925 894 - Closed Sunday evening, Monday, January 1-10, August 1-20 – 60-80,000L. This is a good place to dine when visiting the famous monastery. Be sure to make a reservation- **Chalet della Certosa**, opposite the Certosa - Closed Monday, January.11-24

Iseo

Il Volto, via Mirolte 2, tel. (030) 98 14 62 - Closed Wednesday, Friday at noon, July 1-15 - 60,000 L.

MARCHE

Ancona

Passetto, piazza IV Novembre, tel. (071) 33 214 – Closed Sunday night, Monday, August 10-25 – 55-70,000 L. There is a nice view of the Adriatic from the terrace which is open in the summer – **Osteria Teatro Strabacco**, via Oberdan 2, tel. (071) 542 13 - Closed Monday, May - 40,000 L.

Pesaro

Da Teresa, viale Treste 180, tel. (0721) 30 096 – Closed Monday, November – 60,000L. The restaurant serves fine cuisine in an elegant setting with a view of the sea.

Ascoli Piceno

Gallo d'Oro Corso V. Emanuele 13, tel. (0736) 535 20 – Closed Monday, August. Regional dishes are served in three modern rooms near the Duomo. Specialties: *pollo alla diavola*, fish, truffles – **Tornassaco,** piazza del Popolo 36, tel. (0736) 25 41 51 - Closed Friday, July - 40-50,000 L.

CAFFE'

Caffe' Meleni, piazza del Popolo. Local pastries. Sartre and Hemingway used to come here.

Urbino

I nuovo Coppiere, via Porta Maja 20, tel. (0722) 320 092 – Closed Wednesday, February – 30,000 L. regional specialties – **Self-Service Franco**, via de Possio – Closed Sunday – 15,000 L. Located near the museum, it has reasonable prices – **Vanda**, Castel Cavallino, tel. (0722) 34 91 17 - Closed Wednesday, December 22-January 4 and July 8-21 - 30-50,000 L – **Nené**, via Crocicchio, tel. (0722) 29 96 - Closed Monday, January 7-26 - 20-35,000 L – **Vecchia Urbino**, via dei Vasari 3, tel. (0722) 4447, Closed Tuesday off season – 40-60,000 L. It serves regional cuisine, (the *formaggio di fossa* is remarkable) in a pleasant room in the Viviani Palace.

UMBRIA

Perugia

Osteria del Bartolo, via Bartolo 30, tel. (075) 573 15 61 – Closed Sunday, January 7-15, July 25-August 7 – 60,000L. Very good home-style cuisine and old Umbrian dishes – **La Taverna**, via delle Streghe 8, tel. (075) 572 41 28 – Closed Monday – 40,000L. Country cuisine in a large room with a vaulted ceiling – **Del Sole**, via delle Rupe 1, tel. (075) 65 031 – Closed Monday, December 23-January 10– 35,000L. A beautiful old room with a vaulted ceiling and service on the panoramic terrace in the summer.

CAFFE' – BARS

Pasticceria Sandri, corso Vannucci

32, for pastry buffs – **Caffe' del Cambio**, corso Vannucci 29. It can get pretty crowded in this student cafe.

Assisi

Buca di San Francesco, via Brizi 1, tel. (075) 812 204 – Closed Monday, February, July – 30,000L. It serves traditional Umbrian cuisine in a Medieval palace with a pretty garden in the summer – **Medio Evo**, via Arco del Priori 4, tel. (075) 81 3068 Closed Wednesday, January, July – 45,000L. It has beautiful architecture and meticulously fine cuisine – **La Fortezza**, Vic. Fortezza 2-B, tel. (075) 812 418 – Closed Thursday – 30,000L. Some vestiges of the ruins of the typical Roman house it was built on remain. The cuisine is Umbrian-style.

Spello

Il Cacciatore, via Giulia 42 – Closed Monday, tél. (July 6-20, 35,000L. Pleasant trattoria with a beautiful terrace – **Il Molino**, piazza Matteotti – Closed Tuesday.

Spoleto

Il Tartufo, piazza Garibaldi 24, tel. (0743) 40 236 – Closed Wednesday, August 15-10 – 35-70,000L. This is an excellent tavern serving regional cuisine. The house specialty is *fettucine al tartufo* – **Tric Trac da Giustino**, p. del Duomo, tel. (0743) 44 592 – 20-50 000L. very busy during the "Two World Festival".

CAMPELLO SUL CLITUNNO, 9km from Spoleto – **Casaline**, tel. (0743) 62 213 Closed Monday – 45,000L. After your visite of Tempietto sul Clitunno. Have lunch in this country inn after visiting the Tempietto sul Clitunno. The cuisine is made with local products, and the *crostini* with truffles are marvelous.

Gubbio

Taverna del Lupo, via G. Ansidei 21, tel. (075) 927 43 68 – Closed Monday off season, January. It serves delicious local specialties in a beautiful Medieval tavern decor – **Alle Fornace di Mastro Giogio,** via Mastro Giogio 3, tel 927 5740 – Closed Sunday evening, Monday, February, 60,000L..

Todi

Umbria, via San Bonaventura, 13, tel. (075) 89 42 737 – Closed Tuesday, December 19-January 8 – 40-60,000 L – **Jacopone-da Peppino**, piazza jacopone, 5, tel. (075) 89 48 366 - Closed Monday, July 10-30 - 40/60,000 L.

Trevi

L'Ulivo, 3 km, tel. (0742) 78 969 – Closed Saturday, Monday and Tuesday.

Orvieto

Giglio d'Oro, piazza Duomo 8, tel. (0763) 341 903 – Closed Wednesday – 40-70,000L – **Grotte del Funaro**, v. Ripa Serancia 41, tel. (0763) 343 276 - A regional restaurant – **Dell'Ancora**, via di Piazza del Popolo 7, tel. (0763) 342 766 – Closed Thursday, January – 35,000L. Local home-style cuisine.

LOCAL SPECIALTIES

Dai Fratelli, via del Duomo 11, it has all kinds of cheese and the famous Umbrian sausages and ham.

PIEDMONT VALLE D'AOSTA

Torino / Turin

Vecchia Lanterna, corso Re Umberto 21, tel. (011) 537 047 – Closed Saturday noon, Sunday, August 10-20 – 80-97,000L. This is one of the best restaurants in Italy. The owner, Armando with new flavors, but also does an admirable job with traditional recipes. The wine cellar is superbly well stocked with Italian wines – **Del Cambio**, piazza Carignano, tel. (011) 546 690 - closed Sunday and August-85/110000L- located in the historical center of Turin, birthplace of the unification of Italy, this restaurant has kept all of the luster of the old days when Cavour came to eat here every day. The atmosphere, cuisine, and service are straight out of the 19th century.- **Mina**, via Ellero 36, tel. (011) 696 3608 – Closed Sunday evening, Monday, July – 50,000L. It serves genuine Piemontian home-style cuisine (*antipasti, sformati, finanzeria*) – **Trattoria della Posta**, strada Mongreno 16, tel. (011) 8980 193 – Closed Sunday evening, Monday, July 10-August 20. It is famous for its cheeses and its excellent wine cellar – **Tre Galline,** via Bellezia 37, tel. (011) 436 65 53 - Closed Sunday, Monday noon - 50,000L. Typical Piemontian cuisine – **Al Gatto Nero**, corso Turati 14, tel.

(011) 590 414 - closed Sunday and August - 700000L. Specialties: *assassini.* – **Salsamentario**, via Santorre di Santarosa 7-B – tel. (011) 819 50 75 – Closed Sunday evening, Monday,

August 15-22. There is a large buffet for 35,000 L, just next door to a caterer– **Il Ciacalon** viale 25 Aprile, tel. (011) 661 09 11 – Closed Sunday, August 11-24, located near the fairgrounds, beautiful restaurant with a simple friendly atmosphere – **Ostu Bacu**, corso Vercelli 226, tel. (011) 265 79. Closed Sunday. Typical Piemontian cuisine served in a rustic family atmosphere.

CAFFE' – BARS

Caffe' al Bicerin, piazza della Consolata 5. has had famous customers such as Alexander Dumas who perhaps came to try the famous *bicerin*, a house specialty made from chocolate, coffee, milk, and sugar cane syrup.

Caffe Il Florio, via Po, called "caffe dei condini" because it used to be a meeting place for the most conservative people of the time. Try the *Sabaione, gelato al gianduia.* –

Caffe' Mulassano, piazza Castello 15. his large cafe has a lot of atmosphere, and delicious *tramezzini* .

Caffe' San Carlo, piazza San Carlo 156. opened in 1822, and used to be the meeting point of the European intellegensia.

LOCAL SPECIALTIES

Stratta, piazza San Carlo 191 specialties: *caramelle alla gioca di gelatinases*, "marrons glacés", *amaretti, meringhe con panna montata* - **Peyrano**, corso Moncalieri 47, is a laboratory for the famous Turinese chocolates, *givu*, *diablottini*, and the most famous *giandujotti*, also sold at the pastry shop Peyrano-Pfatisch, corso V. Emanuele II, 76 – **Cantine Marchesi di Barolo**, via Maria Vittoria sells Piedmont wines *Barolo Barbera, Barbaresco, Gattinara, l'Asti Spumante* of course, and the *grappe*.

Carmagnola

29 km from Turin

La Carmagnole, via Sottotenente Chiffi 31, tel. (011) 971 26 73 - Dine in an old palace, reservations a must.

Lozanzé

46 km from Turin

Panoramica, Lungo Tanaro, 4 tel. (0125) 66 99 69 - closed Saturday noon, Sunday evening, Christmas.

This is still one of the best restaurants in Piedmont.

Alba

Il Vicoletto, via Bertero, 6, tel. (0173) 36 31 96 – Closed Monday, July20-August 15 – 50/80,000 L. Gastronomic cooking, specialtie: *langarola* – **Osteria dell'Arco**, piazza Savona 5, tel. (0173) 36 39 74 - Closed Sunday, Monday at noon except from September 25 to November 25 - 30/45,000L – **Daniel's**, corso canale, 28, tel. (0173) 44 19 77 - Closed Christmas and New year. August 1-15, Sunday except from October to December - 45/60,000L. Typical cooking in a typical house - **Porta san Martin**o, via Enaudi 5, tel. (0173) 36 23 35 - Closed Monday, August 20-September 20- 45/60,000L. Truffles in season.

Asti

Gener Neuv, Lungo Tanaro 4, tel. (0141) 557 270 – Closed Sunday evening, Monday, August, Christmas 85,000L. This is one of the best places for traditional Piedmont cuisine – **L'Angolo del Beato**, via Guttuari 12, tel (0141) 531 668, Closed Wednesday, August – 50,000L. A beautiful old house, reservation advised – **Il Cenacolo**, viale al Pilone 59, tel. (0141) 531 110 – Closed Monday et Tuesday at noon, January 10-20 and August 5–20 – 40,000L. Savory regional cuisine is served in this intimate reasturant. Reservations required.

IN CASTIGLIOLE D'ASTI
15km from Asti
Guido, Piazza Umberto I 27, tel. (0141) 966 012 – Closed at noon, Sunday, August 1-24, December 22-January 10 – 100,000L. Elegantly reinvented specialties of Langhe are served here. By reservation only.

Canelli

29 km from Asti
San Marco, via Alba 136, tel. (0141) 82 35 44 - closed Tuesday evening, Wednesday, from July 20 to august 13. A la carte. Great cuisine, you will need a reservation.

Cannobio

Del Lago, in Carmine Inferiore 3 km away, tel. (0323) 705 95 – Closed November, February - 60-100 000L réservation. This restaurant on a lake offers very good classical cuisine.

Aosta

Le Foyer Corso Ivrea 146, tel. (0165) 32136 - Closed Monday evening, Tuesday, July 5-20, January 15-31 – 50,000L. Local specialties are served in this friendly comfortable restaurant. **Vecchia Aosta**, piazza Porta Pretoria,4, tel. (0165) 3611 86 - Closed Tuesday night, Wednesday, June 5-20 and October 15-30-30/40,000L. Reservation.

In Saint Christophe,

Casale, 12 km from Aosta, regione Candemine, tel. (0165) 541 203, closed Monday, holidays, January - 75000L. The house specialties and wine cellar are worth the trip.

Breuil-Cervinia

Les Neiges d'Antan, 4 km away, tel. (0166) 948 775 – Closed Monday, July, October, November – 35-90,000L. This is the best restaurant with the best wine cellar in Cervinia. The charming hotel is also mentioned in this guide – **Cime Bianche**, tel. (0166) 949 046 – 30-50,000L, is on the ski slopes in the winter, and serves regional cuisine in a pretty mountain decor, with a superb view on the Matterhorn – **Le Mattherhorn**, tel. (0166) 948 518. is in the center of town, and serves pizzas, steaks, and fish – **Hostellerie des guides**, is open from 7 am to midnight, and is famous for its Irish coffee.

Courmayeur

Pierre Alexis 1877, via Marconi 54, tel (0155) 84 35 17 – Closed October, November, Monday (except August), Tuesday at noon from December to March – **Al Camin**, via dei Bagni, tel (0165) 844 687 - Closed Tuesday off season, November, Mountain atmosphere and home-style cuisine – **Leone Rosso**, via Roma 73, tel : (0165) 845 726 – Closed Tuesday in low-season, November. Mountain decor but elegant atmosphere.

Caffe' Della Posta, via Roma 41. It is a hundred-year-old bar where you can drink traditional Alpine alcohols and cocktails, comfortably installed in plush sofas. (*Grappas*, *Genepi*).

Entrèves

4km from Courmayeur

La Maison de Filippo, tel. (0165) 89 668 – Closed Tuesday, June 1-July 15, Nov., 50,000L. You must make a reservation for this famous tavern.

Planpincieux Val Ferret

7km from Courmayeur

La Clotze, tel. (0165) 869 720 – Closed Wednesday, June, November 45,000L. Good regional cuisine.

La Palud Val Ferret

5km from Courmayeur

La Palud-da-Pasquale, tel. (0165) 89 169 – Closed Wednesday, November – 30-40,000L. Regional and mountain specialties.

Plan–de–Lognan Val Veny

12km from Courmayeur

Le Chalet del Miage, Closed July, September. Mountain-style cuisine.

Cogne

Lou Ressignon, rue des Mines 22, tel. (0165) 74 034. It has excellent cuts of meat, *fonduta, carbonara* (meat cooked in beer) and also delicious cheeses and desserts.

Verres

Chez Pierre, via Martorey 43, tel. (0125) 929 376 – Closed Monday and Tuesday except August - 50-80,000L. This adorable litttle restaurant, 22 miles (37km) from Aoste, has a friendly atmosphere and regional cuisine.

PUGLIA / APULIA

Alberobello

Il Poeta Contadino, via Indipendenza 21, tel. (080) 721 917 – Closed Sunday evening, Monday, January, June – 50-80,000L. Excellent cuisine – **Trullo d'Oro**, via

Cavallotti 31, tel. (080) 721 820 – Closed Monday, January 7-February 8 – 25-60,000L. It is picturesque, with a country-style decor and regional cuisine.

Castel del Monte

Ostello di Federico, Castel del Monte, tel. (0883) 56 98 77 - Closed Monday, 2 weeks in January and two in November - 40,000L. Specialties: *tortieri di riso e patate, cannelloni di baccalà e ricotta...*

Bari

Nuova Vecchia Bari, via Dante Alighieri 47, tel. (080) 521 64 96 – Closed Friday, Sunday evening –

50,000L. Pugilian cuisine is served in this rustic former oil press house – **La Pignata**, corso Vittorio Emanuele 173, tel. 523 24 81 – **Deco',** largo Adua 10, tel. 524 60 70. Elegant.

Polignano al Mare

Grotta Polazzese, via Narcisso 59, tel. (080) 740 0677 – 65-90,000L. It serves lobster and fish dishes inside a natural grotto in the summer.

Martina Franca

Da Antonietta, via Virgilio 30, tel. (080) 706 511 – Closed Wednesday off season – 25,000L. Flavorful cuisine **Rosticceria Ricci**, via Cavour 19. Excellent cuts of meat – **Trattoria delle Ruote**, via Ceglie 4,5km, tel. (080) 883 74 73 – Closed Monday – 30-45,000L. A nice place with limited seating so be sure to make a reservation – **Caffe' Tripoli**, piazza Garibaldi, is a wonderful old cafe serving pastries and almond paste – **Bar Derna**, piazza Settembre 4. Delicious pastries.

Ristorante In, piazza Magli 6, tel. (080) 705 021 - Closed Tuesday night, Wednesday, two weeks in November - 50,000L. Specialtie:

galantina d'anatra al pistacchio .

Lecce

Gino e Gianni, via Adriatica à 2 km, tel. (0832) 4399 210 – Closed Wednesday – 45,000L. Traditional cuisine in this theatrical-looking town **Il Satirello**, tel (0832) 3768 672 - Closed Tuesday. It is in an old farmhouse with a beautiful garden when the weather is warm, 9km from the road to Torre Chianca.

Taranto

Il Caffé, via San Tomaso d'Aquino 8, tel. (099)452 5097 – Closed Sunday, Monday lunch time, two weeks in August – 50,000L.

SARDAIGNE

Alghero

Le Lepanto, via Carlo Alberto 135, tel. (079) 979 116 – Closed Monday off season 50,000L. After your visit to the Grottos of Neptune, you will undoubtedly be delighted to have a lobster Lepanto or to try other regional specialties here – **Al Tuguri**, via Majorca 113 or **Dieci Metri**, vicolo Adami 37.

Santa Teresa Gallura

Canne al Vento, via nazionale 23, tel. (0789) 754 219 – Closed October, November, Saturday off season *Zuppa galurese, antipasti del mare*, seafood delicacies cooked with love.

Nuoro

Canne al Vento, viale Repubblica 66, tel. (0784) 201 762. It has a nice selection of meat and fish.

Monte Ortobene

7 km from Nuoro

Dai Fratelli Sacchi, tel. (0784) 31200. The Sacchi brothers warmly welcome their guests with savory cuisine.

Dorgali

Il Colibri, via Gramsci 44, tel. (0784) 960 54, Closed December-February, Sunday from October to May – 20-30,000L. This is a good place to stop off for a Sardinian meal on your way to visit the Dolmen Mottore and the Grottos di Ispinigoli.

Olbia

Leone et Anna, via Barcelona 90, tel. (0789) 263 33 – Closed January, Wednesday off season Sardinian cuisine, fish, and some Venetian specialties.

Ristorante dell' hotel Gallura, corso Umberto 145, tel. (0789) 246 48.

It has served fish and seafood dishes cooked with delicious simplicity for more than fifty years.

Cagliari

Dal Corsaro, viale Regina Margherita 28, tel. (070) 664 318 – Closed Sunday, August – 60,000L. If you spend a night in Cagliari before moving on down the coast, you can come here for high quality authentic Sardinian cuisine – **Antica Hostaria**, via Cavour 60, tel. (070) 665 870 – Closed Sunday, August. It is one of the nicest restaurants in Cagliari. Antonello Floris has skillfully adapted traditional recipes, and his wife Lilly makes great desserts.

Isola San Pietro-Carloforte

Al Tonno di Cosa, via Marconi 47, tel. (0781) 855 106. It serves delicious local cuisine (*tonno alla carlofortina*, "casca" regional couscous) on a terrace overlooking the sea – **Miramare**, piazza Carlo Emanuele 12, tel. (0781) 85 653, Carlofortan, Sardinian, and Arab specialties.

Porto Cervo

Il Pescatore, sul molo Vecchio, tel.

(0789) 92 296 – Closed October-May, open in the evening only – 65,000L. You can have dinner by candlelight on a flower-covered terrace – **Bar degli archi**, piazzetta degli Archi. People come here for breakfast, a sandwhich at noon, and a drink in the evening – **Pevero Golf Club**, Pevero, tel. (0789) 96 210 – Closed November-April – 80,000L. This is one of the nicest golf courses. The cuisine served in the clubhouse restaurant is elegant and light, just like the clientele.

Isola la Maddalena

La Grotta, via Principe di Napoli 3, tel. (0789) 737 228 - Closed November 30-50,000L. Seafood – **Mangana**, via Mazzini, tel (0789) 738 477 – Closed Wednesday, December 20-January 20 – 45-60,000L. There are all-fish meals here, too.

Oristano

Il Faro, via Bellini 25, tel. (0783) 700 02 – Closed Sunday, July 11-25; 60,000L. Inventive cuisine based on regional recipes.

Palermo

Renato l'Approdo, via Messina Marina 28, tel. (091) 630 2881 – Closed Wednesday, August 10-25 – 50-70,000L. One of the best restaurants on the island, featuring dishes made from old Sicilioan recipes. – **La Scuderia**, viale del Fante 9, tel. (091) 520 323 – Closed Sunday evening – 55,000L. It has one of the prettiest terraces in town. Dinners here are exquisite – **Charleston,** Piazza Ungheria 30, tel (091) 321 366 – Closed Sunday, June – September - 80,000L. Very good cuisine in a beautiful Liberty-style decor – **Al Ficondindia**, via Emerico Amari 64, tel. (091) 324 214 – Closed Thursday 25,000L. A country tavern serving local regional cuisine - **Gourmand's**, via Libertà 37-E, tel (091) 323 431, elegant, and fine cuisine. Smoked fish is a house specialty.

IN MONREALE,
8km from Palermo

La Botte, contrada Lenzitti 416, tel. (091) 414 051 – Closed Monday, July, August – 45,000L. Delicious cuisine. Don't miss the superb cathedral.

IN MONDELLO,
11 km from Palermo

Charleston le Terrazze, viale Regina Elena, tel. (091) 450 171, opened from June to September. On the most elegant beach of Palermo. It is the summer quarters of the *Charleston* of Palermo, with an superbly elegant terrace on the sea – **Gambero Rosso**, via Piano Gallo 30, tel. (091) 454 685 Closed Monday, November – 45,000L. This trattoria serves good seafood dishes.

CAFFE' – BARS

Caffe' Mazzara, via Generale Magliocco 15. Tomaso di Lampedusa wrote many chapters of "the Cheetah" here - **Bar du Grand Hotel des Palmes** The hotel has been dropped from our selection because the rooms are overpriced, but the superb salons are still worth a visit.

Cefalù

La Brace, via XXV Novembre 10, tel. (921) 23 570 – Closed Monday, December 15-January 15. This small restaurant offers traditional Italian cuisine.

Messina

Alberto, via Ghibellina 95, tel (090) 710 711. Alberto Sardella has served marvelous cuisine here since his return from the U.S. 30 years ago. One of his specialties is *spiedini di pesce spada* – **Pippo Nunnari**, via Ugo bassi 157 - Closed Monday, June – 50,000L.

Taormina

La Griglia, corso Umberto 54, tel.(0942) 239 80 – Closed Tuesday, November 20-December 20 – 40,000L , serves carefully prepared country-style regional cuisine – **a' Zammàrra**, via Fratelli Bandieri 15, tel. (0942) 24 408 - Closed Wednesday, January - 45,000L – **Rosticepi**, via S. Pancrazio, 10 – tel (0942) 24149, is the trattoria of Toarmina – **Giova Rosy Senior**, corso Umberto 38, tel. (0942) 24 411 – Closed Thursday, January. There is a large cart of antipasti and fish on a lovely jasmin-covered terrace – **Ciclope**, corso Umberto, tel. (0942) 625 910 – Closed Wednesday. 25-35,000L. One of the best Sicilian-style trattorias – **La Chiocca d'Oro**, via Leonardo da Vinci, tel.(942) 28 066 - Closed Thursday and November - 30-45,000L

Catania

La Siciliana, via Marco Polo 52-A, tel.(095) 376 400, Closed Monday, August 15–31 - 70,000L. One of their specialties, the *Rippiddu nivicatu*, is a miniature Etna **Costa Azzura**, via de Cristofaro à Ognina à 4 km, tel. 494 920 - Closed Monday. A beautiful terrace for the summer; seafood – ACIREALE 16km, **Panoramico**, Sta Maria Ammalati. Closed Monday. View of Etna and wonderful *pastaciutta al raguttiino di mare*, the "castellane di Leonardo".

Siracusa

Archimede, via Gemellaro 8, tel.

(0931) 69 701 – 40-60,000L. Trattoria – **Darsena**, riva Garibaldi 6, tel. (0931)66 104 – Closed Wednesday – 25-50,000L. Seafood – **Don Camillo**, via Maestranza 92-100, tel (0931) 67 133 – Closed Sunday - 50,000L – **Jonico-a Rutta e Cauli**, riviera Dionisio il Grande, tel. (0931) 65 540 - Close Thusday, Christmas - 40,000-65,000L.

Agrigente

Le Caprice, strada panoramica dei Tempi 51 – Closed Friday, July 1-15, It overlooks the Valley of the Temples – **Taverna Mosé**, contrada San Biagio 6, has a terrace with a view on the Junon temple. They serve spaghetti that Pirandello is said to have liked!

Eolie-Lipari

Filippino, piazza Municipo, tel. (090) 981 1002 – Closed Monday except in summer, November 15-December 15 – 45,000L. Traditional cuisine, and the best fish on the island – **E Pulera**, via Stradale Diana 51, tel. (090) 981 1158 – Closed November-May – 35-65,000 L. You can dine under a charming pergola. Reservations are a must.

Eolie-Vulcano

Lanterna Bleu, Porto Ponente, via Lentia, tel. (090) 985 2287 – 40,000L. The best one on this small untamed island, good fish

Eolie-Panarea

Da Pina, via S. Pietro and **Trattoria da Adelina**, the two best restaurants.

Eolie-Salina

Da Franco, à Santa Marina. Typical cooking.

TUSCANY

Firenze / Florence

Enoteca Pinchiorri, via Ghibellina 87, tel. (055) 242 777 – Closed Sunday, Monday at noon, August, February, Christmas and New Year's 125-150,000L. This upscale expensive restaurant is beautifully decorated, has a lovely flower-covered patio, one of the best wine cellars and some of the finest cuisine and in Italy – **Trattoria Coco Lezzone**, via del Parioncino 26r, tel. (055) 287 178 – Closed Sunday, Tuesday evening,

August, Christmas – 45-80,000L. You will find simple perfection here is a row of small rooms where regulars and locals rub elbows with international celebrities. The manager announces the delicious specialties of the day one after another as they are prepared. You don't have to try them all, but you will be tempted to – **Da Gannino**, piazza del Cimatori, tel. (055) 214 125 – Closed Sunday, August. This typical little osteria near the Signoria has service on the small square in the summer – **Il Latini**, via Palchetti, tel. (055) 210 916, Closed Sunday, August – 30,000L. Hidden on a back street, people stand on line a glass of wine in hand while waiting to be seated in

this noisy convivial restaurant. There is a common table, *prosciutto* and *vitello arosto*, a house specialty. – **Il Cibreo**, via dei Macci 118r, tel. (055) 234 1100 – Closed Sunday, Monday, August, Christmas 60,000L. It serves Italian-style nouvelle cuisine in a trendy atmosphere, not far from Santa Croce – **Trattoria Cammillo**, borgo San Iacopo 57, tel. (055) 212 427 – Closed Wednesday, Thursday, August 1-7, Christmas. This is one of most popular trattorias in town, serving traditional Florentine-style cuisine with a few innovations, such as the curried *tortellini* – **Mamma Gina**, borgo S. Iacopo 37, tel. (055) 2396 009 – Closed Sunday, August – 30-40,000L. Traditional cuisine – **Sostanza**, via della Porcellàna, tel. (055) 212 691 – Closed Saturday, Sunday, August – 40,000L. Tiny restaurant-grocery re with good local specialties.

Cantinone del Gallo Nero, via San Spirito 6, tel. (055) 218 898 – 25,000L. It has great *Crostini*, *Chianti*, and *Tiramisu*. It is in a cellar a few yards away from and opposite

Cammillo, and the entrance can be a little hard to find – **13 Gobbi,** Via del Porcellana 9 r, tel. (055) 2398 769. Enjoy local cuisine around tables with benches in this softly lit restaurant – **Sabatini**, via de Panzani 9-a, tel. (055) 210 293 – Closed Monday 70,000L. The house antipasti will give you a taste of good classic Tuscan cuisine – **Da Noi**, via Fiesolana, 46 r, tel. (055) 242 917 – Closed Sunday, Monday, August, Christmas – 50,000L. This small elegant restaurant serves creative cuisine and seafood – **Dino**, via Ghibellina 51 r, tel. (055) 241 452 – Closed Sunday evening, Monday, August – 35-50,000L. One of the oldest restaurants in Florence, where each day Tuscan tradition is renewed with products fresh from the market – **Cantinetta Antinori**, piazza Antinori 3, tel. (055) 292 234. Hidden in the courtyard of the Antinori palace near the town hall. People come here for simple meals and good Tuscan wine – **Buca Lipi**, via del Trebbio 1 r, tel. (055) 213 768 Closed Wednesday, August – 30-50,000L. This picturesque cellar serves local cuisine – **Buca Mario**, piazza Ottaviani, 16 l, tel. (055) 214 179 – Closed Wednesday et August – 30-50,000L. Typical regional cuisine and wine – **Le Fonticine**, via Nazionale 79 r, tel (055) 282 106. is a large country-style restaurant with walls covered with paintings, Tuscan cuisine, and a few Emilian delicacies. The only drawback is that the tables are a little too close – **Campannina di Sante**, piazza Ravenne, tel (055) 68 8343. It has a nice view of the Ponte Vecchio and the Signoria tower. It serves only fish dishes. There is a very pretty walk you can take in the evening along the Arno to the da Verrazzano bridge – **Antico Fattore**, via Lambertesca 1, tel. (055) 238 12 15 – Closed Sunday, Monday, August – 35,000L. Family trattoria near the Uffizi Museum serving traditional Tuscan specialties – **Fagioli**, Corso Tintori 47 r, tel. (55) 244 285 – Closed Saturday, Sunday, August, Christmas – 30-40,000L. Typical regional specialties prepared by a real Tuscan – **Giubbe Rosse**, piazza della Repubblica, 13 – A very nice gallery-restaurant.

CAFFE' — BARS

Rivoire, piazza della Signoria. It has a large terrace on the most beautiful square in the world, a nice place to have sandwhiches and pastries and relax after visiting the Offices. It is famous for its *gianduiotti* and the *Cantucci di Prato* which is great with a glass of *Vino Santo* – **Gilli,** piazza della Repubblica. It has a Belle Epoch interior, and a large ter-

race on the busiest square in Florence, sheltered by palm trees **Giacosa**, via Tornabuoni 83. ice place to have cappuccino and pastries. It is always crowded – **Vivoli**, via Isola delle Strinche – Closed Monday. Very good ice cream and pastries. **Dolce Vita**, piazza del Carmine. The meeting place for hip young Florentines – **Paszkowski**, piazza della Repubblica 6, concert cafe and restaurant.

SHOPPING

Pineider, piazza della Signoria 13r, used to supply Napolean and Verdi with paper, and has continued to make stationery and desk sets for the rich and famous, and esthetes who come here to buy ink or to have their stationery monogrammed **Officina Profumo Farmaceutica di Santa Maria Novella**, is in a 14th century chapel, and sells per-

fumes, cologne, elixirs, and soap. You can visit the superb back rooms by appointment – – **Taddei**, via Sta Margherita 11, pretty hand-crafted leather goods store – **Boutique de la Leather School**, also sells items made in the neighboring schools – **Bottega Orafa di Cassigoli e Costanza**, via degli Ramaglienti 12 and **Gusceli Brandi-marte**, via Bartolini 18, personalized handcrafted jewelry – **Bizzarri**, via Condotta 32r, sells hardware and herb. The Via de' Tornabuoni is where you can find boutiques. For silk and traditional Florentine Renaissance brocade, try, **Antico Sattificio Fiorentini**, via Bartolini. For embroidered handkerchiefs, or house linens, go to **Loretta Caponi**, borgo Ognissanti 10-12r - **Procacci**, via de' Tornabuoni, sells quality groceries, **Gastronomia Palmieri**, via Manni 48 r and **Gastronononomia Vera**, piazza Frescobaldi 3r, has sausages and ham, wine, cheeses and other Tuscan products.

Prato

Il Piraña, via Valentini 110, tel. (0574) 25746 – Closed Saturday noon, Sunday et August – 70-80,000L. Fine cuisine in a modern elegant decor – **Trattoria Lapo**, piazza Mercatale. Simple and inexpensive – **Tonio**, piazza Mercatale 161, tel. (0574) 21 266, Closed Sunday, Monday, August.

Siena

Cane e Gatto - **Osteria Castel Vecchio**, via Pagliaresi: two good trattorias on a small street across from the art museum – **Guido,** Vic. Pettinaio, 7 tel. (0577) 28 00 42 – Closed Wednesday, January 10-25, July 15-30 - The most genuine cuisine – **Al Mangia**, or **Il Campo** piazza del Campo 43 – 45-50,000L. Its location on the famous Place del Campo makes it worth the visit, but it is not a tourist trap – **Nello La Taverna**, via del Porrione 28, tel. (0577) 289 003 – Closed Monday, February – 25- 50,000L. Taverne frequented by

Siene families, with fine cuisine and a selection of Tuscan wine. – **Osteria Le Logge**, via del Porrione 33, tel. (0577) 480 13 – Closed Sunday – 40-50,000L. Excellent cuisine – **Grotta Santa Caterina da Bogoga,** via della Galluzza 26, tel. (0577) 282 208 – Closed Sunday evening, Monday, July – 30,000L. Country-style cuisine and atmosphere – **Antica Trattoria Botteganova**, strada Chiantigiana, tel. (0577) 284 230 – Closed Sunday, Monday at noon, 20 days between July and August – 40,000L. This very pleasant restaurant is worth the trip: the cuisine and service are meticulously well done.

CHIANTI COUNTRY

Fiesole

5km from Firenze

Trattoria Cave di Maiano, in Maiano 3 km away, via delle cave 16, tel. (055) 591 33 – Closed Thursday, Sunday evening, August – 35,000L. In the summer you can dine on large wooden tables on a shady terrace, and in the winter, in a picturesque tavern setting.

Bagno a Ripoli

9km from Firenze

Cent'Anni, via Centanni 7, tel. (055) 630 122 – Closed Saturday noon, Sunday, August – 50,000L. This pretty restaurant has a lovely garden. The traditional Tuscan dishes served here are a family affair. Mamma Luciani does the cooking, her son Luciano makes the pastries, and Silvano takes care of the wine.

Settignano

7km from Firenze

Caffe' Desiderio is an old cafe dating from the end of the 19th century, where you can have coffee, chocolate, pastries, and cocktails while enjoying a superb view of the Fiesole hills.

Serpiolle

8km from Firenze

Lo Strettoio , via di Serpiolle 7, tel (055) 4250 044 – Closed at noon and Sunday, Monday, August. is in a beautiful room in an old villa which still has an olive oil press (which is why it has this name). The atmosphere is elegant, and the seasonal cuisine is served by *cameriere* dressed in black with white collars.

Carmignano

22km from Firenze

Da Delfina, Artimino 6km, via della Chiesa, tel. (055) 871 8175 – Closed Monday evening, Tuesday, August, January 1-15. Mamma Delfina oversees the entire operation, and everything comes from the family estate (vegetables, eggs, and poultry) and is homemade, notably the *pappardelle*.

San Casciano in Val di Pesa

18km from Firenze

MERCATALE, **La Biscondola**, tel. (055) 821 381 – Closed Monday, Tuesday at noon, November – 40-50,000L.

CERBAIA, **La Tenda Rossa**, 6 km, tel. (055) 826 132. Closed Wednesday, Thursday at noon, August 5-28 – 75,000 L. This small family-run restaurant serves savory cuisine prepared with the freshest ingredients.

Monterriggioni

15km from Siena

Il Pozzo, piazza Roma 2, tel. (0577) 304 127 – Closed Sunday evening, Monday, January, July 30-August 15; 40-50,000L. This excellent restaurant

has a wide selection of wines and regional gourmet cuisine.

Castelnuovo Berardenga

à 20 km de Siena

La Bottega del 30, in Villa a Sesta, 5 km from Castelnuovo, tel. (0577) 35 92 26 - Closed at noon, except Sunday, Thusday and Wednesday - 40/80,000L.

San Piero a Sieve

21km of Siena

Villa Ebe, borgo San Lorenzo, tel. (0551) 845 7507 – Closed Monday – 40,000L. The village and the countryside alone are worth the trip, but it's Signora Ebe's fresh pasta that makes this place truly irrestable.

Castellina in Chianti

26km from Siena

Antica Trattoria La Torre, tel. (0577) 740 236 – Closed Friday, September 1-15 – 30-45,000L. The longstanding family tradition of serving fine cuisine made with local products is contuined here

Gaiole in Chianti

28km from Siena

Badia, in Coltibuono,5km, tel. (0577) 749 424 – Closed Monday, November-December 15 – 45,000L. The Benedictine tradition of humanism and fine gourmet cuisine continues here in this very pleasant place.

Colle Val d'Elsa

25km from Siena

Arnolfo, piazza Santa Caterina 2, tel. (0577) 920 549 – Closed Tuesday, August 1-10, January 10–February 10 – 60-85,000L. On the trail of San

Gimignano and Volterra, Arnofolo is a good place to stop off for a meal. The young chef in charge of the kitchen serves traditional and innovative cuisine.

Montepulciano

66km from Siena

Ristorante rustico Pulcino, strada per Chianciano, tel. (0578) 716 905. Dishes with fresh ingredients accompanied by the best wines.

Monteoliveto Abbey Asciano

37km from Siena

Osteria della Pievina, stratale 438, Lauretana.

La Torre, is a tavern in the Abbey gardens, a very pleasant place to wait for the Abbey to reopen after August 1-10, January 10–February 10.

San Antimo Abbey Montalcino

à 41 km de Siena

La Cucina di Edgardo, via Saloni, 33, tel. (0577) 84 82 32.

Poggio Antico, in Poggio Antico, 4 km tel. (0577) 849 200 - Closed Monday - 60/80,000 L. Famous, Reservation – **Taverna della Fattoria dei Barbi**, in Podenovi, 5 km from Montalcino, tel. (0577) 849 357 - Closed Thusday evening and Wednesday, July 1-15 , second week of January - 50,000L.

Montefollonico

60km from Siena

La Chiusa, via Madonnina, tel. (0577) 669 668 – Closed Tuesday, except from August to September, 5 January 5-March 19, November 5-December 5 – 80-120,000L. Here you will enjoy delicious cuisine prepared by a pretty woman, and a good wine cellar, in a charming setting.

Pienza

52km from Siena

La Buca delle Fate, corso il Rossellino 38a, tel. (0578) 74 84 48 -

closed Monday, from January 10 to 20, July 15 to 31. Authentic Tuscan cuisine copiously served in a rustic setting. – **Dal Falco**, piazza Dante Alighieri 7, tel. (0465) 74 85 51 – Closed Friday, July 12-20 and November 10-30 – 25-35,000L. It serves house delicacies in a family atmosphere – **Il Prato**, piazza Dante Alghieri 25, tel. (0465) 74 86 01 – Closed Wednesday, July 1-20. Friendly atmosphere and regional cuisine.

San Gimignano

38km from Siena

Le Terrazze, piazza della Cisterna, tel. (0577) 575 152 – Closed Tuesday, Wednesday noon – 40,000L. Tuscan specialties and a nice view of the Elsa Valley - **Dorando'**, vicolo dell' oro, 2 – Closed Monday. Elegant atmosphere and very good cuisine, right near the Duomo – 50,000L – **La Griglia**, tel. 940005 – Closed Thursday. A nice view on the valley

Arezzo

Buca di San Francesco, via San Francesco, tel. (0575) 23 271 – Closed Monday evening, Tuesday, July – 55,000L. Delicious cuisine in a Renaissance decor thick with atmosphere– **Al Principe**, 7 km from Giovi, tel. 362 046 – Closed Monday, July 20-August 20 – 50,000L. An old trattoria in the tradition.

Cortona

28km from Arezzo

Il Falconiere, in S. M. a Bolena 3 km away. Closed Wednesday - 60,000L – **La Grotta**, Piazzetta Baldini, 3, good traditional trattoria – **Preludio,** via Guelfa, 11 – **Dardano,** via Dardano, 24. Two sympatical addresses.

Lucignano

27km from Arezzo

Osteria da Toto, piazza Tribunale 6, tel. (0575) 836 988 – Closed Tuesday, November, February. This is a nice place in a beautiful village.

Lucca

Buca di Sant' Antonio, via della Cervia 1, tel. (0583) 55 881 – Closed Sunday evening, Monday, July – 50,000L. One of the best restaurants in the region, with a warm intimate decor – **Antico Caffe' delle Mura**, piazzale Vittorio Emanuele 2, tel. (0583) 47 962 – Closed Tuesday, 20 days in January, 10 days in August – 40,000L. This old cafe serves hearty regional cuisine - **Da Giulio in Pelleria**, via delle Conce 45, tel. (0583) 55 948 – Closed Sunday, Monday, August 1-15, Christmas – 25,000L. Flavorful genuine local family-style cuisine – **Solferino**, San Macario in Piano, 6km, tel. (0583) 59 118 – Closed Wednesday, Tuesday evening, two weeks in August, Christmas – **Vipore**, in Pieve Santo Stefano 9 km away, tel. (0583) 39 4107 – 60,000L. Closed Monday, Tuesday evening. This 18th century farmhouse has been transformed into an adorable restaurant with a nice view of the Lucca plain.

Pugnano San Giulano Terme

Le Arcate, tel. (050) 850 105 – Closed Monday, August - Tuscan cuisine in a pretty rustic decor with an lovely pergola – **Sergio** the famous Pisan restaurant, has opened up at the Villa di Corliano, in Rigoli San Guiliano Terme.

Pisa

Al Ristoro dei Vecchi Macelli, via Volturno 49, tel. (050) 20 424 –

Closed Wednesday, Sunday at noon, August 10-20 – 60,000L - Personalized cuisine – **Sergio**, lungarno Pacinotti 1, tel. (050) 58 0580 – Closed Sunday, Monday noon, January – 70-95,000 L. The best place in Pisa, with market-fresh inventive cuisine and delicious desserts – **Emilio**, via Roma 26, tel. (050) 562 131 – Closed Friday – 25-45,000L. Between the Arno and the Tower, this is a nice place to have lunch, with a large buffet of *antipasti* – **Da Bruno**, via Bianchi 12, tel. (050) 560 818 – Closed Monday evening, Tuesday, August 5-18. 25-60,000L. It serves traditional cuisine in a friendly setting - **Lo Schiaccianoci**, via Vespucci 104, tel 21024 – Personalized local cuisine.

Volterra

60km from Pisa

Da Beppino, via delle Prigioni 15, tel. (0588) 86 051 – Closed Wednesday, January 10-20. Traditional trattoria in a historical center – 30,000L.

Etruria, piazza dei Priori 8, tel. (0588) 86 064 – Closed Thursday, November, 45,000L. The restaurant is located in an old palace.

Livorno

La Barcarola, viale Carducci 63, tel. (0586) 402 367 – Closed Sunday, August – 40-60,000L. The best Livornan specialties: caciucco, fish soup, and *loup a la livournaise* in a 1900 palace.

Gennarrino, via Santa Fortunata 11, tel (0586) 888 093 – Closed Wednesday, February - 45,000L. This is a good classic restaurant.

Il Fanale, Scali Novi Lena 15, tel.

(0586) 881 346 – Closed Tuesday – 50,000L. Reservation advised.

Viarregio

Grand Caffé Margherita, lungomare Margherita 30, tel. (0584) 962 553 Closed Sunday and August – 40-60,000L.

L'Oca Bianca, via Coppino 409, tel. 672 05 - Closed at noon except Saturday and Sunday, Thusday and November - 90;000L. The best address in Viareggio.

Saturnia

I Due Cippi, piazza Veneto, 26.

Isola d' Elba

Publius, Poggio (Marciana), tel. (0565) 99 208, Closed October 15-Easter – 35-70,000L. Reputed to be the best restaurant on the island, with a beautiful view of the sea – **Rendez-vous da Marcello**, in Marciana Marina, piazza della Vittoria 1, tel. (0565) 95251 – 45,000L - Closed Wednesday - January 10–February 10.

TRENTINO DOLOMITES

Trento

Chiesa, via Marchetti 9, tel. (0461) 238 766 – Closed Wednesday evening, Sunday, August 10-25 – 60-80,000L. The specialties vary according to the seasons. During the apple season, all the dishes are made with them. In the spring, there are many early vegetables, and in the summer, fine fresh water fish from the lake – **Orso Grigio**, via degli Orti 19, tel. (0461) 984 400 – Closed Sunday January 1-15. Fine French-style cuisine, with a beautiful garden in the summer – **Hostaria del Buonconsiglio**, via Suffragio 23, tel. (0461) 986 619 – Open in the evening only except on Sunday – 30,000L. Rustic and friendly – **Birreria Forst**, via Oss Mazzurana 38, tel. (0461) 235 590 – Closed Monday – 30,000L. Good place for lunch, either at the bar, or in the back room – **Le Bollicine**, via dei Ventuno 1, tel. (0461) 983 161 – Closed Sunday, August – 35,000L. Restaurant and tavern on the road to

Buon Consiglio Castle - IN CIVEZZANO, 6 km from Trento, **Maso Cantanghel**, via Madonnina 33, tel. (0461) 858 714 – Closed Sunday, Easter, August 35,000L. This beautiful old farmhouse located just outside of town, has been nicely restored, and offers carefully prepared cuisine and attentive service.

CAFFE' — BARS

Caffe' Campregher, via Mazzini. Delicious cocktails made with *Spumante,* a sparkling regional wine.

Calavino

19km from Trento

Castel Toblino, tel. (0461) 44 036. Located in a marvelous landscape of mountains and lakes, this beautiful castle on Lake Garde now has a restaurant in one of its most charming rooms.

Riva del Garda

28km from Trento

Vecchia Riva, via Bastione 3, tel. (0464) 555 061 – Closed Tuesday off season – 50,000L. Elegant, with meticulous service and cuisine – **Bastione** via Bastione 19-A, tel (0464) 552 652 - Closed Wednesday, November 4-December 11 – 30,000L. Typically Trentinan cuisine in a warm friendly atmosphere. You will need a reservation.

Madonna di Campiglio

Prima o Poi, Pozze 8, tel. (0465) 57 175 – Closed Wednesday, June. In a small wooden house a few miles from the center of town, the Recagni family awaits you with hearty mountain cuisine – **Rifugio Malghette,** Pradalago, tel. (0465) 41 144 – Closed September 20-Christmas, May-June 10 – 30,000L. This warm friendly castle is located in theAndamello-Brenta Reserve. The best time of year to visit the forest is at the beginning of July when the rhododendrons are in bloom. The mushroom and blueberry risotto and homemade pasta are always a delight.

Bolzano

Da Abramo, piazza Gries 16, tel. (0471) 280 141 – Closed Sunday and August – 45-65,000L. elegant Restaurant – **Chez Frederic**, via Armando Diaz 12, tel. (0471) 271 011 – 35,000L. It serves French-inspired cuisine. Dining in the shaded courtyard in the summer is especially pleasant. – **Castel Mareccio**, via Claudia de' Medici 12, tel. (0471) 979 439. An elegantly rustic castle surrounded by vineyards.

LOCAL SPECIALTIES

Antica Salumeria Salsamenteria

Guiliano Masé, via Goethe 15 has homemade *spek tirolese, salami di selvagina*, and other delicacies.

Bressanone

Fink, Portici Minoni 4, tel. (0472) 83 48 83 – Closed Wednesday, July 1-15. Typical mountain cuisine in an old palace located under the Medieval arcades of the center of Bressanone – **Oste Scuro**, vicolo Duomo 3, tel. (0472) 83 53 43 – Closed Sunday evening, Monday, January 10-February 5 – 40,000L.

Tyrolean cuisine in a Baroque dining room, and on a beautiful terrace in the summer.

Fie allo Scilliar

Tschafon, Fié di Sopra 57, tel. (0471) 72 5024 – open in the evening only, Closed Monday, January 9-22, November 1-14. If you are a fan of French cuisine, you can expect a warm welcome from Therese Bidart. If you come on a Wednesday between October and April, try her extraordinary fish buffet.

Merano

Andrea, via Galilei 44, tel. (0473) 237 400 – Closed Monday, February 4-25 – 45-85,000L. Its reputation has crossed the Dolomites. Reservations are a must for this elegant restaurant **Flora**, via Portici 75, tel. (0473) 231 484 – Closed Sunday, Monday at noon, January 15-February 28 – 55-85,000L. Sophisticated Tyrolean and Italian cuisine.

Terlaner Weinstube, via Portici 231, tel. (0473) 235 571 – Closed Wednesday. Typical restaurant serving regional cuisine.

LOCAL SPECIALTIES

Casa del Miele Schenk, via casa di Risparmio 25. Honey, royal jelly, and an assortment of hand-crafted candles.

Santa Gertrude - Val D'ultimo

28 km from Merano

Genziana, via Fontana Bianca 116, tel. (0473) 79 133 – Closed Wednesday, November-December 26 – 50,000L. One of the best, and certainly one of the highest (2000 meters) restaurants in Italy.

Villabassa

Friedlerhof, via Dante 40, tel. (0474) 75 003 – Closed Tuesday, June – 40,000L. 23km from Brunico, Lovely restaurant with Tyrolean meals and decor, 23 km from Brunico.

Ortisei

Ramoser, via Purger 8, tel. (0471) 796 460 – Closed Thursday – 40,000L. This warm friendly restaurant, one of the best in Val Gardena, serves authentic regional cuisine –

Janon, via Rezia 6, tel. (0471) 796 412 – Closed Tuesday, November – 30,000L. Typically Tyrolean cuisine and good desserts.

V E N E T O

Venezia / Venice

near San Marco

RESTAURANTS:

Harry's Bar, calle Vallaresco 1323,

tel. (041) 528 577 – Closed Monday, January 4-February 15 – 110,000L. The *Bellini, carpaccio,* and *risotto* are house specialties famous all over the world. The best table is the one near the bar. Reservations are a must.

Trattoria alla Colomba, Piscina-Frezzeria 1665, San Marco, tel (041) 522 11 75 – 70,000L. One of the most popular trattorias in Venice. It has excellent cuisine and works by contemporary artisits on the walls – **Antico Martini**, across from the opera, tel. (041) 522 41 21 – Closed Tuesday, Wednesday noon – 75,000L, delicious – **Taverna La Fenice**, campiello della Fenice 1936, tel. (041) 522 38 56 – Closed Sunday, January. It has all the refinement you could hope for, the perfect place to dine after a show at the Fenice – **Al Teatro,** Campo San Fantin 1917, tel. (041) 523 72 14 – Closed Monday – 40,000L. The walls of this pizzeria-tobacco shop are covered with dedications from actors and performers who come after their shows – **La Caravella**, via XXII Marzo, tel (041) 520 89 01 – Closed Wednesday in winter - 75,000L **– Vini da Arturo**, calle degli Assassini 3656, tel. (041) 528 69 74. Only seven tables which you must reserve if you want to stand a chance of having the excellent meat served here – **Da Raffaele**, San Marco 2347, tel. (041) 523 23 17. You can dine near a large fireplace in the winter. In the summer the tables are set up along a picturesque little canal on a gondola route. – **Do Forni**, calle dei Specchieri 457, tel. 523 77 29 - closed Thursday in winter and end of November-beginning of December.- 60-90000L.

CAFFE' ET BACARI

Florian, piazza San Marco 56 – Closed Wednesday. Travelers and Venetians have appreciated its sumptuous interior and large terrace on the shady side of Saint Mark Square since 1720. Specialties: cocktails, the

Bellini in summer, the *Tintoretto* in winter – **Quadri,** piazza San Marco. is across the square on the sunny side, and is also very elegant – **Caffe' Lavena**, piazza San Marco 134. Despite the fact that it is 200 years old, the Lavena holds its own with its two illustrious neighbors – **Caffe' Paolin**, campo San Stefano, 2692 San Marco. has a large sunny terrace on the campo where you can enjoy the best ice cream in town or a *spritz* (*Prosecco* and *bitter*) - **Vino Vino**, Ponte delle Veste 2007A, is a small bar popular with gondoliers who come here to take a break, just a few steps away from the Fenice Theatre. There is a good selection of Italian wine, which you can enjoy along with a dish of *pasta e fagioli* – **Enoteco Volto,** calle Cavalli, 4081 San Marco 4081 – tel. (041) 522 89 45. is the ideal place for lunch. You can have delicious little sandwiches on rye bread along with an *ombre* (white venetian wine), or other equally good wines such as *Brunello, Barello,* or *Barbaresco.* There is also a wide assortment of beers – **Al Bacareto**, San Samuele 3447, crowed.

near Rialto

Poste Vecie, Pescheria Rialto, tel (041) 721 822. Near the Rialto fisch market. A vrey good place.

Trattoria Madonna, calle de la Madonna 594, tel. (041) 522 38 24 – 40,000L. One of the most typically Venetian trattorias, but it can be difficult to find a table here – **Al Graspo de Ua**, calle de Bombaseri 5094, tel. (041) 522 36 47 – Closed Monday, Tuesday, July 25-August 10 – 70,000L. It has a picturesque decor and lives up to its reputation as the best seafood restaurant in town.

San Polo

Osteria da Fiore, calle del Scaleter, tel. (041) 72 13 08, Closed Sunday, Monday, Christmas, August – Seafood - Reservation advised.

Ai Mercanti, Pescheria Rialto, tél (041) 524 02 82, Closed Sunday - 60,000L – **Da Ignazio**, calle del Saoneri tel. (041) 523 48 52 Closed Saturday - 60,000L – Specialtie: *baccalá mantecado.*

near Cannaregio

Osteria Al Million S. Giovanni Crisostomo, 5841 – Closed le Wednesday. One of the oldest baccari in Venise. Try *Soave* or *Prosecco* if you like while wine, or *Valpolicella*

or *Bardolino* if you prefer red, to go with you *molecche* (soft crab) or *cichetti* – **Vini da Gigio**, near Ca' d'Oro, tel. (041) 528 51 40 - Closed Monday - 45,000L – **Ca d'Oro** or alla Vedova, calle del Pistor, a classic bar behind Ca d'Oro.

BACARI

Do Mori, calle dei Do Mori, near the Rialto brige. The one place you must not miss in this quarter. Careful, it closes at 13:00 for lunch. – **Do Spade**, calle Le do Spade, an extension of des do Mori street. Counter service.

near Dorsoduro Accademia

RESTAURANTS

Ai Cugnai, Dorsoduro San Vio. Typical trattoria – **Ai Gondolieri,** Dorsoduro 366 – San Vio, tel. (041) 528 63 96 – Closed Tuesday – 90,000L – Specialtie: meat – **Agli Alboretti,** Dorsoduro, Accademia, tel. (041) 523 00 58 – Open in the evenig only, closed Wednesday – 60,000L.– **Le Riviera**, di G. Canton, Dorsoduro 1473, tel. (041) 522 762 - across from Stucky Mills, is run by a former Maitre d‘ from Harry’s. The clientele of regulars, politicians and show business initiates reserve their tables on the platform to enjoy the house seafood delicacies.- 50-60000L. **Locanda Montin**, fondamenta di Borgo 1147, tel. (041) 522 71 51 – Closed Tuesday evening, Wednesday – 30,000L. It is located

very close to the Guggenheim Foundation, and serves traditional cuisine. In the summer, the tables are set up under an arbor in the large courtyard – **Linea d'ombra**, Zattere

19, near La Salute, piano-bar in the evening.

between riva degli Schiavonni and giardini

RESTAURANTS

Corte Sconta, calle del Pestrin 3886, tel. (041) 522 70 24 – Closed Sunday, Monday – 60,000L. This subtly elegant restaurant serves truly excellent cuisine. It is the best place in Venice, frequented by a clientele of intellectuals and artists, who have had no trouble keeping it relatively secret, as it is not very easy to find (Vaporetto: stazione Arsenale. On left to 4th bridge and street on right) – **Al Cavo**, campiello della Pescaria

3968, tel. (041) 522 38 12 – Closed Wednesday, Thursday, January, August – 50,000L. Another good restaurant – **Hostaria da Franz**, fondamenta San Isepo 754, tel. (041) 522 75 05 – Closed Tuesday off season, January 50-60,000L. Specialties: seafood. In the summer the tables are set up along the canal. By reservation. (Vaporetto: stazione Giardini).

la Giudecca

RESTAURANTS

Harry's Dolci, fondamenta San Biagio, tel. (041) 522 48 44 – Closed Monday, November 10- March 10 – 70,000L. This is the summer headquarters of ultra-chic Venetians.

L'Altanella. As you walk along the canal on the Giudecca, you will notice the small Virginia creeper-covered terrace of the Altanella, where you can have Venetian family-style cuisine.

Stefano Zanin has sculpted gold-leaf picture frames – **Renato Andreatta** has frames for mirrors or pictures, and masks – **Mondonovo**, ponte dei Pugni, 3063 - Dorsoduro. Giano Lavato makes superb masks, and also does work for the theater.

At the **Legatoria Piazzesi** S. Maria del Giglio 2511 you will find marbled and traditional "carta varese" hand printed stationery, and other Venitian handicrafts, old-fashioned book bindings, and beautiful collectors' items.

Antichita` V. Troïs, Campo S. Maurizio Superb Fortuny fabrics – **Rubelli,** palais Cornerspinelli, Campo S. Gallo. Superb damask, silks, and brocades – **Delphos, et Venetia Studium**, campo S. Fantin, 1997, have dresses, handbags, and Fortuny scarves in a wide assortment of colors, as well as lamps created by Fortuny – Chez **Mazzaron,** sells handmade lace including the famous "Venitian stitch" – **Jesurum,** Ponte della Canonica S. Marco, offers house linens and old lace in an old 12th century church – La **Pantofola** calle della Mandola - S. Marco 3718 sells the velvet shoes which gondoliers used to wear.

Pauly, piazza S. Marco, beautiful glass art objects – **L'Isola**, campo S.-Moise, glass art objects of Carlo Moretti – **Rigattieri,** calle de la Mandola, glass art objects of Seguso, Barovier and Toso, Venini... **Archimede Seguso**, piazza San Marco – **Industie Veneziane** and **Battiston**, calle Vallaresco 1320 have the famous "Harry's Bar" pitchers here.

Codognato, calle del Ascension, sells antique Art-Deco, Cartier, Fabergé, and Tiffany jewelry - **Nardi**, piazza S. Marco, is one of the best jewelers and has a superb series of Othellos, each one of a kind – **M. Antiquités,** sells jewels by Monica Zecchi, silk velvet dresses and capes by Mirella Spinella.

Enoteca Al Volto, calle Cavalli 4081, has good selection of Veneto wines – **Pasticceria Dal Col**, San Marco 1035 has all kinds of traditional Venitian candies.

Murano

Ai Frati, tel (041) 736 694 – Closed Thursday, February. This is the oldest osteria in Murano serving typically Venetian meals.The terrace on the grand canal is particularly pleasant in the summer.

Torcello

Locanda Cipriani, tel (041) 735433 Closed Tuesday, du 10 au 20 March – 70,000L. It has the simplicity and

high elegance of the Cipriani tradition. By reservation.
Ponte del Diavolo, tel. (041) 730 401 Closed Thursday, March-November 15 – 40-60,000L. A pleasant inn serving seafood specialties. In the summer you can dine in a pretty garden.

Burano

Osteria ai Pescatori, tel. (041) 730 650 – Closed Monday, January – 50,000L. Boasts two centuries of activity and fidelity to authentic *buranella* cuisine, a pretty dining room, and a small garden for warm sunny days – **Al Gato Nero-da Ruggero**, tel. (041) 730 120 – Closed Monday, January 8-30, October 20-November 20 – 50,000L. Regional cuisine atmosphere.

Verona

Arche, via delle Arche Scaligere 6, tel. (045) 800 7415 – Closed Sunday, Monday noon, January – 80,000L. Across from the famous Della Scala mausoleum this old tavern is also a marvelous elegant restaurant – **12 Apostoli**, vicolo Corticella San Marco 3, tel. (049) 596 999 – Closed Sunday evening, Monday, January 2-8, June 20–30 – 85,000L. This is the

"must-see" of Verona – **Il Desco**, via Dietro San Sebastiano 7, tel. (045) 595 358 – Closed Sunday, Christmas, Eastern, June – 70,000L. In the historical center of Verona, you can enjoy Italain-style nouvelle cuisine and a very nice wine cellar – **Nuovo Marconi**, via Fogge 4, tel.(045) 591 910 – Closed Sunday, July - 70,000L. an elegant restaurant with fine Italian cuisine and friendly service.- **Re Teodorico**, piazzale Castel San Pietro, tel. (045) 8349 990 – 55,000L. It has a nice view of Verona and the Adige – **Torcoloti**, via Zambelli 24 , tel. (045) 800 6777 - Closed Sunday, Monday evening 50,000L. Elegant atmosphere – **Bottega del Vino**, via scudo di Francia 3, tel. (045) 80 04 535, is a pleasant wine bar with classic cuisine in a cheery informal atmosphere. – **Osteria dal Duca**, via Arche Scaligere 2, tel. (045) 59 44 74. The clientele is made up of regulars who come for the *pastisada de caval* (horse stew), the specialty of Verona – **Osteria all' Oste Scuro**, vicolo San Silvestro 10, tel. (045) 59 26 50 - Closed Saturnay at noon and Sunday, Christhmas, August 20-31 - 40, 000L. Specialties: *la sfilacciata di cavalo et la pastisada.*

Rubiani, piazetta Scalette Rubiani 3, tel. (045) 800 68 30 - Closed Friday and January - 60,000L. Specialties:

risotto ai bruscandoli, coniglio al càffé .

Trattoria Al Camiere, piazza San Zeno 10, tél.(045) 803 0765 - Closed Wednesday evenig, Friday, July. Regional cooking.

C A F F E ’ B A R S

Campidoglio, piazzetta Tirabosco 4. A yuppie bar in a former convent with its original frescos. – **Enotheque Dal Zovo**, Vicolo San Marco in Foro, 7 - has a large selection of wines to taste, *amarone* and *reciota.*

Caffe’ Dante, piazza dei Signori. has a warm friendly atmosphere and opens onto the superb square surrounded by palaces and the Loggia del Consiglio.

Padova / Padua

Antico Brolo, Vicolo Cigolo 14, tel. (049) 656 088– Closed Sunday, August 1-20 – 70-100,000L. It serves cuisine made from fresh products from the market. In the summer you can dine by candlelight in the garden **El Toula’**, via Belle Parti 11,tel. (049) 8751822 – Closed Sunday, Monday evening, August – 65-80,000L. People always love the elegant but conventional Toula’ – **I Michelangelo**, corso Milano 22, tel. (049) 65 60 88 – Closed Saturday noon, Monday, August 10-20 –

45,000L. Reservation advised – **Mario e Mercedes**, via San Giovanni da Verdara 13, tel. (049) 871 97 31 - Closed Wednesday, Christhmas and New Year, August 15-30. 45,000L. Venitian specialties.

San Clemente, Vittorio Emanuele II 142, tel (049) 88 031 80 - Closed Sunday, Monday at noon, December 20-January 2, August. Lunch: 40,000L - Dinner: 85-130,000L. A very famous adress. Specialties: *Storione marinato all'agresto, risotto con cappesante e zucchine.*

CAFFE' – BARS

Caffe' Pedrocchi, piazzetta Pedrocchi. opened in 1831 by Antionio Pedrocchi and was once the most elegant cafe in Europe. Its salons are green, white, and red, like the Italian flag. Don't miss this place.

Dolo

19km from Padoue

Locanda alla Posta, tel. (041) 410 740 – Closed Monday – 55,000L. Seafood restaurant.

Vicenza

Scudo di Francia, Contrà Piancoli 4, tel. (0444) 323322 – Closed Sunday evening, Monday, August – 40,000L. Enjoy Venetian delicacies in a Venetian-style palace, near the piazza Signori in Vicenza – **Cinzia e Valerio**, piazzetta Porto Padova 65, tel. (0444) 505 213 – Closed Monday, January et August – 70,000L. Seafood restaurant – **Gran Caffe' Garibaldi**, piazza dei Signori 5, tel. (0444) 544 147 – Closed Tuesday evening, Wednesday, November – 35,000L. You can either have a drink and a small sandwich on one of the marble tables in a beautiful spacious room on the ground floor, or enjoy classic Italian cuisine in the restaurant upstairs. – **Osteria Cursore**, stradella Cursore 10, tel. (0444) 32 35 04. Friendly and popular.

Treviso

Le Beccherie, piazza Ancillotto 10,

tel. (0422) 56 601 – Closed Thursday evening, Friday noon, July 20-30. One of the oldest and most prestigious restaurants in town, and is doing its part to revive the great culinary tradition of the region – **Al Bersagliere**, via Barberia 21, tel. (0422) 541 988 – Closed Sunday, Saturday noon, January, January 1-10, August 1-10. good Trevisan cuisine. The menu changes from day to day – **El Toula' da Alfredo**, via Collalto 26, tel. (0422) 540 275 – Closed Sunday evening, Monday, August. This is where the famous chain of Toula' restaurants began.

Miane

Da Gigetto, via A. de Gasperi 4, tel. (0438) 960020 – 20,000L. An excellent restaurant in a luxurious country-style setting, serving fine innovative Italian cuisine inspired by nouvelle cusisne, but without the drawbacks of its French counterpart. The wine cellar is excellent, as is the service.

Belluno

Al Borgo, via Anconetta 8, tel. (0437) 926 755 – Closed Monday evening, Tuesday, June – 35,000L. It combines fine cuisine and culture in a beautiful Venetian villa on the border between Veneto and Alto Adigea.

Mel, 14km from Belluno

Antica Locanda al Cappello, piazza Papa Luciani, tel. (0437) 753 651 – Closed Tuesday evening, Wednesday, 2 weeks in July – 30,000L. The old sign still outside this17th century palace testifies to its past as a postal inn. Cuisine based on old recipes is served here.

Cortina d' Ampezzo

Bellavista-Meloncino, in Gillardon, tel. (0436) 861 043 – Closed Tuesday, June, November – 50,000L. A small restaurant, very popular among the regulars at the resort. From the center of Cortina, follow the signs to Falzarego – **El Toulà**, Ronco 123, tel. (0435) 3339 – Closed Monday, December 20-April 2, July 20-August 31 – 90,000L. The elegant restaurant of Cortina – **Baita Fraina**, Fraina, tel. (0436) 3634 – Closed Monday, October, November, May, June – 40,000L. This chalet deep in the mountains has a warm convivial atmosphere and family-style cuisine **Da Beppe Sello,** via Ronco 67 – tel. (0436) 3236 - 40-50,000L. We like the hearty cuisine served in this small three star chalet-hotel, in the pretty Tyrolean-style dining room or on a terrace in the summer – **Il Meloncino al Lago**, lago Ghedina, tel. (0436) 860 376, Closed Tuesday, July, November. It

serves good authentic cuisine in a rustic but elegant chalet in a very beautiful natural setting.– **Da Leone e Anna**, via Alverà 112, tel. (0436) 2768 – 50-60,000L.

CAFFE' – BARS

Bar del Posta, Hotel de la Poste, piazza Roma. Quiet atmosphere and a small bar which Hemingway loved. The *Dolomite* is the house cocktail.

Udine

Alla Vedova, via Tavagnacco 8, tel. (0432) 470 291 – Closed Sunday evening, Monday, August – 45,000L. Savory cuisine in a friendly atmosphere.

Trieste

Harry's Grill, Hotel Duchi d'Aosta, piazza dell' Unita d'Italia, tel. (040) 62 081 – 90,000L. The hotel bar is the meeting point for the town businessmen, and the restaurant is also very popular for its seafood specialties – **Ai Fiori**, piazza Hortis 7, tel. (040) 300 633 – Closed Sunday, Monday, June 15-July 15 – 40,000L. Elegant seafood restaurant – **Suban**, via Comici 2, tel. (040) 54 368 – Closed Monday, Tuesday, 20 days in August – 60,000L. When it opened in 1865, it was a country inn. The town has now surrounded it, but the interior remains unchanged. Try the delicious herb risotto. In the summer, meals are served under a lovely pergola – **Elefante Bianco**, riva Tre Novembre 3, tel. (040) 365 784 Closed Saturday noon, Sunday – 35-75,000L. You must reserve if you want to stand a chance of getting a table – **Al Granzo**, piazza Venezia 7, tel. (040) 306 788 – Closed Wednesday – 50,000L. Try to get a table facing the very picturesque fish market – **Al Bragozzo**, riva Nazario Sauro 22, tel. (040) 303 001 – Closed Sunday, Monday, June 25-July 10. One of the most popular restaurants of the port.

CAFFE' – BARS

Caffe' San Marco opened in 1904 under the Austro-Hungarian Empire. It has been recently restored to recreate the atmosphere of days gone by when it was a literary cafe where Umberto Saba, Italo Svevo, and more

recently contemporary writers such as Claudio Magris and Giorgio Voghera would gather. To celebrate this reopening, the San Marco has teamed up with the Hungaria in Budapest and the Florian in Venice, two other cafes which have played an important role in the cultural life of the center of Europe – **Caffe' degli Specchi**, piazza dell'Unita de' Italia, is on the largest square in Trieste, a good starting point for your visit to the town. Have a drink in the evening and watch the sun go down over the sea – **Para Uno**, via Cesare Battisti 13, has marvelous cappuccino.

INDEX

A

B

C

D

E

F

G

I

L

M

N

O

P

R

S

T

U

V

Z

NOTES

NOTES

NOTES

NOTES

NOTES

NOTES

NOTES

NOTES

NOTES

NOTES

NOTES